AF608133

Inside Israel's Northern Command

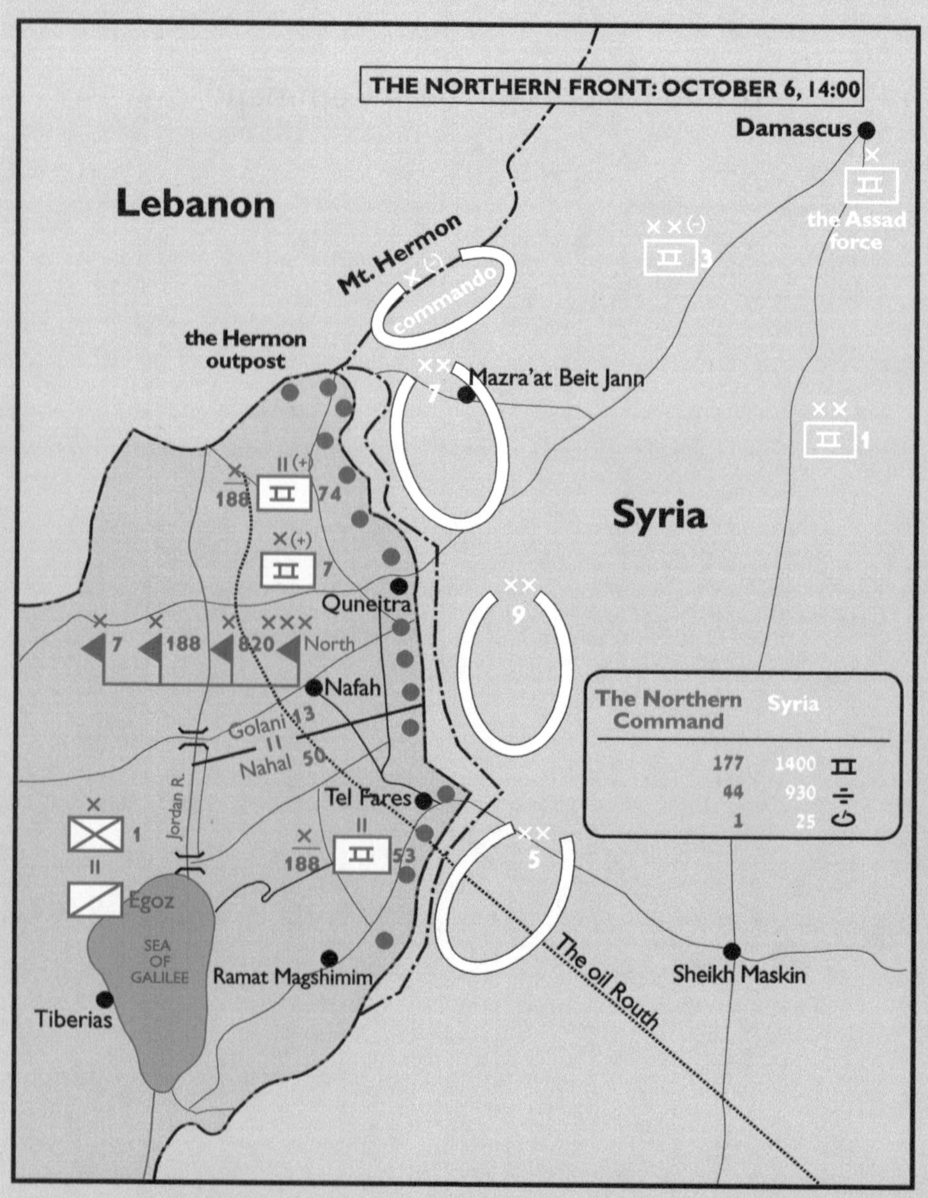

THE NORTHERN FRONT: OCTOBER 6, 14:00
Damascus
Lebanon
Mt. Hermon
commando
the Assad force
3
the Hermon outpost
Mazra'at Beit Jann
7
1
188
74
7
Syria
Quneitra
9
7
188
820
North
Nafah
Golani 13
Nahal 50
Jordan R.
Tel Fares
1
Egoz
188
53
5
SEA OF GALILEE
Ramat Magshimim
Tiberias
The oil Routh
Sheikh Maskin
The Northern Command
Syria
177
1400
44
930
1
25

Inside Israel's Northern Command

The Yom Kippur War on the Syrian Border

EDITED BY
Brigadier General Dani Asher, IDF (Ret.)

Originally published by Contento De Semrik, Tel-Aviv, Israel.

First North American edition published in 2016 by
the University Press of Kentucky

Scholarly publisher for the Commonwealth,
serving Bellarmine University, Berea College, Centre
College of Kentucky, Eastern Kentucky University,
The Filson Historical Society, Georgetown College,
Kentucky Historical Society, Kentucky State University,
Morehead State University, Murray State University,
Northern Kentucky University, Transylvania University,
University of Kentucky, University of Louisville,
and Western Kentucky University.

Editorial and Sales Offices: The University Press of Kentucky
663 South Limestone Street, Lexington, Kentucky 40508-4008
www.kentuckypress.com

Members of the editorial board and initial contributors of the book:

Major General (ret.) Yitzhak Hofi
Major General (ret.) Uri Simchoni
Brigadier General (ret.) Avraham Bar David
Colonel (ret.) Hagai Mann

Photographs and documents courtesy of the Israel Defense Forces
Introductory and closing maps courtesy of Yosef Barzon—Dfus Kal
Inside text maps courtesy of the IDF History Division and Dr. Dani Asher

ISBN 978-0-8131-6737-4 (hardcover)
ISBN 978-0-8131-6766-4 (pdf)
ISBN 978-0-8131-6765-7 (epub)

This book is printed on acid-free paper meeting
the requirements of the American National Standard
for Permanence in Paper for Printed Library Materials.

Manufactured in the United States of America.

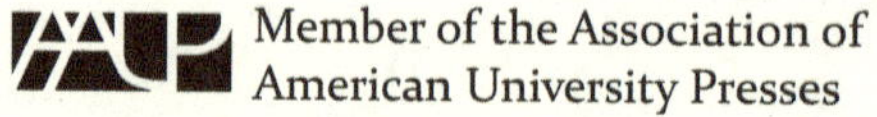

This book is dedicated to the memory of the Northern Command IDF soldiers and officers who fell on the front lines during the Yom Kippur War.

List of Abbreviations and Acronyms

ACB—Armored Command Battalion
AFV—Armored Fighting Vehicle
AOC—Aerial Observation Commander
AP—Aerial Photograph
APC—Armored Personnel Carrier
AVLB—Armored Vehicle-Launched Bridge
CAO HQ—Chief Artillery Officer Headquarters
CCO HQ—Chief Communication Officer Headquarters
CCP—Command and Control Post
CID—Criminal Investigations Department of Military Police Corps
CIPO—Chief Infantry and Paratrooper Officer
CMO HQ—Chief Medical Officer Headquarters
CSC—Command & Staff College
DOW—Died of Wounds
EW—Electronic Warfare
FCO—Frontal Control Outpost (Air Force)
G2—Intelligence/Directorate of Military Intelligence (Aman)
G3—General Staff Branch—Operations Directorate (Agam)
G4—Supply Directorate (Aga)
GHQ—IDF General Headquarters
GOC—General Officer Commanding
HAC—Head of Artillery Command
HAO—Head Armored Corps Officer
HCO—High Command Outpost

HMC—Head of Medical Command
IAF—Israeli Air Force
KIA—Killed in Action
KKL—The Jewish National Fund (JNF)
MAG—*Mitrailleuse d'Appui Général*; Belgian General Purpose Machine Gun
MP—Military Police
Nachal—Fighting Pioneer Youth
NCO—Non-Commissioned Officer
ODG—Operational Discussion Group
PRC—Portable Radio Communication
RAC—Regimental Aid Commander
Radar—Radio Detection and Ranging
RCLR—Recoilless Rifle
Res.—Reserve Service
Ret.—Retired
RMCC—Regimental Medical Corps Company
ROU—Regional Ordnance Unit
RSM—Routine Security Measures
SAM—Surface-to-Air Missile
SPG—Self-Propelled Gun
TOT—Time over Target

Military Ranks and Abbreviations

Private
Corp.—Corporal
Sgt.—Sergeant
Staff Sgt.—Staff Sergeant
Sgt. 1st Class—Sergeant First Class
Master Sgt.—Master Sergeant
Sgt. Maj.—Sergeant Major
Warrant Officer
2nd Lt.—Second Lieutenant
Lt.—Lieutenant
Captain
Maj.—Major
Lt. Col.—Lieutenant Colonel
Col.—Colonel
Brig. Gen.—Brigadier General
Maj. Gen.—Major General
Lt. Gen.—Lieutenant General

TABLE OF CONTENTS

Editorial Notes & Acknowledgments

The Northern Command Headquarters has commanded the forces and operations on the northern border of the State of Israel for many years. That border was a focal point of IDF activity reaching its peak in the fierce fighting during the Yom Kippur War in October 1973. This book deals with the preparation for war, the fighting tactics, the war development and outcome, the way they were perceived by the Northern Command Headquarters, and its commanders at the time.

The Northern Command has been in charge of the "hottest" sectors from the founding of the nation to the present day—the Galilee region border between Israel and Lebanon; the Golan Heights region border between Israel and Syria; the northern section of the border between Israel and Jordan from Beit She'an northward, the Sea of Galilee, the Hula Valley, and the Jordan Valley and its tributaries. The early days of the command have their roots in the crisis during the war against invading Arab armies in 1948—the Israeli War of Independence. This was followed by conflicts over the demilitarized zones in the 1950s and 1960s; the two-year fight over water (1964–1966), and the retaliatory actions after the signing of the Armistice Agreements in 1949. In the 1950s and 1960s, these front lines continued to concern the Northern Command HQ that was stationed in Nazareth. The border region remained highly dynamic between the wars. The different sectors continued to trouble the Northern Command and its branches, as well as the IDF's General Staff, terrorist activity called for preventative actions by the IDF.

During the Six-Day War (June 5–10, 1967), the Northern Command first operated in Samaria against Jordanian forces in the northern section of the West Bank. At the end of the war, it attacked and took over the Golan Heights from the Syrians. From that point on the Northern Command preparatory efforts, as well as those of the Syrians, focused on this region.

During the Yom Kippur[1] War, most of the fighting against the Syrians took place on the front of the Golan Heights. Northern and HQ Commanders cast the command units into combat along with additional units that reinforced the sector. The brunt of the burden, however, was carried by the forces fighting in the line of fire, who resolutely kept the enemy away from the northern settlements, forcing it beyond its lines, and shifting the fighting to within forty kilometers of Syria's capital, Damascus.

This book is not a substitute for extensive historical research, which could only be conducted by historians researching any archives made public from both sides of the border. We, as the commanders of the Northern Command during the Yom Kippur War, chose to bring together selected chapters from the events that took place during that period and set them down in this book. There are three parts to it. The first deals with the issues of advanced forewarning and preparations for war. The second deals with the main war maneuvers—from interception

1 Yom Kippur (Day of Atonement) is the holiest day of the year for the Jewish people. It is traditionally observed by an approximate 25-hour period of fasting and intensive prayer, often spending most of the day in synagogue services.

to the threat on Damascus—and the third describes the various war actions by the various mechanisms within the Northern Command.

The book is based on the testimonies and reminiscences of the Northern Command GOC and his senior staff during the Yom Kippur War. The story of the period before it, as well as the description of the various stages of fighting, is based on official sources from the IDF History Department, chiefly the book by Lt. Col. (res.) Dr. Elchanan Oren about the Yom Kippur War, which is to be published by the end of 2013.

We wish to thank everyone who assisted in and contributed time, talent, and skill to the writing and publication of this book:

Lt. Col. (res.) Avraham Zohar, who coordinated the writing of assignments for the early preparation stages of the book. The seminars he initiated and the tours in the field greatly contributed to the writing of the book.

The writers and researchers who contributed their experience and expertise—Col. (ret.) Roland Aloni; Brig. Gen. (res.) Dr. Dani Asher; Lt. Col. (res.) Dr. Amiad Bresner; Col. (res.) Moshe Givati; Col. (res.) Dr. Shmuel Gordon; Col. (res.) Yehuda Wegman; Lt. Col. (res.) Avraham Zohar; Col. (res.) Benny Michelson; Col. (res.) Ilan Sahar; Lt. Col. (res.) Yossi Abboudi, and Col. (res.) Dr. Hanan Shai (Schwartz).

The staff officers who have each written about their fields—Brig. Gen. (res.) Aharon Ophir; Col. (ret.) Roland Aloni; Brig. Gen. (res.) Dr. Dani Asher; Brig. Gen. (res.) Avraham Bar David; Col. (res.) Hagai Mann; Dr. Danny Nadav; Lt. Col. (res.) Yossi Abboudi; Col. (res.) Avraham Kayam, and Maj. Gen. (res.) Uri Simchoni.

Author Brig. Gen. (res.) Dr. Dani Asher, whose infinite expertise on the material, analytical skills, and tremendous capacity for work made it possible to turn raw material into a book. The editor, Dr. Israel Ben-Dor, who conducted the final Hebrew edit, styled and sifted and gave it its final form.

We hope that this book contributes to preserving the legacy of the Northern Command, its commanders, units, and fighters, from those days of the challenging war that began on Yom Kippur, October 6, 1973.

We wish to thank the people who offered financial assistance, in particular Stef Wertheimer, Menachem Einan, and Modi Ben-Shach.

Thanks go to the previews of Northern Command GOC, Major General Gadi Eizenkot and his staff officers, for their invaluable aid and assistance.

PREFACE

This book deals with the battles of the Northern Command in the northern fighting arena during the Yom Kippur War in 1973. It is common knowledge the command was not alone in this war and fierce fighting took place in areas commanded by the Southern Command Headquarters on the Egyptian front as well.

The experienced IDF were prepared for such a situation. During the Six-Day War in 1967, forces were almost simultaneously active on three fronts, in the south, east, and north, as well as in the air and sea. Building the power of the Israel Defense Forces was designed to address a similar situation if it ever occurred.

Most of the land forces were allocated to the three regional commands before the war: North, Central, and South. The permanent armored division basic formation, with one regular and five reserve brigades was built by the IDF between the wars. It was responsible for the planning and conduct of battle. Three of the divisions—252, 162 and 143—were allocated to the Southern Command, one division—146—parked in the Central Command and the other two—36 and 210 —were arranged in the Northern Command. Every one of the divisions had two armored brigades and a mechanized brigade with additional forces including an armored reconnaissance battalion, an Artillery Group, and an engineering battalion and a Maintenance Support Unit.

In addition, the IDF had independent infantry divisions, most of them belonging to some area with regional responsibility within the borders of their commands. Only some of them—three divisions of paratroopers and one infantry division, the excellent Golani—remained without regional responsibility and could be used as reserves to fight on the different fronts.

There were additional professional forces under the regional command including concentrated artillery battalions, field engineer regiments, transport regiments, armed forces, and military police, who were designated to help and strengthen the maneuvering forces. Intelligence facilities and systems, including military intelligence and electronic war systems from the SIGINT Corps, were activated by the command from their positions in the north, as well. The command stored its units' equipment in emergency warehouses and took care to maintain their operational, planning, and training value, as well as functional weaponry and equipment in the warehouses near the fronts and the regional rear command.

Therefore, the actual authority remaining at the general headquarters was only over a few reserve forces. These were based primarily on Air Force planes that could be moved to the fighting zone from one front to another. Naval forces were successfully activated centrally in the Mediterranean region. Those confined to the Red Sea arena acted independently.

The General Staff kept a few additional reserves under its command. The most prominent among them was the Central Command Division—146—that was transferred to the Northern Command when it became clear the Jordanian Army was not going to take part in the outbreak of war. In addition to that division, a few artillery forces including two battalions of land to land rockets, a long-range artillery battalion, and two battalions of long-range captured artillery[2] were on the General Staff's reserve and were transferred north.

With these forces, the Northern Command initially conducted an arduous war in defending the Golan Heights, fighting the Syrians and later carrying out the Syrian Golan Heights offensive, in the face of expeditionary forces from other Arab countries including Iraq, Jordan, and Morocco. Simultaneously, the command's forces fought against Palestinian terrorists operating from the Lebanese border.

Brig. Gen. (Res.) Dr. Dani Asher

2 Enemy weapons captured during the Six Day War, June 1967.

Foreword

Inside Israel's Northern Command is an important book and a milestone in Israeli military historiography. The book is the most comprehensive and trustworthy account of the Yom Kippur War on the Golan Heights front, and contains a fascinating integration of the web of events, the warriors' and commanders' experiences at the front along with a portrayal of the strategic influences and the considerations of the senior command.

I read the book as part of my preparation for my current position, and I feel, even one year and a half later, that it is not only a reference book but a study and instructional book as well. The first part of the book deals with preparations for war and contains a fascinating account of the preparation process, which was undertaken by the IDF in general and by the Northern Command in particular, in the face of the upcoming war. It has been customary to tag this chapter of our national history with the word "failure," but through the prism of this book, a vigorous, logical military operation shines through, not one of negligence. How does it happen that worthy and capable people take steps that prove insufficient in preparing for a pending, threatening disaster? There is no simple answer, but it does teach a sharp, simple, and clear lesson that can be summarized in one word: modesty. One needs a surplus of intellectual modesty when one comes to examine their basic self-assumptions. The failure in the preparations for the Yom Kippur War cannot be summed up in one clear-cut word: failure. The book reflects a system growing progressively insensitive to reality and becom-ing entrenched in its own work assumptions to such an extent that even signs attesting to the contrary are accredited to inter-pretation. This seems distorted these days.

The second part of the book opens with holding-action battles. There is a feeling that the various writers did their best to convey the essence of those turbulent days with a minimum of judgmental expressions. In my opinion, this sheds light on the weakness of the first chapters in this part. With forty years of hindsight since the war, it is a must and a chance to look at those days with an uncompromising razor-sharp analysis. Nevertheless, the intelligent reader will not need too much imaginative or inventive skills to formulate his understanding of the first two days of the war; the heroism; the inspiration; the weakness and the humiliation that were tied in with those days.

The breakthrough moves into Syria and the fighting, which will later merit the term the "Syrian enclave," are described later in the book. In my opinion, this historical chapter has been somewhat undeservedly forgotten with the background of the brave holding battles. To me, the ability of a beaten and battered army of depleted forces to turn and attack is no less than miraculous. Without the power of leadership exercised by the commanders involved and the incredible bravery of the warriors, this fantastic move would not have been achieved. As one who has had the opportunity to discuss events with many of the commanders who personally took part and carried out this attack, it seems they find it hard, even today, to grasp the enormity of the deed to which they had contributed then. From this aspect, the book is a worthy monument for the action, and serves as an excellent podium for discussing attack and advance battles.

I found the third part of the book to be naturally interesting as it deals with calls for thought that relate to activating the command systems in wartime. One gets the impression that lean staffs and a clear chain of command can lead to high efficiency even when the little that was available was activated despite difficulties and problems. It is a realistic observation that war can lead to that.

Medals of courage awarded after the war and maps are listed in the book, as well.

In summary, *Inside Israel's Northern Command* is an important book for the professional or nonprofessional reader, as well as the inter-ested ones and anyone who finds unsurpassed inspiration in human activity.

Have an enjoyable and informative read!

— *Northern Commander Maj. Gen. Yair Golan*

Introduction

The Northern Command was established as the successor of the 1948 Northern Front, at that time headed by Maj. Gen. Moshe Carmel. Under his command, in the course of Israel's War of Independence, it reached the country's international borders in almost every sector and even went beyond them. The Northern Command is in charge of the operational routine, ongoing defensive activities and the preparation for war with regard Israel's borders with three Arab nations: Lebanon, Syria, and Jordan.

The Command Headquarters, along with its organic units and those placed under its command, has carried the burden of the various assignments along the borders, beyond them, and within Israel for many long years. Stabilizing the borders and maintaining civilian security in the command district make up its central tasks.

During the 1950s, the command units operated mainly against infiltrators who attempted to cross the different borders. They entered in order to steal, rob, kill, and gather intelligence on behalf of Arab nations. These activities were joined by actual military maneuvers over the demilitarized zones, some of which constituted a bone of contention between the Syrians and the State of Israel. Several days of combat against Syrian forces took place in 1951 after their takeover of the Tel Mutila region north of the Sea of Galilee. Other incidents occurred due to the Syrian non-recognition of Israeli sovereignty over the Hamat Gader (El Hamma) region.

The beginning of work to drain the Hula Valley and build the National Water Carrier pipeline (*Hamovil Haartzi*) was nearly jeopardized by the Syrians who attempted to sabotage the operation. There was also occasional gunfire aimed at settlements and farmers who went out on their day's work near the border. Constant Syrian attempts to fish in the Sea of Galilee disrupted the fishermen's work, mainly in the northeastern part of the lake.

The 1955 Operation *Alei Zayit* (Olive Leaves) brought the escalation to a peak when a number of Syrian outposts along the Sea of Galilee were attacked. Syria did not take part in the Suez Canal crisis in October–November, 1956. Northern Command units like the 9th Brigade were moved south and took part in the fighting.

The early 1960s saw the Syrian border heat up once again as Syrian fishermen tried to reach the Sea of Galilee to cultivate the demilitarized areas. The Northern Command carried out retaliatory operations on Syrian targets in Tawfik in the southern Golan Heights in 1960 and in Nukyeab along the shores of the Sea of Galilee in 1962.

The sector flared up once again when the Arab nations decided to divert the water flow from the rivers feeding the Jordan River. The State of Israel could not possibly ignore this act and the Northern Command—backed by tank, artillery, and anti-aircraft units—was ordered to disrupt the activity along the planned diversion route. A series of operations, in which the Israeli Air Force participated as well, resulted in injured workers at the site. The diversion of water failed.

Another wide-range flare up occurred during the Six-Day

War in June 1967. The Northern Command, which had operated against the Jordanian Army in the northern part of the West Bank from the start of the war, concentrated its forces with the assistance of additional forces and embarked on a broad offensive to capture the Golan Heights on the fifth and sixth days of the war.

On June 5, at the onslaught of the Six-Day War, the Syrian Air Force was dealt a serious blow by an Israeli Air Force preemptive strike. And after two days of fighting, on June 9 and 10, including two breakthrough battles which cost many lives, the Golan Heights was captured from under the hands of the Syrian Army from Mount Hermon in the north to the Yarmouk River in the south.

The IDF and the State of Israel obtained their strategic goals on the Syrian front during the Six-Day War. However, growing and unresolved difficulties soon developed in the relationship between the two countries. During the war, over 70,000 residents of the Golan Heights—Druze, Alawites, Circassians, Turkmen, Maghrebis, and Bedouin—left their villages. Only about 8,000 Druze remained in five villages in the northern part of the Golan Heights. In the period following the war, and until the Yom Kippur War, fourteen settlements and two Nachal settlements were established on the Golan Heights: five in the north and eleven in the south.

At the end of the Six-Day War, the IDF began intensive operations to restore combat gear and equipment. Training, accelerated instructional activity, and closing gaps in terms of manpower and equipment all took place. This was in preparation for the forces' future tasks. In the period following the war, the IDF also examined the structure and organization of the forces and began establishing a new framework for the field divisions.

Northern Command carried out two main tracks of activity:

the organization of the fighting forces within the framework of a permanent command division—the 36th Division—and the organization and construction of facilities in the rear of the new front lines, beyond the range of Syrian artillery range, and of observation posts near the line of the border.

The logistics alignment in the Northern Command was in charge of supply and maintenance operations, evacuation of casualties, equipment, transport, construction, purchase, and storage to provide the Command GOC and the division commanders the capacity to perform their tasks. The layout of logistical infrastructure in the command district reflected likely combat scenarios based on situation evaluations by the operational rank.

Immediately following the Six-Day War, the GHQ and Logistics Command alignment dealt with organization along the new borderlines and providing solutions for the following issues:

- An extended stay of the forces in a territory without logistical infrastructure, with special reference to the northern Golan Heights and Mount Hermon—extreme weather conditions the IDF are not familiar with and unprepared for in winter
- The deployment of a medical alignment in accordance with situation assessments and needs of those forces deployed in the territory
- Maintenance of all combat equipment by establishing a series of workshops near the regiments in the field
- Deployment of frontline supply reserves, namely, fuel, ammunition, and food in accordance with operational planning.
- Logistical field-level maintenance, alignment, adjustment to the organizational changes in the structure of the force, and the construction of the permanent division
- System development of transit routes

To control the routes and the command logistical space, during 1971 and 1972, a command transportation battalion and a command maintenance group were established. These units performed basic training exercises in the year before the war.

Since the capture of the Golan Heights, the Syrians rejected the possibility of a political solution and viewed such an option as a significant blow to Syria's status and an international and ideological humiliation. The Syrian solution to the problem had two sole components: the existence of Israel cannot be tolerated and the military option is the only way to deal with the conflict. The liberation of the Golan Heights was to be achieved as part of an overall military solution.

The Syrian Army weakness was the main cause for the gap between their desire to free the Golan Heights and their ability to do it. Until 1970, the Syrian Army worked desperately in order to rehabilitate all that relates to its plans to protect the Golan Heights and the Syrian capital while they began to develop offensive skills as well.

Until the beginning of 1969, the Syrian front was relatively quie until terrorist attacks and infiltration through the Syrian border increased, and by the end of that year, the Syrian Army engaged in fighting by staging commando ambushes in Israeli territory and bombing camps and settlements. The IDF initiated three days of consecutive battles in June 1969 in order to stop the escalation and the front regained its calm. When the agreement to end the Egyptian front War of Attrition[3] was signed in August, it was rejected by the Syrians but fighting did not actually resume. A new period dawned in Syria with Hafez al-Assad's rise to power in November 1970. Upon entering his new position, Assad presented a new direction when he called for the establishment of a united pan-Arab front against Israel.

3 A war between Israel and Egypt (March 8, 1969 – August 7, 1970)

Syria wished to turn the wheel around to the time prior to Israel's conquests during the Six-Day War. The Syrians, who did not accept Israel's existence even within the 1967 borders, were infuriated by its expansion and, like Nasser, stated that "What has been taken by force will be returned by force."

With stubborn patience, Assad began his preparations for war. Various steps to improve the army's fighting capabilities and turn it into a stronger and more modernized army was wholly based on the purchase of combat gear from the USSR and adopting their combat doctrine. New advisors and new military equipment assisted in the absorption and training. These steps allowed for the planning and construction of an organized defensive alignment against the possibility of another Israeli attack, but at the same time, they also served as preparations for an offensive operation. Cooperation between the Syrians and Egypt increased in 1972–1973 in all that related to staging a war against Israel.

Since the Six-Day War, the Northern Command prepared for the possibility of an attempted Syrian "hijack," or of an all-inclusive war, and a defensive system was constructed in the Golan Heights including outposts, fencing, minefields, and an anti-tank trench. The digging of the anti-tank trench began in 1970 after Syrian tanks had attacked an Israeli outpost.

In 1971, terrorist activities from the Syrian border increased once again, and in the second half of 1972, the IDF initiated "combat days" against the Syrian forces, including infantry and armored raids, artillery fire, and aerial bombardments in order to halt the terrorist activity.

In February 1973, apparently due to the start of concentrated Egyptian-Syrian activity in preparation for an attack on Israel, the border resumed its calm. A process had begun that, eventually, after more than six months, led to the Yom Kippur War. The Syrian Army, under the leadership of Hafez al-Assad, who was in control of Syria after the War of Attrition, reached a potency he thought would allow an offensive to restore the Golan Heights to Syrian hands. At the same time, the process of forming a wartime coalition with Egypt under the leadership of Anwar el-Sadat came to fruition. Upon detecting some of the new threats, the Northern Command took steps intended to face the possibility of war.

PART I

Preparation for War

Syria Wants War

Chapter 1

PRIOR TO THE YOM KIPPUR WAR, the Northern Command operated from its headquarters in Nazareth under Northern Command GOC Maj. Gen. Yitzhak Hofi. At the time, the Northern Command was responsible for the region that included the Golan Heights, the Jordan and Beit She'an valleys, and the Lebanese border between Rosh HaNikra on the Mediterranean coast, to the Shabaa Farms at the top of Mount Dov (Jabel Rous) on the eastern section of the border.

In November 1970, the rise of Hafez al-Assad to power in Syria, though he continued the rule of the Ba'ath Party, marked the dawn of a new era. The new political stability allowed him to introduce changes, and his policy was characterized by relative moderation and openness both internally and externally.

As soon as he set foot into his new position, Assad introduced a new orientation when he called for the establishment of a pan-Arab united front against Israel. On the Palestinian issue, Assad worked to draw a distinction between the "Palestinian problem" and the "Problem of the Occupied Territories," the latter of which included the Golan Heights. Efforts were made by the Syrian regime to cooperate with the different Arab nations to create pacts and form ties. Syria strengthened its alliance with Egypt when, following the War of Attrition, it seemed that no political option would resolve Egypt's problems. The Cairo-Damascus axis, based on and formed by this trend, established an axis through 1971–1973, which laid the ground for the Arab nations' entry into the Yom Kippur War.

Syria's political goals, leading up to the Yom Kippur War, remained the same—striving for both internal unification and a position of leadership within the Arab region. At the same time, it was evident that Assad was obsessed with eradicating the stain of the 1967 defeat and restoring the self-confidence of his soldiers, recapturing the territories, and showing the world that given a suitable opportunity the Arabs were capable of holding their own with honor. The need to fight again became an obsession. Without restoring the balance with Israel, there was no hope, in his eyes, of reaching an agreement through political negotiations.

Assad in Syria, like Sadat in Egypt, believed that a change in the balance of power would allow him "another round" against Israel, and this time from a position of a sort of equality and not from a position of weakness and humiliation. No other Arab country felt as strongly as Syria that the very existence of Arab nationality was bound up in the conflict with Israel. Syria wished to turn the wheel back to the period before Israel's conquests during the Six-Day War. The Syrians, who had never accepted Israel's existence within the 1967 borders, were furious in light of its expansion and, like Nasser, believed that "what was taken by force would be restored by force."

Therefore, Assad began his preparations for war with stubborn patience. He operated quietly to prepare the possibility for an attack against Israel. As part of the efforts to prepare for war, Assad addressed the planning and building of military forces. In this, he was assisted by his closest ally among the military personnel from the time of his struggle against his predecessor, Salach Jadid, Syria's Chief of Staff since 1968, Mustafa Tlass. Tlass was appointed Minister of Defense in March 1972.

On different occasions and particularly at conferences of Arab Defense Ministers and Chiefs of Staff, who discussed the preparations of Arab countries for a decisive war against Israel, Syria's representatives claimed that their army was not yet ready for such a war, fearing superiority of the Israel Air Force. It pointed out the need for two additional divisions. The Syrian Army's order of battle during the Six-Day War had included three *Majmuas* (division-sized groups), temporary headquarters that did not yet function as division headquarters. The Syrian order of battle in the Six-Day War included five infantry brigades and an additional coastal defense brigade, two armored brigades, one mechanized brigade, and six reserve infantry brigades, as well as two or three Special Forces battalions and two reconnaissance battalions.

After the Six-Day War, the Syrian Army grew significantly. The control was reorganized into five divisions. Two armored divisions were established—the 1st and the 3rd. The 1st Armored Division was established based on the senior armored brigades in 1968. The establishment of the 3rd Armored Division began in 1971. Likewise, three mechanized infantry divisions were united—the 5th, the 7th, and the 9th, founded in October 1971. The main developmental push was felt in the aerial defense alignment. In less than a year, 1972–1973, five surface-to-air missile (SAM) brigades were formed and a SAM alignment was erected around the capital, Damascus, to defend it. Additionally, in July 1973 a system of positions was constructed on the Golan Heights that allowed SAMs to be brought closer to the front.

In February 1973, Assad secretly visited Moscow. He returned to Syria with a Soviet military delegation headed by

Marshal Pavel Stepanovich Kutakhov, one of the leading Soviet Air Force commanders. Following the visit, the Soviets provided the Syrians with SAM batteries but did not provide them with new MiG-23 fighter jets.

Various steps were taken to improve the Syrian Army's fighting capabilities and turn it into a stronger and modernized army. For example, in 1971, seventy percent of the Syrian budget was allocated to military needs, and most of Syria's economic and human resources were diverted toward preparation for the upcoming military confrontation with Israel. Military improvement was based on purchasing weapons, adopting the Soviet Union's military tactical doctrine, and obtaining the assistance of Soviet advisors who were integrated into Syrian Army units. These steps allowed Syria to plan and construct an organized defensive alignment against the possibility of an additional Israeli offense while also serving as preparations for an offensive action.

There is no doubt that, despite the measures taken, Syria's military strength and political status had still not reached a level at which it could solely initiate an offense against Israel. When the Egyptians decided to launch a war against Israel, Syria was already at the top of its force-building power and had no choice but to join the war as a secondary partner. The Syrian entry into the war, alongside Egypt, was intended to take advantage of the opportunity presented and avoid political isolation and the failure to reach existing and future goals if it were to remain a bystander.

A strategy of a joint coordinated attack on both fronts formed the basis of the joint offensive planning that Sadat and Assad had initiated as early as 1971. In 1972 and 1973, cooperation between Syria and Egypt intensified, with Assad and Sadat continuing their mutual visits to Cairo and Damascus, as well as Moscow. Their defense ministers did likewise, along with planning teams made up of senior officers. In February 1973, new Egyptian Defense Minister Mushir (Field Marshal) Ismail Ali came to Damascus on Sadat's behalf and proposed the launch of a coordinated Egyptian-Syrian attack on Israel. Assad agreed immediately.

On April 23, 1973, the two leaders met again for two days of detailed discussions at the presidential resort in Borg El Arab, west of Alexandria. They determined the main battle lines during that visit.

Through August 21–23, the army heads met at the Egyptian Naval Base at Ras el-Tin for two days of summary discussions and a final examination of the planned maneuvers. Syrian Chief of Staff Yusuf Shakkour and Egyptian Chief of Staff Saad el-Shazly signed an official document that ratified their joint intention to go to war. Syrian Defense Minister Tlass and then-commander of the Egyptian Air Force, Hosni Mubarak, flew from Alexandria to Syria to brief Assad and Sadat, who held a summit meeting at Bloudan, west of Damascus where they reached the decision to go to war in October.

D-Day of October 6 was determined in a secret meeting of the leaders in Cairo on September 12. The H-hour of 14:30 was decided upon in a subsequent meeting between Egyptian War Minister Ismail and Assad in Damascus on October 3. The joint H-hour was set for 14:30, with the open-fire order set for H minus 35 minutes—13:55.

Even if there was agreement regarding the date of the war and the manner of its performance, it seems the partners had not agreed on its goal. While Assad aimed at regaining the whole territory for himself through combat, Sadat merely wished to unfreeze the political deadlock and restart the diplomatic process that had been halted. While Sadat planned an "all-out war with limited goals" (10–15 km), Assad aimed for a war wherein the Egyptian Army would conquer the entire

Sinai Peninsula or at least retake western parts as far as the key regions beyond the mountain passes—the Mitla and the Gidi—at Bir Gafgafa and Bir Thamada. Along this war effort, Assad intended to position his forces for a battle to recapture all of the Golan Heights.

In the summer of 1973, to secure the Syrian southern flank of the front, Assad worked to include Jordan in the planned conflict. Jordan's participation was intended to provide defense for Syria's Southern Branch and prevent a parallel IDF counterattack on the rear of the front and the Damascus region through the north of Jordan. King Hussein agreed to protect the line and prevent IDF activity in his region. In addition, he promised to send two Jordanian Armored Brigades to participate in the battle over the Golan Heights.

Assad also had to secure his army's northern flank at the Lebanese border against an Israeli flanking or counterattack through the Lebanese Beqaa Valley toward Damascus. In August 1973, it was decided in a secret agreement with Lebanese President Suleiman Frangieh that Syrian forces would be allowed to enter Lebanon to defend the mountain passes leading to Damascus from Lebanon's territory. At the same time, and in order to disrupt the IDF forces on this front, an agreement with the Palestinian terrorist organizations—the PLO—was reached so that they would conduct extensive harassment activity along the Lebanese border during the war.

Syrian Order of Battle on the Eve of the Yom Kippur War

- Three mechanized infantry divisions—the 5th, the 7th (reinforced during April-May 1973 by a Moroccan Brigade, which included an infantry battalion and an armored battalion) and the 9th with T-54/55 tanks. The 5th and 7th Divisions each had two infantry brigades, one mechanized brigade and one armored brigade, as well as an Artillery Group and Division units. The 9th Division did not have a mechanized brigade.
- Two armored divisions—the 1st and the 3rd, with T-62 tanks, each with two tank brigades, a mechanized brigade, an Artillery Group and Division units
- Two independent armored brigades—the 51st and the 47th, and an independent mechanized brigade—the 62nd
- 1500 tanks
- 1000 artillery gun barrels
- Seven commando and paratrooper battalions
- Rifaat al-Assad Force—assigned to secure the regime that included two tank battalions and elite infantry forces
- "FROG" SS rocket launchers
- Thirty-six SAM batteries, half of them SA-6
- Air Force—178 MiG-21 fighter jets, 114 other fighter jets, forty-five helicopters
- Navy—nine missile boats, thirteen torpedo boats

The Syrians planned the war as a single systemic maneuver, the finish lines of which were undefined. It is likely that in their initial plan the Syrians intended to reach the Jordan River. It's also possible that they planned to cross it, but it is just as possible that they would have been satisfied with preparing defenses along the cliff line on the western slopes of the Golan Heights.

In planning an offensive against the IDF forces alignment on the Golan Heights, the Syrians assessed that they would have to breakthrough an organized defensive layout. This definition is one of the three categories covered in the Soviet military doctrine employed for evaluating a defense layout and determining the force ratios and the best method of breaking through it. These categories include:

- **hasty defensive layout**—usually established at the end of the offensive phase
- **organized defensive layout**—land, and other, preparations have been made
- **fortified defensive layout**—land infrastructure of the defending forces' layout is deep and complex—consisting of several defense layers—and able to provide prolonged strong protection against an enemy breakthrough.

The classification of the IDF defense layout on the Golan Heights in 1973 as "organized" rather than "fortified" reveals the Syrian assumption that the layout had not been completed. In fact, the layout consisted of only a small number of defense outposts, without depth, and without a continuous, reinforced line of obstacles at the front.

In the Syrians' view, the IDF's organized layout included, alongside the defending forces, ground-based defensive lines such as sites and outposts, firing position lines for tanks and anti-tank devices, positions for artillery batteries, command centers, and obstacles mainly in the form of minefields.

In their attack plan, the Syrians chose an option in the military doctrine that stated that the layout could be broken through by a direct contact offensive. This method allowed the attacking forces to take hold of staging areas within the front's defensive layout, and from this position study the enemy's layout, plan the breakthrough, and attack in a coordinated and organized manner. This is in contrast to a different method that is built upon attacking with a deep movement from staging areas 15–20 kilometers from the contact lines.

Syria camouflaged its full staging within their emergency defensive layouts, from which they leapt to attack, as an unusually broad General Staff exercise, combined with corps exercises intended to commence on October 6. Alongside these attempts to confuse, hide, and mislead at the front, the terror attack on the Jewish refugee camp in Schönau, Austria may also be viewed as an event intended to distract Israel from what was happening on its fronts.

At the same time, the misdirection of the IDF was assisted unintentionally by an aerial incident that occurred on September 13, 1973, wherein twelve Syrian MiG jets were shot down off the coast of northern Syria. This hard blow to Syria's Air Force provided a supposedly rational explanation for the various steps Syria was taking to increase alertness and reinforce its deployment, but the IDF ignored the fact that these maneuvers had begun in August 1973, before the incident took place. Army units and weaponry, artillery, SAM batteries, and bridging vehicles were later transferred from northern Syria and Jordan to the defensive lines on the Golan Heights front.

As early as spring-summer 1973, the Syrians had already begun their defensive and reinforcement maneuvers. Syrian activities recognized by intelligence included:

- Removing forces from the contact line for exercises and organization during the spring and summer. This was in contrast to the routine of many years standing, in which forces were taken off the line ahead of winter.
- Preparing positions for SAM layouts and manning them during September-October 1973
- Preparing positions for general staff artillery batteries and moving 180mm guns and 240mm mortars up to the rear of

the frontal defense layout

- Moving squadrons of fighter jets up to frontal airfields at Blay and Khalkhalah (close to the Golan front)
- Penetrative tours to examine minefields
- Preparatory activity in the civilian sector including storing food, evacuating hospital beds, gathering blood donations, and so on

Transfer of forces and weaponry to the front line was mainly performed during September in convoys that moved at night. This activity reached a peak on the night of September 30. Starting that day, some of the forces were moved forward to the convention and deployment areas and combat teams for the assault were arranged. On D-Day minus one (October 5, 1973), all the first-rank assault forces were stationed in the deployment area and the weaponry was spread out in shooting positions. The 9th and 5th Mechanized Infantry Divisions were each reinforced by an independent tank brigade.

In the two days leading up to the war, the Syrians increased the amount of artillery positioned near the line. An artillery force of approximately 900 mortar and gun barrels of various types and calibers was deployed against the IDF forces on the Syrian side of the Golan Heights. These operated out of 147 batteries consisting of six guns each. An artillery battalion was added to each of the first rank brigades to create a 'brigade task group.' The mid-range Artillery Corps was advanced to a distance of approximately four kilometers from the front line. The support units of the three frontline Syrian Divisions (the 5th, 7th and 9th) were reinforced by support units from the second-rank divisions. Long-range 180mm gun batteries and 240mm heavy mortars from the general staff level reserve were also deployed toward the front lines, mainly intended for use in breaking through fortifications. The heavy mortars were positioned facing the key targets on Mount Hermon and in Tel Fares. Additionally, FROG-7 surface-to-surface rocket batteries with a range of approximately seventy kilometers were deployed to the depth of the front.

Israeli Command Sectors and the Forces under Their Command

The following headquarters were in command of the front lines:

- 820th Regional Brigade—in charge of the Golan Heights, under the command of Col. Zvi Bar
- Miron District Headquarters—in charge of the Lebanese border, under the command of Col. Tzuri Sagi
- 612th Regional Valleys Brigade Headquarters—in charge of the Jordan Valley and the Beit She'an Valley, under the command of Col. Yehezkel Ravid. (When the war broke out the brigade headquarters was transferred to Central Command.)

The regular fighting forces of the Northern Command included the following units:

- Golani Infantry Brigade with four battalions and a Special Forces Unit under the command of Col. Amir Drori
- 188th Armored Brigade with two Centurion tank battalions under the command of Col. Yitzhak Ben Shoham
- 483rd "Egoz" Command Reconnaissance Unit under the command of Lt. Col. Avi Telem
- 334th Artillery Battalion under the command of Col. Arieh (Schwartz) Shacham

The Northern Command HQ consisted of the following headquarters:

- 36th Reserve Division Headquarters under the command of Brig. Gen. Rafael (Raful) Eitan and his deputy Brig. Gen. (res.) Menachem (Men) Aviram
- 210th Reserve Division Headquarters (under establishment) under the command of Maj. Gen. (res.) Dan Lanner and his deputy Col. Moshe Bar-Kochva (Brill) (The Command Headquarters was founded in June 1973.)
- 181st ACB Headquarters (Regional Armored Command Battalion—Sherman tanks) under the command of Maj. (res.) Reuven Ben Alon
- 744th Artillery Command Headquarters under the command of Lt. Col. Avraham Bar David
- 801st Engineering Command Headquarters under the command of Lt. Col. Moshe Peled
- 390th Military Police Headquarters under the command of Lt. Col. Zvi Hershko

Forces Deployed on the Golan Heights for Routine Security:

- **820th Brigade**—regional brigade, responsible for the entire Golan Heights front, with two battalions under its command performing operational activity on the outposts line (eleven manned outposts on the line and on Mount Hermon with twelve combat soldiers in each outpost), as well as a company from the Egoz Reconnaissance Unit (483rd Unit of which one acted on the Golan Heights and the others on the Lebanese border employing routine security weapons systems consisting of a rifle and infrared beacon mounted on a command car for use in routine security nighttime ambushes)
- **188th Armored Brigade**—with two regular tank battalions (totaling seventy-two Centurion tanks), one deployed in

positions on the line near the outposts, the other, concentrated on the rear.

- **334th Battalion** – Golani Brigade's Regular Self-Propelled Mortar Battalion until 1970, commanded by Lt. Col. A. Shacham. The battalion headquarters at the Nafah Base served as an auxiliary headquarters for the 820th Regional Brigade. The battalion had two 160mm self-propelled mortar batteries (a third mortar battery was removed from the order of battle a month prior to the war) and a 155mm SPG battery (based on self-propelled guns from the 212th Support Unit's Reserve Battalion). The three batteries were deployed in permanent positions in the north, center, and south of the Golan Heights. The integration of the 155mm regular gun battery in the short-range mortar battalion was intended to ensure fire coverage toward the outpost sectors, throughout the Golan Heights, chiefly in order to respond to missions encountering enemy fire.

The reserve order of battle included:

- **Three tank brigades** (179th, 679th, 164th)—commanded by colonels Ran Sarig, Ori Orr, and Avraham Baram, the 39th Battalion of the 188th Brigade, commanded by Lt. Col. Yoav Vaspi, and the ACB tanks.
- **Two mechanized brigades** (4th and 9th)—commanded by colonels Mordechi Ben Porat and Yaakov Hadar.
- The infantry battalions and brigade units belonging to the regional brigades (820th and 612th) and the Miron District. On the eve of the war and in light of the IDF's assessment that a war was not imminent, it was decided to reduce and close headquarters, including the Miron District. When the war broke out, the 612th Regional Brigade was assigned to the Central Command Headquarters.

The Artillery Corps' reserve alignment in the north was organized into Artillery Groups:

- The 36th Division's 212th Artillery Group under the command of Col. Benny Arad, which was in the advanced stages of being organized into a permanent five-battalion support unit. The support unit battalions served as the main source of regular artillery deployed throughout the Golan Heights.
- The 210th Division's 282nd Artillery Group (established during 1973) under the command of Col. Moshe Levi, was in its emerging stages. The battalions for the unit intended to support were two 105mm self-propelled Priest battalions, scheduled for conversion to 155mm SPGs in 1974/75, as well as other non-established battalions. The support unit was equipped according to the battalions in the command artillery unit. These were stored on the command bases in Kurdani and Kiryat Motzkin, north of Haifa.

The artillery order of battle of the Northern Command also included the HAC's artillery battalions, most of which towed 155mm battalions, and mortar battalions from the independent brigades and the regional brigades. During combat, units from the GHQ support units also reinforced the command—the CAO HQ Support Unit, including the long-range Target Acquisition Unit, which also operated the MAR-290 MAR-240 rockets, two battalions of 130mm guns captured during the previous war, and a 240mm rocket launcher battalion.

The reserve engineering forces were based on engineering battalions and the heavy engineering equipment unit of the 801st Command Engineering Unit, as well as the combat engineering battalions of the two command divisions.

To maintain the alignment, **Ordnance Corps** units were

deployed at the following workshops during the calm period before the war:

- 188th Armored Brigade's workshop—No. 703 in Nafah for tank service
- 651st Northern Command ROU workshops:
    1. 701st in Bat Galim (Haifa) for vehicle service
    2. 704th in Kurdani (north of Haifa) for vehicle, half-track, APC, and tank service
    3. 704th extension in Biranit (Lebanese border) for vehicle service
    4. 678th regional garage on the Golan Heights for half-track, APC, and tank service with two forward extensions
    5. An additional garage in the Kishon camp in Haifa provided services for the bridging and crossing equipment concentrated in the region.

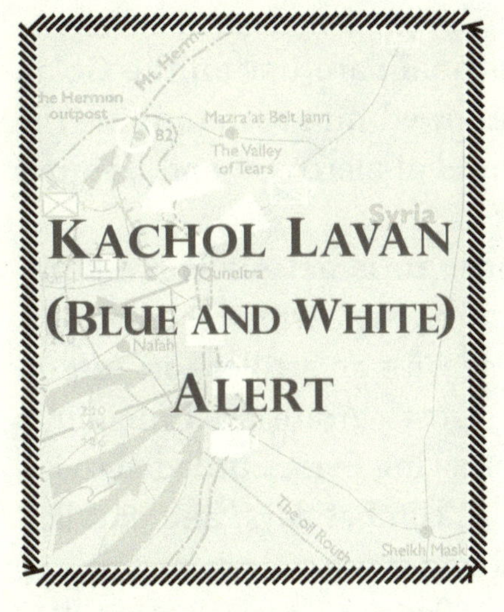

Kachol Lavan (Blue and White) Alert

CHAPTER 2

THE NORTHERN COMMAND, WHICH was responsible for the northern front, was following events across the border and conducted extensive operations to prepare the Golan Heights district and the forces under its command for the upcoming war with Syria. Since the Six-Day War, the command intelligence unit had systematically monitored the Syrian Army's preparations and fortifications on the Golan Heights front. The constant surveillance allowed Israel to recognize operations and unusual activity by Syrian Army units. Throughout the years, the Northern Command and the IDF had obtained a comprehensive picture of the changes taking place in the region, including outpost construction, road paving, bridge building, laying mines, and erection of fencing. The information at their disposal also included reports on the Syrian Army's structure, organization and order of battle, combat doctrine, training, weaponry and many additional details.

The Northern Command GOC, Maj. Gen. Yitzhak (Haka) Hofi, was appointed in the summer of 1972. During his first year, he experienced operations against terrorists on the

Lebanon border as well as occasional flare-ups on the Golan Heights front. This experience allowed him to determine the command's needs, examine its level of alertness, and improve readiness for a future war.

In November 1972, in response to Israel Air Force bombardments of terrorist camps and Syrian Army installations, the Syrians took Israel by surprise with an artillery assault on the full alignment of Israel's outposts. Additional incidents transpired at the end of 1972 following Syria's broad activity. In the north, these were known as 'combat days,' and entailed a series of operations, conducted under the codename Capital, that combined tank and artillery fire with aerial activity for concentrated attacks against Syrian targets. Starting in January 1973, after the most comprehensive of these combined operations, known as Operation Capital D, and apparently due to the start of Syria's preparations for war, the Syrian front was quiet. The Northern Command drew conclusions and improved its readiness in all matters relating to the planning and control of operations like these.

In April 1973, there were increasing intelligence reports of Egyptian and Syrian preparation for war, and IDF alert was raised to a level termed Blue and White (the colors of the Israeli flag). Substantial steps were taken in the Northern Command to improve its preparedness for war. The organization process—orchestrated by Northern Command Chief of Staff Brig. Gen. Uri Bar-On—included: accelerating the establishment of an additional division headquarters; receiving tanks and other weaponry; moving the tank brigades' emergency storage warehouses closer to the front; increasing armament stocks with additional weaponry and ammunition; paving roads and building outposts; digging anti-tank ditches, and laying minefields.

The Command GOC ordered these steps to accelerate the process of equipping the command's reserve brigades in case of an emergency, to allow for quicker access to the combat regions on the Golan Heights, and to improve fighting capability along the lines of contact. The Northern Command sought to complete the deployment by the end of June 1973 to allow for an increased alert toward the summer while adapting to the pace of the construction of emergency storage warehouses. Logistically speaking, the purpose of these changes was to strengthen the logistic alignment in the Northern Command's district and transform it as far as possible into a mobile alignment capable of servicing the forces expected to operate in that district during wartime.

The tank brigades' emergency storage warehouses, which, up until that point, were located in the Haifa Bay and at the rear of the command's district, were moved closer to the front to the Rosh Pina region. The field activity was orchestrated by Lt. Col. Rami Dotan, the G4 officer of the 36th Division. The 36th Division Headquarters was advanced to the Rosh Pina area, along with the 179th Quick Mobilization Brigade with its upgraded Centurion tanks. The 679th "Meteor Engine Centurion" Brigade was also deployed southeast of Rosh Pina. In addition, an emergency storage warehouse was built at the rear of the Golan Heights for the 39th Reserve Battalion, intended to complete the 188th Brigade's order of battle.

The 164th Brigade, the Northern Command's fourth tank brigade, which had upgraded Centurion tanks, was reorganized and placed at a base in the lower Galilee. The Northern Command's 9th and 4th Mechanized Brigades, which had only an outdated Sherman tank battalion and mechanized infantry battalions on half-tracks, were transferred to the rear bases in the Haifa region. At the same time, a 212th Artillery Group of five battalions was moved forward to the Rosh Pina environs.

Moreover, tank ammunition was transferred from warehouses at the rear to the tank brigades' frontline emergency storage warehouses. The stock of ammunition on the frontline bases was increased by twenty percent and stood at 9,000 tons. The construction of "ammunition farms" near the emergency storage warehouses was planned, but the plans did not materialize prior to the war. Ammunition depots for tanks and artillery were also prepared in the heart of the Golan Heights.

In the East, new Bailey bridges were constructed over the Jordan River, parallel to the Bnot Yaakov Bridge and the Arik Bridge over the mouth of the Jordan River at the Sea of Galilee. Some 140 kilometers of new roads were paved from the brigades' warehouses to the Jordan River bridges and from them to the combat zones on the Golan Heights. The relocation of the warehouses and other activity shorted by as much as half the time needed to mobilize the brigades to deploy to the Golan Heights.

All the planned artillery positions were marked and measured by a national measuring network. "Exit points" intended to allow assault aircraft to operate in a missile-defended zone were marked in certain places on the Golan Heights under the authority of the command's artillery headquarters.

Artillery positions for routine security measures were dug, some of which included bunkers for combatants. Permanent lookouts were deployed at controlling sites all along the line and were used by the artillery. All the command's artillery units were patrolling the positions they were scheduled to occupy, as well as the lookouts where operational planning called for them to be deployed. An artillery ammunition depot of 7,000 assorted shells was established at the logistics base in Snobar in the Golan Heights to supply artillery ammunition during isolated incidents and combat days.

In addition, extensive engineering operations were undertaken to improve the defensive capabilities of the forces on the contact lines. These operations included the preparation of fifteen shelters, as well as many positions, and the construction of shooting platforms (ramps) for tanks in the controlling areas of the contact line and in the second line that controlled the anti-tank ditch. Engineering forces worked to deepen the anti-tank ditch and extend it to an overall length of about twelve kilometers, at the entrance to Quneitra, from Outpost 105 to Outpost 109 and the Rapid salient, and from Outpost 111 to Outpost 116. Some sections of the ditch were not completed due to a budget shortage. In the last week before the war broke out, landmines were set in lieu of the ditch work. The anti-tank trenches and minefields were intended to play a crucial role in delaying Syria's breakthrough force, averting, and halting it during the fighting.

In order to improve the command and control capabilities, and due to the sparse system of telephone landlines on the Golan Heights, the Northern Command began laying a new transmission cable and even managed to connect some of the land lines to it on the eve of the war. In addition to the frontline CCP (built on Tel Avital for command of the front and the command bunker) built in Nafah for "combat days," the command also began preparing a frontline command and control outpost for a possible war.

In August 1973, the regular and reserve forces of the command's communication battalion underwent training with an emphasis on the deployment, installation, and operation of the Command CCP. The battalion conducted training for the GOC's CCP using mainly soldiers in mandatory service and acquired extensive and ongoing experience in deploying stationary CCPs in the command's various sectors.

Parallel to all other activity, the command accelerated a plan to establish another division headquarters. Maj. Gen. (res.) Dan Lanner, who had served as Command Chief of Staff during the Six-Day War and commander of the armored forces in Sinai, was assigned to expedite the establishment of the 210th Division Headquarters, which had originally been scheduled to be built in 1974. The division's deputy commander, Col. Moshe (Brill) Bar-Kochva, assumed responsibility for the construction. The new division's headquarters was established at the David Base south of Haifa, which had served up to that point as the headquarters of the 36th Reserve Division, the only division headquarters in the Northern Command since 1954. The 36th Division headquarters, which took on emergency operational responsibility for the Golan Heights, was at that time moved closer to the Golan Heights.

The new division headquarters and its units were established on a tight schedule with increased support and involvement of all the staff officers and command branches. A large portion of the units in the division was built out of the existing units in the command's various alignments, including the command's artillery unit, a battalion of the command's engineering headquarters, logistics and communication units. A year before it was scheduled to operate, the division took part in the war within the IDF's order of battle.

OPERATIONAL PLANNING

CHAPTER 3

DURING APRIL–MAY 1973, AS part of the alert in response to warnings of a possible Egyptian-Syrian attack and after receiving detailed information about the Syrian plan of attack, the Northern Command carefully evaluated the Syrian enemy's possible modes of operation and updated its operative plans. Alongside the offensive plans that, according to Israel's defense doctrine, intended to move the war into enemy territory, GOC and the Operations Branch prepared a series of plans for the defensive gathering, deploying, and activating of forces against a possible Syrian attack. At the same time, there was increasing fear in the command's headquarters that the time of the advance warning, "promised" by the Intelligence Branch, had been significantly shortened.

According to intelligence gathered by G2 (Aman—the GHQ Intelligence Branch) from April 27, 1973, it was clear that the Syrian plan to capture the Golan Heights had been drilled in a Syrian headquarters exercise in December 1972. An attack by infantry divisions across the front, captured a strip of some 8–10 kilometers, followed by attacks the next morning carried out by an armored division on Quneitra and the Bnot Yaakov Bridge, a move intended to reach the Jordan River and complete the conquest of the Golan. At that time, the Northern Command estimated this would indeed be the Syrian plan, and viewed the Quneitra salient as the region in which the Syrians would focus their main efforts, due to the area's proximity to the central Golan and the Jordan River.

Intelligence officials in the GHQ and the command feared the Syrian Army's ability to advance its forces from its permanent bases to the emergency alignment and the line of contact over the course of a single night. They pointed out two main regions through which the second rank Syrian Armored Divisions might penetrate into the heart of the Golan Heights. These were the Quneitra salient in the northern Heights, and the Rapid salient in the south. Shortly before the war, Northern Command Intelligence assessed, based on topographical data and the enemy forces' deployment, the Syrians would make use of both salients at once but more so of the southern one. This would allow the Syrians a greater deployment and more flexible operation of armored forces: toward the west and south, blocking access to the Heights, and toward the center of the Golan Heights. At the same time, the GOC saw a major enemy effort in the Quneitra salient as the greater danger, since Quneitra was a more valuable target relatively easier to amass forces in the sector, given that the distance from Quneitra to the Jordan River bridges was shorter.

The command's defensive plans relied on the GHQ's assertion that Aman would provide advance warning before an enemy attack. This advance warning was meant to allow reserve forces to mobilize and quickly transfer to defensive fighting according to the *Sela* (Boulder) plan, which stipulated that two divisions with about 650 tanks would mobilize to face the Syrians on the Golan Heights within thirty-six hours. In case of a surprise attack, the basic premise determined that "the regular standing army—the armored forces on the Golan Heights along with Air Force aircrafts—will halt (the attack)."

The basic working premises for each of the command's three defensive plans *Hol Yam* (Sand Sea), *Gir* (Chalk), and *Sela* (Boulder) were that:

- The topographical structure of the Golan Heights allowed the Syrians to penetrate into Israeli territory at almost any point along the front, with considerable force, since there was no physical land obstacle that prevented such a breakthrough.
- There was no strategic depth on the Golan Heights that would allow a mobile defensive battle and division maneuvers while temporarily yielding the territory as obligated by the defensive mode of combat. This acknowledges the danger inherent in any retreat to Israel's north and its vital territories.
- The combat weapon was the tank, and due to the Syrian artillery advantage and the inefficiency of Israeli anti-tank weapons, the use of infantry soldiers must be reduced. RSM outposts would be controlled by minimal infantry forces, and their role would be to serve as the command's "eyes" and defend themselves.
- Until the arrival of all the forces allocated for defense, the regular forces, reinforced by up to two tank brigades, would maintain a firm defensive battle by mobile means on the line of outposts and ramps, and perform "armored fist" counterattacks.
- Since Israeli settlements existed on the Golan Heights, a defensive plan must take their existence and positions into account, as well as the need to evacuate them.
- The line of outposts on the front of the Golan Heights was intended, in each of the plans, to serve for only routine security missions and observation. Various other plans addressed the

possibility of major reinforcements or building additional defensive alignments around them. All the outposts were armored and equipped with the weapons required for their protection. At the same time, it was clear that they would be unable to withstand massive artillery fire and a direct assault by the Syrians' numerous armored forces.

- The Syrian advantage in everything related to the use of artillery—in both quantity and firepower—forced the planners to keep exposed infantry forces as far out of artillery range as possible. Since no system of armored outposts was constructed in the depth of the Golan Heights, infantry and mechanized infantry forces were not included in the preliminary alignment in the Heights, except at the armored frontline outposts.
- The Command Headquarters was aware of the fact that the Syrian SAM alignment from the Damascus district south of the border tied the Israel Air Force's hands in a defensive battle, and that the entire Heights would become a missile-defended zone. The *Srita* (Scratch) plan was intended for such an eventuality, and was crucial in halting a Syrian attack until the arrival of reserve forces.
- The Northern Command's operational plans were examined over the years and during the months of Blue and White alert. The GHQ did not conduct war games in a defensive layout on the Golan Heights like the *Eyal Barzel* (Iron Stag) war games in Sinai (the Southern Command sector), which included defensive maneuvers and transferring to offense on the Egyptian front. Instead, the GHQ postponed the planned war game to October 1973. Operational plans were discussed in the commanding staff's regular meetings and presented to the GHQ. The examination of the plans on April 26 and May 8 served as a substitute of sorts for the actual war game.
- The GHQ Chief of Staff summed up the discussions on April

1973, stating: "There's no method and no defense that guarantees it would not be broken through in any spot, but if there were a breakthrough anywhere it had to be handled immediately by concentrating tanks and armored forces. This is why I don't place any importance on an additional infantry line."

- The opening formation as it occurred in the Yom Kippur War had been already defined by the Chief of Staff in the summary of the *Eyal Barzel* (Iron Stag) war game in the Sinai sector in the summer of 1972. He stated that it was possible the IDF would not receive the promised advance warning by Aman, in which case the situation would reach "catastrophe" status. He decided that in such an event, Israel's goal should be to have 200 tanks in the Golan—at the time there were only 350 tanks on the Syrian side—and 300 tanks in the Sinai. In case of disaster, the GHQ Chief of Staff established, the fierce holding action would be performed by the regular forces along with the Air Force until the arrival of reserve forces.

It seems that when this was declared the Syrians had not yet deployed their SAM alignment in the front and the GHQ Chief of Staff did not foresee them doing so. The IAF prepared plans to attack the SAM alignments, assuming it would have sufficient time to do so, but also designed the *Srita* operative plan in case of "catastrophe." According to the plans, Israeli aircraft would strike concentrations of attacking forces by "standoff" and "sneak" attacks, at a low risk to the Israeli aircraft. The ascents toward the Heights from the Hula Valley and the Sea of Galilee were marked with access and attacks routes for aircraft.

Each of the Northern Command's defensive plans, detailed in the 36th Division's orders, could be carried out independently from a standby status based on the existing order of battle on the Golan Heights as part of routine security measures. The silent routine security forces deployed on the Golan Heights included two regular brigade HQs (820th Regional Brigade and 188th Armored Brigade) and the 334th Artillery Corps Battalion.[4] In each of the defensive plans, the front line was divided into two sectors of responsibility with the 820th Regional Brigade (or the 179th Armored Brigade) in the northern sector and the 188th Armored Brigade in the southern sector. Tel Fares and the Nachal Geshur region were made the southern controlling sites for the CCP and HQ respectively, while in the north, the CCP was set up at Tel Avital (Tel Abu Nida) and the HQ in the Kallaa region.

The first two plans intended to join the forces together, supply solutions for the protection of the Golan Heights against a possible small-scale Syrian attack, and even exploit an opening in one of the front's sectors:

***Hol Yam* (Sand Sea) Plan**: This plan for defense and counterattack was based on the regular order of battle alone, which was to include three tank battalions, ten artillery batteries, and the two infantry battalions holding the line's outposts. Deployment should take place within twenty-four hours of the order. This order of battle was recognized as sufficient for "combat days" needs on the Golan Heights.

***Gir* (Chalk) Plan**: This plan was based on the regular order of battle reinforced by reserve units that included two tank brigades, fifteen artillery batteries, and the two infantry battalions holding the line's outposts. According to the plan, the 36th Division was the headquarters responsible for the Golan Heights, divided between the 188th and the 820th Brigades. The plan operated two tank battalions to strengthen the front line, and the

4 See details in "Israeli Command Sectors and the Forces Under Their Command" at the end of Chapter 1.

main armored force was concentrated in two reduced-brigade groupings as a provision for counterattacks and reversals. The *Gir* plan was to be initiated within thirty hours of the reserve call-up. According to the standards of the time, this was the minimum plan that would protect the Golan Heights from a Syrian attack.

In case of an all-out war, the command prepared the ***Sela* (Boulder) plan**, which entailed the Northern Command's complete order of battle. According to the plan, which was intended to be implemented within thirty-six hours of the reserve call-up, the 36th Division would take responsibility for defending the entire Golan Heights using three brigades as well as exploit opportunities into Syrian territory. The new 210th Division, also composed of three brigades, was designed as a command reserve for both defensive and offensive missions. The plan, according to which the Northern Command had a relatively powerful armored force, would also allow for a quick transition from defensive combat to an offensive.

Alongside the defensive plans that were adjusted for three different opening scenarios, the command units also prepared the "Capital" order, whose main focus was the movement and deployment of tanks from their bases to the position on the line, chiefly in preparation for "combat days." This plan allowed regular forces to be deployed quickly along the line, even in case of a "catastrophe" (per the GHQ Chief of Staff) such as a war breaking out without sufficient warning.

The Capital plan called to reinforce the line of contact for war as well, since the 188th Brigade was meant to fight against attacking forces from the tank positions on the line of contact, which controlled the anti-tank ditches and the Syrian tanks' maneuvering area. In every plan, where the 188th Brigade's two tank battalions were positioned on the line of contact, company tank "fists" were left in each battalion sector. The artillery in the Golan included three to four batteries and was reinforced to eleven batteries ahead of combat days. The artillery was to advance its guns on the combat day in order to strike at deep targets, open anti-battery and any other fire needed, including firing to prevent the takeover of an outpost or the anti-tank ditch from being bridged.

Since the battle was expected to take place on the line of contact, the command had no detailed defensive plan for the "catastrophe" scenario to prevent enemy armor from crossing the anti-tank ditch or assault forces from penetrating the line. The *Hol Yam* and *Gir* plans were conceived as intermediate stages that expressed the rate of accumulating forces toward the basic defensive plan, *Sela*. The command planned to complete the accumulation of forces for the *Sela* plan by F-hour (the start of reserve forces mobilization) + thirty-six hours.

The command's logistic plan in the defensive battle initially rested on the logistic independence of the forces given the equipment they had on hand (the first 24–48 hours); an additional 24-hour period based on the equipment in the division; and after that, based on the command's maintenance alignment, the General Staff's frontline maintenance facilities, and the GHQ's supply chains.

Aside from the defensive plans, the Northern Command formulated various attack plans. The *Ben Gil North* plan, for example, was intended as a limited attack in the north on the Heights, while the *Ze'ev Aravot* (Coyote) plan dealt with a general offensive on the Golan Heights with an order of battle comprised of three divisions.

Preparations: Regular Service Forces-Air Force-Armored Corps

Chapter 4

DURING THE PERIOD OF alert in April–May 1973, the commanders realized that the positions of the Syrian Army's permanent bases and assembly areas allowed its forces to move into launch positions on the front line overnight, according to a predetermined plan, while maintaining radio silence. Therefore, the command's headquarters deduced, the possible period of advance warning that war had broken out had shortened significantly. Likewise, intelligence officials and commanders understood that an actual warning might only be received from visual sources, essentially aerial photo sorties and land-based surveillance, which would identify the movement of forces to the front and reveal the removal of camouflage nets from artillery batteries and tanks.

Preparations for Air Force Integration with Defensive Battles

At the beginning of the summer, the General Staff's G2 Research Department believed that the risk of an imminent outbreak of war was decreasing, and the possibility was consistently ruled out. However, an aerial photo sortie in July revealed initial signs of the construction of a new SAM alignment that was both denser and more mobile than the Egyptian one. The alignment constructed between Daraa and Dumeir contained some thirty sites for SAM batteries as well as integrating SA-6 missile batteries. These batteries were mobile enough to easily alter their deployment, increasing the chances they could survive aerial or artillery attacks.

The Northern Command GOC, who received the data from the command intelligence officer, analyzed the change and in discussions with the General Staff, he reported the resulting limitation on the Air Force's ability to act, which had been a crucial feature of the Golan Heights' defensive plan. The GOC stated that the IDF's ground-based alignment in the Golan was a "symbolic" one that depended on the Air Force to assist ground forces. He pointed out the change that had occurred in the sector and the condition created by the Air Force's need to attack the SAM anti-aircraft rockets before joining in a ground war. The operational changes necessitated by the defensive and offensive possibilities this alignment opened up for the Syrians were brought up in the general staff's meetings. Once it was agreed upon to undertake the precautionary measures obligated by this new alignment, it was also decided that a comprehensive exercise should be conducted to examine the integration of the Northern Command's artillery with the Air Force in paralyzing Syrian SAM batteries to a depth of approximately thirty-five kilometers from the borderline.

On the eve of the war, the alignment on the front included twenty-six missile batteries comprising fifteen mobile SA-6 batteries and eleven stationary batteries positioned in the Damascus basin. The Syrians had thirty-six missile batteries, and the front line was entirely a missile-defended zone. The Syrian alignment of missile batteries was backed up by a reinforced alignment of anti-aircraft gun batteries of various calibers, some guided by radar. The anti-aircraft missile and gun batteries effectively closed off the front's entire airspace to operational flight altitudes.

The reinforcement of the Syrian anti-aircraft alignment limited IDF Aerial Operations on the Golan Heights front. Only special sorties intended to ensure that intelligence regarding the Syrian alignment was updated were conducted on the front. There were several aerial photo sorties before fire opened, including aerial photographic coverage of the second line of defense. Low clouds were a hindrance.

The operational plans for attack and defense stated in general terms that the Air Force would assist in the preparation for an operation. It should be noted that attack orders were appeared as an outline and in a non-specific manner. No "target bank" was established for a preemptive strike (excluding artillery targets and stationary targets.)

Methods of utilizing the Air Force in case of a broad or a narrow attack were established in discussions that took place before the war. According to the IDF's *Sela* plan the following priorities were established for the provision of air support: attacking enemy batteries throughout the sector; providing close support for the Israeli forces during counterattacks; attacking enemy headquarters, CCPs and enemy lookouts; attacking enemy frontline armored brigades; and attacking enemy outposts.

In August 1973 the Air Force's operations department issued

a "situation assessment" manual that also established the following order of priorities in the use of aerial force: obtaining aerial superiority by destroying the enemy's air forces and missile alignments; participation in ground battles; attacking strategic targets; intelligence; combat transportation; transportation; evacuating casualties; and so on.

Throughout that period the Air Force designed operational plans and prepared written and organized operation orders in case of war that included: the *Tagar* (Challenge) operation plan for attacking the Suez Canal's missile alignment on the Egyptian front; the *Dugman* (Model) operation plan for attacking airfields and missile alignments on the Syrian front; the *Negicha* (Bunt) operation plan for attacking airfields; and the "Dominick" operation plan for attacking strategic targets deep inside Syrian territory.

Advance intelligence of 36 to 24 hours prior to the opening of fire was taken into consideration for the implementation of all orders for Air Force Operations. This time period allowed the Air Force to first obtain aerial superiority and only afterwards enter ground battles with full force. The Northern Command's operational orders (as well as in those of the Southern Command) called for aerial assistance to be provided only after aerial superiority was obtained.

The IAF Operations Department published the Srita plan for scenario that an enemy initiated war would break out requiring aerial assistance before aerial superiority was achieved. The Srita (Scratch) order addressed methods of employing the Air Force in a SAM missile-defended zone, planning pre- determined, permanent routes for regions where attacks were anticipated, including low-lying routes. The Srita order was only an outline, without predetermined targets for aerial attacks—except, as stated, for artillery batteries. The attack targets had to be determined naturally in the course of the war, wherein the Aerial

Operations Department would them to the squadrons according their priority.

Meanwhile, the Air Force developed the "slingshot" method of dropping bombs from a distance to make it feasible to attack targets in these regions. This method necessitated the establishment of "take aim" positions on controlling points in the Golan Heights according to which attack on possible targets was calculated.

The Northern Command's operational orders (as did those of the Southern Command) discussed using the Air Force for attacking targets in general terms only, without mentioning predetermined or specific targets of attack.

It should be noted that the Israel Air Force HQ gave the Srita order a low priority and viewed it as an unwelcome constraint that would monopolize the Air Force before aerial superiority was obtained and before the missile alignments were destroyed, which might hinder effectiveness of aerial attacks.

The Northern Command transferred targets including sectors and regions where the Syrians were expected to break through the Golan Heights to the Air Force Operations department. When gunfire began the targets were transferred to the 506th Aerial Control Unit 506th, which controlled the aircrafts in the region and was supposed to transmit the targets to them.

Readiness and Alert in the Armored Units

The 188th Division was the only regular armored unit in the Northern Command during this period. Its main mission was to serve as a response force that would immediately respond to a Syrian attack. Since the brigade regularly allocated one of its regular battalions for operational activity under command of the 820th Regional Brigade, which was in charge of the IDF outposts along the "Purple Line," its commanders and soldiers were highly practiced in the terrain of the Golan Heights, the enemy forces' characteristics, and standing orders for integrated combat by tanks and Purple Line outposts. This proficiency deepened through multiple training at the levels of platoon, company, and battalion.

In the year prior to the war the brigade also instituted a top-notch operational and administrative routine that garnered them first place in the IDF in most General Staff inspections.

Brigade commander Col. Aharon Peled (Fedale) and deputy brigade commander Lt. Col. Yossi Peled, who served before brigade commander Col. Yitzhak Ben Shoham and deputy brigade commander Lt. Col. David Israeli, instituted a routine of weekly inspections in the line's tank platoons, conducted by the brigade's complete staff. During these inspections, which the brigade commander and his deputy kept up in all conditions and in any weather, the platoons and the company commanders (after the staff officers had finished "giving them hell," each in his own field) trained for every conceivable operational situation.

In anticipation of "combat days" or a possible Syrian attack, the line of contact in the Golan Heights was organized into an integrated system composed of the 820th Regional Brigade and the 188th Armored Brigade tanks. A special emphasis was placed on turning the infantry combatants in the outposts, the tank crews intended to assist them, and the artillery batteries, into an integrated combat team that would operate at the high level of cooperation of an organic entity, which also had a separate communication network. Tank crews, gunners and commanders studied the sector facing them and targets in case of combat. Crews learned and memorized identification marks of Syrian AFVs, positions, and units. A frontline logistics system was also established, including tank ammunition depots in the rear of the ramps as well as fuel stores and casualty evacuation stations.

In the winter of 1972–1973 the brigade was involved in two "combat days" characterized by static fighting, in the course of which the brigade's tanks destroyed Syrian tanks. Therefore, the forces' training focused on the Capital plan, the master plan for "combat days," that required expertise in precision tank fire. Tank crews pored over all the routes to the positions by day and by night, and practiced joining up with the outposts in the day and at night. They also carried out simulated offensives into Syrian territory in the Golan training fields. All these exercises created a deep familiarity with the Golan Heights region among the tank crews. Crewmembers and commanders who failed the orientation and navigation tests were punished and even dismissed from their positions.

In July 1973 the brigade carried out a brigade-wide exercise, including its reserve battalion. The drill was based on a scenario of a Syrian attack on the central and southern Golan Heights and featured both defense and shifting to offense. The exercise was prepared and managed by 36th Division Commander Brig. Gen. Refael (Raful) Eitan and 179th Armored Brigade commander Col. Ran Sarig. The exercise included all of the brigade's units and was composed of two major stages:

- A methodical stage of defending the Golan Heights, in response to a Syrian offensive initiative, wherein the brigade integrated into the defensive plan of the 36th Division that had been mobilized following early intelligence about the anticipated attack.
- An offensive activity stage in the depths of Syria, which was also the stage exercised in practice, in which the brigade advanced along routes from the Btecha Valley toward the open fields in the Ramat Magshimim region.

The brigade's high level of preparedness revealed itself on a summer night before the war. A Syrian tank operator got into an argument with his commander and stormed toward Outpost 111 in his tank, making the whole sector jump to its feet. The brigade commander, who received notice that "Syrian forces were advancing toward Tel Fares," launched the brigade to the line. In less than half an hour the brigade's CCP was at Tel Fares to control the incident, which wasn't far from inflaming the entire Golan Heights. Fortunately, thanks to the level-headedness of Maj. Gen. "Haka," who instructed the brigade commander to exercise extreme restraint, the incident ended with the capture of the Syrian tank operator, who was transferred to Israel for interrogation.

After other successful "combat days" in the winter, the orderly transfer of the 39th Battalion and the Command Headquarters from the Pilon Base to the Golan Heights in the spring, battalion exercises and a large brigade exercise in the summer, the brigade was well prepared on the eve of the Yom Kippur War.

THE FINAL ROAD TO WAR

CHAPTER 5

When the reinforcement of the Syrian SAM alignment in the Golan Heights was first noticed, the Command Headquarters became aware that the Syrians might launch a significant movement of forces without further warning. This awareness was shared chiefly by Northern Command GOC Maj. Gen. Yitzhak Hofi and intelligence officer Lt. Col. Hagai Mann, who arrived at the command in August, replacing senior intelligence officer Lt. Col. Yehoshua "Shiea" Bar-Masada. They studied possibilities for a Syrian war plan, as they were known to intelligence sources, and discussed the requisite responses.

The Command Headquarters began requesting reinforcement for the order of battle and weaponry in the Golan Heights. The GHQ, including the intelligence branch, stuck to the assessment that Syria did not plan to launch an all-out war without Egypt, and that Egypt, for its part, was not ready at that stage to go to war. Aman justified the unusual Syrian activity as fear of an Israeli attack while the massive reinforcement was, in their opinion, intended for defensive purposes.

Aerial photographs of additional Syrian preparations on the front were viewed and analyzed in August. These included the construction of new positions for heavy artillery and SAM batteries on the Golan Heights front, as well.

Command intelligence knew, from the familiarity of many years, that a thinning out of Syrian forces in the outposts and their relocation to permanent bases and training fields in the rear was to be anticipated in the winter. But lo and behold, the start of September saw additional reinforcement instead, first of the artillery and later of the anti-tank alignment, the infantry, and the Armored Corps. Observation reports testified to the reinforcement of the Syrian outposts. Tracks of Syrian patrols were spotted along the border and in the Golan Heights minefields. In addition, reports were received regarding civilian emergency preparation in Syria. The examination of all the accumulating data and its assessment brought the GOC and staff officers to a state of increased alertness and readiness.

A planned offensive exercise by the Syrian Air Force was reported on September 10. Taking an aerial photo of the exercise and the next day identified comprehensive reinforcement of the Syrian Army's alignment near the front. The reinforcement comprised of armored vehicles and artillery, and also included positions for the deployment of 180mm guns and 240mm mortars. Later on, bridging equipment and breaking through gear were noted being moved up into the Golan Heights sector.

During September, the command ordered increased alertness in its sector and a scrupulous debriefing of the observations alignment. The command repeated its demand to reinforce the regular alignment of forces in the Golan Heights. At the same time, orders for an offensive operation by the 210th Division were issued for the first time—Operation Karchon (Glacier), intended to drive forces toward Syria in a flanking maneuver through the Beqaa Valley in Lebanon.

On the morning of September 13, the Air Force executed an aerial photo sortie along the northern Syrian coast. This was one of many aerial photo sorties carried out in the year prior to the war. The Syrians, as was their wont, launched interception jets to patrol over the airports and did not interfere with the photographing mission. After the operation, however, when the Israel Air Force jets were headed back, the Syrians attempted to intercept the photographing aircraft. The escort jets turned toward them and a dogfight developed wherein eight Syrian MiG-21 jets were shot down and an IAF Mirage was hit and its pilot fell into the sea. Rescue planes were directed to the drop zone, but the Syrians were patrolling the area and attempting to rescue their pilot and capture the Israeli pilot. Interception planes were once again directed to the rescue area, another dogfight developed, and four additional MiG-21 jets were shot down. Thus aerial superiority was obtained in the rescue area and Israeli planes rescued the pilot who had been shot down, as well as the Syrian.

On that day alert levels were increased and the Northern Command prepared for a possible unusual Syrian activity. The Syrians continued the accelerated reinforcement of their front-line alignments, but the intent of the reinforcement was unclear. The commanders adopted Aman's interpretation, which stated that the alignment deployed was of a defensive nature and part of the response to the dogfight. Aman essentially ignored the fact that reinforcement of the Syrian alignment along the border had begun as early as August. It was also expected that the Syrians would respond to the attack on their Air Force in one of the following manners: aerial attacks; bombardment of settlements and outposts; positioning ambushes for attacking vehicles moving along main routes in the Heights; or a surprise attack on a civilian settlement or military base in the Golan Heights.

On September 17, the GHQ held a discussion regarding the termination of the "Kachol Lavan" alert level. The Northern Command representatives asked to reinforce the artillery alignment in the Heights following the reinforcement of the Syrian line with artillery batteries and SAM batteries and in light of restrictions on IAF jets' freedom of movement. Representatives of the Northern Command demanded that the alignment be reinforced by four batteries, including four heavy 175/203mm guns. With the GHQ's approval, the Golan Heights were reinforced with a 175mm battery from the 55th Battalion in Sinai, whose soldiers were flown in and equipped with guns from the Northern Command's Reserve Battalion, based in the Pilon Base. The main objective of the long-range guns was to strike Syrian missile batteries and assist Air Force jets in obtaining aerial control and superiority.

On September 22, another aerial photo sortie was conducted that showed that the Syrian Army was deployed in a full emergency alignment on the front of the Golan Heights. G2's Research Department assessed this deployment, as well, as a defensive one. The Northern Command Intelligence officer, who was aware of the Syrian activity, saw it as a telling sign and as preparation for possible offensive activity. His fears increased. His assessments were backed up by the GOC but not accepted by G2's Research Department.

On September 24, during a GHQ meeting intended to present a strategic assessment for the coming years, Northern Command GOC Maj. Gen. Yitzhak Hofi strayed from the topic. The GOC expressed his concern regarding the dangerous situation that had developed in the Golan Heights following the reinforcement of the Syrian alignment by an umbrella of efficient SAM, which limited the chances of receiving prior warning of offensive actions. The GOC described the "at least potential" threat which the Northern Command would find difficult to preempt. To illustrate the problem, he pointed out a number of facts:

- The Syrians moved from their permanent alignment to positions in the front and returned unbeknownst to the command and Aman, a fact that proved that the warning system in the north, largely dependent on aerial photographs, was insufficient.
- The warning period for the Air Force was shorter in the north than it was in the other sectors. It was easier for the Syrian jets to infiltrate and attack targets in the rear, including military bases and airports.
- The Syrian surface-to-surface FROG rockets threatened urban centers in the Galilee.
- Following the restrictions on the Israel Air Force's activities due to the deployment of the Syrian SAM alignment, the order of battle in the Golan Heights was inadequate for defense.
- The reinforcement of the Syrian Army was greater than the parallel process occurring in Egypt.

In summing up, the GOC added that even though Egypt was, and continued to be, the main enemy, in the event of war the first step that must be taken was to neutralize Syria's ability to attack. The very least needed to achieve this purpose was to target the Syrian Air Force first. The GHQ Chief of Staff maintained his position that the Syrians were incapable of capturing the Golan Heights, and that the IDF were able to receive sufficient warning regarding "the region, without which war cannot be launched." In the summary of this discussion Minister of Defense Moshe Dayan did not portray Maj. Gen. Hofi as arousing **panic**. On the contrary, he ordered an additional discussion of the issue before Rosh Hashanah—the Jewish New Year, which occurred on September 27, 1973).

On September 25, Jordanian King Hussein initiated a meeting with Prime Minister Golda Meir and notified her that the Syrians were "in a launch position for a war against Israel" in which both Syria and Egypt would participate. Command GOC Maj. Gen. Hofi and intelligence officer Lt. Col. Hagai Mann were not informed of this and did not receive this cautionary information.

An additional discussion was held on September 26, Rosh Hashanah eve, attended by the Minister of Defense and his assistant; the GHQ Chief of Staff and his deputy; the head of Aman and the Northern Command GOC. The warning given by King Hussein the previous night was not mentioned. During the discussion Aman presented information that the Egyptians were preparing for a large-scale exercise while the Syrians had completed the emergency alignment of three mechanized divisions on the first line of defense, comprising the majority of the armored reserves and all of the Division artillery. It was also discovered that the 47th Armored Brigade based in northern Syria was scheduled to move into the Golan Heights region. The information regarding the movement of the 47th Tank Brigade from Hama to the Golan Heights reached the command intelligence officer, but its significance as a warning sign for the preliminary stages of war, which had been known to G2's Research Department since June 1972, was not reported to the Northern Command Intelligence officer. In addition (though there was no report of this), the possibility that the second line of defense had also been occupied by the Syrian forces was brought up. Thus, Aman attempted to ground its assessment that Syria was preparing for defense.

In the summary of the discussion, it was determined that the Heights were to be reinforced with an additional regular force. That day a Northern Command technical CCP was deployed in the Nafah Base bunker, intended to provide frontline control of local events in a "combat day" format.

With the approval of the General Staff and despite the optimistic assessment by G2, the order of battle in the Golan Heights was reinforced that same day, Rosh Hashanah Eve. The reinforcement included the 55th Artillery Corps Battalion headquarters with an additional battery of 175mm long-range SPGs, and the 77th Tank Battalion Headquarters from the 7th Brigade with two Centurion tank companies. One of them, Operational Company I, from the 82nd Battalion.

The forces were flown in from their bases in the Sinai desert and were equipped with guns and tanks from the Northern Command's frontline emergency storage warehouses in the Pilon and Jordan bases. The 77th Battalion was equipped at the "Jordan" base with tanks from the 39th Battalion, the 188th Brigade's Reserve Battalion. Its companies, under the command of Lt. Col. Avigdor Kahalani, convened as a reserve force near the Nafah Base in the central Golan Heights. The tank crews and commanders began an immediate and intensive study of the region, including access routes to the outposts and firing ramps controlling the border crossings.

Along with the 77th Battalion, the 7th Brigade's commander Col. Avigdor (Yanush) Ben Gal ascended the Heights with his staff officers and under the instruction of the brigade's intelligence officer they studied the territory and the enemy well. Up to that point the brigade, defined as General Staff reserves, was engaged in planning and exercising on various fronts, mainly in Sinai, and its teams were trained in towing the Roller Bridge toward the Suez Canal. Since 1972 the brigade had also prepared for possible operations in the Golan and in Lebanon. Brigade units were occasionally taken up to the Golan Heights as part of routine security activities and alerts.

Following the discussion Minister of Defense Moshe Dayan, who was chiefly concerned by the dangers posed to civilian settlements, visited the Golan Heights with his assistants. IDF GHQ Chief of Staff Lt. Gen. David Elazar joined the tour later. During the tour the defense minister received reports from the GOC regarding the digging of the anti-tank ditch and the deployment of minefields in the front. The GOC also described the current alignment of the Syrian forces and expressed his concerns regarding the way in which the command might receive warning of possible Syrian activity. The GOC went on to describe the deployment of regular forces in the Heights following their reinforcement:

- Two infantry battalions in the front line outposts.
- Five tank companies on the line and three more companies concentrated in the rear (including two tank companies from the 77th Battalion of the 7th Brigade, from which the battalion commander planned to construct three reduced companies).
- Five artillery batteries: two 160mm self-propelled mortar batteries, a 155mm SPG battery, and two 175mm SPG long-range batteries from the 55th Battalion.
- A MAR-290 surface-to-surface long-range rocket unit to be positioned in the posts at night.

At the end of the tour the defense minister met with representatives of the settlements, then with journalists, at Ein Zivan, and concluded that "there [was] no special reason to perceive a deterioration in the situation, but nothing had occurred which would allow us to relax and weaken our diligence." The reinforcement on the eve of Rosh Hashanah, and the publication of the defense minister's statement regarding his concern, served as testament to the impression the GOC's warning had made on the minister and the GHQ Chief of Staff.

Around that same time, the GOC ordered measures of alert, including doubling the tank force on the line by dividing the Heights between two battalions from the 188th Brigade. In each sector, a tank company was established as a reserve force. The 53rd Battalion of the 188th Brigade was recalled from leave. On that day, a battery of MAR-290 surface-to-surface long-range missiles was brought to the Hermon region.

The Syrians continued reinforcing their alignments on the front lines of the first defensive strip. In several places, observers noticed that the Syrians had placed tank platoons in front of possible breakthrough areas into the Golan Heights. Two squadrons were transferred to airfields closer to the front.

When the holiday passed the alert was cancelled but the command staff remained fearful. On the evening of September 30 an additional situation assessment was conducted by the GHQ Chief of Staff. In this discussion as well, when it was stated that the Syrian Army has completed its emergency alignment along the two defensive strips, Aman determined that Syria's aim was defensive. The assertion that Egypt and Syria would not go to war was voiced once again. At this time the command intelligence had no information regarding the Syrian forces' seizure of the second defensive strip.

The GOC, who was present in the discussion, maintained that an immediate intelligence solution was required in order to provide warning at night, as well, and added that he would like to see a full additional tank brigade in the Golan Heights. The GOC stressed once again that in this new reality the Syrians must be neutralized in case of attack, *before* the Egyptian Army was neutralized. The commander of the Air Force agreed with the GOC regarding the need to change priorities and agreed that the jets would be directed against Syria first.

On the night between September 30 and October 1, the 179th Tank Brigade, the command's "rapid mobilization" brigade, performed a recruitment exercise in its emergency storage warehouses.

On that night, as soon as it got dark, the Syrian Army

mobilized numerous convoys on several routes within its territory, more than on previous nights. This phenomenon of convoy movements at dark "with convoy lights" had begun a few nights earlier and there was no explanation for it. The command intelligence officer supposed that this was either logistical backup for the reinforced alignment or activity meant to accustom the IDF to routine increased activity on the front. The Command Intelligence's feeling that a Syrian attack was approaching increased. The GOC received continuous reports regarding Syrian activity, as did Branch 5 of the Aman Intelligence Directorate's Research department. The command intelligence officer took several steps: he prepared and debriefed an aerial scout from the command intelligence and coordinated a survey and observation flight for the next day at first light; two observation teams of six reserve soldiers from the command intelligence's long-range observation unit were called up for reserve duty "to reinforce observations in the RSM outposts"; the Mount Hermon outpost was reinforced by field NCOs from the command intelligence department and from the regional brigade's intelligence; in coordination with Branch 5 of the Aman Research department; an aerial photo sortie was ordered from a fighter jet; and the 820th Regional Brigade's intelligence officer, Maj. Moshe Temler, received orders to personally brief the RSM outposts about increased vigilance to identify the destination of the Syrian convoys.

As stated, the head of Aman Research Branch 5, Lt. Col. Avi Yaari, called the command's intelligence officer at his home October 1 at 04:00 and reported the warning that had reached the Aman Research department "...that a good and reliable source that you (the Northern Command Intelligence officer) are unfamiliar with stated that at dawn this morning the Egyptians will launch a war and cross the Canal and the Syrians will join them." Lt. Col. Avi Yaari claims that he also told the

Northern Command Intelligence officer to "wake the command up."

It seems Lt. Col. Yaari was unaware of the fact that the Northern Command had already been in a state of peak tension and alert, and that a week earlier Maj. Gen. Hofi had demanded tank and artillery reinforcement for the Golan Heights, basing hid demand on an assessment by the command intelligence of the enemy's situation and against the position of the Aman Research department.

It was actually reasonable to expect the Aman Research department to "wake up" upon receiving the announcement. A great deal of valuable and instructive information was concentrated at the Aman Research department, but Aman did not change its assessments and continued claiming, persistently and blindly, that the Syrian Army's aim was defensive, in spite of King Hussein's warning on September 25, the arrival of the 47th Tank Brigade to the Golan Heights, and foreign intelligence assessments from September 29, which were not transferred to the command intelligence.

The notice was in accordance with the events that took place in the Golan Heights region, and particularly the enemy activity on the night between September 30 and October 1, events that were believed by the command intelligence officer to be a Syrian attack preparation. The command intelligence officer immediately transmitted the news over the phone to the GOC Maj. Gen. Hofi, who was, at that time, attending the 179th Brigade's recruitment exercise. In light of this information, GOC Hofi decided to make use of the planned surprise recruitment exercise and place an additional force in emergency readiness. Maj. Gen. Hofi asked for the approval of G3 Operations (the GHQ Operations Department) to keep the whole brigade on alert, but as dawn lit the sky and war did not break out, he was only given authorization to keep the 96th Battalion tanks fully equipped. The battalion remained mobilized for two additional days and was released only after Aman thought that war was not expected. The battalion's tanks remained in the emergency storage warehouses, fully equipped and armed. At the same time, following the decrease of artillery alertness in the Golan Heights by G3 Operations, the MAR-290 Unit returned from its positions in the north to the base in the center of the country.

An hour after the notice was transmitted to the GOC, the command's G3 officer, Lt. Col. Uri Simchoni, who was with the Command GOC at the recruitment exercise, called the intelligence officer and said that G3 Operations, whom he had called with a request to confirm the mobilization of reserves and reinforcement of the Golan Heights, were unaware of any warning or notice that the war was going to break out in the morning. In the meantime, based on the command intelligence officer information and assessment, orders were issued by the command G3 officer regarding how to act in the field.

On October 1 at 07:00, the assistant to the head of the Aman Research department, Brig. Gen. Arieh Shalev, called the command intelligence officer and angrily asked him, "Why are you spreading panic in the command?" Without giving the command intelligence officer a chance to explain the situation and events, Brig. Gen. Shalev declared, "I'll summon you for an inquiry."

The GHQ convened for the weekly meeting that day. Once again the GHQ Chief of Staff used the term "catastrophe" when he ordered that the Golan be reinforced by up to a full tank brigade if there was news of a Syrian intent to attack. He added, "These are the orders of magnitude, meaning, a force that can prevent catastrophe, not a force that can prevent a one-time surprise..." The Northern Command GOC once again demanded that the mobilized tanks forces be increased.

The discussion was summed up by the GHQ Chief of Staff,

and he ordered "an immediate alert against Syria" for fear of a "one-time eruption" in which the Syrians might exploit openings or carry out an attack, which would be eradicated by the IDF within 24 to 48 hours. After the discussion, the GHQ Chief of Staff instructed his deputy, Maj. Gen. Israel Tal ("Talik"), to strengthen the alignment in the Golan Heights, including the return of the MAR-290 rocket launcher unit.

On that day, the forces on the Golan Heights were reinforced by the 405th SPG regular battalion from the 146th Division's 213th Artillery Group, under the command of Maj. Arieh Mizrachi, who came up from his permanent base at the Bilu Base. The 405th regular battalion was equipped with M-109 155mm self-propelled guns. The battalion went up to the Golan Heights and deployed in positions in the center and south of the Golan Heights. The battalion commander was later appointed the RAC of the 7th Armored Brigade.

Two additional tank companies from the 77th Battalion, equipped on the 179th Brigade's fully geared tanks from the reserve storage warehouses in Pilon, also went up to the Heights. The reinforcement completed the tank inventory in the Golan Heights with 113 tanks. A day later the Heights were reinforced by two field engineering companies brought into position and bolstered minefields on the front line. At the same time, the GOC ordered to increase alert and observations and prepare for a Syrian attack or attempt to exploit an opening.

The Israel Air Force doubled its aerial photo sorties and photographed the Syrian alignment along the front line and within its depth on October 2, as well as on the 4th and 5th of the month. Additional reinforcement of the Syrian alignment could be observed by the sorties, particularly on the artillery alignment, which was also being moved forward. The 47th Armored Brigade, which arrived from Hama, was positioned in the south of the Golan Heights (in the region of the 5th Division).

Likewise, command intelligence aerial photograph interpreters had already noted, based on the October 2 aerial photo sortie, that two armored divisions had left their permanent bases. The command intelligence officer estimated that the 1st and 3rd Armored Divisions (about 450 tanks) were moving toward assembly and deployment areas, and, therefore, the Syrian's intentions were offensive. Based on the same photographs the Aman Research department interpreters determined that the armored divisions were deployed in a second defensive strip alignment and Aman held to its stance that the Syrian intentions remained defensive. Even after it was made clear that the alignments in the second defensive strip were not occupied, the Aman Research department's Branch 5 continued to maintain the position that the Syrian Army's intent was defensive.

On October 2, the command intelligence officer was summoned to a meeting with his Brig. Gen. in order to clear up the "...panic he spread in the command..." —in other words, to be reprimanded by the head of the Aman Research department's assistant and the head of Aman. In this meeting, attended by Researce Branch 5 head Lt. Col. Avi Yaari, Brig. Gen. Arieh Shalev clarified that the report transferred to the Northern Command Intelligence officer by Lt. Col. Yaari was an "exercise report" related to the "Tahrir 41" exercise that took place in the Egyptian Army on October 1, and had no bearing on the activity taking place in the field, certainly not in Syria. Brig. Gen. Arieh Shalev added that Lt. Col. Yona Bandman head of Branch 6 (Egypt) was supposed to call the command intelligence officer and clarify that this was an exercise report—something that "for some reason" was never done.

The command intelligence officer emphasized to Brig. Gen. Arieh Shalev and Lt. Col. Avi Yaari that his assessment differed from the assessment of the G2 Research department as expressed in Aman's compilations, and that the Syrian Army forces in the front strip and the massive reinforcement in artillery and SAMs, the identification of bridging equipment in the Golan Heights and other revealing signs, showed that the threat of attack was immediate. According to his statement, "The notice was complementary to that night's activity and was in accordance with the events. The head of Branch 5, who had only 30 hours earlier told the command intelligence officer to "shake up the command," did not participate in the conversation at all.

At the end of the meeting the command intelligence officer was under the impression that his words had been disregarded, taken apathetically and lightly shaken off. Brig. Gen. Shalev stressed once again that there were no signs indicating that Syria was headed for war, and the Northern Command Intelligence officer ended the meeting by stating, "**The signs attesting to Syria's inclination for attack are finished**," meaning that no additional signals were necessary since the Syrian Army had completed its preparations for war.

The difference of opinion between the command intelligence and the Aman Research department was expressed in a phone call in which the GOC pointed out the significance of dispatching hundreds of tanks from the 1st and 3rd Syrian armored divisions from their bases to the assistant of Aman Research department head Brig. Gen. Arieh Shalev. While the command claimed that the two divisions were moving toward the assembly and staging areas, Aman claimed that the staging was for defensive purposes of Damascus and the defensive alignments in the second defensive strip that were occupied by Syrian forces. Though Aman retracted the false data, it did not change its assessments and repeatedly claimed that the Syrian inclination was defensive.

It was learned from other sources that starting Friday, October 5, the villagers near the border were not allowed to work their fields. Though the report pertained to the 5th Division sector, command intelligence interpreted this as an order that applied to all the villages near the border. Aman Research department's Branch 5 reports didn't carry any reference to this warning.

On Thursday October 4, the GHQ Chief of Staff and his deputy held a meeting with the GOC and the command's staff officers on ways to improve fortifications and obstacles on the Golan Heights lines before winter. The possibilities of adding minefields, building additional tank ramps, and extending the anti-tank trench were brought up, as well as the possibility of flooding areas with the Golan Heights' reservoir waters. In the evening of that same day the command intelligence officer updated the GOC and reported information from a surveillance source regarding the speedy evacuation of Soviet citizens and their families from Egypt and Syria. This information about preparations to evacuate advisors' families matched up with all the other information coming in, and was assessed by the command intelligence officer as a warning and a clear sign that war was imminent.

On October 4, Mossad head Maj. Gen. (res.) Zvi Zamir was summoned for a meeting with a senior agent in Europe. The alarm code was for a war alert. The next day (October 5), and following a discussion with the GHQ Chief of Staff, a Level C alert was declared in the IDF at about 11:00, cancelling all leaves and issuing a No. 2 “Confirm” order which included operational orders for deployment and also indicated readiness for an all-inclusive public mobilization of reserve forces. On that day and on Saturday morning all the unnecessary soldiers were transported from the Golan Heights, including military governance soldiers and the UN Liaison Unit.

The command initiated comprehensive reinforcement and deployment of regular forces. The 7th Brigade Command which had planned to go down to the Sinai the evening before, was ordered to go up to the Golan Heights with all its units. The brigade's command, along with the 82nd Tank Battalion's commanders and teams under the command of Maj. Haim Barak, and the 77th Battalion from the Armored Corps School, where the Armored Corps School guides and teams from the 500th Brigade were stationed, under the command of Lt. Col. Meshulam Rates, were flown north to the Mahanayim airfield—near the Golan Heights. The teams were equipped with additional tanks from the 179th Brigade's emergency reserve storage units, and went up to reinforce the armored force on the Golan Heights. The 7th Brigade's 75th Mechanized Infantry Battalion, which included the brigade's reconnaissance company, was driven north, with the APCs on carriers, and convened in the "Jordan" base area. The recruits company was driven to the "Pilon" base to assist in the preparation of the vehicles for war. The 77th Battalion was advanced to the Nafah junction on the same day.

The 188th Armored Brigade's 53rd Tank Battalion was brought back from the recreational base and convened in the south of the Golan. The 188th Brigade, under the command of Col. Yitzhak Ben Shoham, was deployed in two battalion sectors, and the sectors' border was south of Outpost 110. The 74th Battalion commander took two companies from the 53rd Battalion under his command and transferred his companies on the line to the command of 53rd Battalion commander Maj. Oded Erez.

On the morning of October 6, the 74th Battalion's tanks were deployed along the line under the command of Lt. Col. Yair Nafshi. Company H under the command of Lt. Eyal Shacham was in Mas'ade and in outposts 104 and 105; Company F under the command of Captain Avi Runis was at Jukhader and in outposts 114 and 116; Company G under the command of Lt. Uriel Akavia was at Hushniya. The operational command of the 74th

Battalion was located in Mas'ade (the battalion's administrative base was in Nafah).

The 53rd Battalion's tank companies under the command of Maj. Oded Erez deployed with: Company C under the command of Lt. Uzi Urieli in Hushniya; Company B under the command of Maj. Avner Landau at Waset junction; Company A under the command of Captain Zvi Rak at Quneitra. The operational command of the 53rd Battalion was located in Hushniya (the battalion's administrative base was in Aleika, where the brigade's main permanent headquarters was also located).

No changes were made in the deployment of the brigade's forces along the line on the morning of October 6, mainly so as not to "heat up the sector." Thus a situation was created wherein two 53rd Battalion companies were located in the northern Golan Heights (from Outpost 104 in the north to Outpost 110 south of Quneitra) under the command of the 74th Battalion. On the other hand two 74th Battalion companies were located in the south of the Golan Heights (from Outpost 110 in the north to Outpost 117 east of Ramat Magshimim) under the command of the 53rd Battalion. Mount Shifon (Tel Abu Khnzir) served as a rear boundary between the two battalions.

The artillery battalion soldiers and officers from the Artillery Corps school (Training Base No. 9) were flown in, equipped with 155mm SPGs from the Pilon command warehouses, and quickly departed to take positions in the south and center of the Golan Heights.

About 200 ammunition shells were transferred to positions where artillery units were deployed and either piled on the ground or left on board the ammunition trucks. An alternative was prepared for each position, and the transfer from one to the other was practiced. The units also patrolled access routes between the positions and the ammunition base in Snobar to make the reinforcement of positions with ammunition possible, if the need arose.

The command also issued warnings for mobilization that put the logistics into motion among both the general staff and field ranks. The logistic preparations for the forces on the line included loading various kinds of ammunition, preparing munitions departments, and deploying the frontline medical alignment. In the tank battalions five half-tracks were loaded with ammunition and five were loaded with fuel. The inventory levels maintained by the regular brigades ensured logistical independence for at least 24 to 48 hours.

In the afternoon of October 5, the Northern Command CCP was deployed in the Nafah regional brigade's bunker alongside the 820th Regional Brigade's CCP, whose command was transferred on that day from Col. Tzuri Sagi to Col. Zvi Bar. Starting Friday afternoon the GOC, the G3 officer, the intelligence officer, the HAC, the command's communication officer and additional officers all operated from the Nafah CCP. The frontal command outpost at Mount Knaan was scheduled to open only after the CCP's reserve soldiers arrived.

On October 5 at 14:30, the commander of the Air Force Maj. Gen. Benjamin (Benny) Peled convened a commanders forum in which he updated and stressed that in his estimation, a war was about to break out. In this forum he even stressed that if the Syrians launched a war on the front and broke through the IDF line in the Golan Heights, where forces were meager, the Air Force would be called in to attack at the northern front even before the SAM artillery alignment did. It was also stated that the Syrian SAM alignment was to be attacked once approval was given.

The command instructed its forces to prepare for possible Syrian action. In the commanders briefing that night, Northern Command GOC Maj. Gen. Yitzhak Hofi notified the brigade commanders that an artillery "combat day" with Syria might break out the next day. Two battalions from the 188th Brigade and additional forces already on the Golan Heights would participate in the ensuing combat. Another scenario he predicted was a Syrian attempt to exploit an opening through the Quneitra salient to capture the city of Quneitra or through the Rapid—Qudna salient toward Tel Fares.

The 188th Brigade reinforced by the 77th Battalion was placed on alert for local counterattacks. The 7th Brigade, whose forces had not yet completed their ascent to the Golan Heights, was placed on alert as the main counterattack force. The counter attacks under the code name CABARET were planned to prioritize the Quneitra salient, the Rapid salient, the "Petroleum Road" and the region of outposts 104-105 in the north, all according to the Syrian attack effort.

On the night of October 5–6 the head of the Mossad, who flew abroad for this purpose, received confirmation that war was indeed about to break out. On October 6 at 04:30, the GHQ Chief of Staff received notice that an Arab attack (Egyptian-Syrian) was to commence on that day at 18:00.

On Yom Kippur, October 6 at 05:00, the GOC called the intelligence officer into his room and reported that the head of the Mossad had transferred a notice during the night that, "The Egyptians and Syrians will launch an attack against Israel today at 18:00." The GOC added that he was on his way to attend a General Staff meeting, going by a light plane that was awaiting him at the Mahanayim airfield. Before departing the GOC instructed the G3 officer to prepare "order groups" in Nafah ahead of his return from the meeting with the General Staff.

The command intelligence officer conducted a phone inspection with his assistant at the Command Headquarters in Nazareth which made it evident that no warning or notice had been received through intelligence channels. In accordance with the information delivered to him by the GOC, the intelligence officer instructed his deputy to undertake all preparatory actions necessary to supply intelligence aides such as maps and aerial photographs to the units expected to be mobilized.

By October 5, the Command CCP began receiving reports of unusual Syrian activity. These included reports of tank movements, removal of camouflage nets, and other diverse activity. An aerial photo sortie from October 5, which was only deciphered at dawn on October 6, revealed that the Syrian alignment on the front had been strengthened. The photos revealed additional heavy artillery battalions—some of them at a range of six kilometers from the border in positions covering the whole Golan Heights and its access routes. The sortie also revealed a 240mm heavy mortar battalion intended to crush the line's outposts.

On the afternoon of October 5, Aman received a report stating that Soviet advisors in Syria and Egypt had been evacuated because warlike activity was about to erupt in the region. This warning was not transferred by Aman to the command intelligence officer, who was already in the CCP in Nafah. In an immediate military compilation distributed on October 6 at 03:40, the G2 Research department continued its attempt to establish a situation report wherein Syria was not headed for an attack on Israel. According to the compilation, "What stands out in the Syrian alignment along the first defensive strip, as pointed out in the current AP, is an alignment at a high degree of battle alert. It is difficult for us to determine whether this relates to this strip alone, since we do not have an image of the alignment along the second defensive strip—where the armored divisions should be deployed."

At 07:15, the GHQ Chief of Staff held a discussion with the GOCs and branch commanders. The head of Aman described the Arab plan of attack. In the Golan Heights, he said, the infantry brigades would attack all along the border to a depth of six to eight kilometers, followed by the infantry divisions' mechanized and armored brigades at night. At dawn the armored divisions would be aimed toward the Jordan River.

The GHQ Chief of Staff recommended that the IAF attack the Syrian Air Force in a preemptive strike (weather conditions made an attack on the missile alignment at the front impossible). This was approved by the GHQ Chief of Staff, but was subject to approval by the political echelon. The attack was planned for 11:00, and then postponed to 12:00. The jets were fueled and armed accordingly, squadrons were briefed and the targets were established. Everything was ready for government approval. But in the hours before noon, following a government meeting a preemptive strike on the Syrian Air Force was not approved.

That morning the 36th Division headquarters' technical CCP also arrived in Nafah, under the command of Brig. Gen. Refael (Raful) Eitan, who was scheduled to take command of the Golan Heights. Doctors were stationed in combat units and frontal observation officers from the artillery units took controlling positions in the Hermon outposts, in the 105th Outpost in Hermonit and in Outpost 110. Battalion commanders from the 55th artillery battalions and the Training Base No. 9 Battalion were positioned on Tel Fares and Tel Avital. A main lookout for the regional brigade including the 820th Brigade's assistant intelligence officer, Captain Asher Klichman (Sadan), was also positioned at Tel Hermonit; the outpost at Tel Avital was reinforced by a force from the Golani Brigade under the command of the 13th Battalion commander Lt. Col. Zeev Oren. A 50th Battalion CCP, under the command of Deputy Battalion Commander Maj. Menachem Zatorski, went up to Tel Fares.

At the same time and in accordance with the order of the GOC, all the line's outposts were reinforced with four additional combatants. The 107th Outpost, on the Damascus-Quneitra route, the main route to the heart of the Golan Heights, was broadened to twenty combatants. The Hermon outpost was not reinforced. On that morning evacuation helicopters were moved up to the Ramat David Air Force base and the Golan Heights were closed off to civilian movement.

Preparations on the Hermon

From the time the IDF took over the Hermon's shoulder on June 12, 1967, up to the Yom Kippur War, the strategic importance of Mount Hermon to the State of Israel was acknowledged in accordance with events that occurred during those six stormy years in the military as well as the political arena. The strategic importance of an observation warning outpost leaned on the capacity for early-warning intelligence gathering; real-time intelligence gathering; conducting electronic warfare against ground/air-based enemy forces; the ability to aim artillery during "combat days," or in the event of all-out war; the ability to launch artillery rockets at strategic targets in the Damascus region; its status as a secure northern position during defensive or offensive fighting; the possibility to use the Hermon ridge and western slopes for a strategic outflanking maneuver toward Syria; the ability to manage operations on Syrian and Lebanese territory from it; and the control it provided over Israel's main water sources.

At first, an observation outpost and a relay station were established in Mitzpe Horan, which lies at the eastern edge of the Hermon's shoulder at an elevation of 2100 meters. Over time, a fortified multi-corps facility was constructed, where units from Aman, the Air Force and the communication corps carried out gathering, observation, relay and electronic warfare missions.

Its location allowed a visual observation of the most of the Golan Heights, both the Israeli and the Syrian side. The advanced electronic equipment installed allowed the 848th Signals Intelligence Unit (Sigint) to gather important information.

The 102nd Outpost, or the "Israeli Outpost," as it was called was isolated in its sector with only a single narrow access road leading to it from the Golan Heights and Mount Dov. It was constructed with an underground level that included bunkers for living quarters, ammunition, water and food, connected by tunnels to the guard and surveillance posts, and two stories above ground that housed the studies, laboratories, medical clinic, mess hall, generators, guarding and surveillance posts. When the war broke out the outpost was in the process of renovation so no combat positions, connecting tunnels, or a command position had yet been constructed. Though the outpost was part of the 13th Battalion's sector and the soldiers on guard belonged to this battalion, it was under the command of Lt. Gadi Zidover from the 820th Regional Brigade, whose operational subordination was not properly defined. On Yom Kippur there were sixty soldiers in the outpost: 13 combatants from the 13th Battalion and the rest soldiers from professional units, Artillery Corps officers, NCOs from command and RC intelligence, and the outpost's headquarter staff from the 820th Regional Brigade. Some of the soldiers and officers arrived at the outpost as late as October 4-6, 1973. The professional unit soldiers were only equipped with personal weapons and some had no weapon at all. Most were unpracticed in the outpost's drills and unfamiliar with the sector.

Though a Level C alert had been declared in the IDF by Friday October 5 at approximately 10:40, a "Lock" command had been issued to the entire standing army, and, despite the fact that on Saturday morning the 820th Regional Brigade instructed the 50th Battalion from the 35th Brigade and the 13th Battalion from the 1st Brigade that held the outposts line to reinforce them with additional combatants and prepare for opening fire, for some reason, the Hermon outpost was not shored up and its routine security measures continued as usual. This included a morning foot patrol to scan the route from the outpost to the lower ski lift station, performed by Golani soldiers under the command of the platoon commander 2nd Lt. Hagai Punk. Only two soldiers remained on guard in the outpost. At the end of the patrol the soldiers returned to the outpost, excluding three who took positions at an observation point on a hill to the north of the upper ski lift station which was then under construction. In the outpost itself the observation post and two guard posts were manned. Three observation posts were set up in the morning, as they were every morning, between Mount Dov (Jabel Rous) and the lower ski lift station: Yifat, Tali and Hedva, also manned by soldiers from the same company, but during the day they were under the command of 902nd Nachal Battalion's for regular security operations employment at Mount Dov. A little before 14:00 an EW blocking company from the 374th Communication Corps Unit under the command of Moshe Sapir arrived at the "Tank Bend," and began positioning itself and its gear as per the Northern Command's instructions. Due to faulty coordination their arrival was unknown to the outpost commander or to the Hermon company commander, who sat at the Mas'ade employment base.

Completing Defensive Preparations

Until noon on Saturday, October 6, the regular forces deployed in the Golan Heights region included the 820th Regional Brigade with two infantry and paratrooper battalions under its command; the reduced 188th Tank Brigade (71 tanks); the 7th Tank Brigade (107 tanks); 11 Artillery Corps batteries and the artillery assistance and liaison alignment. The forces were deployed thus:

Infantry

The 820th Regional Brigade under the command of Col. Zvi Bar (Barzani) with two regular infantry and paratrooper line battalions under its command:

- **13th Infantry Battalion** from the 1st Brigade under the command of Lt. Col. Zeev Oren and his deputy Maj. Ilan Biran manned six of the northern sector's outposts from the Hermon to Outpost 110.
- **50th Airborne Infantry Battalion** from the 35th Brigade under the command of the Lt. Col. Kobi Bendal (who was injured in a parachuting accident on the eve of the war) and his deputy Maj. Menachem Zatorski manned five outposts in the southern sector, from Outpost 111 to observation Outpost 117.

Armored

188th Armored Brigade (excluding the 39th Reserve Battalion) under the command of Col. Yitzhak Ben Shoham with seventy-one tanks, deployed with two battalions in platoon positions in the front and company concentrations in the rear of the line's outposts:

- **The 74th Battalion** under the command of Lt. Col. Yair Nafshi was deployed in the northern sector.
- **The 53rd Battalion** under the command of Maj. Oded Erez was deployed in the southern sector.

The 7th Brigade under the command of Col. Avigdor (Yanush) Ben Gal, with 107 tanks in battalion concentrations:

- **The 82nd Battalion** (33 tanks) under the command of Maj.

Haim Barak at Sindyanna.

- **The 71st Battalion** (about thirty tanks) under the command of Lt. Col. Meshulam Rats at Waset junction.
- **The 75th Mechanized Infantry Battalion** headquarters under the command of Lt. Col. Yos Eldar and his deputy Maj. Yossi Melamed, with the reconnaissance company at the Jordan Base.
- **The 77th Battalion** (44 tanks) under command of Lt. Col. Avigdor Kahalani remained under the command of the 188th Brigade in the Nafah region.

ARTILLERY

- **334th Battalion** under the command of Lt. Col. Arieh Shacham: battery A—Buq'ata; battery B—Birket Ram; battery C - Mas'ade.
- **405th Battalion** under the command of Maj. Arieh Mizrachi: battery—Hermonit; two batteries—Shaa'bnia and on the Waterfalls Route in the southern sector.
- **Training Base No. 9 Battalion** under the command of Lt. Col. Ben Ami Cohen: battery—Tel Mahfi; battery—Ein Zivan; battery—Tel Fares.
- **55th Battalion** under the command of Lt. Col. Shraga Ben Zvi: two batteries on the KKL route in the central Golan Heights.

Additionally, batteries of surface-to-surface MAR-290 rocket launchers were also deployed throughout the Golan Heights region in positions within range of Damascus, with elements from the reconnaissance battalion.

On the morning of Saturday, October 6, all the IDF's eleven batteries were on top alert in a new deployment, in fortified positions and in exposed positions, in three battalion sectors across the Golan Heights front. Each of the batteries was linked to outposts in its sector in order to respond to their demand for fire. Facing them, about 157 Syrian batteries were deployed at that time.

The 334th Battalion headquarters was positioned in the Nafah CCP as the assistance headquarters for the 820th Regional Brigade, and in practice functioned as an assistance headquarters for the entire Golan Heights. The 405th Battalion headquarters functioned as the 7th Brigade's assistance headquarters, while the two additional battalion commanders in the Golan Heights, Lt. Col. Ben Ami Cohen and Lt. Col. Shraga Ben Zvi, were positioned in Tel Fares and Tel Avital for observation and control of the support fire, for the infantry and armored battalions' companies and platoons on the line's outposts and ramps.

At the same time, artillery lookouts were deployed in the Hermon outpost, the Tank Bend in the upper Hermon and other controlling sites, and frontal observation and artillery liaison officers were positioned in the different units. They were also equipped with radios to contact aircraft for assistance in case the firing started. An aerial artillery observation was positioned at the Ramat David Air Force base.

The fire plan prepared at the time was based on each battery occupying four targets at once—one gun for each target. The high priority targets were the Syrian artillery batteries that threatened the settlements and IDF bases in the region. In addition, every battery was assigned "dangerous fire missions" to assist the outposts on the line.

On Friday the command and units of the 1st Golani Brigade were called back from a brigade convention due to take place at Tel Aviv's Convention Center. The battalions began organizing themselves in their permanent bases and mobilizing reserve completions. Brigade commander Col. Amir Drori instructed the forces to gather in Rosh Pina for a brigade assembly. Two companies from the 17th Battalion (the Squad Commander's course) were flown out to defend Sharm el-Sheikh and the Shlomo region.

Once the G3 granted approval on the morning of Yom Kippur, the mobilization and logistics system went into operation. The command mobilized the complete combat and assistance alignment of the 36th and 210th Divisions, including completions for the 188th Brigade. The mobilization also included the command units including the artillery battalions of the 744th Artillery command unit, the 801st Field Engineering Command Headquarters' field engineering battalions including the heavy equipment, the command's maintenance units and completions for the command's 371st Communication Battalion.

At 10:30 the head of the medical command instructed hospitals in the northern region to prepare for war. The hospitals began making lists of patients to be evacuated, a process that went into effect an hour after the war broke out. By 19:00 about 75 percent of hospital beds were cleared and a total of 1700 beds were made available to the medical corps. Doctors and medics were deployed in the Golan Heights as part of the medical alignment's reinforcement (see details in the medical corps chapter of Part III).

In the morning, after the mobilization order was issued (060900), the mobilization effort by the adjutant factors increased in the GHQ, the command, the divisions and the brigades. The GHQ and command logistics alignment dealt mainly with coordinating efforts for mobilization, giving orders to the logistics facilities to begin issuing the emergency supplies, and release vehicles which were being repaired or refurbished in maintenance centers and garages. The mobilization of the GHQ and command's logistical reserves commenced at the same time.

The timetable for mobilization and equipping was based

on giving priority to the fighting ranks over the administrative ranks. According to these priorities a plan was also established for issuing fuel and ammunition to the combat units and the Division logistical units that stipulated that the first priority was the combat rank, meaning the battalions and the brigades, and that the Division and other ranks came second.

The reserve brigades were not mobilized and equipped in accordance with familiar, established procedure. The reduced regular staff in the brigades did their best to prepare the equipment to be handed out to the reserve soldiers. Some of the emergency storage warehouses of the brigades that had been transferred to the frontline bases in the months leading up to the war lacked pallets for ammunition or enough places to store the standard ammunition for all the units.

When the first commanders arrived the first and most important mission was to make sure that the tanks were armed and ready for departure. An example of this may be seen in the words of the 679th Brigade commander Col. Ori Orr: "Bring ammunition trucks now, as soon as possible, from the Ein Zeitim bunkers, and clear the roads for them up to the tanks and make sure they arrive. This is the most important thing right now!"

The Northern Command HQ was aware that it might be forced to evacuate the Golan Heights settlements. The evacuation plan was prepared by the command's regional defense headquarters, and its details were kept secret to prevent the settlements from resisting the evacuation. On the morning of October 6 the GOC addressed the GHQ Chief of Staff and it was agreed that women and children would be evacuated from the settlements that same day. The evacuation order was brought down to the 820th Regional Brigade, which immediately began the operation, managed by the command's regional defense officer Col. Zvi Raski. Buses headed for settlements in the southern Heights collected and evacuated women and children even after the war actually broke out, and some were evacuated under cover of darkness while the Syrians were bombing. The settlements in the north of the Heights were also evacuated in darkness and under bombs, in the settlements' own vehicles. The order to evacuate the men as well, given at dawn of October 7, was met with resistance by the residents, who delayed the evacuation.

The Air Force began disarming its jets from attack bombs to install defensive air-to-air combat ammunition, reasoning that jets would be launched to defend the territory and patrol against expected enemy aerial attacks.

At 10:10, the GOC issued a series of commands in Nafah wherein he announced that an all-out war was about to be launched by Syria and Egypt against Israel, on the Golan and Sinai fronts, and that the war was expected to erupt at 18:00. He also ordered the evacuation of women and children from the Golan Heights settlements. The GOC ordered the reinforcement of the number of combatants in each outpost, up to 16 to 20 soldiers for each outpost.

At 10:45 the OGC requested the GHQ Chief of Staff's approval to send a battalion and a reconnaissance company from the Golani Brigade up to the Golan Heights. The GOC also approved the transfer of teams from the 179th Brigade to be equipped on the 164th Brigade's tanks in its warehouses at the Golani junction. The 164th Brigade, which was newly formed and whose combat soldiers had not yet grown familiar with the Golan Heights, was transferred for combat on the southern front in place of the 7th Brigade. Upon its ascent to the Golan Heights the 7th Brigade was partially equipped with tanks from the command's quick mobilization brigade, the 179th.

When the GOC once again left Nafah for the GGHQ, he left the command of the Golan Heights front in the hands of 188th Brigade commander Col. Yitzhak Ben Shoham. Maj. Gen. Hofi preferred to refrain from changing the alignment of forces and leave "tank fists": tank companies in each sector with the 7th Brigade as the command's reserve.

The 7th Brigade commander summoned the battalion commanders for a briefing in which he presented the H-hour and instructed the battalion commanders to make their final preparations for battle: the units were deployed and camouflaged, an anti- aircraft alert was announced and the battalion commanders were called in to receive a series of brigade orders at Nafah at 14:00.

While the 7th Brigade commander was briefing his battalion commanders to prepare for war, the 188th Brigade commander was briefing his battalion commanders for an extended combat day. He did not change his opinion, even after the GOC's instruction and even after his intelligence officer, Maj. Moshe Tzur (Tzurich), notified him that around 11:00, according to Aman reports, a war would break out and it would not be a combat day.

7th Brigade commander Col. Avigdor Ben Gal and 188th Brigade commander Col. Yitzhak Ben Shoham agreed to replace the 77th Battalion, which was under the command of the 188th Brigade, with the 82nd Battalion. The 188th Brigade commander, who assumed that what would take place would be only a combat day, agreed to the exchange, in spite of the fact that the 82nd Battalion under the command of Maj. Haim Barak included only thirty-six tanks, compared to the forty-four tanks of the 77th Battalion, which was more experienced and already familiar with the Golan Heights region. In spite of this agreement, the 7th Brigade commander was prevented from instructing the 82nd Battalion commander to transfer to the command of the 188th Brigade. The 82nd Battalion commander, Maj. Haim Barak, did not transfer to the 188th Brigade's communication network, since he was not told that he was under the command of this brigade.

At about 13:00 the GHQ Chief of Staff briefed the Northern Command GOC about halting the Syrian offensive in the evening, with a minimum of losses. He was told that this mission would continue through the night hours and the next day. He was also told that the Air Force intended to attack the Syrian airfields first, weather permitting, and only then attack the missile alignment despite the fact that the prime minister had not approved the preemptive attack. Thus, the GHQ Chief of Staff added, the ground forces would only be granted limited assistance in the first 24 hours. Only afterwards would the Air Force begin attacking ground targets on the front line with full force. The Navy, meanwhile, got its vessels ready in advance in the Mediterranean and Red sea combat zones, aimed against the Syrian and the Egyptian fleets at their ports. In that briefing the GOC described the command's offensive plans and estimated that they could move from defense to offense according to "Ben Gil North" or "Ben Gil South," starting on Monday morning.

Upon the departure of the GOC to the GHQ at the end of the orders group, the staff officers set up in the crowded command bunker in Nafah. At around 13:40 announcements began coming in from the surveillance outposts that camouflage nets were being removed from the Syrian tanks and artillery guns.

At 13:35 a commanders' discussion was held at the Air Force commander's office about the tense situation and the Air Force's missions. At 13:55 announcements came in that Syrian jets were taking off from the Dumeir airfield. At that time the GHQ Chief of Staff's briefing ended. The commander of the Air Force immediately ordered "going up in the air to defend the ground in the Golan Heights and Ramat David Air Force Base and thwart the attack..." Then the Syrians opened artillery fire and an aerial assault all along the Golan Heights front.

The Golan Theatre and Main Routes

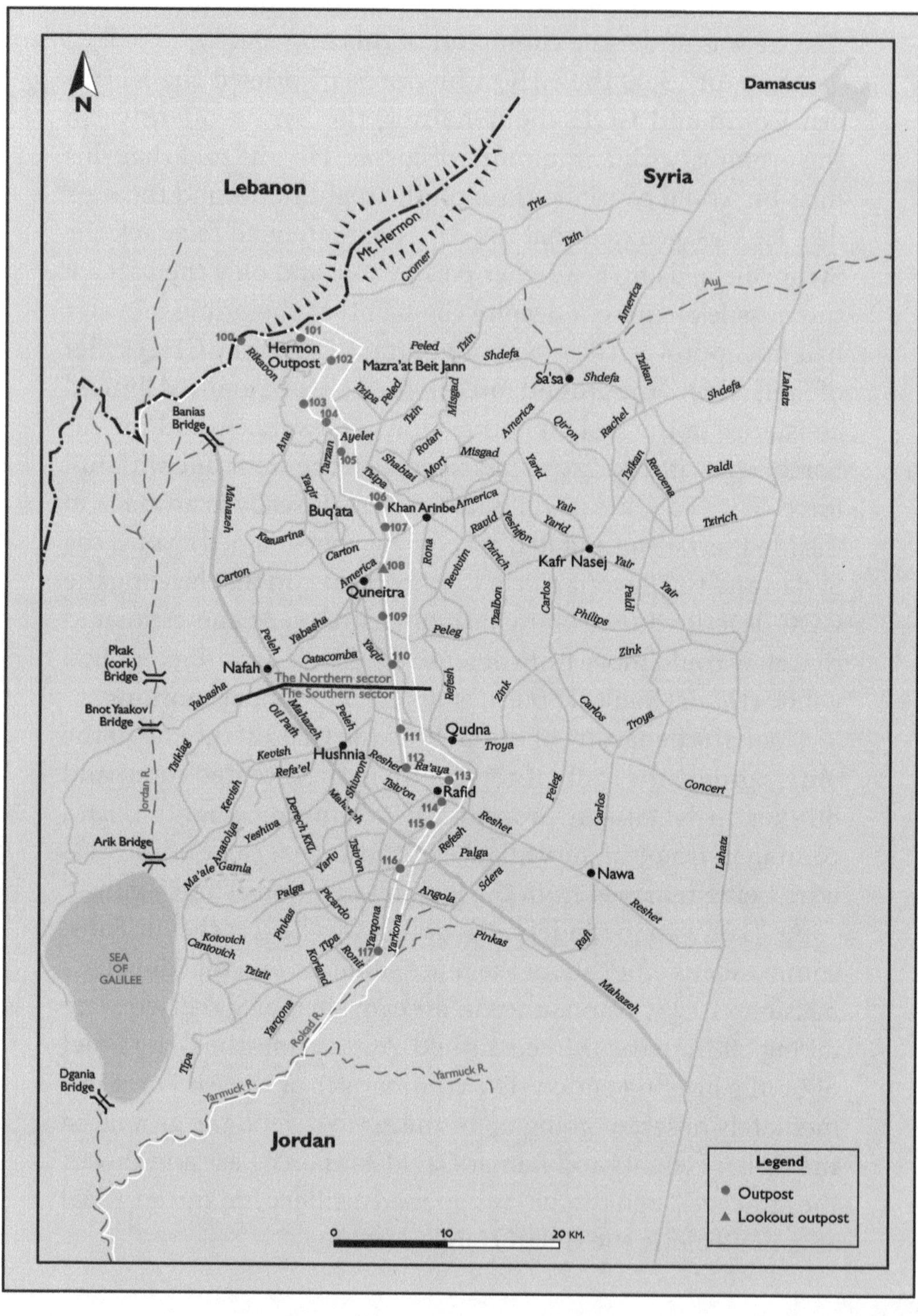

The Syrian Attack Plan (Estimated)

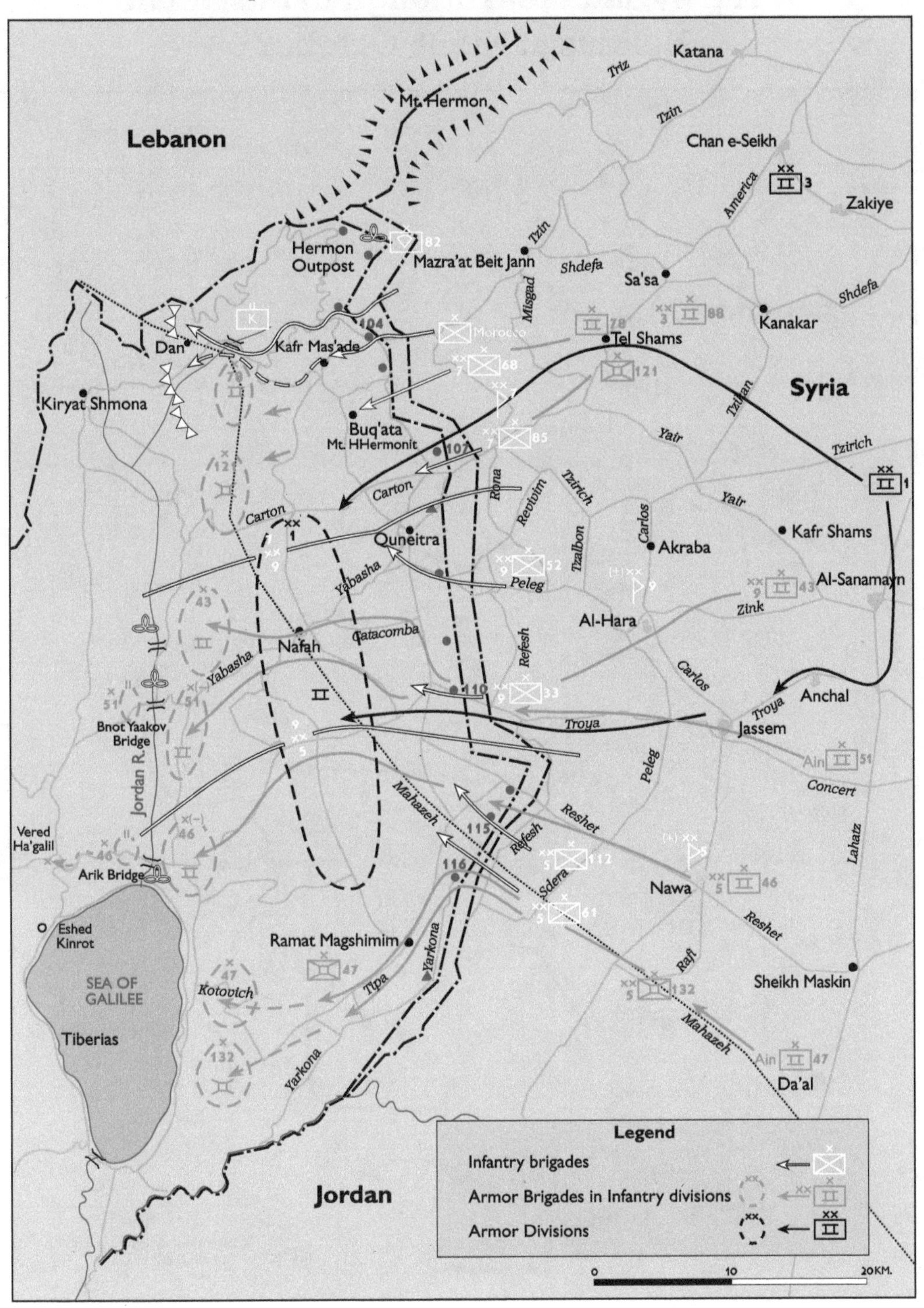

The Syrian Breakthrough in the Golan Heights at Night, October 6-7

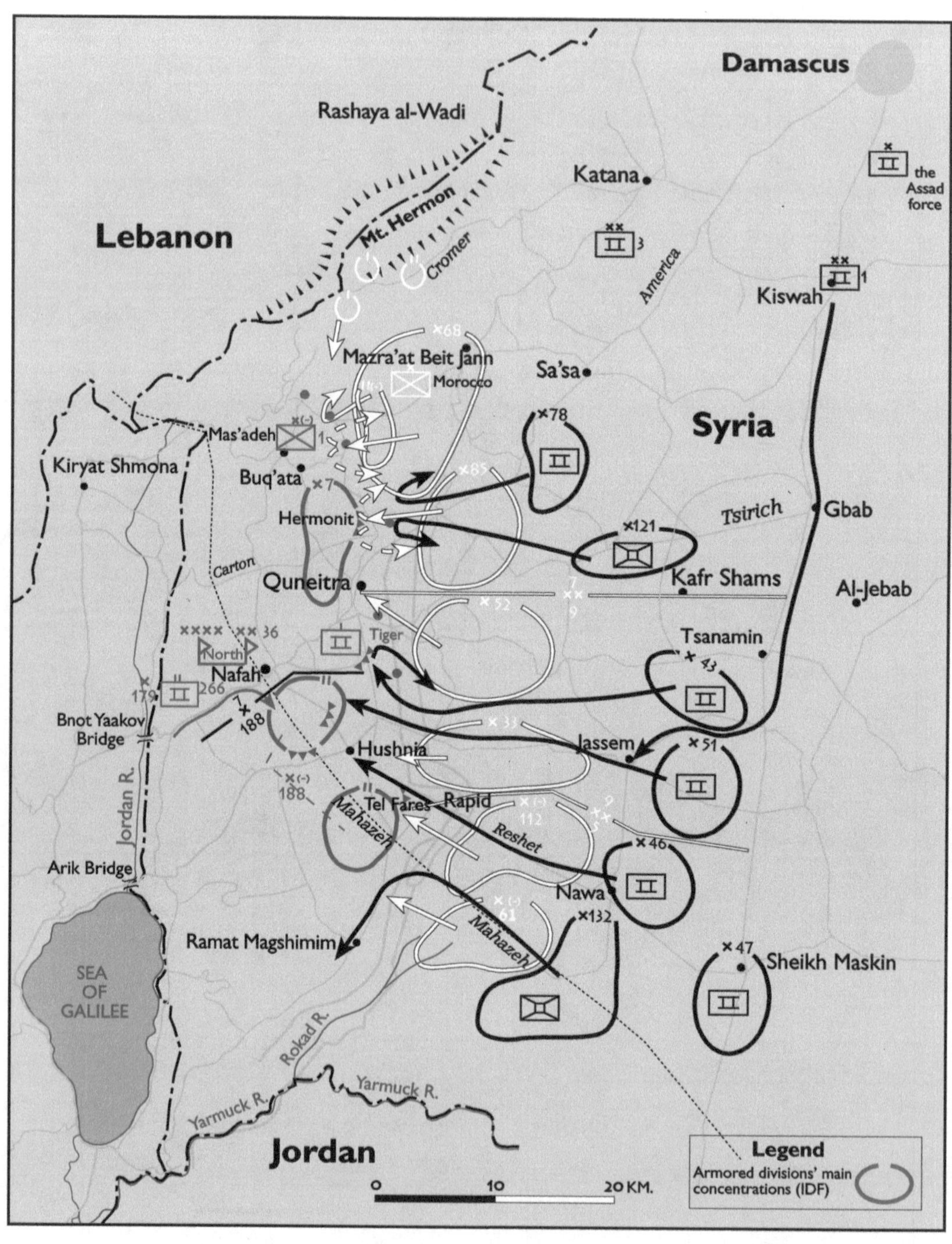

Deployment of Syrian and IDF Forces on the Golan, 13:55 October 6, 1973

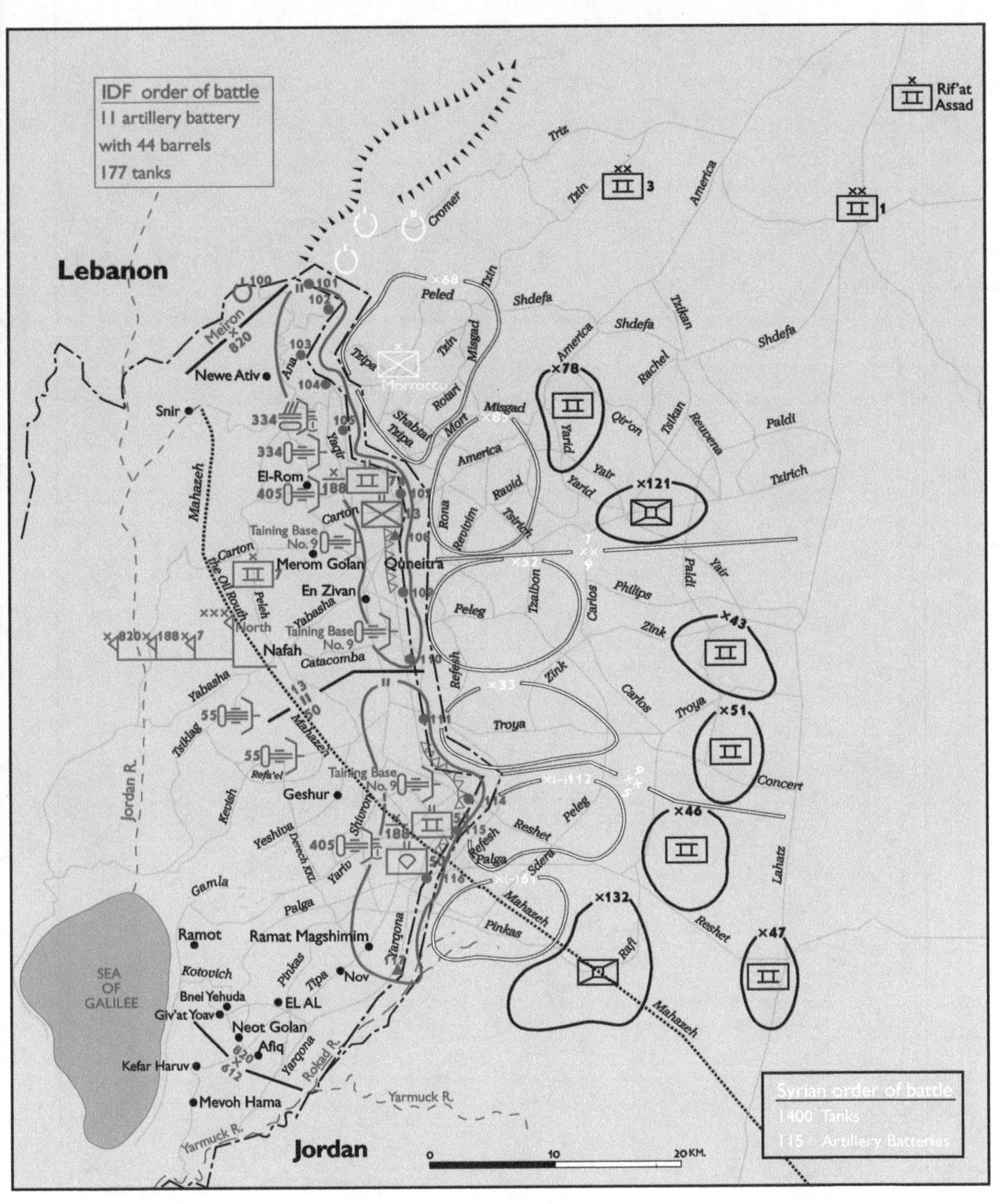

The Situation on the Golan, noon October 7

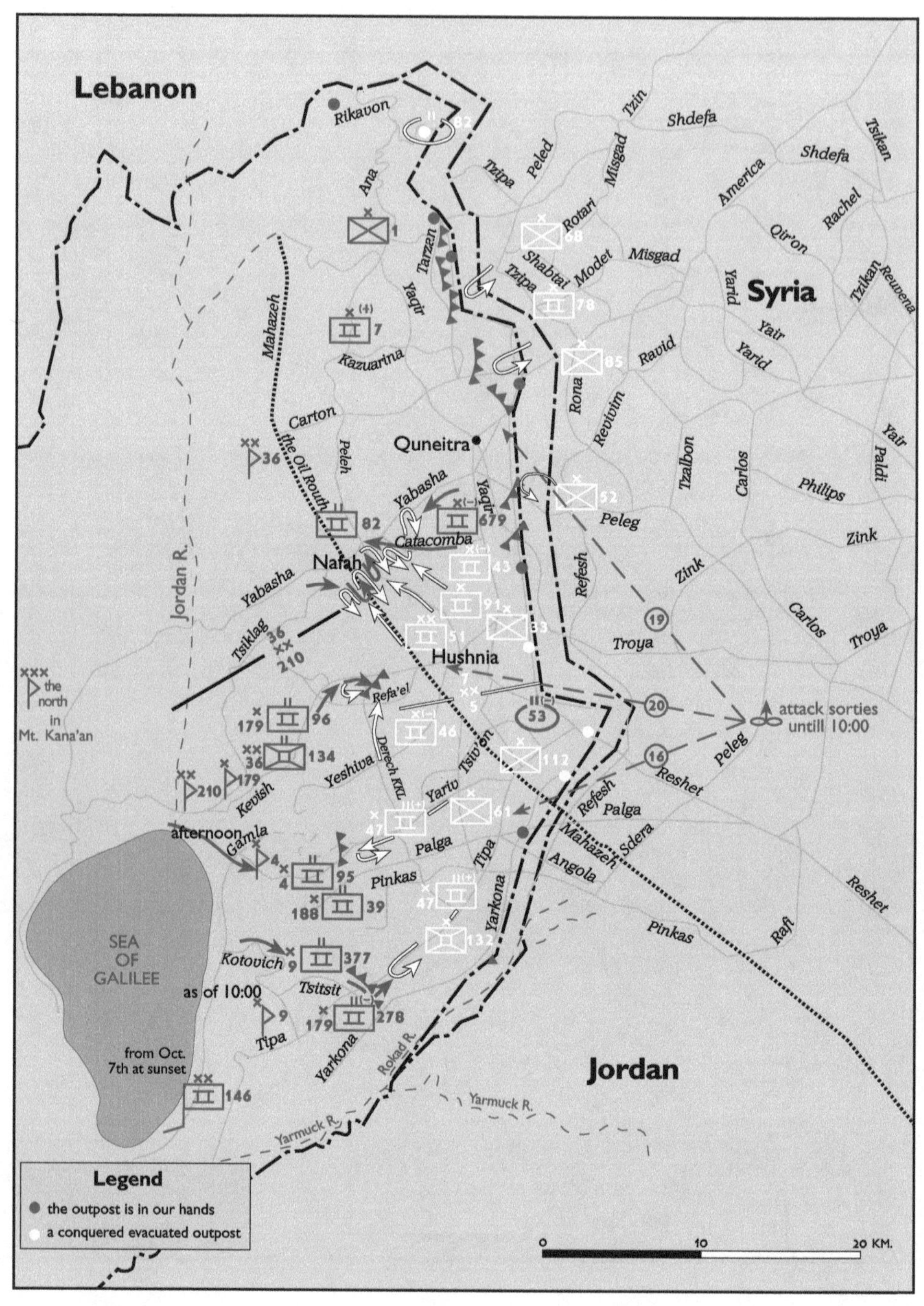

Fighting on the Golan, October 8

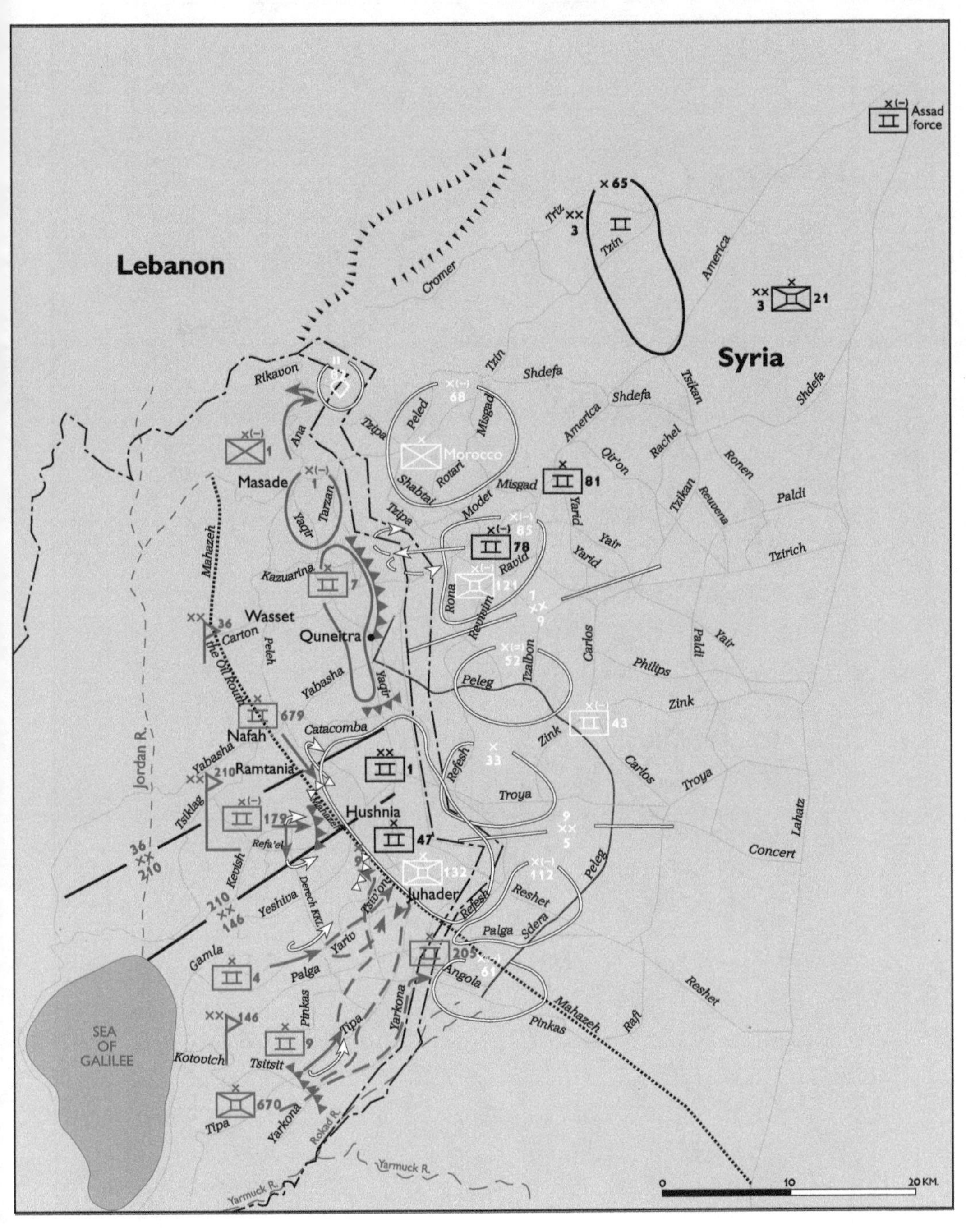

Fighting on the Golan, October 9

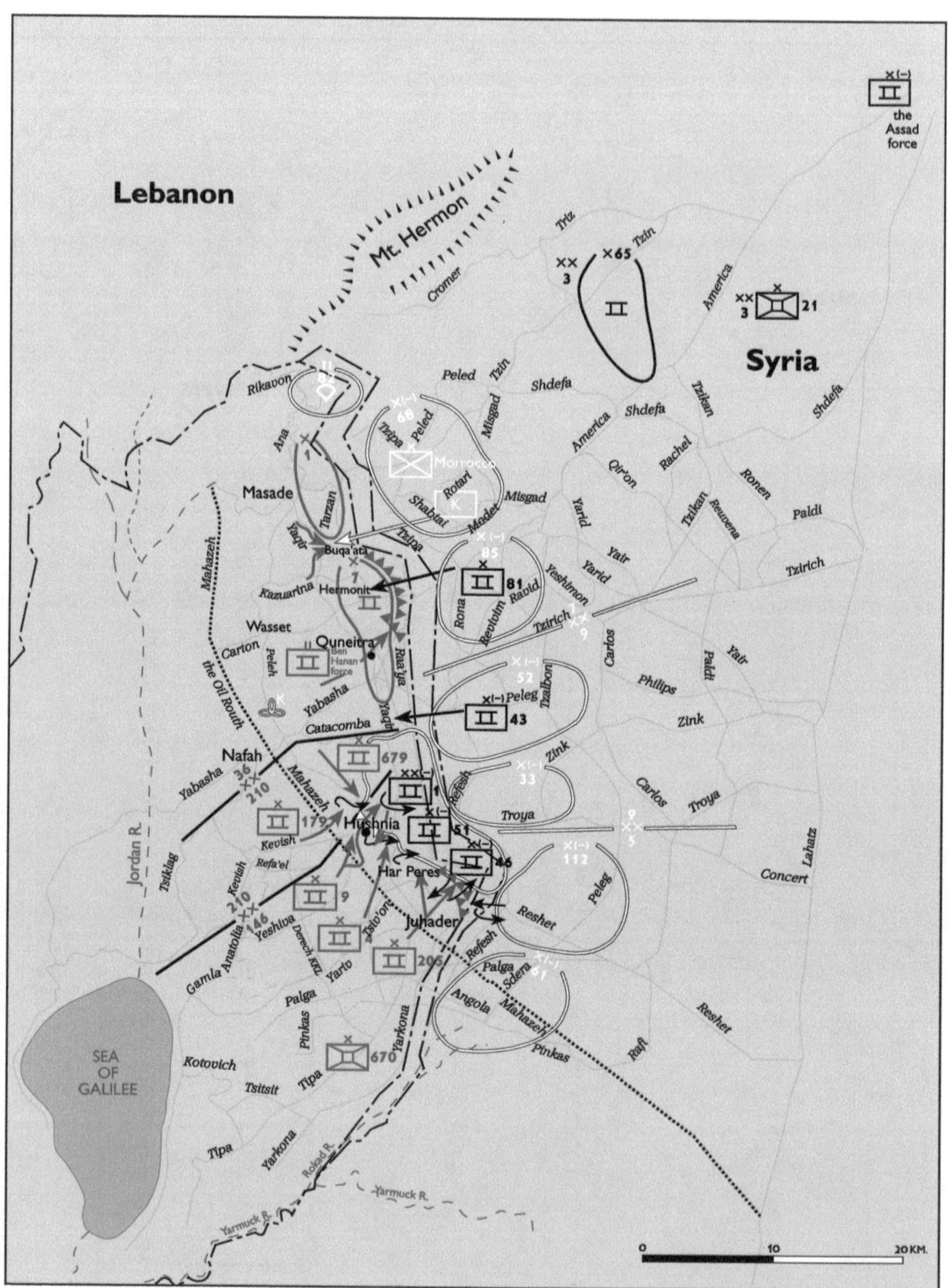

Air Force Attacks in Syrian the Depth of Syria, October 9-10

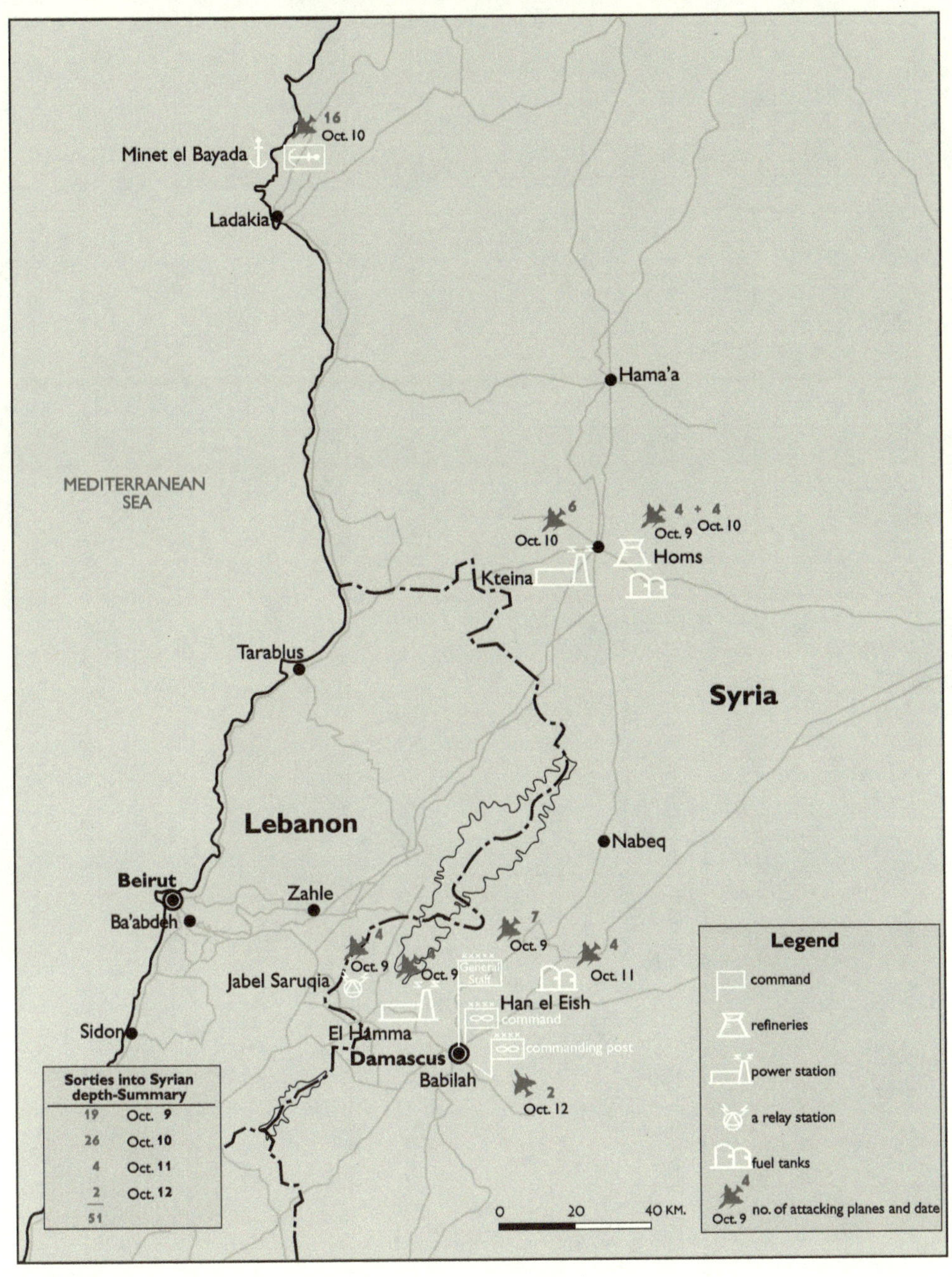

PART II

From Desperate Holding to an Offensive Towards Damascus

The Northern Command Staff During the Yom Kippur War

- Commander (GOC)—Maj. Gen. Yitzhak (Haka) Hofi
- Chief of Staff—Brig. Gen. Uri Bar-On
- Deputy Commander—Col. (res.) Issachar (Iska) Shadmi
- General Staff (G3) Officer—Lt. Col. Uri Simchoni
- Intelligence Officer—Lt. Col. Hagai Mann
- Supply Corps Officer—Lt. Col. Haim Levav
- Adjutant Officer—Lt. Col. Nathan Shpak
- Artillery Commander—Lt. Col. Avraham Bar David
- Engineering Commander—Lt. Col. Moshe Peled
- Communication Commander—Lt. Col. Avraham Kayam
- Supplies Commander—Lt. Col. Aharon Shmueli
- Ordnance Commander—Lt. Col. Yishayahu Halfon
- Medical Corps Commander—Lt. Col. Dr. Gabriel Dineri
- Military Police Commander—Lt. Col. Zvi Herman Hershko
- Education Officer—Lt. Col. Hillel Meir
- Rabbi—Lt. Col. Rabbi Israel Ariel
- Women's Corps Officer—Lt. Col. Nili Eldar
- TD Officer—Col. Zvi Raski
- Field Security Officer—Maj. Eliezer Nadan

At the peak of the war Brig. Gen. Yekutiel "Kuti" Adam was appointed assistant to the GOC. Lt. Col. Menachem Einan was appointed assistant to the G3 officer, and from October 23 served as the G3 officer (after Lt. Col. Uri Simchoni was appointed as the Golani Brigade commander in place of Col. Amir Drori who was injured). On the third day of the war Col. Avraham Arnan volunteered and served as assistant to the intelligence officer.

The Northern Command Order of Battle Before the War

The Northern Command Headquarters

Regional brigades

Golan Heights - 820	Colonel Zvi Bar
The Valleys - 612	Colonel Yehezkel Ravid
Meron Region - Lebanon	Colonel Zuri Sagi

General Chief of Staff Reserve – Central Command

146th Division Headquarters	Commander: Brig. General Moshe Pelled Deputy: Brig. General Avraham Rotem
205th Brigade	Colonel Yossi Peled
670th Brigade	Colonel Gidi Gordon
213 Artillery group	Colonel Daniel Avidar
Maintenance group	Colonel Menahem Zehavi
288th Reconnaissance unit	Lieutenant-Colonel Zvi Dahab

Northern Command Divisions

36th Division Headquarters	Commander: Brig. General Raphael Eitan Deputy: Brig. General Menachem Aviram
179th Brigade	Colonel Ran Sarig
679th Brigade	Colonel Ori Or
9th Brigade	Colonel Mordechai Ben Porath
212th Artillery group	Colonel Benni Arad
Maintenance group	Lieutenant-Colonel David Shechner
134th Reconnaissance Battalion	Lt. Colonel Hanani Tavor

Northern Command Divisions

210th Division Headquarters	Commander: Major General Dan Laner Deputy: Colonel Moshe Bar-Kochva (Brill)
188th Brigade	Colonel Itzhak Ben Shoham
164 Brigade	Colonel Avraham Baram
4th Brigade	Colonel Yaacov Hadar
282 Artillery group	Colonel Moshe Pelled
Maintenance group	Lieutenant-Colonel Haim Titelboim

Independent Northern Command Units

1st Brigade - Golani	Colonel Amir Drori
Egoz - Reconnaissance unit	Lieutenant-Colonel Avi Telem
181st Command Armored battalion	Lieutenant-Colonel Reuven Ben Alon

Command Units

744th Artillery Headquarters	Lieutenant-Colonel Avraham Bar David
801 Field Engineering Headquarters	Lieutenant-Colonel Moshe Peled
371st Communications Battalion	Lieutenant-Colonel Avraham Kayam
390th Military Police Unit	Lieutenant-Colonel Zvi Herman Hershko
Command Ordnance headquarters	Lieutenant-Colonel Yishayahu Halfon

From the Command Operations Log

מיומן המבצעים של הפיקוד

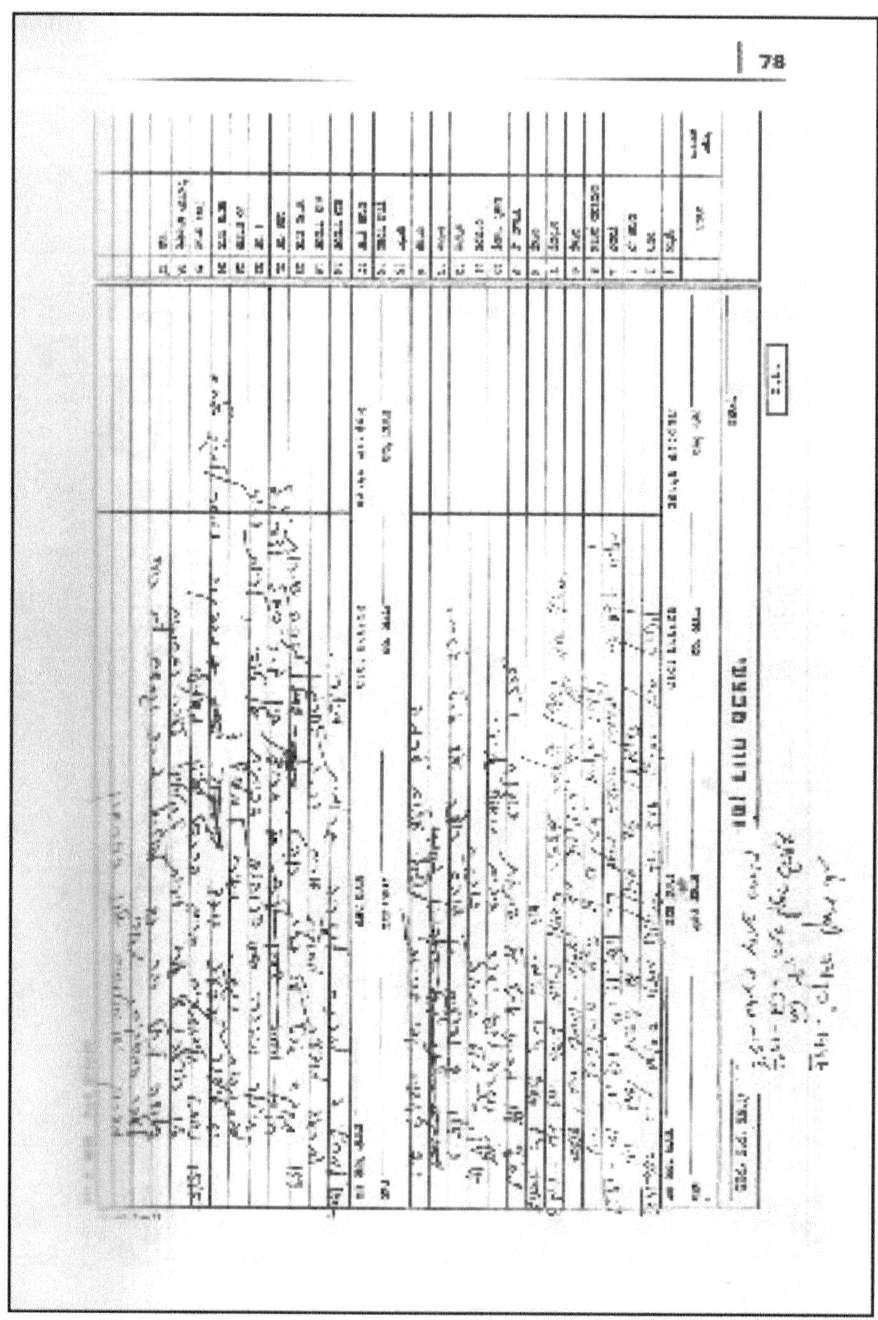

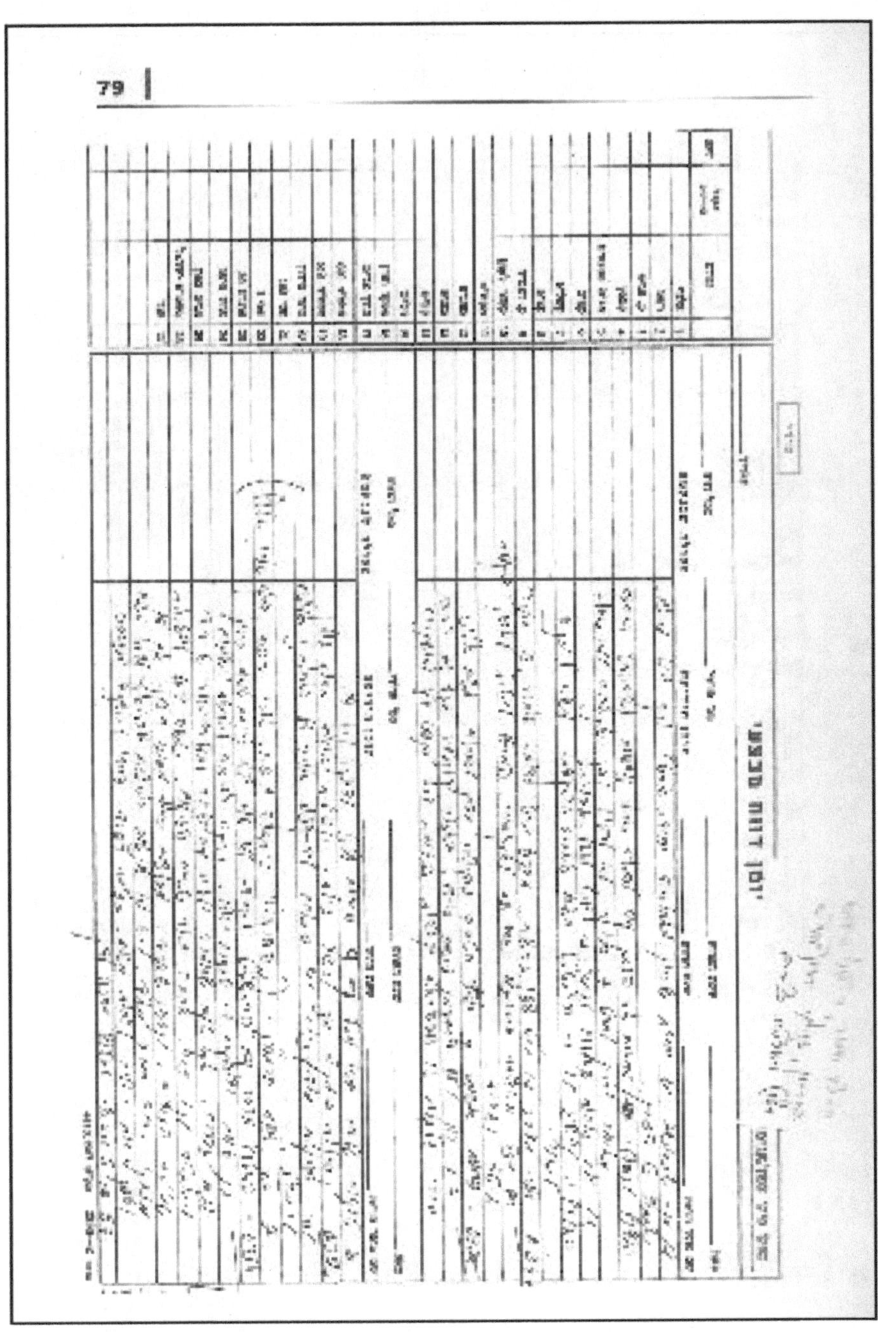

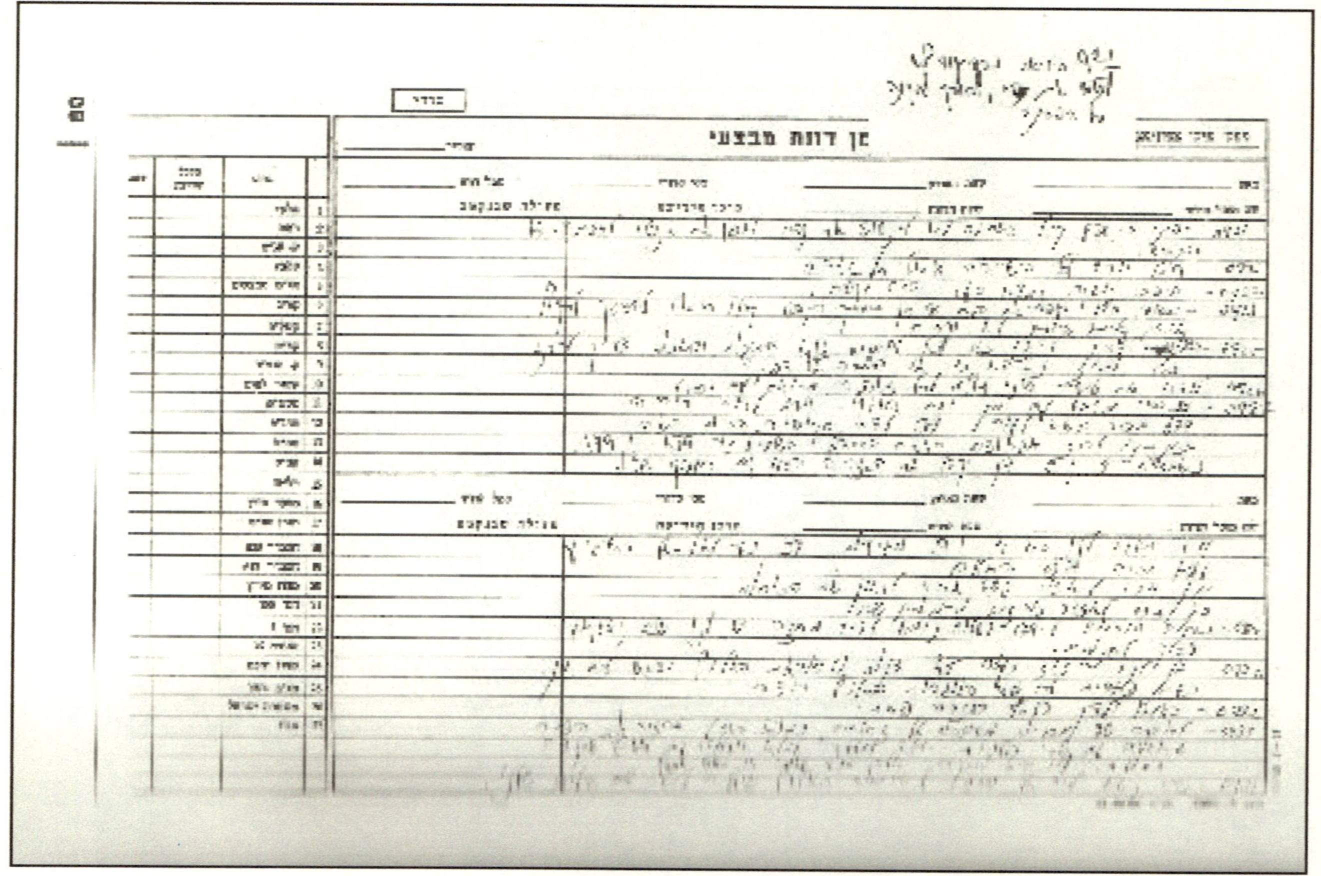

Halting the Syrian Attack

CHAPTER 6

The Syrian Attack Plan and Its Implementation

The Syrian attack at noon on Saturday, October 6 1973, was planned as a single campaign, whose predicted continuation was a preparation for defense at the end lines against possible IDF counterattacks. The Syrians planned to launch one Campaign to be completed within 24 hours in order to preempt the arrival of the IDF reserve forces at the Golan Heights. In practice, the attack lasted from October 6 to October 9.

The Syrians aimed at conquering the Golan Heights, destroying the forces deployed there and stabilize defensive lines along the Jordan River or on the western slopes of the Golan Heights, with the three mechanized infantry divisions on the first line and the senior 1st Armored Division as a second line and a reserve force in the back. The new 3rd Armored Division was intended to serve mainly for defensive missions as a GHQ reserve force or to make some of its forces available to the attacking ranks. The method selected was breaking through the front line in three parallel and balanced Division routes of effort: in the north by the 7th Division, in the center by the 9th Division and in the south by the 5th Division.

Prior to the war the command intelligence analyzed the possibility of a Syrian breakthrough the Quneitra salient in the north and the Rapid and Qudna salients in the south. Due to the command analysis and the IDF's division of the Golan Heights into two brigade responsibility sectors, many were mistaken to assume that the Syrians concentrated their efforts in the southern sector. The topography of the area with the Hazeka ridge in the center, split the Central Division's efforts to the south—the Qudna salient and to the north—the Quneitra south salient.

The 47th Independent Tank Brigade was spotted in the 5th Division's region and at the southern border of the 9th Division's region, in front of the Qudna salient about a week before the war broke out. The 51st Independent Tank Brigade was spotted there even earlier. This meant that a large armored force was located in the southern region, greater in force than the one concentrated in the northern region. An analysis of both the force and the ground brought the command intelligence officer to assess that the enemy will concentrate its main effort in this sector. The GOC did not reject this assessment but viewed the possibility of using force in the Quneitra salient as a dangerous enabling the enemy to reach the Bnot Yaakov Bridge in the shortest way possible and threaten the Galilee.

The 1st Armored Division was intended to reinforce the successful offensive effort as a secondary GHQ rank, and offer assistance as a reserve force to complete the breakthrough and conquer territories in the region in case the first rank forces failed to do so. Its insertion could take one of two possibilities either through the Quneitra salient or through the Qudna salient, according to the progress of the battle. Since the effort in Qudna was eventually more successful the second rank division and the 1st Division passed through it to reinforce the center of the Golan Heights.

The Syrian Army employed airborne commando forces, jets, artillery fire, and anti-tank fire as part of the offensive. The commando forces, jets, and artillery fire were intended to strike quality targets including intelligence installations and headquarters. The designated anti-tank forces, which were teamed up with the first rank units, were intended to assist in the attack on IDF tanks and create areas of anti-tank defense within the captured territory.

The Syrian plan to capture the Israeli Hermon Mountain

The plan to capture the Hermon shoulder and the Israeli Outpost on it prepared by the Special Forces Headquarters and placed chiefly on the 82nd Paratrooper Battalion and was verbally handed down to the battalion officers by the commander of the Special Forces and the 82nd Battalion commander only on Friday, the 5th of the month, without mention of D-Day. The plan included the following stages:

- Situating the blockade on the Tank Bend on the only road to the outpost on D-Day (October 6) from H minus 6 hours (08:30) with the 87th GHQ Reconnaissance Battalion force led by a platoon commander, to arrive at the position from the Syrian outpost on foot.
- A preparatory bombing of the Israeli outpost by the Syrian Air Force jets from the onslaught of the preparation for firing (13:55).
- At the end of the aerial operation artillery shelling would commence to cover the assault landing by helicopters of two blocking forces and an 82nd Battalion suppressive force, later

to cover the rest of the 82nd Battalion movement from the Syrian Hermon outpost to the Israeli outpost.

- Movement of the 82nd Battalion from the Syrian Hermon in eight combat groups (Majmuas) under Battalion Commander (Captain) Naqib Suliman Hassan, from the H-hour until its attack at H plus one hour.
- An assault landing of the blocking and covering force by three helicopters west of the Israeli Hermon outpost. The force is to land at 14:05 at elevation point 2072 and split into three secondary forces as follows:
- The first force—made up of a paratrooper squad and an additional B-10 RCLR team, a Goryunov machine gun team and two engineering soldiers under the command of the 1st Company Commander Mulazim Awwal (Lieutenant) Achmed Rifa'ai Ismail el-Jojo, would land from the first helicopter and position for blocking on the bend in the road south of the upper ski lift station ("the North Bend" according to Syrian terminology).
- The second force—made up of a paratrooper squad and two engineering soldiers under the command of a platoon commander- would land from the second helicopter and move on foot to the Tank Bend to reinforce the GHQ blocking force there. This helicopter would also carry the B-10 RCLR force intended for the covering force.
- The third force—made up of a paratrooper squad and another Goryunov machine gun team under the command of the anti-tank company commander—would land from a third helicopter, joining up with the RCLR force and move together toward the hill west of the Israeli outpost to serve as a covering force to cover the capture of the outpost.
- An assault landing by helicopter of a force composed of 16 "Missions' company" combatants under the command of a platoon commander in the 1st Company of the 133rd Battalion,

near the outpost to serve as a penetrating force, to allow the 82nd Battalion forces to capture it at H-hour plus one hour.
- Completion of the capture of the outpost and organization of a defense on the Hermon shoulder.

The commando forces were also intended to isolate the battlefield, simultaneously or prior to it, by capturing the Bnot Yaakov Bridge, the Pkak Bridge (south of Lake Hula), and the Arik Bridge (on the north coast of Lake Kinneret) all of them bridges over the Jordan River. The attacking forces were notified of the cancellation shortly before the intended implementation.

Once it was no longer necessary to join up with the landed forces, a different Syrian view of the mission was made possible. The change allowed for a limited depth of the missions placed on the mechanized infantry divisions in the first operative rank. Instead of meeting up with the forces landed on the Jordan line it was now possible to suffice with capturing the cliff line in the upper Golan and stabilize the defensive lines there against the IDF reinforcing forces, mostly from the reserve alignment.

The brigades' arrows, seen on operational maps captured during and after the war, reach the region of the Bnot Yaakov Bridge and the Arik Bridge respectively at the end of the daily mission of the 51st Independent Armored Brigade which operated alongside the 9th Division, and of the 46th Armored Brigade of the 5th Division, which served as second rank brigades. Apparently due to the changes the missions were reduced and the brigades were only ordered to reach the slopes in the Snobar and Katzbia areas.

The Syrian fire opened at 13:55—at H minus 35 minutes simultaneously with the Egyptians in an artillery preparation participated by 157 batteries of various weapons of about a thousand guns and an aerial assault against various targets, including headquarters and installations in the north, including the Hermon outpost.

Three infantry divisions, including the 5th and 9th that were reinforced by an additional tank brigade and a total of over 600 tanks and the 7th Division reinforced by the Moroccan Brigade, operated on the front. Each one of the divisions attempted to break through in two sectors at once, to strike the mobile and stationary IDF forces in the controlling positions and in the outposts, and to break the local counterattacks. It seems the breakthrough forces did not insist on capturing the outposts when they discovered a possibility of bypassing them and continued their advancement west. Paratrooper, airborne commandoes, and infantry forces isolated the Hermon Sector, attacked and captured the outpost positioned there.

The Syrians combined an aerial attack in the opening offensive, attacking targets in the north of Israel and the Golan Heights. Fifty-eight assault jets participated in this attack, which lasted from 13:55 to around 16:20. The Syrian attack was coordinated with the Egyptian attack on the canal front, and the Syrian TOT for the aerial attack was 15 minutes earlier than the Egyptian TOT.

The Syrian Air Force aerial attack at the onslaught of the war had just two limited missions, whose impact on the front was minor. Eight MiG 21 jets attempted to attack targets in the Kfar Giladi region. A Hawk SAM battery positioned in Birya launched missiles at them without hitting them but the Syrian jets shelled the area without causing damage. Israeli Air Force Mirage III jets patrolling the area shot down the MiG jets and in a long chase managed to shoot down a MiG 21 jet near the Rayak Lebanese Air Force Base. The rest of the Syrian jets attacked military targets on the Hermon, Mas'ade, Birkat Ram (apparently to weaken it for the capture of the Hermon), Quneitra, Tel Avital, Tel Fares, and Nafah.

The attacking jets were escorted by MiG 21 jets, one of which was shot down by Syrian anti-aircraft fire near Damascus. The Nafah Base was attacked from the air. The jets attacked concentrations of vehicles and structures in the region. Two Israeli soldiers were killed and six others were wounded in this attack. There was no report of damages or casualties in the other places attacked. The outposts along the line were air raided and their handling was left to the artillery, which bombed the outposts and targets in the depth of the Golan Heights immediately following the aerial assault. The massive bombing caused damage to the signals intelligence unit's antennas and disrupted its capacity to gather intelligence, as well as creating a heavy smoke screen over the battlefield. Immediately following the aerial assault a helicopter airborne Syrian force began the capture of the Hermon. An additional Syrian force carried by six helicopters was intended to land in various regions of the Golan Heights. The helicopters returned to base without carrying out their mission due to weather conditions.

During the day the Syrians launched several rounds of surface-to-surface FROG rockets at targets in the region of the Ramat David Air Force base in the north of Israel. The SAM batteries, which mostly managed to evade the Israeli Air Force attacks, struck many IAF jets and thus the Air Force assistance to the holding defense was ineffective.

Up to the evening of the first day of combat Syrian success was apparent in the sector of the 5th Division, under the command of Amid (Brig. Gen.) Ali Aslan, which broke through the Tel Fares—Tel Saki region, and in the sector of the 9th Division's main effort—the Qudna salient—under the command of Amid (Brig. Gen.) Hassan Tourkmani. The secondary effort by the 9th Division (52nd brigade) north of the Hazeka ridge and south of Quneitra was halted as well.

The effort by the 7th Division under the command of Amid

(Brig. Gen.) Omar Abrash, in the "Valley of Tears" (85th Brigade) and north of it facing Mas'ade (the 68th Brigade and the Moroccan 1st Brigade) was halted. The Hermon outpost fell into the hands of the 82nd Paratrooper Battalion.

The placement of second rank brigades was carried out in sectors where the breakthrough succeeded. Four mechanized and armored brigades of the 5th and 9th Divisions including over 300 tanks were introduced into the campaign on the evening of October 6 and advanced west under the cover of night. The two southern brigades (the 132nd Mechanized Brigade and the 46th Armored Brigade),that fought in sector of the 5th Division entered the southern region between Tel Fares and the Ruqqad Canyon and advanced up to the Waterfalls Route, while fighting the few forces of the 188th Brigade.

The 51st and 43rd Tank Brigades, operating under the 9th Division, penetrated through the Qudna region and encountered Israeli forces. The 51st Brigade continued its mission and operated from the Hushniya region to the north and west, along the Petroleum Road toward Nafah. The 43rd Brigade, whose armored advanced forces were destroyed in an ambush by the 7th Brigade southern force, The Tiger Force, in the region of Alonei HaBashan, retreated and regrouped in the center of the Syrian Golan Heights.

In the sector of the 7th Division and in the north of the sector of the 9th Division all of the Syrian first rank attempts to break through the IDF's alignments and obstacles were halted by the 7th Brigade reinforced by the 74th Battalion from the 188th Brigade and forces from the Golani Infantry Brigade.

On October 7, the second rank complementary forces of mechanized infantry divisions were sent into battle. The 47th Tank Brigade reinforced the advancing force of the 5th Division and reached the El Al region, Ramat Magshimim and the cliffs overlooking the Sea of Galilee in the Gamla incline region. The

78th Armored Brigade and the 121st Mechanized Brigade from the 7th Division, reinforced by a tank battalion from the Rifaat Assad force unsuccessfully attempted to break through the Valley of Tears sector once again.

As a supplemental maneuver the 1st Armored Division was placed into battle, the second rank GHQ Division composed of about 250 T-62 tanks, as well. The division under the command of Aqid (Col.) Tewfiq Juhni was directed through the Qudna salient to the heart of the Golan Heights in the region of Hushniya and Nafah. The 820th Regional Brigade headquarters and the 36th Division's CCP were both stationed at Nafah.

In the afternoon hours on Sunday, the Syrians felt that they had almost completed their missions in the southern sector, since they were blocked in the central sector, and since their efforts to break through the defensive lines in the northern sector of the Golan Heights failed. A deputy brigade commander or battalion commander from the 47th Tank Brigade who got lost and reached the edge of the cliff in the Gamla incline region reported that he could see the Sea of Galilee and was reprimanded for advancing too far west.

The main efforts were now directed at bridging the gap. At this stage no Syrian effort to continue advancement to the west toward the bridges over the Jordan River and the shores of the Sea of Galilee could be detected.

Both the successful Syrian efforts and the unsuccessful ones came up against the IDF's regular army or the initial reserve forces and were stopped in their tracks.

October 6—The First Day of Defense

At 13:45, the frontal observation officer at Outpost 110 in the center of the Heights reported the removal of camouflage nets from the Syrian tanks and artillery batteries in the region. This was simultaneously reported by all the observation posts of the RSM outposts. Ten minutes later the Syrians launched a 35-minute long fire preparation, which incorporated hundreds of guns, mortars, rocket launchers, and jets. From that moment, a few minutes before two o'clock in the afternoon, events unfolded quickly. Syrian artillery began softening the IDF outposts along the line as well as many targets deeper in Israeli territory including CCPs, bases and road junctions. The Syrian anti-battery fire was directed at the few IDF artillery batteries deployed in their established position on the line. Artillery fire was also directed at the IDF's observation posts on the hills and on the Hermon in order to silence and screen them. The Tel Fares observation post was shelled by 240mm mortars with the intent to destroy it. Additional shells were apparently fired toward the Hermon outpost as well. A number of 180mm artillery shells were fired at Mount Knaan deep within Israeli territory. Additional shells fell near the Mahanayim airfield. The massive Syrian artillery preparation did indeed destroy intelligence installations and blinded some of the positions, making it difficult to locate and take aim from them, disrupted the ability to listen to Syrian communication networks and prevented observation from the outposts. The interrupted fragments of reports from the engaged forces to the headquarters, concentrated at the bunker of the regional brigade in Nafah, did not offer a clear picture of the situation.

All of the IDF's artillery batteries were put to action in response to the Syrian artillery, including forty-four guns. According to plan, these were first directed at anti-battery targets, chiefly the Syrians' mid-range artillery batteries. It was only afterwards, following the demands made by the forces in the outposts along the line and with the direction of the artillery liaison officers in the tank battalions, that the firing was also aimed at the breaking through Syrian forces. Due to the large number of targets the battery fire was divided into firing companies, and even single guns, directed at the different targets. The fighting in the first stages was mainly carried out by the tank platoons and companies and by the outposts. The front tanks reached positions on the front and struck the Syrian spearhead tanks.

Once the battalion commanders understood the picture a situation report for the brigade began forming in the 820th line brigade headquarters and in the 188th Tank Brigade headquarters that operated parallel to each other out of the command bunker in Nafah. The partial picture formed enabled a command level first assessment of the situation whose senior representative in the Nafah bunker at that stage was the command G3 officer Lt. Col. Uri Simchoni.

When fire opened the command G3 officer reported to the GOC at the GHQ in Tel Aviv that fire was opened all across the line and that a Syrian tank offensive against the northern outposts 104 and 105 was sited. In the report Lt. Col. Uri Simchoni added that he assumed this was not the main effort but merely a distraction or diversion.

Already at the first wave of the attack Syrian Air Force jets attacked Nafah and hit several soldiers as well as the electrical system, which disrupted and complicated the work of the various headquarters in the bunker of the joint command.

Immediately upon the opening of fire, Israeli Air Force jets were launched to intercept the Syrian jets and attack the invading Syrian forces. The basic need to activate the Air Force in order to halt the Syrians, rather than initially to obtain aerial superiority as the original plan set out, forced the Air Force to allocate forces for the fighting in the Golan practically from "the first shot."

A first formation of jets took off at 14:15 and attacked targets in the Quneitra sector. The aerial attacks lasted until 17:45, under conditions of a "hot" missile-defended zone, following the advancement of Syrian missile batteries to the west. Thirty-two attack sorties were carried out, mostly from the Air Force base in Ramat David. The jets attacked in the Hermon, the Quneitra salient, and the Rapid Road junction. The jets attacked artillery batteries and performed against forces on access routes. The Syrian Air Force operated against the IDF jets to defend the Syrian forces and territory. Sixteen of its aircrafts were shot down, including one or two helicopters that were shot down by ground fire near Tel Fares.

Col. Rafi Sivron, the commander of the aerial CCP who arrived in Nafah, was concerned by the possibility that the helicopter he brought with him will not manage to get away. Sivron located his CCP—two trucks with soldiers and communication equipment. He got a small room for them to establish a CCP for the planning and control of the jets and helicopters.

In the absence of the Command GOC, who was at the GHQ, it was unclear who commanded the fighting on the Golan Heights. Prior to his heading for the Kirya (General Staff Headquarters) in Tel Aviv, he instructed the commander of the 188th Brigade, who was the senior over the brigade commander of 820th on the Golan Heights, to take command until his return.

Major General (res.) Uri Simchoni / A Personal View [5*]

The Yom Kippur War was the most important event from every possible aspect. Nothing after that was ever the same both on the personal level and the national one. For me personally the first crisis, the one of leadership, occurred the moment firing began when I was sitting near the CCP bunker in Nafah on 6 October, 1973 five minutes before two o'clock in the afternoon. Great doubts only come after absolute faith. When the order of things collapses, those who believe lose faith in the leaders who were an integral part of their world view. They lose it forever. I remember that moment rather clearly.

From early childhood my entire development, my complete belief system and values both on the kibbutz and later in the army, was built on the notion that those up there—in government, in the movement, in the Ministry of Defense—were people who knew best what needed to be done as all was well until now. We needed to listen, to be disciplined, to perform things as best we could and in the end hear a good word or get a smile from those people and be content that we have experienced a moment of grace. Until October 6 1973, there was no reason to tilt this good order. But when I saw black smoke engulfing the Golan Heights from vista to vista, when I heard the thundering guns all across the front, I understood that a terrible error had occurred. The order to mobilize reserve forces was only issued at ten in the morning, and it was now two in the afternoon. It would take many hours for the first reserve force to reach the Golan Heights. There is no chance that the regular forces could hold on for so long. It was clear that a terrible mistake was made here and that the country was in grave danger. Up there—as it turned out—they

5 * From his book: *A White Whale*, Gilad Simchoni (ed.), Glory Publishing, Binyamina (2006: 63-65.)

know nothing. In the 30 years that have passed since I didn't find any reason to alter the abrupt change in my view then. Up there they don't know anything.

Once I fail to accept leadership something in that bond of blind commitment between leader and individual is broken; a solid blind commitment that existed until then and is now lost forever.

Even on Saturday October 6, when we already knew that a war was about to break out in the afternoon hours and we began to mobilize the reserve forces, I did not comprehend or understand—as I'm sure others did not either—the kind of war that was about to take place. This was unlike anything any of us had ever seen before. In our perception a war was a war we had seen—like the Six-Day War, like the Sinai in 1956; a war with a different volume of fire, a different rhythm of movement, a different size of force, a clash with a different intensity, a different number of casualties, a different danger. The Yom Kippur War was unlike anything any the participants had experienced before. It's necessary to understand what intensity is. All of the firing caused by the First and Second Intifadas, the First and Second Wars in Lebanon—does not compare to the intensity of the barrage of fire inflicted upon us during the first hour of the Yom Kippur War. The entire Golan Heights shook, dust clouds remained in the air for three days.

Luckily for me, the war took place in an area I knew very well. I had been the command G3 officer for over a year, and prior to that the Egoz Battalion commander and Golani's intelligence officer. I had the capability to manage things. In fact, since we ascended to the Golan Heights on the last day of the Six-Day War—excluding one year when I was a student at the School of Staff and Command—I did not leave the Northern Command for even a day. I knew the Golan Heights like the back of my hand. I spent most of my time in the field, closely escorting all work in north—the building of outposts, tank ramps, roads, minefields, and artillery positions. I did not need maps or aerial photographs. I could talk to anyone, wherever he was, and know what he could see, what area he was controlling, and what areas were hidden from him. This knowledge greatly assisted me in the coming days.

When the fire commenced and the horizon darkened from the smoke I called the GHQ and asked to speak with the GOC. I was told he was meeting with the GGHQ Chief of Staff and that he couldn't be disturbed.

"Then I want the GHQ Chief of Staff," I said, "It's **urgent**.*" The GHQ Chief of Staff came on the phone.*

"A war broke out," I reported.

"How do you know it's a war?" he asked.

"I **can see**,*" I said. And thus, the conversation ended.*

Assessment of the Regular Forces at the Beginning of the War

When firing began, the 188th Brigade commander still believed that he was dealing with an expanded "combat day" and therefore ordered the activation of the Capital plan. The brigade commander ordered that a tank company be kept as a reserve force in each sector, as well as the entry into observation positions near the firing positions, to be prepared to capture them and return fire. Within fifteen minutes the tank platoons reached the observation and firing positions, in spite of heavy Syrian shelling of the outposts, ramps, and access routes.

The 74th Battalion was organized for opening fire wherein:

- Three tank platoons from Company H under the command of Eyal Shacham were placed near outposts 104, 105 and 107. The company headquarters with two tanks was at Mas'ade.
- Company A under the command of Captain Zvi Rak was

centered in the former Syrian "Front Headquarters Building" in Quneitra.

- Company B under the command of Maj. Avner Landau was stationed in Waset junction as a reserve force.

On October 6 at 12:00, the 74th Battalion commander Lt. Col. Yair Nafshi received a report from Hermonit and the Hermon outpost of a Syrian preparation and the removal of camouflage nets from tanks and artillery. He ordered to increase alertness. The brigade commander approved his request to advance Company B to the Mansura Junction.

With the battalion commander's order "Engage Capital," close to the opening of fire, the tanks moved into positions: a tank platoon from Company A moved toward Outpost 107 positions; a platoon from Company B was sent to Outpost 105 along with the 74th Brigade deputy commander Maj. Nissim Yosef.

Lt. Col. Yair Nafshi left behind in his permanent base his night vision gear, light mortars, and devices for preventing the glare of the morning sun assuming that he was dealing with one combat day, and moved toward the "Booster" hill north of Quneitra. He ordered his concentrated companies to move into their sectors and assume firing positions in accordance with the plan. The battalion commander was in touch with the outposts and the artillery throughout the defensive battle, using local communication networks.

When the war broke out the 53rd Battalion commander instructed his forces to move according to the Capital plan. The forces deployed as:

- Company F under the command of Captain Avi Runis, with five tanks under the command of the company commander in Jukhader, a platoon at Outpost 114 and a platoon at Outpost 116. The two platoons took the ramps in outposts 114 and the ramps north of 117. The company commander and another tank at Outpost 115 while the deputy company commander moved with a platoon into controlling positions over the Petroleum Road.

- Company C under the command of Captain Uzi Urieli, excluding a company transferred to the deputy battalion commander left Hushniya and was deployed wherein the deputy company commander moved into the Petroleum Road and joined up with Company F. The company commander deployed with five tanks between Outpost 114 and Outpost 115.
- Company G under the command of Uri Akavia, including seven tanks, left Hushniya and split as well: one platoon with four tanks under the command of Deputy Battalion Commander Shmuel Askrov and the company commander moved to Outpost 111 and another platoon under the command of the deputy company commander moved to Outpost 112 on the Rapid Route.

53rd Battalion Commander Maj. Oded Raz positioned himself in the region near Tel Jukhader, south of Tel Fares. The sector was divided between the battalion commander and his deputy who was responsible for Outpost 11 and northwards, facing the Qudna route.

At 14:30 a thirty tanks and Armored Vehicle-Launched Bridges (AVLBs) Syrian force attacked the "Troya" route, in the Tel Qudna sector. A force of seven tanks, commanded by the 53rd Battalion deputy commander, managed to strike the Syrians from its positions at Outpost 111 and Tel Abas and halt the Syrian attack.

To the south, on the Petroleum Road sector, Company C forces from the 53rd Battalion including eight tanks, and Company F, encountered Syrian infantry forces that had crossed the anti-tank trenches at 14:00 and overtook the ramps at 115 C and

115 D. the Syrians controlled the anti-tank trench, Outpost 115 and from there toward the Petroleum Road and Tel Jukhader arena with anti-tank, tank, and artillery fire. In the region of Outpost 116 as well, the 53rd Battalion Company F opened fire on a Syrian force of fifteen tanks, managing to strike ten of them and halt their progress.

At 14:45 the 53rd Battalion deputy commander—who was later injured and evacuated to the hospital in Safed, returned to the battalion and was evacuated again when he was mortally wounded—reported that the Syrians were continuing to transport AFVs to his sector and though he managed to destroy thirty Syrian vehicles he requested tank backup to assist the holding effort. At 15:00 pressure was apparent on Company C that was engaged at the Petroleum Road. The Syrians moved AVLBs forward to bridge the anti-tank trench. These tanks became the central target but the strikes against them did not halt the Syrian attack due to its overwhelming force.

At 15:30, the 53rd Battalion commander instructed the Company C commander to move toward the Petroleum Road after most of the tanks there were hit. At the same time, the 53rd Battalion commander asked the 188th Brigade commander to back him up with tanks.

At that time, the command G3 officer reported to the GHQ Deputy Chief of Staff that an additional Syrian effort was apparent in the Qudna salient.

In the region of Outpost 104 in the northern sector, a Syrian force of fifteen tanks accompanied by AVLBs crossed the border route at 14:20 and reached the anti-tank trench. The 74th Battalion deployed along the line battled with the Syrian forces. The Syrian breakthrough attempts in the sector were mostly halted by the 74th Battalion forces and by infantry forces around outposts 104, 105, 107 and 109. In two places—north of Outpost 107 and north of Outpost 109—the Syrians succeeded in bridging the anti-tank trench but not in crossing it. The 74th Battalion commander reported that he is overcoming a light Syrian effort in the al-Achmadia region.

With the opening of fire through an order series the 7th Brigade commander decided to advance to the "Booster" Ridge to scout and get a clearer impression of the situation on the battlefield first hand.

At 14:27 the command G3 officer took charge. In the absence of the GOC who was in Tel Aviv with the GHQ Chief of Staff, he ordered the reduced 7th Brigade (excluding the 82nd Battalion) to move east toward the Quneitra salient and the northern sector of the front. The 188th Brigade, whose commander continued commanding his forces from the Nafah bunker, transferred its northern battalion, the 74th Battalion, to the 7th Brigade, and received the 7th Brigade 82nd Battalion which was positioned in Sindyanna in its place.

The Golan Heights were divided into two responsibility arenas, where the 7th Brigade (excluding the 82nd Battalion) was in charge of the northern sector while the 188th Brigade (excluding the 74th Battalion) was in charge of the southern one. Upon this issued command a situation arose where three of the Golan Heights five tank battalions were allocated to the northern sector (the 71st, 74th, and 77th Battalions) while two were allocated to the southern sector (the 53rd and 82nd Battalions). From that moment on all the command regular forces were engaged in combat along the front line until the arrival of the first reserve forces.

Fighting by the 188th Brigade Forces in the Southern Sector

Following the assessment at that stage that the Syrian effort in the north of the Heights was the more dangerous one which was apparently based on full and accurate reports regarding Syrian movement by the regional brigade assistant intelligence officer from Hermonit, the 188th Brigade commander ordered that the 74th Battalion reserve company be employed toward that sector. In this manner the 188th Brigade northern sector remained without reserves a short time after the onslaught of the war. No reserve was left to begin with, in the 53rd Battalion sector since all the companies, including the battalion reserve company, moved to the line when battles began.

As early as 14:30 the 188th Brigade commander ordered that the 7th Brigade commander advanced the 82nd Battalion toward Hushniya junction (Pele Road junction) but the order was not carried out. When the command G3 officer noticed that the battalion was not in fact transferred to the command of the 188th Brigade he instructed the battalion commander, over the battalion network, to move toward Hushniya and enter the 188th Brigade network. The 82nd Battalion commander, who continued listening to both brigade networks, understood that he was the force intended for counterattacks in the southern sector under the command of the 7th Brigade commander. It was only at 15:00 that the battalion was transferred to the command of the 188th Brigade. Unlike the situation in the Quneitra salient, the 82nd Battalion was not deployed as a second line of defense for the 53rd Battalion. At 16:00 the 188th Brigade commander ordered the 82nd Battalion commander, who advanced his battalion near Hushniya, to send a company toward the Petroleum Road to assist in the fighting of the 53rd Battalion. Company B, under the command of Chesner, moved to Jukhader. Fifteen minutes later the 82nd Battalion commander sent Company D under the command of Captain Danny Levin, along with the 82nd Battalion deputy commander Maj. Danny Pesach, toward the Petroleum Road.

Chesner's Company B reached the Jukhader road junction and, following the 53rd Battalion commander's instructions, left a tank platoon in the area under the command of Company C commander and moved toward Outpost 111 at the Qudna salient. Following the battalion commander's orders, Company D left one platoon headed by the deputy company commander under Company C and the rest of the company moved toward Outpost 114.

At 16:54 the command G3 officer ordered the 82nd Battalion commander to transfer the rest of the battalion, that was Company A, toward the Qudna salient in order to assist the 53rd Battalion deputy commander—who reported that five of his seven tanks had been hit and the company commander killed —in order to halt the penetrating Syrian enemy.

The command G3 officer ordered the 82nd Battalion commander directly, and he advanced with Company A toward the region south of Outpost 111 and as of 17:30 had destroyed nearly thirty Syrian vehicles, most of them tanks. The 82nd Battalion commander was surprised to learn that upon his arrival at the line of contact, around 17:30, Chesner's Company B emerged north and moved toward Outpost 111, following the order of the 53rd Battalion commander.

At 17:30 the commander of Company F was informed that Syrian tanks were penetrating north of Outpost 116. He moved to the region and saw that a force of sixty tanks and APCs was advancing over an AVLB toward the outpost and north of it. The Israeli tanks quickly ran out of ammunition. Outpost 116 faced constant Syrian attacks with artillery aid from 175mm batteries, until it was joined by forces from the

205th Brigade on October 8.

At 17:00 the commander of Company C attempted to conquer the ramps captured by the Syrians. The attack incorporating his 10 tanks failed but the Syrian effort to bridge the anti-tank trench was transferred to the region south of Outpost 115.

The 82nd Battalion directed to the southern sector was split up into companies that operated from 16:00 in the region of the Petroleum Road, the Rapid Route, and the Sha'af a-Sindian region. By the evening hours the 53rd Battalion had managed to halt and hold back the Syrian breakthrough. The only place where the Syrians managed to quickly overtake the anti-tank trench was at the Petroleum Road, and by 16:00 this was the only Syrian achievement in this sector. At the same time, the Syrians continued their heavy pressure, and the few tanks in the deputy battalion commander's force at Outpost 111 were hit one by one. The situation of Company F operating against the Syrian 5th Division's breakthrough areas was also dire, and it suffered an ammunition shortage.

By 18:00 the 188th Brigade commander had an optimistic situation report. The assessment was that, except for a few passages where the Syrians managed to bridge the anti-tank trenches, most of the Syrian offensive failed. The tank battalions of the 188th and 7th Brigade s caused the Syrian forces serious damage and the assessment was that many dozens of tanks, out of the hundreds that participated in the assault, were hit and destroyed.

At the same time the following situation unfolded: in the Qudna sector—Outpost 111—the 82nd Battalion halted the Syrian south of 111 which was reinforced by a tank company. In the Petroleum Road sector the Syrians managed to capture the anti-tank trench and its controlling ramps but their attempts to advance were halted.

As darkness fell the situation was discovered to be less

favorable and even out right dire. Relative to the intensity of the attack and the size of the forces thrown into battle between 14:00 and 18:00 the Syrian accomplishments were few. Yet, the grinding of Israeli forces was extensive, particularly in the southern sector. At 17:30, only forty-five tanks remained in this sector under the command of the 188th Brigade, with only fifteen belonging to the 53rd Battalion and the rest belonging to the 82nd Battalion.

Fighting by the 7th Brigade Forces in the Northern Sector

The 7th Brigade commander Col. Avigdor (Yanush) Ben Gal ordered his forces to move toward the line of contact. At the same time, the brigade commander ordered the 77th Battalion commander Lt. Col. Avigdor Kahalani to transfer tank companies to the 75th Mechanized Infantry Battalion, thus making it a tank battalion.

As stated above, at 14:30 the command G3 officer ordered the 7th Brigade to transfer a battalion to the southern sector and move to the northern one. The 82nd Battalion was directed to the south, by the brigade commander, to join up with the 188th Brigade commander, and the rest of the brigade, including approximately seventy tanks, moved to the region between the slopes of the Hermon and Outpost 110 in the center of the Heights.

Following a preliminary situation assessment at the 7th Brigade CCP, and after receiving first reports from the 74th Battalion (placed under the command of the 7th Brigade) regarding the efforts by the Syrian forces, the 7th Brigade commander decided to prepare for defense based on the areas and ramps controlling the killing fields west of the anti-tank trench and in the depth of the region as follows:

The 77th Battalion under the command of Lt. Col. Avigdor Kahalani, which moved toward the Quneitra salient, was deployed on the Booster hill.

The 75th Battalion commander Lt. Col. Yosef (Yos) Eldar received Company H under the command of Lt. Ami Plant of the 77th Battalion and was deployed south of Hermonit on ramps up to the Tel Jit region.

The 71st Battalion under the command of Lt. Col. Meshulam Rats moved toward the northern sector and was deployed in the sector west of Buq'ata and Hermonit.

Company B of the 74th Battalion was deployed in the rear of Outpost 105 on the route to Buq'ata.

Company A of the 74th Battalion was deployed in the rear of Outpost 109 south of Quneitra.

At 15:15 Lt. Col. Simchoni ordered the 7th Brigade commander to exercise a counterattack against the locations of the Syrian breakthrough near outposts 104 and 107. A Syrian force that managed to break through, undisturbed, in the Valley of Tearssector north of Quneitra was only halted at 16:00 by the 75th Battalion commander's force including the tank company he received.

At 15:25, the 74th Battalion commander Lt. Col. Yair Nafshi reported, from his position on the Booster Ridge northwest of Quneitra, of a Syrian effort developing south of Quneitra in front of Outpost 109. A few minutes later a report came from Outpost 109 itself that a Syrian force of twenty tanks accompanied by AVLBs was crossing the border route north of the outpost and was attempting to bridge the anti-tank trench.

At 15:30 the 74th Battalion commander reported an additional Syrian effort accumulating north of Outpost 107 and including forty Syrian tanks and AVLBs. The 74th Battalion tanks, in the region of outposts 109 and 107 east of Quneitra, managed to strike many Syrian vehicles and halt the attack. In light of the Syrian attempt to bridge the anti-tank trench and penetrate the 74th Battalion Reserve Company in the northern sector was advanced to the line of contact at 15:40 toward Mount Hermonit.

The movement of the 7th Brigade forces into their positions was carried out under artillery fire, in the course of which the 7th Brigade commander ordered the 77th Battalion commander to transfer another company to the brigade command to secure the right flank of the brigade between Quneitra and Outpost 109. A reduced 75th Battalion took positions in the Hermonit region controlling the Quneitra salient from the north. Near dark, the 77th Battalion was deployed on the Booster Ridge and around it and the 71st Battalion was deployed north of the 75th Battalion—between Mount Hermonit and Mount Varda—closing off the salient leading to Buq'ata.

The 71st Battalion under the command of Lt. Col. Meshulam Rates commenced a firefight in the region north of Hermonit already at 16:30. At that time, the first tanks of the 7th Brigade were already engaged in a firefight with the Syrian forces in the sector of the Valley of Tears as they were reinforcing the company of Maj. Avner Landau from the 74th Battalion that was operating in the region on its own up to that point.

Control of the Battle from the Command CCP

Though the GOC appointed the 188th Brigade commander as the commander of the Golan Heights in his absence, the appointment was valid until the moment firing commenced. When the war broke out it was clear that the responsibility for the entire region was transferred to the command and its senior representative in the CCP, the G3 officer Lt. Col. Uri Simchoni. The 188th Brigade commander who remained in the Nafah bunker continued to order all the forces in the region in the first minutes and until the moment the 7th Brigade was activated. From that stage on, his activity focused on the sector the 188th Brigade was in charge of.

It seems that putting the 7th Brigade into action early toward the Quneitra region before enemy efforts were identified as it was the only concentrated tank force on the Golan Heights derived from the GOC's instructions and the G3 officer assessment that this was the most dangerous sector. Captain Asher Sadan's—the 820th Regional Brigade assistant intelligence officer from the Hermonit observation post - accurate reports compared with the absence of reports from the southern salient created a situation where the main effort seemed to be in the Quneitra salient. The G3 officer was guided by two principles—that of the "concentrated effort" and the "capturing key regions"one. The meaning of the "concentrated effort" principle was that the force must be concentrated for the most important mission on the most important place. The principle of "capturing key regions" dictated that forces were not to be split and dispersed as it could lead to weakness in all areas and the was not to be allowed to capture the controlling regions. If the enemy captured the controlling regions the associate forces were to find themselves in inferior territories and suffer heavy losses. It was clear that the regular forces could not halt the attack and the vital controlling regions in the Quneitra salient and the Hushniya salient had to be captured before they were captured by the Syrians. These considerations were the ones that led to the advancement of the 7th Brigade to the Quneitra salient and of the 82nd Battalion to Hushniya. From that point the 7th Brigade concentrated its control of the entire northern sector of the Golan Heights from its CCP.

When the GOC returned from the GHQ to the Nafah bunker around 16:00 he endorsed the decision, which was in accordance with his assessment and decision before the war regarding the Syrian Army's central and dangerous effort in the Quneitra region. The 36th Division commander Brig. Gen. Refael (Raful) Eitan and a few of his staff officers arrived with the GOC along with the former Air Force commander Maj. Gen. (res.) Moti Hod who was appointed commander of the Air Force front CCP in the north.

The picture was optimistic. It seemed then that the first phase of the Syrian attack had failed. Contrary to their plan, the Syrians did not overtake the line of contact and did not penetrate to a depth of six kilometers as they had intended. At the same time all of the command forces were employed in the combat zones. In the southern sector all of the 82nd Battalion companies were on the combat line and there was no one left to man the second line. In the north of the combat front the 7th Brigade forces along with the 74th Battalion, managed to halt the Syrian attack.

Maj. Gen. Hofi reached the conclusion that the deployment had to be altered toward the night after he had examined the development of combat all along the front in the evening. The command prepared for darkness and the second phase of the Syrian attack. This phase was expected to take place between 17:00 and 22:00, and to include the entrance of the armored brigades infantry divisions across bridges placed over the anti-tank trench to a depth of 12 to 15 KM with on the Golan Heights (up to the line of Zaura, Waset, Nafah, El Al), and the advancement of the armored battalions to the junctions and slopes of the Golan Heights.

Even after it was discovered that the pressure on the southern sector was greater than was presumed, the allocation of force did not change. The command attempts to balance the order of battle in the sectors by directing an additional tank battalion south were not carried out. The deployment was not changed. Directing another battalion south from the northern sector during the first night of fighting could have hampered the strength of the defending force in the north even up to total collapse.

At 17:57 and after it became clear that the Syrians were attacking across the entire front, the command ordered the responsibility for the defensive sectors in the front to be segmented between the tank brigades. The 7th Brigade received the command of the northern sector from Outpost 104 in the north to Outpost 110, and the 188th Brigade remained responsible for the southern sector. Col. Tzuri Sagi, the outgoing commander of the Golan Heights regional brigade, gained command over the Miron District on the Lebanese border from Mount Dov (Jabel Rous) to the west. At this stage the 820th Regional Brigade obtained responsibility for continued handling of the line's outposts, the Heights' settlements and preparation of a defensive alignment on the Jordan River's bridges, where the regional defense forces were directed along with those from the 1st Brigade basic training basis.

The Burnout of the Forces in the Southern Sector

Once the GOC reached the Nafah CCP he ordered the 188th Brigade commander to go out on the field. The 188th Brigade commander left the Nafah bunker and to the CCP's APC south along the Petroleum Road to rule the fighting in his brigade sector.

The burnout of the force in the south was not the most problematic factor at that stage. The 82nd Battalion delay in entering the battle—along with its split and decentralized manner of operation—caused gaps in the defensive alignment to remain uncovered. A broad gap was left south of Outpost 116 and another gaps remained south of Outpost 111. When the second phase of the Syrian attack—the attack by the second Division rank's armored brigades—began the 132nd Mechanized Brigade and the 51st Armored Brigade broke through these gaps without any battle. By 20:00 the Syrians had obtained a breakthrough in the southern sector and even reached the region of Hushniya.

Due to the severity of the situation regarding the forces in the southern sector the 188th Brigade commander headed out of the command outpost at Nafah and headed for the command outpost in the Jukhader sector. The delayed departure from Nafah to the southern sector didn't enable the 188th Brigade commander to join up with his forces. He remained in the Umm Dananir road junction and as far as possible managed the defensive battle in the southern sector with the assistance of the intelligence officer and communication officer from there during the night.

At this stage the Syrian brigades penetrated the depth of the Golan Heights in the center and south almost without combat. In the 188th Brigade sector, the Syrian forces managed to move a tank brigade (the 51st Brigade) up to Hushniya, south of Outpost 111. An additional armored brigade (the 46th Brigade) broke through the Petroleum Road south of Outpost 115 and set up west of Tel Fares, its forces destroying two IDF artillery batteries in the region. The 132nd Mechanized Brigade penetrated south of Outpost 116 and reached Tel Saki, heading south toward Ramat Magshimim.

A report of this 132nd Brigade breakthrough reached the 188th Brigade commander from the GOC, who ordered him to stop the Syrians. At 19:00 the 188th Brigade commander ordered the

82nd Battalion deputy commander Maj. Danny Pesach, who was with Company D (minus one platoon) under the command of Captain Danny Levin, to move south toward Outpost 116 and stop the Syrian force that broke through there. The Israeli force which included eight tanks encountered Syrian forces on its way and lost three tanks. Another tank had turned back. The remainder of the force, made up of four tanks, reached Tel Saki. Around that time the GOC ordered the 7th Brigade commander to transfer another battalion to reinforce the 188th Brigade.

The 7th Brigade commander instructed the 71st Battalion, under the command of Lt. Col. Meshulam Rates, which then had fifteen tanks, to descend from its positions and reach Tel Bar-On. When the battalion reached the area the brigade commander delayed it, being apprehensive of the Syrian pressure in the Valley of Tears, north of Quneitra, to increase. The command did not know about the 7th Brigade commander decision to leave the 71st Battalion in his region, and an exchange of words over this issue took place between the 188th Brigade commander, the command, and the 7th Brigade, until around 20:30 when, in light of the 7th Brigade commander's report of his condition, the GOC approved of leaving the battalion in the 7th Brigade sector.

At around 20:00, in response to reports received from most units regarding a shortage in tank ammunition, the 188th Brigade main headquarters at the Aleika base sent an ammunition convoy under the command of deputy brigade commander Lt. Col. David Israeli, which moved south along the Petroleum Road in order to meet up with the brigade commander's CCP. Following information of an incursion by Syrian tanks in Qudna and the Petroleum Road, the brigade commander ordered the convoy to return to Nafah. Ammunition and the provisions of logistical aid to the units that had been engaged in intense combat since midday was delayed.

Around 22:00, the actual situation was made clear to the brigade, wherein the Petroleum Road sector held exceedingly reduced forces and the situation was not much better in the other sectors. At this time the 188th Brigade had about fifty functioning tanks at its disposal, some without ammunition, compared to about 240 Syrian tanks. Greatly reduced forces remained in the Petroleum Road sector, the Zvika Force, under the command of Lt. Zvika Greengold who had only two tanks and a small reserve force from the 179th Brigade for part of the night.

The Deployment and Defensive Fighting at Night in the Northern Sector

In the evening the 7th Brigade commander built another brigade force under the command of the 77th Brigade deputy commander Captain Eitan Cowley, with the addition of the "Tiger" company under the command of Captain Meir Zamir who settled south of Quneitra to secure the brigade southern flank.

After receiving an update from the 74th Brigade commander about the events taking place in the sector the 7th Brigade commander decided to distribute the forces in the following manner, in order to halt the Syrian effort at the Quneitra salient:

- A reduced 75th Battalion would be deployed between Hermonit and Tel Mahfi on the "Casuarina" route and destroy Syrian forces in its sector;
- The 77th Battalion, minus one company, will move to Quneitra from the south and ascend to the "Booster" sector;
- The 71st Battalion will advance from Dalwa to the Waset road junction.

The Syrian breakthrough in the northern sector, which started around 15:00, included three Syrian infantry brigades and the Moroccan Brigade that attacked in the 7th Brigade sector. The 85th Brigade, 68th Brigade, and the Moroccan Brigade attacked in the region of outposts 104–107. The 52nd Brigade from the 9th Division attacked in the southern Quneitra region and Outpost 109. The attacks were executed with the cover of heavy artillery of about twenty-five batteries for each brigade. The Syrian breakthrough was executed in two attack waves where each infantry brigade had a reinforced armored battalion. The defensive alignment of Israeli forces included the line's outposts, the anti-tank trenches, and the tank ramps in the front and the depth of Israeli territory. In light of the field's characteristics and the situation assessment, the Syrians channeled their forces into four main passages" the Valley of Tears passage in the center of the sector, the Mas'ade and Buq'ata regions in the northern sector and south of Quneitra in the region of Outpost 109. The Syrians managed to bridge the anti-tank trench and cross it on all these locations.

However, the Syrians were blocked by the 74th Brigade tank platoons on the first line of outposts after successfully bridging and advancing west. Other Syrian forces breaking through between the outposts were later blocked by the tank platoons of the 7th Brigade that lined up in the depth of the first line.

The Syrians continued attacking through the night, taking advantage of the night vision aids at their disposal. The Israeli tanks, in comparison, were only equipped with "Xenon" spotlights which served as targets for the enemy's fire. The Israeli artillery only supplied a small number of illumination shells. Syrian tanks located the Israeli tanks from a distance and even managed to infiltrate the brigade units, including accompanied by infantry APCs equipped with anti-tank weapons.

The main burden of fighting that night was carried by the

74th Battalion on the front line and the three battalions from the tanks of the 7th Brigade that halted the Syrians that managed to infiltrate between the outposts. During the night's battles the artillery fire and Syrian tanks injured 75th Battalion commander Lt. Col. Yosef (Yos) Eldar (in the Valley of Tears) and Company G commander Albert Menachem (west of Quneitra) and both were evacuated to receive medical treatment. Seventy-seventh Battalion commander Lt. Col. Avigdor Kahalani took the place of Yos Eldar, while deputy brigade commander Captain Eitan Cowley took command of the company. The Syrian artillery fire ended near midnight and was renewed at dawn, when it was aimed by Syrian artillery officers positioned in the Hermon outpost that they had captured.

Operating Fire Sources in the Command

The command that pushed for the participation of the Air Force in the fighting managed to get aerial assistance of thirty-five jet sorties operating in the missile-defended zone during Saturday. These were directed, as part of the Srita (Scratch) operation, against Syrian armored and infantry forces, mainly in the south of the Golan Heights but in the north and near the Hermon outpost as well.

The artillery on the Golan Heights was managed by the 334th Battalion commander from the Nafah bunker and by the command artillery commander Lt. Col. Avraham Bar David. The employment of artillery was mainly based on intelligence reports and regulated from the line's outposts, rather than by ranging from the observation posts at the mound heads which had turned ineffective by the smoke rising over the combat zone. On the first day of fighting the Golan Heights was engulfed in smoke, not only from the incoming and outgoing shells, but also from the brush fires that spread catching thorns and dry vegetation that remained from the summer before the war. The IDF's artillery fire was mainly aimed at the broken through sectors on the Petroleum Road and Quneitra salient. Fire was also aimed at the Syrian and Moroccan forces penetrating in the north of the Heights. The 160mm mortar batteries and 155mm batteries from the 334th Battalion were also directed at the Syrian forces attacking the Hermon outpost. Under cover of the mortar shells the soldiers attempted to evacuate from the outpost. When the battle developed the batteries were also employed in "firing on our own outposts" to strike the Syrian forces moving toward them. The frontal observation officer intended to operate from the Tank Bend in Hermon left for his position and continued ranging toward targets in the north of the Golan Heights. Lt. Col. Ben Ami Cohen and his staff, who operated from the summit of Tel Fares, ranged artillery guns against the Syrian efforts in the southern sector. A 175mm battery deployed on the Golan Heights was also used to strike the FROG surface-to-surface rocket battery.

In the afternoon hours the batteries began reporting a shortage in ammunition, and the push of additional ammunition to the positions began, mainly from the ammunition base in Snobar which was made available to the command. The Syrian anti-battery fire which had been inaccurate during the first hours of fighting improved and some batteries were forced to leap to alternative positions.

At early nighttime hours there was a shortage of illumination shells. All the ammunition in the batteries, battalions and the Snobar ammunition base had been used. At the same time the head of artillery command was engaged in mobilization and allocation of fire units, as well as in pushing artillery ammunition to the firing batteries, after they had fired about 3000 shells and 900 mortars by 21:00. The first two battalions from the 212th Support Unit of the 36th Division, and a battery of 175mm guns that managed to mobilize and set up had already begun to assist the fighting forces from positions west of the Jordan River until they ran out of all the illumination shells.

Situation, Assessment and Activity at the Level of Command at the End of the First Day of Fighting

The following was the situation report that began forming in the Command CCP at the end of the first day of battle:

The commanders controlled the battle in the northern sector of the Golan Heights. The armored forces held the key regions; the brigade and battalion commanders' control of the forces was effective and the forces were employed within their framework and did not collapse in spite of constant Syrian pressure. The tanks of the 7th Brigade, deployed in the controlling areas and ramps, were prepared in advance and halted the Syrian columns attempting to cross the anti-tank trench. Armored Syrian units which managed to cross the trench and minefields were hit on their way west.

In the southern sector the command was mistaken when it did not instruct the brigade commander to concentrate the forces already in the afternoon hours of October 6 to a defined brigade site in the Tel Fares-Hushniya region, an area which is the key region in the southern section of the Heights. A defined brigade site would have lasted until the joining up of forces for the counter attack. The senior command was not on the field, and the battalion framework arriving to reinforce the sector, the 82nd Battalion, was immediately split and dispersed. The platoons deployed in the field failed at halting the Syrians that crossed the obstacles in the front and broke through with their forces toward the Tel Fares and Hushniya regions, the Petroleum Road and Ramat Magshimim. The first Syrian forces arrived at the Hushniya region as early as 20:00.

Simultaneously to combat management on the front, the command dealt with the completion of the mobilization and equipping process and efforts were made to speed up the mobilizing reserve units and send forces, however small, to reinforce the regular forces on the Golan Heights. The launch of the Egyptian—Syrian attack on Yom Kippur, which is the only day of the year when all reserve soldiers are at home or near it in the synagogues when they are available for immediate mobilization, caused a situation where, starting Saturday night, more and more small reserve forces gathered in the openings of routes heading up to the Golan Heights. The first forces were sent to the capture the openings of the routes descending from the Golan Heights toward the Jordan River bridges and the shores of the Sea of Galilee. The command positioned officer units (G3 and maintenance) along the routes going up to the Golan Heights thus directing the forces and managing to report the forces' rate at going up the Heights to the front in the east.

On the night between Saturday October 6 and Sunday October 7, the 36th Division took over responsibility for the sector, and the forces operating on the Golan Heights that were transferred to its command. Up to that point and until the mobilization of the division's logistical alignment, its equipping, and the start of its operation, the maintenance of forces in the Golan was managed by the command G4 Branch. The command had its own transportation alignment at its disposal, along with a command maintenance company for control, a vehicle and tank maintenance alignment in the workshops deployed in the region, a medical alignment partially mobilized in the period between Rosh Hashanah and Yom Kippur, and a communication equipment maintenance alignment as part of the command communication battalion.

Immediately upon mobilization, reserve forces began filling the ranks of the regular and mobilizing brigades: the 188th, the 7th, the 179th, and the 679th brigades using the ammunition piles located around bases throughout the eastern Galilee.

A first reserve force of about one tank Company from the 179th Brigade, under the command of 266th Battalion commander Lt. Col. Uzi Mor, left the Pilon Base and headed for Nafah and the Petroleum Road. A platoon force under the command of a deputy company commander from the 679th Brigade, Lt. Nitzan Yotzer, crossed the Arik Bridge and prepared for a blocking in the Katzbia region along the Yehudia route.

At that time a Golani force on half-tracks began moving from Rosh Pina to Kiryat Shmona and toward the Hermon with the intention of joining up with the outpost with which communications had been cut off. When the force was near the Neve Ativ settlement the GOC ordered to halt the advancement and prepare for the defense of the northern Golan Heights, securing key fields and vital junctions with the use of infantry forces reinforced by anti-tank equipment, under the command of the 36th Division. Platoons from the brigade were positioned to secure the Jordan River bridges, a force under the 51st Battalion deputy commander, composed of two companies reinforced by RCLRs was sent to the Gamla rise to halt advancing Syrian forces and meet retreating forces from the Tel Fares region.

During the night the GOC ordered the advancement of every possible force to the salient openings on the Golan Heights. Previously, at 19:10, he instructed the 36th Division commander to avoid battles of attrition and evacuate outposts which are in danger of being placed under siege. The GOC also ordered to exploit every gap in the fighting to advance fuel and ammunition to the fighting forces. At 20:40 the GOC Maj. Gen. Hofi ordered the artillery to skip back to rear deployment positions and at 21:22 he instructed the 36th Division commander to construct a reserve force from the mechanized infantry companies' auxiliary forces.

The impression of the Northern Command regarding the situation on the front was grave. The difficult situation of the 188th Brigade in the southern sector was made clear after midnight. Fear that the entire southern Golan Heights would fall intensified. This difficult impression was enhanced by the apprehension that the 3rd Armored Division would enter attack in the Quneitra salient.

Late at night and upon the arrival of additional staff officers from the 36th Division to the Golan Heights, the division under the command of Brig. Gen. Refael (Raful) Eitan took responsibility for the continued fighting in the front. At night, the Command CCP evacuated the Nafah bunker. The GOC left at midnight and his staff officers: the G3 officer, the intelligence officer, HAC, and communication officer left on at around 03:00 in one Carmel car to the command outpost at Mount Knaan. The aerial CCP under the command of Maj. Gen. Moti Hod also moved to Mount Knaan, and from the morning of October 7 began operating Air Force jets. From the Knaan outpost and the central headquarters in Nazareth the command continued to handle the mobilization and operation of the reserve alignment to stabilize an additional line of defense in the route openings east of the Jordan River and the shores of the Sea of Galilee under the direct charge of the Chief of Staff, Brig. Gen. Uri Bar-On.

The 188th Brigade Fighting at Night

In the southern sector, from around 22:00, the situation was stable excluding one Syrian attempt to attack Outpost 115, as well as scattered artillery fire. In general there were no serious clashes in this region at this time. The Company C tanks positioned in the Jukhader junction under the command of the 53rd Battalion occasionally opened fire and managed to strike Syrian AFVs.

On the eve of the first day of fighting the 188th Brigade commander left the Nafah bunker, as mentioned before, and went out into the field in a mobile brigade CCP. It was one of the few CCPs in the IDF that was already mobile on APCs. The CCP moved east on the Petroleum Road aiming at meeting up with the brigade commander's tank—which should have reached the junction from the 53rd Battalion tank park in Hushniya—at the Petroleum Road. Until the arrival of the tank the CCP set up in the Umm Dananir junction in the narrow gap between the fence of the oil pipeline and the Petroleum Road. One of the main matters that bothered him was the planned meeting with the administrative convoy that was already making its way from Nafah toward Umm Dananir. While waiting for the supply convoy and the brigade commander's tank, information of armored battles taking place in Hushniya were received and could be heard behind the position of the CCP. News regarding the penetration of Syrian forces from the Haspin region was received as well. The brigade commander reached the conclusion that the brigade CCP had mistakenly entered a Syrian forces pincer movement that was beginning to close in on them.

Lt. Zvika Greengold, a deputy company commander in the 74th Battalion who had been on leave before leaving the army, returned to the brigade and organized a tank force and teams that he found at the brigade workshop in Nafah, then called the

CCP and declared that he had formed a tank task force.

Zvika positioned his force west of the Hushniya—Petroleum Road—Katzbia junction, in a place that eventually turned out to be a key point which allowed for an efficient defense of Nafah. Only in later conversations was it discovered that the Zvika Force was very small, unlike the prevailing thought at the time that it was a whole company. The brigade commander who thought so as well even attempted to coordinate a joint offensive by the 82nd Battalion and the Zvika Force.

The Zvika Force, which at one time had only a single tank, entered a gun battle with the 51st Syrian Brigade armored spearhead, which arrived at the Mashta junction, in the crossroads of the road to Quneitra and the Petroleum Road. The Syrians, who did not expect any Israeli force, halted the flow of their advancement.

On arrival of the brigade commander's tank from Hushniya, there was the apprehension that additional Syrian forces that had arrived at Hushniya were behind the CCP. The brigade commander could not organize the backwards attack by the 82nd Battalion together with the Zvika Force. Therefore, the brigade commander decided to retreat with his small CCP to Mazraat Quneitra, to create a "stop line" with the 53rd Battalion commander's tanks. Later at dawn, he planned to return to Nafah through the Waterfalls Route and Btecha Valley despite the problematic issue of moving away from the battlefield. Topographical conditions justified that apprehension but a permanent relay station located on Mount Knaan before the war allowed for the full control of the brigade forces through all stages of their movement to the Btecha Valley and their going up back to the Heights.

In the late night hours the 7th Brigade commander received a report from the 188th Brigade regarding a one battalion Syrian Armored Force moving from Jukhader along the "Reshet" route toward Quneitra. On Sunday at dawn a "Tiger" company under the command of Captain Meir Zamir was sent to join up with the 188th Brigade commander in the intersection of "Reshet-Troya" routes northwest of Outpost 111. The company's mission was to stop a Syrian force which had penetrated this route with the intent of attacking the 7th Brigade south of Quneitra. The company commander Captain Meir Zamir—"Tiger" on the communication network—laid his forces in an ambush on the "Reshet" route. The company waited until most of the Syrian forces had entered the ambush area to only then open fire. During the progressing battle the company destroyed about forty Syrian vehicles. This was the 43rd Tank Brigade of the 9th Infantry Division which included about 100 T-55 tanks and about 40 APCs. The Syrian brigade was halted. The brigade spearhead was destroyed and the rest of the brigade withdrew deep into the Syrian territory.

During the night artillery fire was directed at the Syrian forces attacking the Israeli outposts, mainly in the southern sector of the front. At that time the 40th Battalion fire units were employed in assistance of the 7th Brigade forces halted in the Valley of Tears. The night artillery also included illumination shells to locate Syrian forces breaking through.

Some of the batteries skipped back to rear positions understanding that they could be run over by the advancing Syrian forces. Two batteries belonging to the 9th Battalion training and the 405th Battalion deployed in the southern Heights west of Tel Fares were hit by the fire of the advancing Syrian forces. Five SPGs pulled out west toward the Gamla incline in a convoy under the command of the 405th Battalion Deputy Commander Maj. Uri Manos. Other batteries, in the central and northern Golan Heights, skipped to alternative positions and were provided with ammunition. Some of the ammunition trucks headed for the batteries were hit by Syrian tank fire breaking through to the depth of the Golan Heights in the Hushniya region. GHQ ammunition convoys began arriving and were received by the HAC forces that thrust them, at times, all the way up to the gun batteries.

Arrival of the First Reserve Forces

At 02:55, the GOC ordered the 210th Division's reserve forces be sent up along the Yehudia and Gamla routes toward the southern sector. The GOC repeated his message to the 36th Division commander that "we must gain time until the reserve forces arrive." At 03:03, the GOC ordered the evacuation of the Golan Heights settlements, after the women and children had already been evacuated earlier, some time before firing commenced. The Golani Brigade forces that were set to attack the Hermon, were stopped at 04:02 for fear that the battle will run on into daylight hours. At 04:12, the GOC repeated his order to avoid battles of attrition as well as to evacuate combatants from the outpost on foot and not by tanks that could get hit. At 04:14, the commander defined the goals of the defensive battle as follows: the intent was to block the enemy invasion in the south of the Golan. The main effort was to focus on preventing the entry of Syrian forces into Israeli territory. The G3 officer was briefed by the GOC, who stated that the KKL (JNF) road (the Waterfalls Route) and Snobar had to be in their hands. The GOC also ordered the allocation of reserve forces from the 179th and 9th Brigades, and the 188th Brigade Reserve Battalion, to the southern routes going up to the Golan Heights.

At 23:00, a force of eight Centurion tanks under the command of 266th Reserve Battalion commander Lt. Col. Uzi Mor from the 179th Brigade, arrived at Nafah and joined up with Zvika's tank.

The force encountered Syrian tanks near Mashta junction after midnight. The Syrians, who were equipped with infrared lighting, hit three Israeli tanks and the battalion commander was injured and evacuated. The other tanks were hit as well and the company commander Amnon Sharon was captured. Once again Zvika Force was left with mere two tanks.

The Syrians attempting to advance a force toward Katzbia encountered a tank platoon from the 679th Brigade under the command of deputy company commander Nitzan Yotzer in the Katzbia rise at 02:00. The company reached the location after the commander of the 36th Division requested the 679th Brigade commander to send any force he had to that location.

At 03:00, two additional companies from the 266th Battalion arrived at Nafah. One company under the command of Maj. Baruch Lanchner moved along the "Pele" Route parallel to the Petroleum Road and a second company under the command of the 188th Brigade deputy commander Lt. Col. David Israeli joined up with the Zvika Force.

The deputy brigade commander conducted a successful defensive battle and halted the Syrians until 09:00. At dawn, the 266th Battalion deputy commander's force established fire contact with the 51st Syrian Brigade branch protection force and by 09:00, it only had three tanks left. The deputy battalion commander was killed during the battle.

At the end of the first night of fighting, the Syrian forces had taken control over an area of more than ten kilometers deep into the southern sector. In the northern part of the southern sector, the Syrians reached Hushniya and moved on from there toward Katzbia. In the south, the Syrians reached Ramat Magshimim even capturing the settlement. Of the 53rd and 82nd Battalions, which could not withstand the pressure of the Syrian forces flowing west, small subunits and single tanks remained. Few IDF forces remained in the field and conducted a defensive battle, including all the outposts on the line, which were under siege but had not been captured.

Golani Forces join up the Fighting in the Front

Already at near dawn of October 7, the Golani Brigade commander attempted to reach the soldiers under siege in the Hermon outpost, after the GOC had accepted the brigade commander's suggestion at 18:07, Col. Amir Drori attempted to join up with the outpost.

The force headed out of Rosh Pina at 01:50 on October 7, and reached the Neve Ativ area at 04:01. But then the GOC commanded the 1st Brigade commander to immediately halt the advancement for fear of a Syrian breakthrough in the Hader—Mas'ade sector, and ordered him to prepare a blocking on the "Majorca"—"Yakir" route instead, meaning the whole sector between Majdal Shams in the north and the village of Buq'ata in the south, more accurately in the sector of outposts 103–105, wherein the 13th Battalion in the sector would transfer to the command of the brigade commander. The brigade commander was unaware of the combat situation on the Golan Heights and tried to object to the order assuming it would be preferable to attack the Syrian force in the Hermon as soon as possible before it managed to reorganize. His objection was rejected. The force stopped in its tracks and began moving back over the Sa'ar Bridge toward the village of Mas'ade. At 04:21, the 1st Brigade commander was ordered to prepare for a holding and at 05:19 forces of the 1st Brigade were already deployed in their sector and ready to defend against Syrian forces attack.

The Activity in the Command and GHQ at Dawn on Sunday

Toward morning, the GOC instructed the regional brigade commander to prepare the bridges over the Jordan River for detonation for fear of a Syrian takeover, and to position infantry and anti-tank forces to defend them and the slopes leading from the Golan Heights toward the Jordan River. The GHQ, who was also apprehensive of the fate of the crossings over the Jordan River, instructed the command at 06:00 to construct a second line of defense on the Nafah-Aleika route and gather forces to halt a Syrian invasion at the other route openings.

Simultaneously the GOC pressured the GHQ Chief of Staff to allocate additional aerial forces to the sector, in light of the extensive Syrian breakthrough in the south of the front. In the meantime Maj. Gen. (res.) Moti Hod joined the planning and control of the aerial force, who, as stated, had become the commander of the Air Force FCO in the Northern Command.

The Israeli Air Force planned to have its full capacity on the Egyptian front. Squadrons' briefings for attacks and jets' fueling and arming went accordingly. Throughout the night of October 6–7, the wings and bases of the Air Force prepared for the Egyptian front extensively. However, information regarding the serious situation of Israeli forces on the Golan Heights and the depth of the Syrian breakthrough in the south of the Heights was coming in throughout the night. These reports came in more frequently at 03:00 and at 03:56, the Northern Command GOC, Maj. Gen. Hofi, reported to the GHQ Chief of Staff: "... the situation is not good. There is a flow of (Syrian) tanks in the direction of Ben Shoham [188th Brigade commander Col. Yitzhak Ben Shoham]. An order was issued to evacuate settlements... there are many damaged tanks. We will do everything within our power to delay the flooding of routes and battles of attrition. (I) Request a massive aerial support, if not—our situation will be very serious..."

At 04:15, the GHQ Chief of Staff reported to the Air Force commander on the serious condition of the forces on the Golan Heights. In response to his question of what the Air Force could do to assist, the Air Force commander replied that it was feasible to allocate one Sky Hawk squadron for attacks on the Golan Heights that would start its attack in the early morning hours. At this stage the GHQ Chief of Staff still approved the plan to deploy the Air Force solely on the Egyptian front as planned.

However, information regarding the dire situation on the Golan Heights continued flowing in to the HCO. At 05:35, the GHQ Chief of Staff Lt. Gen. Elazar and his deputy Maj. Gen. Tal went to the Air Force control outpost and emphasized the severity of the situation on the Golan Heights. In response to the GHQ Chief of Staff question of whether the Tagar("Challenge") operation for the attack on the canal missile alignment could be carried out in the morning and the "Dugman" ("Model") operation for the attack of missiles in Syria in the afternoon the commander of the Air Force replied in the negative.

At 06:05, the Minister of Defense, Moshe Dayan, reached the Northern Command CCP to closely examine the situation since it seemed critical. At 06:42 the minister spoke with the Air Force commander after failing to reach the GHQ Chief of Staff and described the situation on the Golan Heights in especially grim terms and mentioned that "if there aren't quartets (formations of jets) by noon they (the Syrians) will penetrate the Jordan Valley." Following this conversation the Air Force commander instructed the immediate allocation of jets to the attack on the Syrian forces along the Petroleum Road and in the south of the Heights, and said among other things, that: "...the Rapid Route descends to the Jordan Valley, to the Btecha Valley, so now the minister says that only the Air Force can stop them. The effort is now to halt the Syrians on the Golan Heights."

There was a consultation at the Air Force control outpost between the GHQ Chief of Staff and the commander of the Air Force after this talk. It seemed that, in the meantime, the Northern Command GOC also managed to convince the GHQ Chief of Staff to alter the Air Force earlier plan. It was decided in the meeting to move the Air Force main effort to the Syrian front.

At 06:57, when the Air Force was busy with of the preparatory flight for Tagar("Challenge") and jets were attacking the Egyptian Air Force in its bases an Israeli Air Force command order was issued to the squadrons regarding the altering of the mission as follows : "operate Dugman 5 B, H-hour 11:30, cancel Tagar second flight."

Once this order was issued the air and ground teams worked intensively to equip the jets to perform the new mission, while at the same time over 120 jets were attacking airfields in Egypt and anti-aircraft batteries in preparation for "Tagar."

The Air Force commander ordered that every available plane be directed to the attacking of the Syrian forces, mainly in the southern route of the Golan Heights where there were no armored IDF forces. It was clear that fighting under the threat of missiles caused substantial losses of pilots and jets that had to avoid missiles during attacks. Jets were hit and others were launched to defend the ground forces from attacks by Syrian jets.

The Fall of the Hermon Outpost

CHAPTER 7

A HEAVY ARTILLERY BOMBARDMENT OF the outpost began at approximately at 14:00 on October 6. All the people at the outpost gathered in the central hall and, due to the bombardment, no observation post was manned. When the firing began, a half-track headed for its designated position at the Tank Bend to assist the aiming of artillery fire in the northern Golan Heights, left the outpost carrying a front line observation officer, a technical aid and a driver from the 334th Artillery Battalion. While they were on the road the outpost was attacked by six Syrian MiG 17 jets, immediately followed by three Mil Mi-8 helicopters, two of them carrying about thirty paratroopers to hill 2072 south of the upper ski lift station. The main Syrian force quickly deployed in positions above the road bend south of the upper ski lift station in order to block access to the outpost. Several paratroopers advanced toward the outpost and positioned themselves as a suppressive force. A third helicopter carrying sixteen paratroopers who were to position themselves for the blocking at the Tank Bend crashed while attempting to land east of the bend. Only three paratroopers were saved and they joined their friends near the upper ski lift station. Once the Syrian paratroopers identified the front line observation officer's half-track they opened fire at it but the vehicle continued moving. A jeep carrying the GHQ's EW company commander and a driver heading for the outpost witnessed the landing of the Syrian forces and quickly returned to their unit deployed in the Tank Bend, with the Syrians firing at them all the while. Three Golani combatants in the upper ski lift observation post saw the Syrian helicopters land and after failing to fire at them due to a malfunction in their machine gun, abandoned their position which had a communicator, after a few minutes and went down to the lower ski lift station where they joined up with a platoon from their company holding the place without alerting the outpost of the Syrian landing.

While the Syrian block under the command of Lt. Achmed el-Jojo was taking position, the rest of the 82nd Battalion advanced on foot from the Syrian Hermon outpost to the Israeli outpost, organized in eight platoon combat teams (Majmuas). At around 15:15, when the first two Majmuas drew near the outpost the Syrian artillery ceased firing and the suppressive force opened fire from small arms at the outpost. At that time a fourth helicopter neared the outpost from the southwest, and sixteen commando warriors jumped out, some joining the storming of the outpost and some positioning themselves as an additional suppressive force.

When the bombing of the outpost stopped and the sound of the small arms outside could be heard in the central hall, the commander of the outpost Lt. Gadi Zidover, the platoon commander Punk and four additional Golani combatants went out to the combat platform through the upper western opening. They noticed dozens of Syrian soldiers advancing on the road toward the gate of the outpost, and a suppressive force lying on a rampart outside the fences of the outpost. In the absence of combat positions, the commander of the outpost and combatants deployed on the blast zone to the right of the opening and opened fire from the MAG machine gun and their personal weapons. This took the Syrians by surprise and their advancement toward the gate was halted. The MAG operator was killed immediately and the outpost's sergeant operated the MAG in his place. The outpost commander saw that combatants were quickly running out of ammunition and went down to the central hall to call 820th Brigade commander Col. Zvi Barzani. He explained the situation and requested that he quickly employ "firing on our own outposts." The brigade commander approved his request and the 334th Artillery Battalion commander Lt. Col. Arieh Schwartz, the commander of the brigade's fire support, began handling it. The Golani combatants continued firing at the Syrians and prevented their entrance into the outpost until the bombardment by the IDF forces began at around 15:45. The brigade commander then ordered the outpost commander to withdraw into the outpost until the bombardment ended and to break out only following his command. Due to a misunderstanding the combatants did not leave the outpost and continued defending its openings from within.

The Syrians stormed into the yard of the outpost and even penetrated through the upper western opening in to the outpost's upper level, throwing shrapnel and smoke grenades and firing batches of gunfire at the workrooms. Their entrance into the outpost was hesitant and slow, and was accompanied by much shooting and calls in Hebrew and Arabic for the people of the outpost to surrender. Some of them came down the staircase leading to the central hall and threw grenades at it. They reached the central hall but did not dare to clear the rooms or the tunnels heading out of it. They must have operated a smoke generator working on a small motor. The hall filled with smoke, dust and sound of explosions and shooting, which caused panic and hysteria, chiefly among the non-combat soldiers. The thick smoke caused a sensation of suffocation among the soldiers and once they thought the Syrians were employing gas, chaos broke out in the central hall. Soldiers ran around in panic, looking for cover in the tunnels leading out of the central hall. Some were in a state of shock and remained frozen in place in the rooms next to the central hall. Between 16:00 and 17:00, when the Syrians penetrated the upper level of the outpost, a few soldiers returned fire from different corners of the central hall toward the staircase and prevented the Syrians from coming down. The commander of the outpost attempted to gather the people from the different tunnels and rooms of the central hall toward one of the tunnels. At this stage the connection was cut off between the outpost and the outside world.

At around 17:30 the commander of the outpost and several combatants attempted to break out through one of the tunnels to evacuate through it and move toward the upper ski lift station, but they encountered Syrians and retreated. From that point most the men in the outpost gathered in the same tunnel, excluding the doctor and three Golani combatants, one of them was killed and another injured. Five others hid in two bunkers on the lower level. Due to the fact that some of them did not know the outpost at all and were unfamiliar with the maze, they split into two separate groups in the darkness but were close to each other. Around 19:00 the Syrians ceased clearing the outpost interior and a relative calm prevailed.

At about 16:50 the "Hedva" observation post, which was positioned across from the Lebanese village of Shabaa, received a radioed order to return to Mas'ade through the lower ski lift station and its men began moving on the road leading to the lower ski lift station in their APC. At around 17:00, when the APC was nearing the Si'on River bend, where the "Tali" observation post was located on board an 81mm mortar half-track, heavy fire was directed at both from the ridge above them. The APC was hit by an RPG rocket and stopped in the middle of the road. Three combatants were killed instantaneously and the rest were injured and took cover. The commander of the "Tali" observation post, who was standing exposed in the half-track, was shot in the back by a bullet but his driver started up the vehicle and raced down to the lower ski lift station. The attacking Syrian force was apparently the GHQ's 87th Reconnaissance Battalion which was supposed to set up at the Tank Bend overnight but got lost on its way and positioned itself above the road between the lower ski lift station and Mount Dov. The Syrians fired for a long time and left without descending to the road. When darkness fell, around 17:35, after the Syrians left the place, the "Hedva" commander reported the encounter and the injuries over the radio to the 902nd Nachal battalion's company headquarters at Mount Dov, and requested evacuation. This was reported to the 820th Regional Brigade's CCP at Nafah. The rescue force, consisting of a doctor, a medic and five combatants, was organized within an hour. The force moved on board two APCs and advanced slowly, carefully, and without lights. It reached the encounter scene at about 18:30, treated and evacuated the wounded along with the casualties from the field. From that point until the end of the war no IDF force entered the area between Mount Dov and the Hermon's shoulder.

At around 19:30, following orders by the 820th Brigade's commander, Hermon Company commander Lt. Yiftach Sagiv, left Mas'ade for the lower ski lift station with an APC and a tank platoon from the 71st Battalion appended to him, in order to examine the situation of the outpost and evacuate the wounded that had arrived in the afternoon. The force got to the lower ski lift station around 21:00. After the company commander saw that everything was in order in the lower ski lift station and reported this to the battalion headquarters. The brigade commander ordered him to keep the tank platoon there to defend him. The company commander left the place of his own initiative to evacuate the wounded to Nafah. When he arrived there near midnight he entered the command bunker and reported what had occurred on the Hermon to the GOC and the other commanders present.

At around 21:00 the commander of the Israeli outpost decided to try and escape from the outpost to the lower ski lift station. Due to the severed communication among the people at the outpost, the only ones who managed to escape were him, five officers, and eleven soldiers. They crossed a minefield, went down to the Bolaan Valley and moved west toward the upper ski lift station. A little before 23:00, when they began descending the rocky slope toward the bend in the road leading from the upper ski lift station to the Tank Bend, they were identified by the blocking Syrian force which opened fire at them. A Golani platoon commander and five of his soldiers stormed down the hill. Three of them were killed on the spot, including the platoon commander, and two were injured and captured the next morning. Additional officers and soldiers took cover and returned fire. The front line observation officer was critically injured and later died of his wounds. The remaining eleven soldiers managed to escape the encounter, some lightly wounded, and scattered in the area. During the night and the next day only ten of them managed to safely reach the line of Israeli forces. A soldier from the Air Force Unit outpost, who accidentally reached a Syrian 183rd commando battalion alignment deployed at elevation point 1616, was caught the next day, shot and killed.

Efforts of the 1st Brigade to Recapture the Hermon on the Night of October 6–7

While eleven soldiers from the outpost who escaped an encounter with the Syrian blockade attempted to reach Israeli forces at the lower ski lift station and the Golan Heights, and the rest of the outpost's soldiers hid inside it, a force from the 1st Brigade made its way toward the Hermon, after the GOC agreed with the suggestion made by brigade commander Col. Amir Drori at 18:07 to make an attempt at joining up with the outpost. The force included the brigade commander's half-track, the 51st Battalion's CCP with the 51st Battalion's companies A and B on board 15 half-tracks, the 69th Reconnaissance Company on board eight half-tracks and the brigade headquarters' Medical Evacuation Unit in an ambulance. The force, heading out from Rosh Pina, October 7 at 01:50, reached the Neve Ativ region at 04:01. However, the GOC ordered the 1st Brigade commander to immediately halt his advancement for fear of a Syrian breakthrough in the Hader—Mas'ade sector, and instead instructed him to prepare for a blocking in the sector of outposts 103-105, when the 13th Battalion in the region would transfer to the command of the brigade commander. The brigade commander was unaware of the combat situation in the Golan Height and attempted to appeal the order since he assumed it was better to attack the Syrian force in the Hermon as quickly as possible, before it managed to reorganize. His appeal was rejected. The force stopped in its tracks and began moving back over the Sa'ar Bridge toward the village of Mas'ade. At 04:21, the 1st Brigade commander received an order to prepare for a blocking and at 05:19 forces of the 1st Brigade were already deployed in their sector and ready to defend against the anticipated attack by the Syrian forces.

While the reduced 51st Battalion and 69th Reconnaissance Company prepared for defense in the Mas'ade region, a convoy descending from the lower ski lift station arrived there at around 07:00. It included a tank platoon from the 71st Battalion, an infantry platoon of the 13th Battalion that was manning the lower ski lift station on board two BTR-152 APCs, the front line observation officer's half-track, and a radio jamming company from the 374th Communications Corps Unit with three vehicles. They had received an order from the command at dawn, through 13th Battalion commander Lt. Col. Zeev Oren, to descend to the lower ski lift station. The three tanks were "adopted" by the 1st Brigade and remained under its command. This convoy also included the five survivors from the Israeli outpost. At that time there were no IDF forces left on the Hermon excluding thirty-six soldiers still trapped in the Hermon outpost. Two wounded from the encounter remained on the ridges of the Hermon that had already been captured by the Syrians. Six of the soldiers who escaped were still making their way down the mountain. The convoy held the three observers who escaped from the upper ski lift station as well.

The Syrian Takeover of the Outpost and the Capture of its Men—October 7–12

At around 06:00 on Sunday, October 7, while thirty-six of the soldiers in the outpost were still hiding in its tunnels, the two soldiers that were injured near the upper ski lift station while attempting to escape and were captured by the Syrians were brought to the yard of the outpost. Following a preliminary inquiry they were treated by a Syrian medic and removed to the valley outside the outpost. At about 09:00 the people of the outpost hiding in the northeastern tunnels heard gunfire. Apparently, the Syrians fired IDF weapons they had captured during the encounter near the upper ski lift station at night and so some of the people believed that these were IDF soldiers who had come to rescue them and were fighting the Syrians. The four people hiding in the communication bunker also heard the shooting and decided to go out to the yard of the outpost through the position that served as an ammunition bunker and which the Syrians had blown up early in the morning. A radio operator peeking through the opening noticed soldiers dressed in olive colored uniforms, one of them carrying an Uzi submachine gun and wearing a helmet with IDF markings. Thinking these were Golani soldiers he went out into the yard and shouted: "Golani, Golani, don't shoot!" when his eyes adjusted to the blinding light outside he noticed these were Syrian soldiers. He immediately turned back with the Syrians firing after him. The four returned to the tunnel with Syrians throwing smoke grenades after them and, they retreated to the communication bunker and hid there until the 12th of the month.

The Syrians did not know where the rest of those trapped were. They called them to surrender through the generator openings and the main entrance and directed flashlights into the tunnels. They announced that anyone who didn't come out was going to be killed. An argument grew between the men in the outpost trapped in one of the tunnel, whether to come out and surrender or not. The Golani platoon sergeant, Corporal Yitzhak Shalom, announced determinedly: "it's better to die than fall prisoner" and decided to try and break out through the northeastern position. At around 11:00 he began leading the group through the tunnel connecting the generator cells to the position. The platoon sergeant left for the outpost's roof first, followed by a Golani combatant, an intelligence soldier and a radio operator. They moved through the tunnel bent over, and immediately upon their exit were identified by the Syrians positioned on the roof of the outpost, near the main entrance and on the anti-aircraft hill north of the outpost. Apparently, in response to calls to surrender in Arabic, the platoon sergeant opened fire and threw two grenades at the Syrians. The three were killed in the short battle. The other men who came out as well lay low in the tunnel while Syrians fired at them but missed. When the other people saw that there was no hope of getting away alive they decided to surrender. During the surrender the Syrians killed the radio operator, who was waving a white cloth. The Syrians held their fire and ordered them to raise their hands and descend from the roof to the outpost's entrance. They instructed the surrendering men to put down their weapons and remove their helmets.

At about 11:30 two Syrian soldiers entered the doctor's room on the upper level and captured him along with the two Golani soldiers who were with him, one of them injured. In the late afternoon hours, after the personal belongings of all the twenty-six captured were taken from them and they were tied in pairs with telephone cords and were led on foot toward the Syrian outpost along the same route in four separate groups. They were escorted by about thirty Syrian soldiers from the 82nd Battalion. An injured Golani soldier who had difficulty walking and lagged behind was executed with a burst of gunfire and his body was left in the field. From the Syrian outpost the prisoners were transferred in trucks to a Special Forces training base at Kabun near Damascus, where they remained for ten days.

Five soldiers were left in the outpost itself: the G4 soldier hiding in the emergency bunker and the four soldiers hiding in the operations bunker. In the nearby maintenance bunker they found five combat rations and a plastic water container, which lasted them until they were captured on the 12th of the month. They heard news through a transistor radio they had found, and gathered from it that the kibbutz members on the Golan Heights returned to their settlements, so they decided to hide until the IDF forces recaptured the outpost. During the first three days they heard the Syrians clearing the outpost again and again every morning and evening by fire and grenades. After a relative calm in the outpost the five soldiers tried to escape several times but when they came up toward the central hall they heard the Syrian guards and returned to their hideout. On Friday the 12th of the month, at around 11:30, the Syrian soldiers entered the tunnels near them to search for food, discovered them by chance, and captured them. A few minutes later the Syrians discovered the G4 soldier and captured him as well. The five prisoners were transferred through the Syrian outpost to the Kabun training base. All thirty-one prisoners were taken to an olive grove where they were photographed by journalists on the 15th of the month. The next day all POWs were transferred to the al-Mezzeh prison.

The Battle Outcome

During the battles on the outpost proper, near the upper ski lift station and at the Si'on River bend, 16 commanders and combatants were killed and twelve were injured. In the Israeli outpost seven combatants were killed and four injured, and in the encounter near the upper ski lift station four combatants were killed and three were injured. In the encounter at the Si'on River bend three combatants were killed and four were injured. Thirty-one were captured and two combatants were executed by the Syrians after their capture. The Syrian losses were: 15 killed —12 combatants and the three crewmembers of a helicopter- and three officers wounded in the attempt to enter the outpost from the start of the war until dawn of October 7. The Hermon outpost fell into the hands of the Syrian Army. For the IDF, serious intelligence damages was caused, following the loss of the observation point and surveillance installations, the loss of classified equipment and the information the Syrians obtained from a few POWs

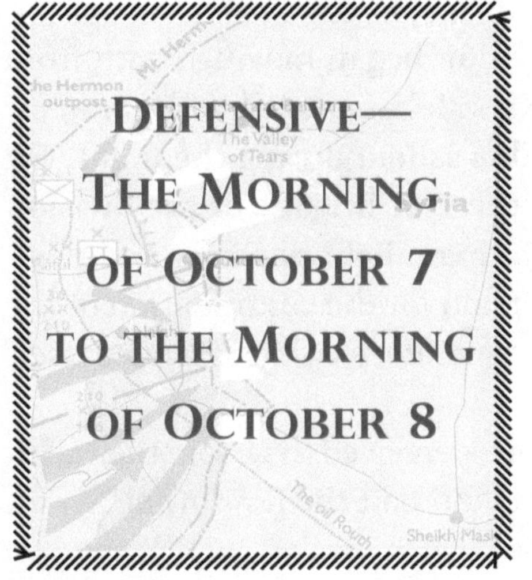

Defensive—The Morning of October 7 to the Morning of October 8

Chapter 8

Command Level Situation Report and Activity

On the morning of October 7, an evaluation at the GHQ was that the situation on the Golan Heights was critical and the Syrians were actually on their way to the cliffs overlooking the Jordan River and the Sea of Galilee. Reports showed that forces of the Syrian 5th Division that had broken through both sides of Tel Fares were moving to the west and south heading for the Gamla incline and the El Al strait. Forces of the 9th Division that had attacked the central Golan Heights were in control of the Hushniya road junction and attacked west on the route descending from Katzbia to the Arik Bridge as well as toward Nafah. In the northern Golan Heights forces of the 7th Division continued attacking the line of contact.

The Syrian GHQ reserves—the 1st and 3rd Armored Divisions—were deployed in forming up areas in the depth of the front, apparently already having done that before the war, as was evaluated by the Northern Command Intelligence and wasn't identified on the October 2 aerial photograph. Upon the opening of fire, the 1st Division began moving south from the gathering areas near the Kiswah bases south of Damascus, and set up in front of the Qudna salient during the night. On Sunday morning, October 7, the 91st Brigade of the division began passing through the Qudna salient passages and positioned itself in the Tel Fazra region for the continuation of the offensive while the division commander's CCP positioned itself on Tel Fazra itself.

IDF commanders, at that time, perceived that from the Nafah line to the south no IDF force could halt the flow of the Syrian offensive.

Four channels of activity were dealt with during the day at the Mount Knaan CCP Command Headquarters and in the main headquarters in Nazareth:

- A top effort to quickly send up reserve forces along the different routes in order to take over the route openings descending to the Jordan River and Sea of Galilee.
- The drawing of a situation report for the defensive alignment on the Golan Heights in an attempt to locate and halt the Syrian offensive efforts.
- The forwarding of demands to the GHQ level, with regard to the reinforcement of the northern front with both aerial forces and armored ones and planning their integration in combat.
- The controlling of the initial activity to establish rear defensive alignments on the slopes of the Golan Heights in the region of the Bnot Yaakov Bridge and west of the Jordan River.

Aerial battles developed at dawn and Syrian jets were shot down a few of them were hit by anti-aircraft fire from the ground and others were intercepted by the IAF jets. The Syrian attempt to deploy forces from helicopters in the Tel Fares sector failed after one of the helicopters was shot down by fire from the ground fire that didn't stop their advancement none the less.

Simultaneously, repeated requests for aerial support were made. It was coordinated by the Air Force Headquarters and the FCO, and the command artillery headquarters, which made its G3 officer, Maj. Gidon Etzion, available to the aerial CCP. Fifty-five aircrafts took part in the aerial assault which began in the early morning hours on the second day of the war. Escort planes secured the assault jets. Weather conditions, SAM alignment and the Syrian anti-aircraft fire all hindered the assault.

Jets attacked targets in the Hushniya region, Tel Fares, and north of Quneitra. A first group attacked at 05:59 in the Achmadia junction near Outpost 107. The jets continued attacking Syrian forces on the Golan Heights in all sectors—south and north. The Air Force attacked in the Ramat Magshimim region, Achmadia road junction, near the El Al River, at the Rapid Road junction, in Hushniya, and Tel Fares, and carried out aerial interdictions against forces moving along the routes. Successful strikes on the center of a convoy of Syrian forces were reported on the routes leading to the southern Golan Heights. In the northern sector assaults were carried out near Quneitra, in the Mount Yosifon (Tel Abu Yusuf) region, at Khan Arnabeh, in the Hermonit region, and near Birkat Ram. Convoys heading west along the routes were attacked there as well.

The command reports during the night caused the GHQ to assess that the situation on the Golan Heights was more severe than that on the front at the Suez Canal. Minister of Defense, Moshe Dayan, accompanied by Maj. Gen. Rehavam Ze'evi ("Gandhi"), was positioned at the Mount Knaan Command CCP as early as 06:00. The effort to hold the southern and central regions with the assistance of the Air Force, the employing of the 679th Armored Brigade as a blocking force in the first stage and as a central force for breaking the Syrians later on, as well as the issue of defending and preparing the Jordan River bridges for blocking and detonation were discussed with the GOC as part of the defensive battle. At the same time the Command GOC informed the GHQ Chief of Staff of his apprehension that the 3rd Syrian Armored Division would be placed into the northern sector against the 7th Brigade forces, and requested maximum aerial support for the northern front.

Following this information the GHQ Chief of Staff decided prior to 06:40, to allocate the GHQ's reserve force—the 146th Division from the Central Command—to the Northern Command. At 06:54, simultaneously with the flow of reserve forces to the front, the GOC started to prepare the counterattack, so it could be partially carried out that same day. At Command, the staff attempted to prevent the dispersal of forces and began rallying them for the counterattack.

At that time, the GHQ Chief of Staff ordered the GOC to establish a second line, particularly along the central route—the Nafah-Aleika route—to defend the slopes descending to the Jordan River and Sea of Galilee. The Minister of Defense, affected by the severity of the situation on the Golan Heights, confirmed the transfer of reinforcement north and strengthened the tendency of the GHQ Chief of Staff and the Commander of the Air Force to alter their basic plan and transfer the main aerial effort to the north.

At seven in the morning the GHQ Chief of Staff decided to cancel the second stage of attacking missiles in the south and directed the Air Force to attack the Syrian missile alignment on the Golan Heights. The strike against the Syrian SAM alignment as part of operation "Dugman 5," which started at 11:30, was intended to allow the Air Force the freedom of movement in the region and integrate it into the halting of the Syrians in the area which was so shallow. The failed operation caused the main aerial effort to be moved to the southern front against the

Egyptian forces[6] in the afternoon. At these hours only about forty attack sorties were allocated for the assault of the Syrian ground forces on the Golan Heights.

The RSM outposts on the lines of contact served as a main information gathering agency and reported enemy movements and the types of vehicles crossing the lines near them, though their efficiency was diminished due to strong artillery fire and dense smoke enveloping the field. These reports—mainly thanks to those transferred from the Hermonit outpost—however limited by local factors, helped locate the enemy efforts none the less. The outposts withstood artillery bombings and with the assistance of tank platoons even pushed the Syrian attacks back and caused losses to the forces moving near them. Apprehension, regarding the outposts left behind, arose. As early as 04:16 the GHQ Chief of Staff allowed the Northern Command to evacuate any outpost in danger of being seized. The 820th Regional Brigade ordered the evacuation of outposts 111, 114, 115, and 116 occupied by the 50th Nachal Paratrooper Battalion. The 53rd Tank Battalion from the 188th Brigade evacuated most of them to Tel Fares. The tanks could not reach Outpost 116, which was detached and surrounded. The commander of this outpost reported everything that was going on in his sector, aimed artillery and drove away Syrian forces attempting to enter the outpost.

In the northern sector, the Golani 13th Battalion was in charge of the outposts that continued their fighting and weren't evacuated, with the exception of the Hermon outpost which had already been captured during the first hours of the war.

6 See details in Chapter 19.

The First Reserve Forces' Way up to the Golan Heights

The reserve forces were pressured to organize quickly and go up to the Golan Heights upon mobilization. The Command Chief of Staff Brig. Gen. Uri Bar-On and the 36th Division deputy commander Brig. Gen. Menachem (Men) Aviram coordinated the activity and spurred the forces to move up quickly. This was happening without a parallel construction of the organic units, an ammunition and equipment shortage and even without going through "target alignment". Regarding the urgency of sending forces the GOC said: "...we lived with the urgency that we had to drive the forces as quickly as possible in order to halt (the Syrians)."

When the reserve forces and administrative ranks began arriving Brig. Gen. Uri Bar-On went out into the field on his own to prioritize the forces going up the routes to the Golan Heights in order to prevent their blockage by ranks unnecessary at this phase.

The forces moved east from the emergency storage warehouses and were directed to the route openings while in motion, in order to block the advancing Syrian forces. The command G3 officer gave the deployment order. Immediately after the allocation of forces to the Nafah region, he emphasized the southern sector that had been broken through. The command logistics supply and ordnance units, under the command of Lt. Col. Haim Levav, Lt. Col. Yishayahu Halfon, and Lt. Col. Yehuda Borovsky, assisted during the organization and mobilization (see details in the logistics chapter of Part III). The order of arrival was in accordance with the priorities in equipping and the distance from the emergency storage warehouses and the Golan Heights. Among the first forces to go up to the Golan Heights on October 7 were the 96th, 266th and 278th Tank

Battalions from the 179th Brigade; the 57th, 93rd, and 289th Battalions from the 679th Brigade; the 39th Battalion from the 188th Brigade; the 95th Battalion from the 4th Brigade and the 377th Battalion from the 9th Brigade. The 134th Reconnaissance Battalion from the 36th Division joined the 179th Brigade, and the command Artillery Corps units mobilized on caterpillar tracks from Kiryat Motzkin[7] to the Golan Heights.

The Reserve Units under the Control of the Command Going up the Golan Heights on October 7

- The 266th Battalion of upgraded "Shot Kal" Centurion tanks, from the 179th Brigade, under the command of Lt. Col. Uzi Mor, equipped at Pilon, went up the Golan Heights toward the Nafah region and incorporated into battles over the Petroleum Road and in the Nafah region, as early as the first night of combat.
- The 96th Battalion of upgraded "Shot Kal" Centurion tanks, from the 179th Brigade, under the command of Lt. Col. Israel Levin, equipped at the Naftali base at the Golani junction on the 164th Brigade tanks, went up the Golan Heights through the Arik Bridge on the Yehudia route, the brigade was in charge of as early as 05:30.
- Forces of Centurion tanks equipped with Meteor engines from the 57th Battalion from the 679th Brigade, under the command of Lt. Col. Moshe Harel went up the Golan Heights at 07:00 to the Bnot Yaakov Bridge route and were directed to the salient south of Quneitra.

7 This is near the Mediterranean coast.

- Forces of Centurion tanks equipped with Meteor engines from the 289th Battalion of the 679th Brigade, under the command of Lt. Col. Raful Shefer, went up at 07:30 on the Bnot Yaakov Bridge route and were directed at the salient south of Quneitra.
- Additional forces from the 679th Brigade including the 93rd Battalion of Centurion tanks equipped with Meteor engines, under the command of Lt. Col. Ran Gottfried, reached the Golan Heights by noon and joined the battle on the outskirts of Nafah.
- The 278th Battalion of upgraded "Shot Kal" Centurion tanks, from the 179th Brigade, under the command of Lt. Col. Yossi Amir, crossed the Jordan River over the Arik Bridge. The battalion was directed to the El Al strait at 10:00 and prepared for defense. A company from the battalion reinforced them on the Yehudia route.
- The 39th Battalion of upgraded "Shot Kal" Centurion tanks, which was the reserve battalion of the 188th Brigade, under the command of Lt. Col. Yoav Vaspi, went up through the Arik Bridge to the Gamla route where it encountered frontal Syrian forces in the afternoon.
- The 95th Tank Brigade of Sherman M-50 and M-51 tanks, from the 4th Mechanized Brigade, under the command of Lt. Col. Yaakov Noifeld, advanced on caterpillar tracks from the Kurdani Base[8] across the Arik Bridge and was also directed to the Gamla route, the brigade was in charge of.
- The 377th Tank Brigade of Sherman M-50 and M-51 tanks, from the 9th Mechanized Brigade, under the command of Lt. Col. Ben Zion Padan, advanced on caterpillar tracks from the Haifa region and arrived at the El Al strait, the brigade was in charge of, at around 14:00.

8 On the Mediterranean coast.

- The 134th Reconnaissance Battalion from the 36th Division of upgraded "Shot Kal" Centurion tanks, APCs and jeeps, under the command of Lt. Col. Hanani Tavor, crossed the Arik Bridge to the Yehudia route and joined the 179th Brigade at around noon.
- The command artillery forces, advancing on their tracks arrived at the Golan Heights from Kiryat Motzkin and used civilian gas stations along the way to refuel.

The mechanized infantry on half-tracks, also equipped at the emergency storage warehouses, were second in priority with all that referred to equipping and advancing to the front. Upon their arrival in the area of the Jordan River bridges they were ordered to wait and deploy where they were. The 4th Brigade Mechanized Infantry Battalions remained in the region of Vered HaGalil while the 9th Brigade Mechanized Infantry Battalions were gathered in the region of Givat Yoav. In a number of cases their half-tracks were transferred to elite infantry units that arrived in the region, as well.

The 820th Regional Brigade reserve forces, who completed the mobilization process at their base in Rosh Pina during October 7, were not sent up to their deployment regions on the Golan Heights. The brigade's 438th Anti-Tank Battalion deployed guns to defend the Bnot Yaakov Bridge. Artillery units including guns and mortars were transferred to the southern sector of the Golan Heights following the forces. The 32nd Infantry Battalion secured the Bnot Yaakov, the Arik and the Pkak Bridges while the 33rd Infantry Battalion and the 34th Infantry Battalion were transferred to reinforce the deployment along the Lebanese border in the Miron District, against anticipated terrorist activities.

To summarize, the Northern Command first reserve forces entered combat within 12 hours of their mobilization, and within 24 hours all reserve forces were either engaged in the war or preparing for it.

The situation, which the IDF commanders believe to be a stunning Syrian success, was not perceived in the same way by the Syrians themselves. The attacks of the three mechanized infantry divisions which commenced with optimal opening conditions were only partially successful. Their ability to reach their goal to quickly align along the cliff line in advantageous positions against the IDF's reserve forces seemed unattainable in those hours. The IDF's reserve forces halted the advancement of their forces by coming far sooner than they had predicted.

The Syrian command decided to change the direction of the attack in the central Golan Heights following the picture of partial success and the disruption of the campaign plan. The 1st Division commander, with his forces near Hushniya, got the assignment to rearrange for a new attack toward the Nafah junction, apparently aiming at threatening the defensive force in the northern sector, the 7th Brigade, on his neck and thus relieve the 7th Division which had so far failed in its efforts to break through.

The Syrian forces allocated for this purpose were the 91st Brigade of the division already situated near the Qudna salient, and the 51st Brigade which was up to that point under the command of the 9th Division and was fighting against deputy commander of the IDF's 188th Brigade who was then in charge of the Zvika Force and Company B from the 226th Battalion, of the 179th Brigade.

Reserve Brigades Enter Combat

The morning of October 7 was marked by the onslaught of a fierce Syrian attack in all sectors of the front. The 1st Armored Division which had penetrated through the Qudna salient toward the Hushniya region was now joined in battle by the mechanized divisions' second rank of armored and mechanized forces.

The evident dimensions of the Syrian breakthrough necessitated the construction of rear alignments to prevent the enemy forces from approaching the Jordan River and the Sea of Galilee. On Sunday morning the GOC ordered the 820th Brigade commander to prepare the Jordan River bridges for detonation. The order was carried out before noon. At the same time, the 36th Division began constructing a rear anti-tank bastion in the region of the Upper Customs House under the command of the deputy division commander. The bastion was made up of the 317th Reserve Paratrooper Brigade Reconnaissance and Anti-Tank Battalion's recoilless cannons. These were later joined by Sherman tanks of the 181st Armored Battalion. Fighters from the GHQ Reconnaissance Unit were also integrated with the preparations for the defense of the controlling areas and in anti-tank ambushes with personal anti-tank weapons. Additional forces from the 1st Brigade were positioned to secure the Jordan River bridges.

The reserve forces entered combat on the different routes against the columns of Syrian tank advancing west. On the Katzbia route, the 179th Brigade commander Col. Ran Sarig entered combat against the Syrian 46th Brigade tanks. On the Gamla route, the 39th Battalion entered battle with the assistance of tanks of the 4th Brigade and defeated the tanks of the Syrian 47th Brigade. At the El Al strait, the 278th Battalion from the 179th Brigade under the command of Yosi Amir blocked columns of the Syrian 132nd Mechanized Brigade, which attempted to advance to the south and west.

Tanks of the 179th and 679th Reserve Brigades began arriving in the center of the Golan Heights through the Katzbia incline and the Bnot Yaakov Bridge did so as a result of the command intention to channel forces to the central and southern sectors. The first to arrive on the scene on the Golan Heights were the 179th Brigade units. Brigade commander Ran Sarig, along with twenty tanks from the 96th Battalion, moved up the Yehudia route toward Hushniya. At 05:30, he joined up with the tank platoon of the 679th Brigade and at 06:42 entered combat against forces of the Syrian 46th Brigade. In the fighting on the KKL (JNF) route the 179th Brigade destroyed over 20 Syrian tanks.

The force, now with thirty-two tanks, managed to take over the region of the road leading to Hushniya. The 134th Reconnaissance Battalion from the 36th Division under the command of Lt. Col. Hanani Tavor, with about twenty additional tanks joined the fighting force. Brigade commander Col. Ran Sarig was injured during the battle and was evacuated. Until the arrival of the deputy brigade commander, he was replaced by the brigade G3 officer, Captain Giora (Birman) Biran. The 268th Battalion under the command of Yosi Amir arrived near Katzbia at 07:00 and was then ordered by the command G3 officer to ascend the Golan Heights with the two companies of nineteen tanks, that were with him through Maale Yoav, and capture the anti-tank trench in the bottleneck of the El Al strait, which he reached at around 09:00. The force positioned itself in the strait and at 11:30 attacked the tank battalion carrying the 132nd Syrian Mechanized Brigade and destroyed it.

When the 9th Brigade commander Col. Mordechi (Motke) Ben Porat arrived in the scene with the 377th Sherman Tank Battalion he took command over. By evening about twenty additional Syrian tanks were destroyed and the force settled for a night camp east of El Al. the brigade mechanized infantry battalions were positioned in the back.

Artillery Support Operation

On Sunday morning the 212th Artillery Reserve group of the 36th Division, under the command of Col. Benny Arad, assumed responsibility for the operation of artillery on the Golan Heights where it received the 334th Battalion under its command, as well as batteries from the 405th Battalion and the Training Base No. 9 Battalion deployed in the center and north of the Golan Heights. The 334th Battalion headquarters transferred to assist the 188th Brigade operating in the south of the Golan Heights. The battalion itself concentrated in the Mount Odem region and continued in assisting the holding efforts in the northern sector.

The long-range artillery gun batteries, and later the batteries of the 412th Battalion as well were put into action along with the 55th Battalion and were employed during the fighting for command missions largely aimed at striking Syrian SAM batteries in accordance with the demands of the Air Force.

Parallel to the management of fire on the Golan Heights the HAC HQ began an effort to mobilize and deploy the Northern Command reserve artillery alignment. When the mobilization and equipping were completed the first reserve units began moving toward positions on the Golan Heights. Some had begun firing from positions west of the Jordan River. Fire at Outpost 116 was carried out by a 412th Battalion 175mm battery deployed in the Kfar Hanasi region.[9]

9 To the west of the Jordan River in the north.

Most of the artillery units were left at the Kurdani and Mansura Bases and only a small portion was transferred to the Pilon and Yiftach bases in the organization of the forces of the Northern Command on the eve of the war. This entailed the necessity to travel by caterpillar tracks from the Haifa Bay region to the Golan Heights which caused a delay in the deployment of the artillery alignment. The forces moving on the main roads refueled at civilian gas stations along the way.

The ones first to arrive naturally were the 120mm mortars on modified half-tracks, which traveled faster. These short range battalions deployed first, following the command of the 36th Division deputy commander Brig. Gen. Menachem ('Men') Aviram to defend the bridges over the Jordan River. Only after a while were they given the opportunity to go up the Golan Heights. More time passed before they netted, came to their senses, and began finding their way around.

The artillery support cluster of the 36th Division operated two 155mm M-50 SPG battalions, as well as a 160mm self-propelled mortar battalion and a 120mm self-propelled mortar battalion equipped at the Pilon emergency storage warehouses in addition to the regular forces the 36th Division.

The 282nd artillery support cluster of the 210th Division under the command of Col. Moshe Levi was in the initial stages of establishment and assumed command over the artillery, including two 105mm self-propelled Priest battalions, a 155mm M50 SPG battalion, a 120mm self-propelled mortar battalion, as well as a towed 155mm battalion from their storage warehouses in the Haifa Bay region. The cluster, which showed up on Sunday morning to plan maneuvers in the Miron District, assumed responsibility for the southern Golan Heights. At noon on Sunday, where it began its operations with the remainders of the 405th Battalion's and Training Base No. 9 battalion's batteries of four M109 Howitzer SPGs and one M-50 SPG, and the two long-range batteries of the 55th Battalion's that had retreated west. Simultaneously the headquarters of the Artillery Group concentrated additional artillery forces for the region, as well.

In one case weapons were hit by direct Syrian fire aimed at the 827th Battalion's Priest 105mm SPGs going up the slope to the east on the Yehudia route. The towed battalions deployed west of the Jordan River and were brought onto the Golan Heights at a later stage.

The HAC HQ—who had in the meanwhile skipped to the Mount Knaan command outpost, which did not have any facilities or systems—made sure that the fire units were already equipped with maps and communication orders when they headed for the front.

At night fall the order of artillery forces in the region was that of approximately ten battalions, after having only eleven batteries deployed on the Golan Heights at the outbreak of the war. All of the Northern Command artillery units, excluding one towed 155mm battalion, had gone up the Golan Heights and were deployed in their positions. These were all employed to assist the units on the line and the reserve forces constantly engaged in halting the Syrian forces that continued moving west. The soldiers, who did not have their cannons, of two 155mm SPG battalions, assisted in administering the artillery ammunition. Due to the heavy traffic on the routes it was agreed upon with the Command Chief of Staff that the routes would be cleared of the division ranks. Artillery ammunition was pushed into a backlog positioned at the entrance to Hazor and supplied the artillery positions from there.

Additional battalions from the GHQ's reserves - including the 412th 175mm SPG Battalion under the command of Lt. Col. Aharon (Aldo) Zohar, two battalions of previously captured enemy 130mm guns that were not initially intended for the northern front, and even the 270th captured BM-11 240mm enemy rocket launcher battalion—were sent north. The first battery of the 412th Battalion reached the 647th Battalion's emergency storage warehouse in Pilon, where it was equipped with the cannons of the two other batteries in the battalion, prior to the onslaught of the war.[10] The battery deployed between Pilon and Yiftach and from there assisted during the early stages of the war. Afterwards it went up to the Golan Heights and operated independently on the Yehudia route.

An artillery targeting ranging acquisition unit under the command of Menashe ("Leviathan") Loutin also arrived on the Golan Heights. From the eve of the war on the northern front the battalion operated the MAR-290 rocket launchers, the floodlights, and the targeting ranging acquisition alignment. To assist the battalions and batteries in navigating to their positions during the night, the command deployed artillery floodlights from the ranging battalion on the Margaliot ridge. These floodlights projected a narrow beam of light into the sky which allowed the forces, receiving the exact coordinates of the floodlights, to more easily navigate into their positions in conditions of the darkness, dust and smoke.

The 210th Division Organization

The 210th Division command, which had completed its organization, was initially directed to the Lebanese sector. When the severity of the situation on the Golan Heights became clear, division commander Maj. Gen. Dan Lener and his deputy Col. Moshe Bar-Kochva (Brill) were ordered to prepare for defense west of the Jordan River, gather heavy engineering equipment,

10 For more on this see Part 1.

and create obstacles along the routes descending to the Jordan River, which the division ceased handling when it moved to the Arik Bridge region and at 12:00 got the command over the southern Golan Heights.

An approximate two-kilometer region line, between the 210th and the 36th Divisions, was established to the south of the Bnot Yaakov Bridge—Quneitra route and parallel to it. The 210th Division CCP was positioned at the "Katche" ranch on the road to Yehudia. The order of battle allocated for the division included the 188th and 179th Tank Brigades and the 4th and 9th Mechanized Brigades. These brigades with very small forces were all engaged in battles at that time. The 7th and 679th Tank Brigades and the 1st Golani Infantry Brigade remained under the command of the 36th Division in the northern sector of the Golan Heights.

The Northern Sector Fighting

The defensive battle carried out by the 7th Brigade and Golani, under the command of the 36th Division, continued in the northern sector throughout the day. Syrian forces of the 7th Division failed at breaking through the lines of defense threw wave after wave of attack into battle. The 7th Brigade conducted a brigade battle across the entire front in its sector, transferring company forces from sector to sector in order to seal breakthroughs and reinforce combat and pressure zones created in the field. The line's outposts held by forces of the 13th Battalion were reinforced by forces and supplies from the battalion and the Golani Brigade. The outposts engaged in firefights with the attacking forces, successfully cooperated with the tank platoons operating nearby.

The Syrian forces attacking in the northern sector were the

"second wave" of the division which included the 78th Armored Division and the 121st Mechanized Brigade from the 7th Division, as well as a T-62 tank battalion from the Rifaat al-Assad Force arriving from Damascus with a battalion of forty tanks. In the 7th Brigade southern sector, around Outpost 109, the 52nd Infantry Brigade forces continued fighting. In the northern part of the sector the Syrians resumed attacks, employing mechanized and tank forces from the 68th Infantry Brigade south of Outpost 105 and in the area of Outpost 104 and random attacks by forces from the reinforcing Moroccan Brigade. The attacks were massively supported by artillery aimed by Syrian observation officers operating from the captured Israeli Hermon outpost. Syrian Air Force jets took part as well.

In the morning, the 820th Brigade commander issued an order to evacuate the northern sector outposts, but after the 13th Battalion commander Lt. Col. Ze'ev Oren objected claiming that his outposts were holding on and were "eyes" for events taking place along the line of contact, the order was cancelled. At 07:35, an order to evacuate Tel Avital, after burning the documents, was issued by the command but this was also cancelled within minutes.

At dawn, the 77th Battalion captured the tank ramps controlling the valley between Tel Jit and Hermonit and was engaged in firefights with Syrian tanks and APCs all day. When heavy pressure formed on the force at "Hermonit," Kahalani transferred half of Company F under the command of Captain Yair Svet to it. The company commander was killed in the battle and the deputy company commander 2nd Lt. Daniel Georgi, took his place. The brigade commander then ordered the 77th Battalion's deputy commander to leave a tank platoon east of Quneitra and advance toward the 77th Battalion commander. He also sent a reserve force tank platoon under the command of the brigade operations officer Lt. Avinoam Baruchin.

North of Hermonit the 71st Battalion under the command of Lt. Col. Meshulam Rates halted Syrian infantry 68th Brigade forces attack attempts. Due to the terrain factors of many hills and mounds, Rates split his force to prevent the infiltration of Syrian tank and infantry forces.

Throughout that morning, the "Tiger" company under Zmir's command destroyed the forward force of the Syrian 43rd Tank Brigade south of Quneitra. The losses suffered by the Syrian Brigade were due to the professionalism and operational capabilities of Zamir's company. About forty vehicles, half of them tanks and half APCs from the 43rd Brigade advance force were hit and the brigade was forced to retreat.

During the day, Syrian forces attacked the "Booster" with APCs. It held a tank platoon under the command of Amnon Lavi, with a tank force under the command of 74th Battalion commander Lt. Col. Yair Nafshi below. They were assisted by a tank platoon from Quneitra. The 74th Battalion's tanks continued operating alongside the outposts throughout that day, when each body of tanks operated in coordination with the outpost and got ammunition and fuel from the battalion. The 74th Battalion had about twelve tanks on this day and the days that followed.

The Syrian offensive stopped after a three-hour battle, excluding firefights and artillery shelling which lasted all day. About ninety Syrian tanks were hit that day in the battle in the Valley of Tears.

On Sunday evening nineteen tanks from the 82nd Battalion arrived at the 7th Brigade under the command of Lt. Eli Geva after the battalion commander Maj. Haim Barak was wounded and his deputy Maj. Danny Pesach was killed.

The 77th Battalion commander, Kahalani, organized his forces after "refilling": Lt. Ami Plant's company was made up of tanks from other companies; Amnon's company improved tanks from Menachem's company, which disintegrated; 2nd Lt. Daniel Georgi commanded four tanks remaining from Captain Yair Svet's company. The battalion was joined by Lt. Ephraim Laor. There were about twenty tanks with the 77th Battalion that evening.

At night, Company Commander Lavi's force moved from the "Booster" to the 77th Battalion in the Valley of Tears and the tanks of the 74th Battalion took its place. The "Tiger" company was once again a brigade reserve force.

The battlefield silenced at midnight. Two men of every crew remained on guard while their friends had a nap after the fierce combat.

The Fighting in the Southern Sector and the Battle over Nafah

The situation in the southern sector during the second day of fighting was markedly different. During the day, the Syrians attempted to insert additional forces in order to exploit their successful breakthrough and achieve the targets defined in the attack plan. At this stage, the command was already aware of the fact that the southern sector had collapsed and the IDF forces in this region did not manage to halt the Syrian offensive.

Despite the fact that no outpost was captured, the 820th Regional Brigade issued an order to evacuate the outposts in the southern sector at around 08:00. The 53rd Battalion commander evacuated the 50th Paratrooper Battalion combatants from outposts 114 and 115 moving with them on board tanks toward Tel Fares. Outposts 110 and 111 were evacuated at 09:00 on board tanks from Company A of the 82nd Battalion that moved to Tel Yosifon for refueling and ammunition. Both Outpost 116 and the Tel Saki observation post remained surrounded and could not be evacuated. The outposts were under fire by infantry and armored attacks and thus could only get artillery fire assistance aimed at "our own outposts," which was carried out.

After a 06:30 report by the Tel Saki outpost that the Syrian forces were actually in Ramat Magshimim and moving toward the battalion headquarters in El Al, the 50th Battalion's new commander Maj. Yoram Yair (Ya-Ya) ordered the company at Nachal Golan and the battalion headquarters in El Al to retreat west. He himself, along with the communications officer, intelligence officer, and operations sergeant, remained in El Al.

At around 10:00, the sound of tank tracks approached from behind the 50th Battalion commander, who thought they were Syrian tanks. These were twenty upgraded "Shot Kal" Centurion tanks from the 278th Battalion of the 179th Brigade moving east capturing the 1500 meters-wide El Al strait before it was captured by Syrian tanks. The Syrian forces moved from Ramat Magshimim south. They were stopped north of El Al by reserve units from the 179th Armored Brigade, and later by the 4th Mechanized Brigade, and driven back into the Ramat Magshimim region.

Nearing midnight on the first night, the 188th Brigade commander gave up on his plan to attack with the 82nd Battalion and Zvika Force, rightfully concerned that his CCP would be surrounded and retreated toward Mazraat Quneitra. His intention was to relinquish control of the Petroleum Road toward dawn and, along with the force of the 53rd Battalion commander prevent the passage of Syrian forces toward the Gamla incline.

Toward 04:00, only four tanks remained on the Petroleum Road and the Pele Route east of it. The 188th Brigade deputy commander Lt. Col. David Israeli entered the Petroleum Road with eight tanks from the 266th Battalion. The brigade deputy commander positioned the forces along the route and detained the Syrian advancement until 09:00 in the morning.

At 05:45, after the 53rd Battalion commander repeated requests, the 188th Brigade commander approved his leaving positions, evacuating the outposts in his sector and move toward Mazraat Quneitra. At first light, the 53rd Battalion began to carry out the order, but when the battalion forces moved from their positions a Syrian force began advancing south of Tel Jukhader in a northwestern direction, cutting through their retreat route. The battalion commander Maj. Oded Erez, with fifteen tanks, was forced to move toward Outpost 115 and from there to Outpost 114. He turned to the command G3 officer, explaining his situation, and reported that he was out of ammunition. The command G3 officer ordered him to go up to the shoulder of Tel Fares, above the quarry, and set up in the position until night fall. On his way the 53rd Battalion evacuated the people from the outposts on board the tanks and gathered in Tel Fares.

When he realized that the 53rd Battalion could not reach him, the 188th Brigade commander decided to prepare for the halting of the Syrian armored forces south of Nafah. At that time, the 179th Brigade forces were getting closer to the Katzbia incline. He assumed that he could concentrate forces, including the 82nd Battalion moving back for refueling, and carry out a defensive or counterattack in the Nafah-Katzbia region together with the 179th Brigade. He descended to the Btecha Valley and around 09:00, the 188th Brigade commander's CCP arrived at Nafah. At the mouth of the Petroleum Road, the CCP met the brigade G3 officer, Maj. Benny Katzin, who implored the brigade commander to take him on with him to the CCP. The brigade commander, who decided to move along the Petroleum Road alone in his own tank, added the G3 officer on board.

The brigade commander ordered the brigade communications officer and intelligence officer to remain at the mouth of the Petroleum Road, and tune the radio frequency of every reserve tank from the 179th Brigade arriving at the route with that of the brigade. Three company-sized combat teams, including about thirty-three tanks and Chesner's seven additional tanks, were organized out of the 188th Brigade and 266th Battalion tanks in the sector south of Nafah, as well as the additional tanks dripping in one by one to the Petroleum Road throughout the morning, including those from the 82nd Battalion. The brigade commander and his deputy operated these combat teams against superior Syrian forces until the noon hours.

The Battle over Nafah

Around 11:00 the Syrian offense got a new momentum in a new direction. The 1st Armored Division commander positioned in Tel Fazra landed an attack by the 51st and 91st Brigades toward the Nafah region. The 46th Tank Brigade of the 5th Division turned north on the Waterfalls Route—the "KKL (JNF) Route" as it was called at the time—and attacked in the direction of the Waterfalls junction. The attack was halted when the 179th Brigade preceded the 46th Brigade for control of the junction from the Tel Zabach ridges to the northwest.

In the central sector the Syrians were significantly successful. The 188th Brigade commander's force managed to block an attack by the 51st Tank Brigade on the Petroleum Road, but the force of twelve tanks of the 82nd Battalion deputy commander could not stop the 51st Brigade attack in the western branch. He was killed while retreating to Nafah.

The 82nd Battalion commander with seven tanks encountered the Syrian 91st T-62 Tank Brigade near Sindyanna. The Syrian attack forced him to retreat toward Nafah. The battalion commander was injured and Company A commander Eli Geva replaced him. The company was also hit by anti-tank fire from a Syrian reconnaissance force arriving at Tel Yosifon and was evacuated with the assistance of Company B tanks of the 82nd Battalion, which had arrived at Tel Yosifon for refueling and rearming along with the combatants from outposts 110 and 111. At about 14:00, when Company A's tanks ran out ammunition it moved along with Company B, with the approval of the commander of the 7th Brigade to "refuel" at Waset junction in the sector of their parent brigade. The 266th Battalion's deputy commander on board the company commander's tank joined up with the 93rd Battalion at the Nafah quarry, where both were hit; the deputy battalion commander was killed and the company commander was evacuated after his driver was killed.

Around 13:20, the 188th Brigade commander discovered that there were Syrian tanks on the Nafah Base. He reported this to Raful. The division commander was then outside the Nafah bunker and positioned on the Pele Route, near Tel Shiban, five kilometers north of Nafah.

Raful ordered Col. Yitzhak Ben Shoham, commander of the 188th Brigade, to attack the Syrians from the rear. In response to the GOC's question at that time the brigade commander reported that he was bringing vehicles back toward Nafah. In fact the 188th Brigade commander saw that Syrian tanks were surrounding his force and were at the Nafah Base. The brigade commander could not contact the 82nd Battalion deputy commander who was killed at 12:30. The brigade commander decided to leave a few tanks for the holding on the Petroleum Road and returned to Nafah with a force of five tanks, together with the deputy brigade commander, to attack the tanks on the base. Many Syrian tanks were destroyed by his force on his way there. At 14:11, the deputy brigade commander David Israeli was killed near Nafah. The brigade commander ordered all the vehicles at 14:23: "Everyone turn right and storm our base, over and out." The brigade commander and G3 officer were both killed during the assault. From that moment on the 188th Brigade was left without its chain of command.

It seemed that the Syrian offensive in the Nafah region was about to succeed. Tanks of the 51st Syrian Brigade managed to penetrate the base, after defeating the force of the 82nd deputy battalion commander; the 91st Brigade tanks pushed the 82nd Battalion commander force and arrived east of the Nafah Base and frontal Syrian forces reached the Sindyanna ridge. A Syrian anti-tank force reached the slopes of Mount Yosifon.

19 tanks from the 82nd Battalion very short on fuel and ammunition were on the Pele Route near Nafah and on Mount Shifon. Without communication with the 188th Brigade commander who had been killed, Lt. Eli Geva, the actual battalion commander addressed the 7th Brigade commander who was not aware of the serious situation in the Nafah region and ordered them to retreat toward Waset. Thus there was no Israeli force left in Nafah excluding scattered individual tanks on the base. This allowed the Syrian 91st Brigade to advance free of interference to the Dalwa ridge northeast of Nafah. The Syrian force could either move toward the Bnot Yaakov Bridge, or surround the 7th Brigade and carry out a one strike attack on it.

From the early morning hours reserve forces from the 679th Brigade began going up along the main route from the Bnot Yaakov Bridge to the Golan Heights. The 679th Brigade commander Col. Ori Orr left his emergency storage Unit at 03:00, as was discussed with the 36th Division commander. The brigade commander went up the Golan Heights with twenty tanks five of which, all of the old "Meteor engine Centurion" model, were stopped due to mechanical failures.

At 07:00, the brigade commander met the 36th Division commander Brig. Gen. Refael Eitan on the road outside the Nafah

Base. The division commander ordered the brigade commander to move toward Quneitra in order to seal the salient south of Quneitra between the 7th Brigade and the 188th Brigade. He stated that the Syrian 7th Division was due to attack there. The brigade commander moved and deployed with the two battalions of the twenty-five tanks force on the ridges to both sides of the city of Quneitra.

On October 7 at approximately 14:00, when the Command GOC sensed danger after the Syrian tanks had trampled the fences of the Nafah Base, he directly ordered the 679th Brigade commander to go back on his track and outflank the Syrian effort. At that point the 679th Brigade was split in its operations, with the brigade commander's tank force near Quneitra while the 93rd Battalion was still in Aleika with eleven tanks.

At 14:30, after the 188th Brigade commander and G3 officer had been killed, the fate of the battle over Nafah was hanging by a thread. The 679th Brigade commander ordered the 289th Battalion commander to leave a 6 tank blocking toward Quneitra. The rest of the battalion tanks moved along the route of the road to Nafah and encountered Syrian forces near Dalwa. In the ensued battle the Syrian were halted on the ridgeline controlling the Ein Zivan—Bnot Yaakov Bridge route. Additional Syrian forces arriving at the fences of the Nafah workshop from the direction of Tel Abas and the Petroleum Road were halted by individual 679th Brigade tanks that had randomly arrived at the region. A few combatants headed by 820th Brigade deputy commander Lt. Col. Pinchas (Pini) Kuperman got together and operated "Bazookas" (Anti-tank rocket launchers) against the Syrian tanks. The 679th Brigade commander moved with fifteen tanks south of the Quneitra—Nafah road, between Tel Shifon and Tel Yosifon and carried out an attack on the Syrian tanks in the Sindyanna region at 15:30.

After a several hours long battle, where about forty Syrian

tanks were hit, the 91st Brigade retreated toward Ramtania. Thus the threat on the rear and from the Nafah key region on the 7th Brigade was removed. Thus an unobstructed route toward the Bnot Yaakov Bridge was offered.

The battle over Nafah was decided by tanks from four different units—the 188th, 7th, 179th, and 679th Brigades. This was the last of the battles that had begun 24 hours earlier, at the end of which the reserve forces halted the Syrian offensive on the Golan Heights. The Syrians were too late in their maneuver toward Nafah even though it surprised the IDF commanders. Toward noon hours there were already enough reserve forces to halt them in a series of battles, where the IDF tactical level commanders struck the Syrians in almost every combat encounter. At 17:17 the command log reported the Dan Lener of Syrian retreat orders for their forces in the Nafah region.

Aerial Struggle

At 11:30, in accordance with the rushed planning, operation "Dugman 5" to attack the Syrian missile alignment was carried out. The failed operation left the entire Golan Heights under the Syrian threat of anti-aircraft missiles, forcing the Air Force fighter jets to attack under these conditions up to the end of the war, suffering losses as a result.[11]

On October 7, the Syrians carried out 44 attack sorties, accompanied by sixty-two MiG-21jets, as well as 11 helicopter sorties. They lost 18 jets and one helicopter—13 were shot down during dogfights, 2 by anti-aircraft fire, and four by self-downing. There were no injury reports among the Israeli forces from

11 See details in Chapter 19.

these aerial assaults. The Syrian aerial assaults were carried out in one flight at a low altitude, dropping all munitions and immediately flying east to avoid interception by the Israeli Air Force jets. This method of attack is inefficient and its outcomes are usually minor. At times the bombs were dropped on their own forces and at times the bombs were dropped without aiming in order to avoid a chase.

Reserve Forces Positioning in the Southern Golan Heights

The 210th Division reserve forces, the 9th Brigade under the command of Col. Mordechi ("Motke") Ben Porat and the 4th Brigade under the command of Col. Yaakov (Feffer) Hadar were directed at reinforcing the southern sector and pushing the Syrian 5th Division forces out.

Of the routes going up to the Golan Heights, only the Gamla incline remained without an Israeli armored force. For this reason the command positioned a Golani Infantry Company with RCLRs on the Gamla incline. After the 4th Mechanized Brigade completed its preparations the brigade headed out and at around 14:00 the column of old "Sherman" tanks and half-tracks reached the Gamla incline. Prior to it, the 39th Reserve Battalion of upgraded "Shot Kal" Centurion tanks from the 188th Brigade reached the Gamla incline, under the command of Lt. Col. Yoav Vaspi. The 4th Brigade commander, who "annexed" the battalion, advanced his vehicles to the head of the armored column. At about 15:00 the battalion captured the highest passage from the Gamla incline and reached the diversion route, where it encountered tanks from the Syrian 47th Brigade. The Israeli force destroyed 12 Syrian tanks without suffering any losses. The remainder of the Syrian force retreated east toward Mazraat Quneitra. The 4th Brigade advanced several kilometers east and returned to the incline for a night camp.

The 188th Brigade Reorganization Activity

When the influx of reserve tanks onto the Petroleum Road ended the remaining officers of the 188th Brigade CCP joined up with the 36th Division commander's CCP, who once again positioned himself in Nafah's command bunker. Raful was happy to receive the assistance offered by the intelligence and communication officers, who as regular officers were familiar with the sector, the forces, and the war maneuvers. Raful was the last to leave the command bunker after tank guns began firing on structures on the base. While he turned west toward Tel Shiban, the intelligence and communication officers turned to the brigade headquarters base in Aleika, where the two of them came up with the idea to utilize the old Syrian minefields deployed along the route connecting Aleika with the Upper Customs House and the arrival of a company of RCLR jeeps in the region, in order to prepare for another defensive battle to halt the Syrian forces if they advance toward the Upper Customs House after capturing Nafah. Since the Syrians were halted in Nafah by the 679th Brigade this idea was never put to the test.

The brigade CCP vehicle was positioned in the entrance to the Aleika base and was joined up by the administrative staff. The brigade staff began to contact the brigade forces to find out what was left of it once it was discovered that the brigade commander had been killed. They found out that only the 53rd Battalion was badly damaged, and that there were many remaining forces that operated under the 7th Brigade and the reserve brigades that started arriving on the Golan Heights, including the 39th Battalion which had been transferred to the command of the 4th Brigade.

At about 20:00 the brigade communications officer, Captain Hanan Schwartz, called up the command G3 to update them that the brigade had not been destroyed and asked that a new commander be appointed for it. That same night Lt. Col. Yosi Ben Hanan arrived at the brigade and took command of the forces. The brigade staff transferred from the Aleika base, where Maj. Gen. Dan Lener's 210th Division headquarters had begun setting up, to the Jordan base, 5 kilometers to the south.

At the Jordan base the brigade staff worked to restructure the brigade by gathering individual combatants, building tank crews, and getting together twenty tanks for the force. Simultaneously, the staff continued to follow the brigade state of affairs. The command of the remaining tank force was assumed by Lt. Col. Yosi Ben Hanan, who had formerly been the commander of the 53rd Battalion, immediately upon his arrival at the brigade. Thus the grain from which the brigade would emerge anew was formed less than 48 hours after the brigade headquarters had been hit.

At 22:30 a column of tanks belonging to the 53rd Battalion commander, moving back with the approval of the Command Headquarters, advanced toward the 188th Brigade 39th Battalion, then operating under the command of the 4th Brigade. The 188th CCP attempted to coordinate the movement of the 53rd Battalion tanks west, with the movement of the tanks of the 4th Reserve Brigade east. The command G3 officer failed to prevent mutual fire in spite of his efforts and these tanks fired at the 53rd Battalion tanks, which were carrying regular infantry soldiers evacuated from the outposts, including Lt. Col. Ben Ami Cohen, commander of the Training Base No. 9 battalion, combatants and observers positioned at Tel Fares. One tank was hit by the firing and the 53rd Battalion operations officer was killed.

Positioning and Operation Plans Stabilization of the Reserve Division

A slightly more optimistic situation report began unfolding in the GHQ as of the noon hours since the Syrian offensive was halted and the line stabilized. In the GHQ Deputy Chief of Staff's operational discussion group that started at 13:30, Maj. Gen. Tal stressed that "The main direction is to restore the balance on the Golan Heights by stabilizing the defense lines and concentrate refreshed forces toward morning to conduct a counterattack."

After completing its organization, the 146th Division - the GHQ's reserve force from Central Command—began moving north (mostly on caterpillar tracks), from the Central Command ESUs to the gathering areas in the Tzemach region during the day. Only one tank battalion was transported on board carriers. At this stage, the division under the command of Brig. Gen. Moshe ("Musa") Peled included: the 205th Tank Brigade of Meteor engine Centurions, under the command of Col. Yossi Peled that departed from the Ofer Base; the 670th Mechanized Brigade under the command of Col. Gideon Gordon that left its Sherman tank battalion in the southern Jordan Valley; the 288th Division Reconnaissance Battalion with upgraded Centurions, APCs and jeeps under the command of Lt. Col. Zvika Dahab; the 213th Artillery Group under the command of Col. Dani Avidar, and the division units. The division additional tank brigade (217th) was allocated to the southern front prior to that on the first day of fighting.

At noon, during the fighting in Nafah, when the 146th

Division was heading for the Golan, the command considered several options for its operation: putting it in the defense of the route openings toward the Hula Valley, in case the halting of the Syrians at Nafah failed; employing it as a counterattack force in the central arena or implementing it for counterattacks along the southern route. Gradually the concept that was preferred was the third one of counterattack.

Even prior to the arrival of the division commander at the command outpost in Mount Knaan the command staff integrated the preferred mode of operation, which was to employ the division as a main force for counterattacks. The command intention was initially to carry out a counterattack against the southern routes. There were two main considerations. The first, the division was arriving from the south enabling a quick operation. The attack from the south was the most convenient along the shortest routes entailing a shorted organization time. The second one was that the route openings going up to the Golan Heights from the south were under control of the command in addition to significant forces positioned in key areas the attack could be launched from (the 9th Brigade in El Al and the 4th Brigade in the Gamla incline). Therefore, at 12:12 the Command GOC ordered the 146th Division commander to go up along the southern Golan Heights routes and participate in the destruction of the Syrian outpost in the Rapid salient.

When the commander of the 146th Division arrived at the command outpost in Mount Knaan at 14:30 the fighting in the Golan was at its peak. The different forces were busy with blocking attempts against the Syrian columns in El Al, the Gamla incline, Katzbia and the entrances to Nafah. The division commander, along with the intelligence officer Lt. Col. Moti Katz and the Artillery Group commander Col. Dani (Feinstein) Avidar, met with the GOC. Following, the command G3 officer detailed the situation report for the forces on the Golan Heights. The officers present were updated regarding the forthcoming missions, derived from the different possibilities of the unfolding situation in the combat regions. One possible mission was the assuming of responsibility over the building of a defense rear line along the Jordan River to prevent further Syrian advancement. The other preferred option was the activation of the 146th Division along the southern routes, as a main counterattack force either from the center or the south of the Golan Heights, in order to outflank the Syrians and break their main war effort. The division commander was briefed to plan the counterattack through El Al and the Gamla incline.

The division commander who wished to see firsthand what was happening in the field went up along the Givat Yoav route with his intelligence officer to observe the southern Golan Heights. Seeing it he understood that the situation in the field was not as dire as had been reported to him. Clearly the openings of the routes going up to the Golan Heights were all formidably held by reserve forces of the IDF, the situation had stabilized, the Syrians had been halted and were unable to exploit their earlier success. The situation on the ground had finally convinced the division commander that the Syrian flank could be counterattacked and brought down. The command order of attack was received by the liaison officer appointed by the GOC, Col. Yehuda Golan (Ashenfeld), former Golani Brigade commander, who served in this important role in the days to come.

That day Lt. Gen. Bar Lev headed for the Northern Command while the GHQ Chief of Staff headed for the Southern Command, to examine the counterattack plans scheduled for October 8. At 18:30 Lt. Gen. Haim Bar Lev, as the representative of the GHQ Chief of Staff, reached the Northern Command. Upon arrival the command holding battle was nearing its end. Nearly 200 Israeli tanks faced about 350 Syrian tanks in the central and southern Golan Heights.

The heavy apprehension that the central and southern Golan Heights would fall into Syrian hands was then replaced by the assessment that the Syrian forces attacking and threatening the openings of the Golan routes had exhausted their strength. This, in spite of the fact that the threat to the heart of the Golan Heights had not passed and the fear that the Syrians would once again attempt an attack with fresh armored forces, remained.

At 19:00 the 146th Division commander returned to the command outpost in Knaan where he met with Haim Bar Lev. The plan accepted by the command planning group at 19:33 established that the 146th Division would attack from south to north. According to the GOC, the plan was intended to disrupt the Syrian main breakthrough route to the west. As he said: "If there is a Syrian collapse, all for the better, and if not was will be harsh." At that time, the Syrian forces occupied an area that spread from the Purple Line to the Sindyanna village in the north and Ramat Magshimim in the south, including the southern part of the Petroleum Road. According to the Syrian GHQ's assessment, due to their difficult situation the Syrians requested the Iraqis that they accelerate the arrival of their forces into the combat arena on the Golan.

On October 7, 20:20, at Mount Knaan, the command plan for a counterattack on the morning of the next day was set in the presence of former GHQ Chief of Staff Lt. Gen. Haim Bar Lev. The command plan for counterattack was based on three parallel efforts:

- **The 146th Division main effort** arriving from the south to be joined by the 4th and 9th Brigades that were on the line of contact with the Syrians and would be directed to all routes of the southern Golan Heights (El Al, Gamla incline and the "border" route) against the Syrian 5th Division forces and the 1st Armored Division.
- **The 210th Division effort** along with the 179th Brigade with

forty tanks along the Yehudia route toward the "Hushniya pocket." The division was to serve as an "anvil" for the main effort.

- **An effort from the north by the 36th Division** with the 679th Brigade forces on the Petroleum Road and Sindyanna route toward Hushniya.

The Command GOC emphasized that the 146th Division should be brought into the battle full force, and not "trickled in." The GOC added an order for an artillery and massive aerial force assistance. New sector boundaries were set in order to allow for the counter attack to come from the south. The border between the 210th Division in the center and the 36th in the north was parallel to the Ein Zivan—Bnot Yaakov Bridge route and two kilometers south of it; the border between the 210th Division and the 146th Division was south of the Yehudia—Hushniya route.

The command attack H-hour was to be determined by the 146th Division capabilities and the main effort plan completion. Brig. Gen. Moshe Peled, who was certain of his division capabilities, recommended that the attack started at 07:00 the next morning, as was decided. A number of deceptive operations, under the responsibility of the Command Headquarters, were simultaneously integrated into the plan.

At 20:30 Lt. Gen. Bar Lev called the GHQ Deputy Chief of Staff from the Northern Command and reported the command attack plan for the following day, stating that he thought the situation could be restored to its previous state "...and maybe a little more."

Following the counterattack order, the 146th Division began an orderly and quick battle procedure. The main headquarters was positioned on the Poriya ridge above Tiberias and was engaged in organizing the forces and secured the next day orders. During the night of October 7-8, the 146th Division headquarters was busy with gathering its forces in the Tzemach—Ein Gev region, refueling them, and organizing them for entry into battle. The headquarters operated simultaneously to establish contact with the brigades fighting in the region that were transferred to its command, and coordinate the forces' operation with the counterattack in mind.

During the second day of fighting all of the Syrian forces that had penetrated the Golan Heights region were blocked. Success was the result of a high fitness level, determination and improvisation skills of the regular units and reserve forces, at all levels. Thus the command holding battle had come to an end. The regular force was successful in preventing any Syrian attempt to break through the Quneitra salient but was unable to block the Syrian effort in the south. During the first 24 hours the reserve forces were engaged in a race against time with the Syrian—that had penetrated the depth of the Golan in the central and southern sectors—and managed to capture the inlet of the Golan and its plateau and halt the advancement of Syrian forces. At the base of their operation was both their relative proximity to the front and the command decision to send forces of any size, even without completing the operational and logistical preparations, without target alignment, with improvised battle gear and partial arming.

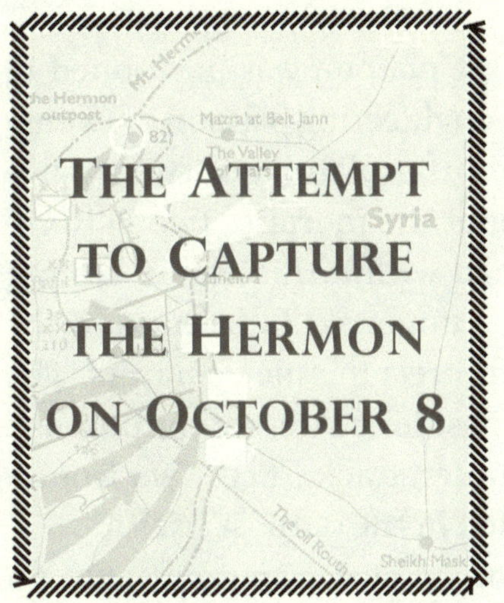

The Attempt to Capture the Hermon on October 8

Chapter 9

The Syrian Army Positioning on the Hermon Shoulder, October 7–8

After 400 combatants of the 82nd Paratrooper Battalion completed the takeover of the Israeli outpost on the 7th of the month which deployed from the upper ski lift station to the Israeli outpost, preparing to intercept an IDF counter attack.

A company, most of which deployed west of the road reinforced by a supplementary battalion weaponry, deployed south of the upper ski lift station the combatants were deployed on the slopes descending from the road bends and built individual positions for themselves by piling stones between the large boulders characteristic of the region. An RCLR crew was in a firing position in a trench they found east of the road. The engineering soldiers deployed an exposed string of mines on the road about 350 meters north of the "Tank Bend."

The two other companies deployed in the controlling areas west of the outpost and south of its access road from the landing pad area to hill 2072. One platoon was positioned in the Israeli outpost, along with an engineering platoon of twenty combatants and the battalion mortar platoon of twenty-five combatants appended to it without the mortars. Two B-10 recoilless rifles were also positioned within this region aiming at the route of the road from the upper ski lift station to the outpost so were four anti-aircraft Strela missile operators. The battalion commander's CCP was positioned west of the outpost, and a platoon next to it as a counterattack force. Two frontal observation officers were stationed in the outpost itself.

Southwest of the 82nd Battalion, at elevation point 1614 on the Hermon shoulder, the 183rd Commando Battalion was deployed at dawn, October 7, for a rushed defense. This battalion served as the northern branch force along with the 68th Infantry Brigade and the Moroccan expeditionary force for the 7th Division breakthrough effort. Its mission was to apparently capture Outpost 103 in Majdal Shams and advance from there through Yafouri Valley to block the Majdal Shams—Mas'ade road and was later intended to move through the Banias to al-Ghajar. On the night between the 6th and 7th of the month it moved west on foot from the Hader region through the Hermon slopes, and positioned itself at elevation point 1614. In the afternoon, on October 7, its reconnaissance platoon apparently attacked Outpost 103 in Majdal Shams and retreated to the battalion range. On the morning of the 8th of the month the battalion was still deployed for a perimeter defense of elevation point 1614 rocky domes and did not advance west, since a day earlier the northern breakthrough effort by the 7th Division on the Hader—Mas'ade road was halted.

The Morning of October 8, 1st Brigade Battle Procedure

As stated, from the 6th of the month at 15:58, when contact with the Israeli Hermon outpost was severed, the Northern Command clearly understood that the outpost had fallen into Syrian hands but what had happened to the soldiers there was left unknown. From that time to the end of the war the recapture the Hermon was kept on the agenda. The strategic importance of the Hermon on one hand, and the moral obligation to rescue whoever remained in the outpost on the other, burdened the IDF commanders at all levels.

As early as an hour after contact with the outpost was severed the command G3 officer Lt. Col. Uri Simchoni suggested that an infantry offensive on the outpost be planned. The Command GOC, Maj. Gen. Yitzhak Hofi, who agreed with him, instructed the 317th Reserve Paratrooper Brigade under the command of Col. Haim Nadel—which was already in its mobilization stage and allocated to the command—to plan the offensive. The 1st Brigade commander who arrived at the Nafah CCP asked for mission to be granted and the GOC approved. From that moment on the brigade commander focused mainly on this mission, troubled by the unrelenting thought that the sooner the assault on the Hermon was carried out, the easier the mission was going to be since the Syrians would not have enough time to adequately prepare for such an attack.

During October 7, forces from the 13th Battalion assisted by the 12th Battalion and the reconnaissance company participated in the defensive battle of the northern sector outposts under the command of the 1st Brigade commander. The insistence by the 1st Brigade commander that the outposts be indeed successful in halting the Syrians prevented the retreat of IDF forces from the northern sector in spite of the command order. Two companies from the 51st Battalion, along with the battalion commander CCP, prepared for defense in the Mas'ade junction region. Occasional bursts of gunfire were heard from the area of the Hermon outpost, leading the 1st Brigade commanders to suspect that the Syrians had not yet captured the outpost. The de-briefing of the mortars NCO, who was in the group of seventeen who managed to escape the outpost and who met with the 1st Brigade commander at around 07:00 near Mas'ade, heightened the brigade commander's sense that the Hermon had to be quickly attacked in order to rescue those trapped in it. An additional appeal at about 11:00 to carry out an attack on the Israeli Hermon outpost by the brigade commander and his deputy to the GOC was turned down.

At noon, when the 17th Battalion commander Lt. Col. Dubi Dror reached the northern sector with two squad commander course companies, the brigade commander ordered 51st Battalion Commander Maj. Yudk'a Peled to brief the 17th Battalion commander and his company commanders about the recapturing of the Hermon outpost. From Saturday night the 51st Brigade commander was busy with, among other things, studying the structure of the outpost with diagrams received from the defense ministry's building inspector. When, toward nightfall, the 51st Battalion commander briefed the commanders of the 17th Battalion in Mas'ade he focused mainly on the structure of the Israeli outpost and the method of clearing it, rather than on the makeup of forces that would participate in the attack, the access routes, and the difficulties they were expected to encounter. The commanders had no intelligence information regarding the Syrians or their deployment. The briefing of the commanders was given on a 1:50,000 ratio map.

At dawn of October 8, the last two survivors, an Air Force Unit commander and a reserve observation soldier, who had managed to escape the outpost on Saturday evening, arrived at

Outpost 103. The commander of Outpost 103 called the brigade commander who questioned them on the spot. Their testimony that several dozen IDF soldiers were still in the outpost made him decide that a rescue offensive had to be carried out immediately. At 06:47 the brigade commander called up the Command GOC on the wireless and updated him regarding the survivors that had arrived in Majdal Shams and requested consent to attack the Hermon. The Command GOC approved the attack.

Once the approval was given, the brigade commander, in consultation with the 51st Battalion commander, decided that the forces to carry out the attack would be: the 51st Battalion with its battalion commander CCP, Company B and a Medical Evacuation Unit; the 17th Battalion with its battalion commander CCP and two additional squad commander course companies with one reduced squad; two tanks from the 71st Battalion platoon, under Deputy Company Commander Lt. David Teeni, appended to the 1st Brigade and the brigade commander's CCP. At about 07:00 the brigade commander updated the 17th Battalion commander over the radio of their departure for the offensive and ordered him to bring his two companies to the region of the Sa'ar Bridge. The 51st Battalion commander, who had already been updated about the offensive, decided after consultation with the brigade commander, that his Company A would remain in its blocking mission on the Mas'ade junction, and subordinated third tank of the tank platoon to it.

At the same time, after completing their organization in Rosh Pina the 13th Battalion Company B and a staff company from Training Base Brigade No. 1 arrived at Mas'ade, both under the command of the training base commander. The brigade commander destined them to the mission of defending the Mas'ade junction. The brigade commander also intended to leave half of the Golani Reconnaissance Company at the Mas'ade junction under the command of the deputy company commander, but following the advice of the previous reconnaissance company commander, who was escorting the brigade commander's CCP, it was decided that half the reconnaissance company be appended to the 51st Battalion in their movement on foot. The 51st Battalion commander instructed the Company B commander, who was in the center of Majdal Shams with his company, to wait in the western exit of the village and join up with the brigade column.

At about 07:30 the brigade commander held a quick briefing for the 51st Battalion commander, the 17th Battalion his company commanders, the deputy reconnaissance company commander, and the tank platoon commander. The briefing took place near the double bridge over the Sa'ar stream. In the ten minute briefing, the brigade commander explained that the 17th Battalion would advance on its half-tracks toward the Israeli outpost along the road path. Two tanks will lead the column, while the reduced 51st Battalion and half of the reconnaissance company will advance on foot along the ridge route. Most of the briefing dealt with the structure of the outpost. The commanders were told that the first force to reach the outpost will have the mission of clearing it. The briefing was suddenly interrupted by a Syrian bombing with the brigade commander instructing the commanders to get on their half-tracks and start moving. Due to the drive to the go up as quickly as possible the company commanders did not brief the combatants of the essence of their mission. The commanders had no information about the enemy, its order of battle, the location of its positions, its weaponry, and so on. Though the brigade was not granted any artillery or aerial support, the brigade commander assumed he would be able to get them during their advancement. Mutual assistance between the two forces was limited due to the structure of the terrain.

The half-tracks the brigade received or "borrowed" from

the emergency storage warehouses were partially equipped and technically deficient. They were missing machine guns, gauging instruments, machine gun ammunition, and especially machine gun mounts, so that the unit's organic MAG machine guns could not even be positioned. The 17th Battalion was missing anti-tank rifle grenades, and it departed without an organic Medical Evacuation Unit. The half-tracks had almost no permanent radios, excluding portable AN/PRC-25 radios. For this reason the 17th Battalion companies couldn't operate on the two company networks and one battalion network when they entered battle, instead all of the battalion forces operating on the battalion communications network.

The Battle Process

At 08:00, the 1st Brigade forces began advancing up the road leading from Mas'ade to Majdal Shams and from there to the lower ski lift station. The forces were fired at by heavy Syrian artillery fire aimed at the road crossing the village of Majdal Shams as they progressed. Most of the shells fell between the village houses and on the ridges above it and did not hit the forces or hinder their advancement. The two leading tanks moved at the head of the column, followed by the half-tracks carrying the 51st Brigade Company B, the Reconnaissance Company, and the 17th Battalion. When the 51st Battalion column reached a point about 1500 meters from the village, where the road crosses the dirt road going up to Neve Ativ, currently the point where the "Maale Golani" road begins, the column stopped to allow the combatants to disembark their vehicles and get ready to advance up the ridge on foot. The two tanks, the brigade commander's CCP, and the 17th Battalion forces continued their slow drive up the road.

At about 08:15, close to the beginning of the advancement on foot, the 51st Battalion commander briefed the Company B commander and the reconnaissance company deputy commander about the mission, the route and advancement order, and the communications arrangements. The communication transfer was conducted on the battalion communications network, and just the battalion commander had an additional communicator on the brigade network. Several minutes later, the forces began moving in the following order: the reconnaissance company force with thirty-three combatants under the command of Deputy Company Commander Lt. Shauli Lev moved first along the trail leading up the ridge. The advance force moved in a broad deployment across the ridge east of the trail, on which the rest of the force moved in a graded column. The battalion commander's CCP advanced at a distance of several dozen meters behind the reconnaissance company force, and Company B was about 200 meters behind the CCP in graded columns, under the command of Lt. Dubi Schechter with fifty-six combatants. A Medical Evacuation Unit under the command of the battalion physician, Lt. Dr. Sidi Yehezkel, moved last in the column.

During the climb up the ridge, greatly dispersed occasional Syrian artillery shells continued falling in the area. The brigade commander's instruction was for the forces to attempt to locate the enemy during their advancement. Evidently, the mission was to move while scanning the ridge, with the goal of eventually capturing the Israeli Hermon outpost, where several dozen Israeli soldiers might still be trapped. The weather was cool, the sky was cloudy, and a medium wind was blowing. Low clouds moved passed occasionally, obstructing the field of vision.

At about 09:45, after an hour and a half of climbing up the steep incline, when the advance force arrived within 350 meters of hill 1614, small arm fire was carried against it from the north.

In retrospect, it was discovered that the reduced 51st Brigade had encountered the 183rd Syrian Commando Battalion, which was positioned on the domes surrounding elevation point 1614. Within a short while several combatants were injured due to the inferior area they were in, including Maj. Avraham Hido, who was the deputy battalion commander before the war and joined the battalion when the war broke out. In a battle that lasted until about 16:00, the battalion commander first attempted to outflank the Syrian force with a right flank from the east with the reduced Company B, with the reconnaissance company combatants serving as a suppressive force to the front. The outflanking failed. During the moving back stage the company's medic was killed and three combatants were wounded. A platoon was sent later to execute a left flank from the west, once again with the reconnaissance company combatants covering them, but the force commander, an attached officer, Captain Yeri Netel, was killed, and the force turned back.

From the Tank Bend, the brigade commander sent a force of sixteen combatants under the Company B deputy commander, Lt. Moti Rosen, down the Hermon shoulder to carry out a rear attack on the Syrian force. The force managed to draw closer to the Syrians without being revealed and opened surprise fire on them, causing many casualties, but a combatant was killed and three more were wounded in the fire exchange. At about 12:30 the 51st Battalion began receiving artillery aid, mediated by the deputy brigade commander Lt. Col. Ruv-ke Eliaz, from a 334th Battalion 155mm SPG and 160mm self-propelled mortar battery deployed near Buq'ata village.

At about 14:30, under cover of artillery fire, the battalion stormed the Syrian force from the southwest and managed to take over elevation point 1614 and chase away the last of the Syrian soldiers that remained there. Company B commander was wounded while storming. At the same time the battalion was ordered to retreat to the Bus Lot following the failure of the 17th Battalion attack near the upper ski lift station. Four combatants were killed and thirteen were wounded in the battle over elevation point 1614. The Syrian losses were estimated at about twenty killed and an unknown number of wounded.

While the 51st Battalion was climbing up the Hermon shoulder the mechanized column including the two tanks continued advancing up the road toward the Israeli outpost. Behind the tanks the 17th Battalion forces moved in the following order: Company C under the command of Captain Yaakov *Sela*, the reconnaissance company squad commander course company with thirty-three combatants on board three half-tracks. The 17th Battalion commander's CCP was in the fourth half-track, followed by the brigade commander command half-track. Company B moved behind it, under the command of Modi Ben-Shach with about eighty combatants on board seven half-tracks. The company had in fact already completed the squad commander course on the eve of the war. One of the half-tracks had the brigade physician, Captain Dr. Shraga Maybloom, on board with two medics from the brigade infirmary and "light medical evacuation" equipment.

The force advanced up to the lower ski lift station without incident. In the parking lot south to the lower ski lift station the tanks deployed and fired with machine guns at all the structures that stood empty since they were evacuated by the 13th Battalion combatants at dawn on Sunday. The structures were scanned and it was discovered that the Syrians did not reach the outpost. The Israeli flag was on mast and was taken down to be raised on the Israeli outpost after its recapture. A caterpillar truck bulldozer belonging to the civilian contractor working on the upper ski lift station was started following the brigade commander's order, and was added to the column to remove any obstacles along the route. At 09:20, the brigade commander reported to the Northern Command Operations room that he had passed the lower ski lift station with the mechanized column and was on his way to the upper ski lift station.

The Syrian commander of the block at the upper ski lift station identified the mechanized column once it passed through the Bus Lot region; he briefed his men for the possibility of an attack and reported the movement of the forces to the 82nd Battalion commander. The battalion commander ordered him to enter a state of red alert. Due to the terrain of the region and the limited visibility that morning, the column disappeared from his view, until he identified it again when it came up from the lower ski lift station toward the Tank Bend, the B-10 RCLR team fired at the tanks as they reached the sharp curve where the road crosses the Gubta stream, about 750 meters from the Tank Bend—"the Quarry." The two shells missed their target exploding on the stream slopes. Only the 17th Battalion commander's half-track returned machine gun fire in the general direction the shells had been fired from, since no one identified the source of the firing. The column continued its movement until the two tanks and two Company C half-tracks passed the Tank Bend and stopped about 100 meters north of it. The column stopped there to let out a force from Company C to scan the ridge and secure the flank. The Company B deputy commander force was also let off and was sent to assist the 51st Battalion after being personally briefed by the brigade commander.

While the mechanized column moved toward the Tank Bend, a couple of jets from the 110th Squadron attacked the Syrian forces positioned on the Hermon. The jets remained in a holding pattern over the north of Israel for a long time. They were directed by the aerial advisor at the Northern Command Operations room following the request of the command artillery commander. After they left the attack flight route a "Strela" missile was launched at one of them and missed. The attack was not coordinated with the 1st Brigade commander, and he didn't know that it was carried out. At that time the sky was especially cloudy and it was possible that the jets attacked the Syrian Hermon outpost instead.

At about 10:00, when the 51st Battalion advance force was engaged in a firefight with the Syrian force deployed at elevation point 1614, and the Company B deputy commander force began moving down the slope to assist the battalion, the 17th Battalion commander ordered the Company C commander to move on foot from the Tank Bend with two teams from its company, up the ridge above the road leading to the upper ski lift station, to secure the mechanized column's flank, which planned to gradually advance from the rear. About twenty-two company combatants including the company commander began moving on foot up the dirt road across the ridgeline leading toward elevation point 2072. At that hour low clouds began covering the region, with a limited visibility of a few dozen meters. A team led by a platoon commander deployed to the right of the ridgeline and a team led by another platoon commander deployed to its left. The company commander moved with his radio operator in the center and a little to the rear. After several minutes of climbing, when the first team had already gone about 200 meters up the ridge and the area in front began descending into a sinkhole—the advance force combatants suddenly identified a group of soldiers moving below and to the right, about 10–15 meters away. When they identified these to be Syrian soldiers they quickly ran to capture the controlling area. The Syrians followed suit while opening fire toward them. The Syrians stormed forward several times, while tossing grenades at the force's combatants who took cover. In the close range battle the Syrians were halted and several of their soldiers were injured. An additional group of Syrians directed RPG-7 rockets and accurate sniper fire at them from a controlling group of boulders they found cover in. The force was caught in the crossfire not being able to either advance or raise their heads. They were utterly exposed.

The Syrian force encountered by the Company C combatants was the 82nd Battalion commander counterattack force with twenty combatants. The force was equipped with AK-47 "Kalashnikov" assault rifles, RPD machine guns, RPG-7 anti-tank rocket launchers, anti-tank grenades and hand grenades. The battalion commander sent the force after the commander of the Syrian block at the upper ski lift station reported the mechanized column had reached the Tank Bend, the Syrian force took positions in a cluster of boulders about 500 meters north of the Tank Bend, which controlled the fire and observation over the string of mines placed on the road by the Syrians two days earlier.

From the moment of the encounter the two Company C teams operated separately from each other. The first team commander and his team sergeant advanced forward with about half the team, who were trapped in a short range battle with a small Syrian force and were injured. The Syrians stormed toward them and were halted mainly thanks to the actions of the team's MAG operator, who was killed in the battle. After they ran out of ammunition the first team's combatants pulled back. The casualty was left in the field due to accurate Syrian fire. The company commander attempted to advance with the rest of the first team's men the whole time but was twice injured during the advancement. His request for artillery aid was declined. Feeling that he had lost control of the battle and following the accurate Syrian fire, he requested permission to retreat. His request was only granted after about an hour and fifteen minutes of fighting.

Men of the second team moved between the ridgeline and

the road and heard the gunfire encountered by the first team. The team commander jumped forward with his sergeant to see where the shooting was coming from. After advancing 100 meters up the ridge, they were fired at from the heap of boulders controlling the road. They called the team members to join them and began jumping forward while offering mutual cover, until they identified Syrian soldiers firing and tossing grenades at the men of the first team and the half-tracks standing on the road. The commander of the team, his sergeant, and a MAG operator stormed the Syrians. In their storming they were caught up in the Syrian alignment. At a very short range battle they managed to kill and injure about ten Syrian soldiers, but the team commander and two combatants were killed and were left in the field. The sergeant and the rest of the team continued storming north and reached the western slopes of hill 2072 where they conducted medium range fire battles with the Syrians positioned on the hill slopes. After a while the team's combatants retreated toward the Tank Bend evacuating the wounded. Due to the fierce firing, two combatants from the team, who were killed on the hill slopes, could not be reached and remained in the field. Since the commanders were hit and the battle complicated, chaos broke out on the battalion radio network. Hysterical reports and requests from combatants and radio operators asking for the wounded to be rescued practically jammed the network. The force commanders transferred communication to the brigade network but the stat of the battle could not be figured out. The requests by the artillery liaison officer for artillery assistance for the 17th Battalion forces were answered by the firing of only a few shells for targeting the upper ski lift station, after which the battery was directed to a different battle in another sector. At about 11:30 the brigade commander approved the retreat of the Company C force to the Tank Bend Of the twenty-two Company C combatants that went up the ridge, four combatants and commanders were killed, and nine were wounded. The four casualties were left in the field with the brigade commander's approval, since they could not be evacuated under the heavy fire. The wounded were evacuated to the Tank Bend during the battle, and from there they were carried on board half-tracks to the brigade medical company deployed west of Mas'ade.

While the two Company C teams were fighting up the ridge leading to elevation point 2072, the brigade commander ordered the 17th Battalion commander to advance with the tanks and Company B on half-tracks toward the upper ski lift station. A string of mines placed on the road and the blocking fire by the Syrians halted the advancement of the column. The 17th Battalion commander Lt. Col. Dubi Dror was killed during the mine clearing along with his intelligence officer and the 334th Battalion artillery liaison officer. The brigade physician and operations officer were injured. Two tanks and three half-tracks continued moving forward under the command of the head instructor Maj. Arieh Peled after the mines were cleared. About 500 meters past the Tank Bend they encountered Syrian anti-tank fire and sniper fire from the blocking force and were halted. In the survival battle conducted by the Company B commander near the upper ski lift station eight combatants were killed and many wounded.

A platoon from Company B, sent parallel to the movement of the mechanized column to assist Company C, climbed up the ridge without coordinating with the Company C commander, met up with just a few of the reconnaissance unit combatants and reached the slopes of hill 2072. An appended officer, Lt. Ephraim Shneur, and two combatants caught in the Syrian alignment were killed and remained in the field. The rest of the platoon was forced to retreat down the hill with its wounded when the brigade commander gave the retreat order. Under cover of a thick fog which enveloped the battlefield, all the AFVs turned back, and all forces retreated to the Tank Bend, and later on from there to the Bus Lot, the brigade commander remained in the Tank Bend until the 51st Brigade completed its fighting at hill 1614, and until the 17th Battalion Company B deputy commander returned with his injured. Even though the staff company from brigade Training Base No. 1 was ordered to remain in the Mas'ade region, it advanced behind the mechanized column and reached the lower ski lift station. It retreated to the Bus Lot along with all the company force. Until around 16:15 only 12th Battalion commander Lt. Col. Yaakov Shachar's CCP remained in the Tank Bend with his Company A who had been called up during the battle to reinforce the mechanized column.

The Battle Outcome

The goal of capturing the Israeli Hermon outpost and rescuing those trapped in it was not reached. During the battle, twenty-three commanders and combatants were killed and fifty-five were injured. At the end of the battle, the bodies of four combatants, from the 17th Battalion remained in the field; a combatant was left behind with the consent of the brigade commander and the bodies of the officer and two combatants, who stormed elevation point 2027 and whose absence was only verified in the gathering area in the Banias, were left behind, as well. The brigade commander consented that the bodies of the four combatants from the reconnaissance company be left behind as well since heavy Syrian fire made evacuation impossible. Syrian losses in the battle were: two killed and four wounded in the 82nd Battalion of the upper ski lift station blocking force, and at least seven were killed and seven wounded, three of them officers from the reinforcement force. About twenty soldiers were killed in the 183rd Battalion.

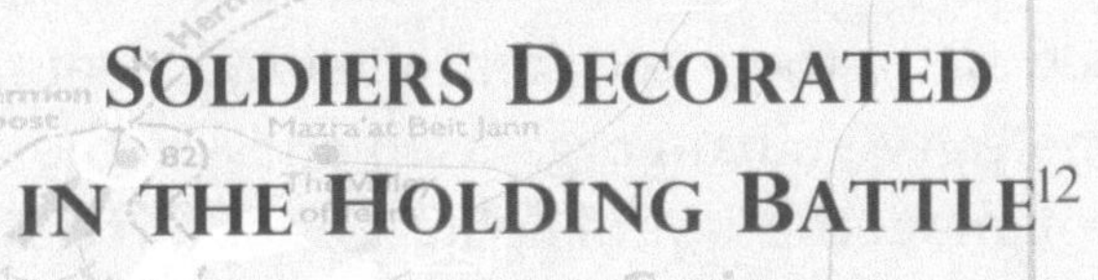

SOLDIERS DECORATED IN THE HOLDING BATTLE[12]

Corporal Avi-Tal Shlomo *2149101*

Description of action:

Corporal Shlomo Avi-Tal was with the force fighting in Tel Saki on the Golan Heights. They were outnumbered by enemy forces and Corporal Shlomo Avi-Tal was trapped wounded inside the bunker. However, when he saw there were many injured he assumed command, organized the wounded, treated them, and defended them. He also made sure to contact the battalion headquarters and they were rescued two days later. In his action, he displayed great bravery, prudence, resourcefulness and comradeship.

For this action, the Medal of Courage was awarded to him

Iyar 5735, May 1975, **Mordechai Gur, Lieutenant General, GHQ Chief of Staff**

12 Details regarding decorated soldiers taken from the website "Beoz Rucham" ("By Their Courage").

Lieutenant Avraham Elimelech *2128799*

For showing bravery, initiative and tenacity
Description of action:

During the Yom Kippur War Lieutenant Elimelech Avraham served as an outpost commander on the Golan Heights. When the war broke out, the outpost was bombed and Syrian armored forces moved along the route controlled by the outpost. Lieutenant Elimelech Avraham organized and led the men in the outpost throughout the days of fighting as he directed IDF tanks against the Syrian armored forces. In spite of serious Syrian infantry attacks on the outpost, a shortage in ammunition and weapons malfunctions, he maintained prudence and served as a model for his soldiers. In these actions, Lieutenant Elimelech Avraham showed bravery, prudence, and tenacity.

For this action, the Chief of Staff Citation was awarded to him

Tishrei 5736, September 1975, **Mordechai Gur, Lieutenant General, GHQ Chief of Staff**

Captain Aharon Netanel, of blessed memory, *2119060*

Description of action:

On October 6, 1973, Captain Aharon Netanel, of blessed memory, served as deputy company commander in a battalion. His company was deployed in the southern sector of the Golan Heights, split into platoons. When battles began, he participated in halting the advancement of the Syrian armored forces along the Petroleum Road, and after he was cut off from the force, and the tank he commanded was hit, he retreated on foot through a Syrian-held area. Between the advancing Syrian tanks, he reached the Upper Customs House, where he boarded a reconnaissance unit tank from the reserve division to continue the halting and breakthrough battles with them. In the breakthrough battle into Syria, in front of Khan Arnabeh, he was injured and killed. His actions showed courage, resourcefulness, and tenacity and were served as an example for others.

For this action, the Medal of Distinguished Service was awarded to him posthumously.

Iyar 5735, May 1975, **Mordechai Gur, Lieutenant General, GHQ Chief of Staff**

Captain Urieli Uzi *2098695*

For showing bravery, initiative, and tenacity

Description of action:

On October 6, 1973, Captain Uzi Urieli served as commander of a tank company fighting on the Golan Heights. He got an order to advance toward the Petroleum Road but encountered a Syrian tank force that captured the area around Jukhader. The force under the command of Captain Uzi Urieli attacked the Syrian positions—but when it failed to capture them, they blocked Syrian attempts to advance along the route. The force was outnumbered by the Syrian forces and blocked their advancement until Sunday, October 7, while inflicting losses on the enemy. In these actions, Captain Uzi Urieli showed bravery, prudence, and tenacity.

For this action, the Chief of Staff Citation was awarded to him

Tishrei 5736, September 1975, **Mordechai Gur, Lieutenant General, GHQ Chief of Staff**

Major Askarov Shmuel *2038141*

Description of action:

On October 6, 1973, Captain Shmuel Askarov served as deputy brigade commander. When the battles broke out, he moved at the head of a seven-tank force to block the "Qudna" route on the Golan Heights. Upon reaching the positions, he engaged dozens of enemy tanks and vehicles and conducted an exemplary holding battle. He was injured and evacuated to the hospital. On October 8, 1973, he escaped from the hospital, still injured, and returned to his unit. He organized a new force of thirteen tanks of the remaining people from his original unit and went into battle in the Mount Hermonit region, where he was seriously wounded. During the battles, he knew how to overcome moments of crisis, encourage his soldiers, his bravery and leadership serving as a source of strength for his subordinates.

For this action, the Medal of Courage was awarded to him

Iyar 5735, May 1975, **Mordechai Gur, Lieutenant General, GHQ Chief of Staff**

Major Ben David Amos, of blessed memory, *950177*

Description of action:

On Sunday, October 7 1973, Maj. Amos Ben David, of blessed memory, left with the battalion's advance force and fought with few tanks, risking his life, against superior enemy forces and destroyed them by exploiting the terrain and the element of surprise. In this action he stopped the advance of the Syrian enemy along the Quneitra—Bnot Yaakov Bridge road. At the end of the day, he remained alone with his tank. He joined the brigade night camp, and entered holding positions at night, which he kept until morning. The following day on Monday, October 8, 1973, he pushed the Syrian enemy penetrating toward Nafah and pursued it even though he was running out of ammunition. On Tuesday, October 9 1973, he led a tank force through enemy lines and saved a reconnaissance force from total destruction at the hands of a Syrian commando force. The next day, he fought on the flanks of many Syrian tanks and destroyed many of them south of Tel Yosifon, and on Thursday before the breakthrough, he talked with his combatants and raised their morale. He was killed during the breakthrough itself. Maj. Amos Ben David, of blessed memory, excelled in his superior bravery, prudence, resourcefulness, and great mental reserve that he bestowed on his subordinates, and thus, granting them confidence and faith.

For this action, the Medal of Courage was awarded to him posthumously

Iyar 5735, May 1975, **Mordechai Gur, Lieutenant General, GHQ Chief of Staff**

Second Lieutenant Bok Shimon, 2125064

For exhibiting bravery and persistence

Description of action:

On October 6, 1973, Second Lieutenant Bok Shimon served as a tank commander in a company fighting near Quneitra, on the Golan Heights. The company carried out a night ambush and Second Lieutenant was on the enemy's route. A large Syrian tank force moved between the company's five tanks and 2nd Lieutenant Bok Shimon destroyed nine Syrian tanks from an extremely short range. He destroyed many more enemy tanks before the war was over. Second Lieutenant Bok Shimon revealed courage and persistence in all his actions.

For this, the Chief of Staff Citation was awarded to him

Nisan 5736, April 1976, **Mordechai Gur, Lieutenant General, GHQ Chief of Staff**

Major Eshel Ilan *304119*

For exhibiting bravery, initiative, and tenacity

Description of action:

During the Yom Kippur War Captain Ilan Eshel commanded a force of four tanks and one APC in the Golan Heights battles. On October 7, 1973, Captain Ilan Eshel went up at the head of the force toward the Petroleum Road at Hushniya junction. Captain Ilan Eshel and his force captured a controlling area and while moving and exchanging fire with larger enemy forces, and making intelligent use of the field, he held the territory, blocked the enemy, and destroyed enemy forces. Later on, greater enemy forces attempted to outflank the force and engaged them in firefights. Captain Ilan Eshel's tank was hit during the battle. He was seriously wounded and his crew was killed. He managed to rescue himself from the burning tank and remained alone in the field. The next day he was rescued by IDF forces that had recaptured the area. In his actions, Captain Ilan Eshel revealed bravery, initiative, and tenacity.

For this action, the Chief of Staff Citation was awarded to him

Nisan 5736, April 1976, **Mordechai Gur, Lieutenant General, GHQ Chief of Staff**

Corporal Bitterman, Moshe, of blessed memory, *2171810*

Description of action:

On October 8, 1973, an infantry force went up the Hermon for an attack. Corporal Moshe Bitterman, of blessed memory, was a MAG operator in the company commander's half-track. During the climb, fierce fire was directed at the unit. Corporal Moshe Bitterman, of blessed memory, got up, in spite of the fierce fire, and fired his machine gun at the enemy. He fired several times, while changing his position in the half-track and exchanging ammunition, prudently and efficiently—until he was hit and killed.

For this action, the Medal of Distinguished Service was awarded to him posthumously

Iyar 5735, May 1975, **Mordechai Gur, Lieutenant General, GHQ Chief of Staff**

Sergeant First Class Bluman Yoav, of blessed memory, *2121723*

Description of action:

Staff Sergeant Yoav Bluman, of blessed memory, served as a platoon sergeant in a tank company that participated in the holding battles on the Golan Heights. On the evening after Yom Kippur, during battle, his tank was hit and he was evacuated. In the rear he organized another tank and joined the unit defending the Nafah Base. His second tank was hit during this battle and he was once again evacuated. From Nafah he rode to the distant Kurdani Base and brought another tank. With two officers who had remained without tanks as his crewmembers from the battalion, he joined the force fighting force in the Mount Shifon region, and the next day when they encountered a bazooka ambush his tank was hit and he was killed. In his actions, he displayed bravery and tenacity, which, to a large degree, allowed the battalion to meet its mission.

For this action, the Medal of Courage was awarded to him posthumously

Iyar 5735, May 1975, **Mordechai Gur, Lieutenant General, GHQ Chief of Staff**

Colonel Ben Shoham Yitzhak, of blessed memory,
302034

Description of action:

Col. Yitzhak Ben Shoham, of blessed memory, served as a brigade commander on the Golan Heights when battles broke out. On October 7, 1973, on the Petroleum Road, he fought to block the heavy Syrian pressure directed toward Nafah. Though the brigade had dwindled and the forces remaining were tired and beaten—he fought until his last breath persistently, bravely, showing exemplary leadership, thus making a decisive contribution to the blocking capacity in that sector. He was killed during the battles of that day.

For this action, the Medal of Courage was awarded to him

Iyar 5735, May 1975, **Mordechai Gur, Lieutenant General, GHQ Chief of Staff**

Sergeant First Class Berkovitch Daniel, of blessed memory, *2120609*

Description of action:

On October 6, 1973, Sergeant First Class Daniel Berkovitch, of blessed memory, served as a platoon sergeant in a battalion fighting on the Golan Heights. During the battle the deputy brigade commander, the company commander and two platoon commanders were injured. The injured deputy battalion commander ordered Sergeant First Class Daniel Berkovitch, of blessed memory, to take command. Sergeant First Class Daniel Berkovitch, of blessed memory, commanded the force bravely and prudently, and continued his stubborn fighting, directing reinforcements toward him, and reporting on the enemy's status in spite of the losses. Afterwards he joined up with a reserve division fighting in the Hushniya region. He fell in the battle on Tel Yosifon. In all his actions, he revealed bravery, resourcefulness, and exemplary leadership.

For this action, the Medal of Distinguished Service was awarded to him posthumously

Iyar 5735, May 1975, **Mordechai Gur, Lieutenant General, GHQ Chief of Staff**

Sergeant First Class Bashari Amir, of blessed memory, *2128234*

Description of action:

Staff sergeant Amir Bashari, of blessed memory, was a platoon sergeant in a tank company that participated in the holding battle on the Golan Heights. On the evening after Yom Kippur Staff sergeant Amir Bashari, of blessed memory, was situated in a firing position against the storming Syrian forces. He exposed a whole convoy of Syrian tanks moving in the valley and engaged them in very short-range combat, destroying about ten enemy tanks all by himself. In spite of the danger, he remained in the same position, until he was hit and killed. In this action, he revealed great bravery, prudence, and resourcefulness.

For this action, the Medal of Courage was posthumously awarded to him

Iyar 5735, May 1975, **Mordechai Gur, Lieutenant General, GHQ Chief of Staff**

Lieutenant Colonel Eldar Yosef 478359

Description of action:

When the battles broke out Lt. Col. Yosef Eldar commanded an improvised tank battalion fighting in the Mount Hermonit region. During the holding battle, he fought from an APC due to a shortage of tanks and stood on the front line, was wounded and evacuated. After receiving initial medical treatment, he "escaped" from the hospital and assumed command of his unit once again. On October 16, 1973, he was wounded again but refused evacuation, and only after the holding battle ended did he agree to be evacuated. A month later, he returned, once again, to command his unit in the battle of attrition. His behavior, bravery, and tenacity served as an example for all combatants.

For this action, the Medal of Distinguished Service was awarded to him

Iyar 5735, May 1975, **Mordechai Gur, Lieutenant General, GHQ Chief of Staff**

Sergeant Gonin Yaakov, of blessed memory,
2141076

Description of action:

On October 8, 1973; in the first battle over the Hermon, Corporal Yaakov Gonin, of blessed memory, served as a machine gun operator in the reconnaissance unit advance force moving on the road. When they encountered a Syrian force he maintained his prudence, and together with four other combatants fought in the position for several hours, while the Syrians constantly attempting to surround them. During the short-range battle carried out under a heavy fog, Corporal Yaakov Gonin, of blessed memory, hopped from one position to another, and when the Syrians attempted to storm his position, he got up firing with the machine gun from the hip, breaking their storming attempt. On one of his jumps, he was hit by a bullet in the head and killed. Thanks to his bravery and his strenuous and efficient work, the Syrian force storming attempt on the vital Israeli position was prevented.

For this action, the Medal of Courage was awarded to him posthumously

Iyar 5735, May 1975, **Mordechai Gur, Lieutenant General, GHQ Chief of Staff**

Lieutenant Gur Yosef *2133532*

Description of action:

Lieutenant Yosef Gur served as an outpost commander on the Golan Heights. When the battles began the Syrian enemy stormed the outpost with tanks, APCs, and infantry forces. Courageously, resourcefully, and prudently he managed to repel the enemy for two whole days—though the enemy had already succeeded in penetrating a number or areas within the outpost. Lieutenant Yosef Gur served as a model for his men and encouraged them to keep fighting, while he himself was injured he continued holding on, until the arrival of the Israeli forces.

For this action, the Medal of Courage was awarded to him

Iyar 5735, May 1975, **Mordechai Gur, Lieutenant General, GHQ Chief of Staff**

Sergeant Gissin Eitan, of blessed memory, *2168377*

Description of action:

On October 9, 1973, in Buq'ata, the company entered a Syrian commando ambush. The deputy company commander's vehicle was hit and four soldiers were killed. Sergeant Eitan Gissin, of blessed memory, climbed up on the APC that was hit, without receiving an order to do so, exposed to Syrian fire, and took a MAG machine gun and ammunition, laid down and began firing. He lost his eyesight due to the shooting but nevertheless did not lose his prudence and volunteered to go into the burning APC, feeling his way inside, in order to radio the situation to the rest of the company. He came out of the APC carrying weapons and grenades. He was later hit and killed by a bullet. In his actions, he demonstrated extraordinary bravery, prudence, resourcefulness and tenacity.

For this action, the Medal of Courage was awarded to him posthumously

Iyar 5735, May 1975, **Mordechai Gur, Lieutenant General, GHQ Chief of Staff**

Captain Greengold Zvi 2084377

Description of action:

On October 6 1973, Captain Zvi Greengold was in his kibbutz after completing his former position, a short time before the war, and not having yet received his appointment to a different position. When he found battles were erupting he returned to his former unit on the Golan Heights, organized a force of three tanks and headed out to block the advancing enemy armored forces toward the Nafah junction. He remained alone after two tanks were lost in the battle, facing repeated Syrian attempts to advance toward Nafah. He fought on his own for hours, while all the command networks believed him to be a tank force commander named the Zvika Force. He was later joined by a reserve unit which attempted to advance, but was forced to retreat due to the large number of injured soldiers. During this battle, Captain Zvi Greengold's tank was hit and he was wounded. Despite his being wounded, he transferred to a tank of another reserve unit and took command. Later in the night, he remained on his own once again and for several hours blocked the Syrian breakthrough attempts until he was joined, toward morning, by a deputy brigade commander with additional tanks. In the morning when they received notice that a Syrian force was arriving from a different location toward the Nafah Base, he was n ordered to move toward the base quickly. Together with another tank, they held off the Syrian tanks that had reached the fences surrounding the base. After the battle, he was evacuated to the hospital but returned a week later to continue fighting. His firm stand, while exhibiting unmatched bravery, delayed and prevented the Syrian advancement toward the Jordan River.

For this action, the Medal of Valor was awarded to him
Iyar 5735, May 1975, **Shimon Peres, Minister of Defense**

Lieutenant Dgani Shmuel, of blessed memory,
2084334

Description of action:

On October 6 1973, Lieutenant Shmuel Dgani, of blessed memory, served as a tank platoon commander in the outposts' line of the Golan Heights. During the holding battles the tank under his command was hit, and he was injured and evacuated. After receiving medical treatment, he returned to battle and commanded a tank platoon at the outposts' line. In a valorous battle, he managed to halt the Syrian Armored Force advancement toward the Achmadia junction. In this battle, he was injured and died. In his fighting, he displayed great bravery, prudence, resourcefulness, and leadership.

For this action, the Medal of Courage was awarded to him posthumously

Iyar 5735, May 1975, **Mordechai Gur, Lieutenant General, GHQ Chief of Staff**

Lieutenant Duvdevan Yehuda *2125763*

Description of action:

On October 7, 1973, during the holding battle on Hermonit, Lieutenant Yehuda Duvdevan evacuated wounded and casualties from tanks that were in firing positions—in spite of Syrian enemy tanks firing, artillery and infantry attacks, including the short range firing of anti-tank weapons. Thanks to his actions, executed with exemplary prudence, bravery and resourcefulness—the thinning tank unit continued maintaining its positions and avoided drawing back tanks during those difficult moments, when each tank was crucial for the halting of the Syrian storming.

For this action, the Medal of Distinguished Service was awarded to him

Iyar 5735, May 1975, **Mordechai Gur, Lieutenant General, GHQ Chief of Staff**

Captain Doron Amichai, of blessed memory,

2119643

Description of action:

Captain Doron Amichai, of blessed memory, served as a deputy tank company commander during the holding battles in the northern sector of the Golan Heights. On the night of October 7, 1973, he went out to rescue the crews of two tanks that were left in the field captured by the enemy. During his movement forward he noticed Syrian tanks passing him, but continued his mission and, with great prudence and resourcefulness, rescued the teams and towed the tanks back toward his forces. During the fighting, his tank was hit but he continued fighting on board another tank. He was later killed by a direct hit. In his actions, he revealed bravery, prudence, resourcefulness, and tenacity.

For this action, the Medal of Distinguished Service was awarded to him

Iyar 5735, May 1975, **Mordechai Gur, Lieutenant General, GHQ Chief of Staff**

Staff Sergeant Weinstein Avinoam *2139361*

For exhibiting bravery, prudence and tenacity
Description of action:

On October 8, 1973, during the first battle on the Hermon, Staff Sergeant Avinoam Weinstein, the medic, fought on the front lines. When soldiers were injured, he treated them under the enemy's fierce and accurate fire. When he treated the fifth wounded soldier, he was hit in his leg but insisted that he not be rescued. He injected himself with morphine and crawled to a concealed area from which he escaped. In this act, Staff Sergeant Avinoam Weinstein demonstrated bravery, prudence, and tenacity.

For this action the Chief of Staff Citation was awarded to him

Tishrei 5736, September 1975, **Mordechai Gur, Lieutenant General, GHQ Chief of Staff**

Captain Zohar Shalom *96242*

Description of action:

On October 6 1973, Captain Shalom Zohar served as a reconnaissance platoon commander in one of the battalions of the first force entering combat on the Golan Heights. When the battalion commander was wounded, Captain Shalom Zohar took charge and led the tank force against the enemy, though he had no prior information regarding what was happening in the field. After many Israeli tanks were hit he entered the combat zone and evacuated the injured, prior to the arrival of medical assistance. In his actions, he revealed bravery, resourcefulness and exemplary leadership.

For this action, the Medal of Distinguished Service was awarded to him

Iyar 5735, May 1975, **Mordechai Gur, Lieutenant General, GHQ Chief of Staff**

Lieutenant Colonel Zamir Meir *980307*

Description of action:

During the Yom Kippur War Captain Meir Zamir commanded a tank battalion in battles on the Golan Heights. In the holding battles his company received missions and executed them in an exemplary manner without suffering losses. The company destroyed about sixty enemy tanks, thus contributing to the halting of an enemy brigade attempting to breakthrough south of Quneitra. On October 9 1973, Captain Meir Zamir commanded his company in the decisive battle in the Valley of Tears. In this battle against superior enemy forces the company managed to destroy many enemy tanks without suffering any losses. In the breakthrough battles Captain Meir Zamir led his company heading the breakthrough division, and in these battles the company also managed to destroy many enemy tanks and successfully withstood all Syrian counterattack efforts. Throughout the days of combat Captain Meir Zamir led his company intelligently and bravely, while inflicting heavy losses on the enemy and maintaining the his force intact. In these actions, Captain Meir Zamir displayed intelligence, resourcefulness, bravery, exemplary leadership, tenacity, and mental strength.

For this action, the Medal of Courage was awarded to him

Iyar 5735, May 1975, **Mordechai Gur, Lieutenant General, GHQ Chief of Staff**

Sergeant Haviv Eliahu, of blessed memory, 2139361

For exhibiting bravery, initiative, tenacity, and comradeship

Description of action:

On the fourth day of the Yom Kippur War, an infantry company entered a battle over Buq'ata to block a Syrian force that penetrated the area. Sergeant Eliahu Haviv, of blessed memory, served as a machine gun operator on one of the half-tracks in the northeastern section of the area, and operated his weapon highly efficiently hitting many enemy soldiers maintaining a high morale though some of his close friends were injured. When there was a need for volunteers to scan an important building in Mazraat Beit Jann he did not hesitate to volunteer. Sergeant Eliahu Haviv, of blessed memory, fell on October 15, 1973 when he was hit by an artillery shell. In all his actions, Sergeant Eliahu Haviv, of blessed memory, displayed bravery, initiative, tenacity, and comradeship.

For this action the Chief of Staff Citation was awarded to him posthumously

Tishrei 5736, September 1975, **Mordechai Gur, Lieutenant General, GHQ Chief of Staff**

Captain Hotzev Haim, of blessed memory, 2025769

Description of action:

During the Yom Kippur War Captain Haim Hotzev, of blessed memory, served as a tank company commander in battles on the Golan Heights. When the war broke out Captain Haim Hotzev, of blessed memory, organized eight tanks, and with this force headed out to fight against superior enemy forces.

On October 7, 1973, his tank was hit in the battles. Captain Haim Hotzev, of blessed memory, transferred to another tank. He prudently continued fighting though most of the tanks under his command had been hit and he remained with only two tanks against the enemy forces that continued attacking at very short ranges. Captain Haim Hotzev, of blessed memory, continued fighting until he fell. In his actions, Captain Haim Hotzev of blessed memory displayed initiative, bravery, and exemplary tenacity.

For this action, the Medal of Distinguished Service was awarded to him posthumously

Nisan 5736, April 1976, **Mordechai Gur, Lieutenant General, GHQ Chief of Staff**

Lieutenant Hanani Binyamin, of blessed memory,
2112022

Description of action:

On October 7, 1973, the Tel Saki outpost on the Golan Heights remained surrounded by large Syrian forces. At this stage there were already many injured among the combatants in the outpost and their commander asked for urgent assistance. Lt. Binyamin Hanani, of blessed memory, heard the requests for help over the radio. He suggested the battalion commander that his platoon be sent to join up with the assaulted outpost, though he clearly knew the Syrian forces blocking the way were especially significant. The force under the command of Lt. Binyamin Hanani, of blessed memory, went on the mission, encountered a Syrian force, and in a fierce battle was killed, as was nearly his entire platoon. In his action, he displayed comradeship, bravery, and tenacity.

For this action, the Medal of Courage was awarded to him posthumously

Iyar 5735, May 1975, **Mordechai Gur, Lieutenant General, GHQ Chief of Staff**

Lieutenant Tal Gil, of blessed memory, *2076446*

Description of action:

On the second day of fighting on the Golan Heights an Israeli tank was hit and its commander was injured and fell on the turret. Under enemy fire Lt. Gil Tal, of blessed memory, advanced toward the tank that had been hit and rescued its commander. That same day another tank was hit and its crew was also rescued by Lt. Gil Tal, of blessed memory, Later on, in one of the attacks in the south of the Syrian Heights, Lt. Gil Tal, of blessed memory, and his unit entered a minefield and many tanks were damaged. Lt. Gil Tal, of blessed memory, continued managing the battle from the minefield, while drawing his unit back. He was later killed at Umm-Butna. In his actions, he revealed bravery, prudence, and leadership.

For this action, the Medal of Courage was awarded to him

Iyar 5735, May 1975, **Mordechai Gur, Lieutenant General, GHQ Chief of Staff**

Captain Yachin Shmuel *2117607*

For exhibiting intelligence, bravery, prudence and tenacity

Description of action:

During the Yom Kippur War Lt. Shmuel Yachin commanded a tank company near a Golan Heights outpost. When the war broke out armored enemy forces attacked and attempted to breakthrough into Israeli territory in the sector of the outpost. From October 6–8, 1973, Lt. Shmuel Yachin engaged in firefights with his platoon against the superior Syrian enemy, inflicting serious losses and hindering their advancement, while wisely keeping the platoon intact. In his fighting, Lt. Shmuel Yachin instilled great confidence in both his combatants and the infantry soldiers and prevented the enemy from capturing the outpost. In these actions, Lt. Shmuel Yachin revealed intelligence, bravery, prudence, and tenacity.

For this action the Chief of Staff Citation was awarded to him

Nisan 5736, April 1976, **Mordechai Gur, Lieutenant General, GHQ Chief of Staff**

Captain Kochav Avraham *2085789*

Description of action:

Captain Avraham Kochav's company was among those halting the Syrian force in the northern sector. During the fighting, most of the tank commanders in his unit were killed, and its force was weakened. He remained in his positions and encouraged the remaining forces to continue hitting the storming enemy in spite of this. On October 9, 1973, at the end of the enemy's main assault in the Hermonit sector, there was a turn in favor of the Syrians and Captain Avraham Kochav returned the retreating tanks in his sector to front battle positions, thus halting the Syrian effort and destroying it, while his unit only had six tanks. In his actions, he revealed bravery and exemplary leadership.

For this action, the Medal of Courage was awarded to him

Iyar 5735, May 1975, **Mordechai Gur, Lieutenant General, GHQ Chief of Staff**

Captain Lavi Amnon *2059615*

Description of action:

During the Yom Kippur War Captain Amnon Lavi served as commander of a tank company on the Golan Heights battles. On October 6, 1973, Captain Amnon Lavi fought with four tanks in the Hermonit region. On the night of October 9, 1973, he engaged in fierce battles against Syrian tanks and infantry attacks who attempted to break through the valley route in the Hermonit region. The next morning an additional large-scale Syrian attack commenced. Captain Amnon Lavi, with only three tanks, stood against the superior Syrian armored forces that attempted to outflank his tanks, and engaged them in firefights destroying several enemy tanks. During the battle, Captain Amnon Lavi advanced with his tank to the valley mouth and blocked enemy advancement. He continued fighting even after his tank had been hit in the battle and some of his crew-members were wounded. In his actions, Captain Amnon Lavi revealed bravery, prudence, and exemplary tenacity.

For this action, the Medal of Distinguished Service was awarded to him

Tishrei 5736, September 1975, **Mordechai Gur, Lieutenant General, GHQ Chief of Staff**

Staff Sergeant Legtivi Eliahu *951767*

For exhibiting resourcefulness and tenacity

Description of action:

On October 7, 1973, Staff Sergeant Eliahu Legtivi served as a tank gun operator in one of the battalions that encountered Syrian armored forces on the "Yehudia" route. Since his gun sights were not coordinated, due to the hasty departure at night, he himself executed battle calibration and began firing at enemy tanks. During the holding battles he managed to strike about thirty tanks, when he operated the cannon himself occasionally, thus relieving the company commander from fire corrections, which allowed the company commander to dedicate himself to managing the battle. With these actions, Staff Sergeant Eliahu Legtivi revealed resourcefulness and tenacity.

For this action the Chief of Staff Citation was awarded to him

Tishrei 5736, September 1975, **Mordechai Gur, Lieutenant General, GHQ Chief of Staff**

Captain Mevorach Yitzhak, of blessed memory,
2113477

Description of action:

On October 6 1973, Captain Yitzhak Mevorach, of blessed memory, received an order to stand with an APC south of Tel Fares on the Syrian Heights. At 18:00, he was ordered to join the rest of the company. On his way back in the dark he suddenly saw a Syrian tank aiming its cannon at him. Without losing his wits he hit the tank, rescued the APC, and even managed to warn the other APCs advancing on the route. On October 9 1973, in Buq'ata, the company entered a Syrian commando ambush. Captain Yitzhak Mevorach, of blessed memory, quickly organized a rescue force and went in to assist in the fighting and evacuate the wounded. After his squad was hit several times, he continued fighting on foot, while organizing and treating his injured soldiers and gathering those killed. In an additional Syrian anti-tank strike, he was struck and killed. In his actions, he revealed bravery, prudence, leadership, and resourcefulness.

For this action, the Medal of Courage was awarded to him posthumously

Iyar 5735, May 1975, **Mordechai Gur, Lieutenant General, GHQ Chief of Staff**

Captain Mansour Mansour, of blessed memory, *2088697*

For exhibiting bravery and tenacity

Description of action:

Prior to the break out of the Yom Kippur War Captain Mansour Mansour, of blessed memory, was on vacation from a company commander course and stayed in his village. On Yom Kippur, when he found out that war had broken out he hurried, of his own initiative, to join up with his former unit which he had left several weeks earlier. Captain Mansour Mansour, of blessed memory, assumed the position of deputy company commander and participated in holding battles on the Golan Heights. On October 9 1973, in a battle in the Buq'ata region he commanded a force while advancing on a half-track. In heading out for attack leading the force, he was injured and fell. In his actions, Captain Mansour Mansour, of blessed memory, revealed bravery and tenacity.

For this action the Chief of Staff Citation was awarded to him posthumously

Tishrei 5736, September 1975, **Mordechai Gur, Lieutenant General, GHQ Chief of Staff**

Major Noy Rafael *485813*

Description of action:

During the Yom Kippur War Major Rafael Noy fought in battles on the Golan Heights as a brigade Operations officer. On October 9 1973, during the storming to capture Hushniya the leading tanks encountered fierce enemy resistance that included heavy artillery fire. Some of the force lost direction and the assault was threatened. Major Rafael Noy jumped out of his moving half-track, and advanced on foot under heavy fire, before the leading tanks and using marking flags to direct the force for the continued attack, highly contributed to the success of the assault. In this action, Major Rafael Noy revealed resourcefulness, great bravery, and exemplary tenacity.

For this action, the Medal of Distinguished Service was awarded to him

Nisan 5736, April 1976, **Mordechai Gur, Lieutenant General, GHQ Chief of Staff**

Sergeant First Class Naidas Zvi, of blessed memory, 2120608

Description of action:

On October 6, 1973, Sergeant First Class Zvi Naidas, of blessed memory, served as a platoon sergeant in a battalion in the northern sector of the Golan Heights. In a fierce battle, he faced Syrian armored forces, and when he discovered that his commander Lt. Dgani, of blessed memory, was hit and his tank caught fire, he reached the burning tank, under fire and barrages of artillery, to rescue his crewmembers. In this attempt, his tank was directly hit killing him and his entire crew. In his act, he revealed bravery and exemplary comradeship.

For this action, the Medal of Distinguished Service was awarded to him posthumously

Iyar 5735, May 1975, **Mordechai Gur, Lieutenant General, GHQ Chief of Staff**

Lieutenant Colonel Nafshi Yair *455203*

Description of action:

Lt. Col Yair Nafshi commanded his battalion in the northern sector of the Golan Heights. During the most difficult hours of blocking, he fought for four days in the outpost and prevented its fall. He also assisted in conducting the brigade battle by observing and reporting the enemy's staging areas. Throughout the days of holding, he managed to prevent the collapse of the Quneitra enclave and though he was surrounded he went on with his assistance. With his courage, prudence and tenacity he unified his scattered unit, instilled a fighting spirit and tenacity in his soldiers—and thus prevented the fall of the outpost, which later served as the offensive springboard.

For this action, the Medal of Courage was awarded to him

Iyar 5735, May 1975, **Mordechai Gur, Lieutenant General, GHQ Chief of Staff**

Staff Sergeant Tobavi Itzhak, *2129038*

For exhibiting persistence, courage, initiative and comradeship

Description of action:

During the Yom Kippur War, Staff Sergeant Tobavi Itzhak served as a tank commander in the fights on the Golan Heights. On October 6 1973, his tank was hit and lost its maneuverability. Despite its malfunction he and his crew remained in the tank alone at the Quneitra Junction and fought against far superior Syrian forces and destroyed a few of their tanks. Despite dire conditions, Sergeant Tobavi gathered wounded crews from other tanks in the area and made sure they were evacuated to the gathering evacuation location. Later on, during the battle in the Tel Shams area, Staff Sergeant Tobavi Itzhak was wounded but continued commanding over his tank until he was replaced by another combatant. In his deeds, he revealed persistence, courage and comradeship.

For this action the Chief of Staff Citation was awarded to him posthumously

Tishrei 5736, September 1975, **Mordechai Gur, Lieutenant General, GHQ Chief of Staff**

Captain Svet Yair, of blessed memory, 2067521

Description of action:

Lt. Yair Svet, of blessed memory, was the commander of a tank company in the holding battles in the Golan Heights. On October 7, 1973, he went up to the firing positions and from short ranges of 200 to 500 meters hit enemy tanks, and managed to inflict serious losses on his enemy. During the fighting, a tank in his company was hit and the team was seen jumping out. Lt. Yair Svet, of blessed memory, came closer to the team to see what had happened, and was hit and killed when he stopped. Lt. Yair Svet, of blessed memory, served as a model and an example for the entire company, with his courage and prudence. Under his influence, the soldiers stood their ground and continued fighting.

For this action, the Medal of Distinguished Service was awarded to him posthumously

Iyar 5735, May 1975, **Mordechai Gur, Lieutenant General, GHQ Chief of Staff**

Lieutenant Sela Shmuel, of blessed memory,

2121728

For exhibiting bravery and prudence

Description of action:

Upon the encounter with the Syrian force in the first battle over the Hermon, Lt. Shmuel Sela, of blessed memory, skipped, together with two additional soldiers, and came very close to the Syrian positions. They engaged them in a sniper battle and prevented them from storming the reconnaissance force fighting nearby. During one of the skips, Lt. Shmuel Sela, of blessed memory, was hit and killed. In his actions, and fighting, Lt. Shmuel Sela, of blessed memory, revealed bravery and prudence.

For this action the Chief of Staff Citation was awarded to him posthumously

Tishrei 5736, September 1975, **Mordechai Gur, Lieutenant General, GHQ Chief of Staff**

Second Lieutenant Ozeri Yitzhak *2137812*

Description of action:

During the ascent to the Hermon, the battalion commander requested that an EOD soldier join him in the command half-track. Second Lt. Yitzhak Ozeri volunteered and joined him. During the advancement, the force encountered fierce fire and a string of mines on the road. Second Lt. Yitzhak Ozeri jumped out of the half-track together with the battalion intelligence officer and cleared away the mines under crossfire. During the last night, when evacuation of the vehicles with the wounded was approved, 2nd Lt. Yitzhak Ozeri went down and helped the wounded up under continuous fire exchange and when the mines hindered the half-track from turning back, 2nd Lt. Yitzhak Ozeri got off and directed the half-track from the ground as he moved on foot. In these actions, he revealed bravery, prudence, and exemplary behavior.

For this action, the Medal of Distinguished Service was awarded to him

Iyar 5735, May 1975, **Mordechai Gur, Lieutenant General, GHQ Chief of Staff**

Sergeant Ezer Zion *2149179*

Description of action:

Sergeant Zion Ezer was a soldier in an outpost on the Golan Heights. When the Syrians attacked the outpost, and after the outpost commander had been injured, he assumed command and encouraged the other soldiers to keep fighting. In these actions, he revealed bravery, initiative, leadership, and exemplary tenacity.

For this action, the Medal of Distinguished Service was awarded to him

Iyar 5735, May 1975, **Mordechai Gur, Lieutenant General, GHQ Chief of Staff**

Captain Akavia Uri, of blessed memory, *2083149*

Description of action:

On October 6, 1973, Captain Uri Akavia, of blessed memory, served as the commander of a tank company on the Golan

Heights. When battles broke out, he took positions in the area of the outpost controlling the Qudna route that the Syrians intended to break through. The force encountered an enemy tank unit and while conducting an accurate and rapid firefight Captain Uri Akavia, of blessed memory, managed to defeat them. In this battle, the enemy sent additional forces to outflank the outpost. When Captain Uri Akavia, of blessed memory, was sent by the deputy battalion commander to block this effort, he made contact with the enemy and during this fight, he was hit and killed. In these actions, he revealed bravery, leadership, and resourcefulness.

For this action, the Medal of Distinguished Service was awarded to him posthumously.

Iyar 5735, May 1975, **Mordechai Gur, Lieutenant General, GHQ Chief of Staff**

Lieutenant Fine Ephraim *2146164*

Description of action:

Lt. Ephraim Fine served as a platoon commander in an infantry company fighting on the Golan Heights. On October 7, 1973, when the company reached Nafah, it split into units to stand at the Petroleum Road, block the path for Syrian tanks, and prevent the landing of helicopters. Lt. Ephraim Fine remained at the entrance to Nafah with two "Bazooka" units of which the soldiers were shell-shocked thus leaving him to manage with just one sergeant. He managed to halt the entry of Syrian tanks with the three bombs he had and by firing a heavy machine gun. He later drove out to get a vehicle to evacuate the wounded. In his actions, he revealed bravery, resourcefulness, and exemplary prudence.

For this action, the Medal of Distinguished Service was awarded to him

Iyar 5735, May 1975, **Mordechai Gur, Lieutenant General, GHQ Chief of Staff**

Lieutenant Palti Shai, of blessed memory, *2129234*

Description of action:

On Monday, October 8, 1973, the battalion was ordered to capture the Hermon outpost. Lt. Shai Palti, of blessed memory, rode in the command half-track. While going up the Hermon, the force encountered fierce fire and a string of mines on the road. Lt. Shai Palti, of blessed memory, jumped out of the half-track and began clearing the mines away under crossfire. The force continued advancing slightly, and then encountered RPG fire 20 meters away. Lt. Shai Palti, of blessed memory, was hit and killed. In his action, he revealed bravery, prudence, initiative, and resourcefulness.

For this action, the Medal of Courage was awarded to him posthumously

Iyar 5735, May 1975, **Mordechai Gur, Lieutenant General, GHQ Chief of Staff**

Sergeant Tzadok Yosef *2126727*

Description of action:

On October 6 1973, Corp. Yosef Tzadok participated in the force arriving as reinforcement to a Golan Heights outpost. When the war broke out armored enemy forces attempted breaking through into Israeli territory through the outpost. Corp. Yosef Tzadok grabbed a bazooka of his own initiative and fired at the enemy tanks. On October 7, 1973, Corp. Yosef Tzadok destroyed a Syrian tank attacking the outpost with a bazooka. On October 9 1973, five Syrian tanks attempted to outflank the outpost and advance toward Israeli territory. Corp. Yosef Tzadok operated the bazooka while exposed to enemy fire and destroyed four tanks. He was injured during the fighting later on. In his actions, Corp. Yosef Tzadok revealed resourcefulness, bravery, prudence, and exemplary tenacity.

For this action, the Medal of Distinguished Service was awarded to him

Nisan 5736, April 1976, **Mordechai Gur, Lieutenant General, GHQ Chief of Staff**

Lieutenant Colonel Zurich Moshe *463001*

For exhibiting initiative, resourcefulness and tenacity

Description of action:

During the Yom Kippur War, Maj. Moshe Zurich served as a brigade staff officer. When the war broke out, he participated in battles in the southern sector of the Golan Heights. Around Nafah he directed the forces going up to the Golan Heights and participated in the battle over Nafah. Together with additional staff officers from his unit, he organized new tank team forces and quickly sent them off to the battlefield. During the fighting, he joined another unit and took part in the holding and breakthrough battles on the Golan Heights. At the end of the battles, he returned to his original unit and reorganized it. In his actions, Maj. Moshe Zurich revealed initiative, resourcefulness, and tenacity.

For this action the Chief of Staff Citation was awarded to him

Tishrei 5736, September 1975, **Mordechai Gur, Lieutenant General, GHQ Chief of Staff**

Lieutenant Colonel Kahalani Avigdor 478446

Description of action:

Lt. Col. Avigdor Kahalani commanded a tank battalion in the Yom Kippur battles on the Golan Heights. During the four days of holding, until October 9, 1973, he operated in the Quneitra and Mount Hermonit sector. On October 9, 1973, the number of commanders and tanks hit in the Golan Heights increased and some positions were captured by the Syrian enemy only a few dozen meters from Israeli forces. Lt. Col. Avigdor Kahalani was sent from a different area of the sector with a few tanks to replace a unit that had been fighting all night and was forced to restock ammunition and reorganize. He was appointed commander of the sector and was placed in charge of the other tanks that remained in the area. Lt. Col. Avigdor Kahalani led the force when he encountered and destroyed four Syrian tanks a few dozen meters away. He then organized all the remaining tanks in the sector that belonged to different units being under constant pressure of the advancing Syrian decisively superior forces. Lt. Col. Kahalani, with his leadership and personality, provided a model for his soldiers who were on the brink collapse. He stormed the Syrian enemy first, with one of his subordinate commanders. The entire force followed him and managed to recapture the controlling Syrian positions, which were key positions of the entire sector. After the shooting positions were recaptured the Syrian force, of dozens of tanks, was destroyed, and the final assault on the Golan Heights was broken. In these actions, he prevented the breakthrough of the front in the northern sector of the Golan Heights. Lt. Col. Kahalani revealed extraordinary leadership and personal courage in a difficult and complicated battle whose outcome change the nature of the campaign on the Golan Heights.

For this action, the Medal of Valor was awarded to him
Iyar 5735, May 1975, **Shimon Peres, Minister of Defense**

Captain Kotef Asaf *471960*

Description of action:

During the Yom Kippur War Captain Asaf Kotef participated in battles on the Golan Heights as a reconnaissance team commander on board jeeps. On October 10, 1973 in the battle over Tel Fares, an enemy tank positioned itself on the top of the mound and prevented its capture. Captain Asaf Kotef arrived at the area, assisted the evacuation of the wounded, and then outflanked the tank in the field, which had not been cleared of enemy soldiers, firing his personal weapon at the crew of the Syrian tank and tossed hand grenades at them. When he ran out of grenades, he returned to his forces, equipped himself with ammunition, returned to the tank and hit its crewmembers. This enabled the capturing of the mound. On the night of October 18–19, 1973, he participated in the recapturing of Tel Antar. He commanded a force of two jeeps and a half-track and cleared the trenches and positions captured during the night by the enemy commando forces. This enabled the recapturing of the mound. Throughout his days of fighting, he also engaged in observations and obtaining information, evacuating wounded and ranging artillery fire. In his actions, Captain Asaf Kotef revealed bravery, self-sacrifice, tenacity, and comradeship.

For this action, the Medal of Courage was awarded to him

Tishrei 5736, September 1975, **Mordechai Gur, Lieutenant General, GHQ Chief of Staff**

Captain Kimovitch Avraham 2084771

For exhibiting bravery, tenacity, leadership and prudence

Description of action:

On October 6 1973, Captain Avraham Kimovitch served as a deputy company commander in a battalion situated in the northern sector of the Golan Heights. When the battles broke out, he commanded a tank platoon and excelled in doing it. After the holding battles ended, he continued breaking through into Syria and was appointed deputy company commander in another company. When the company commander was injured, he took command. His intelligent conduct and careful consideration instilled confidence in his men. In his fighting style, Captain Avraham Kimovitch revealed bravery, tenacity, leadership, and prudence.

For this action the Chief of Staff Citation he was awarded to him

Tishrei 5736, September 1975, **Mordechai Gur, Lieutenant General, GHQ Chief of Staff**

Captain Kenan (Cowley) Eitan 2045882

Description of action:

Captain Eitan Cowley was deputy commander of a tank battalion that participated in battles on the Golan Heights. On October 6–9, 1973, he withstood the Syrian attack in the Mount Hermonit sector. His leadership convinced the tank crews to maintain their positions against the heavy enemy pressure, though many of the battalion tanks were hit, Eitan kept his sound spirit and continued manning the position and firing at the advancing enemy. He was among the storming forces throughout the days of fighting always leading them. In spite of his being physically exhausted, he organized and managed the battalion logistical and medical alignment. His courage, prudence, and resourcefulness were exemplary.

For this action, the Medal of Distinguished Service was awarded to him

Iyar 5735, May 1975, **Mordechai Gur, Lieutenant General, GHQ Chief of Staff**

Captain Klog Avraham, of blessed memory, 974623

Description of action:

Captain Avraham Klog, of blessed memory, served as a tank platoon commander in battles on the Golan Heights when the Yom Kippur War broke out. On October 8, 1973, after a Syrian attack Captain Avraham Klog, of blessed memory, organized his platoon for a quick counterattack, captured positions in a controlling area, and halted the Syrian armored forces attack. Later on during the fighting Captain Avraham Klog, of blessed memory, was injured by shrapnel in his back and was bandaged refusing to be evacuated. In his movement by tank to join up with one of the units to participate in the attack against the Syrian forces, he was injured and died. In his actions, Captain Avraham Klog of blessed memory showed bravery, prudence, and exemplary comradeship.

For this action, the Medal of Distinguished Service was awarded to him posthumously

Tishrei 5736, September 1975, **Mordechai Gur, Lieutenant General, GHQ Chief of Staff**

Captain Rosenzweig Moshe, of blessed memory, *2078392*

Description of action:

Captain Moshe Rosenzweig, of blessed memory, was a company commander in a tank battalion fighting on the Golan Heights. During the holding battle, he fought in an exemplary manner and continued fighting even after he was injured, first above his eye and later in the shoulder. In spite of his grueling injuries, he continued leading his company, and even headed the battalion commander's rescue operation. He entered an area controlled by Syrian fire and rescued the battalion commander and his crew who had been struck by a direct hit. After the rescue, he was injured for the third time and was killed. Captain Moshe Rosenzweig, of blessed memory, was a model commander and friend in the battlefield, and excelled in his bravery, resourcefulness, and prudence.

For this action, the Medal of Courage was awarded to him posthumously

Iyar 5735, May 1975, **Mordechai Gur, Lieutenant General, GHQ Chief of Staff**

Captain Runis Avi, of blessed memory, 2094003

For exhibiting bravery, prudence, resourcefulness and leadership

Description of action:

On October 6, 1973, Captain Avi Runis, of blessed memory, served as a commander of a tank company. When the war broke out his company, in holding positions, was split in the southern sector of the Golan Heights. Captain Avi Runis, of blessed memory, was the first to locate the Syrian penetration attempts, and accordingly managed the fight and directed the reinforcements arriving in the region. He located the offensive attempt on an Israeli outpost and stopped it. In an additional Syrian attempt to capture the outpost and with no other option for halting - Captain Avi Runis, of blessed memory, went up to an exposed position with his tank, struck 6 Syrian tanks attacking the outpost, and thus caused the enemy to retreat. He fell in this battle. In his actions, Captain Avi Runis, of blessed memory, revealed bravery, prudence, resourcefulness, and leadership.

For this action, the Chief of Staff Citation was awarded to him posthumously Tishrei 5736, September 1975, **Mordechai Gur, Lieutenant General, GHQ Chief of Staff**

Lieutenant Colonel Rates Meshulam, of blessed memory, 274164

Description of action:

Lt. Col. Meshulam Rates, of blessed memory, commanded a tank battalion in the northern sector of the Golan Heights. In spite of the arduous conditions, he managed to conduct a fierce and effective defensive battle and prevented the fall of the line's outposts and the capture of the El-Rom ranch. On October 9 1973, he led his dwindling force on a frontal counter-attack against the penetrating Syrians in the Mount Hermonit region. While engaged in contact with the enemy he was hit and killed. Lt. Col. Meshulam Rates, of blessed memory, commanded a dispersed force at the start of the battle but managed to unite it in the course of the fighting and get the best combat competence, out of it, while serving as a model with his bravery, prudence, and optimism.

For this action, the Medal of Courage was awarded to him posthumously

Iyar 5735, May 1975, **Mordechai Gur, Lieutenant General, GHQ Chief of Staff**

Staff Sergeant Ratz Yoram *473653*

Description of action:

During the Yom Kippur War Staff Sergeant Yoram Ratz served as a tank commander in the Golan Heights battles. Many tanks from his unit were hit during the fighting. When a number of tanks he was fighting from were hit and immobilized, Staff Sergeant Yoram Ratz refused to turn back and always found a way to return to the front by replacing them with others. In his actions, Staff Sergeant Yoram Ratz served as a model and example to all the commanders in his unit and revealed resourcefulness, bravery, and exemplary tenacity.

For this action, the Medal of Distinguished Service was awarded to him

Tishrei 5736, September 1975, **Mordechai Gur, Lieutenant General, GHQ Chief of Staff**

Major Rak Zvi *987023*

Description of action:

On October 6, 1973, Maj. Zvi Rak was a company commander in the northern sector of the Golan Heights. When the battles broke out, he received command of a region in the center of the Golan Heights. In a fierce and resourceful battle, he managed to halt the Syrian advancement and push them back to the outskirts of Quneitra. After the holding battle, he went on, invaded the line toward Syria, and reached Tel Shams. In the Tel Shams battles, he bravely and resourcefully withstood Syrian attacks where he was badly injured. In his fighting, he revealed bravery, prudence, and exemplary resourcefulness.

For this action, the Medal of Distinguished Service was awarded to him

Iyar 5735, May 1975, **Mordechai Gur, Lieutenant General, GHQ Chief of Staff**

Major Schwartz Hanan *963278*

For exhibiting initiative, resourcefulness and tenacity

Description of action:

During the Yom Kippur War, Maj. Hanan Schwartz served as a brigade communications officer. When the war broke out, he participated in battles in the southern sector of the Golan Heights. In the Nafah region, he directed the forces going up to the Golan Heights. Together with additional staff officers from his unit, he organized new tank teams forces and quickly sent them into the field. During the fighting, he joined another unit and took part in the holding and breaking through battles on the Golan Heights. At the end of the battles, he returned to his original unit and organized it. In his actions, Maj. Hanan Schwartz revealed initiative, resourcefulness, and tenacity.

For this action the Chief of Staff Citation was awarded to him

Tishrei 5736, September 1975, **Mordechai Gur, Lieutenant General, GHQ Chief of Staff**

Major Shacham Eyal, of blessed memory, *2061820*

Description of action:

On October 6, 1973, Maj. Eyal Shacham, of blessed memory, was a company commander in a battalion in the northern sector of the Golan Heights. When the battles broke out, he commanded a northern outpost sector. He conducted a fierce fight, making use of the few tanks at his disposal in the best manner possible and managed to halt the advancement of the Syrian armored forces from advancing toward Mas'ade. He was killed in this battle. In all his actions, he revealed superb leadership, bravery, exemplary resourcefulness and managed to encourage his soldiers even in the darkest hours.

For this action, the Medal of Distinguished Service was awarded to him posthumously

Iyar 5735, May 1975, **Mordechai Gur, Lieutenant General, GHQ Chief of Staff**

Lieutenant Shachar Yuval *2115548*

Description of action:

On October 6, 1973, Lt. Yuval Shachar served as a battalion intelligence officer. In the afternoon hours the battles increased, tanks were hit, and there was a need to evacuate the wounded. Lt. Yuval Shachar took an APC, entered the region of the tank positions, and evacuated the wounded. When it was discovered in the evening hours that there were still wounded in the outpost, and in spite of information that the Syrians were in control of all routes, he once again took the APC, penetrated the Syrian alignment to a depth of four kilometers, passed between dozens of Syrian tanks and APCs, opened fire at the tank commanders, and hit them. He reached the outpost, took the wounded and headed west, once again passing between the Syrian convoys, until he reached the Medical Evacuation Unit. In these actions, he revealed great bravery, prudence, and comradeship.

For this action, the Medal of Courage was awarded to him

Iyar 5735, May 1975, **Mordechai Gur, Lieutenant General, GHQ Chief of Staff**

Sergeant Shalom Yitzhak, of blessed memory, *2128481*

Description of action:

Sgt. Yitzhak Shalom, of blessed memory, served as a combatant in the Hermon outpost when the Yom Kippur War broke out. When the Syrian bombing of the outpost began, he went up to the roof of the outpost with several other combatants and returned fire against the Syrian forces. He went back into the outpost and organized the people with him to block the entrances to prevent Syrian attempts to enter the outpost. The next day he organized the people with him to try to break out of the outpost and fight the Syrians inside the outpost. During the attempt to break out of the outpost Sgt. Yitzhak Shalom, of blessed memory, went up the roof of the outpost, threw two grenades at the Syrians, and tried to operate his personal weapon. He was then hit and killed. In his actions, Sgt. Yitzhak Shalom of blessed memory revealed bravery, prudence, and exemplary comradeship.

For this action, the Medal of Distinguished Service was awarded to him posthumously

Tishrei 5736, September 1975, **Mordechai Gur, Lieutenant General, GHQ Chief of Staff**

Lieutenant Shemesh Avinoam, of blessed memory,

2145495

Description of action:

Second Lt. Avinoam Shemesh, of blessed memory, was commander of a tank platoon that participated in the holding battles in the Golan Heights. On October 7, 1973, the company including 2nd Lt. Avinoam Shemesh, of blessed memory, moved to block the southern opening of Quneitra. In the city's central junction, the company commander was hit in the head. Second Lt. Avinoam Shemesh, of blessed memory, got out of his tank, ran to the company commander's tank, bandaged him, briefed the crewmembers, and prudently led them out of the danger zone, all under heavy and accurate Syrian artillery fire. Second Lt. Avinoam Shemesh, of blessed memory, fell that afternoon, in the Hermonit sector, while blocking the storming Syrians. In his actions, he revealed prudence and exemplary bravery.

For this action, the Medal of Distinguished Service was awarded to him posthumously

Iyar 5735, May 1975, **Mordechai Gur, Lieutenant General, GHQ Chief of Staff**

Captain Ephraim Shneur, of blessed memory,

2078342

Description of action:

On October 8, 1973, Lt. Ephi Shneur, of blessed memory, was appended to the battalion going up to the Hermon. During the battle, it was discovered that the reconnaissance unit's advance force needed rescuing. Lt. Ephi Shneur, of blessed memory, who was not part of the unit, volunteered to lead the rescue force. The force climbed up the mountain under fire. At a certain stage, the anti-tank rifle grenade operator was killed. Lt. Ephi Shneur, of blessed memory, took the anti-tank rifle grenade from him, fired a grenade, and destroyed an enemy position. Afterwards he organized an attack on that same position, under fierce fire, and captured it. He was killed after doing this. In his actions, he revealed bravery, prudence, leadership, and exemplary tenacity.

For this action, the Medal of Courage was awarded to him posthumously

Iyar 5735, May 1975, **Mordechai Gur, Lieutenant General, GHQ Chief of Staff**

Lieutenant Tavori Ofer *2139397*

Description of action:

Second Lt. Ofer Tavori served as commander of a tank platoon that participated in the holding battles and the breaking through of the Syrian enclave. On the night of October 7, 1973, 2nd Lt. Ofer Tavori stood in positions over a route leading to one of the outposts. In spite of constant pressure by the Syrian forces passing through the sector he remained in his position and did not ask to move back. On 8 October 1973, a track in the tank was dislodged and the tank could not be maneuvered. In spite of both fighting conditions in the field and heavy shelling, 2nd Lt. Ofer Tavori kept his calm, rescued his team, and repaired the malfunction by taking the missing parts from a tank that had been hit and bringing them into his tank. In these actions, he revealed bravery, prudence, and exemplary resourcefulness.

For this action, the Medal of Distinguished Service was awarded to him

Iyar 5735, May 1975, **Mordechai Gur, Lieutenant General, GHQ Chief of Staff**

Lieutenant Colonel Vaspi Yoav, of blessed memory, *44536*

Description of action:

On October 7, 1973, Lt. Col. Vaspi Yoav, of blessed memory, headed a tank company up the Gamla incline and destroyed a Syrian tank force, thus blocking the Syrian route descending to the Jordan River and secured the breakthrough route for the Israeli forces' counterattack. During this action, his tank was hit and he continued operating from another tank. The next day, during the advancement, he encountered an enemy anti-tank, infantry and tank alignment. He stormed at the head of the battalion, destroyed the Syrian alignment, took over the Petroleum Road, and thus blocked reinforcement of the enemy on this route. On October 9, 1973, Lt. Col. Vaspi Yoav, of blessed memory, stormed Tel Akasha leading a five-tank force. In spite of the heavy enemy shelling, he captured the mound and blocked off the enemy's route of retreat. On October 16, he was killed during a battle on the Golan Heights. In all his actions, he revealed great bravery, prudence, leadership, and resourcefulness.

For this action, the Medal of Courage was awarded to him

Iyar 5735, May 1975, **Mordechai Gur, Lieutenant General, GHQ Chief of Staff**

The Syrian Army—From Penetration to the Depths of the Golan Heights to the Delay in the Eastern Defensive Alignments

CHAPTER 10

The Syrians Retreat to the Purple Line (October 7–10)

At the end of the second campaign day on October 7, the advance brigades of the Syrian 5th Division reached a line from which they overlooked the openings of the routes going up to the Golan Heights. The 132nd Mechanized Brigade with forces from the 47th Tank Brigade at their rear reached the El Al passage. Forces from the 47th Brigade were positioned at the Gamla incline while the 46th Tank Brigade advance force reached the Katzbia region, south of the Waterfalls junction. It is worthwhile mentioning that these forces were delayed on this line, overlooking the Jordan River and the shores of the Sea of Galilee on that Sunday as a result of the IDF Air Force attacks that caused the Syrians many losses. Many Israeli jets were hit during these assaults by Syrian anti-aircraft units appended to the forces, as well as the SAM batteries. The Syrian delay across the southern and central sectors, mainly in the Nafah region, made it possible for the IDF's armored reserve forces to go up and situate themselves for holding and a counterattack later, as well.

The counter attack by the Northern Command began on the line where the Syrian forces stopped. Against the counter attack, the 5th Division brigades reinforced by anti-aircraft units engaged in a series of delay and retreat battles. The fighting caused the Syrians to retreat in the southern sector, during October 8 and 9, into their fortified defense alignments east of the border from which they attacked the Golan Heights.

The Syrians positioned tanks, anti-tank units, and mechanized infantry forces against the IDF's counter attacking forces. These engaged in a series of mobile battles wherein the Syrian forces skipped back from one line to the next. Mobile and stationary anti-tank forces that held the ground, based on a BRDM-2 AFV battalion carrying Sagger missiles, allowed for relative maneuverability that created a tank defense of sorts in the Waterfalls Route region (west and north of Tel Fares) and on the southern slopes of Tel Yosifon. These took their toll on the IDF tanks and allowed for a relatively orderly and organized folding up into the alignments east of the borderline and into the "Hushniya enclave" which was prepared for defense in the meantime.

During the redeployment- and very near the borderline - local attempts at parallel counterattacks failed as could be seen. The retreating forces were assisted by artillery alignments ranged from the peak of Tel Fares. The capture of this peak stopped the accurate Syrian firing immediately. The Israeli Air Force control over the region's aerial space allowed hardly any Syrian Air Force assistance to the ground forces.

The main frontal breakthrough efforts in the northern Golan Heights—by the 7th Division throughout the front and by the 9th Division in its northern sector—failed persistently. These were now accompanied by outflanking efforts to assist the divisions on the line in breaking through and advancing their forces in the sectors where breakthrough had been unsuccessful. The 1st Armored Division, with its quality forces, was repeatedly placed north into the Nafah region with the intention of reaching the Waset—Schech region to apparently assist in the opening of the northern breakthrough areas from the rear.

Even in the last phase of the attack on October 9—when the attempts to complete the breakthrough all along the front continued—Syrian forces were once again placed against the sectors that remained impenetrable. In a coordinated Syrian GHQ attack, including massive artillery preparation, the Syrians once again unsuccessfully attempted to breakthrough in the sectors where they had thus far failed. This time the efforts included forces of the 81st Tank Brigade, from the 3rd Division, which was annexed to the 7th Division and was once again cast into the Valley of Tears. At night when the Syrian forces prepared for the renewed offensive attempt, the 7th Division commander Brigadier General Omar Abrash was killed when his command car was hit. A Syrian infantry force operating in the sector managed to infiltrate, encounter, and strike IDF forces in the region of Buq'ata north of Hermonit, mainly employing anti-tank launchers.

The remaining forces of the 43rd Tank Brigade of the 9th Division attempted, at the same time, to breakthrough in the salient south of Quneitra and north of the Hazeka ridge. The 52nd Infantry Brigade was unsuccessful in this sector during the first phase. It should be noted that the 43rd Brigade was placed north of the Qudna salient toward the Tel Yosifon (Abu Yusuf) region, on the first night, was seriously injured by the "Tiger Force," turned back, and was once again placed in the north of the division sector, which had not been broken through, three days later. Along with them, the 91st Brigade of the 1st Division equipped with T-62 tanks attempted an additional last effort to cross the Nafah route and advance north toward the rear of the IDF force defending the region of the Valley of Tears. It was also halted by the 679th Brigade.

A commando force flown in on twelve helicopters to the area north of Nafah was apparently employed to assist the offensive effort. Two were shot down by IAF jets, and one by ground fire. The others landed about seventy-five soldiers, who were either killed or captured shortly after touchdown.

The 3rd Armored Division, which appended the 81st Brigade to the 7th Division, remained as a GHQ reserve force in the depth of the Syrian Golan Heights throughout all the attack stages.

Before noon, October 9 it seemed the Syrian Army had lost its capacity to attack. Exhaustion prevailing everywhere, the losses it suffered, the destruction of whole units and the weakness of its Air Force called for a general withdrawal. The Israeli Air Force strategic bombings in the depth of Syrian territory contributed to this Syrian tendency as well.

On the night of October 9—10, the Syrian forces retreating from the Hushniya region, under the pressure of IDF forces from the south, west and north, attempted to stabilize a defensive line on the Hazeka ridges and Sha'af a-Sindian (between outposts 110 and 111). The 1st Division commander withdrew his headquarters from Tel Fazra to Tel Qudna where he commanded the remaining forces from the 51st and 46th Brigades' battle that had operated under the command of the 9th and 5th Divisions during the attack, in addition to his own forces. The 5th, 7th, and 9th Infantry Forces and mechanized infantry forces of the divisions retreated east and most of them had entered there prior to the war defensive layout.

Syrian Air Force Attacks

The Syrian Air Force evidently made an effort to assist with the purpose of allowing the flow of its forces and stabilization of a line against the attacks of the Northern Command. Overall, the Syrians carried out 266 attack sorties at this stage. There was also an attempt to land forces in the center of the Golan Heights and escort attacking jets. Syrian inefficient aerial attacks did not influence either the process of fighting or the repelling of their forces. In one of the Syrian aerial attacks, an ammunition truck and a mortar battery were hit. Eight soldiers were killed and twenty-three more were wounded. A failed attempt to attack the Air Force controlling unit at Mount Meron followed. Three Syrian jets were shot down in pursuit by IAF jets. The Syrian losses amounted to twenty-nine jets, eighteen of them in dog-fights, five by ground fire, and six in crashes and accidents.

Because of the Northern Command counterattack, the Syrians were pushed beyond the Purple Line and recaptured their dug-in positions, which were not seriously harmed during the fighting that had taken place before. Three Syrian Army mechanized infantry divisions occupied their original alignments on the first line of defense. The 1st Armored Division, which penetrated the center of the Golan Heights, concentrated and regrouped its retreating forces in the Qudna—Swysa region.

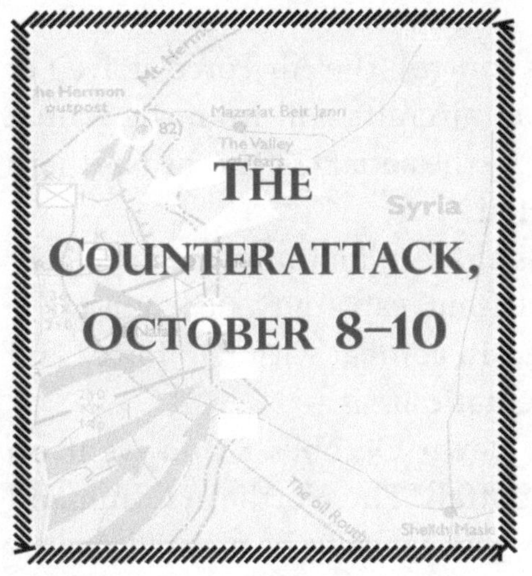

THE COUNTERATTACK, OCTOBER 8–10

CHAPTER 11

Attack Preparation

On the morning of October 8 at 06:00, the "Approval No. 6" order was issued by the GHQ Operations Department that summed up the plan on the two fronts. "The IDF will halt the enemy forces in the Golan Heights and Sinai, destroy most of the enemy forces in a counterattack beginning at dawn on October 8, and will be prepared to exploit success to launch an attack beyond the cease fire lines." Regarding the Air Force, the order stated: "...operation of the Air Force will assist ground forces and establish aerial supremacy."

That morning, Northern Command units began counter-attacking from their defensive positions in the rear south and center of the Golan Heights. The Southern Command offensive failed that day. The situation forced the GHQ to direct most of the aerial support to the Sinai. The Air Force carried out 480 sorties in the Sinai arena and only 190 sorties on the Golan Heights.

Regarding aerial assaults control, the Air Force arrived at the concept that control over aircrafts will from the Ramat David Air Force base directly by the aerial CCP in the Northern Command, Maj. Gen. Moti Hod.

Air Force tendencies at this phase of fighting were to prevent the flow of enemy forces to the front, carry out a close assistance against enemy forces engaged in combat with IDF forces and attack enemy forces in problematic areas.

Aerial assaults began at dawn October 8 and went on throughout the day until nightfall. The Northern Command aerial CCP's plan was for the assistance to be granted mainly in the 146th Division's sectors, to help repel Syrian forces "from the bulge" that had formed due to their control of the southern Golan Heights. From dawn until 08:00, 20 attack sorties were carried out to soften and prepare for the ground attack. Later on, due to clouds gathering over the attack zones, jets' attacks decreased although they had been active throughout the day. Aerial attacks were carried out in the northern Golan Heights, mostly for interdiction on the access routes and attack of the enemy forces.

In contradiction to the Israeli attack plan, the Syrians preferred to focus on defense, while hastily constructing anti-tank alignments in the pocket coming into being around Hushniya. A Syrian attack was carried out only toward Nafah on the Sindyanna route. It seemed the Syrians preferred to avoid their forces burnout by having the next day attack in mind.

The 146th Division that went up as a GHQ reserve from the Central Command brought the 213th Artillery Group headquarters along with it, under the command of Col. Dani Avidar (Feinstein). It was made up of four battalions including: a 105mm self-propelled Priest Battalion, a 160mm self-propelled mortar battalion, a 120mm self-propelled mortar battalion and the 889th Battalion, the only M109 Howitzer SPG reserve battalion. The regular 405th Battalion, originally belonging to this Artillery Group, was already engaged in fighting on the Golan Heights.

The H-hour was postponed from dawn to 08:30 due to the division's attack preparations. This preparation included advancing the 205th Brigade as well as sending up the 889th Artillery Battalion to the Gamla incline, the remainder of the 213th Artillery Group deployed with a 160mm Heavy Mortar Battalion and a 120mm Battalion on the El Al route, and a 105mm self-propelled priest field battalion moving with the 205th Brigade. The division's offensive was supplemented by a constant screen of heavy artillery fire.

The different forces under the command of the three divisions took the initiative and began pushing the Syrians out of the Golan Heights. The 146th Division forces carried the main effort and reached controlling positions over the Petroleum Road in the south of the Golan Heights. The 210th Division and the 36th Division forces remained in their defensive positions.

An additional effort by the Golani Brigade to recapture the Hermon outpost was approved by the command after two Golani soldiers, who had escaped the outpost, revealed that there were IDF soldiers inside. It was carried out parallel to the command counterattack and failed.[13] Forces from the 317th Northern Reserve Paratrooper Brigade requested by the command to enter its sector began gathering in the Kiryat Shmona region where they remained as the command reserve. Upon his arrival, their commander Col. Haim Nadel presented his own plan for capturing the Syrian Hermon outpost.

The command left the management of the counterattack main maneuvering effort in the hands of the 146th Division commander, who was in charge of three brigades, while attempting

13 See details in Chapter 9.

mainly to assist in all that related to the "Fire effort." Improvement in the coordination between the HAC and the aerial CCP (FCO) under the command of Maj. Gen. Moti Hod who was also positioned at Knaan, allowed the integration of artillery in the fight to obtain aerial supremacy. The artillery units were integrated in firing against Syrian SAM batteries that had been identified and advanced to the fighting region. A battery from the 55th Battalion fired at SAM targets while 155mm batteries fired "chaff" shells, for the first time, to disrupt and mislead the Syrian radar alignment.

On October 8, Monday morning, four such battalions were deployed on the Golan Heights. These included additional reinforcements from the command artillery headquarters (HAC) and CAO HQ artillery support from the GHQ's reserves. The battalions deployed in the three division sectors and continued assisting, chiefly in the defensive battles.

Additional 120mm mortar battalions and towed cannons were placed in the secondary sectors in the Meron district, the Lebanese border, and the Jordan Valley.

On the onslaught counterattack on October 8, and the advancing IDF forces back toward the borderline—the Purple Line, field engineering battalions from both divisions were engaged in clearing off obstacles on the travel routes, chiefly clusters of Syrian placed mines. Other forces assisted the ordnance units evacuating tanks out of minefields and Syrian clusters.

At the same time and after the first two days, the three divisions operating on the northern front operated their logistic alignment, and in fact covered the entire territory of the Golan Heights.

The First Day Counterattack Battle (October 8)

On Monday at 05:00, the 146th Division carried out a final series of orders and at 08:00, the division—amounting to a little more than one hundred tanks—launched the counterattack, which led to the reversal in the campaign for the Golan Heights. The attack was accompanied by a screen of rolling artillery fire, which made it difficult for the Syrians to range the Israeli forces and operate their hastily deployed anti-tank alignments against them.

At this time, the Syrians had apparently decided to waive their achievements in the southern Golan Heights and their forces were observed retreating into their territory by the soldiers of Outpost 116. It, therefore, seems that the enemy's mode of battle encountered by units of the 146th Division was that of a fairly organized delay.

The 9th Brigade under the command of Col. Mordechi (Motke) Ben Porat, including the 278th Centurion tanks from the 179th Brigade, attacked in the center and up to the Nov region, where it was replaced by the 205th Division. The division continued the attack with its CCP moving along with it. The 9th Brigade transferred to the left flank, moved north along the Waterfalls Route and turned to the northeast toward Nachal Geshur and Tel Talia. Before Nachal Geshur the brigade encountered a hastily deployed Syrian anti-tank bastion, which was destroyed by a swift response and quick maneuvering by the leading 278th Battalion.

The 4th Brigade under the command of Col. Yaakov (Feffer) Hadar attacked on the Gamla route, chiefly with the 39th Battalion from the 188th Brigade which had been appended to it, and reached the Daliot junction and Mazraat Quneitra. Parallel to the main effort—advancing along the central route of the Southern Golan Heights—the 670th Mechanized Brigade advanced northward along the border route and secured it toward the east with a reduced tank force improvised for it.

In the noon hours, the 205th Brigade under the command of Col. Yossi Peled and the division's reconnaissance battalion under the command of Lt. Col. Zvika Dahab reached Tel Saki and rescued the tank and infantry soldiers trapped there on October 6 and 7th. From there the brigade continued toward Tel Jukhader south of Tel Fares and captured it in the afternoon hours. Most of the forces from the 132nd and 47th Brigade s of the Syrian 5th Division were destroyed that day. By evening, the 146th Division restored the entire Golan Heights to the IDF's control and positioned itself all along the Petroleum Road. From this line, it threatened the southern flank of the "Syrian enclave" positioned for defending the Hushniya region in the central Golan Heights.

The 213th Artillery Group, operating within the counterattack on the southern Golan Heights, advanced slowly behind the 146th Division's advance armored forces moving east on the El Al and Gamla routes, while attacking and repelling the Syrian forces eastward. At that time there were no regular battalion batteries in the southern sector. Being deployed in the Tel Fares region at the start of the war, they were "washed away" by the penetrating Syrian forces.

Artillery battalions that had begun assisting from the shores of the Sea of Galilee in the Ein Gev region split to the two route systems. Some advanced and deployed in the El Al region to assist the primary effort. Others, including the battery left from the 405th Battalion under the command of Deputy Battalion Commander Maj. Uri Manos, assisted the secondary effort on the Gamla route after successfully retreating to the Gamla region and Btecha Valley. Having gone up the back of the Golan Heights, the support unit was once again united in the Waterfalls Route region. The batteries were under Syrian anti-battery fire, apparently ranged from Tel Fares, upon their advancement.

During that day the reduced 210th Division with the 179th Brigade under the command of Col. Ran Sarig, including the organic 96th Battalion and the 134th Reconnaissance Battalion under the command of Lt. Col. Hanani Tavor, attacked toward Slukia, Mashta and Hushniya. By evening, the division was positioned west of Mashta. The 36th Division continued defending against the Syrian attacks in the northern sector, both in the Hermonit sector by the 7th Brigade and the 74th Battalion and in the Nafah sector by the 679th Brigade that included thirty-five tanks, at this stage.

At 10:00, the Syrians broke through the defense in the Nafah sector and once again reached the road outside the base. The 57th Battalion counterattack—which had ten tanks and was directed from the eastern flank by the brigade commander —pushed the Syrians back again. The brigade held the ridges south of the road, once again.

In the afternoon, the brigade was reinforced by the 7th Brigade Company B and embarked on a counteroffensive to capture the Ramtania ridge. The offensive failed, the forces retreated, and the brigade regrouped in the Sindyanna and Nafah region. An additional force from the division—the 181st Command Armored Battalion including thirty Sherman tanks and a Golani company—scanned the rear of the division and destroyed Syrian forces in the Keren base region southwest of Nafah.

Local offensives, blocked without a special effort, took place in the northern sector that was defended by the 7th Brigade. The relative quiet in this region on that day was clouded by a maneuver carried out by the 77th Battalion commander. He was operating under orders from the division commander Brig. Gen. Refael Eitan and the 7th Brigade commander who had ordered him to come down and "scan" the battlefield east of the ramps held by the battalion, where there were dozens of destroyed enemy tanks. The brigade commander's CCP was stationed on the "Booster" hill and watched events in the field, that morning. The 77th Battalion commander with cover from Company H that remained on the ramps, attacked with a company under the command of Lt. Amnon Lavi north of the "Carton" route. They were quickly joined by Company H under the command of Lt. Ami Plant. The Syrians controlled area from the east and opened fire on the force from their line's outposts hitting a number of tanks. They employed artillery and anti-tank missiles against the attacking force. When, at the battalion and the brigade, it was assessed that the operation would cause unnecessary casualties and weaken the battalion, the brigade commander decided to halt the attack and return to the controlling positions over the Valley of Tears. A rescue battle ensued in the area and caused casualties.

In the afternoon hours, Lt. Col. Yosef (Yos) Eldar returned from the hospital and once again assumed command of the line of contact in the Valley of Tears. The 77th Battalion commander moved back to refuel, arm and rest. At the same time, a new situation unfolded in the region of Outpost 109. Reports regarding a Syrian force about to attack south of Quneitra came in. The 77th Battalion was launched to halt the Syrian offensive south of Quneitra but when it reached the area it was discovered that the offensive had been blocked, and the battalion returned for a night camp in the "Carton-Yakir" junction.

Heavy pressure was placed on the 75th Battalion blocking positions at night. The Syrians made every effort to advance tanks and APCs, and capture the areas controlling the Valley of Tears. The force under the command of the 77th Brigade deputy commander Captain Eitan Cowley and the "Tiger" company were sent as assistance to the 75th Battalion. That night the 75th Battalion commander defended the Valley of Tears with a force of only twenty tanks. North of him, the 71st Battalion engaged in a highly challenging battle with Syrian commando forces who positioned anti-tank ambushes in the area south of Outpost 105 and apparently hit seven Israeli tanks. The 71st Battalion deputy commander, Maj. Gidon Wyler, was killed there that night.

A local Syrian attack was also carried out in the region of Outpost 109 south of Quneitra by the 52nd Infantry Division. This was an attempt to break through the obstacle in order to transfer forces from the 43rd Tank Brigade through it. They had returned to battle after suffering heavy losses inflicted by the "Tiger" company on October 6. The offensive, which was an accurate repetition of the previous one, was halted by Company A from the 53rd Battalion. This company had been defending the sector, almost on its own, since Saturday night. It was assisted by a number of tanks from the 679th Brigade, appended to the Golani Brigade by the 13th Battalion deputy commander Maj. Ilan Biran, who defended the town of Quneitra.

The 43rd Brigade advancement toward the sector of Outpost 109 led to a temporary reinforcement of the sector by the 77th Battalion. It returned to the Hermonit sector, after it was discovered that the offensive was blocked by Company A and the enemy's attack was halted unlike the command's fear. The Syrian 7th Division failed, once again, in all its attempts to break through the line of contact in the northern sector.

In retrospect, the command G3 officer spoke of his feelings when the counter attack began, and reports of its initial success were coming in: "I knew, for the first time since firing began forty-two hours prior to our attack, that the war had been decided. Battles were difficult, and went on but the Syrian momentum was over. The wheels had turned and initiative had moved to our hands."

On the night of October 8–9, it was decided at the Command

Headquarters to continue the counter attack at dawn the next day. The divisions' tasks remained the same. At 21:25 the GOC's assistant, Brig. Gen. Yekutiel (Kuti) Adam, dictated the following day assignments. The 146th Division was given the task of capturing the Qudna hills and the ridge with outposts 110 and 111. The 210th Division was given the task of pressing toward Hushniya and the 36th Division was to remain on the defensive. The line of the border between the 210th and 146th Division sectors was established up to Mashta junction for the 210th Division at the crossroads of the Petroleum Road and the Katzbia—Hushniya route and the whole area east of the Petroleum Road for the 146th Division.

That night all the efforts were aimed at restoring the AFVs and forces to a state of fitness, reorganization of the improvised forces and no fighting took place. Putting it clearly, excluding small forces engaged in securing parking lots and assisting in the setup, the vast majority of the division's mechanized infantry and infantry units did not take any part in the fighting, which was based entirely on tanks and artillery.

The command, constantly engaged in the efforts to restore damaged forces, succeeded in assisting the rebuild of a force out of the remaining 188th Brigade. This force was reintegrated as the Ben Hanan force in the 7th Brigade defense battle.[14] In addition, the command requested reinforcements from the GHQ. A tank battalion force made up at the Armored Corps School—under the command of Lt. Col. (Res.) Itzik Ben Ari that was assigned to serve as reinforcement for the Northern Command—began moving north, and was appended to the 7th Brigade the next day. The establishment of an additional battalion force had begun and was also intended for fighting in the command region. All three divisions maintenance participated

14 See page 304

in the efforts to repair damaged AFVs, along with command units and elements from the GHQ G4.

On the night of October 8-9 the Syrians launched surface-to-surface FROG rockets and hit Migdal HaEmek. At dawn, October 9, FROG rockets were launched at the Ramat David Air Force base causing damage and injuries as well as hitting a kindergarten on Kibbutz Gvat. The Command GOC demanded a response and that the city of Damascus be bombed. As a result, a decision to attack strategic targets within the center of Syria was made.

On that day, the GHQ decided—following the failure of the counterattack in the Southern Command on October 8—to prepare for a defensive on the Suez Canal Front and concentrate effort in the north, in light of the success reached on this front, to reach a decisive point and take Syria out of the cycle of war. Following this, effort would be relocated to the Egyptian front.

The Second Day Counterattack Fighting, October 9

At dawn, October 9, in spite of achievements gained the previous day of fighting, the situation was still perceived by the GHQ to be extremely difficult. Regarding the Syrian front the GHQ was apprehensive of an armored Syrian forces attack that had not entered battle thus far. The Minister of Defense still said, "On the Golan there is no retreat... fighting (will continue) until the last man." The GHQ Chief of Staff described the forces in the Golan: "No one is retreating on the Golan Heights anymore. The Syrians will find an army where each person fights the last bullet. We'll see if the Syrians can break such a force. We have 400 tanks, fighting like the Maccabees. Let's hope they don't break and the Golan Heights remains in our hands."

At the same time, at 07:30 GHQ Chief of Staff Dado stated after an optimistic report by Haka: "Dayan no longer states that we must stand in defense on the lowest level of the Golan Heights and hold on until the last man... His position is that we must reach a decisive battle with the Syrians and get rid of the northern front. If Syria is not struck—Jordan and Iraq might join the war. Dayan recommends approving the attack of targets in Damascus..."

Parallel to the continuation of the counterattack, the Northern Command had to withstand a final Syrian offensive on the Golan Heights. The Syrians, who had renounced their achievements in the south of the Golan Heights, saw this day as their last chance to attain any achievements within the Israeli Golan Heights. For the attack the Syrians concentrated two tongs-like efforts aimed at closing in on the northern sector. In the sector of the 7th Division in the north of the Golan Heights and against the 7th Brigade a force of about ninety tanks from the 3rd Division's 81st Tank Brigade and a battalion of about thirty tanks from the Assad force were concentrated. In the sector of the 9th Division, improvised forces from the 1st Division were organized. Included were units from the 76th, 91st, and 51st Brigades that had attacked from south to north in the Hushniya—Nafah sector against the 679th Brigade defending the Nafah region, all fairly worn out by this time. An additional force including the 43rd Tank Brigade of the division, assisted by the 52nd Infantry Brigade, which was clearing the routes for it, was once again concentrated in the sector of Outpost 109 and attacked on the salient south of Quneitra.

On Tuesday morning, the 7th Brigade deployed in the Quneitra salient region at a 12 km wide front with each force focusing on its task and the division reserves positioned as reinforcements and stopgaps or fortifying the assaulted sectors. In total the brigade had between fifty and fifty-four usable tanks. Of these, at least thirty percent had a nearly empty ammunition hull. The Golani Brigade began deploying in the sector of Outpost 104 and Mas'ade village.

7th Brigade—Unit Deployment and Strength

The 75th Battalion reinforced by various forces in position in the Valley of Tears with 20–22 tanks.

The 71st Battalion east of Hermonit on the "Tarzan" route with about twelve tanks.

The 77th Battalion, at the "Carton–Yakir" junction with 7–8 tanks.

The 74th Battalion on the Booster range with four tanks.

The brigade commander's reserves under the command of Lt. Avinoam Baruchin north of "Purple 446" with three tanks.

The "Ace" Company of the 74th Battalion, in the Outpost 109 region and "Peleg—Reshet" junction, with six tanks.

The 7th Brigade commander's CCP—north of "Purple 446."

The Brigade Reconnaissance Company: One half split into teams - under the deputy brigade commander—was pushing ammunition and fuel to the rear of the fighting positions and the second half—under the command of the company commander in the Buq'ata region—was doing the same on the route going up to Hermonit.

Forces in contact with the enemy used up all sorts of ammunition during the night. In the morning, tanks reports stating that they were on the brink of using up their ammunition, their hulls were empty, and they needed to "refill" began flowing in.

At 08:00, an intense artillery shelling began all along the front of the forces' alignment from Outpost 109 in the south to

Outpost 105 in the north. In front of the city of Quneitra the Syrians "rolled" a screen of artillery fire ahead of their forces, advancing from east to west. The fire landed a few hundred meters west of the anti-tank trench and was intended to paralyze the defending forces and allow for the offensive forces to cross the obstacle. The brigade tanks retreated to their rear positions. At 08:30, the final Syrian attack began in all sectors. Having no eye contact with the enemy allowed the Syrians to surprise the 7th Brigade since most of its forces were not in their positions at the time the attack launch. At 08:35, following the pressure of Syrian tanks, the 7th Brigade commander ordered the 75th Battalion commander: "Return your vehicles to forward positions, so they could see everything that's there." At 08:45, the brigade commander ordered the 77th Battalion commander to quickly move and assume command of the forces in the Valley of Tears. Five minutes later the brigade reserve forces, consisting of three tanks under the command of the brigade operations officer, Lt. Avinoam Baruchin, were also rushed into the sector. At that time, the brigade forces in the south of the sector were under Syrian pressure, as well. These were the critical moments of the 7th Brigade fighting in the holding battles. All the reserves and forces at the brigade disposal were allocated by the brigade commander to the sector of the Valley of Tears.

The brigade commander refused to approve withdrawal from the combat positions: "I knew that, when a company commander notified that he was out of ammunition, he still had a few shells left. This time I intended to exploit these last few shells as well." But Yanush—7th Brigade commander Col. Avigdor Ben Gal—and Zamir—"Tiger" force commander Captain Meir Zamir—knew this was only a few minutes slight comfort.

At 09:15, the brigade commander notified the "Tiger" company commander: "Stay put for another 15 minutes. I'm sending immediate reinforcement."

The situation drastically deteriorated and was about to get out of hand. In those minutes, the 7th Brigade commander impatiently expected the arrival of the reinforcements at the 7th Brigade combat zone. Inquiries revealed that the reinforcement was a tank force organized in the 188th Brigade, under the command of Lt. Col. Yossi Ben Hanan.

Yossi was briefed by the brigade commander and the brigade staff regarding the situation in the field at around 10:00. He was assigned the task of advancing along the "Carton" route and closing the "Gap" formed in the "Carton 22" junction, the "Tarzan" route, and the Tel Jit region. Yossi moved quickly to fulfill his task.

The arrival at the "make or break" point of Yossi and the remains of the 188th Brigade of thirteen tanks gathered around him had a significant impact on the 7th Brigade staff and on the fighting forces morale in the critical stages of fighting in the field.

The decisive moments as described by brigade commander Col. Yanush Ben Gal: "I assessed then that we were falling apart, no longer being an organized and fighting brigade unit," Yanush explained. "The commanders had no control over their subordinates. Our tanks, even if they held on, would fight as individuals. There were about twenty to thirty minutes without control, neither by a company commander, nor a battalion commander, nor a brigade commander. Each one was fighting his personal war. Commanders were killed, not everyone could connect with the communications network they needed. This created the impression in me that collapse was imminent. I lost control. I was particularly troubled by the danger that a significant Syrian force would penetrate the holding line and reach the Quneitra—Mas'ade road. It doesn't matter in the breakthrough comes with Kahalani (Lt. Col. Avigdor Kahalani, the 77th Battalion commander) Rates (Lt. Col. Meshulam Rates, the 71st Battalion commander) or through Zamir. If the enemy reached this strategic route, my holding alignment would collapse... I took the radio and was about to instruct Kahalani and the other forces to back down. There was a struggle within me, and in the end, I told myself: we'll wait a little bit longer. I called Raful, commander of the 36th Division, and told him that the situation is dire and we cannot hold on. Raful pleaded us to last a few minutes more, since Yossi Ben Hanan was on his way to me with a new force. These "few minutes" lasted a quarter of an hour. Suddenly, thirteen tanks reached me. On the 9th of the month, when out of the whole brigade there were far fewer than forty-three tanks, 13 was a huge number, a lucky number. In the end, Yossi came with eleven tanks, and two more joined later after they had been repaired. In these fifteen minutes, Kahalani courageously improved the situation in the central and valley sectors beyond recognition. With Ben Hanan, I could plug up the gap formed in the sector of the "Carton" road route, and 71st Battalion commander Rates in the north of the Valley of Tears.

It was a premature joy. The battle was still raging. The 77th Battalion commander was still unable to fully capture the controlling positions over the valley. The 71st Battalion tanks had not yet taken up their positions. The Syrian forces continued the advancement and going west.

At 09:50, the 77th Battalion commander notified the 71st Battalion commander: "I am currently on your left. The enemy is in the entire salient. Guard it, I'm on the ridge to your left." that minute the 71st Battalion commander's tank was hit and the battalion commander Lt. Col. Meshulam Rates was killed.

The fall of the 71st Battalion commander was a serious blow. This was a critical moment in the decisive battle. The brigade commander and staff did everything within their power to introduce the forces into the Valley of Tears, coordinate them, and combine them with the tanks already there under the command of the 77th Battalion commander.

An hour after the force commanded by Yossi Ben Hanan had arrived, additional reinforcement, named "Ptzira" ("File"), and arrived there as well. This was a Sherman tank company from the command armored battalion. The company was directed at capturing the Booster hill. The force was briefed by the 74th Battalion commander and went up to fulfill its task.

The Syrian forces withstood heavy artillery fire during those critical stages. Between 08:30 and 11:30, 21 batteries were firing to assist Israeli forces in the Valley of Tears. At this stage, all the artillery in the region was given over to the commander of the brigade fire support, Maj. Arieh Mizrachi. The RAC and the CCP alongside him were aware of the brigade situation and employed everything at their disposal through the artillery liaison officers in the battalions and through the 74th Battalion commander Lt. Col. Yair Nafshi. The latter assisted in all stages of fighting to employ the artillery against enemy forces. The artillery impact on the Syrian forces was highly effective as they abandoned their vehicles to retreat on foot in many cases. It was a force multiplier that was efficiently and intelligently utilized on the Syrian tank chains during the critical phase of war.

The battle lasted another half hour in this sector, when Yossi advanced with his ten tanks east until he engaged the enemy forces in the region of Outpost 107 on the front and with Lt. Col. Yair Nafshi's force to his south, positioned on the Booster Ridge.

Around 12:00 information regarding hysterical conversations between the Syrian battalion commanders and the 81st Brigade commander, such as: "Many teams are abandoning the tanks and fleeing. We cannot send them back to the tanks. The situation is difficult. We are being pressed by the enemy. Many of our tanks are on fire."

The 7th Brigade got a painful blow when its reconnaissance

company was seriously damaged that day. The company was engaged in transporting ranks, smoke marking the line of Israeli forces, evacuating wounded and performing random infantry tasks. In the noon hours the company was sent by the brigade commander to assist in the rescue of the 12th Battalion forces of Golani entangled in a battle against a Syrian infantry force that had penetrated into Israeli territory north of Hermonit near Buq'ata. Battalion commander Lt. Col. Yaakov Shachar was killed in this battle.

The evacuation of the Golani force was completed but the reconnaissance company's APCs met an additional enemy force on the road route south of Buq'ata. The force stormed and suffered heavy losses, starting a rescue chain. These only ended when tanks were called into the area and opened fire on the Syrians. Most of the company was destroyed.

In the sector of Outpost 109 south of Quneitra, the 43rd Brigade attacked the region of passages over the obstacle north of the outpost. Tank fire and the local maneuvers of the 53rd Battalion Company A prevented their success and the brigade retreated east several hours later.

In the Nafah—Sindyanna sector the Syrians, assisted by heavy artillery, attacked the 679th Brigade waiting for them in the areas controlling the routes arriving from Ramtania and Hushniya. The forces waited until the Syrian tanks reached an efficient range and within a few hours, the battle was won. The retreating Syrians left tanks and much equipment behind.

At the same time, Golani and GHQ Reconnaissance Unit forces, who were on a task securing the rear in the sector quickly destroyed commando forces landing from Syrian helicopters near Nafah. At the same time additional helicopters were observed and one of them was shot down in the 7th Brigade sector. It seemed the Syrians wished to support their attack by operations in the rear of the IDF forces, but all landing attempts failed. The final Syrian offensive effort in both branches of the northern sector turned out to be a complete failure.

The counterattack by the 146th and 210th Divisions against the Syrian forces in the Hushniya region was renewed in the morning parallel to the 36th Division defense in the north.

In the sector of the 146th Division, the 205th Brigade attacked toward Tel Fares. The attacking forces met with resistance and local counterattacks in the Rapid region, which made it difficult for them to continue the offensive, as they were already very small in relation to their original order of battle. Eight Phantom jets, unable to attack the Syrian GHQ in Damascus due to poor visibility, were directed to the attacking the rear of the 5th Division east of Rapid, causing it serious damage and easing the pressure off the 205th Brigade.

In the afternoon hours, the 288th Division Reconnaissance Battalion that was under the command of the 205th Brigade captured Tel Fares that controls the division combat zone. Once the hill was captured, the strength and accuracy of the Syrian artillery were significantly and immediately hindered, thus artillery fire hits on the division's forces decreased greatly. On the other hand, the capturing of this vital area greatly assisted the IDF forces observation and ranging capabilities in the region. From the top of the hill, Syrian batteries deployed east of the border could now more easily be located and targeted. The 213th Artillery Group ranging and meteorology alignment was employed for the first time and accuracy improved. The 213th Artillery Group was integrated into the fighting and assisted the forces on the different routes, mainly in the phases of disengagement and retreat from the Al-Hanut and Tseida regions, from the Petroleum Road and the Umm Lucas region, from the Tel Asbach region and from the Qudna route.

Parallel to this, the 4th Brigade forces advanced from the west and took over the region between Tel Fares and Hushniya. This caused both an additional Syrian retreat in the same sector and battles between the retreating Syrian forces wishing to head east and the 205th Brigade forces standing in their way near Tel Fares and the Rapid junction. Later on however, on October 10 and 11th, the attempts by the 146th Brigade forces to continue advancing east to the borderline were blocked by Syrian mines and anti-tank fire.

The 210th Division's 179th Brigade continued attacking from Katzbia toward Hushniya until the 146th Division's 9th Brigade appeared from the southwest and to its right. In the afternoon, the 9th Brigade failed in its first attempt to capture Tel Talia, south of Hushniya, which was held by a Syrian anti-tank alignment. A repeated attack, outflanking with the 278th Centurion Battalion and the Sherman Battalion caused the capture of the hill and the village of Hushniya next to it. The brigade made contact with Tel Fazra where the Syrian 1st Division's CCP was positioned. Syrian forces in Hushniya were now entirely encircled.

At the same time the Ramtania ridge in the 210th Division's sector was attacked and captured by the 679th Brigade to south of the 36th Division. The 146th Division's 9th Brigade from the south and the 210th Division's 179th and 679th Brigades from the west and northwest finally encircled the Syrian forces. At the end of October 9 the Syrians found themselves in a "pocket" formed around Hushniya, and the 210th and 146th Division forces controlling the Petroleum Road and the Rapid-Quneitra route. The enemy decided to finally retreat from the Israeli Golan Heights and its forces began an orderly retreat at that point. The 1st Division commander was last to leave the region under cover of night and escaped falling prisoner at the very last minute.

That is when the Golan Heights settlers insisted on returning to their farms. In the south of the Golan Heights, the men were allowed to return to their settlements as early as October 8—excluding Nov and Ramat Magshimim. The residents returned to the northern settlements on the 9th of the month and a few days later their families returned as well.

Aerial Support

On October 9, 125 Syrian jet sorties attacked Israeli forces in the Rapid and Quneitra sectors. Likewise, the Syrians attempted to land Special Forces west of the line of contact. Three Iraqi squadrons were already operating from Syria.

On the morning of October 9 the Israeli Air Force could finally assist the ground forces with 144 attack sorties that were carried out in their support on the Golan Heights compared to 350 in the Sinai arena. The ground assaults in the Golan Heights were in the Rapid—Hushniya region and in the Quneitra—Khan Arnabeh region.

Jets were directed to the northern sector at dawn, after it was discovered that the Syrians had placed a concentrated attack there and the pilots attacked convoys and artillery mainly east of the Purple Line (on the Quneitra—Damascus route) and near Khan Arnabeh. Fifteen flights with fifty jets were directed to this sector. The aerial assaults prevented the Syrians from sending forces to the front line, while the 7th Brigade fighting prevented them from obtaining any ground achievements.

Parallel to the aerial assaults in the northern Golan Heights the Israeli Air Force jets attacked in the southern sector, starting at 08:00 and gradually directing attacks to the east, toward Tel Fares and the Rapid junction.

At noon, the Israeli Air Force began an attack on strategic Syrian targets, including the GHQ and the Air Force

Headquarters in Damascus, and infrastructure targets in the region of Homs in retaliation to the FROG strikes on its Ramat David Base.

Four quartets of Phantom jets taking off to attack the Syrian GHQ could not cross the Hermon line due to weather conditions. The command aerial CCP decided to direct these jets for an attack in the southern Golan Heights. From 12:20, the jets attacked tanks concentrations on the road between Tel Fares and Nawa east of the Purple Line, in the Rapid junction region and beyond. High altitude bombings were carried out and the pilots reported accurate hits which were supported by reports from the ground in addition to the fleeing Syrian forces.

A single jet sent in an attempt to try to locate the Iraqi expeditionary forces reinforcement of the Syrian front was unable to locate them.

Artillery Fire Support

The artillery forces deployed throughout the Golan Heights continued offering support for the defensive battle on October 9 and 10. The battalions gathered in the Artillery Groups' areas of operation. Forces of the 212th Artillery Group gathered in the north of the Golan Heights in the rear of Mount Bar-On and Mount Odem and in the Buq'ata region. The long-range 412th Battalion joined and operated alongside the other artillery support battalions. Forces of the 282nd Artillery Group concentrated in the center of the Golan Heights in the region between Nafah and Ein Zivan, and the 55th Battalion two long-range batteries operated alongside them, in addition. Forces of the 213th Artillery Group concentrated in the south of the Golan Heights in the Tel Fares—Jukhader region. Battalions were diverted from one division sector and assisted in another division. Artillery batteries deployments in the different sites were hit by Syrian anti-battery fire and were forced to skip to alternative positions.

In addition, artillery units assisted the Air Force jets in the attempts to strike the Syrian SAM batteries. The artillery batteries were integrated into the attack plans and fired "chaff" shells. At the same time, the Syrian Air Force concentrated on attacking artillery batteries. The batteries, which were usually forewarned were only lightly hit and continued to function. The battery guns hit the Syrian jets in a number of cases and one of them caused the capture of an Iraqi pilot.

One of the problems faced in battle was a lack of designated ammunition for the M-109 SPGs which were not initially intended for the fighting in the north. The Northern Command factors worked to concentrate suitable ammunition and drive it to the batteries where convoys of ammunition of all types arrived and unloaded ammunition. To allow the transfer of ammunition along the routes a command ammunition center had been established in the entrance to Hazor on Sunday at noon and was operated by the HAC. The Command Chief of Staff, Brig. Gen. Uri Bar-On, cleared transportation routes in the field prioritizing artillery ammunition.

From Restoring the Situation to Exploiting Success

During October 9, the achievements in repelling the Syrians led to intensive command staff work in all aspects relating to the move into an offensive. The Command GOC and staff assessed that the forces and supporting alignments needed time to prepare for an offensive that could only be renewed on October 11.

On the night of October 9–10 the GHQ assessed that the Syrians were about to yield. They had only 450 tanks left; had lost the attack option; whole units were destroyed and only a few SAMs remained. The Syrians turned to the Iraqis to expedite the forwarding of their forces. Depth bombings by the IAF in Syria aroused fears for the collapse of the regime.

Therefore, the GHQ Chief of Staff decided "To bring the Syrians to accept a cease fire" by breaking them, through depth bombings and the directing of the main Air Force efforts on to the Syrian front, toward an attack into Syria. Near midnight, the GHQ Chief of Staff instructed the Northern Command GOC to have the attack under way but complied with his request for the command forces to have an additional respite until the morning of October 11. He ordered the capture of Tel Qudna the following day to keep the momentum of the counter attack and maintain constant pressure. He also instructed the supply logistics to repair as many tanks as possible since there were only 250 functioning tanks in the command region.

Meanwhile, the GOC instructed the divisions in accordance with to the GHQ Chief of Staff's directions to continue the counter attack the main element of which was a "tongs movement." He defined the command tasks for the next day as "taking over the 'Purple Line' which was the border line in the Golan Heights and seize the opening in the Qudna region." The tasks of the divisions were:

The 146th Division was to complete the capture of the Sha'af a-Sindian ridge, cross the border and capture Tel al-Achmar and Tel Qudna.

The 210th Division was the capture of the Tel Hazeka ridge up to Outpost 110.

The 36th Division was to continue their holding of the line in the northern sector and stabilize it.

The Third Day Counterattack Fighting October 10, Back to the Purple Line and the Failure of Exploiting Success

The command order instructing the crossing of the line of contact in only one sector was understood by the 146th Division to an action of three brigade attacks in three different sectors without any mutual assistance between them. It is important to emphasize that the brigades' order of battle at this stage was very, numbering 20–30 tanks each. The tank crews and commanders were completely at the end of their tether after four whole days of fighting. Situation was such that, for example, the 670th Brigade included a mix of nineteen tanks, none of which belonged to the brigade before the war. When the brigade was ordered to transfer tanks to other units in the division it remained with only **six tanks**, all under the command of the brigade commander who was in charge of a reduced company that was assigned no less than a task fitting a whole brigade.

The command intended **the 670th Brigade**, for a defense in the southern sector but it was ordered by the division to attack the Al-Hanut outposts toward the Ruqqad canyon.

The 205th Brigade intended to defend the Petroleum Road base was ordered—in light of the brigade commander's conversation with the Northern Command G3 officer—to attack with one battalion and an additional battalion north of it toward Tel Asbach and Tel Qudna and east on the route according to the "Kiton 10" operation layout. It was an armored raid previously carried out in 1970 by the 188th Brigade under the command of Col. Moshe Bar-Kochva.

The 9th Brigade was ordered to attack and capture the village of Qudna with the 4th Brigade from the Sha'af a-Sindian ridge cover.

All the division attacks beyond the Purple Line failed.

Believing the enemy had collapsed the small forces met with minefields, anti-tank fire and artillery operated by the Syrian defensive alignments, which stayed intact and were completely unharmed during all the previous days of fighting. The Syrian line units that had remained at full strength—excluding their tanks that had been destroyed when they participated in the breakthrough into the Israeli Golan Heights—fought valiantly and carried out their fire plans against the Israeli forces who carried out a daylight, frontal attack without assistance, straight into the killing zones of the Syrian defensive alignments. "Exploiting success" became a stinging failure, particularly for the units that had been hitting the Syrian forces relentlessly since the onslaught of the war.

In the south, the 670th Brigade attack toward the Tseida outpost failed immediately upon its launch at 07:00. The tanks stumbled upon mines and were hit by anti-tank fire. Four were rescued and two were blown up to avoid their falling into enemy hands. To the north, the 205th Brigade 94th Battalion attack began at 09:30. The battalion, which only had nine tanks, attacked on the Petroleum Road east and was hit instantaneously. From then on, the force was busy rescuing itself. The 125th Battalion (also from the 205th Brigade) attacked north of Tel Fares toward Tel Asbach and captured it. Tel Qudna to the north, which was not engaged by the 9th and 4th brigades, sent anti-tank fire at the battalion tanks going up the hill. They were struck immediately. The 4th and 9th Brigades were, at that time, advancing from their meeting areas. The battalion was busy rescuing itself until evening and returned to Israeli territory with only four tanks.

The 288th Reconnaissance Battalion attacked near Tel Fares, captured the small Tel Mahir ridge east of it, and held it all day. But this local achievement was not enough to assist the task of capturing the distant Tel Qudna.

The 4th Brigade with forty-five tanks fully achieved its task and captured the entire Sha'af a-Sindian ridge. This effort was carried out relatively late compared to the 205th Brigade forces that needed to get cover for their attack from the south toward Tel Qudna. Later on the 39th Battalion of the brigade, which only had five tanks, captured Tel Akasha. The 9th Brigade was ordered to capture Tel Fazra and—through the Qudna salient, which was held by the division's forces—attack the village of Qudna. The brigade's 278th Battalion, which only had eleven tanks, captured Tel Fazra, suffered counterattacks, retreated, and recaptured Tel Fazra. The battalion commander was ordered to attack the village of Qudna from there with assistance from the field engineer unit of the division, but this attack was cancelled after a consultation with the division commander after thirty enemy tanks had been identified inside the village.

On that day, a final local battle took place in the 679th Brigade sector. The brigade attacked from the direction of Sindyanna and captured the Kalaat al-Tawil ridge west of Tel Yosifon that was still held by Syrian infantry and anti-tank forces. These remained in their positions despite the fact that most of the Syrian units had already cleared the area. The Syrian infantry fighting, who took advantage of the rocky terrain and its natural covers, cost the brigade a number of damaged tanks, casualties and wounded before the task was finally completed.

Brigades from the 210th and 36th Divisions were required to be prepared for an immediate attack beyond the Purple Line in the northern sector. But under the commanders' pressure, who requested time for rest and reorganization, the attack was postponed to the following day, October 11. It seems that the failure of the 146th Division's attack, prior to that, helped in the forming of that decision.

The fire units, teaming up with the 282nd Artillery Group, gathered for the counter attack in Mashta junction. These included the 328th 155mm SPG Battalion, the 827th 105mm Priest Self-Propelled Battalion, the 313th 160mm Self-Propelled Mortar Battalion, the 527th 120mm Self-Propelled Mortar Battalion, and these were now joined by the 873rd 130mm Battalion. The 210th Division's forces were assisted from there in fighting north of the "Hushniya enclave" toward Tel Yosifon and later toward the Hazeka ridge until meeting up with Outpost 110 at Tel Akasha. The front forces continued ranging and hitting the Syrian forces retreating east with artillery.

The takeover of the length long Purple Line was finally completed. All the Syrian forces that had penetrated the Israeli Golan Heights were either destroyed or had retreated east. The last enemy blow that day was inflicted on the 179th Brigade camp that was densely deployed at the foot of the Hazeka ridge. An accurate barrage of "Katyusha" rockets hit a number of tanks and an APC. One rocket penetrated the hull of one of the APCs directly and killed everyone inside it.

Prior to being held back at attempting to take over the Qudna region, the commander of the 146th Division's expanding the sector of attack and advancing from the Purple Line east along the "Petroleum Road" and on the Tseida region south of it was approved by the GOC. The static Syrian forces who had returned to fighting out of their familiar defensive positions blocked the attempts by the 205th and 670th Brigades at attacking east on October 10, as were attempts by the 9th Brigade to attack in the Qudna sector in the afternoon. The division therefore remained on the Purple Line alignments.

The capturing of the Hazeka ridge by the 210th Division's forces and the clearing of the city of Quneitra by forces from the 317th Brigade under the command of the 36th Division brought about a "return to (the) previous state." The Northern Command forces managed to push the Syrians in the southern Golan Heights to the Purple Line, and reposition themselves in all the areas they were in prior to the outbreak of the war with the exclusion of the shoulder of the Hermon.

At the end of the command counterattack the GOC sent the following cable to the GHQ Chief of Staff:

I am pleased to inform you that, after four days of arduous battles,

The Northern Command, with massive Air Force support, has managed to break the Syrian Army that had lost hundreds of tanks in the battles.

The ceasefire line in the Golan Heights is in our hands.

We exploit this success and are attacking past the ceasefire line.

October 10, 1973 **Y. Hofi, Maj. Gen.**
10:00 AM **Northern Command GOC**

Before noon on Tuesday, October 10, the GHQ Chief of Staff circled over Nafah in his helicopter and saw the Syrian tanks on the fences of the base and the Golan Heights after the holding battles. Later on, the GHQ Chief of Staff examined the ways to continue the momentum of the attack with the Northern Command and go beyond the Purple Line after the retreating Syrian forces.

The GOC warned, at that point, that the Syrians were not collapsing and that they were redeploying in their organized defensive alignments east of the borderline, defended by mines. The GHQ Chief of Staff completed his visit with a general warning to prepare for attack the next day. At the same time he was apprehensive of Israeli forces going insignificantly beyond the Purple Line, not overpowering the Syrian Army, suffering many losses, to eventually deploy on a line that would be difficult to defend and would require the investment of many forces for its defense.

At 12:35, the head of Aman said that Russian carrier planes were headed for Syria. Prime Minister Golda Meir approved the bombing of Syrian airfield runways, including in northern Syria. The Israeli Air Force attacked four Syrian Air Force bases on October 10, intending to paralyze them and prevent take offs. The Aleppo airport in the north of Syria, where Soviet planes from the "Russian Airlift"—apparently replenishing the stock of SAMs had landed, was attacked and paralyzed, as well. The radar station in Shahba, which reported aerial movements, was also targeted and hit. Other strategic targets: the Katana power plant, refineries in Homs, and a military seaport and Navy base in Minet el-Beida were also attacked. The aerial assaults began at dawn that day. In addition to the bombing of depth targets, the Air Force continued its aerial assaults in the north of the Golan Heights and its south, and mainly carried out interdictions on convoys along the routes to prevent the flow of reinforcements to the front.

The Air Force carried out 310 attack sorties in the front during the three days of the counter attack. Over half of the pilots reported favorable hits on and around the target regions. Another section did not observe the results or did not report at all. Five jets were shot down. One pilot was killed and four were rescued.

During all fighting stages, terrorist organizations attempted to launch an additional front on the Lebanese border. Using reinforcements that flowed into the sector from their bases in the depths of Lebanon, the terrorists directed their activity at firing rocket launchers and mortars to the "Galilee Panhandle" settlements. The 130 operations that were carried out were firing beyond the border and placing demolition charges and mines. The Meron district command headed by Col. Tzuri Sagi took responsibility for the entire Lebanese sector, including Mount Dov. After receiving reinforcements, he had four infantry battalions—two from the 820th Regional Brigade and two from the Meron district command, an anti-tank battalion, a heavy mortar battalion, a reconnaissance company, two border police companies, a Nachal company and four reserve companies from the 300th Brigade to secure installations. To prevent penetrations he had ranging and observation equipment at his disposal, as well as the "Egoz" company combatants with their special equipment.

The increased activity in the Meron district command sector and preventing the terrorist's efforts that reached a peak of thirty-nine operations of firing across the border, in the days through October 7–10, allowed the command to focus on managing the fighting on the main front on the Golan Heights.

Maj. Gen. Yitzhak (Haka) Hofi

A Syrian tank and bridge in the Quneitra salient

A Syrian tank that fell off a tank bridge

IDF forces in the breakthrough phase
on the Quneitra-Damascus-route

The 679th Brigade commander Col Ori Orr (right) and his
deputy LT. COL. Levi Mann

The 820th Regional Post-Tactical Command Headquarters at Nafah. In the center brigade commander Col Zvi Bar, behind him, his deputy LT. COL. Pini Kupperman, on the right: Cap Giora Goldberg the operations officer

A quick planning at Division 36—front left division commander Brig. Gen. Refael (Raful) Eitan, on the right: Artillery Group commander Col Benny Arad and, in the back wearing camouflage gear, is the intelligence officer LT. COL. Danny Agmon

Planning at Division 36. From left to right: Maj Miaara, the Signal officer, Brig. Gen. Refael (Raful) Eitan, and LT. COL. Danny Agmon the intelligence officer

The Chief of Staff, Lieutenant General David Elazar on a visit to the post-tactical Command Headquarters with Commander of the Northern Command, Maj. Gen. Yitzhak (Haka) Hofi

The commander of the Northern Command, Maj. Gen. Yitzhak (Haka) Hofi showing the counterattack map to Lieutenant General Haim Bar Lev, on October 7. From left to right: The command intelligence officer (wearing sun glasses) Lt. Col. Hagai Mann, head of History Department Col Avraham Eylon (Lantesh), Maj. Gen. Yitzhak (Haka) Hofi, Maj. Gen. Moti Hod commander of the Air Force front CCP in the north, Lieutenant General Haim Bar Lev, General Staff (G3) Officer—Lt. Col. Uri Simchoni (pointing at the map)

At the same event: left to the Northern Command Officer is Signal Officer Lt. Col. Avraham Kayam, on his right are Lt. Col. Haim Levav and Lt. Col. Hagai Mann, to Haim Bar Lev's right is deputy Northern Command commander Col Yisca Shdemi, to his right (sitting) is Brig. Gen. Yekutiel "Kuti" Adam and above him is Lt. Col. Menahem Einan

A visit by Yitzchak Rabin (in civilian clothes) and Maj. Gen. Aharon Yariv at the Command Headquarters. Sitting from left to right: Maj. Gen. Moti Hod, Maj. Gen. Aharon Yariv, Yitzhak Rabin, Col. Yisca Shdemi and Col. Benny Inbar.

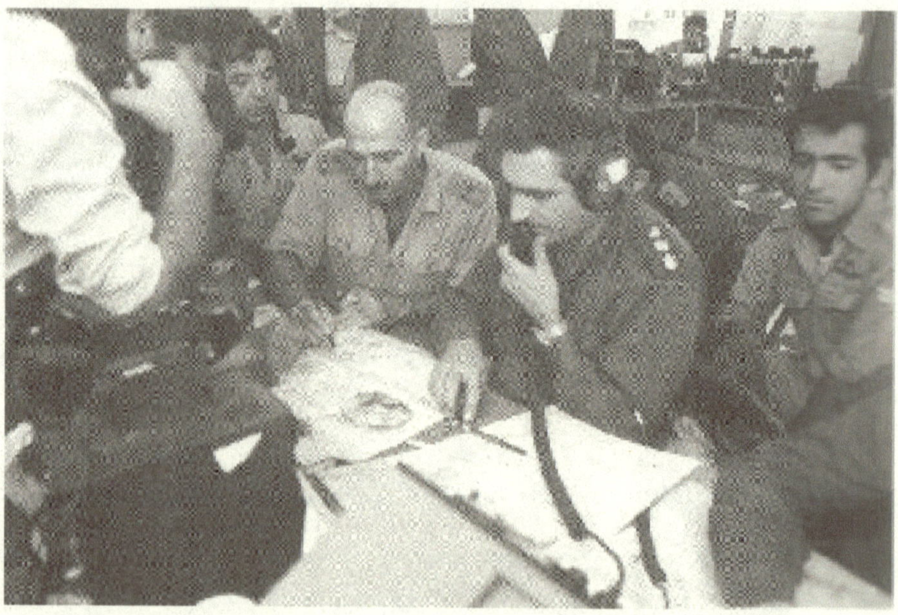

Air Force Post-Tactical Command Headquarters. From left to right: Col. Newtek Eldar (smoking a pipe), Maj. Gen. Moti Hod and Col. Raffi Sevron

Maj. Yoav Golan, the Golani Brigade G3 officer, passing the command over the brigade on to LT. COL. Uri Simchoni following the battle over the Hermon

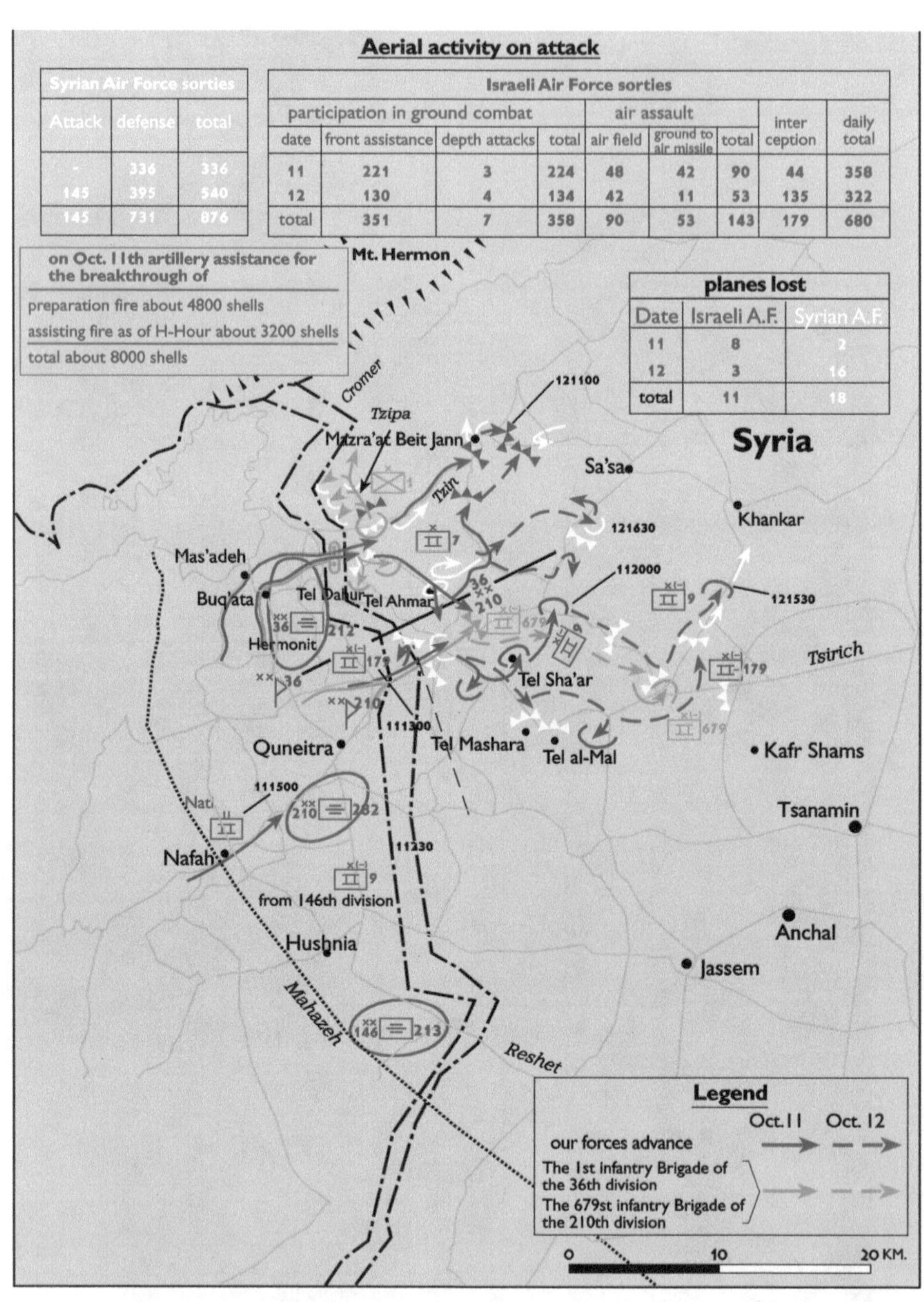

Aerial activity on attack

Syrian Air Force sorties		
Attack	defense	total
-	336	336
145	395	540
145	731	876

Israeli Air Force sorties								
participation in ground combat				air assault			inter ception	daily total
date	front assistance	depth attacks	total	air field	ground to air missile	total		
11	221	3	224	48	42	90	44	358
12	130	4	134	42	11	53	135	322
total	351	7	358	90	53	143	179	680

planes lost		
Date	Israeli A.F.	Syrian A.F.
11	8	2
12	3	16
total	11	18

The IDF Breakthrough on the Golan Heights, October 11 -12

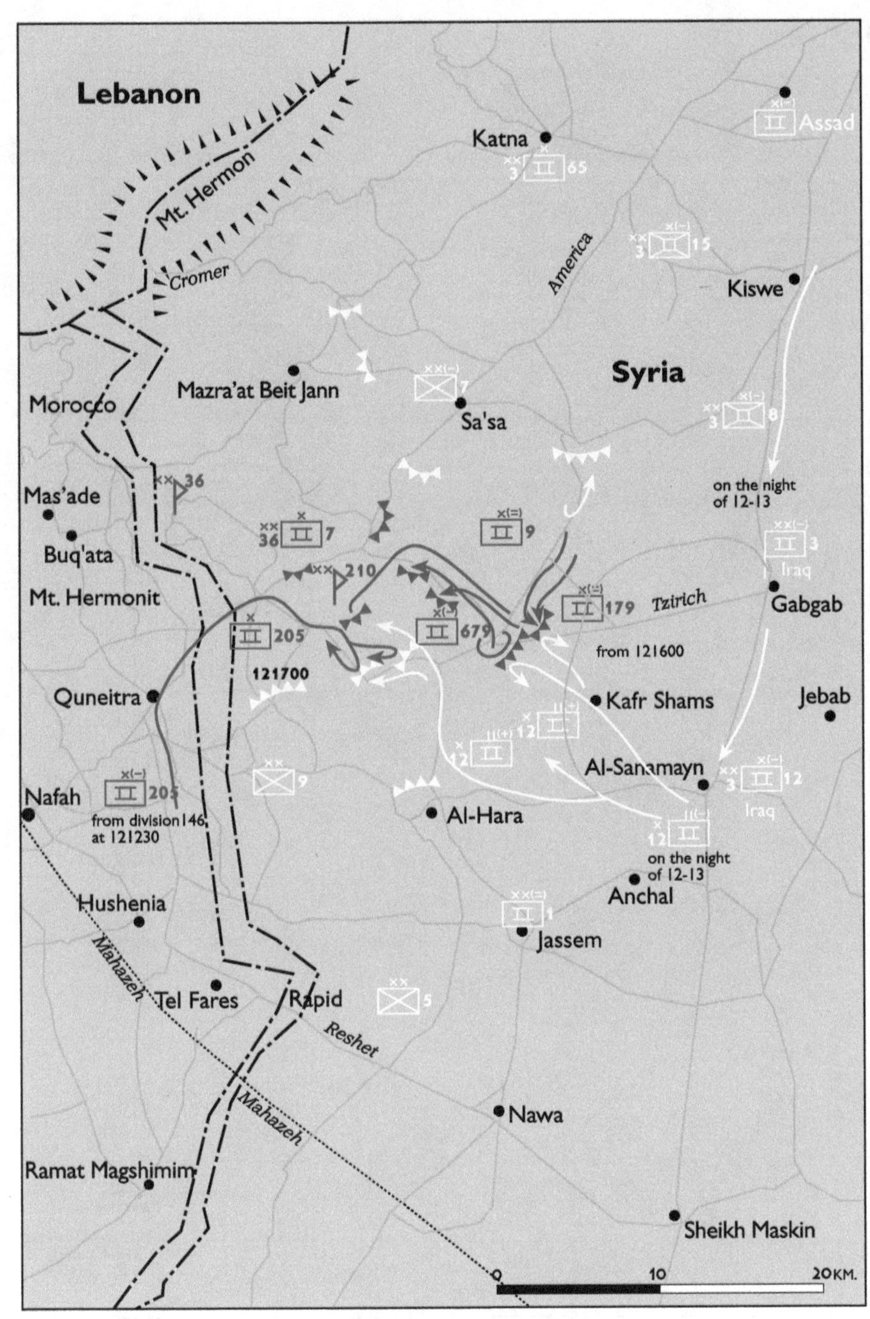

The Iraqi Attack, October 12

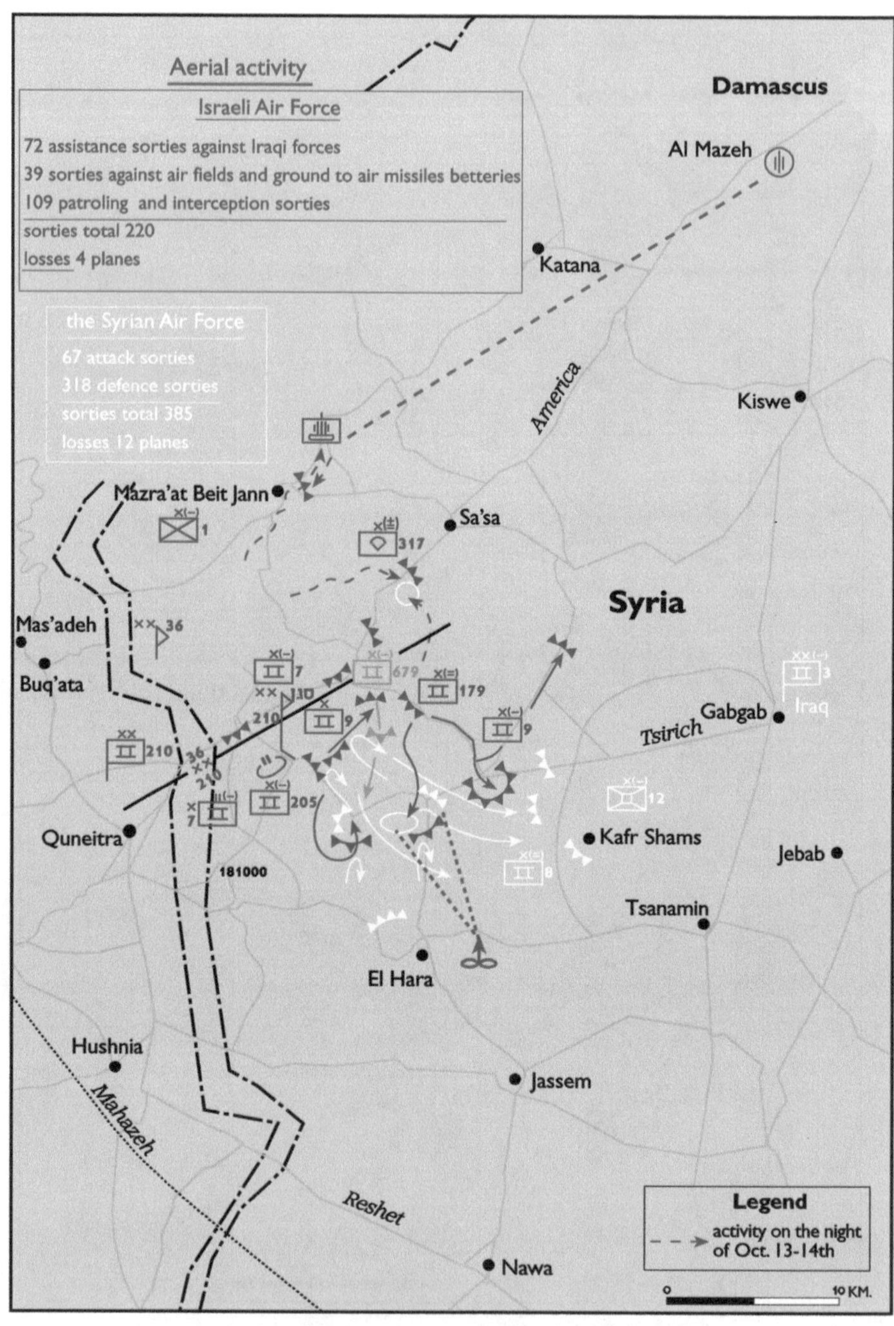

The Fighting in the Enclave, October 13

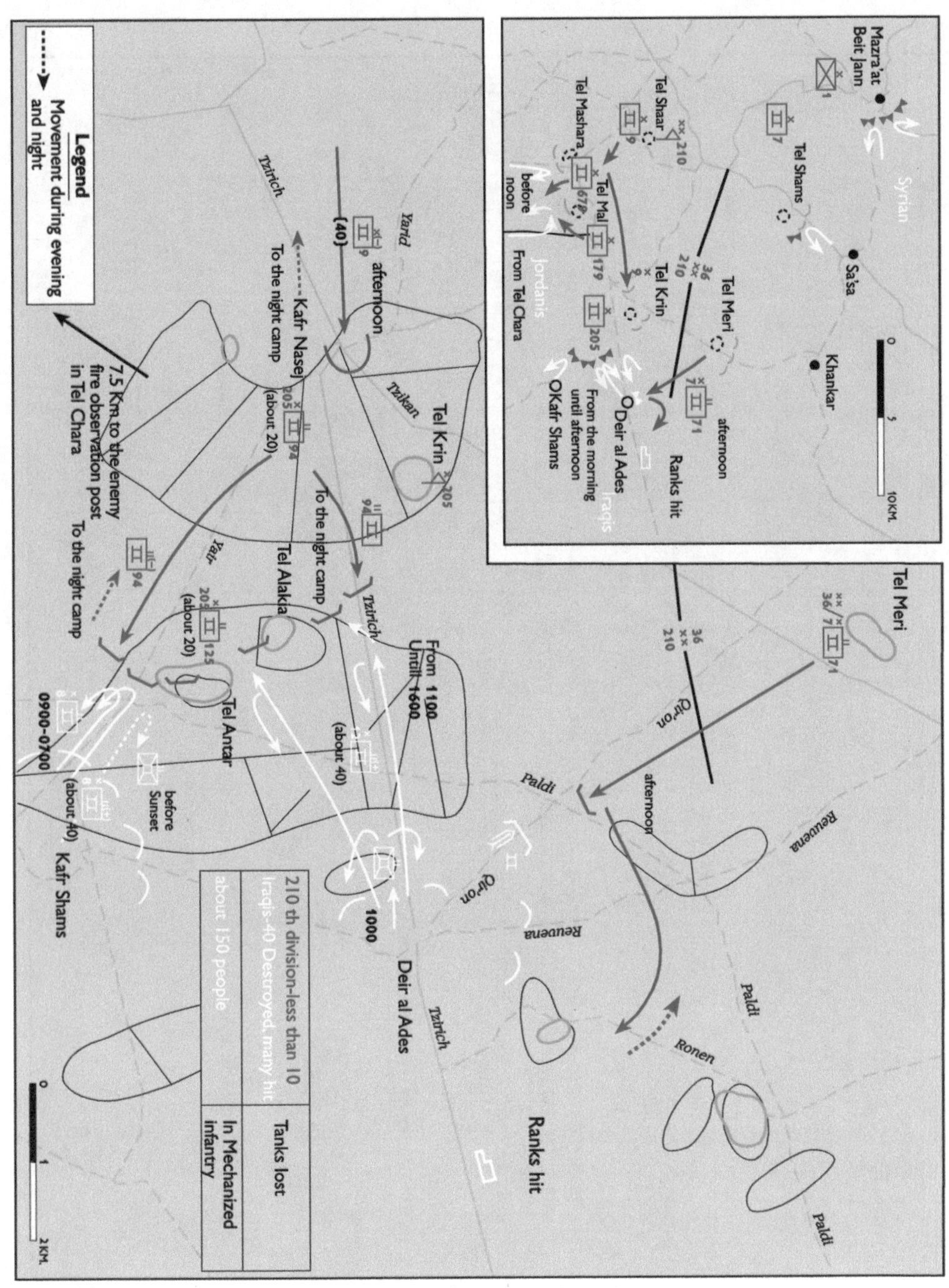

Enemy Attacks in the Enclave on October 16

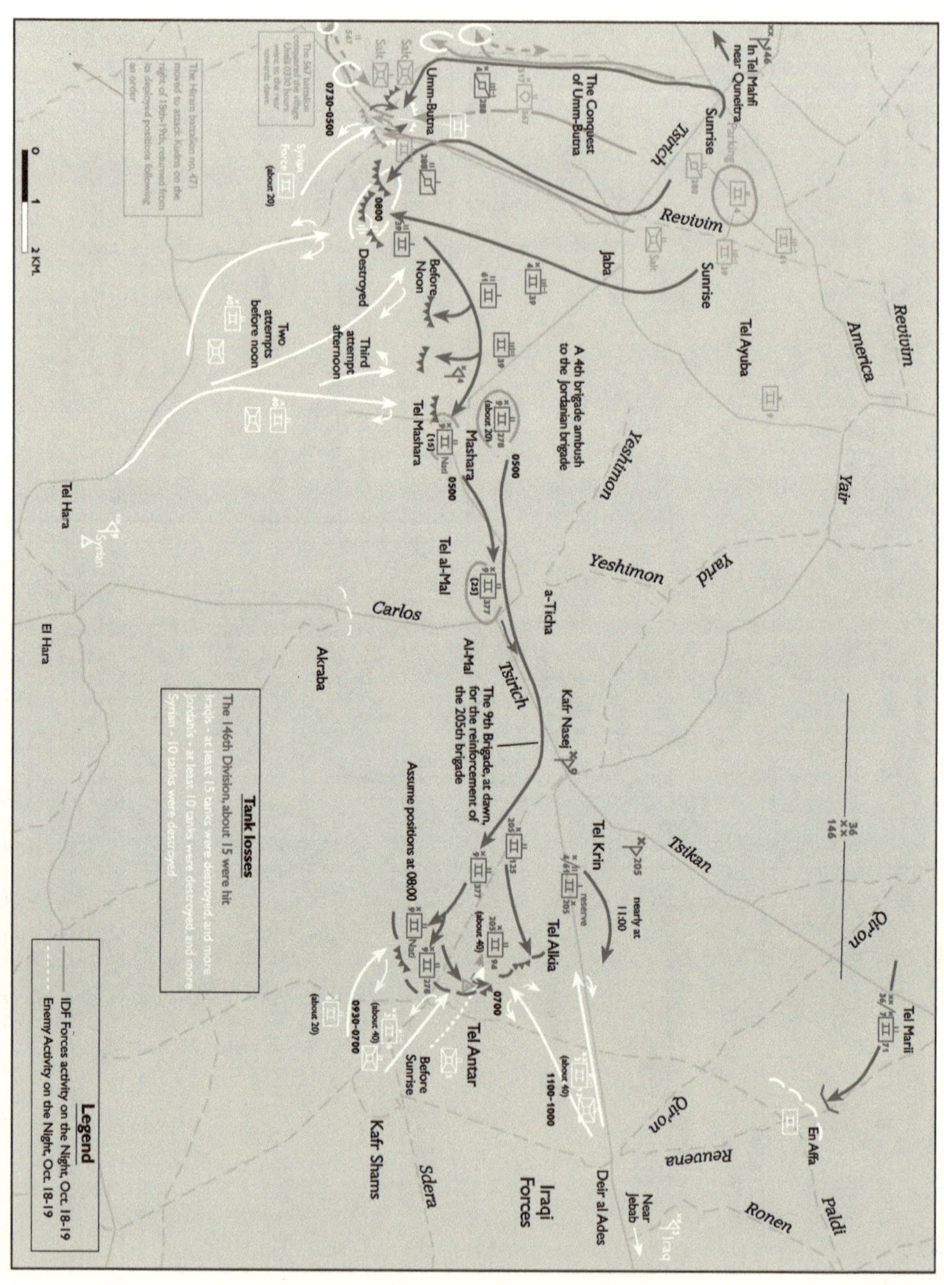

The Fighting in the Enclave, October 18 -19

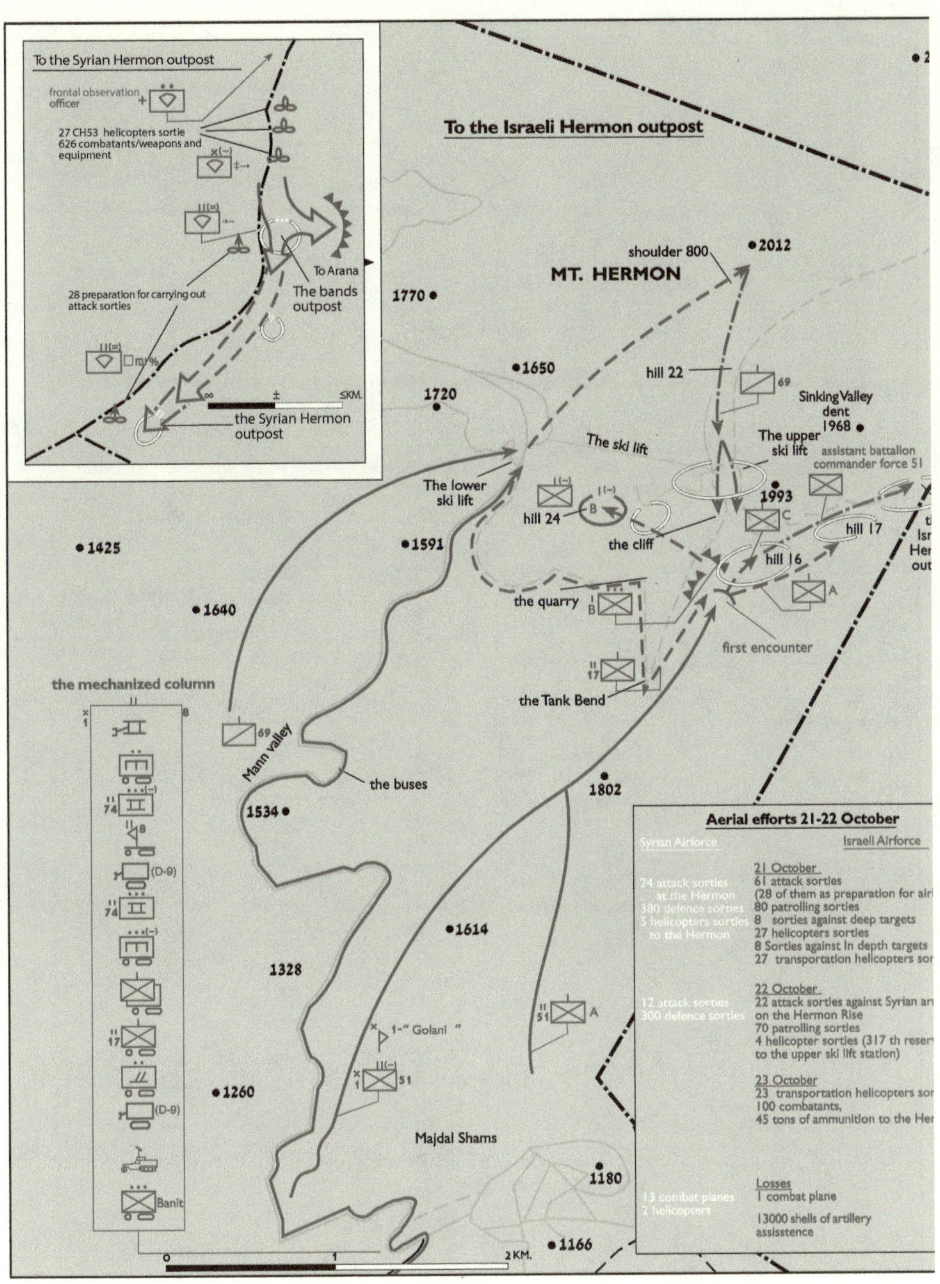

Capture of the Hermon, October 21-22

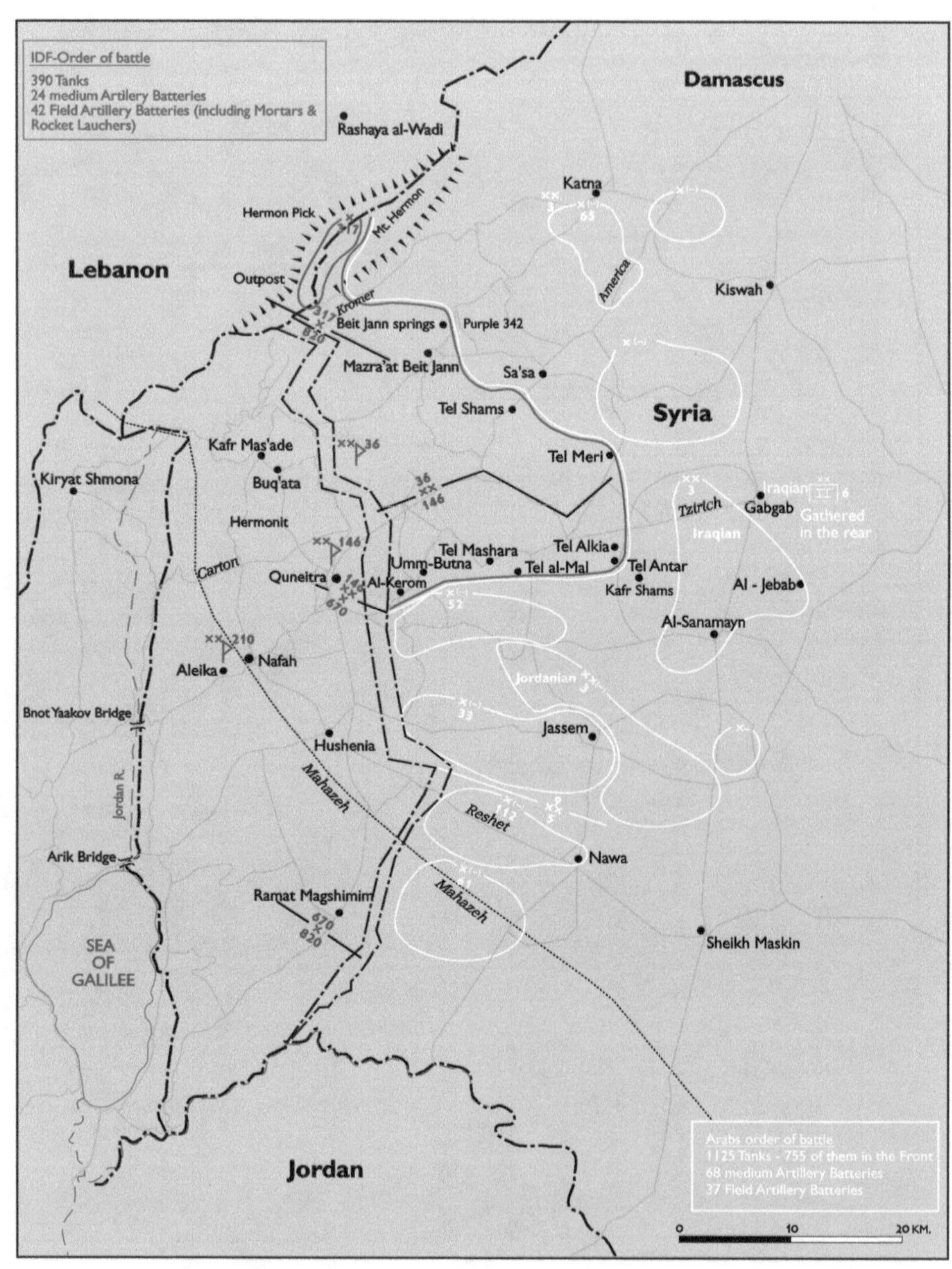

Ceasefire Lines in the Northern Front

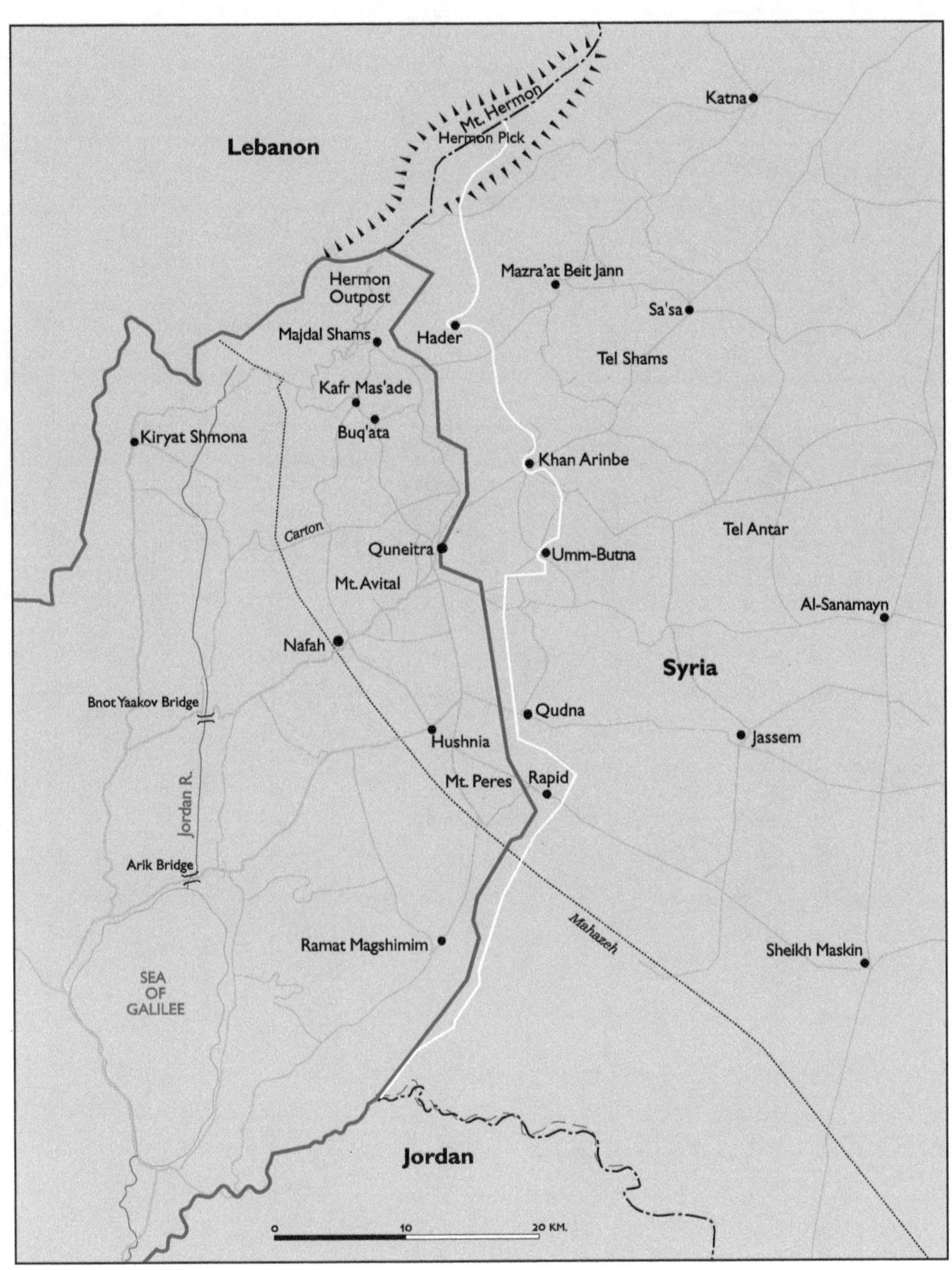

Partition Lines on Golan Heights, May 1974

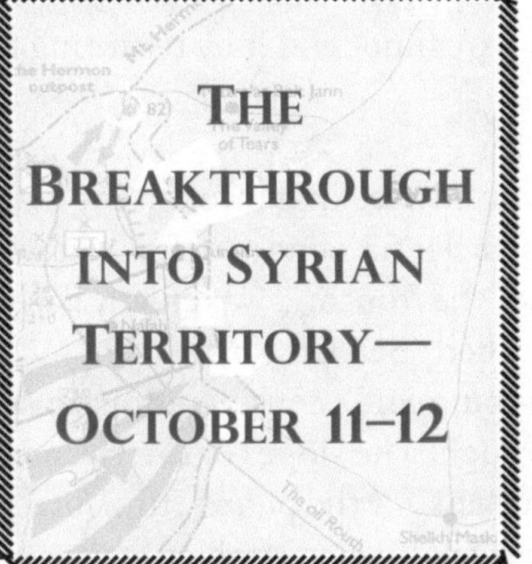

The Breakthrough into Syrian Territory—October 11–12

CHAPTER 12

THE NORTHERN COMMAND PLANNED the breakthrough eastward as early as October 10.

It was based on the GHQ's decision to have the war on enemy territory, on the Syrian front, in order to take Syria out of the war cycle and deter Jordan from entering the war and opening an additional front against Israel.

The command's offensive goals were to:

- Exploit the success, destroy as many enemy forces as possible, and maintain constant pressure on the Syrian Army to hinder its reorganization.
- Upgrade the ceasefire line and take over the terrain to allow the command's forces to threaten Damascus and obtain a decisive position.
- Be in a more comfortable situation to face the Jordanian and Iraqi expeditionary forces if, and when, they entered the arena.
- Push the threat of another round of fighting further away. The GOC expressed it by saying that after such a war, and

after what we had suffered, we cannot end it by returning to the Purple Line.

Shifting to the offensive involved breaking through the Syrian's fortified and laden with obstacles first line of defense. It was planned in the northern flank of the front and was chiefly based on an existing operative plan called "Ben Gil North."

The terrain determined the command's considerations in selecting the sector for breakthrough. The slopes of the Hermon in the north allowed a safe left flank for the penetrating forces. Breaking through in this sector enabled control and takeover of the short, main route toward Damascus while exercising an immediate threat on the Syrian capital.

The plan was to concentrate aerial and artillery efforts at dawn. The 36th Division, composed of the 7th Brigade and the Golani Brigade, planned to break through between the Hermon and the Quneitra—Damascus road. The 210th Division, composed of the 179th and 679th Brigades and the 317th Paratrooper Brigade, was to follow the 36th Division, or carry out another breakthrough on the road route. The operation targets were Sa'sa and Mazraat Beit Jann. The 146th Division was placed in charge of carrying out operations to create the impression of another breakthrough going on in the center of the Golan.

On October 10 at 16:00, a discussion regarding the extent of the offensive in the Golan Heights was held in the GHQ. In the discussion, partially attended by the Minister of Defense, the GHQ Chief of Staff presented two alternatives. One was either an attempt to reach a strategic decision in Syria or enter defensive positions along the Purple Line and the other was to transfer a division to the Sinai. The possibility of moving a division from the Sinai to the Golan Heights was presented, as well. "If the move ends with a tangible threat on Damascus and the Syrians request a ceasefire, it would be worthwhile," the GHQ

Chief of Staff stated, adding "But if it ends in some kind of a ceasefire followed by a war of attrition it would be dire."

The Minister of Defense and GHQ Deputy Chief of Staff sided with the alternative of entering defensive positions in the Golan Heights. "If this is the situation," Dado claimed, "and it means that no improvement is anticipated in the coming days, what Dayan had said earlier should be accepted, namely to accept the ceasefire and deploy along lines that are easy to defend." Dado rejected this possibility and preferred the capture of territory in either the Golan Heights or the north of the Suez Canal sector, toward a hold of the situation on both arenas.

The GHQ Chief of Staff's plans regarding the continued fighting on the Syrian front were presented by the Air Force commander at a commanders' discussion held at the Israeli Air Force at 19:00. With relation to the Air Force attacks, Maj. Gen. Moti Hod, who participated in the discussion, stated: "... opposite Quneitra is the sector line he (the GOC) is going to deploy from, north... Haka doesn't have the strength to go to Damascus... only the Air Force can help him. He thinks the Air Force can give him what it did yesterday and today (meaning the aerial attacks of October 9 and 10)."

Four Syrian SAM batteries were positioned in the sector of the planned breakthrough threatening to hinder the jets' attacks. Therefore, the plan was to attack them first to obtain a SAM missiles free zone and allow a relatively free defensive activity zone for the Air Force's jets.

On October 10 at 19:15 the Command GOC ordered the two division offensive the next day. The command's mobile CCP that was meant to command the offensive, was to be deployed at Tel Avital (Abu Nida). The command's offensive orders' group was held in Nafah that day before evening.

The main plan prepared by the 36th Division that now included the 7th Brigade main tanks force again with 100 tanks, was to break through at daylight along two routes, with maximum aerial and artillery fire support. The breakthrough required detecting the IDF minefields in Israeli territory as well as those of the Syrians and the passage near them.

The 210th Division planned for the two alternatives prepared for it, the first was its passage following the 36th Division and the second was an independent effort along the Quneitra—Damascus route. Upon approval of the plans, it was decided that the division would operate as a first stage diversion force and would be prepared to breakthrough in either of the two alternatives. This plan allowed the command to keep a reserve force that could maintain the momentum of the breakthrough in case the 36th Division was blocked. The additional planned breakthrough was intended to split the defending enemy efforts. Moreover, it was planned for the two breaking through divisions to offer mutual assistance, under the command's control. The 146th Division was intended to remain along defensive lines in the south of the Golan Heights. The H-hour was established at 11:00.

In an additional discussion with the Minister of Defense, GHQ Chief of Staff, Dado, stated that he had no delusions, assessing that the force concentrated in the Northern Command was insufficient if it needed to bring about the ultimate collapse of the Syrian Army and break through the route to Damascus, even though it was the best alternative. The GHQ Chief of Staff's decision to attack full force the next day was final. The Northern Command GOC continued planning and preparing the forces for an offensive despite these misgivings.

The High Command Outpost's senior officers were invited to a war cabinet discussion at 22:00. Dado presented his recommendation to initiate an offensive in the Golan, though he could not, with any certainty, assess that the outskirts of Damascus would be reached or the war would be decided. The issue was resolved when, during the discussion, a telegram from Israeli Ambassador to the United States, Simcha Dinitz, arrived stating that Leonid Brezhnev[15] suggested to Richard Nixon[16] that they submit a joint resolution of a ceasefire to the UN Security Council. The US President announced that he would respond the next day. At this point the Minister of Defense withdrew his objection to the offensive as well and it was approved by the cabinet. At 01:10, Dado notified Haka: "We'll go back and have a war, Yitzhak."

The GHQ's ODG began on October 11 at 02:15, where the Northern Command's plan for the offensive was presented. Before morning, the Northern Command was assigned the task of advancing in the general direction of Damascus, without detailing final campaign goals.

Following the policy determined, the Air Force Operations Department issued orders that included increased effort aerial assaults in the breaking through sector from the early morning hours of D-Day (October 11). It was divided into three subsectors with a wing allocated to each one: the region of the Quneitra—Damascus route up to Sa'sa, the north of the Quneitra–Damascus route up to Mazraat Beit Jann and south of the Quneitra- Damascus route in the region between Achmadia and Maschara.

Attacks were to be carried out from a high altitude in order to secure favorable results. Many other means including electronic warfare, pre-missiles warning and efficient attacks were to be employed. Attacks on Syrian airfields in several waves meant to disrupt the Syrian Air Force plans and force it to defend the area

15 The General Secretary of the Central Committee (CC) of the Communist Party of the Soviet Union (CPSU), presiding over the country from 1964 until his death in 1982. (December 19, 1906 –November 10, 1982)

16 The 37th President of the United States, serving from 1969 to 1974. (January 9, 1913 – April 22, 1994)

with most of its planes, thus keeping them over Syrian airfields, was planned as well. Another plan was to continue attacking strategic targets to bring the war onto "the Syrian home" and take Syria out of the cycle of war. The intent that these attacks signal the Jordanian authorities to stay out of the war—failed.

At 05:00, Dado reached the Northern Command CCP, and met with the Northern Command GOC and divisions and brigades commanders in the Golan Heights at Tel Shiban, to approve the attack plans an hour later. "This sector must be decided," Dado said, "... I don't think you have the strength to reach Damascus, but you do have the conditions to reach a turning point that would end the war... today is the decisive battle and it will happen." The GHQ Chief of Staff stressed in the briefing that it was a general advancement toward Damascus without defining the final campaign goals. This issue was left for later decisions and assessments in light of the advancement and breakthrough achievements. The Minister of Defense, who had briefed the GOC, stressed the importance of maintaining momentum of the breakthrough to be continued unceasingly throughout the night. He did not mention campaign goals either but stressed the political importance of the military threat on Damascus when he said: "Every additional meter in the direction of Damascus is politically important."

Enemy and Terrain in the Breakthrough Sector

Ground obstacles within the chosen terrain limited the tanks optimal tactical operation, despite its advantages for breakthrough that did assist in obtaining the strategic goal. In the south, the rocky terrain covered with basalt rocks and stone fences made moving difficult but did allow for the deployment and maneuvering of armored forces. A number of volcanic mounds enabled observation and control over a longer distance. In the north, the Small Leja was assessed as intractable for armored forces, and small groves made it difficult to control and deploy the tanks.

The enemy forces' assessment in the area was another consideration that led the Northern Command to prefer breaking through in the northern sector. Intelligence assessments revealed that the Syrian armored forces with about 300 to 400 tanks remained in the region between the "Purple Line and the outskirts of Damascus after the battles. This assessment was supported by the command intelligence. Additional concentrations of rear armored forces were on the outskirts of Damascus intending to defend the capital.

The Syrian 7th Infantry Division was deployed to defend the route leading into Damascus from the slopes of the Hermon Mountain. In the first days of the war the division failed in its offensive tasks and suffered many more losses than the other Syrian infantry divisions had and its commander was killed. After the division was hit during the offensives on the Golan Heights, it redeployed in its own sector of the Syrian defensive alignment. The division defensive layout alignment was made up of linear trenches, blockhouses, minefields, and anti-dank defenses including anti-tank trenches, entrenched T-34 tanks, and anti-tank missiles. The division deployment was with two infantry brigades on the first line and an armored brigade and a mechanized brigade on the second line. The division main task was to prevent a breakthrough on the Quneitra—Damascus route, which the Syrians assessed the IDF would use as its main advancement effort. The blocking of other existing routes, such as in the northern part of the sector, was carried out by a Moroccan brigade with one tank battalion. Since it was new in the sector it was assessed to be weaker in its resistance, especially after it had been damaged during its failed breakthrough attempts at the beginning of the war.

The Breakthrough Plan of the Command

The changed H-hour was approved in the GHQ Chief of Staff's briefing held on the morning of October 11. The GHQ Chief of Staff believed the breakthrough should have an early start complied and agreed to postpone the 36th Division H-hour to 11:00 to allow its units to complete their organization and make use of more daytime hours for the aerial preparation. The angle of the sun rays at that designated hour meant that it would be blinding the Syrians, which was an advantage.

The division plans were presented to the GOC on the morning of October 11. The approved 36th Division plan changed the command plans and was as follows:

The 36th Division effort would break through in two directions: A northern effort would break through near Outpost 104 and move in a northeastern direction toward Mazraat Beit Jann and a southern effort would break through west of the Jubata al-Khashab village, advance through Tranja and Khalas and capture Tel Shams.

The 210th Division would break through following the 36th Division, or break through in a graded manner on the Quneitra—Damascus road, advance to Sa'sa, and be ready to move to the southeast of the sector toward Khankar.

The 146th Division was placed in charge of the southern and central sectors of the Golan Heights. It was given the task of preparing to break through into Syrian territory in the central sector and carry out operations that would not go beyond the Purple Line to give the impression that the IDF were attacking in this sector as well.

Artillery fire preparation would commence H-hour minus three and would serve the attacking forces with maximum fire support. For this purpose fifteen artillery battalions were concentrated in the Northern Command, with ten of them included in the 36th Division 212th Artillery Group, which was meant to function as the main command effort, and five in the 210th Division 282th Artillery Group.

The Air Force had been operating against airfields, missile bases, and other targets in the depths of Syria from October 9 and during October 10. Toward the breakthrough battle, almost the entire Air Force was transferred to operate in the breakthrough arena and as of dawn, October 11, it operated intensively against enemy targets on the front line.

Fire Preparations for the Breakthrough Stage

At dawn on Thursday, October 11, jets in hundreds of sorties began attacking the Syrian defensive alignment, as well as depth targets including missile batteries and airfields.

The attack on the Blay, Saiqal, Khalkhalah, Dumeir, and Mezzeh airfields began at dawn, at 05:45 in an operation called Negicha Gdola—Great Ramming. At 09:20, the Nasiriyah airfield was attacked. At 11:00, the international Damascus airport was attacked, and at 12:00, the Dumeir and Khalkhalah airfields were attacked again. Many Syrian jets were shot down during dogfights over the airfields. The Syrians carried out dozens of patrol sorties to defend and secure their fields but refrained from attack sorties on the front, in spite of the IDF armored breaking through and their forces' serious condition on the front.

The missile batteries in the north of the sector were attacked in several waves as well. Two of them were hit and two more skipped east.

The fuel tanks at Khan al-Aish east of Damascus were attacked at 14:55, and twenty of the twenty-three tanks in the place were destroyed. Fire and smoke could be seen from afar.

Each wing in its sector was ordered to attack in a sequence determined by the Air Force Headquarters, where, starting at dawn, an attack was carried out every 10–15 minutes. Every returning flight would report the outcome, the concentration of armored or artillery forces and warnings of clusters of anti-aircraft fire to the flights following them.

Tranja, from Tel Dahur to Hader, Kharfa, Mazraat Beit Jann, Jaba, Maschara, Umm-Butna, Khan Arnabeh, and on the route between al-Visia and Sa'sa were attacked. So were targets in the Hermon Sector. The aerial high altitude attacks were accurate in most sorties. Artillery batteries, vehicles, armored forces, and outposts were attacked and many aerial sorties were carried out to paralyze enemy movements. However, no aerial attack was carried against the Iraqi forces.

In the south of the Golan Heights the Air Force continued its attacks to paralyze the front line and prevent any likelihood of a renewed Syrian offensive. Fewer sorties were carried out in this sector in comparison to the northern one.

As of October 10 fire units were deployed in positions near the borderline to assist in the preparations for the breakthrough battles in the north of the Golan Heights. Thirteen battalions from all three Artillery Groups operating on the Golan Heights, including those from the 213th Artillery Group cluster, which remained in charge of the southern Golan Heights, were gathered for this task. The long-range 130mm batteries and 175mm batteries closely supported the forces. Being responsible for pushing ammunition to positions the command transferred civilian trucks and semitrailers directly to them upon arrival from bunkers in the center of the country.

The 36th Division breakthrough plan in the north of the Golan Heights included a two hour artillery preparation aimed at targets in the breakthrough area and Syrian artillery batteries in the region. The 40 minutes operation of eight flight aerial support flights was also integrated into the preparation. The main fire during the breakthrough was planned as a sort of "Fire Box." The Box was meant to "roll forward" and remain ahead of the armored columns and on their flanks, mainly aimed at striking anti-tank missile launchers.

When the 36th Division attack commenced a light aircraft was sent up to serve as an aerial observation above the forces. It was intended to improve the ability to identify enemy artillery units and silence the Syrian anti-battery fire. When the Dornier Do 27 aircraft approached the line missiles shot it down over Outpost 107. The pilot, artillery liaison officer and the two aerial scouts from the command intelligence on board were all killed. It was the one attempt to range targets[17] made during the war to employ an aerial observation from a light aircraft.

The artillery opened direct fire by thirteen battalions, firing 5000 shells until H-hour. The breakthrough by the 36th Division columns into the field began simultaneously. The division northern effort with two tank battalions and an infantry battalion captured the areas controlling the vital passage in Mazraat Beit Jann, at the foot of the Hermon Mountain. The Khalas camps region was taken over by three battalions as part of the southern effort. The Golani Brigade forces cleared targets near the borderline.

17 See Chapter 16.

Changes in the Attack Plan

Initial reports of Syrian soldiers escaping in the northern sector and the impression left by the swift advancement of the 36th Division led to the assessment that the Syrian Army was collapsing. The 36th Division quickly broke through the Syrian alignment suffering only minor injuries as they penetrated the depths of Syrian territory. When it was evident that the 36th Division breakthrough was successful, the 210th Division was waiting for orders at the Quneitra salient. Both the Command CCP and at the 210th Division headquarters the assessment that the area along the Quneitra—Khan Arnabeh route was not protected, prevailed. The command got reports of Syrian soldiers fleeing from the outposts. Division tanks operating as a reconnaissance-in-force advanced toward the border, fired at targets. The move was left unanswered by the Syrians.

The GHQ Chief of Staff, who was at the Northern Command CCP, and placed high importance on rapid advancement, believed that this development had to be exploited fully in order to shorten the time frame and advance quickly along the road route. At 12:40 he recommended advancing the 210th Division attack, intended to begin at 14:00, and for it to operate in breaking through the main road route and not follow the 36th Division.

The GOC agreed with the GHQ Chief of Staff. He ordered the commander of the 210th Division to begin breaking through the Syrian alignment on the main road at 13:00. It seems that one of his considerations was the advantage of operating each division on a separate route. At 13:00, being aware of the "Nati" reserve force coming in late he ordered the transfer of the 9th Mechanized Brigade reinforced by a tank company from 4th Brigade with a total of fifteen Centurion tanks and thirty Sherman tanks of the 146th Division to the 210th Division.

At 12:40 the 210th Division was ordered to break through. With distant cover by a force from the 679th Brigade, two tank battalions from the 179th Brigade advanced east on the Quneitra—Damascus route and north of it toward the Khan Arnabeh region. The forces were hit by artillery fire, mines, anti-tank cannons missiles. Many tanks were damaged. The Command GOC ordered the 36th Division commander to assist the 210th Division from the flank with artillery and send infantry forces from his division to capture the anti-tank range in Khan Arnabeh. Syrian resistance was fierce and the Israeli forces suffered heavy losses. Additional forces were brought in to evacuate and strengthen the effort. These included the 679th Brigade, and the 9th Brigade following it with a battalion from the 317th Paratrooper Brigade. The forces arrived at the Ma'atz junction toward evening and managed to evacuate forces and clear the Khan Arnabeh municipality and the route crossing it.

In hindsight, the result achieved by this decision was contrary to the one aimed at by the GHQ Chief of Staff and the Northern Command. Instead of exploiting achievements of the 36th Division and avoiding another breakthrough, the 210th Division was involved in grueling battles with the attacking forces suffering heavy losses. These delayed the offensive momentum.

The command did not adhere to the principle of avoiding several parallel breakthroughs. This principle derives from the fact that a breakthrough battle entails heavy losses. In the opinion of Lt. Col. Uri Simchoni: "One must operate like water. Once a crack is formed, a corner breaks and a weak spot is revealed. Everything has to flow through the breakthrough that was formed, straight into the depth, and there each one can split toward its targets. Unnecessary breakthroughs should not be carried out. The front line that had not been broken through can always be captured later from the rear, though it is likely that this will not be necessary. Whoever is left behind, whoever has been passed, ceases to be an influential factor... We should have read the battle differently, and once the first breakthrough succeeded, we should have instructed the 210th Division to move toward it tasks following the 36th Division. We would have saved many lives this way."

At that time, the 146th Division remained in the southern sector, preparing to carry out another breakthrough. The Command GOC held a talk with the division commander ordering him "to carry out operations that would give the impression that we were attacking in the central sector, as well." The division forces took positions and engaged in firefights with the Syrians but did not advance.

Prior to his return to the GHQ, Dado instructed Maj. Gen. Hofi to halt the advancement to be continued the following day. He expressed his impression of that day in his words to the GOC: "Very good job."

The GHQ and the Northern Command on the Night of October 11–12

An intelligence assessment revealed, in a discussion held at the GHQ on the night of October 11–12, that there were about 330–340 tanks on the first line of defense on the Syrian front and that the Syrians were deployed at a range of one armored brigade and one mechanized one in the northern sector. The GHQ Chief of Staff thought that the Northern Command had another day of fighting despite the political assessments that a ceasefire was expected. The GHQ Chief of Staff authorized the Northern Command to advance in the direction of Khankar and Sa'sa. In case of a Syrian alignment collapse it was to advance until an actual encounter took place or they reached Katana.

Despite the difficulties in breaking through along the main road route, a sense of satisfaction prevailed in the Northern Command due to achievements gained the hours before. A decision, to avoid the risk of a night operation, maintain what had been obtained and gather strength to continue the offensive momentum the following day with the majority of the command's forces, was reached. At night the Command Headquarters ordered the 146th Division to push into the southern sector, break through and reach Sheikh Maskin to confine the enemy's armored forces and prevent its transfer to the northern sector preempting a possible Jordanian interference. This was based on accurate data regarding the movement of a Jordanian expeditionary force brigade into Syria. An instruction to try and see if the Syrian defensive alignment was unstable and complete the task without getting involved in crucial combat was added to the order.

After a government discussion, the GHQ Chief of Staff briefed the Northern Command GOC about the political tendencies and limitations placed on continued operational activity. The Northern Command had one more day of fighting as, according to the political assessment, a ceasefire was pending. In accordance with this policy the GHQ Operations Department issued the "Approval No. 9" order," which stated that the IDF will continue the offensive in the Golan Heights to destroy the Syrian Army while, at the same time, holding in the central and southern commands as of 120600. The tasks assigned to the Air Force were to assist the ground forces, attack Syrian airfields and economic targets, attack Egyptian airfields and military targets in the region of the Suez Canal and defend Israel's airspace.

In a discussion with the Minister of Defense, Moshe Dayan, in the Command CCP, it was agreed to concentrate the effort in the north of the Golan Heights to advance toward Damascus as much as possible. The Command GOC established the Khankar—Sa'sa line as the campaign target and the divisions were ordered at 09:12 to advance to that region. The GOC ordered all the command forces to focus on the "supreme effort upwards" and avoid not get caught in additional grim battles.

The command ordered the 146th Division, which was in a secondary effort in the south and center of the Golan Heights, to reinforce the 210th Division with the 205th Tank Brigade as early as 10:40. The division forces that had already launched an offensive on the Syrian alignments in the southern sector could not exploit the local success and at about 13:00 they halted their maneuvers and retreated to stabilize the defense line based on the Purple Line alignments.

At the same time, the 36th Division northern effort took over the Mazraat Beit Jann region. Despite a local Syrian counter-attack, the village was captured during the noon hours. The Command GOC reported to the GHQ Chief of Staff at 12:25 that artillery blocked the 36th Division at Mazraat Beit Jann. The division failed at its southern effort to capture Tel Shams.

The Air Force continued attacking the Syrian airfields in four waves on October 12. Eight airfields were attacked—beginning at dawn and lasting until dusk—and paralyzed for some of the time while the Syrians carried out hundreds of defense sorties over their territory. A missile battery at Khan-a-Sheikh was attacked and hit. A Syrian Air Force control outpost in Babila was attacked which disrupted the Syrian aerial battle call, and Sukhoi Su-20 jets, on their way to attack various targets on Israeli territory, did not carry out their task. The Air Force continued to attack Syrian forces and assist Israeli forces on the front. Targets were attacked in Beit Jann, Tel-a-Shams, Khan-a-Sheikh and Katana.

The 210th Division continued its advance toward the Nasej village junction and from there toward Khankar. At that time, the 679th Tank Brigade was reinforced by the "Nati" force with twenty tanks which was one of two battalions established by the HAO HQ that were moved to the Northern Command. The other was the Ben Ari force that became the Lt. Col. Amos Katz 71st Battalion after its commander, Lt. Col. Meshulam Rates was killed in action. The Nati force was sent to the north by the GHQ and directed by the command to reinforce the 210th Division. The brigade captured the Nasej village junction. The 17th Brigade, also reinforced by a number of tanks, encountered an anti-tank force in the Tel Maschara region, continued east and was worn out on its way to Khankar. The forces continued to the Tel Merai region with reinforcement from the 9th Brigade. The advancing division, with the 205th Tank Brigade, was halted when a large tank pioneer Iraqi expeditionary force appeared before them.

The Surprise Arrival of Iraqi Forces

At noon, October 12, 1973, an observation position at Tel Shaar, manned by the 210th Division assistant intelligence officer, Captain Itamar Tzizik, identified an armored enemy force advancing toward the division forces from the southeast. Lacking any information from other sources the arrival on the scene of the 12th Iraqi Armored Brigade from the 3rd Armored Division was a surprise.

As early as the night of October 6–7 it was clear at the intelligence branch that contacts between the Syrian and Iraqi presidents were made and the Iraqis had decided to join the war in principle. Iraq that decided to send an aerial force to Syria also planned the delivery of a ground force at a scale and timing that had not been made sufficiently clear. During October 7, the

Iraqi 8th Mechanized Brigade commander received an order to begin advancing toward the Syrian border at night.

The arrival of Iraqi officers in Syria the very next day was made known on the night of October 7–8. They were to coordinate the joining up of an Iraqi force. The Iraqis' request for Syrian tank carriers was declined. On October 8, and following the IDF's counterattack and the failure in breaking through the Israeli alignment in the northern Golan Heights, the Syrians approached the Iraqis with a request to send a large scope of forces as quickly as possible.

On the night of October 8–9 reports regarding the flow of the 3rd Iraqi Armored Division forces into Syria came in. The next day the Northern Command Intelligence estimated after calculating time, distance, and the number of carriers the Iraqis had at their disposal that the first Iraqi forces had already arrived in Syria. This assessment was not integrated into the counterattack and offensive toward the Syrian Golan Heights plans probably because there was no reliable information regarding location and potency of the expeditionary force.

The next day, October 9, the command was unaware of the arrival of the Iraqi 8th Mechanized Brigade in the Damascus region. A reduced 12th Armored Brigade arrived in the region as well, apparently during the night of October 10-11. Information regarding the arrival of an armored brigade size Iraqi force in Syria that same night was flowing in at the GHQ. The following day the force concentrated in the rear of the central front in the Fqia region, where the headquarters of the Iraqi 3rd Division had arrived as well. In an aerial photo sortie on October 11, a concentration of AFVs, whose Division affiliation was unclear, was identified in the Al-Sanamayn—Ghabaghib region. An attempt to connect these AFVs with an Iraqi force was not accepted at the GHQ level. This evident disregard led to a failure at taking preparatory measures. The very fact of an Iraqi force at the strength of at least one brigade on the Golan Heights front was accidentally revealed as a result of an encounter with the enemy on October 12 and thus reached the awareness of the GHQ, the command, and the fighting forces by surprise.

The Air Force was required to operate in the depth of the territory and on the access routes to strike the expeditionary forces on their way from Iraq. These actions were not carried out, excluding one single aerial patrol which bore no results. A paratrooper reconnaissance unit ground force, under the command of Captain Shaul Mofaz, was activated by the GHQ through the Chief Infantry and Paratrooper Officer only on the night of October 12–13, when some of the Iraqi forces had already reached the region of the front. Two tanks were apparently hit by the paratrooper force that arrived in a helicopter.

The 210th Division brigades halted their advancement and prepared to face the Iraqi force in the Kafr Nasej—Tel al-Mal region. In the talk between division commander, Maj. Gen. Dan Lener, and the GOC's assistant, Brig. Gen. Yekutiel "Kuti" Adam, he reported the deployment and requested a quick aerial intervention. At 16:10 he even defined the situation as intricate.

The Command Headquarters that had been taken by surprise handled the operation of an aerial attack force against the advancing columns. Starting at the noon hours the Air Force attacked the Iraqi armored forces that had just arrived at the front. The pilots reported favorable results.

At dark, and once the affiliation, strength, and direction of the Iraqi force had been clarified, the command ordered the divisions to deploy for defense and be ready to face the enemy at dawn, October 13.

That day at 07:30, the GHQ's ODG took place—an intelligence review and a situation assessment report mentioned that the Syrians were advancing forces to the front exploiting the Iraqi forces on the scene; a Jordanian Armored Brigade had entered Syria; additional forces from Saudi Arabia were expected; Syria was formulating an assessment to hold on, thanks to the abundant equipment arriving in the Soviet airlift and the reinforcement of forces.

The GHQ Chief of Staff summed up the discussion and directed the Syrian front operations as follows: destroy the Iraqi forces arriving at the front; examine the possibility of capturing Sa'sa and advance Damascus to within artillery range.

The Air Force continued the assaults in the region of the front and attacked the Syrian and Iraqi forces, among them two SAM batteries that had arrived with the airlift near Jassem. Favorable results were reported. The Air Force continued attacking and paralyzing airfields for periods of time, which caused the Syrian Air Force to remain on the ground.

At this stage, during the first three days of fighting, the Air Force carried out 463 attack sorties on the Syrian front line. The attacks were carried out from high altitudes utilizing other attack methods that obtained good results. Eleven Israeli aircrafts were lost during these attacks, two pilots were killed and six were captured.

On October 13 at 01:30, Dado spoke with Haka even prior to the battle with the Iraqis. He stressed the importance of reaching Sa'sa and suggested attacking through the Leja toward Tel Shams. The Northern GOC preferred to avoid getting involved in a breakthrough battle against the fortified Tel Shams believing that Sa'sa was best to be reached in an outflanking maneuver through Khankar.

On the same morning, the front stabilized on the Enclave on the Syrian Golan Heights. Northern Command forces were not able to advance east. At night the key territory of Tel Shams was captured by a reduced 567th Battalion from the 317th Brigade. That night two 175mm cannons were advanced to forward positions in "Small Leja." At 23:30 the force fired 20 shells at the al-Mezzeh airfield, southwest of Damascus, and skipped back.

The Syrian Army Defensive Battle in its Defense layout

All the Syrian forces were forced to retreat east of the Purple Line following the success of the counterattack in the southern sector. The weight caused the remains of the 1st Division to retreat east and deploy in the rear of the 9th Division forces in the center of the Jassem—Swysa region.

Once in their familiar defense layout the Syrian infantry and anti-tank forces felt more secure. The infantry brigades that took part in the first stage of the division offensive now returned and captured their alignments in the outposts on the front. With them, the static anti-tank forces entered the anti-tank battle houses and the hulls of tanks on the front and were reinforced by additional forces, mainly of Sagger missile operators. Breakthroughs in the minefields were sealed once again and new sections were laid to prevent free movement of the IDF forces on the routes heading east. The Syrian armored and mechanized forces that managed to escape gathered in the rear of the front and tried to rehabilitate and reorganize.

Defense dispositions in the depth of Syrian territory that had been prepared in advance for a defensive battle now served the retreating Syrian forces who quickly stabilized new defensive lines. The remaining 7th Division forces, those of the 78th and 121st Brigades that were reinforced by tanks and commando forces now captured a ground alignment from Mazraat Beit Jann to Tel Shams and Tel Krin where they planned and carried out the next stages counterattacks and those of the expeditionary forces that had arrived in the Ghabaghib region in the meantime. The northern forces of the 9th Division, the 52nd Brigade and the remainders of the 43rd Tank Brigade captured alignments against the advancement of the IDF forces along the lines south of Umm-Butna, Tel al-Mal and Tel Maschara. The 3rd Syrian Armored Division, lacking some of its forces, stabilized a second defensive line on the Sabrani River and alignments in its rear, to prevent the IDF forces to break through eastward to the Damascus region.

During October 10, the Northern Command forces were instructed to advance east. The 146th Division leading the counterattack intended to exploit the success, advance on a broad front and chase the retreating enemy after having completed all the regions' takeover on the Golan Heights up to the Purple Line. A number of efforts—throughout the nearly entire 5th Division defensive front north of the Ruqqad Canyon and up to the region of the Qudna route—were carried out by battalion forces, particularly from the 205th Brigade. All breakthrough attempts failed. The Syrians, in their familiar defensive dispositions, could make better use of the familiar territory and restricted maneuverability of the IDF armored forces, as a result.

The IDF armored forces encountered minefields and were hit by anti-tank and artillery fire that was directed at them in an area that limited their maneuverability. The 146th Division was forced to relinquish its plan of its continued offensive and the main focus now shifted north toward the planned breakthrough attempts by the 36th and 210th Divisions.

On the morning of October 11, the 36th Division, heading east, broke through the obstacle on the line of contact in the region of Jubata al-Khashab with relative ease. The outposts on the front alignment that was held by the worn out forces of the 68th Brigade and the Moroccan Brigade had been broken through without any special setbacks. The Druze 68th Brigade commander, Aqid (Col.) Rafiq Halawi, who had failed in his defensive task after failing in his offensive task, was court-martialed and was put to death.

The 210th Division forces moved to break through along the main road route from Quneitra to Damascus in the Khan Arnabeh region where an organized alignment occupied by the infantry forces of the 85th Brigade was waiting for them. This alignment operated successfully while employing anti-tank equipment of various types against the tanks and APCs moving along the route and moving within the minefields north of it.

The subsequent breakthrough into the enclave came up against Syrian forces as well. Key areas and essential passages were held by infantry units reinforced by tanks and anti-tank units. Routes were blocked and water carriers were blown up. Missiles that were fired along the advancement routes damaged additional tanks. Near the vital targets of Tel Shams and Mazraat Beit Jann there were also commando forces that had placed ambushes and operated as tank hunters. A mobile Syrian anti-tank battalion, operating "Sagger" missiles from its BRDM-2 AFV, participated in the defense of the vital region of Tel Shams, as well.

On October 12–13th the Syrian Air Force made an additional effort to assist the ground forces and advanced MiG-17 jets from the north of Syria to an airfield near the front intending to counterattack Israeli forces. After failing to participate in the battles of the previous day, when IDF forces broke through their lines and advanced in the enclave the Syrian jets made a supreme effort to halt the IDF forces on October 12. That day, the Syrians carried out 127 attack sorties. The aerial attacks were carried out at a low altitude and in one flight, and the jets immediately fled east to avoid being shot down by IAF jets. Nine Syrian jets were shot down in dogfights. One jet was shot down by Israeli forces and another crashed for an unknown reason. Six soldiers were killed in the Syrian attacks and two tanks, two half-tracks, and one truck were hit. Patrol aircrafts did not accompany the attackers. They performed instead mainly defensive patrols above their airfields that had been attacked throughout the day.

Their attacks had no real impact on the advancement of Israeli forces, but it must be added, that the Syrian Air Force carried out the largest number of sorties in a single day.

Arab Expeditionary Forces

The Iraqi government, which had been taken by surprise at the war outbreak, decided it was going to take part in it, as early as October 6. The initial decision was to send a squadron of combat jets to Syria. Simultaneously, a state of alert was announced in the armed forces and the divisions regularly stationed near the Syrian border were given a warning order regarding a possible advancement to the west. On the morning of October 7, it was decided to send additional aerial forces as well as armored divisions to Syria. The Iraqi GHQ decided to send the 3rd Armored Division to the Golan front in light of the decision of the political rank. This division was part of the Iraqi forces' "armored fist" which included the 6th Armored Division and another division that was established at that time. The divisions, scattered in different bases across Iraq, were given an order to move on board carriers and advance directly from their bases. They were also ordered to make themselves available to the Syrian command immediately upon their arrival in Syria.

On the morning of October 8, the first brigade—the 12th Brigade—began its long journey westward. Two days later, the armored Iraqi evacuation units entered the Damascus basin region. At that time, with Syrian explicit authority and request, the first forces deployed in the center of the Golan Heights front to halt the IDF forces and carry out a parallel counterattack. On October 12, the forces included two battalions from the 12th Armored Brigade, "Alma'atsam" and "Ktiba," the 2nd Mechanized Infantry Battalion from the 8th Mechanized Brigade, as well as several Artillery Groups and other forces.

The Jordanians, who reassessed the situation on the battlefront after the IDF's breakthrough eastward, were apprehensive of possible pressure placed on them to join the war and open an additional Arab front. To relieve this pressure they decided to redeploy. The course of action that was agreed upon in the Jordanian government was based on a partial inclination to respond favorably to the Syrian call for help and send an armored division to the Golan Heights. This force was to be subordinated to the Syrian command. Thus the Jordanians found a way to fulfill their obligation to "Arab unity," avoid the opening of an additional front against Israel and ease both internal and external pressure. The Jordanian 40th Armored Brigade began moving north to assist the Syrians in the holding efforts against the IDF forces breaking through. Israel failed in its efforts to prevent this assistance via political channels. Hussein kept his promise to the Syrians. At his meeting with Israel's prime minister, Mrs. Golda Meir, on September 25, prior to the war, he failed to mention the commitment he had taken upon himself.

Command Units Breaking Through the Syrian Enclave (October 11–12)

Organization and Reinforcement of the Forces Breaking Through

Both the 36th and 210th Divisions planned for the breakthrough had been through several days of arduous battles. Compared to the previous days intense fighting, October 10 was a sort of more relaxed maneuvers and far less intensive. The tank inventories for the two divisions were reduced, the organization of their units had been disrupted during the previous days, and reinforcement efforts had been under way including the repair of those tanks deemed possible for re-use and reorganizing them.

The 36th Division, under the command of Brig. Gen. Refael (Raful) Eitan, had a single armored brigade unit—the 7th Brigade. It was reinforced on October 9 when the "Ben Hanan" force joined him. The brigade prepared for the shift of the war onto enemy territory on October 10. Syrian attacks ceased that day and the brigade forces were gathered in battalion camps in the rear of the controlling areas overlooking the anti-tank trench. That day and up until breakthrough, the brigade got the "Katz" force—later called the 71st Battalion—which was organized by Lt. Col. Itzik Ben Ari. The force had about thirty Centurion tanks and was manned with commanders and teams that had returned to Israel from abroad, wounded soldiers that had recovered, as well as remaining forces of the 71st Battalion. Lt. Col. Amos Katz, who had returned from the United States, assumed command of the force. It included a reduced 74th Battalion Tank Force from the 188th Brigade, which operated in the northern sector from the start of the war, under the command of Lt. Col. Yair Nafshi.

October 10 was dedicated to repairing tanks, organizing forces, observing the field, planning the breakthrough, and going through other various preparations. Following these actions the concentrated force of the brigade grew and amounted to about one hundred tanks. The division received the regular infantry brigade—the 1st Brigade—Golani - that had gathered three of its battalions toward the offensive—under its command. An additional infantry force in the division was an infantry company from the 269th Unit.

On October 10, the 210th Division under the command of Maj. Gen. Dan Lener, which included the 179th and 679th Reserve Tank Brigades, was still occupied with clearing the field of the anti-tank units that had covered the retreating Syrian forces, near the Purple Line. The number of tanks in the division was relatively small and was made up of the reduced 179th Brigade—including the 96th Tank Battalion and the 134th Division Reconnaissance Battalion—with forty-four tanks and the 679th Brigade, organized into four reduced tank battalions, with about 60—mainly "Meteor engine Centurion" tanks. The division was intended for reinforcement by the "Nati" force under the command of Lt. Col. Netanel Golan that got organized at Armored Forces Training Base on October 9 and was manned by soldiers returning from abroad, and had twenty-eight upgraded "Shot Kal" Centurion tanks. But as the force had only begun moving on board carriers on the night of October 10-11 it failed to supply the expected backing. In the division, October 10 was dedicated to AFV repairs and organization, as well as initial scouting to study the field. The 471st Paratrooper Battalion was attached to the division under the command of Lt. Col. Hezi Shelach.

The Divisions Battle Procedures and Preparations for the Breakthrough

The 36th Division

Already on October 10, the division commander thought that the influence of the Syrian defeat in the battle in the Valley of Tears ought to be exploited to continue breaking through beyond the Purple Line. However, the condition of the division tanks and the need to organize the forces removed this possibility from the agenda. He tended, in the initial stages of planning the offensive, not to operate in the area of the Quneitra—Damascus road, which was well organized for defense, and rather attack the "less predictable for an Israeli offensive" Syrian line in the northern sector with the division full force. The division plan, crystallized in the afternoon hours of this day, determined that five small battalions would be organized within the 7th Brigade, which was the division sole tank brigade. It was to operate in two efforts, with each effort operating in a separate sector and having a separate goal, thus:

The northern effort, which included the 77th Tank Battalion and the "Katz" force, would break through half a kilometer south of Outpost 104 against a Syrian observation outpost, capture Tel Achmar and advance northeast toward Mazraat Beit Jann.

The southern effort, which included the "Ben Hanan" force, the 75th Battalion, would break through north of Outpost 105, advance and capture the villages of Jubata al-Khashab, Tranja, and Khalas, and capture Tel Shams.

The 74th Tank Battalion was intended to cover the southern break through effort and later serve as a reserve brigade force.

The Golani Brigade was ordered to move behind the southern effort and the 269th Unit's company joined the northern effort.

The division artillery was planned to carry out preparatory fire for three hours before H-hour, and a screen of rolling artillery fire advancing about 300 meters ahead of the advance forces when the breaking through began.

Crossing the Syrian minefields beyond the Purple Line posed a special problem. This problem arose during the planning stages and turned out to be more acute than before as the IDF had also placed mines in the border region during the alert period before the war. The division took several measures to assist in overcoming these obstacles. A Centurion tank with a mine trawl system along with a Sherman tank bulldozer, a bomb disposal unit, and information regarding the accurate locations of the Israeli mines was attached to each force. In light of the anticipated difficulties in crossing the minefields, another option arose following a successful breakthrough in one of the efforts. The other forces would advance through the formed breakthrough if they were unable to break through by themselves.

From October 10, the division and its units began preparations for breakthrough according to the plan made by the division. The 7th Brigade commanders on the lookout from the observation point at Hermonit did not clarify the exact location of the mine areas and could only sustain a general overview of the fighting sector. At 22:00 in an order series at the 7th Brigade, the brigade commander briefed the force commanders, unfolding the different possibilities in all that related to crossing the minefields. Order series and briefings were issued at the battalion level closer to H-hour.

The 36th Division attack plan, considered the Central Command effort and diverted from the command's initial guidelines for planning, was approved by the Northern Command GOC. The plans for the command and the 210th Division were adjusted and changed accordingly.

The 210th Division

On October 10, the division captured the entire Israeli territory west of the Purple Line in the central sector of the Golan Heights and joined up with Outpost 110, which had been cut off since the beginning of the war. In an order series in Tel Yosifon at 11:00 the division issued the breakthrough orders that was to take place between outposts 109 and 110. Briefings and scouting were held as well but the Northern Command decided to postpone the breakthrough since its scope of breakthrough was limited rather than go deep into Syria territory.

The division attack plan and preparations for the breakthrough underwent changes that hindered an optimal implementation of the required actions. A division order series took place after the Northern Command established the initial plans for the break through into Syria, on the evening of October 10. Three possible courses of action were suggested in general terms, without mention of specific tasks.

The three possible courses of action as follows:

The entrance of one brigade following the 36th Division on the northern route.

Breaking through in the Jubata al-Khashab route and capturing the Khan Arnabeh region.

An independent breakthrough that would exploit the impact of the 36th Division maneuver on the Quneitra route—capturing the Khan Arnabeh region.

The division plan regarding the preferred second possibility was as follows: The 679th Brigade would break through in the region of Outpost 105 and advance south toward Khan Arnabeh. The 179th Brigade would wait in the region of Outpost 107 on the Quneitra—Damascus road and operate following an order to attack Khan Arnabeh.

At dawn, October 11, the commanders of the forces went on a reconnaissance patrol in the planned breakthrough sector. At 08:00, two tank platoons from the 134th Reconnaissance Battalion conducted a reconnaissance-in-force along the borderline from Outpost 109 north, while firing at the Syrian alignment along the main road route. The Syrians did not respond.

Following the command's approval of the 36th Division plan that was granted at 08:00, and an additional plan to break through along a route passing Jubata al-Khashab entailed the removal of the second possibility. The division commander was instructed by the Command GOC to either enter after the 36th Division or conduct a gradual breakthrough toward the 36th along the Quneitra—Damascus road route.

Having less time on their hands as a result of the changed plans, the division began breakthrough preparations on the route of the Quneitra—Damascus road. At 10:00, a division order series was conducted in which the main task was to advance in the direction of Sa'sa, capture it and move toward Khankar. The estimated H-hour for breakthrough was 14:00. The brigades were given the following tasks:

- The 179th Brigade with the addition of the "Nati" force, scheduled to arrive, would break through on the Quneitra—Damascus road route.
- The 679th Brigade would cover the 179th Brigade breakthrough and be prepared to move ahead of the 179th Brigade and turn south.

In the short period remaining before the command's H-hour

(11:00) plans were made in the brigades, observations were posted and tanks patrolled near the borderline without being fired at.

The Breaking Through and Fighting on October 11

Breaking Through in the 36th Division Sector

At 07:15, the aerial and artillery preparation began and the division forces moved toward the breakthrough areas without interference by enemy jets. At 11:15, the 36th Division forces began moving into Syrian territory, crossing the mines under a screen of rolling artillery fire.

The support for the breakthrough was based on the Artillery Groups deployed in the Buq'ata region. It was mostly allocated to the two breaking through wherein:

The 7th Brigade had two batteries from the battalion Training Base No. 9 and the 405th Battalion battery under its command. It was directly supported by two 334th Brigade batteries and two 871st Battalion medium range batteries.

The 1st Brigade had the 335th Self-propelled 120mm Mortar Battalion under its command and was directly supported by the 822nd Priest 105mm SPG Battalion and one 871st Battalion medium range battery.

The 412th Battalion 175mm cannons, which had been converted to 203mm ones due to lack of ammunition, the 846th Battalion 130mm guns and the 270th (240mm BM-11) Rocket Launcher Battalion remained for the division general support.

As part of the partial artillery preparation, the batteries

fired thousands of shells at the Syrian alignments in the hours before noon. The preparation of aerial assaults was planned, integrated, and carried out in collaboration with the artillery. When the 36th Division forces penetrated in the region of Jubata al-Khashab and Tel Dahur, a screen of "rolling artillery fire" was operated ahead of them. The artillery fire accompanied the forces advancing into the enclave up to Mazraat Beit Jann and Tel Shams. Throughout the entire breakthrough maneuver the captured Hermon outpost was kept under fire and efficiently smoke-screened.

The division had operated on two parallel routes and in two efforts that were both led by the 7th Brigade. A screen of rolling artillery and Air Force fire advanced before the force, the breakthrough force reached the Hader junction and later advanced toward Mazraat Beit Jann.

The central problem in the breakthrough stage was the going through the minefields. The advancing forces broke through the minefields based on prior information and familiarity with the frontal minefields. Intentions to employ mine trawl systems and armored bulldozers encountered problems, and the force broke through at the edge of the minefield, while some of its vehicles did activate mines. The 641st Field Engineer Battalion moved after the first tank company, marked the breakthrough, and continued advancing. A more orderly route from the breakthrough point into the depth of the captured territory was prepared by the battalion heavy engineering equipment unit at a later stage.

The northern effort was made up of the 77th Battalion leading it and was reinforced by a mine trawl tank, a bulldozer tank, a mechanized infantry platoon, and a bomb disposal platoon. The "Katz" force moved behind it. The mine trawl and bulldozer tanks were stuck and could not reach the breakthrough region of the minefields. Syrian artillery began bombing the advancing force. Tanks broke through the minefields. After two of them triggered mines and under Syrian tank fire, a path was cleared through the field, and the force began going beyond the Purple Line into Syrian territory. The 77th Brigade moved along a rocky and difficult route dense with trees, toward the fortified Tel al-Achmar and captured it without resistance. The northern effort advanced quickly on the road toward Mazraat Beit Jann while firing at enemy tanks and anti-tank guns that attempted to hinder their advancement and destroy them. The 77th Battalion engaged in fire contact with Mazraat Beit Jann and captured regions controlling the village from the west. Artillery fire was aimed at the "Katz" force that deployed south of it and firefights with about ten Syrian tanks that were in the village and hiding between the trees ensued and lasted through the afternoon hours. A few tanks were destroyed. Syrian helicopters were seen landing in the village and reinforcing it with commando forces. In the initial plan the "Katz" force was to capture the village but it was decided that the offensive would be delayed until artillery fire and aerial support could be offered.

In light of the accomplishments of the 210th Division, which passed Khan Arnabeh, the 36th Division ordered the 7th Brigade to delay the offensive on the village since controlling the nearby junction was sufficient at this stage. A later decision was to carry out the offensive on the village the following. The 12th Infantry Battalion was transferred from the southern effort and joined the northern one. At dark, the 77th and 71st Battalions arrived and deployed west and south of Mazraat Beit Jann, and entered night camps.

The southern effort, made up of the "Ben Hanan" force and the 75th Battalion with the cover of the reduced 74th Battalion first encountered and crossed the Israeli mines in the southern effort without waiting for the overdue mine trawl and bulldozer tanks. The leading tanks crossed the Purple Line and advanced on the stone fences to avoid triggering mines. Syrian artillery fire at the force and two tanks did hit mines. The 75th Battalion commander's tank and another one began opening a passage through a tough terrain strewn with basalt stone fences, understanding that such a difficult surface would allow for a mine free passage. They found a passage between two minefields and the forces began moving. Later on, they reached the Syrian outposts route. The tanks moved north of Jubata al-Khashab, advanced toward Tranja, and captured it. They deployed east of the village and began their advancement in the open yet challenging field before the Khalas camps while exchanging fire with a number of enemy tanks.

Following the difficulties in the 210th Division offensive, the southern effort was given the task of advancing south toward the main road route to assist the division activity. After the 210th Division had successfully broken through the passage to Khan Arnabeh, the task was cancelled. The southern effort forces continued a coordinated offensive of mechanized infantry forces, covered by tanks, and captured the Khalas village itself and its camps. The 75th Battalion captured the village of Kharfa.

The 1st Brigade moved behind the southern effort. The 12th Battalion cleared the village of Jubata al-Khashab and was then sent to the northern effort. The 51st Battalion, assisted by tanks, cleared the Syrian outpost at Tel Dahur.

At night, the Syrians attacked the 7th Brigade forces with armored and infantry units and were pushed back with the assistance of a GHQ Reconnaissance Unit Infantry Force securing the brigade battalions night camps. The next morning, the division deployed for two brigade battles in two different sectors. The northern force, the 71st Battalion under the command of Lt. Col. Amos Katz captured Mazraat Beit Jann with cover by the 77th Battalion. The 71st Battalion commander was injured in combat and was replaced by the operations' officer Captain

Amos Loria. Two hours later the battalion commander returned and resumed his command over the battalion until the capturing of the village was completed.

The southern brigade effort encountered difficulties in capturing Tel a-Shams. Aware of the importance of the hill, its control over the Damascus route and its entire surroundings the Syrians defended it with a reinforced tank force, mobile anti-tank missiles, artillery, and jets. The area was a fortified and well protected bastion, encircled by minefields and other obstacles. The attack by the Ben Hanan force along the "America" route with cover by the 75th and 74th Battalions did not succeed and was halted within the hills' "killing field." The Ben Hanan battalion was forced to retreat.

The brigade reorganized. Its intelligence officer, Maj. Ilan Sahar, found an alternative route within the "Small Leja" on the aerial photograph that would enable an attack on the hill from an unexpected direction. The force under the command of Lt. Col. Yossi Ben Hanan exploited that newfound route and managed to go up the hill from a northwestern direction. An anti-tank missile attack struck four tanks and the battalion commander Yossi Ben Hanan was seriously wounded and remained in the field. It was only thanks to a daring operation by the GHQ Reconnaissance Unit, under the command of Maj. Yoni Netanyahu and the cover and support of all the firepower the brigade had, that he was rescued and flown to the hospital by helicopter.

In the following days the brigade forces, reinforced by Golani and paratrooper forces, defended Tel-a-Shams. The Syrians attacked the hill with renewed vigor but all their attacks were warded off. In those days, eighteen of the brigade soldiers were killed, and many were wounded and evacuated, including the 75th Battalion commander and his replacement. Fifteen to twenty tanks were hit as well.

The 210th Division

Two Artillery Groups—the 212th and the 282nd—support the offensive with intermittent fire. The operation began at 12:50 and fire went on for about 25 minutes. The artillery aid operated again at 13:37 and its fire ceased at 14:14. The changes in the division plans determined a change in the artillery aid and the fire plan was prepared in the morning hours that day. Air Force jets operated in the 210th Division sector, as well. A reduced battalion from the 679th Brigade that took positions in the "Booster" region offered direct cover for the force breaking through.

The fire units were moved during the afternoon hours to assist the 210th Division forces that had encountered difficulties in the breakthrough in the region of Khan Arnabeh. The 282nd Artillery Group—made up of four fire units including the 873rd Self-propelled medium range battalion, a 130mm battalion, a 203mm battery from the 412th Battalion, and the 155mm towed 828th Battalion—led the preparation and artillery support of the forces breaking through in the brigade sector. Some 4770 shells were fired between 12:50 and 13:15, intended to hit the Syrian outposts and alignments on both sides of the "America" route, which is the short route to Damascus. All the long-range 130mm ammunition the IDF had was used up at this point.

The plan of the 179th Brigade, operating at the head of the division force, was to breakthrough along two routes: the 134th Reconnaissance Battalion along the northern route while exploiting the breakthroughs that had apparently been formed when the Syrian forces moved during their offensive and the 96th Battalion on the road route. At 13:00, the 179th Brigade began the offensive. Near Outpost 107 the brigade encountered clusters of Israeli mines placed on the main road. After clearing them, the 134th Reconnaissance Battalion thrust forward and immediately turned from the road in a northeastern direction.

The 96th Battalion, delayed on its way due to the need to overtake the covering force on the Booster hill, continued advancing along the road route. Even before establishing contact with the enemy, the brigade was flooded by a barrage of artillery fire that hit three tanks. The brigade gave up on the 679th Brigade cover since the dust and smoke rising from battlefield and its far range made it inefficient. The brigade renewed its advancement at 14:20 and passed the anti-tank trench without artillery support. The brigade commander's decision to break through by himself was approved. A few of the reconnaissance battalion tanks blended with the 96th Battalion tanks and the reconnaissance battalion advanced toward the target. Massive fire from Khan Arnabeh and Tel Zahi and tanks that hit mines caused damage. By 14:40, all the reconnaissance battalion tanks excluding the battalion commander's tank were hit. The northern effort by the 179th Brigade went off track.

The 96th Battalion advanced quickly along the road route and met with efficient anti-tank fire from T-34 tank turrets dug in the ground, as well as anti-tank missiles and tanks from the region of Khan Arnabeh. The battalion tanks were getting hit and at 14:40 the brigade commander, who was advancing with the battalion, reported that both his forces suffered many losses. The reconnaissance battalion, which had been blocked in the area north of the Quneitra—Damascus road, was busy evacuating injured and tanks. Several tanks from the 96th Battalion continued moving rapidly on the road and six of them reached the Khan Arnabeh—Jaba junction and began firing at the Khan Arnabeh region from the rear. The brigade commander suggested that the 679th Brigade entered a quick offensive to exploit the brigade achievements and stabilize them.

The division did not have a clear picture of the battle during the offensive due to dense smoke and dust rising in the sector but casualty reports and the retreating wounded revealed the tight situation. The actual situation became evident only later, after the 179th Brigade commander reported the stat of his forces.

The assumption that the Syrian military was in a state of collapse in the northern sector was far removed from the reality encountered in the field during the 179th Brigade offensive. The 210th Division encountered many difficulties upon entry into an offensive in a sector that was well organized for defense. The GHQ Chief of Staff suggested that the Command GOC consider pulling out the 210th Division. The GOC also believed that putting the 210th Division into battle was premature and considered the possibility of evacuating the attacking force. At that time, he instructed the 36th Division to direct an effort south to assist the 210th Division forces fighting on the main road route. After the 179th Brigade reported that its tanks had arrived at the Khan Arnabeh junction, the misgivings regarding the progressing offensive dispersed and the command decided to keep on going. The 210th Division commander instructed the 679th Brigade to advance quickly along the road route toward Khan Arnabeh and Tel Shams to exploit the success gained obtained by the six tanks from the 179th Brigade that had arrived at Khan Arnabeh.

Although the division order was to act quickly, the brigade planned its steps cautiously in light of the bitter experience of the 179th Brigade and decided that destroying the enemy's anti-tank weapons was to have first priority over an accelerated movement forward. The brigade divided into a covering force and a breaking through force. The first force was made up of a tank battalion, which took positions at an efficient range and was instructed to fire at static anti-tank cannons positions, tanks and infantry forces equipped with anti-tank weapons as a first priority of action. The breaking through force was made up of two tank battalions, which were planned to advance along the road route, without getting off it for fear of mines. The brigade began the offensive at 15:00. The covering force, though under heavy artillery fire, worked efficiently against the entrenched tanks south of the road, but its capacity to operate against targets on the road was limited. A first battalion from the force breaking through advanced while avoiding pits on the road detonated by the Syrians and moving past damaged tanks from the 179th Brigade. A second battalion began advancing following it. The brigade commander's half-track was hit by anti-tank fire and the brigade commander moved to a tank. The fierce head on Syrian resistance dwindled. The force breaking through continued advancing, reached Tel Shaar and captured it reaching the hills about 6-8 kilometers east of Khan Arnabeh. The covering force left its positions and also went into the breakthrough area. It turned northwest at the Khan Arnabeh junction, identified Syrian tanks retreating from Khan Arnabeh and fired at them. The 36th Division opened fire on the force advancing toward the 7th Brigade. It was stopped after the commanders coordinated their communication.

The 471st Paratrooper Battalion advanced to Khan Arnabeh to clear the region and began evacuating the wounded. An APC loaded with mines was hit, the mines exploded and the route remained impassable. By evening, the brigade managed to reach Ma'atz junction but the road route remained closed to both traffic and supplies.

The 9th Brigade—made up of a Sherman tank battalion with thirty tanks and a upgraded Centurion battalion with about fifteen tanks—arrived at the Achmadia junction at 16:20. Following the 210th Division order it was instructed to move on the main road following the 679th Brigade, capture Tel Shaar and advance to Ma'atz junction. At 17:00, the brigade began moving slowly due to artillery fire and difficulties crossing the route following the evacuation of the wounded. At nightfall the brigade captured Tel Korum, continued advancing and at 19:00 captured the Ma'atz junction without resistance.

Closely after the breakthrough, the fire units were advanced into positions in the enclave. The 328th Battalion was advanced along the "America" route, immediately following the forces breaking through, and succeeded in assisting the advancing forces from its new position. A first convoy, with three semitrailers carrying hundreds of shells, was brought in to enable that battalion to fire large amounts of ammunition.

At dark, the offensive operations in the northern front ceased and the attacking forces set up for the night to defend themselves and allow for maintenance according to the situation of each division or unit.

The Maneuvers during October 12

The 36th Division planned to advance toward Sa'sa in two efforts on October 12. The northern effort was to capture Mazraat Beit Jann and advance on the road leading to Sa'sa. The southern effort was to capture Tel Shams, on the main road route, and continue toward Sa'sa.

Battalions of the northern effort set up at night camps. An arriving supply convoy came near the village and nearly entered it. About 400 meters away from the village the forces managed to stop its movement and turn toward the battalions that refueled and filled up ammunition and other supplies. The southern effort forces set up night camps in the region of the Khalas camps. At night, a force that included a tank platoon and two APCs conducted a patrol. The 7th Brigade CCPs set up for the night in the Tranja area.

The 210th Division plans for October 12 were to move east

toward the village of Nasej and from there north to the village of Khankar. When night fell, the village of Khan Arnabeh had not been cleared and Syrian infantry forces there disrupted the transfer of ranks and the evacuation of the wounded, which were prioritized in moving along the route. The 179th Brigade, with a small number of tanks at Khan Arnabeh, was busy rescuing and evacuating wounded and tanks as well as being reorganized. The division engineering battalion was brought into the field to allow the rescue of tanks from the minefields. The 679th Brigade force with thirty fit tanks set up at night camp while the crewmembers remained inside the tanks. The infantry force added a company to secure the brigade tanks and stop attempts to harm the tanks by Syrian soldiers carrying short-range anti-tank weapons. The delay in opening the main road route and the failure of the supply convoy to arrive had an adverse impact on the brigade functioning. The brigade tanks, upgraded Centurions, needed refueling badly. The 9th Brigade forces set up in night camps and struck Syrian tanks and vehicles that were unaware of having encountered Israeli forces and were traveling on the road route. The supply ranks did not reach the 9th Brigade either and the tanks were almost out of fuel. The 471st Paratrooper Battalion combatants and the 91st Mechanized Infantry of the 9th Brigade dealt with evacuating and clearing the village of Khan Arnabeh. Clearing meant fighting Syrian anti-tank forces that were in the village. During the night, the "Nati" force reached the Golan Heights and was due to join up with the division forces the following morning.

The Battles on October 12

The 36th Division Battles

The division planned to reach Sa'sa in two moves: the first from the direction of Mazraat Beit Jann and the second through the Quneitra—Damascus road.

At dawn forces of the northern effort assumed recapturing positions in front of Mazraat Beit Jann, which was a densely built area surrounded by groves and plantations, and was reinforced by commando and tank forces overnight. Ensued fire exchanges were inefficient due to the 77th Battalion tanks being blinded by firing against the sun. Ten Syrian tanks were identified in the village and the village itself seemed deserted, later after the sun had come up. The Syrian artillery bombed the 77th Battalion tanks at dawn and several Syrian tanks were hit in the exchange of fire. Syrian jets attacked the 77th Battalion the same time.

At 10:00, the "Katz" force began attacking Mazraat Beit Jann with limited artillery support, while being covered by the 77th Battalion. The storming tanks of the offensive needed to cross a bridge over a narrow valley, which necessitated their moving in a column on the road leading into the village, while positioning the battalion for cover. The offensive met with powerful resistance. While moving, the attacking force was targeted by fierce artillery fire and attacks by Syrian jets, which also attacked the covering tanks. During the movement toward the target, the battalion commander was wounded and the operations officer took over and continued managing the battle. When the attacking force reached the bridge, three tanks were hit by anti-tank fire. The battalion continued the offensive and managed to capture the areas controlling the village. Later on a tank company captured the junction east of the village after crossing a forested area, destroyed about ten tanks. The capturing of the village was completed at 14:00. The "Katz" force lost fourteen men and seven tanks. During the first hours after the fighting, the northern effort forces set up in the Mazraat Beit Jann region to defend against Syrian counter attacks, which did take place in the days that followed. Mazraat Beit Jann was used by the Syrian Army as a "cork" to stop the IDF advance to the east. Again, a civilian location turned into a military position by its own army.

The southern effort forces began attacking Tel Shams at dawn. The 75th Battalion took positions against the missile alignment northeast of the main road route and the Ben Hanan force began advancing toward the hill along the main road route. Tank fire, at a 3,000-meter range and anti-tank fire, was opened at the force at the foot of the hill. The force was in an inferior territory when the battle developed. About twenty enemy tanks were destroyed. Following a fierce battle the force left the inferior territory with five hit tanks. The 7th Brigade was under the impression that the Syrians viewed Tel Shams as vital and organized it well for defense against attack attempts from the road route. The advancement in the southern effort stopped.

The 7th Brigade assessed that there was an option to exploit routes in the Leja region that were considered intractable for tanks to outflank Tel Shams from the north and attack it where it was less defended. A clear disadvantage in this maneuver was that the movement in the field was limited to a narrow route without the possibility of deployment. A force of eight tanks left the brigade under the command of Battalion Commander Ben Hanan to attack Tel Shams by exploiting passages through Leja. The force was 1,500 meters away from the mound when it opened fire, and destroyed many vehicles and a number of AFVs. The force stormed the hill and was attacked by anti-tank missiles after about thirty minutes of firing. Four tanks were damaged and the battalion commander was seriously injured, remained in the field, and was evacuated at nightfall. The attack was halted and the remaining force retreated and escaped.

The 1st Brigade was engaged in opening routes and clearing the Hader village and its surroundings. One battalion from the reduced 317th Paratrooper Brigade, which was added to the division, was given the task of clearing the hills in the rear of Khan Arnabeh.

Putting the day's achievements of capturing Mazraat Beit Jann aside it seemed that the division advancement met with fierce resistance that day and could not the meet its desired goals.

The 210th Division Battles

The command intended to deepen the effort from the Quneitra—Damascus road to the south. Therefore, it directed the 210th Division toward Nasej with the intent of advancing east to Ghabaghib. This inclination was later reinforced in light of the difficulties met by the 36th Division in its operation.

The Khan Arnabeh village turned into a section of the Syrian Army first line defense fortifications turning into an essential part of the Syrian defense despite the fact that it was, at least officially, a civilian village. The start of the division operation was delayed due to the ongoing clearing of Khan Arnabeh, the need to open a supply route as well as Syrian jets attacks - which struck a tank in the 179th Brigade and an ammunition truck in the 679th Brigade. The division planned to reach Khankar and expand the sector of activity toward the southern hills, on the morning after Minister of Defense's visit to the division

Command CCP, knowing that the division would receive the 3205th Brigade. The tasks ahead were:

- The 679th Brigade would move first on the Ma'atz route and on the route south of it and capture the Nasej village junction.
- The 9th Brigade would follow the 679th Brigade up to the village of Nasej and lead toward Khankar.
- The 179th Brigade would move toward the Tel Maschara junction, capture the junction and advance toward the Nasej junction.

In the morning, the 679th Brigade received a small amount of ammunition and at 06:00, it was reinforced with about twenty tanks from the "Nati" force. It now had fifty tanks. The brigade departed at 09:15 to capture the Nasej village junction. The "Nati" force, leading the attack, met with Syrian tank fire from the ridges controlling the junction area. Five tanks were hit and the force commander was seriously injured thus stopping the advancement. The remaining force, mostly made up of crews and commanders that did not know each other prior to that task, had to be reorganized. Two tank battalions from the brigade moved forward—one toward the "Nati" force and a second from the south in a right flank. About twenty Syrian T-55 tanks were identified and a fire battle ensued. The Syrian tanks were hit and began retreating. At 13:00 the brigade forces captured Tel Krin, the Nasej village and the junction. The brigade that remained in place due to a fuel shortage, engaged in fire contact with the enemy to the north while waiting for the arrival of the supply convoy and the reorganization of the "Nati" force.

Intensive operations to rehabilitate the 179th Brigade went on during the night. The "Nati" force reinforced it with eight tanks thus gaining a 24 tank and 15 APCs strong force by morning. Its organization included a tank battalion and a APCs battalion.

Early in the morning, the brigade moved to Tel Shaar and Tel Korum to replace the 9th Brigade. Later on, the brigade left for Tel Maschara and came up against a powerful anti-tank region. After two hours of heavy fighting and intense Syrian resistance the brigade commander was authorized to disengage and go past the Tel Maschara junction from the north. On its way, the brigade encountered twenty-five Syrian tanks at a range of 2,000 to 2,500 meters. The brigade had eight usable tanks left. It stopped in place and awaited the 9th Brigade.

Upon refueling, the 9th Brigade headed south at 10:15, broke through the enemy alignment at Hamrit, reached Nasej at 14:00 and turned north. The brigade stormed the Syrian tanks halting the advancement of the 179th Brigade and made them flee. The 179th Brigade, which recovered and had repaired a number of tanks, joined the advancement of the 9th Brigade toward Khankar. At 16:00, when the two brigades passed Tel Merai and the division forces began deploying for capturing Khankar, they were ordered to halt.

The 146th Division

The division order of battle was thinned out due to the command's ambition to attain maximal goals in the northern sector offensive on October 11. The main reason behind it was the fact that the 210th Division had entered the offensive sooner than had been planned and before it had received the intended reinforcements. Accordingly, at noon, an order was issued to take the 9th Brigade out of the division order of battle and subordinate it to the 210th Division. After the removal of the 9th Brigade, the division total order of battle included the 205th and 4th brigades, and the 670th Brigade reinforced by the 181st

Armored Command Battalion.

On the night of October 11–12, the division was assigned the task of apply pressure in its sector to examine the durability of the Syrian defensive disposition and attempt to break through into its depth. The command saw this effort as a movement in response to the imbalanced Syrian forces and not as a breakthrough. The 146th Division planned to move east in the Qudna—Tseida region in the first stage. A command order series, detailing the two-stage offensive was conducted on the morning of October 12.

- The 4th Brigade would leave a cover in the Sha'af a-Sindian ridge, advance from Outpost 110 east beyond the prior to the war Syrian outpost line and attack Qudna from the north.
- The 670th Mechanized Brigade, reinforced by three tank companies from the 181st Armored Command Battalion, would attack Tseida and Al-Hanut from the south.
- The 205th Brigade would cover the two brigades to advance east toward Sheikh Maskin at the next attack stage.

Process of the attacks:

The 4th Brigade—left one battalion in the Purple Line outposts and began attacking with two battalions moving under fierce bombing on rough terrain. The brigade reached the Quneitra—Bir Ajam route and continued advancing along a more convenient route. The brigade got a retreat order and returned to the "Purple Line."

The 670th Brigade—the 181st Armored Command Battalion was assigned the capturing of Al-Hanut and Tseida and two mechanized infantry battalion were supposed to break through on two routes. The armored command battalion tanks got caught while moving through a cut up, rocky terrain and the battalion launched the offensive with only two companies. They encountered heavy artillery fire and anti-tank fire a kilometer beyond the Purple Line in Syrian territory. The tank of the battalion commander and that of the company commander were hit, the battalion commander was injured, the company commander was killed and several tanks were on fire. The tanks from the third company that had arrived advanced along a different route toward Al-Hanut and captured it. A mechanized infantry battalion that reached the battlefield evacuated the wounded. The brigade forces were preparing to continue the attack on Tseida when a division order came in to retreat from Al-Hanut. The damaged tanks were towed leaving behind two tanks that could not be evacuated.

At 08:00, while the 146th Division offensive was in progress, the Minister of Defense visited the Command CCP. He believed that the 146th Division operation in the southern Golan Heights did not serve the political goals and demanded that all efforts in the north be concentrated at capturing as many additional territories as possible toward the upcoming ceasefire. Relating to a possible Jordanian military interference he declared that, if it were to occur, the Air Force was going to deal with it. Come what may, it was in the hands of a government decision.

He recommended reinforcing the division following his visit to the 210th Division commander CCP. In a discussion attended by the Minister of Defense, the GHQ Chief of Staff and the GOC it was agreed to reinforce the forces operating in the offensive on the northern front by transferring the 205th Brigade of about fifty upgraded "Shot Kal" Centurion tanks to the 210th Division. At 10:40 the Northern Command GOC ordered the transfer of the brigade, intended to secure the southern flank of the 210th Division and allow it to advance north.

With the removal of the 205th Brigade from the 146th Division, exploiting the accomplishments of the 4th and 670th Brigades was made redundant and they received an order to go back over the Purple Line and prepare for defense.

As of noon, October 12, the division was arranged with the 670th Brigade deployed on the line and the 4th Brigade concentrated in the rear as a force for counterattack.

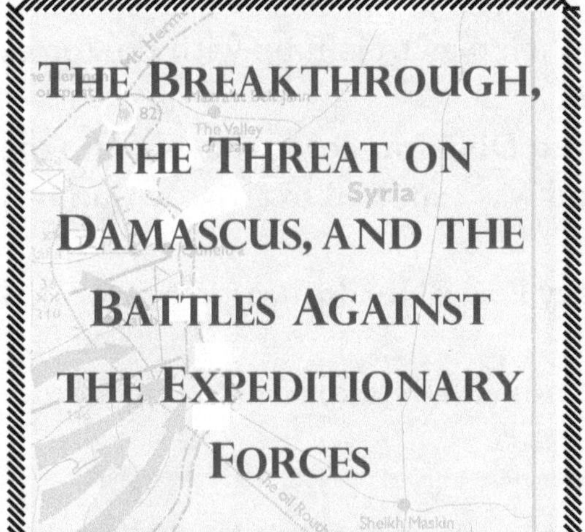

The Breakthrough, the Threat on Damascus, and the Battles Against the Expeditionary Forces

CHAPTER 13

Renewal of the Attack East

The command forces spent October 13 preparing for the renewal of the advancement east, which had been halted following the arrival of the Iraqis expeditionary force. The Syrians used the Israeli forces delay in combat o concentrate the ever increasing forces in their arena:

- **The Syrian 7th Division** dismantled during the breakthrough battle and only its small force remained in the Tel Shams bastion.
- **The 90th Infantry Brigade** was transferred south from Homs and deployed west of Damascus.
- **The 12th Division** that was the Iraqi expeditionary force's advance brigades—with about sixty tanks and eighty APCs—deployed on the southern flank of the 210th Division and additional forces from **the 3rd Iraqi Armored Division** began gathering around it, including **the 8th Mechanized Brigade**. Additional infantry and armored brigades, along

with artillery, were on their way to join up with the forces that had already arrived.

- **A second Iraqi Armored Division** began moving into the Golan Heights arena and was expected to arrive within two or three days.
- **The Iraqi expeditionary Force Headquarters** was located in Suwayda.
- **The 40th Jordanian Armored Division** crossed the border at night and parked at Daraa.

The Soviet planes and ships, beginning to be damaged in the airlift activities into Syria, aroused their concern. The IDF strikes on Syrian infrastructure and the attacks on Damascus accelerated the delivery of Russian weapons. By that day, over ninety Antonov An-12 transport aircrafts flights had been made from the Soviet Union to Syria, as well as thirteen Antonov An-22, and twenty-eight Antonov An-12 flights to Egypt.

Egypt and Syria continued vigorously to recruit pan-Arab support for the war effort against Israel with varying success degrees according to the Arab country.

Reassessing the situation, the Israeli Northern Command aspired to continue the tendency for a decisive battle in the northern arena while paying attention to Soviet sensitivity and the upcoming ceasefire.

The Northern Command orders issued on October 13 were to continue the offensive east and south, to stabilize a line based on the Aawaj River on the Khanker—Sa'sa line, advance toward Tel Hara in the south and bomb the Kiswah bases.

That day, however, attention of the senior command was focused on the expected Egyptian armored offensive in the south the next morning thus the move to a counter attack in the Southern Command was delayed to October 15.

The Northern Command continued its pressure to the east,

intending to arrive within artillery range of Damascus. Therefore, it instructed forces from the 7th Brigade who had been assisting the fighting against the Iraqis, to return to their division. It planned to capture Tel Shams on foot. Likewise, the plan was to capture outposts at the foot of the Hermon with infantry forces and continue helicopter raids to delay the Iraqi expeditionary forces in the Qutayfah region.

The Minister of Defense and the GHQ Chief of Staff arrived at the Northern Command CCP on the night of the 13th and affirmed the continued offensive move in the northern arena.

Following the detection of the Iraqi forces and the advancement of their columns toward the 210th Division forces, the division with its four reduced brigades on the morning of October 13, prepared to contain the Iraqi force. The entrance of the Iraqi force in the Box caused the eradication of the "wedge" that strove to the heart of the enclave with considerable effort including a substantial artillery fire strike.

A day earlier, and until October 13, five battalions were directed and deployed into positions in the Ma'atz junction under the 210th Division 282nd Artillery Group. These positions allowed for the close support of the division forces planned to advance up to the region of Khankar. Artillery had a decisive role in the defensive battles against the Iraqi forces attacking in the afternoon and night hours in the Tel Shaar region that day. Concentrated artillery guns of between seven and eight artillery battalions launched over 2,000 shells into the attacking Iraqi armored columns and caused their retreat. Artillery continued tailing and hitting the retreating forces in the following morning hours.

The command instructed that two units from the 412th Battalion with two guns each be placed in the Small Leja in the Kharfa region on the night of October 12–13th to fire at strategic targets in the Damascus region. The artillery force penetrated the depth of the field with close assistance of the GHQ and the Golani reconnaissance units, where they fired about forty shells, in twenty minutes time, toward targets on the Al-Mezzeh airfield on the outskirts of Damascus. To make it difficult for the Syrians to range the firing force, all artillery guns on the Golan Heights fired at the same time intending to show the Syrians that their capital was in danger. Additional firing into the depth of Syrian territory was carried out the following night by two guns from the Mazraat Beit Jann region.

The 212th Artillery Group carried out an intensive artillery effort on October 13 against the Syrian forces on the hill and around it toward an additional offensive attempt by the 36th Division forces to capture the controlling area in Tel Shams. The fire strike included the massive employment of rocket launchers by the 270th Battalion causing the Syrian forces retreat, and a relatively easy capture of the hill with hardly any injuries. The key area of Tel Shams on the Quneitra—Damascus route was captured on the night of October 13–14th by the 567th Battalion from the 317th Paratrooper Brigade, under the command of the 36th Division. The command installed an assigned headquarters, "The Kastel Force," under the command of the 36th Division, to hold the hill due to its tactical importance and following several Syrian counter attacks.

The entrance of Iraqi expeditionary forces into battle as early as October 12, followed by the entrance of the Jordanian 40th Armored Brigade into the arena alongside the beaten Syrian forces brought about a decisive change in the balance of power in the Northern Command region. As of the morning of October 14, the focal center of the war shifted to the southern arena toward the presumed Egyptian offensive with their armored divisions. The IDF blocked the armored offensive on the Suez Canal Front successfully and Egyptian forces suffered many losses. There was no significant activity in the Syrian arena that day. Nevertheless, forces from the 7th Brigade captured Tel Aris, Tel Fatma and Tel Merai advancing east of Ma'atz junction on the Golan Heights.

Though the IDF's main fighting effort shifted to the southern arena initiating the campaign to cross the Suez Canal, the Northern Command continued pressing east with an offensive intent. It still had the two tasks of reaching the Aawaj River to remain within effective artillery range of Damascus and of recapturing the Hermon.

The Northern Command had, from that point to the end of the war, between 300 and 400 tanks. There was an increase in the number of enemy tanks after Iraqi and Jordanian forces joined the Syrians. Therefore, the number of tanks facing the command forces in the enclave increased on October 18 to 520 tanks, including 150 Syrian, 70 Jordanian, and 300 Iraqi tanks.

The GHQ Chief of Staff instructed the GOC, Maj. Gen. Hofi, not to wear out his forces but try to expand the enclave southwards and toward Damascus so as to allow the striking of the Syrian capital with long-range 175mm guns.

The 212th Artillery Group and the 282nd Artillery Group deployed in new positions in "artillery ranges" where main and alternative positions were prepared for all the batteries. These positions, most of which were scouted by Syrian frontal observation officers from the slopes of the Hermon and the mounds on the Golan Heights, were fired at with anti-battery fire and were occasionally forced to skip. During the different stages of battle, the batteries were protected in the enclave by infantry forces. These were attached to the long-range batteries and those deployed in forward positions. The routine support of the armored and infantry forces on the front continued. The support units assisted the division forces but aimed the fire according to need regarding the neighboring division region, as well.

The 212th Artillery Group battalions assisted in defending the Tel Shams region against Syrian counter attacks. The artillery battalions continued to fire at various targets on the enclave's borders and toward concentrations of Syrian, Iraqi, and Jordanian forces that carried out repeated attack attempts on Israeli alignment forces. The anti-battery fire directed at the Syrian and Iraqi batteries was fired after being ranged by an optical gunfire locator network deployed by the 212th Artillery Group targeting and ranging support unit alignment.

Finding captured enemy ammunition in the enclave allowed for an additional allotment of ammunition to the two 130mm gun battalions that had run out of ammunition. Thousands of additional shells were found in the Syrian positions and were fired at their alignments and artillery positions.

The 282nd Artillery Group battalions, firing about 2600 shells, and the enemy's artillery exchanged fierce fire throughout October 14. On October 15, the artillery support's fire units accompanied the armored raid against Tel Antar and the Iraqi forces in the region by firing over a thousand shells. On October 15, the IDF began crossing the Suez Canal on the southern front toward continued fighting on the Canal's western bank and close in on the Egyptian third army. This operation became the IDF's main offensive effort. This implied that the forces in the Sinai were prioritized for aerial support and three artillery battalions including the 55th Battalion with the 175mm and the 270th with 240mm BM-11 rocket launchers battalion were transferred to the southern front.[18]

Artillery units of the two divisions assisted the forces on the defensive lines in striking the Iraqi, Jordanian, and Syrian forces that launched another counter attack on October 16 on the Golan Heights. This attack, mainly aimed at the hills to the

18 See details in Chapter 17.

south and east of the enclave, was halted.

The Syrians continued firing anti-battery fire toward the southern sector and forced the batteries occasionally to skip to alternative positions. On October 19, the support headquarters returned to its assigned facility in the Nafah Base as the artillery support headquarters for the entire region.

Inside the enclave, the eight battalions operating under the command of the 213th Artillery Group supported in an activity to expand and improve the outposts in its southern region. The battalions took part in curbing an additional Iraqi-Jordanian counter attack the same day. Immediately following this the Artillery Group cluster went down to the southern bank of the Suez Canal to secure the corridor for crossing the canal with the rest of the 146th Division command forces and the 352nd Self-propelled mortar battalion with its command.

Simultaneously, attempted penetrations and shootings on the Lebanese border took place. The mortar battalions under the command of the Meron district support headquarters deployed observations and fired at targets in the region.

At 08:40 on October 15, the GHQ's ODG emphasized that many weapons were coming into Syria; the preparation of new fighting forces had begun in the depths of Syria and the Syrians felt that the fighting could keep on with the Iraqi and Jordanian forces arriving in Syria. In this ODG, the GHQ Chief of Staff decided to attack the Iraqi forces, continue fighting while maintaining what had been accomplished, stabilize a line and plan to capture the Hermon. The order to attack the Iraqi 3rd Division forces, in the afternoon hours before it regrouped and an additional tank brigade arrived, reached the Northern Command. The order added that the command was to stabilize a line of defense on the Aawaj River, plan the capture of Khankar and Sa'sa, and obtain artillery range of Damascus.

The planning of the offensive against the 3rd Iraqi Division forces and striking their tanks, which were deployed near Kafr Shams and Deir el Ades, was assigned to the 210th Division on the morning of October 15. Beginning at 13:00 forces from all four of the division brigades took part, tanks were destroyed, and Tel Antar and Tel Krin were captured. Jets that were initially intended for the offensive encountered a screen of SAMs and thus could not help.

At this stage, the main effort of the Air Force was transferred to the Egyptian front. The Air Force commander's policy was to attack intensively on the Egyptian front while keeping pairs of jets in the air at every one time on the Syrian front to deter and attack when necessary. The Aerial Operations Department, adhering with the Air Force commander's orders, planned the activity of the Israeli Air Force on the Syrian front. Simultaneously, there was a planned offensive on the Mezzeh airfield, fuel tanks in Latakia and Tartus, a tank repair workshop in Harasta, and additional targets.[19] Following the demands of the command aerial CCP, targets in Mazraat Beit Jann, the Sa'sa region, Tel Shams, near Qudna, the Tel Hara region and the Hermon were attacked as well.

The Syrian Air Force's activity at this stage was mostly defensive. Hundreds of patrol sorties were carried out over their airfields. At this stage, they even went as far as to operate Dolphin jets that were training jets of a "Fouga" jet quality to defend the region. This pointed at the Syrian Air Force great distress in its aerial strength. On the other hand, activity on the front was scanty. A few attack sorties carried out had no impact on the front.

On October 16, the Syrian, Iraqi, and Jordanian forces conducted an integrated and coordinated counter attack toward

19 See details in Chapter 19.

the south and east of the enclave. The 210th Division four brigades faced the offensive once again, this time having advance intelligence pre-warning. The command operated the 71st Tank Battalion from the 36th Division 7th Brigade, which advanced in a deep flank toward the northern side of the Iraqi force and engaged in a tank battle north of Deir el Ades in coordination with the division. The movement of the force assisted in breaking the Iraqi offensive by evening. At the same time the division brigades that were deployed toward the south in the Tel al-Mal region, hit the tank columns of the Jordanian 40th Armored Brigade on their advance to the north.

At night, 175mm cannons bombed the Artouze and Katana bases south of Damascus.

Four days of the offensive ended in the northern arena wherein the IDF managed to break through the first Syrian defensive line, break out of it, encounter the Iraqi expeditionary force and halt it, fight the Jordanian expeditionary force and advance to a range of about forty kilometers from Damascus. In the 10 days that followed the Northern Command turned to defense from its new alignment while improving positions and repelling counter attacks by the various Arab armies on the Golan Heights.

The command forces continued the efforts to improve positions and stabilize defensive lines but the main effort was now invested in fending off counter attacks. Shifting the IDF's focal point to the Egyptian front, followed by the transfer of forces from the Northern to the Southern Command reduced the order of battle and allowed for only a limited number of initiated operations.

The division field engineering battalions, that had split their forces into companies and platoons, were given the task of assisting in clearing away mine clusters from the routes, overcoming water crossings that had been bombed, and preparing bypass routes. The field engineering forces were also integrated in the activity of placing mines on the flanks of the advancing forces and near them, to secure night camps. The companies and platoons were integrated into closely securing the night camps as a mechanized infantry force near the tanks. Another task that kept recurring was rescuing and evacuating AFVs that triggered mines.

The fortification effort based mainly on the division battalion heavy engineering equipment companies began when the external borders of the enclave were captured over controlling hills and between. Some of the tasks were carried out under massive artillery fire, which caused more than a few casualties among the workers and damaged to their vehicles.

The enclave was held by two divisions—the 36th Division in the north, and the 210th Division in the south—while the impaired 146th Division stabilized the defensive lines in the south of the Golan Heights.

The 146th Division was ordered to prepare a system of engineering obstacles intended to prevent a parallel counter attack by the Syrians or their partners in this sector, in a wide range engineering operation alongside the command offensive in the north of the Golan Heights. The command effort was invested there at this stage. The frontal obstacle was reinforced by additional minefields. The anti-tank trench was dug deeper and made longer. The dirt batteries in its rear were made higher. The command gathered its two field engineering battalions, the 602nd and the 261st, as well as the command of the 570th Heavy Engineering Equipment Battalion for this operation. A company of NCOs from field engineering Training Base No. 14, which was part of the 751st Battalion of the 146th Division field engineering battalions, participated in the operation. Placing 21,000 mines in a relatively short period exerted the main effort. A large scope and a high pace construction works were carried out as well.

On October 17, the 146th Division replaced the 210th Division in the enclave. The 670th Mechanized Brigade along with the 820th Regional Brigade assumed responsibility for the southern Golan Height sector and the RSM outposts along this line as an independent force under the Northern Command.

In order enable to transfer the 213th Artillery Group headquarters to replace the 282nd Group and continue the parallel operation of two Artillery Groups in the region of the enclave, the 334th Battalion headquarters was transferred to the Nachal Geshur region on October 17 where it served as the sector's support headquarters for the south of the Golan Heights. In the region that was under the responsibility of the 670th Brigade, a sort of improvised Artillery Group cluster deployed. The support unit included the 826th Medium Range Battalion, which abandoned the 155mm towed battalions it had converted to and returned to its SPGs left by the Training Base No. 9 Battalion forces (who returned to their base to complete the courses they participated in); the 829th Priest 105mm SPG Battalion, the 325th and 352nd 120mm Self-propelled Mortar Battalions, and the 175mm Battery from the 55th Battalion that remained on the Golan Heights.

When the 146th Division command replaced the 210th Division command in the enclave, the latter entered the Golan with the 179th and 679th Brigades and the renewed 188th Brigade forces under the command of Col. Dan Vardi. They needed a rest after having fought constantly since October 6. The 4th Brigade replaced them on the front.

The 210th Brigade that evacuated to the rear of the Golan Height began rehabilitating its two brigades, with command assistance. The 679th Brigade remained in the region as a command reserve unit while the reduced 179th Brigade was transferred on October 20 to reinforce the Southern Command in its offensive on the western bank of the Suez Canal. Through October 13–19 enemy forces carried out numerous counter attacks with Iraqis and Jordanians joining in with the Syrian forces. The attack goal was to prevent the expansion of the captured area and hinder the advancement of Israeli forces toward Damascus as well as prevent the Syrian Army complete destruction.

The attacks, that attempted to sever the alignment of the defensive forces, were directed at key areas and controlling territories in the Mazraat Beit Jann region at the foot of the Hermon, Tel Antar, Tel Krin and Tel Shams in the center, and Tel Maschara and Tel al-Mal in the south of the enclave. All these attacks failed and left the command forces in their positions. The main effort in the field was devoted to establishing control, improving positions, and responding to enemy attacks.

On the morning of October 18, the Northern Command Headquarters gave the 317th Paratrooper Brigade direct responsibility for the capturing the Umm-Butna and Tel Qudna regions. The offensive goals were to push the enemy forces away from the main maintenance route in the enclave, improve the borders and prevent Syrian control and observation from Tel Qudna which controlled the central and southern sectors on the Golan Heights. Opening an additional route into the enclave, south of Quneitra toward Umm-Butna and Jaba junction, was also planned.

The two operations were planned to take place in a brigade framework. The offensive toward Umm-Butna progressed slowly due to the slow advancement on foot and the enemy artillery fire. The village was captured toward morning, but forces replacing the paratroopers met with a Syrian counteroffensive that caused many injuries leading to its repulse. The forces had already departed as planned and were in their deployment positions when the offensive over Tel Qudna was cancelled.

On October 19, after the battle on Umm-Butna, an additional offensive by the coalition forces began before noon. Iraqi forces with eighty tanks attacked in the Tel Antar and Tel Alkia sector again, Jordanian forces with a brigade, along with Syrian forces, attacked toward Tel Maschara and Umm-Butna twice. Ten Jordanian tanks were hit during the battles and the Jordanian force retreated. An additional attack by a tank battalion from the Jordanian 40th Brigade toward Tel Maschara caused the Jordanian forces to retreat with damaged tanks.

In the Tel Antar and Tel Alkia sector, the Iraqis bombed the mounds at night. Under heavy artillery cover, an Iraqi mechanized infantry force succeeded in capturing Tel Antar until it was repelled toward 07:00 by a tank force from the 205th Brigade. After the defensive battles the 205th Brigade remained with as little as fifteen operable tanks and was replaced on the line by the 9th Brigade. About forty enemy tanks were destroyed in the battles of that day: ten Syrian, twenty Jordanian, and ten Iraqi tanks.

The Arab coalition forces multiplied over the next few days: the Jordanians added the 92nd Tank Brigade and additional units. The Jordanian expeditionary force had 180 tanks, 120 APCs, and forty artillery guns. The Iraqi expeditionary force increased its force by two divisions by the end of the battles. A Saudi Arabian armored vehicle battalion had arrived on the scene as well.

There were ongoing attack preparations both in the IDF forces and the "Three coalition armies" but aside from a Syrian tank battalion attempted attack toward Tel Merai on October 21, ending with eight damaged Syrian tanks, and artillery fire and raids by Special Forces, no offensive was carried out until the end of the war. The Northern Command forces remained in the enclave region until the end of the war until the Israeli—Syrian separation arrangement was reached in June 1974.

The completion of the deployment assignments for the defense of the front in the enclave and the southern sector left a part of the field engineering and heavy engineering alignment idle. The Northern Command decided to build defensive alignments in the depth of the Golan Heights, on the slopes going down to the Jordan River and the Sea of Galilee. Extensive construction works, including that of batteries and tank ramps and the digging of anti-tank trenches, as well as preparations for laying minefields were underway.

The Battle against the Iraqi Expeditionary Forces on October 12–13

While the 210th Division forces continued their activity to develop the breakthrough effort, the division CCP at Tel Shaar noticed dust columns rising for kilometers on end on the division southern flank, in the region east of Tel Hara. The division intelligence assessment, based on general information, was that it was an Iraqi force on its way to Syria.

The 679th Brigade, which was rearming and refueling at the time, was ordered to stop its organization and prepare for retrain the enemy's armored forces. The brigade deployed with two battalions in controlling positions on the route to halt the enemy advancement, whose identity had not yet clearly been ascertained. The brigade's 3rd Battalion, the Nati force under the command of Lt. Col. Nati Golan, had not yet completed its organization. The Iraqi 12th Armored Brigade, reinforced by an additional mechanized infantry battalion from the 8th Brigade, was the one observed. It entered a battle with Israeli forces at 15:00. The brigade moved along two avenues, with the east avenue, named the Ktiba Unit (Majmua), advancing toward Kafr Nasej, and the 679th Brigade, under brigade commander Aqid (Col.) Salim Sacher al-Imam and with 45 T-54 tanks and a mechanized infantry battalion. The Iraqi tanks, with different battle color markings on their vehicles than those of the Syrian ones, came into fire range of 600–1000 meters and tank battles ensued. While in battle, the Iraqi Brigade commander incorporated focused artillery fire. The pressure on the 679th Brigade was heavy and the brigade commander, Col. Ori Orr, brought the "Nati" force into battle after it had completed its organization. The Nati force on the scene prevented an Iraqi breakthrough that remained in their positions while exchanging static fire until 19:00.

The 210th Division command, unaware of the exact strength of the Iraqi force, overestimated it, gave a comprehensive withdrawal order to all its forces, fearing a greater force Iraqi attack on its southern flank. This order was a particularly bitter pill to swallow for the 9th and 179th Brigades that had just finished capturing Tel Merai and were advancing toward Khanker. Most of forces retreated until they ran out of fuel and stopped near Tel Shaar.

The 205th Brigade with sixty tanks, under the division command in the morning hours, was supposed to assist in the capturing of Khankar. It joined the division in the region of Khan Arnabeh, and when the Iraqi force arrived, the division commander decided to have this brigade secure the southern flank. The brigade commander, Col. Yossi Peled, got the order in the division CCP, and with a hasty battle, procedure was to capture Tel al-Mal and Tel Maschara. The brigade left its organization area in Kafr Jaba at 16:00 after being ordered by the brigade commander over the radio and advanced quickly with two battalions in front—on both sides of the road—and a rather reduced battalion behind on the route leading to Tel Maschara.

At the same time, the Alma'atsam Unit of the Iraqi 12th Brigade under the command of Raid (Maj.) Zuhir Qassam Shukri was moving toward the 205th Brigade. This unit, made up of a mechanized infantry battalion and a tank battalion of forty-five tanks, intended to reach Tel Shaar. The two forces, both after a hasty battle procedure, moving toward each other were unfamiliar with the territory.

At 19:00, the eastern Israeli 125th Battalion forces encountered the Iraqi force in the Al-Mal region and engaged in a short range of a few hundred meters firefight. Tanks of the 94th Battalion intermingled with the Iraqi tanks, the battalion companies were split, contact between the brigade commander and the battalion commander, Lt. Col. Guy Jacobson, was lost as well as the contact between the battalion commander and his companies. Since the Iraqi AFVs had an advantage in night vision equipment, the brigade commander ordered his forces to disengage and retreat toward Kafr Jaba, to reorganize. The first battalion reached the reorganization area without incident, but the 94th Battalion tanks, with its split and scattered units in the chaos of battle, arrived slowly, alone, in pairs or in isolated platoons. The withdrawal lasted for two hours and was carried out under artillery cover. At that stage the 205th Brigade was ordered to prepare for defense of the Jaba region.

Raid Shukri, commander of the Alma'atsam Unit, decided to exploit the withdrawal of the 205th Brigade and his advantageous night vision and continued the momentum of the offensive. Despite lack of communication with the brigade and Syrian Liaison officers to assist in navigation and artillery fire, the Iraqi unit continued advancing, captured Tel Buzuk and the Maschara region, and, eventually, at 22:00 gathered in the a-Ticha village.

An estimate of the situation took place in the 210th Division command in the evening hours of October 12. Following the unexpected encounter with the Iraqi force, it was decided to gather the division four armored brigades for an ambush in the Tel Shaar—Ma'atz junction region and wait for the impending attack with most of the available forces. This concentration of forces was also needed in light of the fuel and ammunition supply situation in the division units and enabled the refilling of tanks and AFV hulls under cover of night. A decision to change the location of the CCP and go down to Kafr Jaba was reached when the Alma'atsam Unit continued advance was observed from the mound, parallel to the planning group in the Tel Shaar division CCP.

The Northern Command also instructed the 36th Division to halt its advance and participate in the effort against the Iraqis by securing the left flank, a task which the 74th and 75th battalions on the Quneitra—Damascus road were directed to. The 210th Division was reinforced by an Artillery Group. The 210th Division intended to move to counter attack and recapture the territories left behind during the hasty withdrawal of that day upon the destruction of the advancing Iraqi force.

When the 210th Division completed the alignment of its brigades and the preparations for the Iraqi offensive a sort of division N-shaped alignment formed and was called the Box by the division. On October 13 at 03:00 the Alma'atsam Unit continued advancing northwest, employing the infrared night vision equipment installed on its vehicles. The 210th Division forces were ordered to abstain from firing until they clearly identified the battalion forces attacking at dawn. The Iraqis continued their advancement unaware of the 210th Division deployed forces.

At dawn, the 9th Brigade's 377th Sherman Tank Battalion identified about forty AFVs approaching its front from the direction of Tel al-Mal. When the leading vehicles came within a distance of several hundred meters the Sherman tanks opened fire at "battle range," while the upgraded Shot Kal Centurion tanks moved into firing positions on the Iraqi's eastern flank. About fifteen Iraqi tanks were hit.

Other Iraqi tanks came down the route from Tel Maschara and encountered the 205th Brigade fire at the west flank of the Box. On the eastern flank, the 179th Brigade was advanced toward Kafr Nasej. The 679th Brigade advanced and joined the firing on the Iraqi flank parallel to this, but halted following a division order to allow the Air Force to operate against the Iraqis. The Air Force attacked depth targets in the Akraba—Maschara region but in spite of the twenty-eight sorties the Alma'atsam Unit was not damaged at all.

At 07:00, the Iraqis began disengaging, with the 210th Division forces pressing behind them. The 679th Brigade moved in the center toward Maschara and the 179th Brigade toward A-Ticha. With their cover, the 9th Brigade under the command of Col. Mordechi Ben Porat advanced and recaptured Kafr Nasej at 08:45. The 205th Brigade received the 7th Brigade's 75th Battalion under its command, with twenty tanks, and headed out at 07:20 to capture Tel Maschara. The Syrians fired rockets and controlled artillery fire. The brigade captured Tel Maschara and the village by 09:55 with a southern flank, and with cover by the 679th Brigade, which carried out covering fire at the enemy from the north. The mound itself was captured on foot and was cleared by a paratrooper company from the 471st Battalion of the 317th Brigade. Capturing Tel Maschara took longer than expected. The Iraqi 12th Brigade force managed to retreat in an orderly manner, leaving about forty damaged AFVs and vehicles in the field. Exploiting the success following the Iraqi retreat allowed the 210th Division to capture the entire region of Tel Maschara, Tel al-Mal, Tel Krin, and Tel Merai. From that point on, the 210th Division southeastern flank was under increasing threat by Iraqi forces.

October 13–15

Preparing to renew the advancement to Sa'sa the 36th Division instructed the 317th Paratrooper Brigade to capture Tel Shams in a night operation. At the same time, a long-range artillery force was to be introduced into frontal positions to fire at the outskirts of Damascus. The 317th Paratrooper Brigade commander, Col. Haim Nadel, came up with a plan to attack Tel Shams with a paratrooper battalion from the north to be assisted by a tank company from the main road. The plan was changed by the division commander, Brig. Gen. Refael Eitan, before evening. He ordered the parallel storming of the mound and the anti-tank bastion from the south with the general direction being from the southeast. The brigade's CCP together with a tank platoon and an infantry company were to advance in the Small Leja, in the route used by the Ben Hanan force the day before, in order to isolate defenders on the mound from the rear, and assist the main effort if the need arose in accordance with the brigade commander's plan. The change introduced by Brig. Gen. Eitan was due to both the steep topographical structure of the mound to the north and the Syrians familiarity with this direction following the previous failed offensive attempt. Likewise, passing the main road could needlessly endanger the flank of the attacking forces.

After a hasty battle procedure, the forces began advancing from Tel Achmar at 19:00. The reduced 567th Paratrooper Battalion arrived on half-tracks at 21:00 and headed for the target on foot, reached the deployment areas around midnight and prepared for storming. After artillery preparation, including a barrage of rockets, two companies stormed the anti-tank bastion and one company came down the mound itself. They captured their targets by 14:04 facing weak Syrian resistance.

The brigade force that arrived near midnight at the fork in

the rear of the mound blocked it off from the Syrian Army reinforcements and even destroyed three Syrian tanks attempting to escape the targeted region. At dawn the force opened the road toward the rear up to the Halas intersection. Thirty Syrian soldiers were taken prisoner and about sixty were killed in this battle. The Israeli forces had four wounded.

Parallel to the paratrooper offensive on Tel Shams, the IDF advanced a force of two M-107 175mm guns of a 35 Km range, from the 412th Battalion into the region of the Small Leja. It fired 20 shells at the al-Mezzeh airfield south of Damascus after 23:30. Following the termination of shooting they skipped back to their waiting positions.

The Golani Brigade placed an ambush in the Maghar-el-Mir region east of Mazraat Beit Jann and ranged artillery at the Syrian site in the region that night. One ambush was placed near the Hina village on the way up to the Syrian Hermon. The two ambushes did not encounter any enemy forces. The brigade's 12th Battalion deployed to defend Mazraat Beit Jann where it restrained Syrian counter attacks.

That same night, the 35th Brigade Reconnaissance Company under the command of Captain Shaul Mofaz set out once again to raid the Iraqi advance routes. The reconnaissance company force was landed by a CH-53 helicopter on the Damascus—Homs road in the Qutayfah region. After landing the force discovered that it had landed in the wrong location and began advancing toward the planned position of the ambush. While moving, the force encountered Syrian soldiers, stormed them, and one of its men was injured. The mistaken landing location disrupted the planned timetable and the force was ordered to abort its task. Meanwhile, the force was exposed and the Syrians began closing in on it, lighting up the field with aerial flares. The force positioned for defense in intractable territory and waited for the Syrians to move away. Then a helicopter flown by the 118th Squadron commander, Lt. Col. Yuval Efrat, came and rescued them.

At noon, October 15, the 210th Division began maneuvers meant to destroy the 3rd Iraqi Armored Division. The 679th Brigade carried out a deep flanking maneuver in the zone northwest of Tel Krin to west of Kafr Shams. It encountered anti-tank bastion fire at Deir al Ades. The 205th Brigade advanced west of it to secure its flank while taking positions east of Tel Krin toward Tel Alkia.

The 179th Brigade advanced from Tel al-Mal in a southeastern direction while engaged in battle with enemy AFVs that were in contact with the 679th Brigade.

The 9th Brigade pressed from Kafr Nasej east and before evening exploited a lack of vigilance in the enemy alignment and captured Tel Khankar and Tel Alkia. Storming the mounds cost the brigade four damaged tanks but the surprised Iraqi Brigade deployed east of them retreated. The Syrians and Iraqis carried out artillery fire, including rockets at the forces and at targets in the division rear east of Tel Shaar.

The division lost seven tanks and destroyed several dozen enemy AFVs. At night fall the division command decided to disengage. The 205th Brigade prepared for defending Tel Antar and Tel Alkia in place of the 9th Brigade that moved toward the lineup location near Tel Shaar. The 679th and 179th Brigades entered night camps to reorganize from Tel al-Mal to the north.

The Iraqis tried to counterattack at night and regain control over the territories they had lost during the day. Their attempts were repelled by tank fire assisted by artillery flares. The IDF cannons attacked depth targets including the Kiswah bases once again, that night.

The Iraqi forces were reinforced on the night of October 14-15th by the reduced 6th Armored Brigade, which gathered in Kiswah—a third tank battalion from the brigade was waiting for tank transporters in the H-3 region—and the 5th Division 20th Infantry Brigade, which also arrived at Kiswah, while one of its battalions deployed at Deir el Ades. The Jordanian 40th Brigade advanced to Tel Hara and prepared to join the fighting against the IDF forces. After the battles on the 15th of the month the Iraqi 12th Armored Brigade was taken out of the battlefield after it had suffered losses of more than 50 percent in three days of fighting against the IDF forces. The brigade didn't resume active participation until the end of the war and the 6th Armored Brigade deployed in its place.

The Arab Counter Attacks on October 16

Forces from the Arab armies gathered in the Syrian arena carried out their first offensive on IDF forces on the morning of October 16. It was carried out from the south and east and was mainly aimed at the 210th Division forces. The Iraqi and the Jordanian expeditionary forces were supposed to coordinate the offensive between them. The task was assigned to the Iraqi 3rd Armored Division the Jordanian Brigade was subordinated to. In effect, however, the Iraqi 6th Armored Brigade and the Jordanian 40th Armored Brigade carried out an uncoordinated, split offensive.

The IDF forces were aware of the impending offensive, achieved through surveillance reports, and the two divisions within the Syrian enclave were in a high alert level at dawn. The 210th Division deployed with the 679th and the 179th Brigades in front. The 9th Brigade was concentrated as a reserve force and a division counter offensive force from the rear.

The 40th Armored Brigade moving forward from Tel Hara north to Tel al-Mal and Tel Maschara began at 09:00. The

Jordanian employment of Centurion tanks similar to the ones in possession of the IDF confused the Israeli forces and made identifying the enemy difficult.

The goal of the 40th Brigade was to capture Tel Maschara. The brigade eastern battalion combat team advancing on the route to Al-Mal turned northwest. At a range of 2000–2500 meters from Tel al-Mal it exposed its flank to the 179th Brigade tanks, which had pre-positioned itself on the slopes of the mound. With large green flags on the antennas these were clearly Jordanian Centurions, since the IDF did not use this marking.

The 179th Brigade hit about twenty Jordanian AFVs from its positions on the slopes of Tel al-Mal. This was before the Jordanians managed to capture positions or turn their turrets. The Jordanians continued moving west and entered the range of the 679th Brigade tanks, which had headed south and deployed in controlling positions in advance. During the southern maneuver, the brigade forces hit the Jordanians again. The 91st Mechanized Infantry Battalion of the 9th Brigade reinforced by a tank company secured the fighting sector in the Jaba—Tel Korum region. The Jordanians surprised by the firing of the IDF forces, stopped and began retreating to the deployment area in the Tel Hara region.

The Jordanian 40th Armored Brigade attacked with three armored battle teams made up of tanks and APCs. They lost 10 tanks and 13 APCs. Even though it was planned otherwise, the attack went on without coordinated Syrian or Iraqi artillery assistance and without a parallel Iraqi offensive.

The Jordanian 40th Brigade offensive was expected to turn west and cross the Purple Line into the Golan Heights when it began in the morning. The command ordered the 146th Division to place a force south of Quneitra, without crossing the line to the east. Therefore, the division was reinforced by the 53rd Tank Battalion—the "Pliz" ("Brass") force under the command of Col.

Dan Vardi. After 09:00, when the Jordanian direction was clearly to the south and not west, command ordered the return of the forces.

The 53rd Battalion returned to the 36th Division but the 39th Battalion of the 4th Brigade, which was positioned in the region of Outpost 109, was ordered by deputy 146th Division commander, Col. Avraham Rotem, to advance carefully up to the Syrian border road, to improve positions against the Jordanian force and on its flank, as opposed to the command orders. The battalion found itself frontally breaking through the first Syrian lines of defense in the sector of the 9th Division, which included minefield obstacles and artillery fire killing zones.

The battalion was heavily shelled on the outskirts of A-Rihania after 11:00. The battalion commander, Lt. Col. Yoav Vaspi, was hit and killed by shrapnel. Two tanks triggered mines. A half-track from the field engineering platoon, which came to assist in breaking through the minefields and evacuating the tanks, got a direct artillery hit and exploded. The battalion retreated immediately after the GOC's interference. The damaged tanks could not be evacuated until the night hours due to the fierce fire.

In the Iraqi sector, a tank force began moving at 07:00 from Kafr Shams to the southern flank of Tel Antar. The tanks were discovered at a distance of 1,000 meters, five were destroyed and the others retreated. A brigade level offensive was launched an hour after the Jordanian offensive, at 10:00. An APC force discovered at Deir el Ades was hit by artillery and machine gun fire and retreated east. The 6th Armored Brigade offensive on Tel Antar and Tel Alkia began an hour later. The tanks advanced in a broad deployment accompanied by APCs carrying infantry and field artillery forces. The armored forces were repelled at close ranges and the brigade's mechanized infantry battalion, which was also involved in the fighting, stormed from the south.

The repelling of the Iraqi attacks was carried out by the 205th Brigade who held the mounds, the 179th Brigade that had finished fighting the Jordanians and operated from the direction of Al-Mal and the 9th Division operating north of the mounds. The battle went on until 16:00. Before evening another Iraqi mechanized infantry force from the 8th Brigade was repelled while advancing from Kafr Shams to Tel Antar with the intention of assisting the armored forces of the 6th Brigade. The Iraqis operated about ninety tanks in two battalions, two infantry and eight artillery battalions. During the battle the Iraqi Brigade lost about 25 percent of its fighting force, including several dozen tanks. In the evening it retreated to tend to its dire defeat. Lt. Col. Tuvia Toren, the commander of the 125th Battalion of the 205th Brigade was killed.

The 7th Brigade, 71st Tank Battalion from the 36th Division was put into action, in coordination with the 210th Division, when the battle east of the mounds was raging in the afternoon hours. The battalion advanced in a deep flank from Tel Merai to Deir el Ades, on the Iraqis northern flank and launched a battle against the 20th Infantry Battalion tanks and anti-tank units 1.5 kilometers north of the village. Some of the Iraqi AFVs were destroyed and some retreated. Here, again, a village turned into military position. The battalion advanced to the village which was the center of the Iraqi Brigade site and met with efficient anti-tank Cobra missiles and artillery direct fire. The Iraqi posts were between the village houses and in Syrian positions thus making it difficult to identify the sources of the shooting. The battalion commander decided to bypass the village from the east with cover of other forces, and when he was about three kilometers northeast of the village, he encountered a column of trucks leading an infantry battalion from the Iraqi 20th Brigade. He hit many trucks moving east on the road to Ghabaghib. During its operation, the battalion hit a Saudi Reconnaissance

Unit, which was quick to disengage. The threat posed by the 71st Battalion over the northern Iraqi flank assisted in breaking the offensive. The Iraqis withdrew, leaving behind dozens of damaged vehicles.

After the Iraqi 3rd Division attacked from the south, the Syrians joined the offensive in the north of the sector against the 36th Division in the Tel Shams—Mazraat Beit Jann region. This offensive was repelled after the enemy lost dozens of tanks.

The Battles on October 17–18

It was discovered that the Syrian Army was gradually rehabilitating with flowing massive deliveries of AFVs and jets from the Soviet Union. Twelve Soviet ships had already arrived at the Syrian ports and the tanks deployed in the second line of defense. Jets were assembled in northern Syria and Soviet and North Korean pilots flew them to southern airfields. A Saudi Mechanized Brigade equipped with AML armored vehicles had arrived in Syria and was deploying in Daraa. The heads of government in Damascus declared that Syria was not going to request a ceasefire, due to the Soviet overwhelming support with weapons and fighting gear.

On the night of October 16–17, the IDF long-range artillery bombed bases south of Damascus again, this time in Artouze and Katana. Some 130mm towed guns, from the GHQ's reserves, were advanced to Syrian positions and fired captured Syrian ammunition.

Before dawn, October 17, forces from the Iraqi Special Forces Brigade attacked the 205th Brigade, 125 Battalion night camp on the south slope of Tel Antar with anti-tank rocket grenades, suffered losses and were repelled.

During these days, the Syrians attacked repeatedly with battalion size forces of tanks and infantry. A Syrian force managed to break through Mazraat Beit Jann and was halted by infantry anti-tank fire and a parallel counter attack. At the same time the Golani Brigade captured the village of Beit Jann and the ridge north of it.

The Syrians attacked Tel Shams on the road to Damascus, Tel Merai on the road to Khankar, and Tel Aris between them, with infantry and tank forces once again. On October 16-17, a Saudi AML battalion participated in the attack on Tel Merai. Most of it was destroyed. In order to improve the command and control of the Tel Shams sector the Castel force was established under the command of Col. Yosef Castel, including the 13th Infantry Battalion form Golani and the 74th Tank Battalion.

On the 17th and 18th of the month, the Syrians deployed the 62nd Mechanized Brigade in Khankar and reinforced the Iraqi sector by placing the Syrian 85th Infantry Brigade in Deir el Ades and the Iraqi 12th Mechanized Brigade in Ghabaghib. At dawn October 18, the Iraqis attempted to carry out a night raid from the direction of the Shams and Deir el Ade's villages with the Special Forces brigade but the raiding forces were discovered and retreated after suffering losses, leaving two soldiers behind.

The IDF carried out initiated operations which included Golani Brigade operated ambushes in the region of the Arna village and Mazraat Beit Jann, and appending frontal observation officers in the Hina region to range artillery at the Syrian outposts. At night, October 17–18th, the 317th Paratrooper Brigade placed two ambushes, south and east of Khankar, and struck a jeep. A force raiding an artillery battery discovered that the battery had skipped.

A Second Counterattack, October 19, 1973

The senior Syrian Command issued orders for a coordinated counter attack on October 7 intended for the 18th of the month, but its execution was postponed to the following day due to delayed planning and preparations.

The Arab order of battle included the Jordanian 40th Brigade deployed in the Tel Hara region—together with forces from the Saudi Armored Vehicle Brigade—and the Iraqi Force deployed between Sanamayn and Kfar Shams. This force included:

- The reduced 12th Brigade that had been beaten in battles between the 12th and the 15th of the month and engaged in recuperation and reorganization.
- The 6th Armored Brigade that completed its organization and deployment after battles on the 16th of the month.
- The 8th Mechanized Brigade already damaged in previous battles.
- The 20th Infantry Brigade which was also damaged.
- The 5th Mountain Infantry Brigade.
- The Special Forces brigade.
- Artillery assistance including three towed medium range battalions of 122mm long and 130mm guns and a 122mm SPG Battalion.

The Jordanians operated at first under the Iraqi command but after their disappointment on the 16th and King Hussein's visit to the 40th Brigade two days later they were placed under the Syrian 9th Division.

Activity of Command Forces toward Capturing Key Targets

Intensive activity was scheduled for the night of October 18–19. Two battalion operations by the 317th Brigade's paratroopers were planned to capture Tel Qudna and the village of Umm-Butna. These two attacks were intended to improve the deployment of the Northern Command forces for defense. Capturing Tel Qudna was meant to improve the control of the Rapid salient, prevent the Syrians from scouting the depths of Israeli territory in the west and allow the IDF to achieve this over Syrian territory to the east. Capturing Umm-Butna was intended to expand the base of the enclave and open an alternative maintenance route south of the Quneitra—Damascus route. A number of raids were planned as well.

The 567th paratrooper battalion under the command of Lt. Col. Elisha Shelem was assigned the capturing of Umm-Butna in the sector of the 4th Brigade of the 146th Division by the 317th Paratrooper Brigade. The task of capturing Tel Qudna in the sector of the 670th Brigade was assigned to the 471st Battalion under the command of Lt. Col. Hezi Shelach. A joint H-hour was established on October 18 at 22:00. The paratrooper brigade presented its plans to the 146th Division command and the 670th Brigade command in the afternoon. The 471st Battalion planned to attack Tel Qudna on foot and after capturing the controlling areas was meant to be replaced by armored forces that would deploy for defense. The paratroopers left on time but were ordered to return as the GHQ Chief of Staff changed his mind deciding that capturing the mound was not worth the anticipated loss of lives.

The 567th Battalion was meant to capture Umm-Butna on foot from the direction of Tel Korum in the north, and at the same time allocate a company for the capture of two Syrian border outposts along the outposts route. Two mechanized forces intended to advance behind it from Jaba and Khan Arnabeh. Their task was to clear the area between the Purple Line and Umm-Butna. Each force was made up of a number of tanks, a mechanized infantry company and a field engineering platoon on half-tracks.

The 146th Division was made up of an improvised force named: Salat ("Salad") with a battalion order of battle intended to replace the paratroopers at Umm-Butna immediately following its capture and prepare for defense in the village and its surroundings. Lt. Col. Egozi, commander of the 91st Mechanized Infantry Battalion of the 9th Brigade, commanded the force and included a company from his battalion—a mechanized infantry company from the 42nd Battalion of the 4th Brigade—as well as a tank company from the 61st Battalion, transferred from the 4th Brigade under the command of the operations officer. Battalion commander Lt. Col. Moshe Meler was in the company commander's tank with an IV- infusion due to dehydration.

The two paratrooper infantry forces performed as planned, but were delayed due to the difficult terrain that slowed down their moving through, the enemy artillery fire, the misleading first artillery target ranging inaccuracy and the difficulties in identifying their targets.

The 567th Paratrooper Battalion entered the village quietly, after 23:00 and found a Syrian force with the strength of one tank and one infantry companies. Three of the Syrian tanks were destroyed and the village was captured by 190330. At this point, it became evident that the continued capture of the controlling areas outside the village was delayed and the division and the Northern Command agreed that the paratrooper battalion would not go on to capture the hills southeast of the village. By break of dawn the paratroopers cleared out of the village with their wounded, 3 killed, twenty injured, and sixteen Syrians POWs.

The two mechanized forces moved as planned and assisted in evacuating the paratroopers' wounded under artillery shelling. The paratroopers left before the men of the Salat force could establish themselves in positions due to a misunderstanding. Before dawn, the Syrians landed a local counter attack at the strength of a tank company and with cover of accurate artillery shelling. Battalion commander Lt. Col. Moshe Egozi was killed and the mechanized infantry company retreated from the village without its half-tracks. The tank company lost its commander, and four of its eight tanks were destroyed.

The 4th Brigade rushed to assist the Salat force in a dual battalion raid, with the 288th Reconnaissance Battalion under the command of Lt. Col. Zvi Dahab west of the village and the 39th Armored Battalion Lt. Col. Haim Porat east of it. These forces repelled the Syrians while flooding the 9th Syrian division artillery positions. Ten Syrian tanks were damaged and seven Israeli ones. A rescue team of three half-tracks, under the command of the 42nd Battalion deputy commander and the company commander himself, managed in the meantime with the assistance of concerted artillery fire, to enter the village three times and evacuate most of the wounded and ten of the abandoned half-tracks. At the end of the battle, the 4th Division tanks were set up in a broad deployment east and south of the village.

Parallel to the capture of Umm-Butna, the Iraqis launched an attack to capture Tel Antar at dawn. This attack was carried out by the 6th Armored Brigade reinforced by tanks and a mechanized infantry battalion from the 8th Brigade. At night, the Special Forces brigade carried out a number of raids against the 205th Brigade night camps in the mound region, all of which were repelled. The activity did distract the forces from observing the movement of the 8th Brigade's 3rd Mechanized Infantry Battalion that had begun its advance toward the mound at 03:00. Before dawn, the paratrooper scouts and frontal observation officers decided to come down from the peak of the mound, while the mechanized infantry force that was due to replace them took positions on the rear slope due to the intensity of the Syrian-Iraqi bombardment that covered the storming by the Iraqi 3rd Mechanized Infantry Battalion. This way, the Iraqi Battalion captured the peak of the mound and took positions at dawn. When the Iraqi 6th Brigade commander got the report of the battalion positioning on the mound he ordered the armored battalions to move toward it. This was an outnumbered offensive of about 140 Iraqi tanks against forty tanks from the 205th Brigade. However, the 205th Brigade counterattack managed to return Tel Antar into IDF hands by 07:00 before the Iraqi tanks had managed to develop their offensive while employing the 94th and 125th Battalions.

The IDF artillery, particularly the 160mm Self-propelled mortars, played an important role in breaking the 3rd Iraqi Infantry Battalion on the mound. With this artillery cover and the firing by the 125th Battalion that was positioned on Tel Alkia, directly aiming at Tel Antar, the 94th Battalion stormed the latter and captured it. The Iraqis had about forty dead, who were left on the mound, and a few prisoners. After the 205th Brigade recaptured Tel Antar it discovered the large Iraqi tank force, advancing in deployment from the southeast. The brigade established itself in fine positions and began striking the advancing Iraqi tanks. Their outsized number raised the apprehension that the 205th Brigade would be outflanked from the south. Therefore, the division sent in the 9th Brigade on the southern flank of the 205th Brigade. The two brigades engaged in an armored battle with the Iraqis until the offensive was broken.

Since the offensive by the Jordanian 40th Armored Brigade —at that point subordinate to the 9th Division—only began at 09:00, over an hour after the offensive toward Tel Antar by the

Iraqi 6th Armored Brigade was broken it seems that coordination between the Iraqi 3rd Armored Division and the Syrian 9th Division was weak at best.

The Jordanian Brigade moved to the offensive organized in two tank battalion efforts and was reinforced by the mechanized infantry aimed to attack Tel Maschara and the village of Umm-Butna at the same time, from south to north. This offensive effort was doomed to fail both due of its timing - at the end of the Iraqi attack—and to the deployment of the 4th Brigade, under the command of Col. Yaakov Hadar (Feffer), that was fully alert in its positions after the battles at dawn. The 40th Armored Brigade forces began movement preparations in which the brigade units were arranged into battalion columns, at dawn.

The force began moving from Nawa to Tel Hara at 07:00, along two parallel routes: on the Nawa—Tel al-Mahatz—Nab-a-Sacher—Umm-Butna route and on the Nawa—Nimer—Al-Hara junction—Naba-a-Sacher—Maschara route.

At about 10:30, the 6th Iraqi Armored Brigade launched the second offensive of the day. This one was broken by the 205th Brigade reserve forces of seven tanks that operated in the Iraqi flank in the Tel Krin region, destroying about 10 AFVs. The 36th Division 71st Battalion also joined the battle and attacked the Iraqi force from the northwest, destroying a number of AFVs.

At that point, the 40th Brigade's advance force was identified coming down from both sides of Tel Hara, on the dirt trail from the eastern shoulder, moving north. At this stage, the 146th Division command assessed that the stronger effort was by the Iraqi force. When the direction of the Jordanian attack was made clear, the sector was thinned out.

Two tank companies from the 288th Battalion remained in the Umm-Butna region along with a company from the 39th Battalion. Another company from the 39th Battalion was directed at capturing the Tel El-Mal region in order to bridge the gap between the battalion and the forces halting the Iraqi offensive and the eastern Jordanian offensive.

The tank force in Umm-Butna opened long-range fire on the Jordanian Armored Brigade after it was discovered. Two Jordanian tanks were hit about 15 minutes later. The western Jordanian effort stopped for 30 minutes while the wounded were evacuated by the armored infantry's APCs apparently without identifying the source of the shooting. Upon resuming movement from this region north the tank battalion by passed Tel Hara from the east, and advanced toward Marbaat. Identifying tanks on the battlefield was a problem because both sides were using Centurion tanks.

A battle between tanks ensued during the advance of the Jordanian force, and they retreated. The Jordanians, who carried out the attack while carefully advancing and remaining in fire contact with the IDF forces, lost 17 tanks that day of fighting. The Jordanian 40th Brigade suffered losses and was forced it to retreat as a result of the maneuvering and fire of the 4th Brigade.

During the October 19 offensive the Iraqis and Jordanians exposed themselves in open killing fields but the 146th Division requests for aerial assaults were refused for fear of the Syrian dense SAM defensive alignment.

The division was assisted in the two sectors by its own Artillery Group that was reinforced by the 282nd Artillery Group battalions of the 10th Division that gathered for reorganization. The artillery order of battle included three 155mm medium range battalions, two 105mm Self-propelled field battalions, two 160mm Self-propelled mortar battalions, and two 120mm Self-propelled mortar battalions.

The 146th Division was on the defensive in two of its sectors, throwing all its forces into battle. Fifteen of its tanks were hit that day. The 205th Brigade, who carried the brunt of the battle over Tel Antar, remained with only fifteen functioning tanks by the end of the day. On the night of October 19–20th, the 9th Brigade replaced the 205th on the mounds and the latter headed out to organize in the Jaba region.

The 3rd Iraqi Armored Division, which lost about fifty tanks, about 50 APCs and hundreds of infantry soldiers, that day, did not attack again. Neither did the Jordanian 40th Armored Brigade.

The Syrians attempted to attack Tel Merai with a battalion force, were repelled and lost eight tanks on October 21.

The IDF organized and the 36th, 210th, and 146th Divisions reached a strength of 380 tanks. With this in mind, the Northern Command prepared three offensive plans:

- The recapturing of the Hermon
- An offensive northeast toward Khankar—Sa'sa to intimidate Damascus
- An offensive east to improve the situation in the arena toward the ceasefire
- To destroy the Iraqi expeditionary force and take over the main Sheikh Maskin—Damascus road.

Simultaneously, the command continued elite infantry units' ambush and raid activities beyond enemy lines with no significant impact.

The senior command decided that the Northern Command would focus on the recapturing of the Hermon, with second priority placed on drawing closer to Damascus in the Sa'sa-Khanker region.

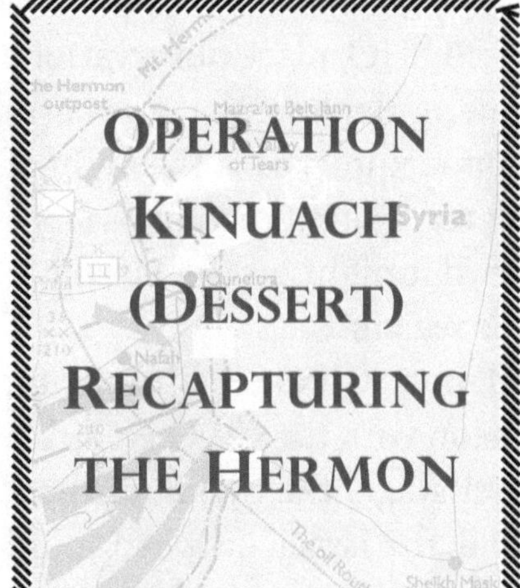

Operation Kinuach (Dessert) Recapturing the Hermon

Chapter 14

Consolidation of the Command Plan and Battle Procedure Toward Operation Kinuach

The recapturing of the Hermon remained on the agenda of the GHQ and the Northern Command. The battle procedure for Operation Kinuach (Dessert) accelerated on the 15th of the month, when Maj. Gen. Yitzhak Hofi met with the GHQ Chief of Staff, Lt. Gen. David Elazar (Dado), to discuss the direction of the command activity. The GHQ Chief of Staff stated, among other things, that the Hermon outpost had to be captured and the CIPO HQ, responsible for the planning of the capture and its carrying out, could be allocated to the command. Maj. Gen. Hofi objected to the operation being carried out that night due to lack of intelligence regarding the Syrian alignment. In the GHQ Chief of Staff's ODG, before noon, the GHQ Chief of Staff instructed the Northern Command to plan the capture of the Hermon outposts with the CIPO HQ, place observations in the region in order to study the enemy deployment, and carry out the operation the first possible opportunity as of the night of October 16–17. Maj. Gen. Hofi ordered a silent reconnaissance task of the 269th Unit to take place that night on the Hermon, which wasn't carried out for various reasons.

On the 16th of the month the deputy CIPO, Lt. Col. Arieh Tzimel, presented GOC Maj. Gen. Hofi with the CIPO HQ plan to capture the Hermon. On the first stage, the Syrian outpost would be captured and on the second, the Israeli outpost would be captured with a helicopter landing force of two battalions from the 317th Paratrooper Brigade. The GOC, Maj. Gen. Hofi, ordered the 269th Unit to carry out a silent reconnaissance in the Hermon and the capture of the Hermon to take place within 48 hours of a warning. In the GHQ Chief of Staff's ODG that took place on the 19th of the month the GHQ Chief of Staff once again stressed both the need to capture the Hermon outposts and the required presence of the 317th Paratrooper Brigade. Therefore, permission wasn't granted to attack Tel Qudna that night. The GHQ Chief of Staff ordered the command to capture the Hermon after the Northern Command missing artillery ammunition was gathered. Later that night the GHQ Chief of Staff held a situation assessment when it became known that the Soviets had made an insistent request that the US Secretary of State, Henry Kissinger, came to Moscow immediately, which implied that a ceasefire agreement was drawing near. In light of the assessment that the end of the battle was a few days away, and that the IDF must attain all possible goals within the next three days, the GHQ Chief of Staff said that it was mandatory to capture at least one of the two Hermon outposts, and if possible, to capture its peak as well. The GHQ Deputy Chief of Staff, Maj. Gen. Israel Tal, updated the GHQ Chief of Staff that the operation was scheduled for October 21 and that 3,000 artillery shells were allocated to the Northern Command, as well as helicopter transportation support, aerial support, and artillery support as required, and that the Air Force was to continue preventing the Syrians from paving a road between the two outposts on October 20. As decided, the CIPO was not to command the capture of the Hermon since he was planned to command the operation to capture Port Said, on the Egyptian front. The Chief of Staff shared this with the Northern Command GOC and instructed him to plan the capture of the Hermon within 48 hours. In light of this, Maj. Gen. Hofi decided that a team led by his deputy, Brig. Gen. Yekutiel (Kuti) Adam, will be in charge of the planning of the Kinuach (Dessert) operation at the command level, as well as controlling it while he was to function as a secondary command. This team had already operated as a planning team parallel to the team conducting the actual combat in the field under the command of the GOC, the Command G3 officer, and the command senior staff officers.

On October 20 at 09:30, a planning group for capturing the Hermon took place in the Northern Command CCP, headed by the GOC and participated by his deputies, the deputy CIPO and staff officers. Maj. Gen. Hofi presented the main points of the operation: the 317th Paratrooper Brigade would be flown to the Syrian Hermon by dark. Under cover of dark the brigade would advance, clear it and be prepared to go down to the Israeli Hermon. The 1st Brigade—moving in two forces and along two routes, with one to advance on foot from Majdal Shams toward the upper ski lift station, and from there toward the Israeli outpost and the second force would be mechanized and go up on the road parallel to the infantry force—would capture the Israeli Hermon. The 269th Unit was to place an observation that night at Mitzpe Shlagim. A company was to go up there on the D-Night to sever the route between the Syrian and the Israeli Hermon, observe, and range artillery fire. The 36th Division was given the task to secure the flank and strike the escaping Syrians. The 1st Brigade assistance would be based on heavy mortars, while the 317th Paratrooper Brigade assistance would be based on 155mm guns. The D-Night was to be the night between Sunday and Monday. Assuming the operation were to last until Monday evening he instructed the establishing of an aerial HQ for helicopters at the Mahanayim airfield to enable the forces to receive supplies during the battle and evacuate the wounded. Regarding the operation command and control, Maj. Gen. Hofi stated that the Command CCP would be divided into two teams, since the command was to initiate an offensive in the enclave toward south on Monday morning. Kuti's team would control the capture of the Hermon, and his team would control the offensive. After the GOC, the deputy CIPO presented the 317th Paratrooper Brigade flight plan including aerial and artillery operation support. At the end of the planning group the GOC, Maj. Gen. Hofi, flew to the GHQ and presented the plan to the GHQ Deputy Chief of Staff, as the GHQ Chief of Staff had flown to the southern front.

At the same time, first group of orders for Operation Kinuach was carried out at 14:00 in the Northern Command CCP, that was attended by the commander of the operation Kuti, the 317th Brigade commander, the deputy CIPO, the 269th Unit commander, the 36th Division representative, the 820th Brigade commander, the Air Force representative in the command, the staff officers, and the G3 staff officers from the 1st and 317th Brigades. The D-Day and the H-hour were set: 21:18—for starting the capture of the Syrian Hermon outpost and for the beginning of movement toward capturing the Israeli Hermon outpost.

The 1st Brigade commander suggested, unlike the order established by the command, that the infantry force planned to go up on the ridge trail of the Hermon shoulder would instead head out of Hadar to Mitzpe Shlagim and attack the Syrian alignment from the northeast, with a secondary force attacking the Israeli outpost from the rear and a Golani Reconnaissance Company holding observations at Mitzpe Shlagimas. In light of the 1st Brigade commander's suggestion, Kuti allowed the brigade to present the capture of the Hermon in detail, both as the command had presented it and as the brigade commander's suggested. The 317th Brigade commander was instructed by Kuti to present a detailed plan for capturing the Syrian outpost and the Bends region, as well as two alternatives for operating his brigade if no helicopters were available. The first was to fly the brigade on board helicopters to Mount Dov, advance on foot to capture the Lebanese village Shabaa to advance to capture the Syrian Hermon from there. The second alternative was to advance on foot from Hader through Mitzpe Shlagim and from there to the Syrian Hermon. Kuti instructed the 269th Unit commander, Lt. Col. Giora Zoreah, to present a plan to advance to Mitzpe Shlagim and from there through the Duvdevan ridge to observe the Syrian Hermon and block the road between the two outposts without referring to the plans of the two brigades.

At the end of the orders group in the Northern Command CCP, the brigade commanders began planning their tasks in accordance with the command order. At the same time a few of their staff officers gathered information and conducted professional planning groups with their counterparts in the staff command. Since Kuti decided in the first orders group that the 1st Brigade commander was to present the two plans for his approval, both the brigade's and the command's, the following day he preceded and presented the brigade's plan to capture the Hermon outpost from the north already at noon on the same day. Kuti rejected it. First because the advance route was too steep and difficult, secondly, the 51st Battalion was going to be split up into forces that were too small, thirdly, the problem of the evacuation of wounded to the rear could arise and lastly, a force from the 269th Unit to go up along this route to position itself west of Mitzpe Shlagim had already been planned. Though the two plans seemed reasonable to the brigade commander, and though he preferred his own plan, he agreed with the command plan.

The 1st Brigade commander and his staff officers returned to the brigade headquarters at Hader junction on Saturday night, where the brigade commander convened the force commanders and updated them on the general outlines of the attack plan dictated by the command. The brigade's orders group was established at 06:00 and afterwards it was planned for the brigade commander to return to the Command CCP in Knaan to present his plan for the GOC's approval. After the 317th Brigade commander Col. Haim Nadel finished planning the flights operation with the Air Force representatives and the CIPO, and his staff officers completed their professional coordination with the command staff officers, he presented his brigade's plan to Kuti who approved it around midnight. Then, the 317th Brigade commander and his staff officers rode to the Mahanayim airfield to prepare the brigade orders group that was planned for 10:00 the following morning. The 317th Brigade deputy commander moved the brigade from the assembly area in Kallaa to the Mahanayim airfield.

At 06:15, on the 21st of the month the first orders group to capture the Hermon was carried out at the 1st Brigade headquarters in Hader, after which the brigade commander and the intelligence officer drove to present the brigade's plan to the GOC. At 07:30 a staff update, headed by the GOC took place at the Command CCP, toward the operation. At 08:30 the command second orders group was carried out and the brigade's plans were approved. At 10:15, the Northern Command GOC updated the GHQ Chief of Staff by phone regarding the plans to capture the Hermon, after it was discovered that the GHQ

Chief of Staff could not participate in the second orders group. At the same time an orders group was held for the commanders of the 317th Brigade force in Mahanayim. At 11:00, five CH-53 helicopters out of the six due to arrive landed at the Mahanayim airfield, and the detailed planning of the flights operation began, with the participation of the helicopter teams, representatives of the 317th Unit, officers from the Air Force CCP in the command and representatives of the paratrooper training base.

The Air Force Activity in Preparation for and during Operation Kinuach

The Air Force was assigned tasks in seven areas. First, the bombing of the Syrian forces on the Hermon ridges in preparation for the infantry forces' operation. The second was the flying in of the 317th Paratrooper Brigade forces and landing them north of the Bends Outpost. The third was flying reserve forces according to the battle progress and the evacuation of wounded. The fourth was the interdiction of Syrian ground forces from intervening in the battle, particularly in the region of the Syrian Hermon, and providing an aerial umbrella for the forces. The fifth was to carry out aerial photo sorties over the Hermon for intelligence needs. The sixth was to carry out observation flights to range artillery (AOC) and the seventh was to maintain an aerial relay during the flights operation. The Air Force allocated the 109th Eagle squadron from the 1st wing to provide offensive support for the operation to capture the Hermon. In a joint planning, the Air Force representative in the Command CCP and the Air Force staff established that the attacks would be carried out from a high altitude and the targeted main area would be the airborne forces landing location, namely, the region of the

Bends Outpost and the Syrian Hermon outpost. The Air Force allocated the 118th CH-53 squadron under the command of Lt. Col. Yuval Efrat to both fly the 317th Brigade forces to the Syrian Hermon and the forces and their gear from Mahanayim. The Air Force offensives and aerial photo sorties over the Syrian forces in the Hermon had begun as early as October 20, in preparation for the operation. As preparation of the artillery on the Syrian Hermon, the 109th Squadron carried out five observation sorties (AOC) between 09:00 and 16:45 on October 21.

Artillery Activity in Preparation for and during Operation Kinuach

The command artillery headquarters planned the artillery support for the forces since Operation Kinuach was a command operation. On the 20th of the month, the HAC, Lt. Col. Avraham Bar David, began gathering as many artillery units as he could for the operation without harming the command capacity to continue holding the Syrian and Iraqi forces on the enclave's lines of contact. The HAC assumed that there would be a need to provide artillery support for the forces toward the operation, particularly from high-trajectory weapons, namely, 120mm and 160mm heavy mortars, due to the mountainous terrain. The need for an artillery response to the Syrian reserve forces that might operate from the Arne sector against the 317th Brigade forces in the Syrian Hermon entailed the deployment of 155mm guns, that are the only efficient ones in that region. In the absence of precise data regarding location of the Syrian forces, the HAC assumed that a screen of rolling artillery fire ahead of the forces would be needed, which would necessitate massive amounts of ammunition. As a result, the Northern

Command GOC notified the GHQ Deputy Chief of Staff and Maj. Gen. Rehavam Ze'evi, on the evening of October 18, that receiving additional ammunition was a prerogative for Operation Kinuach to take place.

The artillery order of battle assembled for the operation stood at fourteen batteries and an additional company as follows: the 334th Battalion from the 282nd Artillery Group with two 160mm Self-propelled mortar batteries and a 155mm SPG battery deployed in the Birket Ram region; the 871st Battalion from the 212th Artillery Group with three 120mm Self-propelled mortar batteries deployed north of Hader; the 313th Battalion from the same unit with two 160mm Self-propelled mortar batteries deployed west of Hader; the 343rd Battalion from the Central Command with three 120mm towed batteries deployed in the Neve Ativ region; a 120mm towed mortar company from the 833rd Battalion deployed south of the Bus Lot.[20]

A special operation map with coded words and artillery targets - to make it difficult for the Syrian intelligence to discover intentions and understand the operation maneuvers - was prepared at the Northern Command Headquarters. RAC 1, Lt. Col. Ben Ami Cohen, who received the map in the command orders group on the 20th of the month, added his own artillery targets to it, in accordance with the forces' travel routes, numbering them with two digit numbers according to the HAC's allocation. Some of the controlling routes in the field on the map got two different digits causing the different forces some problems in identifying targets during the battle.

The concentrated artillery and aerial support preparation was taken on by the command, due to the tight schedule and complexity, since it was necessary to coordinate the Air Force activity with artillery operations. Another issue handled by the

20 See Chapter 17.

HAC was the allocation of liaison officers to the 1st Brigade, which unlike the 317th Brigade did not have an organic support headquarters. For this the HAC mobilized liaison officers from the command reserves, officers able to move on foot in the difficult mountainous terrain established for the brigade, as well as to operate a large number of fire units at the same time, to enable the operation of a screen of rolling fire. In order to overcome the difficulty of ranging the targets on the Syrian Hermon, it was decided that an Artillery Corps officer would fly in a 109th Squadron two-seat Sky Hawk and range from the air from the morning of the operation. Five observation flights were planned in coordination with the Air Force between 09:00 and 16:45. After the officer failed to withstand the physical difficulties of the first flight, the other four flights were carry out d by the pilots themselves, but they could not properly range the targets.

It was decided in the command that the concentrated artillery preparations and aerial support preparations would begin at H-hour minus 12 hours. The H-hour was established at 18:00 on October 21. In reality, they only began at 09:00, when the ranging of targets on the Syrian Hermon began, and continued at 10:30 with the attack by the Air Force jets. Two powerful 60-inch artillery floodlights were positioned to blind the Syrians at night, and disorient them in relation to the direction of the offensive. One floodlight was placed on Mount Odem and one in the Mount Dov outpost. The execution of anti-battery fire was under the command responsibility, with 130mm guns and 175mm guns that fired at Syrian SAM batteries, to enable the Air Force jets to operate without disturbance. In total over 13 thousand shells were fired during the operation.

Maneuvers of the 317th Brigade during Operation Kinuach

On October 21 at 07:00 an orders group for the 317th Brigade force commanders was carried out in Mahanayim. Five CH-53 helicopters landed in Mahanayim at 11:00, out of the six due to arrive. Then the detailed planning of the flights operation began, with the participation of the helicopter teams, Air Force CCP officers in the command, the brigades' G3 officers, and the paratrooper training bases' operations officer who showed up with a group of markers. It was decided that the helicopters would fly in a "flight convoy "to the Syrian Hermon. It was meticulously planned and coordinated in an exact time table between helicopters. Reporting points after takeoff were set, wherein the pilots were to report time of arrival, to only afterwards allow the next pair of helicopters' takeoff. The plan ordered takeoffs to begin at 14:00 from Mahanayim followed by an additional pair taking off every ten minutes. Four landing areas between the Bends Outpost and the summit of the Hermon were set as well. While the battalion briefings were taking place and the brigade prepared for the flights from Mahanayim to begin, the command began ranging targets on the Syrian Hermon with the AOC. The command fire plan including Air Force jets bombings and artillery fire was activated to hassle the Syrians on the Hermon. A short time before the beginning of takeoffs the Northern Command GOC arrived in Mahanayim to bless the brigade combatants before they headed for battle. As of 14:00 the CH-53 helicopters moved paratroopers from the brigade two battalions, the brigade field engineering company, the heavy mortars battalion and the brigade commander CCP. Twenty-seven sorties were made in total, and each helicopter carrying out 4–5 rounds. During the brigade flight operation a C-97 Stratocruiser Anak (Giant) aircraft from the 120th Squadron carried out the aerial relay task. Before and during the flight operation, Skyhawk jets carried out about thirty bombing sorties against the Syrian infantry forces on the Syrian Hermon, against armored forces attempting to reinforce it, and on terrorist bases on the slopes of the Hermon. When the operation to fly the paratroopers began, the Syrians launched twenty-four jets toward the Hermon to injure the landing forces. They also attempted to land commando forces to reinforce their outposts on the Hermon with five Mi-8 helicopters, flying with cover of four Mig-17 jets and ten Mig-21 jets. Israeli Air Force interception jets flew toward them and shot down six Mig-21 jets, two Mig-17 jets and two of the helicopters in aerial dogfights. The rest of the helicopters fled from the region. During the day an IAF F-4 Phantom was shot down, and a Skyhawk jet crashed due to a technical malfunction. At 16:31 one of the CH-53 helicopters landed nineteen combatants under the command of an artillery liaison officer directly on the Hermon summit. At 16:33, the paratroopers identified four Syrian tanks departing from the Arne village, going up the Arnon route toward the Syrian Hermon and reported it immediately to the Command CCP. It was decided to land them with 155mm guns fire and launch assault jets toward them.

Within three minutes, an artillery barrage landed on the tanks. At about 17:00 two jets quartets from the 109th squadron attacked the seven tanks advancing from Arne to the Syrian Hermon and the tanks retreated to Arne. At 17:25, at twilight the last two helicopters landed on the Syrian Hermon, thus completing the flight of 626 soldiers and a 120mm mortar barrel with ninety shells. Immediately upon landing, the 120mm mortar barrel was positioned and ready to assist with lighting shells or high explosives as the case might be. At 17:30 the forces buildup was completed and at 17:45, the 317th Brigade began moving toward the Bends Outpost. At about 18:00, an IDF listening in surveillance uncovered that the Syrians had ordered their forces to go up from Arne toward the Syrian Hermon. The 317th Brigade commander was briefed and was told to get ready to face them.

Battle Maneuvers of the 471st Battalion

Company B from the battalion secured the landing area from the initial flight of the first pair of helicopters at 14:19 landing with soldiers from the battalions Company B and the battalion commander's CCP until the end of the flights stage at 17:25. The rest of the company moved south about 200 meters down the ridge in order to clear away from the landing area, which was occasionally bombed by the Syrians. While the company combatants gathered in the field, Company B sent a group of combatants south to exploit the daylight hours and scout the targets and the continued route of progress and to range controlling points in the field. The brigade commander CCP and the brigade support headquarters also advanced south, and at 16:50 the brigade commander reported to the command that he is positioned on the rear slope of elevation point 2269.

The intelligence summary command operation report stated that the 83rd Commando Battalion was deployed in the Syrian Hermon Sector, possibly with another platoon from the 133rd Commando Battalion. Whether there was a force in the Bends region and its order of battle was not ascertained. Information gathered after prisoners' interrogation at a much later point in time, showed that the 183rd Commando Battalion and two companies from the 83rd Commando Battalion were deployed in the Syrian Hermon. Either way, the Company B scouting observed that the main Syrian forces were in the Bends region and on the ridge south of it. Dozens of Syrian soldiers were seen walking around the field. The Company B commander watching the targets noticed that the Syrian soldiers were gathered on the slope going down toward Arne. He was under the impression that their drive to stay and fight was very low. Shortly before nightfall, the Syrians in the Bends Outpost identified the Company B combatants on the front slope to their north and fired several RPG rockets at them. One of them exploded near a platoon commander that was in observation. He was slightly injured and was evacuated to the landing area. Another officer that was with him took command of the platoon.

At 17:45, during the last twilight sun rays, the battalion under the command of Lt. Col. Hezi Shelach began moving at a right flank toward the Bends Outpost. As planned, Company B moved first, followed by the battalion commander CCP. Behind him were: Company A, Company D, the platoon from the field engineering company and the Medical Evacuation Unit at the far end of the column reinforced by an RMCC platoon. The difficulty of moving in a high altitude thin air and challenging terrain added to the desire to avoid unnecessary casualties toward the end of the war determined the forces' extremely slow advance with close artillery assistance.

Company B arrived at 18:15, under the command of Maj. Uzi Tzur, to the gathering point for the attack of the Bends Outpost. Immediately upon its advance squad crossed the road it met with several light weapon barrages, which killed an officer appended to the battalion. Despite the fire, the platoon charged ahead and destroyed the Syrian force defending the place. The Bends Outpost was captured by 19:05. There were five Syrian dead at the end of the short battle. Immediately following, Company B positioned itself in the outpost and prepared to block the route going up from Arne. All the company's anti-tank rocket launchers were gathered in one platoon which positioned in controlling positions along the route. A high explosive charge was detonated and a deep pit opened in the road to block the route for vehicles, an hour later.

Immediately after capturing the Bends the battalion continued its slow advance toward the southern ridge, with Company A, under the command of Captain Shay Lin, leading the way while slowly scanning the field. The battalion CCP advanced in the middle of the company, to control the screen of rolling fire landing near the front of the company's advance force. The battalion moved along a very steep incline for about three hours without firing a single shot.

A little before 22:00 the battalion's advance force reached its second destination. The battalion commander decided that Company A would continue moving in an attack formation, while deploying covers. At 22:25 the fighting over the destination began. The very close range encounter with the Syrians lasted about an hour and a half, at the end of which twelve Syrians soldiers were dead. Company A had no injuries, mainly thanks to the slow and careful fighting. When the fighting ended, the battalion assembled for the continued movement toward the next target. Since Company D had not yet reached the top of the hill and the brigade commander pressed the battalion commander to continue moving, the battalion commander consulted the commander of Company A and decided that in light of the high fighting morale and the combatants' sense of security, the company would continue leading the battalion to the next target. Company D, under the command of Maj. Refael Dgani, left a force to defend the captured target, with the rest of the company moving close to Company A in order to be ready to fight in its place. Company A's advance platoon commander occasionally reported encountering enemy positions, which had been abandoned shortly before his arrival, along the ridges he was advancing along. Voices of escaping

Syrians were heard from the valley to the east all along. At approximately 01:30, the battalion advance force reached its final destination where the battalion's fight ended.

While the 471st Battalion was about to complete its task, the Command CCP received a report at 00:45 from intelligence sources that the Syrians had called up reinforcements to assist the Syrian Hermon outpost. The force, made up of a tank platoon and an infantry company, began moving from the Sabrani region toward Arne. At about 01:30 Company B commander reported that his company, which was ready to block the route going up from Arne, heard approaching vehicles and reported them being about 150 meters away from him. The battalion commander ordered him to hold his fire and wait until they were 50–60 meters away from him. At the same time Deputy Battalion Commander Maj. Yair Ogen was sent in with a force of twenty combatants to reinforce company B. when the head of the Syrian convoy reached the pit formed in the center of the road, the soldiers got off their vehicles and began advancing on foot. At about 01:45 the blocking soldiers fired their small arms and a barrage of anti-tank rockets. They also fired lighting shells from 52mm mortars a few minutes later and saw a convoy of six trucks ahead of them. One of them managed to turn and escape. The Syrian soldiers escaped without returning fire. None of the fired seven anti-tank rockets hit the trucks due to the difficult firing angle. Bodies of two Syrian soldiers were found during the search through the fighting area later. The unit they belonged to was a 120mm mortar battery. There was one mortar on board each truck with ten shells. Had the anti-tank rockets hit the trucks, a fierce explosion would have resulted. At 02:55 the Command CCP received an additional Aman report stating that Syrian reinforcement retraced due encountering the Israeli forces and the artillery that was fired at it.

Battle Maneuvers of the 567th Battalion

Only 240 of the 300 combatants planned from the battalion under the command of Lt. Col. Elisha Shelem, excluding the assisting company, were flown in since the sixth CH-53 helicopter joined the flights operation as late as at 15:15. These forces included the battalion commander's CCP, companies A, B, and C, half of Company D, a platoon from the field engineering company and the Medical Evacuation Unit. At nightfall, the battalion advanced behind the brigade commander's CCP down the ridge to capture the Syrian Hermon outpost which was its primary task, and later serve as a reserve force for the 471st Battalion. After the 471st Battalion captured the Bends Outpost, the brigade's CCP and the 567th Battalion advanced along the road route while waiting for the 471st Battalion to complete its tasks. At 23:30 the Command GOC talked to the 317th Brigade commander, who assessed that he was about to bring the 567th Battalion toward its destination since the 471st Battalion was on the verge of achieving its final destination. Due to dense darkness and difficult terrain along with the commanders' intense fatigue the 567th Battalion commander was unable to ascertain the Syrian outpost with any certainty. The attempt to identify with the use of artillery fire was unsuccessful as well. An argument developed in the field between the brigade commander and the battalion commander, wherein the former claimed that the 471st Battalion had not yet reached the point agreed upon in the brigade's plan. To settle the argument the 471st Battalion commander was called to the brigade commander's CCP. After additional targeting and ranging the Syrian outpost, it was discovered that the 471st Battalion commander was right, and that he did indeed complete his task as planned. At about 02:30 it was discovered that the 567th Battalion's advance force was already near the Syrian helicopter pad, about 400 meters from the outpost fences. The outpost was then identified.

In accordance with the battalion plans, the field engineering platoon under the command of the deputy company commander, Captain Mordechai Cohen, was assigned the task of making two breakthroughs along the road route and on an additional route to the east. The fences would be broken through with pipe bombs, and Company B, under the command of Maj. Amiram Vilnai and his deputy Captain Ran Eshel, would enter the outpost through the gaps. Company C, under the command of Major Yoram Netzer, was planned to follow it to assist in clearing the outpost. Company A, under the command of Captain Dan Kimmel, and Company D, under the command of Captain, Zeevik Shabtay, were in the reserve and were prepared to assist in the capturing of the outpost. At 02:58, the battalion commander reported that he was at the assembly point for the offensive. No shots were fired from the outpost until then. The battalion commander assumed that it was abandoned already. Therefore, he ordered the Company B commander to enter with through the gate of the outpost with his company and carefully scan it without firing. The outpost was indeed abandoned. At 03:25, the 567th Battalion commander reported that he held the destination, and instructed his men to organize for defense in the existing was at his target and ordered his people to organize for defense in the existing positions.

At about 05:30, the Northern Command learned that the Golani Brigade was waging a fierce battle on hill 2072 and had suffered many wounded. The command examined the possibility of reinforcing it with the command reserve force waiting in Mahanayim, or with forces now on the Syrian Hermon. At 05:42, Kuti spoke with the 317th Brigade commander and updated him that the 1st Brigade was having difficulties and explained the location of its forces. He instructed him to move from the Syrian outpost to the upper ski lift station and updated him that a force from the 269th Unit was west of Mitzpe Shlagim. Kuti warned him of the Syrian forces between the Israeli outpost and the Syrian Hermon and instructed him to advance very carefully. Kuti instructed him to establish a radio connection with the 1st Brigade's G3 officer, who had taken command after the brigade commander was injured. Immediately afterwards, Kuti updated the 1st Brigade's G3 officer that a force from the 317th Brigade was ordered to move to the upper ski lift station to join the brigade's reconnaissance unit.

At 05:58, the GOC ordered to fly in the command reserves from Mahanayim to the upper ski lift station in order to assist the 1st Brigade. Maj. Yoni Netanyahu, deputy commander of the 269th Unit commanding the force at Mitzpe Shlagim, was ordered to transfer to the 317th Brigade radio network. At 06:08, Kuti briefed the 317th Brigade deputy commander, Lt. Col. Mara El-Ami, commander of the Northern Command Reserves, about the situation of the 1st Brigade. Kuti ordered him to fly in with the two companies to the lower ski lift station and from there go up along the road route through the Tank Bend to join up with the 1st Brigade's G3 officer and take command of the battle. He updated him that he had instructed the 317th Brigade to send a force from the Syrian Hermon to the upper ski lift station. At approximately 06:00, the 567th Battalion commander was ordered by the 317th Brigade commander to advance with two companies, one from his battalion and one from the 471st Battalion, to assist the 1st Brigade.

The battalion commander went up to an observation point in the Syrian outpost and examined the movement route. At approximately 06:20, the battalion commander instructed Yoni Netanyahu over the radio to activate a smoke grenade for identification since he intended to range the controlling points on the route with 120mm mortars and wished to know where the 269th force was. Once his location was identified, the 567th Battalion

Artillery liaison officer began ranging source targets along the planned route. Simultaneously, the combatants of the two companies began preparing for a day battle in the mountainous terrain. Their switching their "Uzi" sub-machine guns with the firearms of the other companies' combatants delayed their departure. In the meantime, the battalion commander ordered the field engineering company deputy company commander to create a space in the minefield that surrounded the outpost. During the breakthrough one of the soldiers from the bomb disposal unit stepped on an anti-personnel mine and triggered it off. The deputy company commander standing next to him was injured in the explosion along with him. They were rescued by their friends and the Medical Evacuation Unit in the field treated them.

At about 06:45, the 567th Battalion commander force began moving toward the Israeli Hermon. The movement through rocky terrain was incredibly grueling and the combatants were exhausted. After advancing about two kilometers southeast the force reached elevation point 2170 at 08:00. The advance was aided by the firing of 120mm mortars on the controlling domes ahead for fear that they were occupied by Syrian soldiers. Half an hour earlier observations by the 269th Unit and the 567th Battalion from the Syrian Hermon and the its top identified Syrian soldiers fleeing from the Hermon shoulder east and north through the ("Sinking Hole") Bolaan Valley toward Mitzpe Shlagim on their way to the Syrian Hermon, toward Arne or down the Beit Jann River. At first the fleeing forces encountered the 269th Unit soldiers, who fired at them and engaged them in long distance battles. Some surrendered and some continued fighting until they were killed. At 08:10 small arms fire from a 500 meter range was aimed at the 567th Battalion Commander force. A battle with the fleeing Syrians ensued while the combatants continued advancing toward the upper ski lift station.

The 1st Brigade battle had been won and the scanning of the ridge leading up to the Israeli outpost was being scanned at about 08:15. The landing of the command reserve force at the Bus Lot was completed at that time and it began advancing on board the 51st Battalion half-tracks toward the upper ski lift station. At the same time the 567th Battalion commander force was drawing nearer the upper ski lift station from the north. It was, eventually, unnecessary to bring in the 317th Brigade combatants to participate in capturing the Hermon shoulder and the Israeli outpost. At 10:03 Kuti instructed the 567th Battalion commander to return to the Syrian outpost while establishing radio contact with the 317th Brigade commander. The battalion commander was still exchanging fire with fleeing Syrians. He requested and was granted an approval to continue and engage them. Kuti Adam instructed the 317th Brigade deputy commander to take responsibility over the sector from the Israeli outpost to the Tank Bend once the takeover of the outpost was completed. He was to resume command with the two companies he came with along with the 269th force located at Mitzpe Shlagim and on the Duvdevan ridge. When the Golani combatants entered the outpost at about 10:35 and raised the national flag along the Golani flag from its rooftop, the paratroopers stood near the gates of the outpost and along the ridge and witnessed the moving scene.

The 567th Battalion commander force came across many fleeing Syrian soldiers on the Hermon shoulder on his way back to the Syrian outpost. Some were killed in the fire exchange and some were taken prisoner. The reserve paratroopers were near total exhaustion after over 30 hours of continuous activity in a challenging rocky terrain and constant fighting without food or water. A combatant was killed in one of the encounters with the Syrians. Only in the late afternoon hours did the force return to the Syrian outpost to complete its fighting.

Battle Results

The 317th Brigade met all its assigned tasks capturing the Syrian Hermon outpost, the Bends Outpost, and the summit of the Hermon. One combatant was killed during the capture of the Bends Outpost and one was killed in battle with retreating Syrians south of the Syrian outpost. Two combatants were injured during the landing of the forces and two combatants were injured during the breaking through the mine filed in the Syrian Hermon outpost. The Syrian had six killed in the Bends Outpost and eighteen killed between the Bends Outpost and the Syrian Hermon. Fifteen Syrians escaped the Israeli Hermon and were killed in battle south of the Syrian Hermon. Seventeen Syrians were taken prisoner.

The 1st Brigade Maneuvers in Operation Kinuach

In the operational plan that crystallized during the brief period of time that the brigade had for the battle procedure, the 51st Battalion, under the command of Maj. Yehuda (Yudk'a) Peled, was made up of the companies A, B, C; the assisting company; the Medical Evacuation Unit; the artillery liaison officer, and frontal observation officer. All were instructed to head out of Majdal Shams at the H-hour and advance up the Hermon shoulder along two routes with a screen of rolling fire. Company A, under the command of the deputy battalion commander and an additions frontal observation officer, were to advance in a right flank from Majdal Shams toward elevation point 1802, be ready to capture the Tank Bend or go down north of hill 12 to assist the main force. Company B was to lead up the ridge, capture hill 17 and be prepared to capture hill

19. Company C was to follow Company B and be prepared to capture hill 10 at elevation point 1614 or 12 and later capture hill 16 at elevation point 2072. It was to cover hill 17 from hill 16 and assist Company B in capturing it. Following its passage, Company B was to capture the upper ski lift station. In the final stage, Company A was to capture the Hermon outpost. The assisting company was to split into a battalion reserve force of forty combatants and an evacuation force with thirty combatants, mainly from the RCLR platoon.

The 69th Reconnaissance Company, under the command of Captain Shemaryahu Vinik—with six combat teams of twelve combatants each under the command of an officer that was reinforced by a platoon from the 17th Battalion, a reduced Medical Evacuation Unit and a frontal observation officer—was assigned the task of advancing toward the Bus Lot on half-tracks, from there advance on foot, at 19:00, through the Mann valley and ridge 1640 toward the lower ski lift station, capture it and place a security force. The rest of the company was to climb up toward elevation point 2012 and be ready to assist in the capture of the upper ski lift station or the Hermon outpost from the northwest, or alternatively join up with the 269th Unit force west of Mitzpe Shlagim.

A mechanized armored battalion team No. 8, led by Maj. David Katz, was assigned the task of heading out at 21:00 from the Mas'ade forest, move toward the Bus Lot, open the road to the lower ski lift station and then open the road to the upper ski lift station. The armored battalion team was made up of six tanks from the 74th Battalion of the 188th Brigade; a reduced infantry Company A from the 17th Battalion; an infantry company from the staff of brigade Training Base No. 1; a field engineering platoon from the 36th Division 641st Reserve Field Engineering Battalion on board three half-tracks, two bulldozer tanks, a D-9 bulldozer; a Medical Evacuation Unit and an evacuation tank from the 36th Division; two 81mm mortars on half-tracks (model C); a team of prisoner interrogators from the 154th Unit on a half-track; a casualty identification team from the military rabbinate, and a bomb disposal team and a frontal observation officer. Three infantry forces of six combatants each, under the command of a company commander from the staff of the brigade Training Base No. 1, were to advance in front of the tanks, starting from the Bus Lot, to expose possible ambushes, mines and traps along the road route. The force was to be on the alert to assist the capture of the upper ski lift station and the Israeli outpost. The Banit force made up of fifteen combatants on board five BTR-152 APCs was planned to assist in the transfer of wounded from the battlefield to the RMCC located at Birket Ram.

The 17th Battalion, made up of Company D and the assisting company, under the command of Lt. Gen. Gidon Hameiri was assigned the task of positioning four blockings on the Hermon slopes to strike the fleeing Syrians from the Hermon towards Mazraat Beit Jann. These blockings were to be positioned at the following locations: the Pitma outpost 2,500 meters west of Hader; elevation point 1659 nicknamed *Hamasor* ("the Saw") 2,500 meters northwest of Hader; elevation point 1615 2,500 meters north-northwest of Hader and a Syrian outpost 2,500 meters northeast of Hader. Three 81mm mortars were to be placed in the village itself, with two infantry alert teams, an RCLR squad and the battalion commander's CCP.

The "floodlight" force—made up of two 60-inch Artillery Corps floodlights positioned on Mount Odem and Mount Dov—was assigned the task of lighting the operation sector in order to blind the Syrians and assist Israeli forces in identifying their targets. The artillery aid in the operation, under command's responsibility, was based on: concentrating artillery preparation from H minus 12; allocating direct artillery support to the 51st Battalion and the reconnaissance company throughout the operation and provide a screen of rolling fire ahead of the forces throughout the movement up both when they draw near their targets and during the fighting over them. In the morning hours three 81mm mortars from the 17th Battalion's assisting company began firing from the Hader region at the Israeli Hermon outpost to distract the Syrians. The last day light hours were devoted to final briefings and talks with the combatants. At approximately 16:00—17:00, the brigade commander walked among his soldiers and stressed the importance of capturing the Hermon in light of the impending ceasefire. The command allocated artillery liaison officers and frontal observation officers for the 1st Brigade that did not have an organic assisting headquarters. They joined the fighting units three hours prior to heading for battle. Not having enough time to study the terrain several incidents of wrong firing during the advance occurred.

Battle Maneuvers of the 51st Battalion

At 17:15 the 51st Battalion and the brigade commander CCP headed out of the Mas'ade forest on board half-tracks toward Majdal Shams. At 18:00, the 51st Battalion Company A and CCP of Deputy Battalion Commander Maj. Zion Zluf began going up on foot from Majdal Shams to the Hermon along a separate route. The rest of the battalion with the brigade CCP began advancing on foot up the Hermon shoulder at 18:40. The force of the deputy battalion commander climbed up the steep slopes of the Hermon shoulder toward elevation point 1802, marked on the field organization map as Target 13. The frontal observation officer operated the 160mm Self-propelled mortar battery and the 120mm Self-propelled mortar battery at his disposal in a screen of rolling fire. At the same time, the rest of the battalion advanced while its artillery liaison officer, Lt. Herzl Cohen, operated the three batteries at his disposal in the same manner.

At about 21:40, when the force of the deputy battalion commander was about one kilometer south of Target 13, and the rest of the battalion was still in the area of Target 11—about six to eight phosphorus shells fired from a 120mm mortar landed within the battalion column. Luckily, no one was injured. It was unclear whether these were Syrian shells or misfired Israeli shells. Therefore, the RAC ordered all frontal observation officers to cease fire for a few minutes. It turned out to be an erroneous firing by one of the Israeli batteries. Upon fire renewal, several phosphorus shells were fired at Target 13 and the deputy battalion commander force went up to the target free of resistance. The force went on from there, advanced, reached the Tank Bend and reported Target 14 (Tank Bend) was in their hands and it was waiting to join up with the rest of the battalion at 23:28.

Moving up the ridge on foot, the 51st Battalion main force was led by Company B as the advance force, with the battalion commander's CCP immediately behind it. The brigade commander's CCP moved behind Company C, and the brigade's secondary CCP moved at the end of the column under the command of the brigade's operations officer. Half an hour later, when the advance force reached the area of Target 3, the battalion artillery liaison officer began operating the screen of rolling fire. Fire was also aimed at Mount Habushit which is the ridge between the upper and lower ski lift stations. The artillery teams' exhaustion after over two weeks of nonstop firing caused several incidents of misfiring. At 21:40, when the battalion commander CCP was in the area of Target 11, one of the 335th Battalion 120mm Self-propelled mortar batteries fired from the

Hader region, apparently aimed at an old target by mistake. Therefore, he stopped employing it until the end of the battle. When the mechanized column reached the lower ski lift station at about 01:00, nearly four stray shells landed there, as well.

As mentioned before, the different target numbering on the brigade and the command maps, for organizing the field, seemed to have caused firing mistakes. This fact made the brigade commander divert the fire toward the outpost itself and toward Target 17 to only later bring it closer to hill 16. This was, eventually, the reason that no artillery fire was directed at the main target—hill 16—before it was reached by Company C. The battalion commander, who thought the artillery fire was excessive and feared there would be no ammunition left for the fighting stage, instructed the disagreeing artillery liaison officer to slow down the fire rate. The battalion advance was very slow, both due to the malfunctions that happened during the operation of artillery fire, and due to the careful movement of the advance company, since it was unclear where the front Syrian positions were. In seven hours, the battalion had moved through the four kilometers from the crossroads of the road and the path and up to the Tank Bend. It was a steep ridge ascending from 1,200 to 1,860 meters and was characterized by giant boulders, steep cliffs, and deep lengthwise valleys cutting through it. It reached and joined the deputy battalion commander's force that was waiting there at 01:00.

After the battalion commander short briefing to the company commanders regarding the order of movement ahead, at about 01:30, Company C, under the command of Lt. Yigal Paso, began moving toward hill 2072. The battalion commander CCP moved behind it. Company B, the deputy battalion commander CCP, Company A, the brigade commander CCP, the battalion reserve force, the wounded evacuation force, the Medical Evacuation Unit and the brigade secondary CCP were still waiting at the

Tank Bend. The company moved on the ridgeline up the steep slope toward hill 2072 with two platoons in front and a reserve platoon in the back. The ascent was difficult and very slow. At this stage the floodlights, which had lit hill 2072, were stopped. The very dark night limited sight to a few dozen meters at best. The thousand meters from the Tank Bend to near the top took the company about 45 minutes to cross. The slow advance and the fear of entering combat during daylight hours worried the brigade commander, who continually checked the advance rate with the battalion commander over the radio.

At that time, the brigade reconnaissance unit was near elevation point 2012—about a kilometer and a half north of the upper ski lift station—and the mechanized column had already moved 500 meters up the road from the lower ski lift station. The 269th Unit force at Mitzpe Shlagim joined the brigade communications network. The brigade commander asked the commander of the force, Maj. Yoni Netanyahu, what was going on in the field. Yoni answered that everything had been quiet during the day and no enemy movements had been identified. At 01:42, the brigade commander asked him to open a MAG machine gun fire toward the Israeli outpost for distraction, but Netanyahu said he was out of effective firing range being about 1,800 meters away from the Israeli outpost. Despite their discussion the force did not carry out the shooting, eventually. The brigade commander ordered him to remain on the northern slope of Mitzpe Shlagim so he wouldn't get hit by the 51st Battalion expected firing.

At 02:38, Company C combatants reached the edge of the sector defended by 2nd Company of the Syrian 82nd Battalion on hill 16. The company sector stretched from the western slopes of the hill, the hilltop, and to its eastern slopes. This company was reinforced by soldiers from the 1st and 2nd Platoons of the 133rd Commando Battalion 3rd Company that deployed on the top and western slopes of hill 2072. The company sector also held a B-10 RCLR placed on the western slope and directed at the road leading from the Tank Bend to the upper ski lift station. The Syrians were deployed in positions inside rock clusters and controlled the area effectively. They also built depth positions controlling the forward ones. Most of the positions in this sector were unmarked in the decoded aerial photograph given to the commanders of the 51st Battalion and the reconnaissance company on the eve of the battle. Hill sixteen was known to be the main target on the way to the Hermon since the October 8 attempt and it was precisely the one that did not get artillery fire before contact. Company C began storming it and many commanders and combatants were hit immediately. The battalion commander sent a combat team from Company A at the onslaught of the battle to assist the company's fighting later to be followed by two teams from the assisting company. A team from Company B also assisted evacuating the wounded at a later stage.

While a bloody short range battle was raging on hill 16, the battalion commander decided to change the task of Company B which was meant to storm hill 17. At 03:15, he called the deputy company commander, Lt. Eliezer Michaeli, the company commander's stand-in, and instructed him to advance in a left flank on the slopes of hill 16 and position himself on hill 19 which was about 800 meters east of the upper ski lift station and north of the access road to the Israeli outpost. The battalion commander briefed him out in the field on a map using a flashlight. Once the task was clear to him, he went on his way at about 04:00. On the way the deputy company commander placed one team as a suppressive fire unit and left another team to assist Company C in evacuating its injured. Due to a navigation mistake the deputy company commander began climbing up in a left flank on hill 24, west of the road between the Tank Bend and the upper ski lift station at around 05:00. It was identified by the deputy company commander, in the morning dim light, when the mechanized column had already passed the Tank Bend and began moving north toward the upper ski lift station. Thinking he was north of the road and not west of it, where he actually was, he called the deputy battalion commander on the battalion radio network and asked him to notify the mechanized column not to fire at him.

The deputy battalion commander was busy evacuating Company C's wounded and therefore did not update the mechanized column commander or take notice of the deputy company commander's mistake of the continued climbing up hill 24 from the southwest. At about 05:20, men from the mechanized column, who were standing on the road between the Tank Bend and the upper ski lift station, identified the Company B combatants mistaking them for Syrian soldiers, opened small arms fire at them and injuring three combatants. Most of the company did not take part in the battle and three combatants were wounded by Israeli forces' fire due to the deputy company commander's navigation error. The clarification with the deputy company commander regarding his position, and his demands to cease fire against him and evacuate the wounded kept the radio networks of the battalion and brigade busy and badly hindered the critical stages of the battle.

At 03:55, the 51st Battalion commander updated Company A commander Lt. Shuki Viater over the radio with a new task assigned to him. He was instructed to outflank hill 16 from the right while going down the slope, to capture the two folds east of hill 16 from in south to north direction. When the Company A commander asked whether a left flank with artillery cover attack was possible the battalion commander said that the Syrians were dug in their positions and trenches and all frontal attack attempts by Company C had failed. The battalion commander instructed the assisting company commander, Lt. Mickey Mossberg, that once Company A shifted right he was to advance up the hill and take the Medical Evacuation Unit and wounded evacuation force with him in order to be ready to assist Company A or Company C. While the commander of Company A studied his new task, the artillery liaison officer and RAC were busy ranging the folds east of hill 16 again as it was the battalion commander's condition for Company A to start an offensive toward them. The ranging only ended at 04:25 which was the time the battalion commander had ordered Company A commander to advance he updated him that artillery shells were falling on hill 17 and east of it. If he believed it was endangering him he was to request to stop fire before storming.

At 04:34, A company commander reported that he was on the move. The deputy battalion commander joined in with his command unit. The quick advance was not detected by the Syrians. During the activity echoes of Company C's battle on hill 16 could be heard from the left. Six minutes later the Company A commander asked the battalion commander to instruct the artillery liaison officer to land fire on the front slope where he was supposed to go up the hill in addition to the back slope. The battalion commander did not get his meaning since the artillery fire seemed to him to be on target from his position on the southeastern slopes of hill 16. Since the battalion commander was unsure whether the company commander was indeed about to go up the right fold, he instructed the company commander, in addition to the fold east of hill 16, to also go up the next two folds as well. At about 04:45, the company commander approved that he was sending two teams to every fold. The battalion commander was still uneasy and so he warned the company commander once again to watch out for the Syrian positions on the eastern slope of hill 16. The battalion commander instructed him to place "a formidable fire base that would be ready to fire in a half to the left angle toward these positions." The deputy battalion commander placed the company's suppressive force before the battalion commander called him back to hill 16 to handle the evacuation of the wounded from before dawn.

While Company A moved toward the assembly point, the battalion commander instructed the team under the command of Company C's 3rd platoon commander—which was near the battalion commander's CCP—to place a suppressive force toward two Syrian positions on the southeastern slope of hill 16 and storm them, where fierce fire was constantly under way. The platoon commander positioned a suppressive force e storming ahead under its cover. It took only a short while for most of the team members to be hit including the platoon commander. Sometime afterwards, the battalion commander instructed the battalion's operations officer, Lt. Ran Ginosar, to move a little east with two MAG machine gun operators from the 3rd platoon commander team and employ suppressive fire toward the western slopes of the folds—which Company A was about to storm—in order to allow it to reach the assembly point without being discovered.

At this stage, the artillery liaison officer notified the battalion commander that he was beginning to engage the seven artillery batteries at his disposal with heavy fire on Target 17, while constantly advancing the fire west to the eastern slope of hill 16. He continued doing so until shrapnel began falling on the battalion commander CCP. The RAC, who was near the brigade commander CCP on the southeastern slope of hill 16 under heavy small arms fire, as well, decided to halt the fire and ask each fire unit to shoot control shells to see where each unit was firing. Only then did he renew fire. Therefore, the artillery liaison officer ceased fire and began operating the batteries one at a time while checking data and correcting it. When all the batteries were ready to renew their accurate fire, the artillery liaison officer was killed. Fire failed to renew. The battalion commander believed the artillery liaison officer had ceased fire in accordance with the plan. It took him a few minutes to find out that the artillery liaison officer had been killed. At about that time, one of the battalion commander's radio operators was killed as well and the battalion communications officer was wounded and taken to the Medical Evacuation Unit.

At 04:50, Company A reached the assembly point. The company commander gathered the platoon commanders, identified their location for them, and quickly briefed them before the storming. The company commanders did not know they were about to storm the center of the Syrian alignment, which had about thirty-five rocky positions where the 82nd Paratrooper Battalion's 3rd company was deployed, reinforced by the 133rd Commando Battalion's 3rd platoon. The sector also held a B-10 RCLR. The 82nd Battalion commander CCP was located several hundred meters east of hill 17, near the outpost helicopter pad. He and his staff officers escaped the sector before dawn.

At the assembly point, the company commander readied his company for storming in a two platoon formation in front and one in the back, with the company commander CCP in the center. The company began moving north, up the folds, passing abandoned Syrian positions, and began going up into a small geological dent in the ground which the Syrians planned as a killing field since it was surrounded by positions from the west, north, and east. Going up from the geological dent north toward the ridgeline the company commander decided to start storming with fire up the fold toward the Syrian positions. When the storming began the Syrians opened heavy fire against them from the southwest and northwest. The first barrage of fire hit most of the combatants including the company commander. The rear platoon soldiers, moving in the back, attempted to line up toward the front but accurate fire stopped their advance and they took cover between the rocks. From this point to the end of the battle the company stopped fighting excluding a few individual attempts to silence the sources of fire and evacuate the wounded, at about 08:45. The connection with the company was severed toward the end of the battle except for a few calls by combatants and officers that occasionally got through on the radio network and asked for assistance in evacuating the wounded.

Sixteen commanders and soldiers were killed in Company A's fighting, including the company commander, who was critically wounded at the beginning of the battle. His men could not evacuate him until the end of the battle. He died of his wounds in the hospital two weeks later. Nine commanders and combatants were wounded.

When the deputy battalion commander began returning to hill 16 he heard the battalion commander request the brigade commander to examine the possibility of sending tanks up to hill 16. Though he was not ordered to do so, he acted following the "Call of Battle" and went down with his CCP toward the Tank Bend and attempted to bring the tanks up the steep incline. On his way down, he met the commander of the mechanized column slowly advancing on foot toward hill 16 with a reduced company from the 17th Battalion and updated him of the difficult situation of the battalion. When the deputy battalion commander reached the bend, he saw that the tanks had already passed him by on their way to the upper ski lift station, and the half-tracks were following them without the possibility of turning back. At that point many wounded were gathered in the Tank Bend and the deputy battalion commander began handling the transportation of vehicles to take the wounded down to the RMCC.

Battle Maneuvers of the 69th Reconnaissance Company

The brigade's reconnaissance company left the Mas'ade woods at 17:30 and moved behind the 51st Battalion. Some of the combatants were on board half-tracks and some on board buses. At about 19:00, the company went down from the Bus Lot to the Mann valley on foot and from there climbed up to the Yifat observation point, moving on the eastern slopes of the Namneman ridge. The artillery at its disposal was not employed yet so as not to expose the route of progress at this stage. The observation post was found to be abandoned and the reconnaissance unit advanced east slowly on the Arar fold on both sides of the narrow road leading to the lower ski lift station, with the frontal observation officer directing the two mortar batteries at his disposal toward the region of the lower ski lift station. The artillery fire was stopped at about 22:30, a short while before the advance force reached the hill controlling the lower ski lift station. After scouting the lower ski lift station structures from it with night vision devices the combatants went down there to scan the place. Some of the outpost's cottages caught fire due to the artillery fire. Small arms ammunition, left there by Israeli forces when they abandoned the place at dawn October 7, were exploding occasionally. For fear of being hit by the exploding ammunition the scan was delayed. When it was discovered that the area was deserted, a team under the command of the reconnaissance unit deputy commander was left there.

At about 24:00, the reconnaissance company commander, Captain Vinik, reported to the brigade commander that the place was empty and began climbing toward elevation point 2012, which he reached at 01:15. No artillery fire was employed during the climb. Upon reaching the top he was instructed to advance with his men east of the Duvdevan ridgeline and position himself at a distance of about 1,200 meters north of the upper ski lift station. At 02:38, when the 51st Battalion Company C encountered the Syrian alignment on hill 16, and the brigade commander was at first unsure where the shooting was coming from, he called Vinik up over the radio and asked him to identify the source of fire. Vinik responded that it sounded like from the south to him. He was ordered to try and observe the field and locate the source of the shooting, but the reconnaissance company did not have eye contact with the targets of the 51st Battalion. At 03:20, nearly an hour later, the brigade commander ordered Vinik to advance quickly toward the upper ski lift station and capture it, with the border between his sector and the 51st Battalion's established on the road leading to the Israeli outpost. The reconnaissance company commander and his subordinates did not know the size of the Syrian force facing them nor its exact deployment, though, from the partially decoded aerial photograph they received, they should have been aware of an alignment of eleven rocky posts constructed 200 meters south of the upper ski lift station on both sides of the road, most of which were to the west on the slope below the road. There were, actually, additional positions in the field which were not marked during the decoding, though they could clearly be seen on the aerial photograph.

Opposite the reconnaissance unit was a blocking force from the Syrian 82nd Paratrooper Battalion reduced Company A, under the company commander, which included a paratrooper platoon, a B-10 RCLR team, a Goryunov machine gun team and two field engineering soldiers which added up to about twenty-eight combatants. These were deployed south of the upper ski lift station. The majority of the force was deployed west of the road, and one squadron deployed east, above the road bend. The Syrians were deployed on the slopes under the road bends in personal positions built by piling rocks between the giant boulders. The RCLR team was placed in a firing position inside a dugout prepared by the Israeli postal service east of the road. On the night of October 9–10, the Syrian 133rd Commando Battalion company three was sent down from the Hermon outpost to reinforce the 82nd Battalion on the Hermon shoulder. The battalion staff chief, who joined the company, deployed with his CCP alongside the blocking force. Another squad from the 133rd Battalion was, apparently, positioned on the shoulder between hill 2072 and the upper ski lift station.

At about 04:00, the reconnaissance company advance force reached the top controlling the upper ski lift station from the north. The commander of the reconnaissance company left the main force on the summit and advanced with his CCP and two teams down the ridge where he could closely observe the structures of the ski lift station, which was under construction. The commanders scouted the region with night vision devices but no movement was observed. Then two teams positioned themselves in close cover, one east of the ski lift station and one west of it, and a third team prepared to head down and scan the trenches north of the road, those that were dug in order to lay foundations for the station structure. Suddenly a shot was fired from the southern top of the ski lift structure. Since the source of shooting was not identified and Vinik was, apparently, unsure of the location of the 51st Battalion forces—he asked the brigade commander to fire a green flare for identification. However, though the brigade commander ordered the 51st Battalion commander to fire a green flare to mark the western border of his sector, it didn't happen and, eventually, at 04:05 the brigade commander himself fired a green flare, which Vinik identified.

At approximately 04:15, the third team quickly scanned the trenches of the ski lift structure and found nothing. At this stage it seems, Vinik wanted to scan the road leading from the upper ski lift station to the Tank Bend to be ready for movement along this route when he was asked to assist the 51st Battalion. He ordered two senior teams to go up and scan the rocky south peak of the ski lift station, and he himself began moving down the road leading another team. When the senior team began its gradual climb up to the top, they were fired at from the RCLR position. The combatants threw phosphorous grenades into the dugout, stormed up the hill, and scanned the area behind them, without encountering any Syrians. At the same time Vinik, who was marching on the road, was fired at from the dugout. He managed to fire a few bullets in return before falling down, bleeding profusely. The Syrians, who were unharmed, remained in their position and hit the radio operator and medic who attempted to rescue their commander. One of the combatants fired an anti-tank rifle grenade into the RCLR position, then another phosphorous grenade was tossed toward it and it turned silent. The three wounded were dragged to the rear, placed under a cliff and treated by the doctor and medics. At dawn, the sniping increased from the Syrian positions on the western slopes of hill 16 at the reconnaissance company and another combatant was killed. The reconnaissance company suffered friendly fire from Israeli forces on the slopes of hill 16 and from the mechanized column, as well. From the moment that the reconnaissance company commander was hit until about 09:00, the rest of the reconnaissance company officers did not initiate any action, excluding one attempt at 04:48, following the brigade commander instruction, to move from the upper ski lift station east and reach hill 16 from the north. Likewise, they did not attempt to evacuate the wounded to the lower ski lift station along the ascent route. In fact, the reconnaissance company did not contribute to winning the battle. Their team commanders' calls over the radio and those of the commander who assumed command over the reconnaissance company demanding the evacuation of the wounded and the ceasing of the friendly fire actually interrupted the brigade's G3 officer while he was conducting the battle. In the battle over the upper ski lift station the reconnaissance company lost four combatants, including their.

The Mechanized Column Fighting

At 20:07, the brigade commander ordered the commander of the mechanized column to start moving from Mas'ade. They arrived at the Bus Lot where they remained at about 21:40. At 23:05, the column began advancing toward the lower ski lift station. Fifty meters ahead of it, the combatants from the staff of 1st Brigade training base advanced on the road and its shoulders, slowly scanning for traps or mines. The force arrived without delays to the south of the ski lift station structures a short while past midnight and met the reconnaissance company force securing the area. Brig. Gen. Kuti Adam followed the advance of the brigade in the Command CCP and at 00:51 ordered the 1st Brigade commander not to rush pushing the mechanized column from the lower ski lift station. Therefore, the force waited in place for another hour. The column had already advanced about 500 meters up the road to the Tank Bend without encountering anything unusual. Then the brigade commander ordered it to slow its advance pace and stop when it reached the first channel—the "Quarry" bends—until the 51st Battalion completed capturing the ridge between the Tank Bend and hill 16. The brigade training base combatants advanced from the lower ski lift station, with one infantry unit headed by a company commander advancing on the road. A flank security unit headed by another company commander advanced on the slope to the left, above the road. A unit headed by a third company commander advanced on the slope to the right, below the road. The flanking units advanced slowly on the steep slopes, due to the difficult terrain. At 02:05, the brigade commander approved that the column reach the Tank Bend Several minutes later, anti-vehicle mines laid out across the road and covered in dirt were revealed in the Quarry Bend. The field engineering force exposed them and left them exposed on the left shoulder of the road. An additional string of mines was discovered and cleared away on the road before the Tank Bend When the route opened at 03:14 the column continued its advance.

At 03:15, the brigade commander updated the commander of the column over the radio that the 51st Battalion was fighting over its first target and instructed him to be ready to arrive at hill 16 with one infantry company. The mechanized column continued advancing but at about 03:30, when its lead almost reached the Tank Bend, one of the field engineering force half-tracks moving behind the four tanks triggered a landmine that had been exposed and placed on the road side at the "Quarry" bend. The commander of the column instructed the bulldozer advancing behind the command APC to turn back and clear the route of the damaged half-track to the side of the road. At 03:32, the brigade commander ordered Maj. Katz to go up with a company on foot toward hill 16 and join up with him while his deputy continued advancing on the road. Katz ordered the 17th Battalion reduced Company A to get off the half-tracks and advance on foot with him from the Tank Bend toward hill 16. The tedious and slow advance of the CCP and the company enabled them to reach the brigade commander CCP at around 05:00. The brigade commander updated Katz that the 51st Battalion was stuck in front and that he had to assist the takeover of hill 16. The brigade commander was injured a few minutes later and was taken from the field. Katz did not have a clear picture of the battle but believed that the first priority was to assist in the evacuation of the 51st Battalion wounded, therefore, he ordered the deputy company commander to organize two suppressive fire teams, each led by a platoon commander. One suppressive fire team was sent to capture cover positions toward the folds east of hill 16, while the other force was sent to carry out the same task in the southwestern flank of hill 16. He thought that the cover provided by these fire bases would keep the Syrians in their positions and would allow the evacuation of the wounded to the rear. Anyone not in these teams remained behind cover.

The Syrian positions could not be seen even in the morning light. They continued sending accurate fire. The location of the 51st Battalion combatants was not entirely clear either. The suppressive fire teams began positioning themselves, under heavy Syrian fire, in front and within minutes five soldiers were killed, including one of the platoon commanders, and six were wounded. The suppressive fire team sent at about 05:20 to the southwestern flank of hill 16 deployed to the left of the team commanded by the 51st Battalion mortar platoon commander and began firing in the estimated direction of the Syrians. The territory between the Syrians and them was filled with 51st Battalion soldiers that had been wounded or killed in the previous waves of attack. Many continued shouting: "Golani! Help! Don't shoot!" It seems this force fired at the reconnaissance company combatants positioned on the upper ski lift station by mistake, mainly because the 17th Battalion combatants did not have a clear picture of the battle situation, did not know where the Syrians were positioned and where the reconnaissance company was. From about 05:15—when the two company suppressive fire teams assumed their advance toward the ridgeline while firing at the Syrian alignments and assisting the evacuation of the 51st Battalion wounded and their own to the rear—no offensive action was carried out until 08:15.

Battles—Staff Company from the 1st Brigade Training Base and the Tank Force from the 74th Battalion

The company—led by the brigade training base deputy commander, Captain Eitan Yaron, who served as deputy commander of the mechanized column as well—was made up the staff of three advanced training companies and that of the training staff. The 74th Battalion Tank Force under the command of Deputy Battalion Commander Maj. Yosef Nissim was made up of six upgraded "Shot" Centurion tanks. At about 04:00 the column lead passed the Tank Bend and advanced toward the upper ski lift station. The bulldozer tank moved at the head of the column followed by the field engineering half-track and a pair of tanks. The first tank was commanded by a platoon commander and the second by the deputy brigade commander. The infantry team led by a company commander advanced on the right-hand slope above the road, advancing in a rear column due to the steep terrain. A team headed by a second company commander advanced on the road itself, ahead of the bulldozer tank. A team headed by a third company commander advanced a little to the back on the left-hand side under the road.

The brigade commander called Captain Yaron over the brigade communications network at 04:24 and ordered him to open the route as quickly as possible. At 04:38, the brigade commander rushed him once again to join up with the reconnaissance company at the upper ski lift station ASAP and Yaron reported that the column lead was already about 250 meters north of the Tank Bend. At 05:03, when the tanks were about 500 meters south of the upper ski lift station, they were identified by the 51st Battalion Company B commander, who was climbing hill 24 from the south. He asked his deputy battalion commander to warn them not to open fire at him, but as mentioned previously, he misidentified his location and his request was not understood. The mechanized column wasn't notified of it.

At dawn, the company commander advancing above the road identified heavy fire exchange to and from the upper ski lift station. For fear of getting caught in the crossfire, he decided to go down from the cliff to the road. When he arrived with his men he identified green flares being fired from the direction of the upper ski lift station. The flares were fired by the reconnaissance company men in order to stop the friendly fire directed at them apparently by the 17th Battalion suppressive fire team, located on the western slopes of hill 16. When the company commander over the radio asked who was firing the flares, Yaron answered that it was the reconnaissance company that had already captured the upper ski lift station. At that moment, the Syrian blocking force, deployed in the rocks south of the upper ski lift station, opened fire toward him. The company commander reported this but was told that this was friendly fire. In order to ascertain this he lowered his combatants to the side of the road near the cliff and quickly ran to the western side of the road. The fire toward him continued and he returned to the trench at the cliff. The company commander verified over the radio and was told that this was friendly fire. He once again headed out into the road to identify the source of the fire and was hit in the back by a bullet. With remaining strength he headed back and lay down in a trench by the road. After being bandaged by the team's medic his men put him on a stretcher.

At this stage, they were fired upon from the northwest as well, from the blocking force, and from the rock crest above the road, which was several dozen meters to their northeast. The company commander instructed his men to carry him on the stretcher and quickly run south on the road or leave him in the trench and retreat without him south toward the tanks. His men began running with the stretcher south but after a short while they tripped into the trench. One of the two reserve officers attached to the team trying to lift it up again was hit by two bullets and was killed instantly. The team's medic resuscitation efforts failed and the company commander ordered them to leave him there with the body of the reserve officer. The rest of the men on the team retreated south and joined up with the infantry team advancing on the road. The company commander was evacuated by the brigade supply officer, who reached him with several medics, only at about 09:30.

The two remaining teams continued advancing on the road even before the company commander was hit. The advanced with the bulldozer tank, half-track, and two tanks behind them. At about 05:10 they reached a line of boulders blocking the road. The bulldozer tank began clearing them off the road while the infantry team continued their advance. Suddenly, the bulldozer tank triggered a mine and was hit by two RPG rockets. The operator from the 606th Armored Field Engineering force was killed on the spot. The bulldozer tank was diagonally on the road when it was hit and was now blocking the road completely. The two tanks immediately behind it began receiving small arms fire and anti-tank shells from the blocking force's B-10 RCLR but did not fire back since they were uncertain where the Israeli forces were. At about 05:13 the 74th Battalion deputy commander was hit by shrapnel in his shoulders and was evacuated to the rear. The commander of the first tank reported the deputy battalion commander's injury and was immediately injured himself when an anti-tank shell hit his tank. He was evacuated to the rear, as well. After a few minutes the pair of tanks began firing ahead at the sources of fire, apparently also striking the reconnaissance company combatants in the upper ski lift station. Yaron ordered the rest of the combatants from the brigade training base staff company to get off the half-tracks and advance on foot toward the head of the column. Parallel to the increase of fire directed at the mechanized column, the Company B force was seen going up the ridgeline of hill 24 and the mechanized column opened small arms fire at them. Three of company B's combatants were injured by this fire. The Company B deputy commander understood that the tanks and half-tracks were firing mistakenly at him and decided to fire green and red flares. He occupied the communications network with a demand to cease fire from the mechanized column and to rescue his three wounded. As may be recalled, he kept reporting, throughout the whole incident, that he was on hill 22, which added to the confusion of the battle scene.

When fire was opened against the tanks and infantry force, some of its men took positions on the west shoulder of the road and returned small arms fire toward the estimated location of the Syrian blocking force. The rest of the combatants took cover between the tanks and the cliff, since they were facing accurate fire from the blocking force and from the rock crest east of the road. At the same time the tank commanders were injured as they were exposed in their turrets, firing shells and small arms at the Syrian positions on the slopes of hill 16 and in the area south of the upper ski lift station. From approximately 05:30 to 09:30, the staff of the brigade training base attempted to advance on the road toward the upper ski lift station under tank cover but due to the Syrian blocking force fire directed at them, they could not advance. In those four hours both the combatants from the brigade training base company and the tank crewmembers were constantly injured and evacuated to the rear under tank cover.

From approximately 08:45, they were also evacuated on board the mechanized column commander command APC. Due to the load of talks and cries for help over the mechanized column internal communications network, the infantry force commander did not manage to talk with the deputy column commander. Therefore, at about 08:50 the commander switched to the brigade network, and with brigade's operations officer mediation he began coordinating the advance of his force with the deputy commander of the reconnaissance company. During the bypass attempts to move past the bulldozer tank blocking the road the commander's tank was hit by a sniper, lost control and moved backwards crushing the legs of a reserve officer between the rear of his tank and the cliff.

At about 09:00, Yaron attempted and failed at pushing the bulldozer tank off the road to the slope using another tank to enable the advance of the other tanks toward the upper ski lift station. He intended to assist in the capturing of the Israeli outpost in accordance with the repeated orders of the G3 officer, from there. At that time, the brigade's G4 officer, Maj. Yitzhak Paz, arrived at the place and began handling the shifting of the damaged tank with its wounded still inside. After evacuating them, he tried unsuccessfully to start the tank. Then Paz attached a towing cable to the right side of the bulldozer tank intending to pull it back and to the right, bringing it closer to the cliff and allowing the other tanks to pull forward. The towing tank began moving back, and the bulldozer tank triggered another mine. It turned out that the Syrians had placed a string of mines in the road and covered it with asphalt. This option was marked on the aerial photograph distributed to the commanders during the battle procedure. The deputy commander of the column ordered the tank commander to continue towing the bulldozer tank toward the wall thus allowing for a wide enough opening for the tanks to move through on the road. The tank with a reserve team began its advance forward and triggered a mine. In the attempts to advance the tank it rode off its tracks, blocking the road completely.

During the whole time, the column commanders and the

brigade operations officer tried to convince the reconnaissance company commanders to open fire against the Syrian blocking force from the rear to allow for the opening of the route. After they were assured that the tanks would not fire at them, the reconnaissance company combatants advanced to the edge of the road, opened fire against the Syrians, and persuaded them to surrender with the assistance of a prisoner interrogator speaking Arabic. At about 09:30 the route was opened for infantry movement. Several minutes later, one of the paratrooper companies arrived with the 317th Brigade deputy commander and advanced on the road toward the Israeli outpost on foot reaching it before the flags were put to mast. Four combatants were killed during the mechanized column attempts to advance from the Tank Bend toward the upper ski lift station, two from brigade training base, a tank commander from the 74th Battalion and the bulldozer tank operator from the 606th Armor Field Engineering Battalion. Fifteen combatants from brigade Training Base No. 1 were injured and six combatants from the tank force were injured.

The Battle Process from Dawn to the Conquest of the Israeli Outpost

In the beginning of Company C combat over hill 16, the battalion and brigade commanders' CCPs advanced to the line of fire and found themselves on the southeastern slopes of the hill just before dawn. In the morning dim light the Syrian sniping from the hill east of hill 16 increased. The 51st Battalion commander did not know that the brigade commander's CCP was about twenty meters east of him. The 51st Battalion combatants were scattered between the rocks around the two CCPs, most of them already wounded or dead. At about 05:12, the brigade commander was injured when he rose from behind a rock. The injured brigade commander called the 51st Battalion commander over the radio to transfer the command to him, but there was no response. The brigade commander ordered the G3 officer, Maj. Yoav Levi (later Golan), to transfer the command to the 51st Battalion commander, stop the battle and reorganize the forces, land heavy artillery fire on hills 16 and 17, and then attack again. “Don’t dare not to recapture the Hermon,” the brigade commander ordered before he was evacuated. A few minutes after the brigade commander was evacuated Yoav called the 51st Battalion commander over the battalion network and asked him for a status report. Yoav instructed the battalion commander—who explained that Company A's situation was unclear and that only one of the radio operators was answering him from there—to skip back to assume command of all the forces. Yoav had to repeat the order three times before the battalion commander could understand why he had to skip back and advanced toward the brigade commander’s CCP. Five minutes later, on his way there Yudk’a was injured and was evacuated from the field.

When Yoav understood that the 51st Battalion commander was injured, he assumed command of the battle of his own initiative since it was only natural as a G3 officer who was the most involved in the brigade’s battle plan, though Maj. Katz and the 51st Battalion deputy commander Maj. Zluf were also nearby. The brigade commander and the 51st Battalion commander were themselves in an inferior and fire prone territory and could not make out a comprehensive picture of the battle, therefore Yoav himself had difficulty in understanding what was going on in the field. The chaos on the brigade’s communications network added to the interrupted understanding of the situation. The brigade’s operations officer, Captain Yoad Zlivenski, who was sent by Yoav, at about 05:40, with a small group of combatants from the 17th Battalion and radio operators from the secondary CCP to capture the peak of hill 16 and prevent the Syrians from recapturing it, was instrumental in understanding the battle situation, coordinated the forces and prevented friendly fire. During the two hours that the operations officer's force held the hilltop it was fired at by Syrian small arms, anti-tank, and heavy artillery fire and asked to retreat. Request was denied and they continued holding the spot under Yoav's orders.

From 05:15 to about 08:15, Yoav was in constant contact with the Command CCP regarding the arrival of reserve forces. He operated artillery to assist in the rescue of the 51st Battalion wounded, subdued the Syrians and attempted to advance the mechanized column toward the upper ski lift station to join up with the reconnaissance company and get its assistance in advancing toward the Israeli outpost all under accurate Syrian sniper and heavy Syrian artillery fire. No force, other than the operations officer's force, advanced from the location it had reached before dawn. All the commanders were busy evacuating wounded, landing artillery, and trying to understand where everyone was and in what condition. It is important to mention that not one of the Israeli forces retreated from the positions they had captured. The firm hold of combatants who stubbornly held on to the positions they had reached, along with the heavy artillery support, eventually overpowered the Syrians.

When it was discovered at 08:15 that the Syrians had begun to flee the battlefield, Yoav instructed Katz to organize the forces from Company A of the 17th Battalion on hill 16, the rest of the 51st Battalion under the deputy battalion commander and the battalion's operations officer to begin advancing east on the ridgeline while clearing the Syrian positions. The advance was slow and careful, from crest to crest after placing suppressive fire teams in the front and clearing the Syrian positions. At the same time, as stated, the deputy commander of the mechanized column was unsuccessful in his attempt to advance with his forces toward the upper ski lift station.

The forces had completed the area takeover between hill 16 and the Israeli outpost by about 08:45. During the advance toward the outpost, about ten Syrians who didn't surrender were killed. Twenty Syrians who surrendered were taken prisoner and were immediately questioned by a prisoner interrogator who wanted to know if there were any Syrians in the outpost and if it was booby-trapped. At 09:05, Maj. Katz conducted a hasty orders group on the hill facing the Israeli outpost and established the makeup of the forces that would take over the outpost. At about 09:10 Brig. Gen. Kuti ordered Maj. Yoav not to enter the outpost itself but rather capture the openings for fear of booby-traps. At 10:05 the forces began advancing toward the outpost. Hundreds of small armed cluster bombs from the Israeli Air Force jets bombings of the outpost were scattered in the yard of the outpost which entailed a slow and careful advance. Five more Syrians surrendered at the entrance to the outpost. The takeover was carried out without firing. The main hall was scanned after smoke grenades had been thrown in.

While the Golani combatants entered the yard of the outpost, Brig. Gen. Kuti informed Yoav that following the initial takeover operation responsibility over the Hermon shoulder will be transferred to the 317th Brigade's deputy commander. One company from the command reserve force under the deputy brigade commander that land in the Bus Lot arrived at the Hermon outpost. At 10:35 the Golani combatants began climbing the roof of the outpost. The 51st Battalion intelligence officer and a platoon sergeant from the 17th Battalion climbed up one of the two antenna masts that was damaged by shrapnel and raised the Golani flag and the Israeli flag from them. At 10:38 Maj. Katz announced the following over the brigade communications network: "To all stations of the world, this is eight, the flag has been raised." The battle to conquer the Hermon shoulder and the Israeli Hermon outpost ended. At about 10:40 the GOC appointed the command G3 officer, Lt. Col. Uri Simchoni, as brigade commander in place of the 1st Brigade commander who was injured. Lt. Col. Simchoni's assistant, Lt. Col. Menachem Einan, was appointed the command G3 officer in his place. At 11:15 the GOC Maj. Gen. Hofi and Lt. Col. Simchoni flew by helicopter from Mount Knaan to the Israeli Hermon to meet the commanders of the 1st Brigade and transfer the command of the brigade to Lt. Col. Simchoni.

Battle Results

The battle of the Golani Brigade lasted eight straight hours, ending at about 10:40, when the 17th and 51st Battalion combatants entered the yard of the abandoned Israeli outpost and raised the national flag and the brigade's flag from the antenna mast on its rooftop. Though the Golani Brigade completed the task it had been assigned—conquering the Hermon shoulder and recapturing the Israeli outpost—the toll was very high. Fifty-six combatants were killed and seventy-nine were injured in the battle. From the 51st Battalion forty-two combatants were killed and fifty-two injured, from the 17th Battalion five combatants were killed and six injured, from the reconnaissance company four combatants were killed, from brigade Training Base No. 1 two combatants were killed and fifteen injured, from the 74th Battalion one combatant was killed and six injured, from the 405th Battalion one combatant was killed, from the 606th Battalion one combatant was killed, and from the brigade, command the brigade commander was injured.

The Syrian losses in the battle were estimated at about 50 to 60 killed. Israeli forces took captive sixty-two Syrian soldiers: 45 from the 82nd Paratrooper Battalion and seventeen from the 133rd Commando Battalion. Several dozen Syrian soldiers who escaped the battle zone were killed in the Bolaan Valley by the 269th Unit combatants. Most of the Syrians were killed by the Golani combatants' small arm fire and only a few were killed by the Israeli Air Force bombings and artillery shelling.

The battle was summed up years later by the command G3 officer, Maj. Gen. Uri Simchoni: "The picture of the battle to capture the Hermon altered toward the end of the night; while Golani began their fighting from the bottom to the top the paratroopers had completed capturing the Syrian Hermon outpost. At that moment we had a significant force in the Syrians' unprotected rear. The right thing to do was to instruct Golani to stop where they were, create fire pressure, and switch to deception. Then instruct the paratroopers to capture the Hermon outpost from its exposed rear. We did not do this. We stuck to the original plan, and Golani paid a massive price."

Control over the Hermon shoulder was transferred to the deputy brigade commander of the 317th Brigade at the end of the battle. The capture of the Hermon shoulder, the Syrian Hermon and the Hermon summit right before the ceasefire of October 22 took the last Syrian stronghold in the region of the Purple Line out of their hands and gave the Israeli forces observation positions that controlled the depth of enemy alignments north of the wedge and all the way up to the outskirts of Damascus.

SOLDIERS DECORATED IN THE BREAKTHROUGH PHASE

Lieutenant Colonel Egozi Moshe, of blessed memory, *113878*

For revealing a drive to fight, personal example and bravery

Description of action:

During the Yom Kippur War, Lt. Col. Moshe Egozi of blessed memory, commanded the mechanized infantry battalion in the Golan Heights battles. Throughout the days of fighting, Lt. Col. Moshe Egozi of blessed memory, insisted that his battalion be integrated into the offensive alignment against the enemy, and the battalion, under his command did indeed participate in the clearing of Khan Arenba and the capture of Umm-Butna. The half-track that Lt. Col. Moshe Egozi, of blessed memory, was in suffered a direct hit and he was injured and died. Throughout the days of combat Lt. Col. Moshe Egozi, of blessed memory, was a personal example of bravery and the drive to fight for his subordinates.

For this action the Chief of Staff Citation was posthumously awarded to him

Nisan 5736, April 1976, **Mordechai Gur, Lieutenant General, GHQ Chief of Staff**

Sergeant Eddy Nissim, *2141485*

Description of action:

On October 22nd 1973, during the second battle on the Hermon, Corp. Nissim Eddy served as a platoon medic. After his platoon commander was injured he ran facing enemy positions through open terrain to treat the platoon commander. He knelt, lit a flashlight in front of a Syrian position targeting him with efficient fire until he finished bandaging the platoon commander, and only then took him to the medical evacuation unit. Throughout the battle he treated the company's wounded with exemplary prudence and courage.

For this action the Medal of Distinguished Service was awarded to him

Iyar 5735, May 1975, **David Elazar, Lieutenant General, GHQ Chief of Staff**

Corporal Ohana Yosef, of blessed memory, *2147160*

Description of action:

On October 22nd, 1973 Corp. Yosef Ohana, of blessed memory, participated in the battle over the Hermon. At a stage where there were already many dead and wounded and the situation was dire, Corp. Yosef Ohana, of blessed memory, got up with a machine gun in his hands, returned fired at the sources of fire without cover, thus allowing others to assist and evacuate the wounded. When he ran out of ammunition he went to get more and continued covering his friends who were evacuating the wounded. He maintained in this position for nearly an hour and a half. The Syrians surrendered towards noon. On

November[1] 13th, 1973, during a shooting battle with the Syrians in the Mazraat Beit Jann sector, he was killed. In his actions he revealed bravery, prudence and exemplary tenacity.

For this action the Medal of Distinguished Service was posthumously awarded to him

Iyar 5735, May 1975, **David Elazar, Lieutenant General, GHQ Chief of Staff**

Corporal Atias Prosper, *2146101*

For manifesting bravery, initiative and tenacity

Description of action:

On 22 October 1973 Private Prosper Atias participated in the second battle over the Hermon. When the majority of his force was injured he remained by himself facing the Syrian positions and covered the evacuation of the wounded. Under consistent fire he suppressed the enemy with a machine gun he took from a wounded soldier, and when he ran out of ammunition has assisted in the evacuation of the wounded. In his action Private Prosper Atias exhibited bravery, prudence and comradeship

For this action the Chief of Staff Citation was awarded to him

Tishrei 5736, September 1975, **Mordechai Gur, Lieutenant General, GHQ Chief of Staff**

1 He was killed during the War of Attrition on the Egyptian front – the editor.

Sergeant First Class Eliani Mordechai, *209108*

Description of action:

On October 6th, 1973 Sgt. 1st Class Mordechai Eliani served as the battalion commander's driver. On October 11th, 1973, during a hasty movement into positions, the battalion commander got disconnected from the other tanks. Sgt. 1st Class Mordechai Eliani, of his own initiative, directed several tanks to firing positions. On October 12th, 1973 he bandaged, evacuated and rescued wounded while exposing himself to heavy artillery fire. On the night of October 19th, 1973, in the battle over Umm-Butna, he rescued and evacuated about 6 wounded from the paratrooper force, from the mechanized infantry force, and from his own battalion – all under heavy artillery fire, while placing himself in serious danger. Sgt. 1st Class Mordechai Eliani, who had served in the unit as a volunteer, having passed the age of service in a combat unit, exhibited, bravery, dedication, and exemplary comradeship throughout the battles under heavy artillery fire.

For this action the Medal of Distinguished Service was awarded to him

Iyar 5735, May 1975, **Mordechai Gur, Lieutenant General, GHQ Chief of Staff**

Sergeant Ashkenazi Israel *215935*

For manifesting bravery, initiative and tenacity

Description of action:

During the Yom Kippur War Sgt. Israel Ashkenazi served as the operations sergeant in an APC and participated in battles on the Golan Heights. On October 11th, 1973 in the breaking through battle towards Khan Arenba, Sgt. Israel Ashkenazi was in the APC as part of the rescue force. While in movement the APC triggered a mine. Sgt. Israel Ashkenazi got off the APC with another officer, and began to direct the APCs and clear a route between the mines to rescue them from the minefield under enemy fire. Throughout the days of fighting he exhibited initiative and resourcefulness in difficult situations. In these actions Sgt. Israel Ashkenazi exhibited bravery and prudence.

For this action the Chief of Staff Citation was awarded to him

Tishrei 5736, September 1975, **Mordechai Gur, Lieutenant General, GHQ Chief of Staff**

Lieutenant Colonel Ben Hanan Yosef, *930536*

Description of action:

When the Yom Kippur War broke out Lt. Col. Yosef Ben Hanan was abroad on his honeymoon. When he found out about the war he interrupted his special vacation and returned to Israel on October 8th, 1973. He was assigned the task of assembling a force from the people remaining from the unit damaged during the battle when he arrived. Lt. Col. Yosef Ben Hanan organized the force quickly, and on Tuesday, October 9th, 1973 he participated in the decisive battle to halt Syrian attacks in the region north of Quneitra; a battle that ended in pushing the enemy forces and destroying them. While pursuing the enemy, during battle his face was injured but he continued commanding the force. During the breakthrough, on October 11th, 1973 he led his unit in the advance force deep into Syrian territory in the northern sector of the Israeli forces. During the offensive that night even though he was injured a second time he continued commanding and personally organized the forces for continued fighting in the morning. On October 12th, 1973 he was seriously injured for the third time by enemy jets but he refused to evacuate in spite of an explicit order by the doctor and the division commander. When a certain stalemate formed on the division front in light of enemy resistance, Lt. Col. Yosef Ben Hanan boldly suggested attacking the enemy key positions by outflanking through a territory that was deemed impassable, and volunteered to carry out this offensive leading a small force, though he was weak from his previous injuries. The outflanking was carried out and the force reached its target, while destroying the enemy's tanks and other vehicles. During the capture of the target part of the force was injured, including Lt. Col. Yosef Ben Hanan's tank, and he was seriously wounded for the a fourth time. Lt. Col. Yosef Ben Hanan remained in the field in this condition for four hours while being treated by the tank driver. In spite of his injury he directed the Israeli forces' artillery fire over the radio, as well as the rescue force which reached him after dark. Throughout the days of fighting Lt. Col. Yosef Ben Hanan proved extraordinary initiative and resourcefulness, a will to fight and a keenness to lead the forces, thus instilling his soldiers with confidence and a fighting spirit. In his actions Lt. Col. Yosef Ben Hanan exhibited tenacity, initiative, and superb leadership.

For this action the Medal of Courage was awarded to him

Tishrei 5736, September 1975, **Mordechai Gur, Lieutenant General, GHQ Chief of Staff**

Lieutenant Gavron Pinchas, of blessed memory, *985000*

For manifesting bravery and tenacity

Description of action:

Lt. Pinchas Gavron, of blessed memory, joined a battalion fighting in the Golan Heights. On the fourth day of the war, during the second Syrian counter attack on Mazraat Beit Jann, he along with two friends stormed a house 3 Syrian commandoes were firing from and cleared it. Afterwards he joined the company commander to storm an RPG unit that threatened the house. He was killed during the storming by a sniper's bullet. In his actions Lt. Pinchas Gavron, of blessed memory, exhibited bravery and tenacity.

For this action the Chief of Staff Citation was posthumously awarded to him

Tishrei 5736, September 1975, **Mordechai Gur, Lieutenant General, GHQ Chief of Staff**

Major Goldfarb Uri, of blessed memory, *946085*

Description of action:

On October 7th, 1973 after a fierce battle over the anti tank bastion in front of Tel Fares, Maj. Uri Goldfarb, of blessed memory, towed tanks that were left without fuel in the position and organized their evacuation while advancing on foot. He was exposed to artillery fire for about 3 hours until he brought the entire battalion into the night camp. On October 10th, 1973 he himself managed the rescue of the brigade's stranded tanks while evacuating wounded from the tanks that had been damaged, again under heavy artillery fire. On October 18th,

1973 Maj. Uri Goldfarb, of blessed memory, took command of the battalion and during the day planned and prepared the battalion for the capture of the village of Umm-Butna. On October 19th, 1973 he commanded a tank force that captured Umm-Butna in cooperation with the paratroopers while manifesting exceptional commanding ability and bravery. In the morning of October 19th, 1973 a call for help to evacuate wounded from a mechanized infantry force east of the village was received. Under heavy tank fire 800 meters away from him, Maj. Uri Goldfarb, of blessed memory, went out to rescue the mechanized infantry force. He was then hit and killed. Maj. Uri Goldfarb, of blessed memory, originally a paratrooper who had changed to tanks only a week prior to the war, exhibited an extraordinary understanding and control of tanks and commanding a force, exemplary bravery, dedication and comradeship

For this action the Medal of Courage was posthumously awarded to him

Iyar 5735, May 1975, **Mordechai Gur, Lieutenant General, GHQ Chief of Staff**

Captain Gur-Arieh Gabriel, of blessed memory,
2083356

For manifesting bravery, prudence and leadership
Description of action:

On October 22nd, 1973 Captain Gabriel Gur-Arieh, of blessed memory, participated in the second battle over the Hermon. He was sent, at the head of a team, to capture a number of Syrian positions. The team was hit by grenades, and he himself was hit by shrapnel. Despite his injury, he reorganized the group of soldiers, and together they stormed the positions again. During the storming he was hit by enemy fire and was killed. In his action Captain Gabriel Gur-Arieh of blessed memory exhibited prudence and leadership.

For this action the Chief of Staff Citation was posthumously awarded to him

Tishrei 5736, September 1975, **Mordechai Gur, Lieutenant General, GHQ Chief of Staff**

Staff Sergeant Gal Eitan, of blessed memory,
2012837

Description of action:

When the battles broke out, Staff Sgt. Eitan Gal of blessed memory, served as a tank commander in a tank battalion fighting on the Golan Heights. He always advanced ahead of everyone else and was the first to identify enemy tanks and destroy them. In one of the cases he rescued two Israeli tanks that had triggered mines in enemy territory and were under heavy artillery fire. On October 19th, 1973 his tank was hit near the village of Umm-Butna and in spite of his serious injury Staff Sgt. Eitan Gal of blessed memory, continued to direct his tank until it was evacuated. He died on the way to the hospital. In his actions he exhibited great courage, prudence, resourcefulness and comradeship.

For this action the Medal of Courage was posthumously awarded to him

Iyar 5735, May 1975, **Mordechai Gur, Lieutenant General, GHQ Chief of Staff**

Master Sergeant de-Levi Yehuda, *268992*

Description of action:

During the Yom Kippur War Master Sgt. Yehuda de-Levi served as a battalion master sergeant. On October 13th, 1973 while he was near Mazraat Beit Jann, the battalion was bombed by the Syrians. A number of combatants were wounded and the majority of the force lost contact. Master Sgt. Yehuda de-Levi, along with one of the officers, remained in place, gathered the wounded and evacuated them. When they reached the medical evacuation unit it was discovered that a Sgt. 1st class from one of the battalion's batteries remained alone in the field. Master Sgt. Yehuda de-Levi went into the field that was bombarded by heavy enemy fire and rescued the Sgt. 1st class of his own initiative. Afterwards he brought a team together and returned to the field several times in order to evacuate the Israeli force's casualties left on enemy territory. In his actions Master Sgt. Yehuda de-Levi exhibited resourcefulness, prudence, exemplary comradeship and served as a personal example to others.

For this action the Medal of Distinguished Service was awarded to him

Nisan 5736, April 1976, **Mordechai Gur, Lieutenant General, GHQ Chief of Staff**

Major Dafna Ehud, of blessed memory, *415448*

Description of action:

On October 6th, 1973 Maj. Ehud Dafna of blessed memory, was at home. When he heard of the battles erupting, and since he was had not been assigned to any other unit, he returned to the Golan Heights and organized a company from the remaining tanks and teams of the brigade forces in the southern sector. Maj. Ehud Dafna, of blessed memory, participated in the fierce holding battles. He later continued the break through into Syria at the head of his company, participated in the first attempt to capture Tel Shams and when this failed he participated in the capture of the mound during the night attack. After capturing the mound he blocked the "Sa'sa" road and halted the Syrian infantry and armored offensives. In this battle he was wounded and killed. In his actions and fighting he exhibited great courage, resourcefulness and tenacity despite his physical limitations that resulted from the Six Day War he was a handicapped veteran of.

For this action the Medal of Courage was posthumously awarded to him

Iyar 5735, May 1975, **Mordechai Gur, Lieutenant General, GHQ Chief of Staff**

Lieutenant Colonel Harel Moshe, 460571

Description of action:

During the Yom Kippur War, Lt. Col. Moshe Harel commanded a tank battalion in the Golan Heights holding battles. On the evening of October 7th, 1973 in the battle over Nafah, his tank was damaged. Lt. Col. Moshe Harel rescued his team, and at darkness joined up with the Israeli forces and rearranged his force for continued fighting. On October 9th, 1973 Lt. Col. Moshe Harel commanded his battalion while halting the Syrians in the Sindyanna region. During the battle Lt. Col. Moshe Harel's tank was damaged, he was wounded and was evacuated to a hospital. The next day he escaped from the hospital and reassumed command of his unit in the break through battle in the Khan Arenba sector. His tank was damaged during this battle and Lt. Col. Moshe Harel switched to command from another tank. During the battle he was wounded again and was evacuated. In his action Lt. Col. Moshe Harel exhibited bravery, prudence, and exemplary tenacity.

For this action the Medal of Distinguished Service was awarded to him

Nisan 5736, April 1976, **Mordechai Gur, Lieutenant General, GHQ Chief of Staff**

Major Vinik Shemaryahu, of blessed memory,

2059623

Description of action:

In the week of October 13th - 20th, 1973 Major Shemaryahu Vinik of blessed memory, and his unit conducted incursions and patrols across the border. In these patrols he encountered Syrian forces, captured a few Syrian soldiers, blew up a Syrian tank, and kept conducting these patrols every night. During the defensive battle on an outpost in the northern sector he organized the men in an exemplary manner, knew how to accurately direct fire at the Syrian forces concentrations, maintained the soldiers' alert, encouraged them, and increased their self confidence. On October 22nd, 1973 he participated in the battle over the Hermon where he was killed. In his behavior he exhibited bravery and exemplary leadership.

For this action the Medal of Distinguished Service was posthumously awarded to him

Iyar 5735, May 1975, **Mordechai Gur, Lieutenant General, GHQ Chief of Staff**

Sergeant Vachterman Boris, *2097009*

Description of action:

On October 22nd, 1973 Sgt. Boris Vachterman served as an SPG driver on the Golan Heights. The gun battery was deployed when it got artillery fire from the Syrians. The guns of one team were damaged and a fire spread over the team's ammunition carrier. Sgt. Boris Vachterman volunteered to drive the burning carrier and take it out of the position. When he abandoned the burning carrier he noticed an SPG team nearby that could be injured by the carrier's explosion. He warned the team, got back in the driver's seat of the SPG and drove it away from the danger zone. In these actions Sgt. Boris Vachterman exhibited prudence, bravery, and exemplary comradeship.

For this action the Medal of Distinguished Service was awarded to him

Tishrei 5736, September 1975, **Mordechai Gur, Lieutenant General, GHQ Chief of Staff**

Sergeant Harazi Shmuel, *2154266*

Description of action:

On October 13th -14th, 1973 in the battle over Mazraat Beit Jann, Syrian tanks attacked IDF armored and infantry forces defending a junction outside the village. Corp. Shmuel Harazi, and infantry soldier, struck two enemy tanks at short range, in two different incidents, with an anti tank launcher. In these actions he exhibited bravery, prudence and resourcefulness.

For this action the Medal of Distinguished Service was awarded to him

Tishrei 5736, September 1975, **Mordechai Gur, Lieutenant General, GHQ Chief of Staff**

Major Yahalom Yehoshua, of blessed memory,

472111

Description of action:

During the Yom Kippur War, Maj. Yehoshua Yahalom, of blessed memory, fought in battles on the Golan Heights as commander of a jeep company. In this position he was essentially occupied in evacuating wounded from the front to the rear and in directing Israeli tanks in fighting against enemy armored forces. Later on in the battle his unit company commanders were injured and Maj. Yehoshua Yahalom, of blessed memory, demanded his commander to give him the command of a tank company, though he had no professional training for it. His commander agreed and gave Maj. Yehoshua Yahalom, of blessed memory, command of a tank company. On October 11th, 1973 Maj. Yehoshua Yahalom, of blessed memory, led his company in the battalion's offensive against the village of Khan Arenba. Under heavy artillery fire he continued leading the offensive and at the edge of the Syrian trenches he was hit and fell. In these actions Maj. Yehoshua Yahalom, of blessed memory, exhibited bravery, daring, and exemplary tenacity.

For this action the Medal of Distinguished Service was posthumously awarded to him

Tishrei 5736, September 1975, **Mordechai Gur, Lieutenant General, GHQ Chief of Staff**

Sergeant Yaakov Tuvia, of blessed memory,

2096597

For manifesting bravery and tenacity

Description of action:

Sgt. Tuvia Yaakov, of blessed memory, joined a battalion fighting on the Golan Heights. On the fourth day of the war, during the second Syrian counter attack on Mazraat Beit Jann, he stormed a house where three Syrian commandoes were firing from, and cleared the house with two friends. Afterwards he joined the company commander to storm an RPG unit threatening the house. During the storming he was killed by a sniper's bullet. In his actions Sgt. Tuvia Yaakov, of blessed memory, exhibited bravery and tenacity.

For this action the Chief of Staff Citation was posthumously awarded to him

Tishrei 5736, September 1975, **Mordechai Gur, Lieutenant General, GHQ Chief of Staff**

Lieutenant Yaron Itamar, of blessed memory,

2137904

Description of action:

On October 22nd, 1973 at twilight, during the fighting to capture the Hermon outpost, the fighting force where Lt. Itamar Yaron, of blessed memory, served as a platoon commander, had several critically wounded soldiers who could not be evacuated due to Syrian heavy bombing. A medic who attempted to rescue them was injured. Nevertheless, Lt. Itamar Yaron, of blessed memory, decided to rescue one of the wounded, and while requesting the cover of smoke grenades he crawled towards the wounded soldier. On his way he was hit by a bullet and killed. In this action he exhibited great bravery, prudence, and comradeship.

For this action the Medal of Courage was posthumously awarded to him

Iyar 5735, May 1975, **Mordechai Gur, Lieutenant General, GHQ Chief of Staff**

Lieutenant Lutzki Dov, *2125770*

Description of action:

On October 11th, 1973 2nd Lt. Dov Lutzki joined a tank battalion breaking through into Syrian territory with a mechanized infantry platoon. On October 21st, 1973 the enemy attacked the enclave to recapture it. 2nd Lt. Dov Lutzki was sent by the battalion commander to Tel Merai, the highest forward point in the region, to serve as a frontal observation officer. Tel Merai was heavily and accurately bombarded by the Syrians but 2nd Lt. Dov Lutzki remained in position and continued reporting of the enemy's movements, enabling the planning of the holding battle. Thanks to his endurance under difficult combat conditions and thanks to his persistence and tenacity, it was possible to reinforce the place with tanks and prevent its capture.

For this action the Medal of Distinguished Service was awarded to him

Iyar 5735, May 1975, **Mordechai Gur, Lieutenant General, GHQ Chief of Staff**

Sergeant Litan Gilad, of blessed memory, 2144047

Description of action:

On October 8th, 1973, in the first battle over the Hermon, Sgt. Gilad Litan, of blessed memory, covered the retreat of the force from the ridge with another soldier. When they reached the road it was discovered that one of the soldiers was missing. Sgt. Gilad Litan, of blessed memory, and another soldier volunteered to go up again and locate the absent soldier. However, after failing to find the soldier they met with fierce fire, and returned to the road. On October 12th, 1973, during the break through of an access route to an outpost, Syrian jets injured soldiers of the the bomb disposal unit and infantry force. Sgt. Gilad Litan, of blessed memory, volunteered to be the first to examine the road. When he marked the mines he found and organized the passage of the convoy between them until they reached the border route. On October22nd, 1973 in the second battle over the Hermon, the company commander was injured and remained lying in the road. Sgt. Gilad Litan, of blessed memory, skipped to drag him back into a clear zone where he could be treated. He was wounded during the skip and later died of his wounds. In these actions he revealed exemplary bravery, volunteering spirit, initiative and comradeship.

For this action the Medal of Courage was posthumously awarded to him

Iyar 5735, May 1975, **Mordechai Gur, Lieutenant General, GHQ Chief of Staff**

Captain Maor Uri, *217841*

Description of action:

During the Yom Kippur War, Captain Uri Maor served as commander of a mortar platoon. On October 12th, 1973 Captain Uri Maor's battalion organized to halt the Syrian armored forces on the Golan Heights east of Maschara village. At dark the Syrian armored forces began firing at the battalion forces while employing night vision equipment. At that time, Captain Uri Maor and his platoon were several kilometers away from the battalion area of deployment and due to the need to reach the place quickly he led his platoon in unfamiliar territory, through a village occupied by enemy forces, and reached the combat zone at night. Captain Uri Maor employed his platoon and assisted the battalion in conducting the battle and rescue, employing lighting devices. In these actions Captain Uri Maor revealed bravery, initiative and resourcefulness.

For this action the Chief of Staff Citation was awarded to him

Tishrei 5736, September 1975, **Mordechai Gur, Lieutenant General, GHQ Chief of Staff**

Lieutenant Meushar Avshalom, *2142532*

For manifesting initiative, resourcefulness, and tenacity

Description of action:

On October 11th, 1973 during the fighting against Syrian armored and infantry forces in Mazraat Beit Jann, 2nd Lt. Avshalom Meushar's cannon system malfunctioned: there was no recoil and the spent shells were not extricated. 2nd Lt. Avshalom

Meushar showed initiative and tenacity by ramming another tank or a boulder and thus extricating the spent shells to enable the continued fighting. In this action 2nd Lt. Avshalom Meushar revealed, resourcefulness and tenacity.

For this action the Chief of Staff Citation was awarded to him

Tishrei 5736, September 1975, **Mordechai Gur, Lieutenant General, GHQ Chief of Staff**

Sergeant Machlouf David, of blessed memory,

2132715

Description of action:

On October 22nd, 1973, in the battle over the Hermon, the unit encountered fierce Syrian resistance – and many combatants were injured. Sgt. David Machlouf, of blessed memory, treated many wounded under enemy fire, until he was hit and fell. In his actions he exhibited bravery, prudence, and exemplary comradeship

For this action the Medal of Distinguished Service was posthumously awarded to him

Iyar 5735, May 1975, **Mordechai Gur, Lieutenant General, GHQ Chief of Staff**

Lieutenant Colonel Meler Moshe, 467427

Description of action:

When the battles broke out, Lt. Col. Moshe Meler served as tank commander battalion. He and his battalion participated in pushing the Syrian armored forces that had entered the Golan Heights back to their territory. On October 18th, 1973 he was dehydrated but refused to be evacuated and lay under a tank in the lot and was administered an IV (intra vinous). That night his unit headed out to assist a paratrooper battalion in capturing the village of Umm-Butna. Lt. Col. Moshe Meler's deputy was appointed commander of the force in his place, but Lt. Col. Moshe Meler entered the command tank and travelled with them. When the battle began he replaced his deputy of his own initiative and succeeded in rescuing part of his unit from enemy fire while being injured in the process. In all his actions he revealed bravery, prudence and served as a model and example to his subordinates with his resourcefulness and tenacity.

For this action the Medal of Distinguished Service was awarded to him

Iyar 5735, May 1975, **Mordechai Gur, Lieutenant General, GHQ Chief of Staff**

Major Nissim Yosef, 955562

Description of action:

On October 6th, 1973 Maj. Yosef Nissim served as deputy battalion commander in the northern sector of the Golan Heights. When the war broke out and knowing that there was a shortage in ammunition he made sure it arrived at the front regularly.

While manifesting bravery and resourcefulness he managed to block the advance of the Syrians in his sector, and continued towards Mazraat Beit Jann with the Golani forces fighting there. At the end of the battle he led the force that captured the Hermon outpost where he was badly wounded. In these actions he revealed bravery, prudence, and exemplary leadership.

For this action the Medal of Distinguished Service was awarded to him

Iyar 5735, May 1975, **Mordechai Gur, Lieutenant General, GHQ Chief of Staff**

Major Netanyahu Yonatan, *945940*

Description of action:

Maj. Yonatan Netanyahu commanded a force from a unit attached to an armored brigade forces. He fought with the tank forces day and night and went on raids and ambushes while the armored divisions were busy organizing. On October 8th, 1973 he and his unit destroyed a Syrian commando force landing from helicopters in the rear of the Israeli forces. When a senior officer was wounded in Tel Shams, Maj. Yonatan Netanyahu volunteered to lead the rescue unit after a previous rescue attempt had failed. He completed this task successfully. His bravery, swift action, and tenacity were served as a formidable example for his soldiers.

For this action the Medal of Distinguished Service was awarded to him

Iyar 5735, May 1975, **Mordechai Gur, Lieutenant General, GHQ Chief of Staff**

Corporal Salam Shimon, *2129496*

For manifesting bravery, prudence and resourcefulness
Description of action:

During the second Syrian offensive fighting in Mazraat Beit Jann, Corp. Shimon Salam served as a captured RPG operator. On October 14th, 1973 Corp. Shimon Salam ambushed a Syrian tank that had hit an Israeli tank. When the tank drew near he fired and missed. He changed his position, fired again, and hit. In this action Corp. Shimon Salam exhibited bravery, prudence and resourcefulness.

For this action the Chief of Staff Citation was awarded to him

Tishrei 5736, September 1975, **Mordechai Gur, Lieutenant General, GHQ Chief of Staff**

Sergeant First Class Feinstein Ezra, of blessed memory, *2119451*

For manifesting bravery, prudence and camaraderie
Description of action:

On October 12th, 1973 Sgt. 1st Class Ezra Feinstein of blessed memory, participated in battles on the Golan Heights in breaking through a passage from Hader to one of the outposts. The foot patrol men were injured during the battle. Sgt. 1st Class Ezra Feinstein of blessed memory, organized a gathering location for the wounded, treated them level-headedly and kept their spirits up. When Syrian jets flew over them he protected one of the wounded with his body to defend him from the jets strikes. Sgt. 1st Class Ezra Feinstein of blessed memory, fell in the second battle over Mount Hermon. In these actions Sgt.

1st Class Ezra Feinstein, of blessed memory, exhibited bravery, prudence and comradeship.

For this action the Chief of Staff Citation was posthumously awarded to him

Tishrei 5736, September 1975, **Mordechai Gur, Lieutenant General, GHQ Chief of Staff**

Lieutenant Colonel Padan Ben Zion, *246802*

Description of action:

On October 9th, 1973 Lt. Col. Ben Zion Padan led his battalion towards Hushenia. Triggering a mine he was injured in his face and leg. He refused to be evacuated and continued commanding over the battalion. On October13th, 1973 the battalion, made up of 18 tanks, was deployed at the foot of Tel Shaar, expecting the Iraqi expeditionary force due to arrive from this direction. When the Iraqis arrived they encountered the small force waiting for them and within 30 minutes many of their tanks were destroyed. Lt. Col. Ben Zion Padan commanded the offensive against the Iraqi expeditionary force which was made up of many tanks. He expressed bravery and prudence in this battle against the Syrians, which was halted never to be renewed.

For this action the Medal of Distinguished Service was awarded to him

Iyar 5735, May 1975, **Mordechai Gur, Lieutenant General, GHQ Chief of Staff**

Staff Sergeant Plonski Eitan Zvi, of blessed memory, *2147117*

For manifesting bravery, tenacity and camaraderie

Description of action:

On October 22nd, 1973 Staff Sgt. Eitan Zvi Plonski, of blessed memory, served as a medic in the second battle over the Hermon. Once he heard the company commander and the radio operator were injured, he ran forward to treat them despite fierce fire in the region. One of the combatants tried to stop him, saying there was no chance of reaching them due to enemy fire. Staff Sgt. Eitan Zvi Plonski, of blessed memory, replied that it was his duty to treat the wounded and continued advancing towards them. When he drew near he was hit in the head by a bullet and was killed. In this action Staff Sgt. Eitan Zvi Plonski, of blessed memory, expressed bravery, tenacity, and comradeship.

For this action the Chief of Staff Citation was posthumously awarded to him

Tishrei 5736, September 1975, **Mordechai Gur, Lieutenant General, GHQ Chief of Staff**

Staff Sergeant Friedex Nehemia, of blessed memory, *2121553*

Description of action:

When the Yon Kippur War battles broke out, Staff Sgt. Nehemia Friedex of blessed memory, served as a medic in an infantry force fighting on the Golan Heights. On October 22nd, 1973, during the second battle over the Hermon, many soldiers of the attacking force were injured. Staff Sgt. Nehemia Friedex of blessed memory, treated, bandaged and encouraged the wounded despite fierce fire directed at the field. With grand peace of mind he treated the soldiers without paying attention to the grenades falling around him, until a sniper's bullet hit and killed him. In these actions he expressed bravery, prudence, and exemplary tenacity.

For this action the Medal of Distinguished Service was posthumously awarded to him

Iyar 5735, May 1975, **Mordechai Gur, Lieutenant General, GHQ Chief of Staff**

Major Klein Yaakov, of blessed memory, *951586*

Description of action:

When the battles broke out, Maj. Yaakov Klein of blessed memory, served as commander of a tank company fighting on the Golan Heights. On October 7th, 1973 his tank was hit and caught fire. Maj. Yaakov Klein, of blessed memory, was injured, but level-headedly managed to rescue the gun operator who was fatally wounded. After putting the fire out, he was evacuated to a hospital, "escaped" the very next day, and returned to his unit. On October 19th, 1973, during the attack and capture of Tel Antar, one of the tanks in his company was hit and caught fire. Maj. Yaakov Klein, of blessed memory, jumped out of his tank, put the fire out and rescued the crew. He was killed later. In these actions he exhibited bravery, resourcefulness, prudence, and exemplary tenacity.

For this action the Medal of Distinguished Service was posthumously awarded to him

Iyar 5735, May 1975, **Mordechai Gur, Lieutenant General, GHQ Chief of Staff**

Staff Sergeant Rosenthal Dov, of blessed memory, *2133159*

Description of action:

On October 22nd, 1973, in the battle over the Hermon, company C led towards hill 17. When it was fired upon from hill 16, company C sent an advance force from company A including Staff Sgt. Dov Rosenthal, of blessed memory. They began going up the hill in the dark and encountered a Syrian position. The force returned gunfire flares towards the sources of shooting. Staff Sgt. Dov Rosenthal, of blessed memory, skipped forward to range the snipers. He was hit during his observation by one of the snipers, but rose again to report their location. It was then that he was shot and killed. In this action he revealed exemplary bravery and resourcefulness.

For this action the Medal of Distinguished Service he was posthumously awarded:

Iyar 5735, May 1975, **Mordechai Gur, Lieutenant General, GHQ Chief of Staff**

Sergeant Rosenzweig Zvi, 2167523

Description of action:

On October 6th, 1973 Sgt. Zvi Rosenzweig served as a tank battalion crew member fighting on the Golan Heights. After the force was hit,. Sgt. Zvi Rosenzweig returned to fighting and served as the battalion commander's driver. In the battle over Tel Shams the battalion commander's tank was damaged, and Sgt. Zvi Rosenzweig rescued the wounded battalion commander from the burning tank, though it was in a Syrian controlled area under Syrian fierce fire. He contacted the other forces in the division, reported his situation and directed the rescue force towards him. He bandaged his commander and protected him from the approaching Syrians, until the recue force arrived and thus saved his life. In this act he revealed bravery, resourcefulness, and exemplary comradeship.

For this action the Medal of Distinguished Service was awarded to him

Iyar 5735, May 1975, **Mordechai Gur, Lieutenant General, GHQ Chief of Staff**

Staff Sergeant Ronen Dan, of blessed memory,

2128751

For manifesting bravery, prudence and resourcefulness

Description of action:

On October 13th, 1973, during the company's battle in Beit Jann, the force discovered a Syrian sniper on the hill. The unit including Staff Sgt. Dan Ronen, of blessed memory, came close to the sniper's location, threw a grenade and Staff Sgt. Dan Ronen of blessed memory, fired and killed the sniper. Afterwards, going down to the village, he assisted the company commander in arranging the force. On October 22nd, 1973 he fell in the battle over the Hermon. Throughout the fighting Staff Sgt. Dan Ronen, of blessed memory, revealed bravery, prudence, and resourcefulness.

For this action the Chief of Staff Citation was posthumously awarded to him

Tishrei 5736, September 1975, **Mordechai Gur, Lieutenant General, GHQ Chief of Staff**

Corporal Rittman Dan, *2127026*

For manifesting bravery, prudence and tenacity
Description of action:

On October 22nd, 1973, in the battle over the Hermon, Corp. Dan Rittman covered the advance of his friends towards the Syrian positions. When he ran out of ammunition he fired a machine gun he had found in the field, and later fired an anti tank rifle grenade. In going to treat the wounded he himself was wounded but despite his injury he continued treating the wounded and fighting for two more hours. In his actions Corp. Dan Rittman exhibited prudence, bravery, and tenacity.

For this action the Chief of Staff Citation was awarded to him

Tishrei 5736, September 1975, **Mordechai Gur, Lieutenant General, GHQ Chief of Staff**

Corporal Shmulevitch Alexander, of blessed memory, *2127026*

For manifesting bravery, a volunteering spirit and camaraderie

Description of action:

During the Yom Kippur War, Corp. Alexander Shmulevitch, of blessed memory, fought in a mechanized infantry company in battles on the Golan Heights. The day after the breakthrough into the enclave, the company was heavily shelled by Syrian artillery, which injured a soldier who was out in the open field. Corp. Alexander Shmulevitch, of blessed memory, volunteered to go out with the company commander to the soldier lying there and assist in his evacuation to a safe spot all under heavy fire. Later on, Corp. Alexander Shmulevitch, of blessed memory, volunteered to serve as the company commander's driver, and advanced with him through areas exposed to fierce enemy artillery fire. In the battle over Umm-Butna, during heavy artillery bombing, the company soldiers took to shelter in a place too narrow to protect all of them. Corp. Alexander Shmulevitch, of blessed memory, volunteered to step out and scout the enemy. In this position he was hit and fell. In these actions, Corp. Alexander Shmulevitch, of blessed memory, revealed bravery, a volunteering spirit, and comradeship

For this action the Chief of Staff Citation was posthumously awarded to him

Nisan 5736, April 1976, **Mordechai Gur, Lieutenant General, GHQ Chief of Staff**

Major Sarig Yosef, of blessed memory, 482026

Description of action:

When the battles broke out, Maj. Yosef Sarig of blessed memory served as a tank company commander fighting on the Golan Heights. On October 8th, 1973, while leading the force towards Quneitra, he encountered a Syrian ambush. Though Israeli commanders were injured and tanks damaged, Maj. Yosef Sarig, of blessed memory, managed to prudently push the enemy back. Later on, his company encountered missile fire from the direction of Tel Saki. Maj. Yosef Sarig, of blessed memory directed the tanks to low positions and managed to destroy a few missile carriers. On October 10th, 1973 he led the battalion to successfully capture an outpost held by dozens of enemy tanks. He was killed at the foot of the outpost. In all his actions he revealed bravery, prudence, leadership, and exemplary tenacity.

For this action the Medal of Distinguished Service was posthumously awarded to him

Iyar 5735, May 1975, **Mordechai Gur, Lieutenant General, GHQ Chief of Staff**

PART III

Operating the Command Systems at War

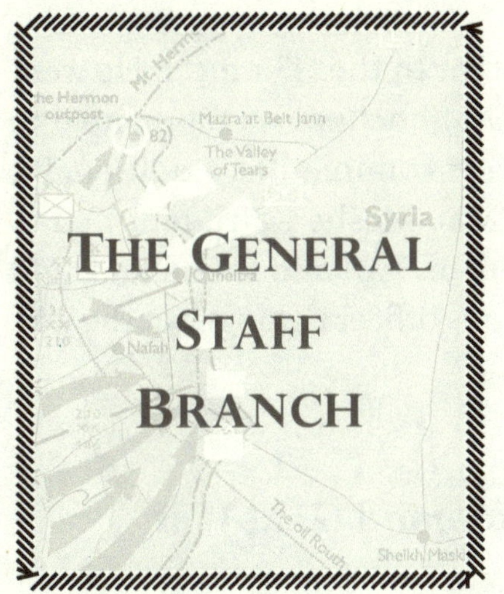

The General Staff Branch

CHAPTER 15

The Northern Command General Staff Branch (G3), headed by Lt. Col. Uri Simchoni had direct responsibility over the core issues of the command tasks. These included the operational tasks in the three sectors on the Lebanese, Syrian and Jordanian borders and the operational activity, training, standby, the order of battle service, the preparation of annual work plans, performance supervision and coordination of the professional staff officers—the HAC, the Command engineering HQ, the command communications office, and the intelligence officer. Intelligence (G2) enjoyed a special privilege since it operated directly with the GOC.

The main positions in G3 were:

Command Operations Officer – Maj. Aharon Vardi,

Deputy G3 Officer – Mordechai Shachar (Schwartzi)

Training Officer – Maj. Yaakov Ohayon

When the war broke out G3 was reinforced by additional officers. Lt. Col. Menachem Einan had arrived from studying abroad and was appointed assistant to the G3 officer. He went on to replace him after Lt. Col. Uri Simchoni was appointed to replace the injured Golani Brigade commander. Additionally, the previous operations officer, Maj. Moshe Kafri, returned to the command G3 from the School of Staff and Command, and served as assistant to the operations officer throughout the war.

Manning of the Command G3 at War

Northern Command (NC):
G3 Officer: Lt. Col. Uri Simchoni
(He was appointed Golani Brigade commander on October 23rd)
NC Deputy G3 Officer: Lt. Col. Menachem Einan
Operations Officer (OO): Maj. Aharon Vardi
Assistant OO (previous OO): Maj. Moshe Kafri
Assistant OO: Captain Baruch Rajuan
Assistant OO: Captain Amnon Golan
Assistant OO: Captain (res.) Gruner Benvenisti
Assistant G3 Officer: Maj. Mordechai Schwartz (Schwartzi)
2nd Assistant G3 Officer: Maj. Dar
Training Officer: Maj. Yaakov Ohayon

Maj. Gen. Uri Simchoni said: “From the beginning of my service as the command G3 officer I viewed the position not solely as that of the classic coordinating body of staff work but as an initiating agent, the one who looks far ahead, that serves as a central axis for brainstorming, introduces issues, separates the wheat from the chaff, and is responsible for the running of ongoing activities and planning for the future.

"I didn’t think bureaucratic aspects of staff work had to be closely monitored and preferred a 'utting through' responsibility contact that enabled us to go straight down to field and unit levels. This perception directed the operations of G3 already in the period prior to the fighting itself and particularly during the first two days of the war. The command G3 received information from the divisions and brigades, and from here, the decisions went down, through orders, into the communications network of the battalions and companies, and even directly to the outpost commanders and the tank platoon commanders.

"The staff work in the Northern Command Headquarters suited the nature of the commanders and senior staff officers. It was a group of officers that had all reached their positions after a long line of positions and professional courses. They were all veterans of the Northern Command that had been there through the Six-Day War and the War of Attrition and had an intimate knowledge of every centimeter in the Golan Heights and a personal acquaintance with every commander. A highly unified staff, both professionally and socially, worked there.

"The special personality of the Northern Command GOC projected onto the staff work. Maj. Gen. Hofi operated with calm and solid self-confidence, used a policy that delegated authority, responsibility, and support to his subordinates, and of a stable and level-headed command which issued clear orders.

"The GOC—('Haka') Maj. Gen. Hofi told me in one of our talks—is like a man standing in the middle of the room, his feet firmly planted in the floor and his hands support the ceiling so it doesn't collapse. The meaning of this image was clear. For everyone underneath, namely us, to function, someone had to hold the roof up above our heads, everything that is above the command. The atmosphere here was one of—**think, initiate, work,** because your back is secure. All these came into being when the war broke out."

In the year prior to the war, the command staff work was highly intensive. Alongside a series of G3 events, regular intelligence patrols were carried out in the depths of the Lebanese territory. Sometimes seven and eight patrols were conducted on the same night to. Aside from the intelligence goals, the training of the commanders and soldiers in command and navigation it meant to offer them an opportunity to breath the special air of "being past the border." About a year before the war, Lebanon was shaken by "The Great Turmoil," wherein the 188th Brigade and Golani forces reached Kafr Kanna. Battles between the 188th Brigade tanks and Syrian tanks took place during two "combat days" on the Golan Heights.

The intensive construction of a border fence along the border from Rosh Hanikra to Mount Dov began at the same time. The G3 pushed and planned, and the command engineering HQ supervised the work, which included the obstacle and fortification activity on the Golan Heights including anti-tank trenches, the outposts, the tank ramps, and the roads along and across the Golan Heights.

The command G3 concentrated the training activity for the command entire order of battle. The command constructed the "Eliakim facility" to improve the training of reserve forces before they go up for routine security tasks on the border. The facility developed quickly and offered gradually more activity. In the year prior to the war each one of the command regular units went through two lengthy brigade training exercises in the summer and the winter. The majority of reserve forces underwent periodic training at the same time.

Placing the emergency storage and ammunition warehouses of the tank brigades closer to the Golan Heights necessitated extensive staff work. Aside from the G3 and maintenance staff in the command, many additional entities took part in it. The 36th Brigade G4 officer, Lt. Col. Rami Dotan's significant contribution should be mentioned as he was the one to carry it out.

The construction of the second armored brigade for the command forces required vast improvising. The 210th Division

Deputy Commander Col. Moshe (Brill) Bar-Kochva pushed and cut processes and managed to have an additional division ready for war.

Weeks prior to the war, the Northern Command, headed by the GOC, pushed toward a different policy than that of the General Staff. Demands to reinforce the northern front stemmed from many discussions in the GOC's office, and from the command intelligence assessments. As a result of the GOC's pressure the Golan Heights was reinforced by the 77th Armored Battalion on the eve of Rosh Hashanah. The demand reached a climax seven days before the war when the command requested that the 179th Brigade not be released after performing its mobilization exercise and be kept mobilized. The plea was denied by the General Staff.

Staff work and methodical early advance preparation before the war created the conditions for the quick and accurate response at its first moments. In spite of the difficult launch conditions, the command units managed to halt the Syrian forces breaking through within 24 hours, and move to counterattack within 40 hours of the onslaught of fire.

A customary Friday morning coordinating staff meeting took place in the GOC's office on that Friday before the war as well. In that meeting, since an alert Level C had been declared at about 10:40 in the IDF, it was decided to advance the Command CCP to Nafah. The GOC, G3 officer—and intelligence officer, along with a number of operations and intelligence NCOs—opened a reduced CCP in the Nafah bunker and reinforced the command Artillery HQ representatives who had been there two days earlier.

The command G3 split into three centers as of Saturday morning even before the firing began. The operations officer remained in the command in Nazareth and dealt with the mobilization of reserves and equipment, pushing the forces to the Golan Heights and issuing orders. The previous operations officer, Kafri, went up to Mount Knaan and dealt with preparing the Command CCP to absorb the staff.

The G3 officer prepared the command orders group intended for Saturday at 10:00 in the Nafah CCP. Later on, and in the absence of the GOC, the G3 officer commanded the forces from the moment the war broke out. The first fire strike landed on Nafah at 13:55. A number of soldiers were injured as a result of the Syrian jets bombing. Others were brought into the packed bunker. The electrical system in the bunker was damaged and there was complete darkness. In addition to the three CCPs that were working in standing positions in the bunker, it was packed to capacity with the regional brigade's administrative soldiers in the bunker as well.

The G3 officer described the outbreak of the war: "Once firing began and I saw its potency it was clear that this was an all-out war. It was clear that our situation was dire. I had no illusions, not even for a minute. The mobilization of the reserve forces was only operated at 10:00, a mere four hours before the war broke out. We were very far from the Sela plan—the defensive deployment plan for the Golan Heights in case of all-out war. I knew that many hours would pass before the reserve units arrived. I also knew that the rapid mobilization brigade did not exist in essence since the 7th Brigade had received most of its tanks. I understood that there was not even a remote chance that the regular alignment on the line of contact would be able to hold. The opening strike was so powerful in volume and surprising. The Golan Heights skies were blackened with smoke of the fires, the thousands of shells, and the dust of the end of summer.

Clearly, steps had to be taken. First of all, the key ground positions, the Quneitra salient in the north and Hushniya in the south had to be captured. The Syrians were not to be allowed to capture them. The reserve forces coming up the Golan Heights had to be rushed.

The GOC, who was in the GHQ in Tel Aviv, appointed the 188th Brigade commander as the senior officer in the region, to stand in for him. This made sense until war broke out. Once firing began the situation changed. Temporary appointments turned insignificant. Everyone had to perform his real role, do the best he could in the most important place for him to be in."

The command G3 began operating the elements and units deployed in the Golan Heights. Commands for the immediate capture of the key areas in the Quneitra salient and the Hushniya region were issued. In managing the battle, G3 wished to hold on and slow down the Syrian advance by utilizing the regular forces, artillery and Air Force until the first reserve soldiers arrived.

The G3 orders were initially issued to the 188th Brigade commander and from him to the forces. This arrangement lasted not loner than twenty minutes as differences of opinion between the commanders caused the 7th Brigade commander to fail to adhere to the 188th Brigade commander's orders, therefore, the forces got their orders directly from the G3 officer.

The command G3 officer suggested that the 188th Brigade commander leave Nafah and command his brigade and the fighting in the southern Golan Heights sector, to which the 82nd Battalion had also been transferred at that point. But the brigade commander said that in light of his appointment as the commander of the Golan Heights he was going to stay at the Command CCP until the GOC returned. When the brigade commander finally headed south, it was already too late. At the critical point in time, the 7th Brigade commander was in the key area of the Quneitra salient at the decisive spot but the 188th Brigade commander was missing from the parallel spot in the southern sector. Thus, Hushniya fell and the way to Nafah was broken through.

In the northern Golan Heights topography limits the enemy's movement to a narrow opening for breakthrough, while the breakthrough option is wider in the southern sector. The difference between fighting in the North of the Golan Heights and the South of the Golan Heights during the first 48 hours was in the application of battle principles. There was one more additional tank battalion in the north of the Golan Heights, which was highly significant. In addition, two principles of war were better maintained in the northern front: the concentration of effort and the capture of key regions. According to the effort concentration principle, the force had to be at the most important place for the most important task. According to the key region capture principle, the enemy had to be stopped its capturing controlling regions or associate forces would be kept in inferior territory and suffer heavy losses.

The commanders controlled the battle in the north. The command armored forces held the key regions; the brigade commander and battalion commanders commanded the forces in the field and the forces operated within their framework and did not disintegrate. In the south there was no senior command in the field, and the battalion framework that had arrived to reinforce the sector—the 82nd Battalion—was immediately split and dispersed.

The command G3 officer thought it was a mistake not to order the brigade commander in the southern sector to concentrate his forces into a brigade site in the key region of the southern Heights—in the Tel Fares—Hushniya region, already in the afternoon hours of October 6. The platoons in the field could not halt the Syrian advance but a brigade site might have blocked their advance toward the target in the

Nafah—Hushniya region.

Once the outpost in Mount Knaan was ready the Command

CCP skipped to it. The entire G3 was transferred to it later on and from this point on operated as an integral branch. All G3 staff work in the first 24-hours dealt with the quick mobilization of the reserve forces and directing them in order to capture key regions, mainly, the route openings in the Golan Heights before the Syrians did. This effort succeeded beyond expectations only thanks to the resourcefulness and initiative of the commanders and reserve soldiers. The staff work relied heavily on numerous improvisations during these stages. These were enabled only due to expertise and familiarity with the territory. Organized staff work began once the situation stabilized. This included planning groups, orders groups, and the issuing of written orders.

In the second 24-hour period, the G3 focused on the command counterattack preparations. Three plans were prepared for its operation once the arrival of the 146th GHQ Reserve Division in the Northern Command was approved. All of them were dependent on the probable developments in the battlefield. In any case, the division was clearly going to be employed for command counter attack. Since the division was advancing north on tracks, the command still had a few hours ahead to consider the various options for its employment.

Heavy battles were going on simultaneously in the Nafah and Petroleum Road region, the Katzbia region, the Mazraat Kanaf region, in El Al and in the Quneitra salient during those hours, Sunday afternoon. The command was kept in the dark regarding the holding efforts success and whether or not a counter attack was feasible as well as whether the Syrians were continuing their advance—a situation that would have entailed sending the division to stabilize a second line of defense. Since the division arrived from the south, the southern route openings were in the hands of the command and there were significant forces in key positions—the 9th Brigade in El Al and the 4th Brigade in the Gamla rise - the command preferred to cast the counter attack along the southern routes.

Toward the end of the second day of fighting—once the situation became somewhat clearer and after it was discovered that the 679th Brigade had managed to block the Syrian offensive on Nafah—"Haka" made the final decision. He decided to attack the next morning through the shortest and simplest path—up the southern routes going up the Golan Heights. The commander of the 146th Division Brig. Gen. Moshe "Musa" Peled reached the command with a few of the division staff officers. They met with the GOC. He was later briefed in detail by the G3 officer to prepare a counter attack through El Al and the Gamla rise. The final decision was reached toward evening. The command order for the attack was received by the division through the liaison officer sent from the command, the former Golani Brigade commander, Col. Yehuda Golan (Ashenfeld). The counter attack, due to start on Monday, October 8, was prepared for and adjusted during the night. After the attack had begun and the first reports of its success were coming in, it was evident that, for the first time since the war had begun, tides had changed—the straining Syrian momentum had vanished and initiative transferred to the IDF. The Israeli side decided the war.

Later on the G3 focused—in addition to the ongoing management of fighting—on planning and organizing staff work toward the offensive into the depth of Syrian territory. Once it was clear counter attack was a success and the Syrians were being pushed back, the GOC decided that going back to former borders was not an option. He instructed the staff to prepare an offensive into Syrian territory. Two alternatives were examined by G3 based on the "Ben Gil" plans in the south and north. Upon choosing the northern path - the short route to Damascus —forces and equipment for it were gathered.

The 36th Division broke through quickly. When it was already evident that the 36th Division was successful, the 210th Division was still in the Quneitra salient awaiting an order. It seemed that the enemy was not prepared to fiercely defend the Quneitra—Khan Arnabeh route. The desire to exploit success immediately, the 210th Division was ordered to break through in its sector. In terms of combat doctrine, it would have been better to avoid additional breakthrough attempts as much as possible. These entailed losses and serious burnout. Once the breakthrough were made, it was better to exploit it to bring additional forces into the enemy's alignment. In hindsight, the G3 officer believes that: "We should have read the battle differently, and once the first breakthrough succeeded we should have instructed the 210th Division to move toward its tasks following the 36th. We would have saved many lives."

After the breakthrough and the pushing of the Syrian, Iraqi, and Jordanian counter attacks, it was decided that this achievement was to suffice and the forces were to be deployed for defense along the existing lines. Alongside fortification efforts, the G3 dealt with planning a rotation between the units to allow for refreshment and rest.

The command decision to recapture the Hermon toward the end of the war led to an extensive battle procedure and the establishment of a command plan. The planning and command effort was divided: Brig. Gen. Kuti Adam coordinated, planned and commanded the operation while the Command CCP headed by the GOC and with the G3's assistance and coordination, continued commanding the entire front. The development of the fighting in Operation Kinuach, toward the end of the night, created a situation wherein, while the Golani Brigade had begun fighting its way up to the outpost, the paratroopers had already completed the capture of the Syrian Hermon outpost. Under the new circumstances, it would have been preferable to instruct the Golani Brigade to stop its advance, suppress the Syrian forces, and have the paratroopers complete the task of capturing the Israeli Hermon outpost. However, the command stuck to the original plan thus inflicting heavy losses on the Golani Brigade.

Operation Kinuach was the pinnacle of a monumental effort that returned the command to the positions it occupied before the war in all its sectors and even deeper in the enclave that was forty kilometers away from the Syrian capital.

INTELLIGENCE

CHAPTER 16

THE NORTHERN COMMAND HEADQUARTERS intelligence branch was in charge of all the intelligence required by the GOC, the staff officers and branches and the subordinate units. It provided information relating to needs of the different fields: terrain, enemy, activity, routine security needs, operational planning and the fighting that went on before and during the war in all three sectors of the Northern Command:

- The Jordanian border from Beit She'an up to the Yarmouk River.
- The Syrian border on Golan Heights from the Yarmouk in the south to the Hermon summit.
- The Lebanese border from Mount Dov and the Hermon summit in the east to the shore of the Mediterranean in Rosh Hanikra.

The command intelligence department dealt with these three arenas different in terrain character and enemy. In addition, it dealt with subversive, hostile terrorist activity, its research and forewarning provisions.

Intelligence officer Lt. Col.Hagai Mann headed the department as of August 15, 1973 when he assumed position after Lt. Col. Yehoshua (Shiea) Bar-Masada had completed his duty in the Northern Command and was appointed both instructor at the Command & Staff College and intelligence officer of the new 210th Division of the command.

During his period on the command, the command intelligence prepared intelligence aides for the possible different fighting conditions: maps, Photostats, route files and terrain files. About two months before the end of his tenure, during the period of the Kachol Lavan alerts of April-May 1973, "warning signs" of the changes in the Syrian enemy's situation became apparent. These raised many unanswerable questions. Following the GOC's demand, the intelligence information data that had been accumulating since the beginning of that year influenced the command situation assessment and brought about initiated actions that allowed the command to better prepare itself for a possible Syrian offensive, at a very short notice or no pre-warning at all.

The "warning signs" accumulating from April to June were supported by reports that added more unanswerable questions. The intelligence department was asked to gather and assess information, in order to provide a reasonable response for the shifts and changes that occurred behind the Syrian border. All aides were constantly updated and distributed to the GOC, the staff officers, the J2 Research Branch and the different units at their different levels. This was done in order to allow them to integrate "the enemy's possible courses of action" as a basis for operational plans.

Once Lt. Col. Hagai Mann was appointed, the department needed an assistant intelligence officer as the previous assistant, Maj. Avinoam Nahum, was promoted and received the rank of Lt. Col. Replacing Lt. Col. Hagai Mann in his previous position as intelligence officer at the chief infantry and paratrooper officer headquarters. The position was filled in the meantime by the head of the hostile terrorist activity sector, Maj. Giora Avni. Pressure on the Aman chief's assistant resulted in the nomination of Maj. Shlomo Tagner to the position as late as September. He arrived from the Command and Staff College.

Command Intelligence Department Structure and Organization

Command Intelligence Officer
Lt. Col. Hagai Mann
Assistant Intelligence Officer
Maj. Shlomo Tagner

Staff

Syria sector Sector Head: **Captain Reuven Fenikel**	Jordan sector Sector Head: **Captain Amir Johannes**	Lebanon sector Sector Head: **Captain Dror Galili**	Hostile Terrorist Activity sector **Maj. Giora Avni**
Alignment Officer: **Captain Arieh Rizel**			
Photography Lab	Maps Stockroom	Aerial Photograph interpreters Head : **Lt. Zvika Horowitz**	Cryptography **Miri Stein, Mary, Leah**

There were twenty-five reserve soldiers, officers and NCOs, to reinforce the department regular alignment, as well as a long-range observation unit with twenty-five reserve soldiers, most of them officers.

The following collecting agencies were at the command on the eve of and after the Yom Kippur War:

- **The RSM Outposts** on the Golan Heights were in a good observation post over the Syrian outposts on the border and over the first strip line of defense. NCOs from the command and the Regional Brigade intelligence occasionally reinforced the observation posts manned by the forces performing routine security maneuvers. Near the outbreak of the war, the Hermon outpost was reinforced by three NCOs from the command intelligence department. Yedidya Tzur went on leave for Yom Kippur on October 4, Avi Shlein managed to escape the Hermon outpost after it was captured by the Syrians, and Yossi Tor was taken prisoner of war by the Syrians and returned to Israel as part of the POW's exchange.
- Aman **Human Intelligence 154 Unit** which was an agents' unit in the northern district gathered information on the different fronts and passed it on directly to the command intelligence. The unit, under the command of Maj. Yehoshua Bar-Tikva, was also in charge of interrogating enemy prisoners in the battlefield and in prison camps during the war.
- **The Central Signal Intelligence Unit 848** in direct contact with the command intelligence was under the command of Itzik Yochanan and operated out of bases on the Golan Heights and the Galilee. During the war, the district representative Captain Oded Sela was assigned to assist the command intelligence officer in everything relating to *network* intelligence. Tactical Mobile Sigint Platoons under the command of Maj. Nissim Atzmon operated alongside the divisions and assisted their intelligence units.

- **A light aircraft aerial observation**, which was at the service of the command intelligence on the Ramat David Air Force base. Where aerial observations were carried out from in accordance with intelligence needs and following the intelligence officer's decision in coordination with the Air Force. Patrol sorties were carried out along the borders and allowed the command intelligence aerial scouts to carry out observations and oblique limited ranges aerial photographs. The information gathered from these aerial patrols was reported to both Aman and the command units sources.
- **Fighter jet aerial photographs** were carried out on occasion following demands by the command intelligence and according to the Aman's plans and initiative. Film development was usually carried out by the Air Force's 121st Intelligence Services Unit. The interpretation was performed by the command intelligence photo interpreter and at the same time by the 399th Aman Central Research's Aerial Photo Interpretation Unit. Air Force intelligence photo interpreter- decoders analyzed the data required by the Air Force including missile alignments and anti-aircraft guns. The analysis results were distributed to all in need of the information.
- **The "Hatzav" OSINT Unit** passed on open sources intelligence information material taken from Arab newspapers, radio, and television broadcasts that had been translated into Hebrew.
- **Most of the Intelligence summaries and reports prepared at the Aman Research Department** arrived at the command as intelligence and not allowed for cross-reference and update of information.

General information and intelligence derived from the material gathered in the Northern Command was distributed to the different units and headquarters, including Aman Research. On the other hand, not all information Aman had and obtained in the period prior to the war, not even that relevant and pre-warning reached the command intelligence.

The command intelligence ability to assess the enemy's situation was limited in comparison to that of Aman because it was based on basic information, ongoing current information and that coming from the higher level, that is, Aman Research reports. This was the case since:

The command intelligence officer did not have all the information Aman Research had.

The intelligence summaries and Aman reports were transferred to the command intelligence as intelligence that had already been evaluated, namely not raw information but rather processed information.

Those engaged in intelligence assessment in the command intelligence were usually few and lower in ranks with insufficient experience.

Nevertheless, the command intelligence was successful in wisely interpreting the manifold volumes of information that arrived from the collecting agencies and assessed that the preparations carried out by the Syrian Army before the Yom Kippur War showed clear signs of attack preparations.

The Command Headquarters intelligence assessments in the year prior to the war - chiefly based on field findings analysis and the capabilities of the Syrian enemy—caused the Command GOC to take action that was found highly effective at the onslaught of the war and assisted in the rapid reserve divisions mobilization, halting the Syrian Army and pushing it back beyond the Purple Line, and at a later stage enabled the IDF forces to be within artillery bombing range of the outskirts of Damascus. Aman Research, Branch 5, disagreed with the command intelligence assessments until the war actually broke out. It kept insisting that the Syrian Army was preparing for defense.

In the late evening hours, on Friday, October 5, a commanders' meeting with the GOC took place in the Nafah Base to discuss the possibility that the Syrian Army would initiate an expanded "combat day" format or attempt to obtain the political achievement of capturing an outpost, a settlement, or the former district city of Quneitra. Its deployment and strength were known to the command.

The intelligence officer was summoned by the GOC on Saturday at 05:30. He was notified of a report handed to the head of the Mossad who was in Europe at the time by a highly reliable source, stating that on that day at 18:00 Egypt and Syria were launching a war against Israel. The intelligence officer immediately checked with his deputy, Maj. Shlomo Tagner, who was at the command main headquarters in Nazareth, and discovered that this report had not reached Northern Command Intelligence either. At that early morning hour, Lt. Col. Hagai Mann ordered the placing of teams on call to be ready to supply intelligence aides to the forces that would surely be mobilized.

At about 10:00 the GOC flew to the Nafah Base by helicopter and in the orders group stated: "Today at 18:00 a war will be launched against Israel by both Egypt and Syria simultaneously." A detailed intelligence review, the enemy's possible courses of action along with data updates by the staff officers were given during the orders group. At the end of which the intelligence officer and his assistants positioned themselves in the Nafah Base cramped command bunker.

The CCP's reduced intelligence team included the Syrian sector officer, Captain Reuven Fenikel, two intelligence NCOs and the teleprinter operator Miri Stein in addition to the intelligence officer. At about 13:40 reports came in from the outposts and observations posts that the Syrians were removing camouflage nets from the tanks and artillery guns. Less than twenty minutes later the entire area of the Golan Heights was covered by barrages of artillery fire from about a thousand guns, tank fire, and aerial bombardment by Syrian jets, across the front and rear of the Golan Heights. The Northern Command was not surprised that war broke out. The only surprise was that the opening of fire was moved up from 18:00 to 14:00.

The operation of the intelligence system during the war required that it be split between the forward alignment, which was initially positioned in Nafah and later, in the course of the war, in the *Armon*[21] command outpost on Mount Knaan, and the main alignment, which continued to operate, prepare and issue intelligence aides, under the assistant intelligence officer, at the Command Headquarters in Nazareth. The work on Mount Knaan suffered due to lack of minimal conditions for proper intelligence work, such as insufficient light, improper communications system and nowhere to hang aides.

In order to assist the intelligence officer in his round-the-clock work, Col. Avraham Arnan, former commander of the GHQ Reconnaissance Unit, arrived at the Mount Knaan CCP of his own initiative, immediately after the war broke out. Col. Avraham Arnan wished to serve as assistant intelligence officer and fulfilled every task he was assigned. He hung up maps, marked intelligence data on, participated in briefings and briefed in planning groups and ongoing situation assessments.

During the war the command intelligence department maintained contact with Aman Research Branch 5 and the divisions' intelligence departments. This is where the processed information was sent to and sent from regarding the status of Israeli and enemy forces in the field. The divisions' intelligence departments were headed by experienced intelligence officers:

21 "Castle" in Hebrew.

the reserve officer Lt. Col. Danny Agmon in the 36th Division, Lt. Col. Yehoshua (Shiea) Bar-Masada in the 210th Division, and Lt. Col. Moti Katz in the 146th Division. Information from the field reached the command from the regional brigade observations as well, particularly those of assistant intelligence officer Captain Asher Sadan (Kalichman) who was at Hermonit, and the 7th Brigade intelligence officer Maj. Ilan Sahar.

A permanent communication line was established between the 848th Sigint Unit northern district Command Headquarters and to the Northern Command Intelligence to improve work processes. The unit positioned network intelligence officer Captain Oded Sela with the command intelligence officer for the course of the war to assist in classifying the large volumes of information. During the organization on October 7, the Command Communication Officer Lt. Col. Avraham Kayam installed radio devices, at the intelligence officer's request, to enable listening to the IDF forces, which in turn made it possible to "read the battle" and intercept data regarding enemy maneuvers.

When the 36th Division began breaking through the Purple Line to the east, although approval was not granted to dispatch a light aircraft aerial observation over the forces was sent. It was intended to improve the ability to identify enemy artillery units and silence the Syrian anti-battery fire. When the Dornier Do 27 approached the line it was shot down by missiles over Outpost 107. The pilot, the artillery liaison officer, and the two command intelligence aerial scouts, Staff Sgt. Eli Agasi and Staff Sgt. Benny Samuel, were killed. This was the only attempt made during the war to employ aerial observation from a light aircraft to range targets.

Even though, the Northern Command Intelligence did not get all the reports and information that Aman had, it assessed that the Syrian operations were in preparation for an offensive.

In contradiction, Branch 5 of Aman Research that was trapped by "the concept" and insisted, decisively and unreservedly, in reports, weekly summaries and talks that the Syrian military activity was defensive for fear of an Israeli offensive.

Intelligence officer Lt. Col.Hagai Mann shared: "The short period I was on board before the war broke out was frustrating and exhausting. The staff work in the Command Headquarters and particularly the backup I received from the Command GOC, made it possible for me to practice my professional judgment. The officers and NCOs, both regular and reserve in the command intelligence department, participated in the strenuous task in the period prior to and during the war.

In retrospect it seems that the valuable and cautionary information that had not been brought to my attention could have supported my assessments that Syria was preparing for an offensive. This includes the information provided by King Hussein; estimates by foreign intelligence sources; the significance of the arrival of the Syrian 47th Tank Brigade at the Golan Heights front; the report regarding the departure of the Russian consultants' families from both Syria and Egypt and the report transferred by the head of the Mossad on the morning of October 6, 1973, from the top agent Babel. My assessments clashed with those of Aman, as it was expressed up to the last report before the first shot was fired. The excuse that the information was halted due to security measures and the need to protect sources does not hold water. There are varied possibilities to transfer information without jeopardizing sources' security. The "top source" report regarding the war due to break out that morning was transferred to me over the phone by Lt. Col. Avi Yaari on October 1, 1973 without mention of the source, is evidence enough of such possibilities."

The final report of the "Agranat Investigative Committee" states, among other:"Northern Command Intelligence Officer,

Lt. Col. Hagai Mann, who was more independent in his assessments discussed the troubling information with the Command GOC which prompted him to demand the reinforcement of the alignment on the Golan Heights... and so disagreed with the Aman Research estimate regarding the two Syrian armored divisions' deployed in the second defensive strip on the Syrian front..."

The "Agranat Investigation Committee" goes on to state: "A debate on equal terms between the view of Aman Research and the field intelligence was lacking. [In this case the reference is to the Northern Command Intelligence department] The atmosphere of consensus and adaptability caused the weakening of the combat intelligence engaged in field intelligence activities, such as observations in the field, patrols and prisoner interrogation. The special significance of this intelligence is in its being "fresh" when it is gathered and could therefore supply immediate and updated information whether by contact of observation, surveillance, or contact in battle regarding the enemy's level of preparedness and intentions." The committee decided: "...within GHQ Intelligence the combat intelligence was pushed into a corner, thus neglecting a suitable confrontation with other information obtained by Aman."

It is worthwhile mentioning that throughout the period of September and early October prior to the war, when Aman's senior intelligence officials were supposedly pondering over the meaning of the "warning signs" in the Syrian arena, the Northern Command Intelligence officer was not invited to meet with the head of Aman. Nor was he invited to meet with the research department even though the Northern Command GOC raised doubts regarding the events in Syria during the GHQ forum and demanded additional forces to reinforce the alignment in light of the command intelligence assessments. This does not include a meeting where he was reprimanded by the Research

Branch head, Brig. Gen. Arieh Shalev, on October 2, 1973. The Northern Command Intelligence officer, who assumed this position on August 15th, 1973 and completed his tenure in June 1976, was not summoned to the discussions that took place after the war where the "lessons of the war" were to be learned.

The Agranat Investigative Committee mentions that aside from the channel between command intelligence and Aman Research to transfer information, there was room for this to take place through commanders and G3, which was not done,... excluding the exception to the rule, the Northern Command GOC, who called up the GHQ after learning following an aerial photograph of September 24th that we do not have the possibility of pre-warn." The Northern Command GOC did raise issues of intelligence, pre-warning, and the problem of the balance of power in discussions held by the Minister of Defense, in GHQ discussions and in a meeting with the Air Force commander after the SAM sites were identified in aerial photographs of the Golan Heights front and were built and manned before the war. This deployment was expected to and eventually did significantly limit the capabilities of operational flights and aerial support to the ground forces.

Intelligence Officers in the Northern Command Brigade and Divisions During the War

188th Brigade: intelligence officer—Maj. Moshe (Tzurich) Tzur; assistant intelligence officer—Captain Haim Vidal

820th Regional Brigade: intelligence officer—Maj. Moshe Temler; assistant intelligence officer—Captain Asher (Klichman) Sadan

36th Division: intelligence officer—Lt. Col. Danny Agmon; assistant intelligence officer—Maj. Immanuel (Joe) Nishri, Maj. Elkana Har-Nof

210th Division: intelligence officer—Lt. Col. Yehoshua (Shiea) Bar-Masada; assistant intelligence officer—Maj. Rachamim (Rachmin) Aharon, Captain Itamar Tzizik

146th Division: intelligence officer—Lt. Col. Moti Katz; assistant intelligence officer—Maj. Shay Hevron

1st Brigade (Golani): intelligence officer—Maj. Yoram Kateli

7th Brigade: intelligence officer—Maj. Ilan Sahar; assistant intelligence officer—Captain Menachem Levi

179th Brigade: Maj. Noah Efrat

679th Brigade: intelligence officer—Maj. Eitan Nadiv (DOW) and replaced by Yonatan (Yoni) Magal

164th Brigade: intelligence officer—Maj. Haim Eliahu fought in Sinai front

4th Brigade: intelligence officer—Maj. Yonatan (Johnny) Heiman (KIA); replaced by Dror Galili

9th Brigade: intelligence officer—Maj. Dan Luz

205th Brigade: intelligence officer—Maj. Shlomo Iliah

317th Brigade: intelligence officer—Maj. Yigal Talami

670th Brigade: intelligence officer—Maj. Ilan Waxelbaum; assistant intelligence officer—Lt. Dudu Tzur

Meron District: intelligence officer—Maj. Yonatan (Yoni) Magal replaced Eitan Nadiv who was injured in the breakthrough battle.

612th Regional Brigade: Cap. Israel Cogot

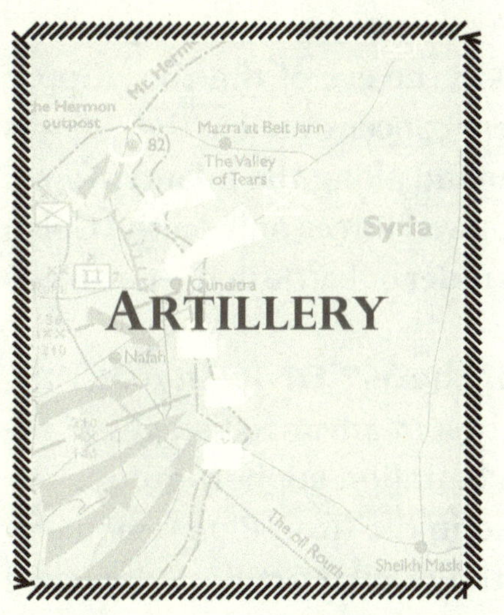

ARTILLERY

CHAPTER 17

THE 744TH ARTILLERY COMMAND Headquarters (HAC HQ)—under the command of Lt. Col. Avraham Bar David and G3 officer Maj. Gidon Etzion—planned, assembled, and deployed the artillery in the Northern Command region. The artillery had an extensive reserve alignment and a reduced regular one.

The order of battle was established after the Six-Day War based on the divisions Artillery Groups. Each division Artillery Group included five battalions: three gun battalions and two 160mm and 120mm S.P. heavy mortar battalions. Each battalion had three batteries of four guns each. Every infantry brigade and regional brigade had one battalion of 120mm mortars. Additional long-range guns (175 mm) and captured 130mm enemy cannon from the Six-Day War with a number of designated rockets were part of the GHQ artillery reserve were employed by the Chief Artillery Officer HQ (CAO HQ).

The artillery alert was chiefly based on the regular force to be reinforced by reserve units during periods of tension or at times the regular force was training. On the eve of the Yom Kippur War the regular artillery alignment concentrated in the rear was deployed in the Northern Command along the infantry forces in the RSM outposts and the armored forces only on the Golan Heights front. The reserve forces order of battle in the north was organized into Artillery Groups:

The **212th Artillery Group of the 36th Division** under the command of Col. Benny Arad was in advanced stages of organization as a permanent five battalion support group. The battalions' equipment was stored in the Rosh Pina region and served as the main source of the regular artillery deployed throughout the Golan Heights.

The 282nd Artillery Group of the **210th Division** recently established in the course of 1973, under the command of Col. Moshe Levi, was in the early stages of establishment. The battalions intended for the support group were two Priest battalions —105mm Self-propelled M101 guns scheduled for conversion to 155mm SPGs—and other battalions were in the planning stages. The support group was equipped based on command Artillery Group battalions. These were stored in the command bases in Kurdani and Kiryat Motzkin north of Haifa.[22]

In addition, the Northern Command artillery order of battle included the HAC's artillery battalions most of which towed French 155mm battalions, and the mortar 120mm battalions of the independent and the regional brigades.

Prior to the Yom Kippur War, the artillery on the Golan Heights included just the 334th Battalion, which had been the Golani Brigade regular mortar battalion until 1970, under the command of Lt. Col. Arieh Schwartz (Shacham). It was operating two 160mm Self-propelled mortar batteries. A third mortar battery was removed from the order of battle a month prior to

22 On the Mediterranean coast.

the war, and operated instead a 155mm SPG battery which was based on guns which were part of the 212th Reserve Artillery Group battalion.

The three batteries were deployed in permanent positions in the north, center and south of the Golan Heights. The integration of the 155mm regular gun battery in the short range mortar battalion was intended to ensure fire coverage toward the outpost sectors mainly in order to respond to nearby danger fire risk tasks throughout the Golan Heights. Likewise, a 155mm SPG reserve battery was deployed on the Golan Heights from time to time. Months prior to the war, the mobilization of the unit was not approved. The battalion headquarters positioned at the Nafah Base served as the 820th Regional Brigade Group headquarters and was responsible for the entire Golan Heights front.

The outpost commanders went through a fresh training session in operating artillery fire in their sector at every forces replacement on the border. Danger Fire risk tasks were marked in the field around every outpost. All the batteries deployed for operations were equipped with additional communications radio system through which they were integrated into the network of the borderline outposts as well, along the artillery networks. Forward observer officers from among the batteries were integrated into the morning patrols along the line of the border. Through them the artillery guns, meant to secure the patrols and respond to any fire request, followed the patrol route of advance.

As part of the increased activity in the command on the eve of the war, all the planned artillery positions were marked and surveyed on the national grid map by a national survey unit. "Exit points" intended to mark ground location for the airplanes to engage targets within the range of the anti-air Syrian deployed missiles and to allow the operation of combat jets to attack ground targets without being exposed to the missiles defended zone, were marked in certain places on the Golan Heights under the responsibility of the command artillery headquarters.

The artillery positions that were used for routine security measures were dugouts or built bunkers for combatants. Permanent long-range observation posts were deployed in controlling sites all along the border and were used by the artillery. Operational planning determined the command artillery unit deployment, the positions they were planned to take and the observation posts they were to be deployed at. An artillery ammunition depot of 7000 shells which as usual were deployed calibers meant to supply artillery ammunition during the onslaught of incidents and combat days was established at the logistics base in Snobar on the Golan Heights.

As early as the beginning of September 1973, and contrary to their custom, the Syrians did not thin out their artillery on the Golan Heights but rather added to it and reinforced it as could be observed through intelligence and artillery observations as well. On September 13th, the command demanded the reinforcement of the artillery alignment in the north following the aerial incident, the flare up in the sector and the continued Syrian forces reinforcement of the front including additional artillery and SAM batteries. With the GHQ's approval, the alignment on the Golan Heights was reinforced by two 175mm batteries and the 55th Battalion command under Lt. Col. Shraga Ben Zvi, which normally were deployed in the Sinai. The two batteries were equipped with the weapons of the Northern Command 647th Reserve Battalion, located in the Pilon Base, and deployed along the Waterfalls Route. The main task of the long-range guns was to strike the Syrian missile batteries, thus assisting the Israeli Air Force jets in attain aerial supremacy. On September 26 a battery of surface-to-surface MAR-290 Ivry rocket launchers was also brought up to the Hermon region.

The continued state of alert and the 7th Brigade coming up to the Golan Heights on Rosh Hashanah Eve led to an additional artillery reinforcement of the regular M-109 battalion, the 405th M-109 SPG Battalion from the 146th Division 213th Artillery Group, under the command of Maj. Arieh Mizrachi, who came up from his permanent Bilu Base which was under the Central Command. The battalion joined the 7th Brigade, went up on the Golan Heights with it and took positions in the center and south. The battalion commander was appointed the RAC of the 7th Brigade.

On the eve of the war, the Golan Heights were reinforced by another battalion of M-50 SPGs based on artillery Training Base No. 9, under the command of Lt. Col. Ben Ami Cohen. This battalion was also equipped with the Northern Command reserve battalion guns taken from the Pilon emergency storage warehouses on Saturday. The Training Base No. 9 M-50 battalion went up and deployed in positions in the south and center of the Golan Heights.

About 200 ammunition shells for each gun were transferred to positions where the artillery units were deployed. These were either piled on the ground or left on board the ammunition trucks. Every battery firing position had an alternative position prepared and skipping from one to the other was practiced. The units also patrolled access routes between the positions and the ammunition base in Snobar to make the ammunition reinforcement of positions possible when the need arose.

Parallel to the IDF forces, an artillery force of about 900 barrels was deployed on the Syrian side of the Golan Heights. It was made up of mortars and various caliber guns, including 122, 152, and 130 mm. These operated out of 157 batteries of six guns each. The artillery in the alignment included the brigades guns and mortars, the Artillery Groups of the three frontline Syrian divisions (the 7th, 9th, and 5th), reinforced by support units from the second rank divisions. Two heavy 240mm mortar batteries were positioned facing key targets on the Hermon and Tel Fares

The Syrians increased the amount of artillery positioned near the line in the two days leading up to the war. An artillery battalion was added to each one of the first rank brigades in order to create a Brigade Task Group. The mid-range Artillery Corps was advanced to a distance of approximately four kilometers from the front line. At the same time, long-range 180mm gun batteries and 240mm heavy mortars from the GHQ level were also deployed at the front line and were mainly intended for breaking through fortifications. Additionally, FROG-7 surface-to-surface rocket batteries with a range of approximately seventy kilometers were also deployed in the depth of the front.

On Saturday morning, October 6, all of the IDF eleven batteries were on maximum alert in a new deployment both in fortified positions and in exposed positions in three battalion sectors across the Golan Heights front.[23] Each of the batteries was linked to outposts in its sector in order to respond to their fire demand. Facing them, about 157 Syrian batteries were deployed at that time.

Additionally, batteries of surface-to-surface MAR-290 "Ivry" rocket launchers were deployed throughout the Golan Heights region in positions within range of Damascus, with elements from the ranging battalion, on the eve of the war.

The 334th Battalion commander and headquarters reported to the Nafah CCP as the artillery headquarters supporting the 820th Regional Brigade, and in fact functioned as an artillery headquarters for the entire Golan Heights from the first moment of the war. Similarly to the debate in the armored forces, there was a debate regarding who was in command of the Artillery Corps.

23 See details of deployment in Part I.

This was settled when the Northern Command HAC assumed command.

The 405th Battalion headquarters functioned as the 7th Brigade Artillery Group headquarters, while the two additional battalion commanders on the Golan Heights, Lt. Col. Ben Ami Cohen and Lt. Col. Shraga Ben Zvi, were positioned in Tel Fares and Tel Avital for observation and control of the support fire for the infantry and armored battalions, companies and platoons, on the line outposts and ramps.

At the same time, artillery forward observation officers were deployed in the Hermon outpost, at the Tank Bend in the upper Hermon and in other controlling sites. Forward observation and artillery liaison officers were positioned in the different units. They were also equipped with communicators to contact aircrafts so as to get aerial fire support in case firing started. An aerial artillery observation officer with a small air plane was positioned in the Ramat David Air Force base to be deployed when needed.

The fire plan prepared at the time was based on each battery engaging four targets at once—a gun for each target. The high priority targets were the Syrian artillery batteries threatening the settlements and IDF bases in the region. In addition every battery had "dangerous close fire tasks" to assist the outposts on the line.

Artillery Defensive Battle on the Golan Heights

At 13:45 the forward observer officer at Outpost 110 in the center of the Golan Heights reported the removal of camouflage nets from the Syrian artillery batteries in the region. Ten minutes later the Syrians launched a 35 minute long fire preparation of hundreds of guns, mortars, rocket launchers, and jets. The Syrian artillery began stifle the IDF outposts along the line and many deeper targets including CCPs, bases and junctions. The Syrian anti-battery fire was directed at the few IDF artillery batteries deployed in their established positions on the line. The artillery fire was also aimed at the IDF observation posts on the hills and on the Hermon in order to silence and blind them. The Tel Fares observation post was shelled by 240mm mortars intending to destroy it. Additional shells were fired, apparently toward the Hermon outpost as well. A number of 180mm artillery shells were fired at the Mount Knaan command outpost and the intelligence base north of Saffed and fell near them. The Syrian artillery preparation did indeed destroy and blind some of the positions making it difficult to locate and target from them.

All IDF artillery batteries were activated in response to the Syrian artillery, including forty-four guns. These were first directed at anti-battery targets, chiefly the Syrians' mid-range artillery batteries, and only afterwards and following the demands made by the forces in the outposts along the line did they fire at the breaking through Syrian forces. The large number of targets split the battery fire into firing companies, and even single guns were directed at the different targets.

The employment of artillery was mainly based on intelligence reports and was aimed from the line outposts, rather than by ranging from the observation posts at the mound heads, which had been neutralized by the rising smoke over the combat zone. On the first day of fighting the Golan Heights was engulfed in smoke, not only from the incoming and outgoing shells, but also from brush fires that spread due to the dry thorns of late summer. The artillery fire was mainly aimed at the broken through sectors on the Petroleum Road and Quneitra salient. Fire was also aimed at the Syrian and Moroccan forces penetrating in the north of the Golan Heights. The 160mm mortar batteries and 155mm batteries from the 334th Battalion were also directed at the Syrian forces attacking the Hermon outpost. Under cover of some artillery shells the soldiers attempted to evacuate from the outpost while the fighting developed the batteries were also employed in "firing on our own outposts" to strike the Syrian forces moving toward them. The Hermon forward observer officer operating from the Tank Bend continued ranging toward targets in the north of the Golan Heights. Lt. Col. Ben Ami Cohen and his team, who operated from the summit of Tel Fares, ranged artillery guns against the Syrian efforts in the southern sector.

In the afternoon hours the batteries began reporting a shortage of ammunition and the push of additional ammunition from the ammunition base in Snobar, made available to the command began. The Syrian anti-battery fire—which had been inaccurate during the first hours of fighting—improved and some batteries were forced to skip to their alternative positions.

The firing of mortars toward the Hermon continued and combatants tried to escape the outpost under its cover. The forward observation officer intended to operate from the Tank Bend in Hermon left for his position and performed tasks throughout the following days of combat. A 175mm battery deployed on the Golan Heights was also used to strike the FROG surface-to-surface rocket battery. During the night artillery fire was aimed at the Syrian forces attacking the Israeli outposts mainly in the southern sector of the front. At the same time the 405th Battalion fire units were employed to assist the 7th Brigade forces holding in the Valley of Tears. Artillery included the firing of illumination shells to locate the breaking through Syrian forces at night.

Already at the early night hours there was a shortage of illumination shells. All ammunition in the batteries, battalions and the Snobar ammunition base had been used up.

Some of the artillery batteries skipped back to rear positions during the night due to the advance of the Syrian forces. Two batteries belonging one to Training Base No. 9 Battalion and the other to 405th Battalion deployed in the southern Heights west of Tel Fares, were hit by the advancing Syrian forces tank fire. Five SPGs pulled out west toward the Gamla rise in a convoy under the command of the 405th Battalion deputy commander, Maj. Uri Manos. Other batteries, in the central and northern Golan Heights, skipped to alternative positions and were stocked with ammunition. Some of the ammunition trucks headed for the batteries were hit by Syrian tank fire penetrating the depth of the Golan Heights in the Hushniya region. GHQ ammunition convoys began arriving and were received by the HAC forces that pushed them at times all the way up to the gun batteries.

On the morning of October 7, the 212th Artillery Group of the 36th Division, under the command of Col. Benny Arad, gained responsibility for the operation of artillery on the Golan Heights. The 334th Battalion was placed under his command, as well as batteries from the 405th Battalion and Training Base No. 9 Battalion deployed in the center and north of the Golan Heights. The 334th Battalion headquarters operated as the support headquarters for the 188th Brigade, which was placed in charge of the south of the Golan Heights. The battalion itself concentrated in the Mount Odem region and continued assisting the holding efforts in the northern sector.

The 55th Battalion long-range artillery gun batteries as well as the 412th Battalion batteries later on were employed during the fighting for the benefit of command tasks, many of which were dictated by the Air Force and aimed at striking SAM batteries.

The first reserve units were recruited in the emergency storage warehouses and began advancing toward positions on the Golan Heights. Some had already begun firing from positions west of the Jordan River. Fire at Outpost 116 was carried out by a 412th Battalion 175mm battery deployed in the Kfar Hanasi region. The 120mm mortar batteries were deployed to defend the Jordan River bridges.

Parallel to fire management on the Golan Heights the HAC HQ placed a special effort on mobilizing and deploying the Northern Command reserve artillery alignment. When mobilization and equipping were completed, the first reserve units began their advance toward positions on the Golan Heights. During the organization of the Northern Command forces on the war eve, most of the artillery units were left at the distant Kurdani and Mansura Bases and only a small portion was brought closer to bases near the Golan Heights. Due to circumstances under which the war broke out, it was necessary to travel by caterpillar tracks from the Haifa Bay region to the Golan Heights,[24] crossing that great distance, some of which in hilly terrain caused a major delay in the deployment of the artillery alignment. The forces moving on the main roads refueled at civilian gas stations along the travel routes. There was one incident of the 827th Battalion Priest 105mm SPGs on their way up to the Golan Heights along the Yehudia route that were hit by direct Syrian fire.

The ones arriving first were naturally the 120mm mortars on faster moving modified half-tracks. These short range battalions deployed first, following the command of the 36th Division deputy commander Brig. Gen. Menachem Aviram to defend the Jordan River bridges. Only after a while were they given the opportunity to enter the Golan Heights. Even more time passed before they became accustomed to the circumstances.

The 212th Artillery Group of the 36th Division set the regular forces in motion. These were made up of two M-50 SPG

24 This is some 100 kilometers away.

battalions as well as a 160mm and a 120mm Mortar Battalion.

The 282ndmm Self-propelled mortar battalion, equipped at the Pilon emergency storage warehouses Artillery Group of the 210th Division under the command over artillery supporting the division. It included, including two 105mm Self-propelled Priest battalions, a 155mm M-50 SPG Battalion, a 120mm Self-propelled mortar battalion, as well as a towed 155mm battalion from their storage warehouses in the Haifa Bay region. The support group, which showed up on Sunday morning to plan maneuvers in the Meron district, was assigned responsibility for the southern Golan Heights at noon that day, where it began operating the rest of the 405th Battalion and Training Base No. 9 Battalion batteries made up of 4 M-109 Howitzer SPGs and one M-50 SPG, and the two long-range batteries of the 55th Battalion who had also retreated west. Simultaneously, the artillery support group headquarters gathered additional artillery forces for the region.

The HAC HQ—who had meanwhile skipped to the Mount Knaan command outpost which did not have any facilities or systems—verified that had been equipped with maps and communication orders while they were heading for the front.

In the evening the order of artillery forces in the region stood at approximately ten battalions. All of the Northern Command artillery units, excluding one towed 155mm battalion, went up to the Golan Heights and deployed in their positions. All were employed to support the units on the line where the reserve forces constantly engaged in halting the Syrian forces, who continued moving west. Soldiers who were waiting for their weapons to arrive of the two 155mm SPG battalions assisted in pushing the artillery ammunition. Due to the heavy traffic load on the routes, the Command Chief of Staff agreed that routes be cleared of division logistic units and ready for supplying artillery ammunition. It was pushed into a stockpile positioned at the entrance to Hazor. Ammunition was supplied to the artillery positions from there.

Additional battalions from the GHQ's reserve were sent north, including the 412th 175mm SPG Battalion under the command of Lt. Col. Aharon (Aldo) Zohar, two battalions of captured enemy 130mm guns which were not initially intended for the northern front, and even the 270th captured enemy 240mm BM-11 rocket launcher battalion. The 412th Battalion first battery reached the 647th Battalion emergency storage warehouse in Pilon, where it was equipped with its SPGs. It was the only battery left in the emergency storage warehouse after the 55th Battalion—which had been in the Sinai and went up to the Golan Heights with only two batteries—was equipped with these guns. It deployed next to its emergency storage warehouse between Pilon and Yiftach, and from there offered support at the early stages of the war. Afterwards it went up to the Golan Heights and operated as an independent battery on the Yehudia route.

One Northern Command 155mm towed artillery battalion was deployed in positions in the Beit She'an valley and was transferred to the Central Command forces later in the war.

An artillery ranging battalion, under the command of Menashe (Leviathan) Loutin, operated on the Golan Heights as well. It had the MAR-290 Ivry rocket launchers, the long-range projectors and the ranging alignment, and operated in the northern front from the eve of the war. To assist the battalions and batteries in navigating to their positions at night, the command deployed artillery long-range projectors from the ranging battalion on the Margaliot ridge. These projectors sent a narrow beam of light into the sky which allowed the forces, receiving the exact coordinates of the projectors location, to navigate more easily into their positions despite darkness, dust and smoke.

On Monday October 8, the 146th Division that went up the Golan Heights as a GHQ reserve from the Central Command brought along with it the 213th Artillery Group headquarters under the command of Col. Dani Avidar (Feinstein). The support group included a number of battalions: a 105mm Priest battalion, a160mm Self-propelled mortar battalion, a 120mm Self-propelled mortar battalion, and the 889th Battalion, the only M109 Howitzer SPG reserve battalion.

On the morning of Monday, October 8, 24 battalions were deployed in the Golan Heights. These included additional reinforcements from the command artillery headquarters (HAC) and CAO HQ artillery support from the GHQ's reserves. The battalions deployed in the three division sectors continued assisting, chiefly in the defensive battles.

Additional 120mm mortar battalions and towed guns were placed in the secondary sectors in the Meron district, on the Lebanese border, the 612th Regional Brigade and in the Jordan Valley.

The Artillery Battalions Deployed on the Golan Heights Front on October 8

Battalion No.	Type Of Weapon	Number Of Weapons On First Day Of War	Affiliation At War Outbreak
405	M-109	12	213th Group / Northern Command
Training Base No. 9	M-50	12	GHQ / 212th Group
334	M-50 160mm mortar	4 8	Command / 212th Group
55	M—107/110	8	Ascended from Sinai from 209th Group
313	160mm mortar	6+6 at 10/10	212th Group
325	160mm mortar	10-12	213th Group
343	120mm mortar	16	
352	120mm mortar	12	213th Group
527	120mm mortar	16	282nd Group
826	M-50	0	282nd Group
871	M-50	9	212th Group
328	M-50	8	212th Group /operating with 282nd Group
412	M—107/110	12	CAO HQ Group
827	Priest– 105	12	282nd Group
822	Priest– 105	11	282nd Group
829	Priest– 105	8-11	213th Group
899	M-109	9	213th Group
873	130mm towed	12	CAO HQ
846	130mm towed	12	CAO HQ
870	130mm towed	12	Northern Command—744th
270	240mm BM-11 rocket launcher		CAO HQ Group

The Artillery Battalions Deployed in the Northern Command Secondary Sectors

Battalion No.	Type Of Weapon	Number Of Weapons On First Day Of Fighting	Ascription at Outbreak of War
330	M-50 converted to 155mm towed	12	212th Group it /positioned at Beit She'an valley
337	120mm towed mortars	12	820th Regional Brigade—deployed in Meron District
833	120mm towed mortars	12	1st Brigade in Meron District
336	120mm towed mortars	12	612th Regional Brigade—deployed in Jordan Valley

The Artillery During the Counterattack

The 213th Artillery Group, operating within the counter attack on the southern Golan Heights, advanced slowly behind the 146th Division advance armored forces moving east on the El Al and Gamla routes, while attacking and repelling the Syrian forces to the east. At that time there were no regular battalion batteries in the southern sector. The regular batteries initially in the war in the Tel Fares region had been hit by the penetrating Syrian forces.

The artillery battalions that began assisting from the shores of the Sea of Galilee in the Ein Gev region split into route systems. Some advanced and deployed in the El Al region to assist the primary effort. Others, including the battery left from the 405th Battalion under the command of Deputy Battalion

Commander Maj. Uri Manos having successfully retreated to the Gamla region and Btecha Valley assisted the secondary effort on the Gamla route. The support group was once again united in the Waterfalls Route region following its going up to the rear of the Golan Heights. During the advance the batteries got Syrian anti-battery fire, apparently ranged from Tel Fares.

On October 8, the Golani Brigade, under the command of brigade commander Col. Amir Drori, attempted to go up the Hermon with two battalions in a counterattack attempt to restore it to Israeli control. It seemed there was no organized artillery planning in the brigade and in the 36th Division operating in the north of the Golan Heights at that time. The Golani Brigade headquarters lacked a fire support headquarters. The artillery liaison officer operating with the force was killed. The brigade had difficulties in getting support from the 120mm mortar company deployed in the lower ski lift station as well.

The artillery situation in the region changed in favor of the division forces upon the arrival of the 146th Division forces in the Tel Fares region at noon, on Tuesday October 9, as part of the counterattack. These were being hit less by artillery fire and could range from the mound top more efficiently where Syrian batteries deployed east of the border could be ranged and attacked from. The ranging and meteorology alignment was employed here for the first time and could send a meteorological telegram to the 213th Artillery Group which improved accuracy.

The 146th Division forces' attempts to continue their advance to the border to the east on October 10-11were halted by Syrian anti-tank fire and landmines. The 213th Artillery Groups were incorporated into the fighting and assisted the forces on the different routes, mainly in the disengagement and retreat phases from the Al-Hanut and Tseida regions, from the Petroleum Road and the Umm Lucas region, from the Tel Asbach region and from the Qudna route.

The fire units teamed up with the 282nd Artillery Group gathered for counter attack at the Mashta junction. These included the 328th 155mm SPG Battalion, the 827th Priest 105mm SPG Battalion, the 313th 160mm Self-Propelled Mortar Battalion, and the 527th 120mm Self-Propelled Mortar Battalion. These were now joined by the 873rd 130mm Battalion. From here, they assisted the 210th Division forces in fighting north of the "Hushniya enclave" toward Tel Yosifon and later toward the Hazeka ridge until meeting up with Outpost 110 at Tel Akasha. The frontal forces continued artillery ranging and hitting the Syrian forces retreating east.

The artillery forces deployed throughout the Golan Heights region continued to assist on October 9–10 and gathered into support groups' areas of operation. The 212th Artillery Support Group forces gathering in the north of the Golan Heights in the rear of Mount Bar-On and Mount Odem and in the Buq'ata region. The long-range 412th Battalion joined up and operated along the other artillery support battalions. The 282nd artillery support group forces concentrated in the center of the Golan Heights in the region between Nafah and Ein Zivan, and the 55th Battalion two long-range batteries operated along with them. The 213th Artillery Group forces gathered in the south of the Golan Heights in the Tel Fares—Jukhader region. Battalions were taken from one division sector to assist in another. The different artillery batteries deployment sites were hit by Syrian anti-battery fire and were forced to skip to alternative positions.

On October 9 the RAC of the 7th Armored Brigade Maj. Arieh Mizrachi utilized all the units from the 212th Artillery Group deployed within the efficient range to block the final Syrian forces offensive in the Valley of Tears region. That afternoon the 334th Battalion and the 412th Battalion assisted the Golani Brigade forces, who were disengaging and evacuating following the failed offensive over the Hermon.

Artillery Groups assisted the Air Force jets in its strike attempts at Syrian SAM batteries. Artillery batteries were integrated into aerial attack plans and fired "chaff" shells as well. At the same time the Syrian Air Force concentrated on attacking artillery batteries. The batteries, which were usually pre-warned were only lightly hit and continued functioning. In a number of cases the battery guns hit the Syrian jets and in one case even caused the capture of an Iraqi pilot.

Status of ammunition grew worse in these stages. One of the problems was a lack of specific ammunition (primers being different from the primers used by the other 155mm guns) for the M-109 SPGs which were not initially intended to fight in the north. The Northern Command factors worked to gather suitable ammunition and push it up to the batteries. Convoys of ammunition on board semitrailers arrived and unloaded ammunition in the positions. To allow its transfer along the routes, a command ammunition center was established at the entrance to Hazor as early as Sunday at noon and operated by the HAC. The Command Chief of Staff Brig. Gen. Uri Bar-On cleared transportation routes in the field prioritizing the artillery ammunition.

Artillery During the Breakthrough into the Enclave

As of October 10, fire units were deployed in positions near the border to assist in the preparations for the breakthrough battles against the Syrian alignments in the north of the Golan Heights. Thirteen battalions from all three Artillery Groups operating on the Golan Heights, including from the 213th Artillery Group, which remained in charge of the southern Golan

Heights, were gathered for this task. The long-range 130mm batteries and 175mm batteries were also part of the close support for the forces. The command—responsible for pushing the ammunition to the positions—transferred civilian trucks and semitrailers directly upon arrival from the warehouses in the mainland.

The 36th Division breakthrough plan in the north of the Golan Heights included a two hour artillery preparation aimed at targets in the breakthrough area and Syrian artillery batteries in the region. A 40 minute operation of aerial support of eight flights was also integrated into the preparation. The main fire during the breakthrough was planned as a sort of "Fire Box." The Box was meant to "roll forward" and remain ahead of the armored columns at their front and flanks and were mainly aimed at striking anti-tank missile launchers endangering the tanks. The engagement of other targets was planned for the breakthrough region at that time.

The breakthrough artillery support was based on the Artillery Groups deployed in the Buq'ata region. The support was mostly allocated to the two brigades breaking through where the 7th Brigade had two batteries from Training Base No. 9 Battalion and the 405th Battalion Battery under its command. It was supported directly by two 334th Brigade batteries and two 871st Battalion medium range batteries. The 1st Brigade had the 335th Self-propelled mortar battalion under its command and direct support from the 822nd Priest105mm SPG Battalion and one 871st Battalion medium range battery. For general support of the division there remained the 175mm guns of the 412th Battalion, which had been converted to 203mm guns due to a lack of ammunition, 130mm guns of the 846th Battalion and the 270th (240mm BM-11) rocket launcher battalion.

In the hours before noon as part of the artillery preparation, the batteries fired thousands of shells at the Syrian alignments.

The operation of aerial assaults was planned and carried out in collaboration with the artillery and was also integrated into the preparation. When the 36th Division forces broke through in the region of Jubata al-Khashab and Tel Dahur, a screen of "rolling artillery fire" was operated ahead of them. The artillery fire accompanied the forces advancing into the enclave up to Mazraat Beit Jann and Tel Shams. Throughout the entire breakthrough maneuver the captured Hermon outpost was kept under fire and efficiently smoke-screened.

The fire units were shifted in the afternoon hours to assist the 210th Division breakthrough effort, which had become complicated in the Khan Arnabeh region. The 282nd Artillery Group, made up of four fire units including the 873rd Self-propelled Medium Range Battalion, a 130mm battalion, a 203mm battery from the 412th Battalion, and the 155mm towed 828th Battalion, led the preparation and artillery support of the breakthrough forces in the brigade sector. Some 4770 shells intended to hit the outposts and the Syrian alignments, on both sides of the "America" route which was the short route to Damascus were fired between 12:50 and 13:15. At that point all ammunition of this caliber that the IDF had for the long-range 130mm guns was used up.

Close after the breakthrough fire units were advanced into positions in the enclave. The 328th Battalion was advanced along the "America" route immediately following the forces breaking through and succeeded in assisting the advancing forces from its new position. To enable it to fire large amounts of ammunition a first convoy of three semitrailers carrying hundreds of shells were brought in with it. Approval was granted to send up a light aircraft aerial observation over the forces when the 36th Division attack began. It was meant to improve ability to identify the enemy artillery units. When the Dornier Do- 27 approached the line it was shot down by missiles. The pilot, the artillery liaison officer, and the two aerial scouts from command intelligence were killed. This was the only attempt made during the war to employ aerial observation from a light aircraft to range targets.[25]

Artillery in the Enclave

From October 12-17, battalions were directed and deployed under the 282nd Artillery Group of the 210th Division into positions in the Ma'atz junction region. These positions allowed for the close support of the division forces planned to advance up to the region of Khanker. The artillery had a decisive role in the defensive battles against the Iraqi forces attacking in the afternoon and nighttime hours of that day in the Tel Shaar region. Over two thousand shells were shot from the artillery guns of the 7th and 8th Artillery Battalions landed in concentrated form over the attacking Iraqi armored columns and caused their retreat. In the morning hours the artillery continued tailing and hitting the retreating forces.

A command order to fire at strategic targets in the region of Damascus, issued on the night of October 12–13th, resulted in two units from the 412th Battalion with two guns each to be brought into positions in the Small Leja in the Kharfa region. The artillery force broke through into the depth of the field closely assisted by teams from the GHQ and the Golani reconnaissance units. They fired about forty shells in 20 minutes at targets in the al-Mezzeh airfield on the outskirts of Damascus. In order to make it difficult for the Syrians to range the firing force, all of the artillery guns on the Golan Heights were fired

25 See Chapter 16.

simultaneously. Its intent was to show the Syrians that their capital Damascus was in danger. Additional firing into the depth of Syrian territory was carried out the following night by two guns from the Mazraat Beit Jann region.

On October 13, toward an additional offensive attempt by the 36th Division forces to capture the controlling area in Tel Shams, a concentrated artillery effort was carried out against the Syrian forces on the mound and around it by the 212th Artillery Group. The massive fire strike included the vast employment of rocket launchers by the 270th Battalion. It caused the Syrian forces to retreat and the mound to be a relatively easy capture with hardly any injuries.

The 212th and the 282nd Artillery Groups deployed in new positions in "artillery ranges" where main and alternative positions were prepared for all the batteries. Most of them were closely observed by Syrian frontal observation officers from the slopes of the Hermon and from mounds in the Golan Heights. Therefore, they were heavily fired at with anti-battery fire and were occasionally forced to skip. During the different battle stages the batteries were secured in the enclave by infantry forces. These were attached to the long-range batteries and to those deployed in forward positions. The routine that included support for the armored and infantry forces on the front continued. The artillery support groups assisted the division forces but moved the fire according to need into neighboring divisions region as well.

The 212th Artillery Group forces assisted in defending the Tel Shams region against Syrian counterattacks. The artillery battalions continued firing at various targets on the borders of the enclave and toward gatherings of Syrian, Iraqi and Jordanian forces that repeatedly attempted to attack the alignment of Israeli forces. The anti-battery fire directed at the Syrian and Iraqi batteries was fired after being ranged by an optical gunfire locator network deployed by the 212th Artillery Group ranging alignment.

Finding additional captured enemy ammunition in the enclave allowed for an additional allocation of ammunition to the two 130mm gun battalions, who at that stage had run out of their initial ammunition. Thousands of additional shells were found in the Syrian positions and were fired at the Syrian alignments and artillery positions.

Throughout October 14 an artillery battle ensued between the 282nd Artillery Group battalions and enemy artillery. During the day the support group batteries fired about 2600 shells. On October 15 the artillery support fire groups supplemented the armored raid against Tel Antar and the Iraqi forces in the region. Once again over a thousand shells were fired.

The two divisions' Artillery Groups assisted the forces on the defensive line in striking the Iraqi, Jordanian and Syrian forces that launched another counter attack on October 16. This attack which was mainly aimed at the hills in the south and east of the enclave was halted.

Three of the artillery battalions fighting on the Golan Heights were transferred south to the Sinai already on October 14. These were the 899th Self-propelled Battalion, the 175mm 55th Battalion (battery and company) and the 270th (240 mm) Rocket Launchers Battalion. These were transported to the southern front and as of October 15, participated in the crossing operation and the advance of IDF forces on the western bank of the Suez Canal until the siege on the 3rd Egyptian field army was carried out.

In order to make it possible to transfer the 213th Artillery Group headquarters to replace the 282nd Artillery Group and continue the simultaneous operation of two artillery support groups in the region of the enclave on October 17, the 334th Battalion headquarters was transferred to the Nachal Geshur region. It served as the sector support headquarters for the south of the Golan Heights. Under its command now deployed a sort of improvised Artillery Group under the responsibility of the 670th Brigade in the region. This support group included the 826th Medium Range Battalion which abandoned the 155mm towed battalions it converted to. It returned to its SPGs left by the Training Base No. 9 Battalion forces who had returned to their base to complete the courses they had been participating in. It included the 829th Priest105mm SPG Battalion, the 325th and 352nd 120mm Self-propelled mortar battalions and the 175mm company from the 55th Battalion that remained on the Golan Heights.

The Syrians continued firing anti-battery fire toward the southern sector as well and forced the batteries to occasionally skip to alternative positions. On October 19, the support headquarters returned to its assigned facility on the Nafah Base to serve as the artillery support headquarters for the entire region.

Inside the enclave the eight battalions operating under the command of the 213th Artillery Group assisted in activity to expand and improve the outposts in the "enclave's" southern region. The battalions took part in holding off an additional Iraqi-Jordanian counterattack on October 19. Immediately following, the artillery support group went down from the Golan Heights with the rest of the division command forces to the southern bank of the Suez Canal on the Egyptian front to secure the corridor for crossing the canal. The 352nd Self-propelled mortar battalion and unit command joined them as well.

Throughout the fighting there were also attempted penetrations and shootings on the Lebanese border. The mortar battalions under the command of the Meron district support headquarters deployed observations and fired at targets in the region.

Artillery in Operation Kinuach and at the End of the War

Toward the end of the war a large artillery force was assembled to assist the Golani Brigade and the 317th Paratrooper Brigade in the offensive march and landing toward the capture of the Hermon outpost and the Syrian outposts on the ridge in Operation Kinuach. Special coded maps, planned by the command, with marked targets ranged along the routes of advance were prepared for the operation. A two-seat fighter jet holding an Artillery Corps officer was allocated to range targets. The command, which was short on ammunition, approached the GHQ and was reinforced with 15,000 shells, of which 13,000 were fired during the operation. A large artillery force was gathered into a sort of improvised artillery support group. Six battalions in total were allocated for the operation, including the 334th, the 871st and the 335th from the 212th Artillery Group.

The Golani Brigade, going up toward the Hermon outpost from the west, was allocated chiefly mortar battalions whose range allowed them to reach the targets.The order of battle included the following units:

The 335th 120mm Mortar Battalion, deployed in the Hader region.

The 343rd 120mm Mortar Battalion, deployed in the Neve Ativ region.

The 833rd Mortar Battalion Company, deployed in the Bus Lot region.

The 313th 160mm Heavy Mortar Battalion, deployed in the S'heita region.

A 155mm gun battery from the 334th Battalion was positioned for general support of the brigade.

Training Base No. 9 Battalion Commander Lt. Col. Ben Ami Cohen, who volunteered to serve as the brigade fire support commander in the operation, allocated "direct assistance" fire units to each advance route: three to four batteries for the 51st Battalion; three batteries for the reconnaissance unit and the remaining three batteries for the Golani Training Base 17th Battalion.

The 317th Paratrooper Brigade flown in by helicopters to the Syrian Hermon region for illuminating the targets employed some of its organic mortars from the 833rd Battalion for support. The command made the 871st 155mm SPG Battalion available to the brigade deployed northeast of Hader to range the planned targets. A 120mm mortar battery deployed in the Mount Dov region employed fire to disrupt the planned route of the helicopter flight north of the Hermon's peak, toward the landing fields in the Syrian Hermon.

The 334th Battalion short range 160mm mortars were apparently planned for general support, mainly for the Golani forces.

The plan was to land fire in the "steamroller method" on predetermined targets near and ahead of the infantry forces arrival there. Points of departure were established along the planned advance routes. Thousands of shells were allocated for the operation in addition to the command allocation.

During the operation the artillery fire accompanied the paratrooper advance until the takeover of all their targets was completed. About 2,700 bombs and shells were fired at their targets enabling the completion of the tasks with hardly any casualties.

The artillery fire accompanied the advance of the Golani force advancing on foot up to the region of hill 16. Following shelling close to the forces, the accompanying fire was halted and diverted east toward the Hermon outpost itself and toward the upper ski lift station which was about five kilometers to the north. With the advance, and following a close engagement with Syrian commando forces, the 51st artillery liaison officer employed fire of seven batteries at a point of departure near the stranded force at dawn. After the artillery liaison officer was killed the RAC continued operating the fire units. After nearly two hours of continuous fire where over 5,000 shells and bombs were fired the force managed to advance and capture the Hermon outpost. This ended the fighting on the Golan Heights front.

The artillery forces remained in their positions in the enclave and on the Golan Heights, from which they had operated, when the October 23rd ceasefire was enforced. They assisted in defensive activities throughout the enclave and during the War of Attrition on the Golan Heights, from here.

The 282nd Artillery Group that had left for organization on October 17 returned a week later and assumed responsibility over artillery forces deployed in the enclave. From that point on, the support unit remained in charge of the artillery activity on the Golan Heights. The reserve battalions that had exchanged among themselves to allow for organization and refreshment, returned home only six months later when the separation of forces agreement with the Syrians was signed.

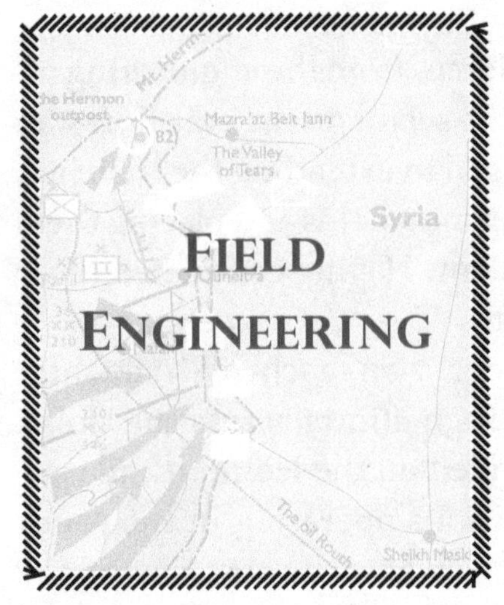

Field Engineering

Chapter 18

The state of alert declared in the Northern Command on the eve of the Yom Kippur War included field engineering necessities and preparations. The main activity in the period between Rosh Hashanah and Yom Kippur[26] was devoted to preparing the ground for the possibility of a Syrian attack all across the front.

Despite ongoing preparation in the years leading up to the war the Golan Heights obstacle was incomplete and there was an urgent need to continue its construction according to existing plans. An important part of the preparatory effort before the war included placing minefields, completing anti-tank trenches and preparing roads, positions, and tank ramps on the front line. Lacking regular field engineering forces on the Golan Heights front entailed that most of the work was carried out by the 801st field engineering corps of the command, under the command of Lt. Col. Moshe Peled (Hadad) and Maj. Shlomo

26 A ten-day period.

Aharonishki, the G3 officer, and forces from the engineering officers' course that had arrived in the sector on the eve of the war. As stated, these forces were engaged in extending the trenches, mainly to the south, in thickening minefields and placing them mainly in the Valley of Tears salient. Having completed these bore fruit when the war broke out.

On the noon of October 6, three Syrian mechanized infantry divisions started their breakthrough efforts across the Golan Heights front. A special force landed on the Hermon and captured the outpost. The two divisions operating in the south and center of the Golan Heights overcame the obstacles on the front, which at that time included just a thin system of anti-tank trenches, minefields, and outposts defended by a small amount of regular forces. They managed to break through and penetrate the depth of the territory. The Northern Division encountered a relatively thicker obstacle, defended by greater forces and was halted. Up to October 9, all breakthrough attempts failed.

The second rank Syrian brigades penetrated through the breakthrough passages and were followed by an armored division intended to thicken and expand the captured territory. The IDF reserve forces going up the Golan Heights in three armored divisions stabilized the lines as early as October 8 before the slopes descending to the Sea of Galilee and the Jordan River and began a counterattack aimed at advancing in the southern sector up to the line of the border the forces were to reach on October 9.

Upon coming up to the Golan Heights, the armored reserve divisions' tank force was followed by field engineering battalions. The battalions traveling on board half-tracks generally moved in the rear for fear of extensive artillery fire throughout the line of contact. The field engineering forces were therefore engaged in mechanized infantry tasks—deployed in the field, secured night camps and advanced provisions to the engaged forces. The field engineering units were instructed to prepare rear fortification alignments only in a few cases, for fear of a Syrian advancement into the depth of the Golan Heights.

The Field Engineering Alignment in the Northern Command

During the Yom Kippur War

The 602nd Field Engineering Battalion—under the command of Lt. Col. Avraham Varshevski,

The 261st Guard Sappers Battalion—under the command of Lt. Col. Moshe Arling,

The 570th Command Mechanical Engineering Equipment Battalion—under the command of Lt. Col. Israel Yehuda,

The 642nd Bomb Disposal Unit—under the command of Maj. Yosef Muzel.

The command was reinforced during the war by bridging tanks and bulldozer tanks from the Armored Corps engineering battalion—the 606th Battalion.

The valleys' sector 612th Regional Brigade that was transferred to the Central Command got a company from the 261st Guard Sappers Battalion.

The divisions had armored field engineering battalions established in the years prior to the war based on the brigades engineering companies. These were:

The 36th Division and the 641st Armor Field Engineering Battalion under the command of Lt. Col. Izzy Hod.

The 210th Division and the 923rd armored field engineering battalion, under the command of Lt. Col. Yehuda Cohen.

The 146th Division of the 751st Armored Field Engineering Battalion under the command of Lt. Col. Eli Arad. The battalion was partially regular, based on officers and soldiers from Training Base No. 14 which was the Military Engineering Training Base.

On Monday afternoon, October 8, following the increasing apprehension of a Syrian advancement, the command engineering force was assigned the preparation of the Jordan River bridges for detonation, and the preparation of blocking areas going down to the Jordan River and the Sea of Galilee to disconnect the routes. The command field engineering force was activated and prepared the Arik, Bnot Yaakov, Pkak, Neot Mordechai, and Banias bridges for detonation. The 570th Command Mechanical Engineering Equipment Battalion began preparing blocking points in the depth of the Golan Heights, mainly in the southern sector in the El Al region. Heaps of gravel and rocks were prepared there to block and disconnect the routes before the arrival of the Syrian forces.

When the counter offensive began on October 8, and the IDF forces advanced toward the border (the Purple Line) the divisions' field engineering battalions were engaged in clearing the travel routes of obstacles, mainly Syrian placed mine clusters. Other forces assisted the ordnance units dealing with tanks evacuation out of minefields and Syrian clusters.

The attempts to cross the Purple Line raised engineering problems due to the need to overcome the obstacles systems, mainly the minefields placed ahead of the Syrian defensive alignment which were part of it. On October 10, battalions from the 205th and the 670th Brigades attempted to cross the border in the southern sector of the Golan Heights and advance east. All attempts failed when the armored advance force entered minefields and was directly hit by the Syrian stationary antitank alignments. The field engineering units that arrived at a later stage of the offensive could only assist in clearing passages through the minefields and evacuating the stranded AFVs. Additional attempts by the 146th Division forces to cross the border on the Qudne route, on October 10 and again two days later, this time with closer engineering assistance, failed. The 751st Battalion Field Engineering force moving behind the advance forces dealt with the rescue of tanks that had triggered the Syrian mine clusters.

On October 11, the Northern Command forces went on an offensive. The 36th Division was the first to break through and penetrate the Syrian alignments in the north of the Golan Heights. The advancing forces broke through the minefields based on prior information and acquaintance with the front minefields. The intention to employ mine trawl systems and armored bulldozers was not implemented. The force broke through at the edge of the minefield and some of its vehicles triggered mines. The 641st Field Engineer Battalion moved after the first tank company, marked the breakthrough, and continued advancing. At a later stage, the battalion Mechanical Engineering Equipment force organized a more orderly route from the breakthrough into the depth of the captured territory.

The 210th Division—which had broken through several hours later on the "America" route, the Quneitra—Damascus route—had to cross a heavier alignment of obstacles. The tank forces leading the offensive were caught in the minefields and in the Khan Arnabeh alignments controlling them. Dozens of tanks and APCs were hit but the division force managed to break through and penetrate the Syrian alignment and enter the enclave. The 932nd Battalion field engineering forces, advancing behind the armored forces breaking through were left with the task of paving routes through the minefields, assisting in the evacuation of wounded, and later in evacuating the damaged AFVs.

When the armored brigades advanced into the depth of the enclave the divisions' field engineering battalions—that had split their forces into companies and platoons to assist in clearing mine clusters from the routes—were given the task of overcoming bombed water crossings and preparing alternative routes. The field engineering forces were also integrated into mine placement activities on the advancing forces flanks and near them, to secure night camps. At night the companies and platoons were integrated into the tight securing of the night camps as a mechanized infantry force attached to the tanks as well. Another recurring task was the rescue and evacuation of AFVs that had triggered mines.

Fortification effort began when the external borders of the enclave were captured on controlling hills and between them mainly based on the companies from the divisions Mechanical Engineering Equipment Battalions. Some of the tasks were performed under massive artillery fire that caused injuries among workers and damage to their tools. The attempts to evade the fire that struck seven heavy engineering vehicles and perform the task at night failed as operating heavy engineering equipment in the dark was impossible.

Alongside the command offensive in the northern Golan Heights, the 146th Division was given the task to prepare a system of engineering obstacles intended to prevent a parallel counter attack by the Syrians or their partners in this sector in a broad ranging engineering operation. This is where the command effort was invested at this stage. The front obstacle was reinforced by additional minefields. The anti-tank trench was deepened and extended. The embankment battery in the rear was raised. The command assembled the 602nd and 261st Command Battalions for the operation along with the 570th Command Mechanical Engineering Equipment Battalion. A company of NCOs from Training Base No. 14, who were part of the 146th Division 751st Battalion, was also involved in the operation. The main effort was the placing 21,000 mines in a relatively short period of time. A large-scale and rapid-construction works was carried out.

The task completion in the front of the enclave left part of the heavy engineering alignment without work. At this stage the Northern Command decided to construct defensive alignments in the depths of the Golan Heights before the slopes to the Jordan River and the Sea of Galilee. A series of extensive construction works began, including that of batteries and tank ramps and the digging of anti-tank trenches. All preparations for the actual placement of the mines were made except the actual placement which was postponed.

The recapture of the Hermon as part of "Operation Kinuach" on October 21–22nd entailed additional engineering activity. An engineering platoon force under the command of a company commander, on board half-tracks, accompanied by two bulldozer tanks and two D-9 bulldozers began breaking through an additional route up the Golan Heights—later to be known as the "Golani rise." On the route of the existing road, alongside the armored force going up an engineering force went up as well. It intended to open the route of the road. Reports and aerial photographs revealed that the route up to the Hermon held obstacles and mines including charges along the roads and other obstructions. The force completed its task and opened the route. During the activity an engineering company commander was killed, sappers were injured and a bulldozer tank and tractor were damaged.

Later on after the ceasefire, the 570th Mechanical Engineering Equipment Battalion began a complex operation of opening a difficult mountain route to the Syrian Hermon outpost. Construction works matched prior assessments and the route was broken through fifteen straight hours of work later. These works included explosions and land preparations employing a large number of heavy tractors.

With the ceasefire an extensive fortification operation ensued within the borders of the enclave. The area was organized for a long stay under attrition conditions. The Northern Command prepared for defense in a broad ranging engineering operation intended first and foremost to provide combatants and equipment relative protection from enemy artillery fire. At later stages actual outposts were constructed, including combat trenches, bunkers and barbed wire fences. Long strips of minefields were placed on their sides and along their fronts, including 47,920 anti-tank and 2,650 anti-personnel mines. The fortification effort included the construction of outposts and shelters for infantry forces holding the summits of the Hermon. Small compressors, jackhammers, explosives, fortification materials, and fencing were flown in on board helicopters for this purpose.

Simultaneously, the breaking through and route preparation to the alignment of outposts began in order to ease movement and preempt foreseen difficulties in the coming of winter. The routes were broken through and were covered by a bed of rock made up of very small volcanic fragments compacted together quarried from the foot of Tel Avital. Many Trucks and depot trucks were allocated to the paving forces. The line of fortifications, outposts and batteries in the south Golan Heights based on the old alignment was renewed by the engineering forces that included a company from the Field Engineering NCOs course.

With the retreat to the former lines following the agreement with the Syrians, the system of obstacles on the front and sides of the alignment was once again improved. This system was made thicker and serves the IDF to this day.

For the expanded activity the Northern Command was

reinforced by Field engineering forces from the Central Command. Civilian contractors were employed for the reconstruction tasks which included the civilian contractor who had originally constructed the Hermon outpost and was brought back to renovate it. About 250 engineering vehicles of different sorts were employed in the fortification efforts during the most intensive period of activity. This intense activity aroused maintenance problems and a shortage in professionals to operate in it.

CHAPTER 19

The Yom Kippur War on the Golan Heights—Background

DURING THE MONTHS OF July to September 1973, the first signs of significant changes in the Syrian alignment along the front as well as their thickening their anti-aircraft alignment were observed. On July 16, 1973, the Israeli Air Force published a special intelligence review entitled: "Changes in the Organization of SAM Batteries in Syria and Their Deployment" after new sites for the absorption of surface-to-air missiles batteries were identified on aerial photographs along the Damascus—Daraa route. The ground data regarding the SAM deployment was presented in this intelligence review, along with the operational significance and limitations derived from it. The identification of the Syrian SAM deployment was one of the significant warning signs that pointed to Syrian offensive intentions. The GOC was aware of the offensive implications of the deployment and warned of it in a GHQ discussion and in conversations with the commander of the Air Force, Maj. Gen. Binyamin (Benny) Peled. On the eve of the war, the alignment on the front included twenty-six missile batteries, 15 of which were mobile SA-6 batteries and eleven were stationary batteries positioned in the Damascus basin. The Syrians had a total of thirty-six missile batteries making the front a completely missile-defended zone. The Syrian alignment of missile batteries was backed up by a strengthened alignment of anti-aircraft gun batteries of various calibers some guided by radar. The anti-aircraft missile and gun batteries effectively closed off the front entire airspace for heights of operational flights.

The strengthening and reinforcement of the Syrian anti-aircraft alignment limited the IDF Aerial Operations on the Golan Heights front where only special sorties were still conducted, intended to ensure that intelligence regarding the Syrian alignment was continuously updated.

A severe aerial incident developed on September 13. The Syrians attempted to intercept the photographing planes and dogfights ensued. Twelve MiG-21 jets were shot down and an IAF Mirage was hit.[27]

The Air Force Tasks in the Northern Command Plans

The Air Force was instructed in general terms to assist in the preparation for the operation with attack and defense. It should be stated that attack orders were written as a general outline with no "target bank" for a preemptive attack excluding artillery

27 See Part I.

targets and stationary ones.

The methods of utilizing the Air Force in case of either a broad or narrow attack were established in the discussions that took place before the war. According to the IDF Sela plan the following priorities were established for the provision of air support: attacking enemy SAM batteries throughout the sector; providing close support for the forces during counter attacks; attacking headquarters, CCPs and enemy lookouts; attacking front armored brigades and attacking outposts.

In August 1973, the Air Force Operations Department issued a "Situation Assessment" manual which also established priorities in the use of aerial force in the following order: obtaining aerial superiority by destroying enemy Air Force and missile alignments; taking part in ground battles; attacking strategic targets; collecting intelligence; combat and general transportation; evacuating casualties and more.

The Air Force Operation orders were written and organized. They included the *Tagar* (Challenge) operation for attacking the canal missile alignment on the Egyptian front, the *Dugman* (Model) operation for attacking airfields and missile alignments on the Syrian front, the *Negicha* (Ramming) operation for attacking airfields and the "Dominick" operation for attacking strategic targets in the depths of enemy territory.

An issued advance intelligence warning of 24 to 36 hours prior to the opening of fire was taken into account in all Air Force operation orders. This time span allowed the Air Force to obtain aerial superiority to only afterwards enter full force into participation in ground battles. The Northern Command as well as the Southern Command operational orders established that aerial assistance would be provided after aerial superiority was obtained.

However, in case of an enemy initiated attack without prior warning and before obtaining aerial superiority and the need to supply aerial assistance arose before aerial superiority was achieved, the Air Force Operations Department published the Srita (Scratch) plan. It dealt with the methods of employing the Air Force in a missile-defended zone, planning established routes for regions where attacks were anticipated, including low routes. The Srita order merely included the outline of the order without predetermined targets of aerial attacks—except, as stated, for artillery batteries. Attack targets were to flow in, in the course of the war, which the Aerial Operations Department assigned to the squadrons according to the list of priorities.

The Northern Command operational orders mentioned the Air Force attack operation in a general manner, without mention of defined, specific targets for the offensive.

It should be stated that the Air Force Headquarters had its reservations regarding the implementation of the Srita order and it was to be employed only under constraints. Employ the Air Force before aerial superiority was obtained and before the missile alignments are destroyed was a grave hindrance to efficiency aerial attacks.

Preparations for the Preemptive Aerial Strike and its Cancellation

On October 5 at 14:30, the commanders Air Force forum was called by the Air Force commander where they were updated of the situation. He mentioned his apprehension that a war was about to break out. He even went as far as to say that if the Syrians launched a war and broke through the front on the Golan Heights where forces were insufficient the Air Force was going to be called in to attack on the northern front even before the SAM artillery alignment was attacked.

He added that they were to prepare for an attack on the Syrian SAM alignment once approval was granted. The raising of the IDF alert level caused the Air Force CCP to report in the Northern Command CCP. The commander of the CCP Col. Rafi Sivron flew north and joined up with the command group in the Nafah bunker when the fire broke out. The CCP equipment arrived on board a flight to Mahanayim, was loaded on trucks and deployed in a narrow room in the Nafah command bunker.

At dawn October 6, a report came in from the head of the Mossad who was in London that a joint initiated Egyptian and Syrian war was about to break out that day. It was assessed that H-hour was going to be at 18:00. In a GHQ discussion held that morning, the Air Force commander suggested attacking the Syrian Air Force in a preemptive attack. Attacking the missile alignment on the front was not possible due to weather conditions. The GHQ Chief of Staff approved but was waiting for the political ranks to approve. The attack was planned for 11:00 and was postponed to 12:00. The jets were fueled and armed accordingly, briefings were held at the squadrons and the targets for the teams were established. All awaited the approval of the political rank which failed to come in. The government decided that the preemptive strike on the Syrian Air Force would not go through.

The Air Force began to disarm the jets and prepare them for an air-to-air defensive combat considering that jets would have to be launched to defend the field and patrol against the enemy anticipated aerial attacks.

At about 13:00 the GHQ Chief of Staff briefed the Northern Command GOC regarding the holding of the Syrian offensive in the evening with a minimum of losses. He was also told that this task would continue through the night and the following day. It was also determined that the Air Force would attack Syrian airfields on October 7 and would then attack the Syrian missile alignment to only afterwards enter full force into the attack of ground targets on the front.

At 13:35 at the Air Force commander's office a commanders' discussion was held, regarding the tense situation and the Air Force tasks. Twenty minutes later reports came in of Syrian jets taking off from the Dumeir airfield. The Air Force commander immediately instructed "...take wing to defend the Golan Heights and Ramat David and impede the attack..." The Syrians opened artillery fire and conducted an aerial assault over the entire Golan Heights front.

Air Force Participation in Ground Battle During Defensive—October 6–7

The Syrian Aerial Assault

The Syrians launched an aerial assault offensive at 13:55 attacking targets in the North of Israel and the on Golan Heights. Fifty-eight assault jets participated in this attack, which lasted from 13:55 to about 16:20. Immediately following the first aerial assault, a heavy artillery shelling began to prepare for a ground offensive. The Syrian attack was coordinated with the Egyptian attack on the canal front with the Syrian TOT for the aerial attack preceding the Egyptian TOT by 15 minutes.

Two limited tasks were assigned to the Syrian Air Force aerial attack at the onslaught of the war which had a limited impact on the front. Eight MiG 21 jets attempted to attack targets in the Kfar Giladi region. A Hawk SAM battery positioned in Birya launched missiles at them hitting two MiG 21 jets. The Syrian jets shelled the area without causing damage. Israeli Air Force

Mirage III jets patrolling the area shot down the MiG jets and managed to shoot down a MiG 21 jet near the Rayak air base in Syria in a long chase. The rest of the Syrian jets attacked military targets in the Hermon, Mas'ade, Birkat Ram apparently to weaken it for the capturing of the Hermon, Quneitra, Tel Avital, Tel Fares, and Nafah.

The attacking jets were escorted by MiG 21 jets, one of which was shot down by friendly Syrian anti-aircraft fire near Damascus. The Nafah Base was attacked as well. The jets attacked concentrations of vehicles and structures in the region. Two soldiers were killed and six others were wounded in this attack. Damages or casualties were not reported from other attacked places. The outposts along the line were not attacked from the air but were shelled by artillery. Two 20mm anti-aircraft companies from the 66th Battalion, deployed on Tel Avital opened fire. Another company from the battalion deployed in Tel Fares was apparently hit by Syrian artillery.

Immediately following the aerial assault a helicopter borne Syrian force began capturing the Hermon. An additional Syrian force on board 6 helicopters, intended to land in various regions of the Golan Heights, returned to their base without carrying out the task due to weather conditions.

Air Force Attacks at the Beginning of the War

Immediately upon the opening of fire Israeli Air Force jets were sent out to intercept the Syrian jets and attack the invading Syrian forces. A first flight of jets took off at 14:15 and attacked targets in the Quneitra sector. The aerial attacks of thirty-two attack sorties lasted until 17:45. Most of them came from the Air Force base at Ramat David. The jets attacked on the Hermon, the Quneitra salient, and the Rapid junction. They attacked artillery batteries and performed interdictions against forces on access routes.

In a GHQ Chief of Staff discussion held at about 21:30, the Air Force commander presented the following day plan with the main effort directed at Egypt in accordance with decisions reached in previous discussions. The Air Force commander recommended carrying out the Tagar Operation to attack missiles on the canal front and attack air fields in the depths of Egypt following the Negicha order. The GHQ Chief of Staff approved the Air Force plans, wherein four assault flights were to be carried out against the Egyptian missile alignment and attack their air fields.

The Northern Command aerial CCP was transferred to the responsibility of Col. Rafi Sivron during the night to the command outpost in Knaan. Maj. Gen. Moti Hod, who had arrived earlier in the afternoon from the GHQ with the GOC, began serving as the Air Force forward commander in the north where jets were operated against organized and defined targets from the early morning hours of the second day of the war.

The Decision to Switch the Main Effort from the Egyptian Front to the Syrian Front

The Israeli Air Force planned to place its full force on the Egyptian front. The squadrons underwent attack briefings, the jets were fueled and armed accordingly, and throughout the night of October 6- 7th, the Air Force wings and bases were under intensive preparations toward the operation against Egypt.

However, information regarding the serious situation of Israeli forces on the Golan Heights and the depth of the Syrian breakthrough in the south of the Heights came in during the night.

At 03:56, the Northern Command GOC, Maj. Gen. Hofi, reported to the GHQ Chief of Staff: "... The situation is not good. There is a flow of tanks in the direction of Ben Shoham—the 188th Brigade commander Col. Yitzhak Ben Shoham. An order was given to evacuate settlements... there are a lot of damaged tanks. We will do everything to delay the flooding of routes and battles of attrition. Request massive aerial support, if not—our situation will be very serious..."

At 04:15, the GHQ Chief of Staff reported the dire situation of the forces on the Golan Heights to the Air Force commander. In response to his question of what the Air Force could do to assist, the commander of the Air Force replied that it was possible to allocate one Sky Hawk squadron for attacks on the Golan Heights which would start attacking in the early morning hours. At this stage the GHQ Chief of Staff still approved the plan to deploy the Air Force on the Egyptian front as planned.

However, reports regarding the dire situation on the Golan Heights continued flowing in to the HCO. At 05:35, the GHQ Chief of Staff Lt. Gen. David Elazar and his deputy Maj. Gen. Tal went to the Air Force control outpost and stressed the severity of the situation on the Golan Heights. The Air Force commander rejected the possibility requested by the GHQ Chief of Staff to have the Tagaroperation for attacking the Suez Canal Front missile alignment in the morning and the "Dugman" operation for attacking SAMs in Syria in the afternoon.

At 06:05, the Minister of Defense, Moshe Dayan, reached the Northern Command CCP to closely examine the situation since it seemed critical. At 06:42 the minister spoke with the Air Force commander after failing to reach the GHQ Chief of Staff and described the situation on the Golan Heights in very grim terms and mentioned that "If there aren't quartets (formations of jets) by noon they (the Syrians) will penetrate the Jordan Valley." Following this conversation the Air Force commander instructed the immediate allocation of jets to attack the Syrian forces along the Petroleum Road and in the south of the Golan Heights and said, among other things, that: "...The Rapid Route goes down to the Jordan Valley, to the Btecha Valley, so now the minister says that only the Air Force can stop them. The effort now is focused on halting the Syrians on the Golan Heights." Following, at a consultation at the Air Force control outpost between the GHQ Chief of Staff and the Air Force commander the main effort was shifted to the Syrian front.

At 06:57, when the Air Force was in the middle of the preparatory flight for Tagar and jets were attacking the Egyptian Air Force at its bases, an Israeli Air Force command order to the squadrons was issued regarding the altering of the task thus: "Operate Dugman 5 B, H-hour 11:30, cancel Tagar second flight."

Once this order was issued the air and ground teams intensively equipped the jets to perform the new task while over 120 jets were simultaneously attacking anti-aircraft batteries in preparation for Tagar and airfields in Egypt.

Air Force Activity in the North on the Second Day of the War

There were repeated requests for aerial support due to the Syrian breakthrough, mainly in the south of the Golan Heights. Support was coordinated by the Air Force Headquarters and the FCO and the command artillery headquarters, which even supplied its G3 officer, Maj. Gidon Etzion, to the aerial CCP. The aerial assault began at dawn on the second day of the war. A first jets flight attacked at 05:59 in the Achmadia junction near Outpost 107. The jets continued attacking Syrian forces on the Golan Heights in all sectors as well.

The Air Force attacked in the Ramat Magshimim region, Achmadia junction, near the El Al River, at the Rapid junction, in Hushniya, and Tel Fares, and carried out aerial interdictions against forces moving along the routes. A convoy of Syrian forces, viewed on the routes leading to the southern Golan Heights, was attacked and successful strikes on the center of the convoy were reported. In the northern sector assaults were carried out near Quneitra, in the Mount Yosifon region, at Khan Arnabeh, in the Hermonit region, and near Birkat Ram. Interdictions were carried out on the routes and struck convoys, as well.

Attacking the Syrian Missile Alignment

At 11:30, in accordance with the rushed planning, operation "Dugman 5" with 120 attack sorties was against the Syrian missile alignment. It softened the anti-aircraft alignment and attack missile batteries. In total one battery was destroyed and one more was damaged. The Israeli Air Force lost 6 Phantom jets in the operation and ten more were hit and were forced to land in their bases. The operation failed. The Air Force, not having taken photographs or made updates, attacked empty sites. The entire Golan Heights remained a "hot" missile-defended zone forcing the Air Force jets to attack under threat of anti-aircraft missiles until the end of the war. Despite these poor opening conditions, the failure of the "Dugman" operation and the jets getting hit, Israeli jets continued attacking the Syrian forces.

During this stage of the defensive battle, the Air Force carried out 129 attack sorties against Syrian forces on the Golan Heights and 120 additional sorties against the missile alignment. Most of the activity, of eighty-four sorties, was carried out in the south of the Golan Heights. Pilots' reports were either good or vague. The missiles launched at them forced them to take evasive maneuvers in order to avoid them thus they did not always notice the results. According to the Command CCP reports the military convoy advancing on the routes in the south of the Golan Heights was halted as a result of the aerial attacks. Thirteen jets participating in the ground battle were hit and fell, five pilots were killed and one was injured.

At this stage the Syrians had lost 19 jets, 13 of which were shot down during dogfights, two by ground fire carried out by the 20mm battery in Tel Avital. Four Syrian jets fell due to "friendly downing."

Air Force Participation in the October 8–10 Counterattack

The Change in the Military Balance

In accordance with the GHQ's plans for the morning of October 8, "Approval No. 6" order was issued by the GHQ Operations Department summing up the plan on the two fronts: "The IDF will halt the enemy forces on the Golan Heights and the Sinai, destroy most of the enemy forces in a counter attack as of dawn, October 8 and will be prepared to exploit success to launch an attack beyond the cease fire lines." Regarding the Air Force the order stated: "...operation of the Air Force for assistance of the ground forces and establishment of aerial supremacy."

Regarding the control of aerial assaults, a view crystallized in the Air Force control outpost to control the aircrafts arriving from the Ramat David Air Force base directly from the aerial CCP in the Northern Command under the command of Maj. Gen. Moti Hod.

The Air Force tendencies at this phase of fighting were to prevent the enemy forces flow to the front, to carry out close assistance against enemy forces engaged in combat with IDF forces and attack enemy forces in problematic areas.

The aerial assaults began at dawn, October 8 and lasted until twilight. The Northern Command aerial CCP's plan was to grant assistance to the 146th Division sectors and help repel Syrian forces "from the bulge" that had formed due to their control of the southern Heights. From dawn until 08:00, 20 attack sorties were carried out to soften and prepare for the ground attack. The jets attacked at all hours of the day, though the attacks thinned due to low clouds gathering over the attack zones. Aerial attacks were also carried out in the northern Golan Heights, mostly for interdiction on the access routes and attack enemy forces.

The next day, October 9, it was discovered that the Syrians were carrying out a concentrated ground attack in the northern sector. Jets were directed there at dawn, and pilots attacked convoys and artillery mainly east of the Purple Line on the Quneitra—Damascus route and near Khan Arnabeh. Fifteen flights of fifty jets were directed toward this sector. A MiG17 was shot down by anti-aircraft fire carried out by the Tel Avital battery. The aerial assaults prevented the Syrians from sending forces to the front and at this stage the 36th Division forces, particularly the 7th Brigade, prevented the Syrians from obtaining any ground achievements.

Parallel to the aerial assaults in the northern Golan Heights the Air Force jets attacked in the southern sector gradually directing attacks to the east toward Tel Fares and Rapid junction starting at 08:00.

Phantom Jet Attacks in the Southern Sector

On the night of October 8-9 the Syrians launched surface-to-surface FROG rockets and hit Migdal HaEmek. One of the rockets struck the Ramat David Air Force base and caused injuries and damage, which resulted in a decision to attack strategic targets in the center of Syria. Weather conditions disabled four quartets of Phantom jets taking off to attack the Syrian GHQ. The command aerial CCP decided to direct these jets to an attack in the southern Golan Heights. The jets attacked tanks concentrations on the road between Tel Fares and Nawa east of the Purple Line beyond the Rapid junction and in its region starting at 12:20. The pilots carried out high altitude bombings and reported favorable results. Similar were results reported from the ground, as well as the obvious fleeing of Syrian forces.

On October 10, the aerial assaults began at first light. At this stage the Northern Command forces had managed to push the Syrians in the southern Heights up to the Purple Line. The Air Force continued carrying out aerial assaults in the north and south of the Heights, and mainly performed interdictions on convoys on the routes, to prevent reinforcements from flowing to the front.

On October 10, the Air Force attacked four Syrian air fields intending to paralyze them and prevent the planes takeoff. The Aleppo airport in the north of Syria, where Soviet planes from the "Russian Airlift" landed, was attacked and paralyzed. The radar station in Shahba, in the Jabal Druze region, was targeted and the station was hit. Other strategic targets: the Katana power plant, the refineries at Homs and a military seaport and base in Minet el-Beida were attacked.

During the three days of the counteroffensive the Air Force carried out 310 attack sorties on the front. More than half the pilots reported favorable results others did not notice the results or did not report at all. Five jets fell. One pilot was killed and four were rescued.

Air Force Participation in Breaking through the Enclave on October 11–13

At 19:00 on October 10, in a commanders' discussion held at the Israeli Air Force, the Air Force commander presented the GHQ Chief of Staff plans regarding the continued fighting on the Syrian front. In relation to the Air Force attacks Maj. Gen. Moti Hod, who participated in the discussion, said: "... Facing Quneitra is the sector border where he (the GOC) is going to deploy, north... Haka doesn't have the strength to go to Damascus... only the Air Force can help him. He thinks the Air Force can give him what it gave him yesterday and today (meaning the aerial attacks of October 9 and 10)."

Four SAM batteries were positioned in the sector of the planned breakthrough, threatening to hinder the jets attacks. Therefore it was planned to initially attack them to obtain a missiles free region and allow the Air Force's jets to reign supreme.

In adherence with the policy established, the Aerial Operations Department issued operational orders that included an increased effort of aerial assault in the breakthrough sector from D-Day, October 11, at dawn. The breakthrough sector was

Divided into three subsectors and each was allocated a wing. They were: the region of the Quneitra—Damascus route up to Sa'sa; north of the Quneitra—Damascus route up to Mazraat Beit Jann; south of the Quneitra—Damascus route in the region between Achmadia and Maschara.

The attacks were planned to be carried out from high altitude in order to obtain good results. The plan included many other means to be employed, including electronic warfare, information of missiles to make the attacks more efficient. An attack on the Syrian airfields in several waves in order to disrupt the Syrian Air Force plans forcing it to defend the area with most of its planes thus holding them over its airfields was added to the plan as well. Another plan was to continue attacking strategic targets to move the war to the Syrian rear and take Syria out of the cycle of war. These were meant to signal the Jordanian authorities to stay out of the war, as well.

Aerial Assaults during the Breakthrough Stage

The attack on the airfields began at dawn at 05:45 in an operation called *Negicha Gdola*—Great Bunt. The Blay, Saiqal, Khalkhalah, Dumeir, and Mezzeh airfields were attacked. So was the Nasiriyah airfield at 09:20, the international Damascus airport at 11:00 and the Dumeir and Khalkhalah airfields at 12:00. Dogfights ensued over the airfields in which many Syrian jets were shot down. The Syrians carried out dozens of patrol sorties to defend and guard their fields but they did not carry out a single attack sortie on the front in spite of the IDF armored breakthrough and the serious condition of their forces on the front.

On that day, missile batteries in the north of the sector were attacked in several waves. Two of them were hit and two more batteries skipped east.

The fuel tanks at Khan El-Aish east of Damascus were attacked at 14:55, and twenty of the twenty-three tanks in the place were destroyed. Fire and smoke could be seen from afar.

Attacks beginning at dawn on these fronts were carried out in the order established by the Air Force Headquarters—each wing in its own sector. It detailed the attack plan so that attack flights left every 10 to 15 minutes. These were to report results to the flights following them, point out concentrations of armored or artillery forces and warning them of anti-aircraft fire concentration.

The attacks were carried out in the regions of: Tranja, from Tel Dahur to Hader, Kharfa, Mazraat Beit Jann, Jaba, Maschara, Umm-Butna, Khan Arnabeh, and on the route between al-Visia and Sa'sa. Targets in the Hermon Sector were attacked as well. High altitude aerial attacks were carried out resulting in favorable reports. Artillery batteries, vehicles, armored forces and outposts were attacked and many aerial interdictions were carried out to paralyze enemy movements.

In the south of the Golan Heights the Air Force continued carrying out attacks to paralyze the front and prevent any possibility of a renewed Syrian offensive. All in all, fewer sorties were carried out in this sector in comparison to the northern one.

Air Force Integration with the Ground Assault

At 00:10, the GHQ Deputy Chief of Staff operational discussion group discussed the IDF activities for that day, October 12. The GHQ Chief of Staff himself was at the Northern Command and later participated in a government discussion. Following the Northern Command GOC was briefed about the political inclinations and limitations for continued operational activity. A political assessment had it that a ceasefire was imminent granting the command one more day of fighting left.

In accordance with this policy the GHQ Operations Department issued the "Approval No. 9" order which determined that the IDF were to continue the offensive on the Golan Heights to destroy the Syrian Army while holding in the central and southern commands as of 06:00.

The Air Force was ordered to assist the ground forces, attack Syrian airfields and economic targets, attack airfields and military targets in the Canal sector and defend Israel's airspace.

The Air Force continued attacking the Syrian airfields in four waves on October 12. Eight airfields were attacked and paralyzed for lengths of time while hundreds of defense sorties were carried out above them. The attacks on the airfields began at dawn and lasted until late afternoon hours. A missile battery at Khan-a-Sheikh was attacked and hit. That day a Syrian Air Force control outpost in Babila was attacked, which caused interferences in the aerial battle call resulting in Sukhoi Su-20 jets unable to fulfill their task. On the front, the Air Force continued attacking Syrian forces and assisting Israeli forces. Targets were attacked in Beit Jann, Tel-a-Shams, Khan-a-Sheikh and Katana.

From the early noon hours, the Air Force attacked Iraqi armored forces that had just arrived at the front in the eastern sector of the enclave. The pilots reported favorable results.

At this stage the Syrian Air Force advanced MiG-17 jets from the north of Syria to an airfield closer to the front with the intention of operating them for counter attacks against Israeli forces. Syrian jets made a major effort to halt the IDF forces, after failing to participate in the previous day battles, when IDF forces broke through their lines and advanced in the enclave. The Syrians carried out 127 attack sorties that day. Aerial attacks were carried out in a one flight, low altitude quick to flee east maneuvers to avoid being shot down by IAF jets. Nine Syrian jets were shot down in dogfights. One jet was shot down by Israeli forces and another crashed for an unknown reason. Six soldiers were killed in the Syrian attacks and two tanks, two half-tracks and one truck were hit. The attackers were not accompanied by aircrafts but rather patrolled above their airfields that had been attacked throughout the day.

The results of their attack had no meaningful impact on the Israeli advancing forces. On the other hand it should be noted that this was the largest number of sorties carried out by the Syrian Air Force in a single day.

Pushing the Iraqi Offensive and Establishing in the Enclave

The arrival of the Iraqi expeditionary force on the Golan Heights caused a change in the Northern Command forces deployment, halted their advancement and changed plans for the continued fighting.

At 07:30, October 13 the GHQ's ODG took place and an intelligence review and situation assessment took place where, among others, the following was expressed: the Syrians are taking advantage of the arrival of the Iraqi force to advance forces to the front; a Jordanian Armored Brigade had entered Syria; additional forces from Saudi Arabia were expected; an assessment was taking root in Syria that it was going to hold on thanks to both the extensive acquisitions arriving in the Soviet "airlift" and the forces reinforcement.

The GHQ Chief of Staff summed up the discussion and instructed the operations on the Syrian front which were to destroy the Iraqi forces arriving at the front, examine the possibility of capturing Sa'sa and advance within artillery range of Damascus.

The Air Force continued assaults in the region of the front, attacked the Syrian and Iraqi forces and reported favorable results. An ambush was placed for an Iraqi convoy at night. Helicopter borne combatants landed near Qutayfah—about twenty-five kilometers east of Damascus—blew up a water carrier and hit an Iraqi convoy which included tanks carried on board carriers and trucks at night. The force was later evacuated on board an Air Force helicopter without incident. In spite of the order to carry out an interdiction against the Iraqi expeditionary force on its advance only one sortie was carried out.

Two SAM batteries which had apparently arrived in the airlift were attacked near Jassem. The Air Force continued attacking and paralyzing airfields for periods of time, which caused the Syrian Air Force to remain grounded in its bases.

At this stage, during the first three days of fighting, the Air Force carried out 463 attack sorties on the Syrian front. The high altitude attacks utilized other attack methods that obtained good results. Eleven Israeli aircrafts were lost during these attacks, two pilots were killed, and six were captured.

Col. Rafi Sivron, the commander of the aerial CCP in the Northern Command, summed up the activity of the Israeli Air Force against the Iraqi expeditionary forces at a soldier's inquiry by saying: "We planned just an attack in a hot missile-defended zone... and then one carries out artillery tasks as one goes along." In the same inquiry Lt. Col. David Yitzhak, commander of the 109th squadron that participated in the attacks said: "When the Iraqis attacked from the south we put in quartet after quartet, followed by another quartet after quartet... and attacked from noon to twilight again one quartet after another all solely in the direction of Tel Hara." With regard to the attack on the Iraqis, GOC Maj. Gen. Yitzhak Hofi said in the Northern Command convention on November 15th 1973: "Battle dust was seen from afar and it very quickly turned out to be a significant Iraqi force going up the southeastern route toward the 210th. We employed a rather limited air support which the 210th Division commander defined as efficient."

Air Force Participation in Establishment within the Enclave

The situation on the Syrian front seemed relatively stable at this stage and the command forces managed to hold off all the enemy attacks on the front and even improve positions and stabilize a line. At this stage the main Air Force effort was transferred to the Egyptian front. The policy dictated by the Air Force commander was that attack on the Egyptian front be increased while keeping pairs of jets in the air on the Syrian front to deter and attack when necessary.

The Aerial Operations Department planned the Israeli Air Force activity on the Syrian front in accordance with the Air Force commander's orders. Likewise, there was a plan to attack air fields in Syria to damage Syrian Air Force capabilities as much as possible. On October 14, the Mezzeh airfield was attacked and paralyzed for many hours where two MiG 21 jets were shot down in a dogfight over it. On October 15, fuel tanks in Latakia and Tartus in the North of Syria were attacked, and twenty storage tanks were destroyed. Fire and smoke could be seen from afar. A MiG 21 jet was shot down in a dogfight over Tartus. The Syrians transferred tanks damaged on the front to a tank repair workshop in Harasta in the Damascus region. The Israeli Air Force attacked this base on October 16. The base commander was killed, serious damage was inflicted on the workshops and work was halted. That day, two road bridges and two railway bridges were attacked as well. No serious strikes on the bridges were observed but traffic on them stopped for a while and continued later much more slowly.

On the front targets in Mazraat Beit Jann, the Sa'sa region, Tel Shams, near Qudna, in the Tel Hara region and in the Hermon were attacked following the demands of the command aerial CCP.

Air Force Participation in Capturing the Hermon Outposts

The Northern Command decided to attack the Hermon outposts within 48 hours where the Israeli outpost was prioritized over the Syrian one, on the night of October 19–20. On October 20, the plan was approved by the Minister of Defense to be approved for action by the GHQ Chief of Staff's ODG. The planning included powerful artillery softening and massive aerial strikes. The 1st Brigade was planned to attack on foot while the 317th Brigade was to be flown in close to the "Bends Outpost" and attack the outposts from there.

An artillery strike was directed at the outpost on the morning hours of October 21 as well as aerial attacks which continued until the afternoon hours. At this stage the Israeli Air Force assembled six CH-53 helicopters from the 118th Squadron under the command of Lt. Col. Yuval Efrat at the Mahanayim base to transport the paratroopers. Prior to landing, 4 jets dropped smoke bombs in the landing area to create a smokescreen to cover up the forces. Interception jets patrolled the region to prevent Syrian jets interference. When the landing began five helicopters made repeated trips and landed 626 combatants. The assault jets continued attacking the outposts toward the landing to soften and prepare them for capture.

The capture of the Israeli outpost was completed the next day at 10:30. Following the capture of the Hermon, the Syrians had no hold left in the territory which had been under Israeli control before the war. At this stage the Air Force jets continued attacking strategic targets in the depths of Syria including treatment plants, power stations, and fuel depots. Air fields were attacked, and dozens of Syrian jets were shot down in dogfights, assault jets and interception jets among them, including Dolphin jets that carried out defensive actions over their airfields.

Summary of Air Force Activity on the Syrian Front

During the Yom Kippur War the Syrian Air Force carried out about 6,300 combat sorties, of them 720 assault sorties on the front which were about 11.4 percent of the overall activity, and the rest to patrol and defend territories over its airfields and deep in Syria. The Syrian Air Force attacks on the front were inefficient: one low altitude bombing flight dropping all its ammunition immediately followed by a turn east and north to avoid being intercepted by Israeli jets. This is a bombing technique with poor results. There was no close or directed support for the fighting forces. At times ammunition was thrown at their own and at Iraqi forces. The Syrian Air Force attacks did not impact the process of the war in any way and did not cause the Israeli forces to alter their deployment nor did it disrupt the Northern Command battle plans.

The Syrians lost 153 jets, 97 of them intercepted in dogfights, 9 destroyed in airfield assaults, 24 were brought down by Israeli missiles and guns and twenty-three jets were hit by Syrian friendly missile and gun fire. Twenty-eight of the assault jets on the front were shot down. As a rule, the Syrian Air Force "wasted" nearly 89 percent of its defensive activity, while the ground forces were on the defensive retreating from the IDF forces and while the Israeli Air Force attacked on the front intensively.

The Israeli Air Force carried out about 3,000 attack sorties which was about 27 percent of total Air Force activity during the Yom Kippur War, including about 1,100 attack sorties on the front in participation in the ground war, about 200 attack sorties against missile batteries, about 300 sorties against airfields and radar stations, about 100 sorties against strategic targets, and about 1,300 sorties to patrol, escort, and defend the field. The Air Force did not succeed in preventing the arrival of long columns of Iraqi and Jordanian expeditionary forces throughout the war. As stated above, only one interdiction sortie was carried out against the Iraqi forces, while the Air Force was not employed against the Jordanian forces at all.

During most stages of the war jets operated in missile-defended zones. The attempts to destroy the SAM batteries lacked updated intelligence. Forty-nine Israeli Air Force jets were hit and fell during the Yom Kippur War on the Syrian front. Twenty-seven of them fell in the ground battle, six were hit by missiles, four by air field and radar attacks, three in attacking strategic targets in the depth of Syria and nine in patrolling and interception tasks (three in air-to-air combat). On the front: fifteen jets including a light observation aircraft on an intelligence and artillery ranging task[28] were hit by missiles, nine were hit by anti-aircraft guns and three fell due to various malfunctions. Thirty additional jets were hit by anti-aircraft fire and landed safely, were repaired and resumed operational activity. Sixteen aerial crewmembers were killed,twenty-four were captured and fifteen were rescued.

In the period between the ceasefire and the separation of forces the Air Force carried out about 500 attack sorties on the Golan Heights, about 600 patrol sorties, and about 120 special sorties to transport, evacuate, and rescue soldiers. In these attacks the Air Force carried out eighteen offensive operations in Syria, mostly in the Hermon Sector, intended to prevent the Syrians from breaking through a path into the region. Tractors and tanks, an administrative base, a lot of mechanical equipment and Syrian soldiers were hit. In this activity the Air Force lost seven aircrafts, including five fighter jets and two helicopters. Six pilots, five electronic warfare operators, four medical

28 See Chapter 16.

team members and one mechanic were killed. Three pilots were taken prisoner.

The Syrians carried out nine attack operations against Israeli forces, most of them on the Hermon and the enclave. One soldier was wounded in these attacks and phone lines were damaged. Forty attack sorties were carried out in these operations. Seven Syrian jets were intercepted in dogfights.

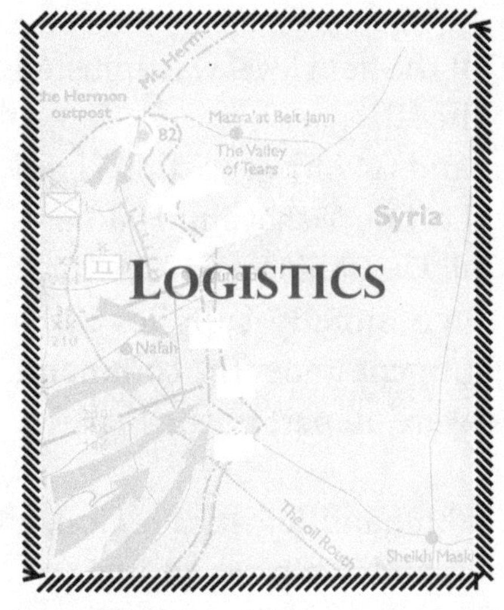

CHAPTER 20

The GHQ and Northern Command Logistics Alignment—from the Six-Day War to the Yom Kippur War

GHQ AND COMMAND LOGISTICS facilities were established, including forward supply facilities, regional workshops, communications installations and medical facilities when the IDF deployed in the new regions. These forward facilities held the inventory required by the IDF region operational plans. The workshops alignment and medical one that had been established were intended to cater to the operational needs of the forces ongoing activity. GHQ/G4 kept the rest of the GHQ inventory in rear bases placed throughout the country.

War preparations included expanding the logistics infrastructure by opening transportation routes, developing the water grid and erecting forward stockpiles. New logistics structures were built on the different fronts, including maintenance facilities in Snobar and in Nafah on the Golan Heights. At the same time, the logistics alignment at the field level was adjusted to fit the organization changes in the IDF.

When the war broke out, command G4 officer Lt. Col. Haim Levav led the command logistics. Lt. Col. Yishayahu Halfon—ordnance corps commander, Lt. Col. Dr. Gabi Dinari—medical corps commander, Lt. Col. Aharon Shmueli—supplies commander and the military police alignment under the command of Lt. Col. Zvi (Herman) Hershko were all part of the logistics branch.

To control the routes and the command logistics region, a command transportation battalion and a command maintenance team were established in the years 1971–1972. These units performed establishment training exercises in the year prior to the war. Lt. Col. Yehuda Borovsky was the commander of the recently established command maintenance team and performed a founding exercise. This body was to serve as a command executive and assisting tool to perform logistics activity at the command level between the GHQ rear and the combat divisions' forward region. As an emblem of Borovsky's intense activity it is noteworthy to mention that the Rosh Pina junction, where the base was located during the war, was called the "Borovsky junction" for a while after the maintenance team commander. Lt. Col. Shaul Solomon was appointed commander of the Command Ordnance Unit in August, but less than a month later, Solomon was appointed commander of the 210th Division Ordnance Battalion, and Lt. Col. Gadi Beter was appointed in his place.

Stockpiles and other facilities such as medical installations and workshops were established in the command region. In the year prior to the Yom Kippur War, particularly after the Kachol Lavan alert of the spring of 1973, emergency storage warehouses were built and expanded. The ammunition inventory in the forward bases was increased by twenty percent and stood at about 9,000 tons. The armored brigades' emergency storage warehouses in the Western Galilee and the Haifa Bay area were advanced toward the anticipated combat fronts.

The Logistics Plan for Defense

The command logistics plan was based on the principle of forces' granted logistics independence in a defensive battle with the following means:

- The forces' unit level organic means allowed for logistics independence for a period of 24 to 48 hours.
- The division level logistics means allowed for logistics independence for an additional 24-hour period.
- The command maintenance alignment, including medical units, a communications equipment base, ordnance units, a transportation battalion, a command supply chain center, reserve vehicle units, mechanical and engineering equipment units, building units, and so on.
- The GHQ forward maintenance facilities, deployed in the northern region and on the Golan Heights.
- Allocation of supply and evacuation routes for the forces in accordance with the operational deployment plan.
- GHQ supply chains.

The Division Logistics Alignment

Between the Six-Day War and the Yom Kippur War, the principal and fundamental organizational change of the logistics alignment at the field level was in the establishment of the permanent division. Its establishment entailed the cancellation of the logistics units at the brigade level. A Maintenance Support Unit was established, including a medical corps, an ordnance services, and a supply battalions and a headquarters with communications and control elements of MPs. At the war outbreak the division organization was not yet completed.

The doctrine of operation states that the Maintenance Support Unit Headquarters be intended to carry out the logistics plan determined by the division staff. A logistics staff remained in the division staff, to plan, coordinate and operate logistics agencies within the battalions or those provided in the division assistance dependent on operational needs. The logistics field ranks chain was graded—logistics agencies were established at the both the battalion and the division level without logistics ranks in the brigade. This change brought about the better use of money, means, manpower and a cutting down of the logistics "tail" trailing the forces. This new format of organization of logistics was studied by the training alignment and was practiced in division exercises prior to the war. Organic logistics units remained in the infantry and paratrooper brigades, as well as in independent tank brigades which were not included in the permanent divisions.

Order of Battle Changes and its Deployment in the Northern Command

These changes and the growing order of battle necessitated changes in the GHQ and command logistics alignment in the Northern Command. A few plans took root simultaneously: a supply center to be built in the lower Galilee—not yet established when the war broke out; a forward extension on the Golan Heights; the establishment of a forward company of an ordnance services battalion; beginning construction of an AFV workshop at the Golani junction as part of the command ordnance services unit and the organization of the command communications battalion and equipment base.

The Northern Command Headquarters reached an agreement with the GHQ regarding the transfer of the armored formations emergency storage warehouse to the eastern Galilee. It was established that the 36th Division would deploy its emergency storage warehouses in the eastern Galilee while the 210th Division, which was at organizational stages, would deploy its emergency storage warehouses in the Haifa region. The tank brigades were transferred to bases near the front and at the same time tank ammunition was transferred from the rear bases to emergency storage warehouses near the front. Tanks and artillery ammunition depots were prepared for in the heart of the Golan Heights.

The GHQ and Northern Command aimed at completing the deployment by the end of June 1973 in order to allow a higher level of alert in the Northern Command toward the summer while adjusting to the construction rate completion of the emergency storage warehouses. As will be shown later, upon mobilization on October 6, work at the bases had not been completed and the 210th Division entered the Yom Kippur War before the establishment of its Maintenance Support Unit.

Mobilization and Organization at the Outbreak of War

On Friday, October 5 1973, the GHQ Chief of Staff announced a C-Level alert and decided to have the reserve mobilization centers on alert.

Mobilization warnings issued at the Northern Command initiated the logistics activity at both the general staff and the field levels. The logistics preparations were expressed in the loading of rank ammunition, preparing ordnance departments, and deploying the forward medical alignment in the forces on the line. In the tank battalions five half-tracks were loaded with ammunition and five with fuel.

The next morning, after the mobilization order was issued, the GHQ and command logistics alignment dealt mainly with gathering mobilization efforts, giving out orders to the logistics facilities to begin issuing the emergency allocations and releasing repaired or rehabilitated vehicles from rehabilitation and maintenance centers and workshops. Mobilization of the GHQ and command logistics reserves began simultaneously.

The timetable for mobilization and equipping was based on prioritizing the fighting ranks over the administrative ones. Thus, a plan was established for the issuing of fuel and ammunition supply to the combat units, battalions and brigades and the division logistics units and only then to the division and other ranks. Reserve brigades mobilization and equipping was not done in accordance with known and practiced procedures. The reduced regular staff in the brigades did their best to prepare the equipment to be handed out to the reserve soldiers. When the first commanders arrived, the first and most important task was to make sure tank ammunition was brought to the tanks, tanks were prepared and command half-tracks and wounded evacuation vehicles were ready for departure. As is expressed in the 679th Brigade commander words—who placed the utmost importance on the transportation of most of the force into battle after being equipped with ammunition—"Bring ammunition trucks as soon as possible, from the Ein Zeitim bunkers and clear the roads for them up to the tanks and make sure they arrive, this is the most important thing right now!"

Ammunition pallets were scarce and there weren't enough places to store the standard ammunition for all the units in some of the brigade emergency storage warehouses that transferred to the frontline bases in the months prior to the war. Units organization, dispatch to the front and refueling along the way were all affected by the quick mobilization. Some of the 146th Division forces equipped with Meteor engine Centurion tanks went up to the Golan Heights on caterpillar tracks and refueled at Tzemach .[29]

Speedy dispatch of any organized force caused some of the ammunition and tank gear to be left behind in the emergency storage warehouses. As a result of the pressure by the mobilizing units in the initial stages of equipping disrupted the plan to issue ammunition in the ammunition center. The GHQ G4 issued advance equipping orders with ammunition from the ammunition bases. In reality upon mobilization the units' arrival was disrupted as well. Some units came to draw ammunition several times. Some emergency storage warehouses were missing enough forklifts. This meant that ammunition was to be manually and rather slowly lifted upon trucks. The ammunition center was to issue about 7,500 tons of ammunition to eighty-three units in the first thirty hours. In reality, 6,300 tons were issued to 240 units in three days including repetitious issuing to the same units which caused units to wait hours on end to be serviced.

In the Northern Command, the advancement of tanks on caterpillar tracks up to the gathering and deployment areas was made possible thanks to the forward deployment of the tank brigades emergency storage warehouse during the year before the war. In spite of difficulties in organization, equipping and

29 It is a civilian gas station on the southern shore of the Sea of Galilee.

advancement, about 400 tanks made their way up to the Golan Heights in forty-eight hours. Forty-eight hours after the war began, the Northern Command was at its full order of battle of about 600 tanks. Initially, at the war outbreak, there were all in all 171 tanks on the Golan Heights.

First Days—Holding

The tanks high fire rate, using up much ammunition, resulted in some tanks depleted of ammunition toward the night of October 6–7. An ammunition convoy was sent from the Nafah Base to meet up with the CCP—command and control post—of 188th Tank Brigade commander Col. Ben Shoham in the Jukhader region near the border. The convoy commander approached a tank positioned on the Petroleum Road in the dark and was surprised to discover that it was a Syrian one. When the brigade commander learned of this encounter where Syrian forces were so deep in Israeli territory he instructed the convoy to return to Nafah and wait there until the situation was clarified and a transfer convoy of fuel and ammunition ranks could reach the forces. The Syrian fire and their penetration all the way up to the Petroleum Road made it impossible to dispatch fuel and ammunition trucks to the forces. Three artillery ammunition trucks moving along the Petroleum Road encountered Syrian forces and were destroyed. The escort jeep with three men was destroyed and all three were killed.

The command HQ and the 36th Division commander rushed the reserve units to organize quickly and go up to the Golan Heights. The brigades were required to move up quickly even if it meant equipping only half a hull of ammunition, missing equipment, failing to perform calibrations as the orders required and even at the cost of disassembling organic units. Numerous mobilizing forces operated in this manner.

The first reserve forces began arriving in the morning hours of Sunday, October 7. Parts of the different units going separately up the Golan Heights, due to quick movement, created logistics problems. For example, in the 210th Division there were tanks of different types: Meteor engine Centurion tanks, upgraded “Shot Kal” Centurion tanks, M-50 Sherman tanks, and M-51 Sherman tanks. This entailed that the ordnance people had to supply different kinds of fuel, petrol, diesel fuel and different oils and varied ammunition to the various kinds of tanks assembled together. This hindered the supplying of the required services. To make matters worse, the division supply company arrived on the field two days later after mobilization and equipping had been completed.

The fighting arena on the Golan Heights is characterized by its multiple routes: longitude routes, from the Galilee to the Golan Heights and latitude routes crossing the Golan Heights from northwest to southeast. This allowed for an allocation of logistics routes for the forces operating in the sector an independent logistics route for each division, where the division could operate along one advancement route. The proximity to civilian settlements and relative proximity to logistics facilities allowed for fairly short supply rounds.

The 188th Tank Brigade was set on the Golan Heights and was the Northern Command organic brigade. When the state of alert was announced, following the assessment that they had to prepare for a “combat day,” each battalion prepared five half-tracks loaded with ammunition and five half-tracks loaded with fuel. After the firing began, the brigade prepared fourteen additional REO M35 trucks (front-wheel drive trucks) loaded with ammunition, from the inventory of the forward facility in Snobar. On Tuesday October 9, the 188th Brigade stopped functioning as a brigade and its logistics officer, Maj. Yermiahu Yosefzon, transferred to the 7th Brigade.

The brigades were refueled and rearmed on the night of October 7–8. The 179th Brigade had no refueling tankers only trucks loaded with fuel drums with one or two manually operated pumps on each truck. This caused both a sheer waste of time since only two tanks could be refueled simultaneously and the crew's exhaustion since they operated the pumps manually. Due to exhaustion tanks were only partially refueled and armed. A heated dissatisfaction over the shortage of fuel and ammunition led to the arrival of mechanized infantry soldiers who did not participate in the battles. Additional fuel pumps were supplied in order to assist the refueling of the tanks from the drums.

During the holding stage, the command logistics alignment was forced to simultaneously deal with two vital tasks:

- Providing logistics assistance to the units fighting on the front: the Regional Brigade forces in the line outposts, the 188th Tank Brigade, the 7th Tank Brigade, the Golani Infantry Brigade and the first reserve forces entering the battle. The 13th and 50th Battalions were routinely managed by the 820th Regional Brigade who attempted to continue commanding them during the beginning of the war. Control in the north remained in the hands of the 13th Battalion commander who got support and supplies from Golani later on during the fighting. In the south the outposts were assisted by the 188th Tank Brigade forces and were evacuated on the second day of fighting.
- Providing logistics support and organizing means for the mobilizing reserve units while mobilizing the reserve alignment of the logistics units themselves (the transportation battalion, the recruited vehicle unit alignment, the Command Maintenance Unit, the transportation alignment, the ordnance and

medical alignments, and so on) the Command Maintenance Unit operated as the executive arm of the command logistics branch to control the logistics region.

After the first two days, the three divisions operating on the northern front operated their logistics alignment and in fact covered the whole area of the Golan Heights in coordination with the Northern Command. It seemed that the GHQ Chief of Staff, Lt.

Gen. Elazar was influenced by the initial organization of the logistics alignment when, in the senior command outpost on October 9, he mentioned that "One of the problems for our forces is also the logistics problem. Our logistics organization is disrupted because we went to war straight from the emergency storage warehouses and the ordnance services battalions and supply companies and all these are in bits and pieces." It is worth mentioning here that the logistics alignment was mobilized, contrary to former decisions, together with the combat units rather than after them.

Logistics Activity in the Combat Divisions

The 36th Division

On the night of October 6–7, the 36th Division assumed responsibility over the forces operating on the Golan Heights sector. Forces' maintenance on the Golan Heights was managed by the command G4 Branch up to that point and until the mobilization of the division logistics alignment, its equipping and the start of its operation. The command had an organic transportation alignment at its disposal, along with a command control maintenance company, a vehicle and tank maintenance alignment in the workshops deployed in the region, a medical alignment partially mobilized in the period between Rosh Hashanah and Yom Kippur and a communications equipment maintenance alignment as part of the command communication battalion.

Immediately upon mobilization, reserve forces began filling the ranks of the regular and mobilizing brigades: the 188th, the 7th, the 179th and the 679th Brigades from the ammunition piles scattered throughout the bases in the eastern Galilee.

On Sunday October 7, 1973, the 36th Brigade's G4 officer Lt. Col. Rami Dotan (later Brig. Gen. and the IDF Head Logistics Officer) ordered that the tank hulls of the mobilizing units and brigade ranks be filled with ammunition.

During the first days of fighting, the division was the first one to organize logistics. The 7th and 188th Tank Brigades had organic logistics means at their disposal, fuel, and ammunition loaded on vehicles, ordnance units and medical units in the battalions, a medical alignment of doctors in the outposts and a medical bunker on the Nafah Base. Three brigade logistics centers were established at the Yiftach base for the 679th Brigade, in the Pilon Base for the 179th Brigade and the 7th Brigade. As of Tuesday October 9, the division put together an ongoing push of ammunition to the 188th Brigade. The brigade ranks were operated by the division G4 Branch with division operation and gathering.

The division G4 officer established a division logistics center at the Korazim base intended to serve as a forward stockpile for the fighting brigades' ranks.

The division medical battalion operated along the Gonen route from Monday, October 8.

The ordnance service battalion operated two forward companies in the Aleika base to treat tanks: one company for upgraded

"Shot Kal" Centurion tanks and one company for Meteor engine Centurion tanks. A forward company for upgraded "Shot Kal" Centurion tanks operated on the Gonen route for the 7th Brigade. During the war, the 36th Division ordnance service battalion treated close to 200 tanks.

The communications equipment maintenance company operated along the routes to repair communications equipment.

The 594th Supply Division Battalion ammunition company began filling up on ammunition in the northern extension of the GHQ ammunition center in the Galilee. Trails of ammunition and fuel tankers sent from the GHQ's logistics center bases in coordination with the Northern Command logistics staff, arrived at the Rosh Pina—Mahanayim junction and advanced from there to the Korazim base under the control of the 36th Division. From the Korazim base the ranks were turned north to Gonen and from there to the Waset junction and south to the Arik Bridge and the Golan rise.

From Thursday October 11, the 36th Division logistics center skipped from Korazim and on October 12, the division forward logistics base was established at Waset junction where the command directed daily supply trails for the brigades. The command also operated refueling stations at central junctions.

Each trail of ranks for the brigades included ammunition, fuel, water, battle rations supplemented by fresh vegetables and fruit, cigarettes, mail, and newspapers. The maintenance control support unit led these trails to meeting points with the brigade ranks.

The smaller than the norm tank inventory due to the many damaged tanks allowed the use of the ranks' front-wheel drive vehicles to transport supplies without employing the supply battalion vehicles, which did not have front-wheel drive. Thus, the supply battalion vehicles were not advanced into the Golan Heights and remained in Ein Zeitim.

Incidents occurred where logistics men were injured while working at tanks rescue and repair, as was the case with the 7th Brigade. On October 10, a tank arrived for repairs. When the ordnance team climbed the tank to examine its systems, a malfunction occurred. It was discovered that the cannon was shell loaded. The shell was launched and hit a fuel truck on the premises. The truck caught fire, immediately exploded and the two soldiers in the driver's cabin, trying to escape, were killed. Arthur Gafni, the 7th Brigade G4 officer, was hit by shrapnel and died on the way to the hospital.

The 210th Division

Following the Kachol Lavan alert of May 1973, the General Staff and Northern Command decided to advance the establishment of the 210th Division under the command of Maj. Gen. Dan Lener. The division logistics officer was Lt. Col. Alex Kiril. Toward October 1973, the division headquarters was at the David Base in the Haifa region with 75 percent of the equipment and hardly any vehicles.

The Maintenance Support Unit Headquarters carried out a skeletal training exercise two weeks before the war and the commanders managed to get to know each other. The Maintenance Support Unit was actually established and organized in the course of the war in a very short period of time, thanks to the intense activity of its commander, Col. Haim Teitelbaum (later Brig. Gen. in the logistics alignment). The support unit began providing logistic services to the division units on Monday, October 8, 1973, complying with the forces' advance routes. The support unit initial gathering was in the Genosar region where it skipped from to the region of the Arik Bridge.

The support unit had a medical battalion, an ordnance services battalion and a supply company replacing the supply battalion, as was required. The medical battalion was different in structure from mobile forward companies therefore moved unlike requirements demanding that companies advance behind armored brigades. Each reserve company had a standard brigade medical company that mobilized with the brigade. The battalion headquarters was established and organized in the course of the war while providing medical services to the forces.

There was no designated equipment for the battalion headquarters. Likewise, the battalion did not have a basic company but rather medical teams arrived at the Arik Bridge within 24 hours, deployed there and absorbed the wounded.

The ordnance services battalion was established based on the 164th, 4th, and 188th Brigades' workshops and had about 100 regular ordnance soldiers from the Northern Command Regular Ordnance Unit. Upon mobilization, apparently on October 8, Lt. Col. Gadi Beter assumed command over the ROU, and Shaul Solomon was appointed the full time commander of the ordnance battalion. It began organizing at the Motzkin base and the designated equipment was received during combat. There were many organization handicaps, among others while the personal equipment of the 164th Brigade workshop personnel was at the northern base, the designated equipment including vehicles and tools, was still near Rehovot[30] and the men had to go there and fetch it. The ordnance battalion first assembled in Genosar and later moved up to the Golan Heights. During the fighting, the ordnance battalion repaired 216 Centurion and fifty-three Sherman tanks and twenty-two Self-propelled guns and heavy mortars. The ordnance units went up the Golan

30 These locations are 130 kilometers apart.

Heights with the forces. The battalions' organic ordnance crews advanced behind the tanks and deployed in the rear of the fighting forces. The supply company was the only one in the IDF that stayed intact following the establishment of permanent divisions and division supply battalions. The company was organized through the 274th Tank Brigade mobilization network intended to operate within the Southern Command which made it difficult to mobilize it and transfer it to the Northern Command. On October 8, the company was allocated vehicles and could begin pulling supplies for the division. The company skipped to the Hukok region the following day where it organized and sent supply trails with ammunition, fuel, water, and food to the Hushniya and Sindyanna regions.

The battle was conducted by the forces commanders in the field without the required logistics support during the first days of battle. Twenty-four to forty-eight hours after, the forces went up to the Golan Heights, based on recruited vehicles the logistics aid elements organized. At this stage, fuel and water tankers were scarce. This was recounted by the division commander, Maj. Gen. Dan Lener: “In fact, the supply of both fuel and ammunition, and the evacuation of the wounded was initially haphazard and improvised and slowly began operating more methodically.”

After organization and equipping, the supply company was deployed in the Genosar region. The division organized a push of supplies according to the forces' demands. Artillery ammunition was pushed directly by the command to the Artillery Group and from there to the battalions under the responsibility of the Artillery Group and not through the Maintenance Support Unit.

On the evening of Sunday October 7, forces in the division reported a shortage of ammunition. The following night convoys organized by the Northern Command logistics branch arrived, including semitrailers loaded with ammunition, drums of fuel, petrol and diesel. In many cases the refueling was done from the drums, using the tanks' standard pumps.

The command convoys reached the meeting points regularly every morning or evening. The Maintenance Support Unit Headquarters made sure to transfer the supplies from the command convoy to the brigade ranks' vehicles. At times, during transportation by the Maintenance Support Unit command units, supplies were transferred directly to the forces. The tanks that had skipped back in a coordinated fashion refilled and continued fighting.

The 146th Division

The 146th Division was the Central Command Armored Division. It was intended to serve as the GHQ reserve force and was equipped with Meteor diesel engine Centurion tanks intended for conversion to upgraded diesel engine "Shot Kal" Centurion tanks. The mechanized brigade was equipped with "Sherman" tanks. The division had a Maintenance Support Unit under the command of Col. Menachem Zehavi.

With regard to the first day organization, Lt. Col. Hagai Shalom, the division ordnance officer (later Maj. Gen. and head of Logistics Headquarters) said: "The mobilization process was carried out Saturday afternoon, October 6 1973. There was chaos. Forces flowed into the emergency storage warehouses to gear up, equip their vehicles and arm. There was a real problem in the distribution of ammunition. While equipping the vehicles ammunition had to be pulled by pickup trucks from the ammunition facility in the Judea Mountains. The pickup trucks were civilian pickup trucks that were mobilized as part of a recruited vehicle unit."

The whole process was supposed to take about four days according to plan. The assumption was that there was no need to accelerate preparations of the GHQ reserves as it was going to be needed at an advanced fighting stage. In effect, the tanks were missing both heavy and small arms ammunition, and advanced on caterpillar tracks from Judea and Samaria, and north through the Jordan Valley. On October 7, the division first units arrived in the Jordan Valley, missing partial ammunition and, in certain cases, with nearly empty fuel tanks. The command logistics officer who met with the division logistics men solved the refueling issue on the spot by recruiting civilian fuel from the Tzemach civilian gas station.

Lt. Col. Haim Levav, the Northern Command logistics officer, stated at a November 1973 logistics convention: "The 146th Division arrived as early as the evening of October 7. We absorbed it in Tzemach. There were immediate issues of refueling since most of the brigade (the 205th Brigade) arrived on caterpillar tracks. There were issues of arming since the brigade was not armed with small arms ammunition and some of the heavy ammunition. And then we had to arm. This division or some of it entered battle the next day on Monday morning."

After the war, the division G4 officer, Lt. Col. Meir Zucker (later Col. Meir Zucker, the Northern Command G4 officer) described the initial logistics alignment in a submitted report. It mentioned that the main shortage was that of fuel. When it was learned that the division was heading north, Zucker asked to arrange refueling with petrol and diesel fuel in the Tzemach region which, in fact happened. "When we arrived, Northern Command refueling tankers were waiting for us."

On the night of October 8–9, in light of the future tasks definition, all the Northern Command forces on the Golan Heights were engaged in logistics preparations of refueling, rearming, treating tanks, repairing and restoring damaged vehicles.

Dozens of tanks were repaired, and the fighting vehicles were ready for combat toward morning. When needed at all hours of day and night the ranks' convoys penetrated the combat zone. The mechanized infantry soldiers accompanying these convoys quickly refueled tanks and transferred shells. At the same time, the men from the technical units moved from one tank to the next to repair combat day damages. This commotion would end toward dawn and all convoys organized quickly and left the field. The 4th Brigade commander, Col. Yaakov Hadar (Feffer), described it: "When the hours passed and the ranks failed to arrive we were worried and began 'nagging' over the radio. It turns out the machine was still creaking. The convoys brought in were too big because the division staff didn't know the exact order of battle for the brigades attached to it in the field. They were treated like standard brigades, which was not the case, and "traffic jams" formed. Scouts even had difficulties finding our lots but in the end the ranks arrived. The sight of the large convoy made us worry that it would not be able to leave before dawn. But toward five in the morning not a single truck was left in the field."

The division supply battalion organized quickly and manpower mobilization operated properly. Vehicles recruitment was problematic an issue. Some recruited vehicles were unsuitable for their task and they were in a poor technical state. There were flaws in the emergency storage warehouse's vehicle as well. Out of thirty-nine fuel tankers only one was equipped with a pump. There were no forklifts and no water tankers.

Due to a trucks shortage for the loading of the complete stock of ammunition allocated for the division, the amount drawn was a third smaller than planned and there was a shortage of small arms ammunition and certain types of tank ammunition. All predictions and planned levels of inventory were surpassed during the days of fighting since utilization was significantly higher during the days of fighting.

Both the division and the command increased the ammunition push to the ranks. For every day of fighting during the holding stage there was a provision of nearly 6,000 tank shells a day, and two artillery ammunition portions. From October 6–24th, the division supplied 1,650 tons of Centurion tank cartridges, 200 tons of Sherman tank cartridges, 650 tons artillery shells and 250 tons small arms ammunition. Fuel was sent to the fighting forces, and particularly the 205th Brigade, twice daily due to the high fuel consumption of the Meteor engine Centurion tanks. The fuel was also supplied to the ranks including refueling by improvised means due to fuel pumps shortage on the tankers. Once every 24 hours a convoy of fuel tankers would be sent by the command to reinforce the division. Diesel fuel– 458,000 liters, petrol—650,000 liters and oils—44,000 kilograms were supplied by the division supply battalion until the ceasefire on October 24th.

The 794th ordnance services battalion operated in the division under the command of Lt. Col. Yaakov Idan (Bocho) who was a senior ordnance man. The forward companies were operated by the division ordnance officer. The tanks maintenance and repair was performed by the ordnance services battalion in the following manner:

A forward company for upgraded "Shot Kal" Centurion tanks was positioned in the El Al region.

A mechanized brigade forward company which provided services for the "Sherman" tanks from the 4th Brigade, the 9th Brigade, and the Artillery Group was positioned about a kilometer and a half north of El Al, on the "Tipa" route.

The basic company was positioned in the Tzemach region and dealt with collecting and the gathering of the AFVs and vehicles arriving through the Jordan Valley, repairing them, allocating them to the armored forces and sending them up to the Golan Heights to fight. The ordnance services battalion headquarters was positioned in Tzemach.

As a rule, and in accordance with the maintenance doctrine of the Armored Corps, the night was used to carry out maintenance activity including evacuation of wounded and dead which could not be carried out during the day, refilling the tanks with fuel, ammunition, and other means, evacuating combat vehicles, and carrying out repairs that would allow their reinstatement into combat the following day. There were more than a few cases where the repairs were performed by "cannibalization," namely, taking required repair parts for one tank from another that could not be repaired under field conditions. The tireless work of the ordnance personnel throughout the night brought dozens of tanks back into battle every morning.

One of the difficult and emotional problems facing the ordnance staff and other workers was going into damaged tanks whose crewmembers had been injured. This involved a personal difficulty for anyone who handled these tanks. Still, it was important to do it and enable its return to the cycle of fighting. Men on the technical unit cleaned and scrubbed the tanks and repaired the damages.

The division medical battalion was organized according to standard and included a basic company and two forward companies. The battalion began moving on Sunday October 7, and positioned in the Yavniel region in the morning hours of October 8. A medical battalion forward company deployed in the El Al region following the 205th Brigade and the casualty evacuation platoon moved behind the brigade, to take the wounded. After being hit by Syrian fire, the company was moved to the rear to the Ramat Magshimim region. A second medical battalion company went up to the Afik junction and evacuated casualties. There were thirty-seven casualties that day. Patrols were conducted in the field as far deep as it could be entered to reach the damaged vehicles following casualty reports in different areas.

On October 9, the forward company positioned in Ramat Magshimim suffered an artillery bombardment and was forced to skip back to the Fiq region. Due to Syrian fire hits the company was replaced by the medical battalion basic company in the El Al region. That day the company suffered eighty-five casualties of them five were dead.

The following day, the medical battalion forward Company A, which was positioned near the supply battalion, was under heavy and accurate artillery bombardment that caused many casualties among the Maintenance Support Unit men in both the supply battalion and the medical battalion. Half the company dispersed in the field or was injured and the company had to be reorganized. That day the medical battalion suffered the largest number of casualties in the division in a single day: 226 casualties of them twenty-nine dead and ten seriously wounded.

Summary

The logistics alignment operated on all levels to supply units' needs after the first days. At times there were difficulties in advancing the ranks to the forces, due to Syrian forces activity or due to a lack of a safe logistics route. The logistics activity overcame the inorganic nature of the units, the arrival of new units, the unification of forces and the transfer of forces from one division to another while making use of the short distances and resourcefulness of men in command positions.

The ordnance workforce operated continuously throughout the war. It carried out nighttime welding tasks that could be easily detected by the bright light created as a result of their work. This placed them in danger. They succeeded in restoring most of the tanks hit. This enabled the daily tanks' order of battle to remain at over half the strength, between 300 to 400 tanks for every day of fighting.

The medical alignment—following the forces, treating and evacuating casualties under fire and being exposed to high personal risk—operated throughout the days of fighting. The treatment and evacuation were along the forces' advance routes and people were treated regardless of their unit affiliation.

The war breakout came as a surprise to the logistics alignment as it did for the entire nation. It is reasonable to assume that the decision to equip the 7th Brigade with the Northern Command rapid response brigade tanks, though economically correct would not have been made had the decision making parties assessed that the war was to break out two weeks later.

The high percentage of over 85 percent reporting of the IDF tanks order of battle on the two main fronts—the northern and the southern—within 72 hours of the mobilization order, with over 1,400 of them advancing on caterpillar tracks, contradicts the claim of poor maintenance level in the emergency storage warehouses. The IDF maintenance alignment succeeded in restoring damaged vehicles and enabled their re-use every day keeping it at about half the tanks order of battle throughout the days of fighting.

The establishment of logistics infrastructures in the period between the Six-Day War and the Yom Kippur War and the advance of the emergency storage warehouses in the year before the war made it possible to cut the forces' time of arrival at the front short. It allowed for the cutting short of supply rotations for the forces.

The tank ammunition inventory levels that was determined based on forecasts and estimates was accurate, unlike that of the artillery ammunition.

The IDF gathered a wealth of captured enemy tanks and cannons. There were close to 1,100 tanks including 200 T-62 tanks, of them about 500 were operational and about 500 guns. The GHQ Chief of Staff ordered, as early as October 9 to establish fighting units equipped with these vehicles.

The true test of a combat support alignment, such as the logistics alignment, is in the end result. In this one, thanks to activity, resourcefulness and courage of the logistics combatants in the face of adverse opening circumstances the alignment fulfilled its tasks.

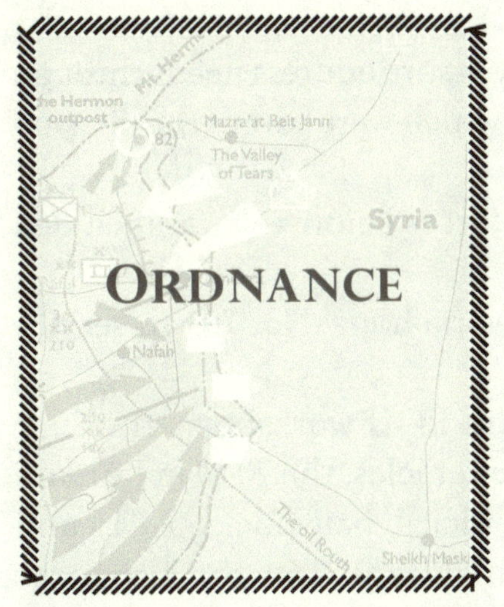

ORDNANCE

CHAPTER 21

THE ORDNANCE ELEMENTS IN the Northern Command region were part of the general effort to provide logistics support to the maneuvering forces. At the head of the Ordnance Corps alignment in the command, stood the Command Ordnance Unit under commander Lt. Col. Gadi Beter. He served as the commander of the forces and advisor to the Command GOC in professional matters. With him was a staff of assistants in charge of the various fields, such as ordnance equipment, vehicles and AFVs, weapons and ammunition, maintenance and control and even the reserve vehicle units intended to reinforce the command.

The ordnance maintenance was based on organic designated forces within the units which were to provide ongoing maintenance at the first rank. The main professional work was carried out well by the Regional Ordnance Unit (ROU) workshops and the brigade workshops scattered throughout the northern region from the Golan Heights to the Golani junction. Upon arrival of the reserve forces reinforcements along with the unit logistics alignment, the ordnance was to address needs through the division ordnance battalions which were part of the division Maintenance Support Unit.

The deployment of ordnance forces before the war included the following workshops:

- The 188th Armored Brigade workshop—No. 703 to service tanks in Nafah.
- The 651st Northern Command ROU workshops: the 701st in Bat Galim (Haifa) to service vehicles, the 704th in Kurdani (north of Haifa) to service vehicles, half-tracks, APCs and tanks, the 704th extension in Biranit (on the Lebanese border) to service vehicles and the 678th Regional Workshop in Snobar for half-track, APCs and tanks with two forward extensions in El Al and Hurshat Tal.
- An additional workshop in Kishon (Haifa) provided services for the bridging and crossing equipment concentrated in the region.

During the war the ordnance order of battle in the northern district was reinforced by the division ordnance battalions - including forward companies to treat AFVs from the tank and mechanized brigades—a basic company and a radio maintenance company. Most of the repairs and maintenance operations were performed by these battalions. The battalions operating on the Golan Heights were:

- The 36th Division 702nd Ordnance Battalion under the command of Lt. Col. Yaakov Silei, which operated within the 811th Maintenance Support Unit.
- The 210th Division 793rd Ordnance Battalion under the command of Lt. Col. Shaul Solomon, which operated within the 813th Maintenance Support Unit.
- The 146th Division 794th Ordnance Battalion under the command of Lt. Col. Yaakov Idan, which operated within the 850th Maintenance Support Unit.

The battalions received forward ordnance companies from different bodies and integrated them into the battalion's work throughout the activity. The ordnance battalion headquarters skipped and operated the forward companies continuously, following the fighting forces. They managed to repair and return the different levels of damaged or malfunctioned vehicles to the combat alignment. Seriously damaged or destroyed vehicles were transferred for reconstruction in the centers operated by the command or the general staff.

The ordnance forces began work at the initial stages of mobilization and equipping in the emergency storage warehouses. The 702nd Ordnance Battalion, which assembled and mobilized in the Mansura base, began maintenance and reconstruction operations at the base to prepare its organic vehicles in the emergency storage warehouse. Recruited vehicles arrived at the base at the same time, which allowed the loading of spare parts and heading out to the organization fields. At noon on Sunday, once the mobilization was completed, the battalion's four companies left along two routes, through Afula and Ahihud, toward the Galilee. The battalion's Company C continued toward Waset. Company B deployed in the Elifelet region and Company A in the Mahanayim junction. The battalion's basic company was deployed in the Hatzor region to later be deployed at the Aleika and Waset junction during the fighting.

The teams repaired vehicles along the fighting routes, including tanks stranded on the way from their emergency storage warehouses to the battlefield. The basic company treated vehicles operating in the rear region. Most of the damaged vehicles were repaired and returned to their units within 24 hours. The battalion's two rescue tanks operating out of Aleika were of assistance in many tasks. Spare parts came from the rear storage bases or via "cannibalization" of other tanks and equipment. The radio maintenance company contributed its share and made it possible to equip every reconstructed and repaired vehicle with functioning radio equipment. During the fighting the battalion treated 333 Centurion and thirty-two Sherman tanks.

The 793rd Ordnance Battalion intended for the new 210th Division had not yet formed at the beginning of the war. It was established immediately and was based on brigade workshops, manpower and means from the Command Ordnance Unit regular alignment. ROU commander Lt. Col. Shaul Solomon was appointed commander of the ordnance battalion in addition to his previous role. The new Maintenance Support Unit commander Lt. Col. Haim Teitelbaum ordered, and was personally active in, the equipping and organizing the unit. The ordnance battalion mobilization began at the Motzkin base. Its headquarters was organized in the Bat Galim workshop. The command ordnance commander Lt. Col. Gadi Beter later assumed responsibility over the ROU.

On Sunday the new unit skipped into the assembly areas near the Genosar gas station where the battalion sent mobilized squads headed by officers that moved behind the forces, located malfunctioning tanks and repaired them. Due to mobilization gear shortage, the battalion skipped six times in four days of fighting, since its arrival and redeployed near the forces. From the end of fighting its companies deployed within the enclave in the captured Syrian territory and maintained the forces on the front. The battalion treated 291 tanks, including 194 Centurion and seventy-five Sherman tanks and twenty-two Self-propelled guns and mortars. Only forty-two remained unemployed during the fighting. At the same time the battalion treated over 600 vehicles.

The 794th Ordnance Battalion of the 146th Division mobilized to its base in the Central Command. The battalion began advancing north on October 7, following the division fighting forces. Its Company A was transferred to the Southern

Command and its Sherman tank department was left in the Central Command. In moving from the Ofer Base to Tzemach, the battalion's Company B performed the maintenance of the 205th Brigade's unfit vehicles discovered along the routes.

Ordnance battalion units were deployed in forward work areas. Company B positioned in El Al was under fire and had one dead and eleven wounded. From El Al the company skipped to a structure in the Mansura village near Quneitra. Company C deployed at the El Al junction and from there continued to deployments in the Hushniya region, on the Quneitra—Marom Golan route and finally in the city of Quneitra itself. The ordnance battalion dealt mainly with providing regional maintenance for the different units scattered in the sector regardless of their unit affiliation. During the fighting in the north the battalion companies treated 1,691 vehicles and AFVs.

Maintenance activity began immediately upon the onslaught of the war. In the first two days of the defensive stage and before the ordnance battalions arrived, the activity was carried out solely by the regular forces at the battalion level or by those operating within and out of the Golan Heights workshops.

At the counterattack stage and up to October 10, the forces operated in a sort of "regional maintenance." The ordnance battalion companies were deployed at key junctions and in close vicinity to the fighting forces. Many tanks were damaged during the counter attack which necessitated their quick return to fighting. The ordnance battalion companies sent technical units to repair tanks in response to various reports and requests. At times malfunctioning tanks came to the ordnance forces themselves. The 702nd Ordnance Battalion commander Lt. Col. Yaakov Sally mentioned that due to their proximity to the front the tanks drove in for repair, the electricians worked throughout the night and fell asleep in the tanks. Technical units repaired damaged tanks concentrated along the routes at times exerting great effort within a short period of time.

After the breakthrough and the IDF forces' establishment within the enclave, the forward ordnance companies established themselves in the field and operated according to the principles of regional maintenance. Tanks were reconstructed in maintenance treatments carried out in 24-hour shifts. Tank companies were taken out of the field. The crews were sent for 24 hours rest, and the ordnance treated the tanks and restored them to service. Tank repair and maintenance was done ceaselessly under arduous conditions and under fire. They worked frantically moving from one unit to the next, searching for units in the dark of night and under fire. They exhibited initiative and improvisational skills in unorthodox repair methods and while employing spare parts from damaged vehicles.

The skill of the ordnance alignment, its efficiency and performance in the battlefield, allowed for ongoing and solid continuity of professional service throughout the days of fighting. The returning vehicles contributed to the balance of the forces which enabled the fighting units to continue fighting and allowed the combatants to turn the tides and win.

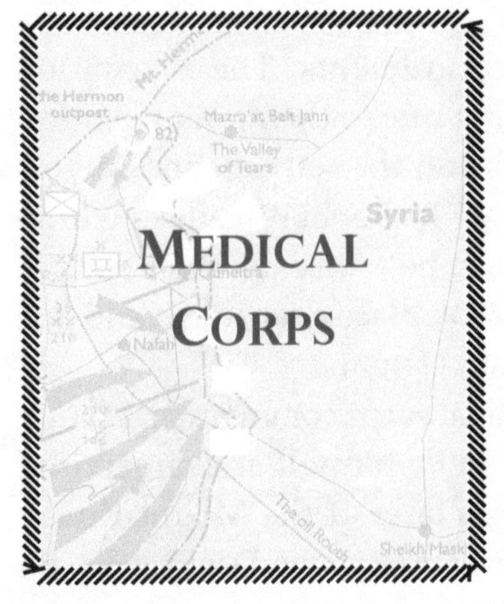

Medical Corps

CHAPTER 22

War Preparation

THE NORTHERN COMMAND 541ST Medical headquarters entered a state of full alert on Friday morning, October 5, when the Lock order was issued by the command G3. All preparations were made for mobilizing the reserve forces after the full regular staff was brought back from the weekend vacation.

Simultaneously, doctors and medics were placed on alert to reinforce the Golan Heights in accordance with the Sela defensive plan. According to which fifteen doctors were required to be on the first line on the Golan Heights—five on the Golan Heights settlements that were evacuated within the first 24 hours, four in the evacuation tanks attached to the Artillery Corps batteries and the other six in the line battalions' headquarters in El Al and Quneitra, in the company headquarters in Rapid, Mas'ade, Nafah and the Hermon outpost. As early as Saturday morning, twenty-one doctors arrived on the Golan

Heights surpassing the Sela requirements. The evacuation tanks could not be operated at first due to their poor technical condition. Some of their doctors and the settlements' doctors were added as a reserve to the 820th Regional Brigade doctor in Nafah. In retrospect this proved to be a wise decision both in light of the difficult battles that took place near Nafah and due to its central location on the Golan Heights.

The Northern Command medical corps commander, Lt. Col. Dr. Gabriel Dinari, reached Nafah by himself and supervised the forces reinforcement. He was later at the Mount Knaan command outpost. The logistics center at the David Base, on the outskirts of Haifa, supplied the medical forces with gear and reinforcement and was connected with the rear hospitalization facilities.

At 10:30 Saturday morning, the medical corps commander instructed the hospitals in the northern region to prepare for war. Hospitals began preparing lists of patients to be sent home that took place an hour after the war had broken out. By 19:00 about 75 percent of the beds were ready. Some 1,700 beds were made available to the medical corps.

The orders to mobilize the 541st Unit entire reserve alignment were somewhat delayed and was issued at 18:30. The 36th Division medical battalion which was the most senior among the medical battalions and the only one whose standards was full and had trained continuously including a skeletal exercise a few weeks prior to the war was mobilized in its entirety on the evening hours of Sunday.[31] At first its forces deployed in the Bnot Yaakov Bridge and Gonen regions. On the first night, the medical corps commander Lt. Col. Dinari made sure to reinforce it with plentiful medical equipment which proved important especially in response to the 7th Brigade 's many casualties. The

31 A day after the war had broken out.

medical battalions of the other divisions participating in the war—the 210th and the 146th—were gradually built while deploying in the Arik Bridge region (the 210th) and the Ramat Magshimim—El Al region (the 146th). These medical battalions completed their standards parallel to the fighting.

The 530th regional RMCC, the 280th field hospital, the 5201st Surgical Company, the 221st Evacuation Company (evacuation vehicle reserve) and the 2nd "X" list units positioned in hospitals and completions for the command medical corps headquarters were recruited on the first night. Men of the 306th Hospitalization and Recuperation base and the POW hospital were mobilized the following night and the 280th field hospital moved to the Meron region.

Medical Aid during Battles

Many more casualties than expected in prewar outlines were the result of the surprise war outbreak. Though in terms of the medical corps, substantial medical forces were quickly concentrated on the Golan Heights these were insufficient during the holding stage when the Golan was "flooded" by enemy forces. The quick Syrian advance toward Nafah, for example, posed serious problems to the reinforced medical staff concentrated at the base, headed by the 820th Brigade's physician, Dr. Hadar.

Until the arrival of the medical battalions on the Golan Heights many wounded were gathered in Nafah and were primarily and treated there under bombardments. Even secondary treatments were offered there in those difficult conditions where the medical bunker was too small to hold all those who required treatment. A few wounded were taken for treatment outside the base. The medical team at the base treated 250 wounded in a little over 24 hours. Apprehensive of the base falling into Syrian hands a decision to transfer the 820th RMCC to the Mahanayim junction was reached on October 7. At the same time the 612th RMCC was positioned in Tzemach so that the flow of wounded evacuated by vehicles could be directed and regulated along these routes.

Some medical forces retreat behind the green line and the nearly complete absence of armored evacuation vehicles left many of the wounded without sufficient medical aid. Civilians assisted in transporting the wounded in their private vehicles haphazardly. Lt. Col. Dr. Dan Michaeli, the 36th Division physician who treated the northern sector's wounded, mentioned that "many tragedies" had occurred in the difficult ground battles in the different sectors. Wounded remained trapped in AFVs, tanks, APCs and half-tracks for 24 hours and more and by the time they were reached they had died. Though there were some Medical Evacuation Unit doctors from the 7th Brigade for and medics who risked their lives and saved many. Some received citations, including Dr, Dan Engelhard, who received the Medal of Distinguished Service.

The story of Dr, Ilan Cohen, a battalion physician, and his improvised treatment of the casualties during the first chaotic 24-hour period of fighting testifies to the situation at the start of the war. Dr. Cohen served as a physician in the 82nd Battalion and went up the Golan Heights from Pilon before the war with the 7th Brigade. His force, on board two half-tracks had five medics with light medical evacuation satchels in the beginning. An ambulance arrived on the morning of Yom Kippur. A short time before the war broke out the deputy battalion commander sent most of the force back to Pilon and took with him the physician with only two medics on the technical half-track. The physician went to war without any instructions regarding evacuation routes of any medical rank. The first call to treat a wounded was answered by his team. After stabilizing the wounded he was evacuated to the rear by the ambulance of another unit passing through the region. The physician continued along the Petroleum Road toward Tel Fares. In the process he treated wounded within APCs and sent them to the rear in their vehicles. Another APC joined him and the two vehicles traveled together. At night they suddenly encountered a Syrian tank ahead of them but while fleeing from it received the order to move to treat the wounded. A medical crew member was hit by enemy fire and they could not reach the wounded they were on their way to. In the morning they found themselves near Tel Fares and met an ambulance filled with wounded some from the 82nd Battalion. The ambulance belonging to another battalion had a physician on board and attempted to evacuate the wounded from Rapid toward the Petroleum Road. On its way it encountered the enemy and returned to Rapid. The two physicians now remained together but were forced to hide in the Rapid bunker apprehensive of a fierce Syrian offensive. At this stage a tank force was sent to rescue the force from Rapid, including the "Mobile Medical Unit." One of the APCs Dr. Cohen was in, was damaged and he transferred to another APC. Among the twenty soldiers with him there were also three wounded. They reached the Arik Bridge after a 10 hour ordeal. They treated the crew of a damaged tank while in motion. One of the wounded moved in the field along with the Medical Evacuation Unit for 26 hours before he finally reached the hospital but his life was saved.

Among the larger units, the 36th Division medical battalion, headed by Lt. Col. Dr, Zvi Strauss stood out. The medical battalion, partially deployed at the Waset junction in the northern sector, treated as many as 600 wounded throughout the days of battle.

On the morning of October 8, a unit was sent from the 280th

Field Hospital to the Kiryat Shmona landing pad. Due to the thinning out of the 280th Field Hospital the 530th RMCC was attached to it. Additional units were positioned in Banias and Snir, and received many wounded from the Hermon battles. Some of the Golani wounded were treated by the brigade RMCC positioned near Mas'ade under the command of Dr. Michael Weiner. A severe shortage in evacuation vehicles, rectified in the following days, was felt in the evacuation of the many wounded who were hit in the attempts to recapture the Hermon outpost. Wounded were taken to the rear on board private vehicles and even trucks.

It should be mentioned that the Hermon outpost physician, Dr. Charles Kovalski, was injured while treating the men in the outpost and upon being captured by the Syrians was also beaten and tortured. The outpost medic, On Hefer, was killed during the battle.

The 146th Division Medical Battalion operated in the southern sector as part of the counter attack. On October 9, the surgical company was sent to reinforce the Tzemach station for the gradation of wounded in case of a continued enemy offensive. On October 10, a force from the division medical battalion was hit by direct bombardment and had to be reinforced by command emergency units due to the casualties on the staff.

The 210th Division medical battalion operated mainly in the central sector. After overcoming the Syrian armored forces the battalion was positioned in the Nafah region, Ein Zivan and east of the Waset junction. In total the battalion forces treated nearly 300 wounded.

With the move to the offensive stage on October 11 and creating the enclave within Syrian territory some of the medical forces advanced as well. The 36th Medical Battalion forward medical company deployed in Khan Arnabeh on October 14 and treated the wounded of the two fighting divisions, the 36th and the 210th. The divisions' medical companies and reinforcements from the 541st Medical Reserve Unit deployed in the east and center of the Golan Heights and treated the wounded brought to them from the sectors breaking through. A few medical staff members showed their courage here as well, including the intern Dr. Uriel Elimelech, who volunteered to reinforce the 679th Brigade medical force, drove a half-track by himself treated many wounded from the armored forces for which he received the Medal of Distinguished Service.

The preferred method of evacuation was that the forward medical company armored vehicle draw the wounded from the Medical Evacuation Units on board the forward medical company's armored vehicle. Lt. Col. Dr. Dan Michaeli even used past proven efficient captured enemy BTR 152 APCs which were equipped with stretchers. Paratroopers from the 317th Brigade battalions used these as well. On the other hand the evacuation tanks brought in from the Sinai and intended for the offensive on Tel Shams, did not help much. They became fortified positions on the Hermon summit upon its recapture, eventually.

Throughout the days of battle there were no actual issues regarding the provision of medical supplies. This was thanks to the establishment and deployment of two forward warehouse units in Meron and Tzemach. On October 12, the unit from Meron was advanced to Nafah. The medical battalions pushed equipment to the forward units and renewed stocks from these warehouses. The demands for equipment and manpower reinforcements were transferred to the HMC by the division physicians. They were personally met by the HMC during the days of battle. The division physicians seldom employed the assistance of the Chief Medical Officer headquarters (CMO HQ). Thus for example, the 36th Division physician, Lt. Col. Dr. Michaeli, approached the corps supplies officer after his medical battalion mobile operating room was damaged by

Syrian bombing. He received a new operating room.

An additional bright side in the treatment of the wounded was the airborne evacuation employed wherever possible. Lt. Col Dr. Dan Michaeli went up to the summit of Tel Dahur overlooking the entire northern Golan Heights and the breakthrough sector in the Syrian territory of his own initiative, where he could personally direct the helicopters toward the many wounded of the 36th and the Golani Divisions. When there was a need to rescue more than two or three wounded arose, he was assisted by his deputy medics' officer, David Margolis. They both independently operated the medical battalion communications network where each brigade physician had his own call sign. In at least one case the 205th Brigade's physician, Dr. Moshe Revach, saved the life of an artillery battalion wounded soldier who was on the verge of dying.

Later on the airborne evacuation activity, from the entire Golan Heights and the breakthrough sector became more efficient, when an officer representing the HMC entered the Command CCP to organize and coordinate all the evacuation requests with the Air Force representatives. Most of the airborne evacuees were taken to the Rambam hospital in Haifa where an additional helicopter landing pad was prepared at the lower end of Freud Street near the seashore. Wounded were then carried by ambulance to the Carmel hospital when pressure increased. The relevant section of the road was blocked off for other traffic. Some of the wounded were flown in mainly to the Safed hospital in emergencies. Airborne physicians supervised the condition of the wounded during evacuation. One physician, placed in each of the evacuation helicopters, was assisted by at least one airborne medic and at times two.

The ground evacuation of the lightly wounded was mainly made to the Ziv hospital in Safed and partially to Poriya but also to the Emek hospital in Afula. Evacuees were later transferred to the forward hospitals, sometimes by air, for continued treatment in Rambam and the government hospital in Nahariya. The overall number of wounded on the northern front was estimated at 2,500. About half were seriously or moderately wounded. Among the lightly wounded many returned to the battlefield after being treated.

On October 10, the 306th Hospitalization and Recuperation base began receiving wounded in the Akko convalescent home. On October 14 and the following week two others were established in the "Meggido" and the Ben Yehuda hotel in Haifa due to the large number of recovering wounded.

Regarding the nature of the injuries it should be mentioned that, at the time, the number of soldiers suffering from shell shock was small. This might have been the result of closely monitoring turnover of the fighting units after the crisis of the holding stage battles. The combatants were brought to nearby Kibbutzim for a day or two. This short period of rest offered them a peaceful time to recuperate and reconnect with combatants later on. Some of the post trauma was, naturally, only revealed over time.

There were many suffering from burns among the victims due to the substantial part played by the armored vehicles in the battles. Though fireproof overalls saved the lives of many including, for example, the 679th Brigade commander Col. Ori Orr not everyone was equipped with them in the early stages of fighting. There were many seriously burned when they were exposed to the fire as well as many orthopedic injuries.

The war cost a total of 783 dead combatants on the northern front. 89 additional soldiers died after the fighting was over and before the separation of forces agreement was signed with Syrian on May 31, 1974.

Military Police

CHAPTER 23

DURING THE FIRST DAYS of the war the military police in the Northern Command, under the command of Lt. Col. Zvi (Herman) Hershko, was engaged in assisting the mobilization efforts and in opening and controlling the routes from the depth of the territory to the routes going up to the Golan Heights. The amount of attacking Syrian forces and the breakthrough of the defensive alignment required a rapid mobilization of reserve forces from the emergency warehouses to the front. The military police, reinforced by its reserve battalion, enabled the arrival of reinforcement forces of tanks, half-tracks and guns sometimes on caterpillar tracks from the Central Command and the GHQ reserves.

Military police from the command and the divisions ensured the way up the Golan Heights for supply trails and at the same time, in the opposite direction the evacuation of the few Syrian prisoners from the front to holding facilities in the rear. Military policemen directed and regulated the movement along the Jordan River bridges even when Syrians forces were about take over the region.

On the eve of Yom Kippur, the Northern Command military police was engaged in its usual tasks of patrolling and assisting soldiers at transport stations from its Haifa headquarters and bases in the region. When HMP HQ was told of the state of alert by the CID commander, who was with the military police at the Haifa base, he checked with the Nazareth base commander, who was close the Command GOC and got word that there were no leaves and that war was imminent. He began organizing orders and maps of the Syrian and Jordanian fronts immediately upon getting the news. "On the morning of Yom Kippur I went up to the command in Nazareth," Lt. Col. Zvi (Herman) Hershko said. "On the way I was ordered over the radio to change direction and head for Nafah. When I got there, I saw four CCPS in one bunker—the Regional Brigade, the 188th Brigade, the 36th Division headquarters and the command. When I saw the chaos there, with the staff officers barely able to work, I assisted the organization following a short conferring with the GOC's Chief of Staff.

I took an MP Unit from the nearby Snobar base and we began sorting those present and put things in order. I asked the Chief of Staff to address the G3 officer and tell him that the HMP wants him since he doesn't know what to do, the G3 officer reported to me that the a war was to erupt that same day, and that I had to operate in coordination with the supplies officer. At that point he approved that I mobilize the full force I required. I called my deputy at the rear base immediately and ordered the immediate mobilization of 100 to 120 policemen in the Haifa and Krayot region. I reported to the G3 officer and mobilized about 100 to 150 policemen and about thirty vehicles... I returned to the Snobar military police, we assembled all the regular service men from the bases of Haifa, Tiberias, Snobar, and Nazareth which is where we actually began our real activity.

First we sealed off the Golan Heights with the regular blockades at the Banias, the Tank junction, Gonen, Gadot, the Arik Bridge, Fiq and Hamat Gader by the regular forces, who were later replaced by policemen from the reserve alignment. The command reserves had three companies: a transport company with 197 men, a POW company and a regional supplement company. Immediately upon their mobilization the reserves replaced some of the regular service men at the Golan Heights blockades and established twenty-seven control posts. It was assumed that the command would receive reinforcements from the center and thus control posts were also established in Hadera and Givat Olga to absorb the forces that had to pass through the Meggido and Golani junctions.

We carried out patrols in the main junctions and those control posts as early as the eve of the war. At a certain stage an order to evacuate settlements as well as bases on the Golan Heights was issued. The base was evacuated to the Rosh Pina region and the Mahanayim junction which was bombed since it was not near ammunition and supplies concentrations. We set up blockades there to prevent civilians' and IDF forces from injury. The Mahanayim junction was manned in spite of the bombing.

POW camps were set up in Birya and afterwards near Rosh Pina as well. In addition to taking care of prisoners, the military police assisted in their interrogation by the intelligence elements. These supplied fast and reliable information to the front. The GOC himself asked whether there were new prisoners, what their rank was and which unit they belonged to. There were a few hundred prisoners, Syrians among them. We also guarded them in hospitals and eventually opened another military police base for this. I remember that one day one of my officers told me over the radio: "Commander, there are prisoners of my origin." I told him that I would immediately find out what his origin was. He laughed. When I discovered he was of Moroccan origin I told him I didn't care what his origin was as long as he was functioning well but I did pass on the information that there were Moroccan prisoners. There were also a number of Iraqi prisoners."

Another activity the military police participated in was a misdirection activity coordinated with field security. For example, field security men accompanied jeeps and the policemen continued talking over the radio, submitting false reports regarding alleged traffic jams along certain routes. It was later discovered that these areas had been bombed. At a certain stage the HMP was urgently summoned to the Northern Command to meet with the Command Chief of Staff. The latter claimed that many junctions and routes were blocked and jammed according to wireless reports. Lt. Col. Zvi (Herman) Hershko was surprised to hear this since he had patrolled there a short while earlier. When he recalled the field security misdirection activity he reported this to the Chief of Staff and calmed him.

The HMP went on to say:" Alongside the military police bases in the command region engaged in traffic patrols and blockades in the rear, the divisions' military police companies operated in the front. The forces dealt with preventing looting. We knew Syrians had entered Israeli settlements, we feared there would be looting of Israeli property by IDF soldiers. We patrolled these settlements as well as the routes. From a certain stage the blockades at the foot of the Golan Heights became blockades to prevent looting, even though there was little of it."

Maj. Shmuel Primo, military police company commander in the 36th Division—the division under Brig. Gen. Refael (Raful) Eitan—went up the bombarded Golan Heights with his soldiers when the fighting began. Here, without auxiliary equipment, he operated along the bombed routes and assisted stranded drivers, civilians included to clear their vehicles. The policemen's night activity included placing signs and directing along the routes to allow the forces to reach their destination and convene toward the breakthrough into the Enclave on the Syrian Golan Heights.

Maj. Yoram Idan, commander of the military police company in the 146th Division—under Brig. Gen. Moshe (Musa) Peled —mobilized with his soldiers on Saturday, October 6. The division, which served as a GHQ reserve, was placed into battle on the Golan Heights. The division military police company accompanied the division supply alignment on the long way from the permanent bases in the center of Israel to the Golan Heights. At first the support unit was positioned near the El Al junction but a few hours after deployment it was heavily bombarded, which caused many injuries among the support unit soldiers, including three military policemen who were injured. There was chaos among the support unit soldiers. Frightened drivers from the ordnance battalion abandoned ammunition trucks with their engines running and took cover far away from them. The deputy company commander, Captain Amnon Shabtai, was among the first to come to his senses, moved from one t to the next and switched their engines off.

Lessons of the event were learned quickly and the company made sure to dig in and take cover every where it happened to be. Doing this ensured that even under heavy bombardments the company's soldiers were not injured.

At the end of the war a decision to send about 50 percent of the company's soldiers on a three week leave was agreed upon. Military policemen who happily arrived at their homes were surprised to receive new mobilization orders within a few hours to join their friends in the Sinai as a decision to transfer the division to reinforce the IDF alignment on the southern front on the banks of the Suez Canal was issued.

Adjutant Branch

Chapter 24

On the war eve, the Northern Command, under the command of GOC Maj. Gen. Yitzhak Hofi, felt that the order of battle on the Golan Heights was insufficient in case it needed to defend the Golan Heights and demanded reinforcements from the GHQ. As a result, the 7th Brigade was transferred to the Northern Command before the war. It was absorbed by the Northern Command entire staff and its staff officers joined up with the command elements.

The adjutant branch under the command of Lt. Col. Nathan Shpak remained on call in the command on the eve of Yom Kippur along with all of the command branches. The command G3 under Lt. Col. Uri Simchoni coordinated the staff work holding ongoing update briefing meetings with all branch representatives. Officer, Maj. Aharon Ophir represented the command adjutant branch in this forum as the manpower commander.

On Yom Kippur the adjutant branch prepared to collect data and assist the absorption of those mobilized publically in the command units and in supplements of the branch command branch units: the Burial Unit, the Canteen Stores Service, the

Postal Services Unit and the Transit Unit. When part of the command, particularly the G3 sector, transferred to Mount Knaan in Safed, they were joined by Lt. Col. Naftali Damti, the command staff officer, and the command manpower officer Aaron Ophir. Most branch officers moved to Mount Knaan later.

The command adjutant representative who was one of the position holders, the command adjutant officer, the staff officer, and the manpower officer took part in discussions and orders groups led by the GOC and his deputy, Maj. Gen. Yekutiel Adam.

The adjutant branch war tasks were professional, diverse, complex and sensitive, and were, among others:

- **Control of mobilized manpower**—absorbing ongoing reports regarding manpower strength from the units and head adjutant emphasizing fighting units and tank crews.
- **Data gathering regarding casualties**—the command adjutant gathered data regarding dead and wounded from all possible sources: units, hospitals, and medical units at the deployed rank and passed it on to the head adjutant.
- **Operating a transit camp**—established at the Pilon Base where the newly recruited soldiers, soldiers who had lost their units and soldiers leaving hospitalization facilities including shell-shocked soldiers were all sent for reassignment. Soldiers were personally attended to for refreshing. They were equipped with personal gear and sent as reinforcements to the units according to a plan prepared by the command adjutant branch.
- **Establishing new units**—according to combat needs, new frameworks were established. The command adjutant branch took part in the reconstruction of units and particularly the 188th Brigade, which had lost its senior command staff along with many of its combatants. The brigade's adjutant officer, Maj. Shmuel Ben-Moshe, did much to rehabilitate the brigade and received the GHQ Chief of Staff Citation for this.

- **Operation of emergency economic measures**—the emergency economy which was in charge of the economical functioning, required people with vital skills. Through the head adjutant orders to take soldiers out of the war and return them to their civilian positions were issued it was a difficult and problematic task to implement, requiring the intervention of a senior ranks to enforce the orders.
- **Release of soldiers to participate in mourning**—soldiers whose first degree relatives were killed in battle were released according to the head adjutant's orders and were carried out by the adjutant branch. There were complicated and complex humane situations. Suffice it to mention the special order issued to take Lt. Col. Avigdor Kahalani out of the fighting force as his brother was killed on the southern front. How and when to carry this order out was decided unanimously with the GOC.
- **Evacuation and identification of the fallen**—the command burial unit under the command Rabbi Lt. Col. Israel Ariel performed the complicated and difficult holy task of evacuating the fallen, bringing them to an identification facility established for this purpose in Amiad and bringing them to temporary burial.
- **Treatment of enemy fallen**—the complex task of burying the enemy's fallen in an orderly manner and registering information which would make it easier for the enemy to identify was carried out under Lt. Col. Nehemia Davidi, who was studying at the university at the war outbreak. This issue, beyond its obligatory status according to IDF orders, was of vital importance in the process of the POWs and fallen exchange agreements.
- **Performing a census of IDF soldiers**—the rapid public mobilization and the changes in the forces' assignments performed during the war caused mass confusion. Therefore,

the head adjutant decided to have a census of all IDF units and feed the updated information into a personal registration file.

- **Education**—an educational program for the command units was activated. Daily orders and combat papers were issued by the education branch, headed by Lt. Col. Hillel Ben-Meir.
- **Women's Corps**—treatment, escort and reinforcement of women soldiers serving in the fighting units and assisting the civilian population in the rear as well was under the command of the women's corps officer, Lt. Col. Nili Eldar.

The command adjutant branch and in the units did their outmost, without an operating theory and an organized doctrine behind their roles during the war. The war aroused many organizational, complex, humane and sensitive problems. The adjutant staff members, as well as others, operated determinedly, ceaselessly and belief to answer problems they were not prepared for.

The head adjutant headquarters under the command of Brig, Gen. Mati Niv, operated commendably to treat the wounded, employ the city officers, handle the economic confinement, carry out payments to the families of the mobilized soldiers, control manpower and coordinate the IDF census during the war.

The manpower branch in the IDF under the command of Maj. Gen. Herzel Shafir assisted as much as it could. The head of the manpower branch had an open, ongoing dialogue with the command adjutant branch.

The war revealed the lack of an adjutant doctrine for the deploying ranks, and the failure to properly construct the adjutant officer through training and the promotion course. An Adjutant Corps was established in April 1974 as a lesson of the war, under the command of Brig. Gen Mati Niv.

SIGNAL CONTROL AND COMMUNICATIONS

CHAPTER 25

THE COMMAND SIGNAL OFFICER Lt. Col. Avraham Kayam was in charge of the control and communications alignment in the Northern Command, his deputy was Maj. Rafi Siman Tov and Maj. Uri Tal was the G4 Signal officer. The system was operated by the signal battalion. The battalion was mostly based on reserve soldiers of over 500 soldiers and officers and about 150 regular service soldiers and officers. The role of the battalion was to supply the GOC and all of the staff's branches with control and communications means, and to serve as a professional and maintenance, guiding and assisting, as well as a source of professional manpower to all of the other communications units in the command.

A training exercise for the communications battalion's regular and reserve forces was held in August 1973 where emphasis was placed on deployment, installation and operation of the Command CCP. The highly successful training exercise helped draw lessons pointing to a shortage of linear communications and radio communications infrastructures in the CCP.

This necessitated dedicating a long period of time for the deployment and installation of the communications system. The battalion held routine exercises for the GOC's CCP based on regular service soldiers, and gained much current knowledge in deploying station CCPs in the different sectors of the command.

When the Yom Kippur War broke out the Northern Command Headquarters operated out of the police building in Nazareth and a station Command CCP in Nafah. At the same time preparations were being made to deploy and install the "Castle" CCP which began operation on Sunday night October 6. A mobile GOC CCP was prepared on board half-tracks and temporary station CCPs were prepared in different sites within the expected combat sectors.

The Command CCP, which prepared for a possible "combat day" against the Syrians on the Golan Heights, deployed in Nafah and the 820th Brigade headquarters a few days before Yom Kippur. The CCP deployed within a bunker surrounded by the GOC's mobile CCP. The control based on linear communicators and radio communicators deployed inside the bunker at the opening stage of the war with the GOC's CCP deployed around the bunker and the communications junctions in the Golan Heights.

Though the CCP was deployed for a combat day it held an extensive communications system which was sufficient for the managing of the first day of the war and up to the move to Knaan late in the evening of October 6. The G4 communications officer (Uri Tal) and several other officers and operators were in the CCP in addition to the command communications officer.

Only on Saturday morning, when the first reports regarding the possibility of a war began coming in did the command personnel - headed by command communications officer Lt. Col. Avraham Kayam - begin shifting the center of gravity toward the planned Command CCP in the police convalescent home on Mount Knaan where, following a hasty organization, the command personnel controlled the fighting arenas from at all stages of the war.

The 36th Division commander took command over the signal battalion manned by Uri Tal along with a team of operators upon the move of the Command CCP. Maj. Menachem Miara stood out among the commanders having arrived at the division a few days before the war to assume the position of deputy communications officer and was in an overlapping process with Bar-Zvi.

The GOC's mobile CCP served Brig. Gen. Refael Eitan to the end of the war.

Before noon on October 6, when it was discovered that a war was imminent and after granted approval for mobilization, intense activity began to operate the CCP. Therefore, Maj. Yanka'le Saltsburg from CCO headquarters, who had served in the Northern Command for many years, was assigned the task of preparing the place. Simultaneously, deputy Maj. Rafi Siman Tov was engaged in mobilizing the reserve force and in prioritizing the reinforcement company intended to deploy and operate the communications system at the Command Headquarters.

Maj. Yanka'le Saltsburg arrived at the command in Nazareth from the center of Israel and together with a small, reduced regular team went up to the command outpost and began preparations for deploying and setting the communications network. While this activity was going on the postal service was asked, through the north telephones officer who was a CCO HQ representative, to operate the phone lines in the command outpost.

The means required for the mobilization were not allocated since the people engaged in mobilizing the reserve forces did not prioritize the command communications battalion. It was rectified after an explicit order was issued by the Command CCP. Thus the late arrival of the reinforcement company caused a delay in the setting up of the Knaan headquarters.

Another problem that arose was the inability of the postal service to meet the obligation to install the telephone lines in the "Castle" where they had to be extended to the CCP and the different offices. By dusk on Saturday there were only two operational lines when the staff arrived from Nafah. One line was to the command operational call center and the second to the Nafah CCP. While the 36th Division CCP was still in Nafah and after the GOC and staff had left, the G3 communications officer Maj. Uri Tal improvised and connected the CCP point-to-point telephone with the HCO point-to-point telephone, allowing for direct calls between the command and the GHQ.

The linear communications' status only stabilized toward Sunday morning. From dusk on Saturday, radio communications was conducted by regular vehicles going up to the CCP with Maj. Yanka'le Saltsburg's regular unit. There was functional radio contact with the 36th Division, the 188th, 7th, and 820th Brigades. During the night of October 6–7 reinforcement groups of reserve soldiers arrived with additional vehicles. At the same time the full communications system for the outpost needs was deployed.

Alongside the ground command a forward CCP was operated for aerial control. This operated closely connected and full coordination with the command artillery headquarters in the war. The Air Force CCP deployed near the Command CCP and had an independent communications system under the Air Force's control, excluding a linear communicator installed by the north telephones officer, assisted by the command communications battalion.

The transfer of written material was conducted by teleprinters to the GHQ and the divisions. Toward the end of the fighting a separate communications system was established in the CCP for Brig. Gem Yekutiel (Kuti) Adam who was the direct commander of the Golani Brigade and the 317th Paratrooper Brigade fighting to capture the Hermon.

The Command Headquarters in Nazareth continued operating in various roles throughout the war and reserve deputy Haim Porat's signal unit provided communications services to the different headquarters elements.

The command operated electronic warfare (EW) to disrupt the Syrian communications systems, in coordination with intelligence factors during the war. Lt. Col. Yossi Barnea, the EW officer in the command operated constantly with a unit from the national EW battalion. His main activity was in planning and coordinating EW operation.

Written transmissions were passed between the command units by the postal rounds, special couriers, and encrypted teleprinter communications. The teleprinter communications was with the GHQ, divisions, and brigades.

Communications maintenance was performed by the command communications equipment base by withdrawing equipment from and by pushing it into the units. Maintenance issues were taken care of by David Shazar, a reserve soldier who volunteered to assist in this important task, and by the command communications maintenance officer, Maj. Alter. Alter dealt mainly with staff work in relation to the units and the CCO and Shazar directly assisted the units and pushed the equipment.

Command and control of the functioning and regularity of communications systems was performed by the signal control center, which was the command communications CCP. The communications control center was manned by command communications staff officers or their representatives. All data flowed there and decisions were taken as to how to act, who to prioritize and who was to receive EW and means. The communications control center instructed the operation of communications backup as required, and served was an address for the different units' assistance, reinforcement and communications requests. It operated in coordination with the CCO HQ and its representative at the HCO in directing assistance and reinforcement requests directed to them.

The work to establish a system of bunkers in Tel Avital for a station Command CCP and a protected communications junction was underway when the war broke out. The bunkers' system was not ready yet. When the planning for the offensive within Syrian territory began, the command communications officer decided that an option for a Command CCP had to be established on the Golan Heights. Accordingly, instructions were given to Yossi Margalit, who went to Nazareth to prepare the communications body that he was to take up to the Golan Heights.

The deputy command communications officer Rafi Siman Tov and Yossi Margalit went up to the Golan Heights and prepared the deployment. On October 10 the latter began deploying the communications junction and installing the communications system for the Command CCP being under fire the whole time. The additional Command CCP was not used but its facilities served to extend the communications "arm" into the Syrian enclave.

The 36th Division

On October 6, the 36th Reserve Division CCP with just the division commander Brig. Gen. Refael (Raful) Eitan and a small number of assistants entered the Nafah bunker. The place was already a center of operation for the 820th Regional Brigade, the 188th Armored Brigade, the Air Force representative and the Command CCP. Lt. Col. Eliezer "Monty" Harari, the former command communications officer, was in charge of operating the division communications along with his vigorous deputy, Maj. Menachem Miara.

When the GOC and staff officers left for the CCP, they employed the command system that remained there, including the Command GOC's mobile CCP. When the Syrians advanced to the base fences, the Division CCP left and deployed in the Tel Shiban region. The division headquarters deployed west of the Jordan River in the Mishmar Hayarden–Mahanayim region.

During the counter attack the headquarters remained in place. The main headquarters skipped to the Tel Shiban region during the offensive. This, while the CCP was advanced to the Mount Bar-On region and later forward to the Tel Dahur region, Jubata al-Khashab.

The 210th Division

The division which was established close to the war, deployed a reduced main headquarters and CCP near Rosh Pina, where it remained in the defensive stages, with the deputy division commander's CCP operating in front on the Yehudia route. Lt. Col. Hagai Gery, who came from the School of Staff and Command, served as the division communications officer. An improvised division CCP operated from a site prepared under the supervision of the deputy command communications officer Rafi Siman Tov on the Golan Heights. Toward the breakthrough, the forward headquarters skipped to the "Booster" region near Quneitra where a light main headquarters was advanced to during the stages that the division operated within the enclave. The deputy division commander's CCP operated from positions in the Tel Shaar region.

The 146th Division

The division, which went up the Golan Heights from the Central Command, deployed its main headquarters in the eastern Galilee on October 8 toward the counter attack. Lt. Col. Pinchas (Pini) Shachar served as the division communications officer. The division commander's CCP advanced behind the forces in the southern Golan Heights from the Givat Yoav region to the Jukhader region. When the division entered the region of the enclave on October 16 the CCP was advanced following the forces to the Tel Mahfi region and later to Tel Korum. In the last stages of the war the main headquarters was advanced to Tel Avital.

Soldiers Decorated Among the Firepower and Combat Support Alignments

Staff Sergeant Agasi Eli, of blessed memory,
2120547

Description of action:

On October 11 1973, Staff Sergeant Agasi Eli, of blessed memory, went on an aerial patrol assignment to support the ground forces during their breakthrough on the Golan Heights. There was a need to take risks far and beyond the call and limitations of duty. The plane he was flying in crossed the front, was hit by a missile and crashed.

Staff Sergeant Agasi Eli, of blessed memory, was killed in this action. In this action he revealed courage and exemplary persistence.

For this action, the Medal of Distinguished Service was awarded to him posthumously

Nisan 5736, April 1976, **Mordechai Gur, Lieutenant General, GHQ Chief of Staff**

Captain Dr. Elimelech, Uriel *950621*

Description of action:

When the Yom Kippur War broke out Lt. Dr. Uriel Elimelech joined up with an armored division on the Golan Heights of his own initiative. During the fighting Lt. Dr. Uriel Elimelech volunteered with the medical evacuation force, which rescued wounded from the battlefield. On the night of the penetration into the enclave while in the region of Khan Arnabeh, the APC crew including Lt. Dr. Uriel Elimelech met up with an Israeli force, which had many wounded. Calmly, while under enemy fire from a nearby Syrian outpost, Lt. Dr. Uriel Elimelech treated the wounded. Later on in the fighting, Lt. Dr. Uriel Elimelech volunteered to carry out the task of transporting ammunition to the tanks. When the Israeli forces broke through toward Tel Antar, Lt. Dr. Uriel Elimelech was among the first forces and treated the wounded under fire. In his actions, Lt. Dr. Uriel Elimelech exhibited a volunteering spirit, bravery, and prudence which contributed to saving the lives of many combatants and served as an example to all around him.

For this action, the Medal of Distinguished Service was awarded to him

Nisan 5736, April 1976, **Mordechai Gur, Lieutenant General, GHQ Chief of Staff**

Major Afek Omri, *932921*

Description of action:

During the Yom Kippur War, Maj. Omri Afek served as a leading pilot in jet offensives on the Syrian and Egyptian fronts. Maj. Omri Afek led a flight in an offensive against the Syrian

GHQ in Damascus. Despite his plane being hit and on fire he managed to land it. In the offensives of the Tanta airfield northwest of Cairo, the wing of Maj. Omri Afek's jet suffered a serious hit but he did not abandon the plane and managed to return with and land. During a nighttime aerial battle he brought down an enemy aircraft in the depths of Syrian territory—all under unusual flying conditions. In all his flights Maj. Omri Afek revealed tenacity, bravery, and superior performance skills and served as a distinguished personal example.

For this action, the Medal of Distinguished Service was awarded to him

Nisan 5736, April 1976, **Mordechai Gur, Lieutenant General, GHQ Chief of Staff**

Lieutenant Colonel Efrat Yuval, *400531*

Description of action:

On October 111973, Lt. Col. Yuval Efrat commanded two helicopters in an operation to land a force in a difficult mountainous terrain beyond enemy lines. After performing the task the helicopters returned to evacuate the force. The field, which was a missile protected zone, was covered in fog and clouds. Lt. Col. Yuval Efrat decided, despite these conditions to go in for a landing with one helicopter, taking a major risk succeeded after three attempts, to land and rescue the entire force. In this action he revealed tenacity, resourcefulness, and exemplary personal bravery.

For this action, the Medal of Distinguished Service was awarded to him

Iyar 5735, May 1975, **Mordechai Gur, Lieutenant General, GHQ Chief of Staff**

Captain Dr. Engelhard Dan, *969060*

Description of action:

During the Yom Kippur War, Lt. Dr. Dan Engelhard served as a battalion physician near the Golan Heights. When the war broke out and reports of the first wounded came in, Lt. Dr. Dan Engelhard began treating the wounded and evacuating them, answering the different forces distress calls. Under enemy fire and at a great personal risk, Lt. Dr. Dan Engelhard saved many lives while reassuring his men and creating a calm atmosphere for those surrounding him. At the breakthrough stage, Lt. Dr. Dan Engelhard joined the forces breaking through and again under fire, continued treating and evacuating wounded. In these actions, Lt. Dr. Dan Engelhard exhibited bravery, dedication, and tenacity, which contributed to the saving of many lives.

For this action, the Medal of Distinguished Service was awarded to him

Nisan 5736, April 1976, **Mordechai Gur, Lieutenant General, GHQ Chief of Staff**

Captain Dr. Eshel Alexander, *969009*

For manifesting bravery, initiative and tenacity
Description of action:

Lt. Dr. Alexander Eshel was a physician in a battalion during the Yom Kippur War and participated in the breakthrough and penetration battles into Syria. On October 9 1973, he rescued, from a tank an injured officer who was suffocating due to a jaw injury. Under artillery fire and while the battle was on, Lt. Dr. Alexander Eshel operated on the officer, opening his windpipe thus saving his life. Lt. Dr. Alexander Eshel treated the wounded and evacuated the dead in spite of fierce fire around him and encouraged the medics in their work. In these actions, Lt. Dr. Alexander Eshel exhibited prudence, resourcefulness, and leadership.

For this action the Chief of Staff Citation was awarded to him

Tishrei 5736, September 1975, **Mordechai Gur, Lieutenant General, GHQ Chief of Staff**

Staff Sergeant Ben-Haim Meir, *2050636*

Description of action:

During the Yom Kippur War, on the Golan Heights battles, Sgt. Meir Ben-Haim served as a medic with the Medical Evacuation Unit. While the Medical Evacuation Unit half-track moved to evacuate a casualty, it encountered a Syrian tank and APCs force in the Tel Abu Hanzir region. Fire was directed at the half-track and the team jumped out of it and disengaged. Sgt. Meir Ben-Haim who was not in command of the half-track stayed near it together with two combatants. They engaged in a difficult battle with the nearby Syrians. The two combatants with him were wounded during the battle. After the Syrians left, Sgt. Meir Ben-Haim remained alone in the field with one dead soldier and one injured. He bandaged the wounded soldier and evacuated him with another soldier in the field. While moving they met up with an Israeli force and were rescued. In his actions, Sgt. Meir Ben-Haim revealed initiative, bravery, prudence and exemplary comradeship.

For this action, the Medal of Distinguished Service was awarded to him

Nisan 5736, April 1976, **Mordechai Gur, Lieutenant General, GHQ Chief of Staff**

Major Ben-Moshe Shmuel, *950193*

For manifesting bravery, initiative and tenacity
Description of action:
During the Yom Kippur War, Maj. Shmuel Ben-Moshe served as a brigade adjutant officer. When the war broke out, Maj. Shmuel Ben-Moshe was engaged in locating his unit wounded and evacuating them. Together with additional staff officers from his unit, he organized new forces of tank crews and quickly dispatched them to the battlefield. At the end of the battles he engaged in the reorganization his unit. In these actions, Maj. Shmuel Ben-Moshe exhibited initiative, resourcefulness, and tenacity.

For this action the Chief of Staff Citation was awarded to him

Tishrei 5736, September 1975, **Mordechai Gur, Lieutenant General, GHQ Chief of Staff**

Captain Ben Ami Arnon, *987720*

For manifesting a volunteering spirit, bravery, and resourcefulness

Description of action:
On October 61973, Lt. Arnon Ben Ami was still abroad. When he heard of the fighting, he returned to Israel and joined a battalion as an artillery support officer, a day before the penetration

into the enclave on the Golan Heights. He quickly integrated into the unit and excelled during the battles. In this position, he made sure his unit received ongoing support while taking personal risks under conditions of heavy bombardment. He continued fighting even after he was injured. In his actions, Captain Arnon Ben Ami exhibited a volunteering spirit, bravery and resourcefulness.

For this action the Chief of Staff Citation was awarded to him

Tishrei 5736, September 1975, **Mordechai Gur, Lieutenant General, GHQ Chief of Staff**

Lieutenant Goldenstein Sorel, *2114179*

Description of action:

On October 7, 1973, Lt. Israel Goldenstein served as an anti-aircraft team commander in Tel Avital. Since only one usable turret remained in the team and since the mound was under heavy bombardment, he left the soldiers under his command in the bunker, while he himself manned and operated the turret. He operated this way for 4 days straight, of his own initiative. In one of the jet offensives he shot down a MiG 21 jet. In his actions, he exhibited initiative, bravery, and exemplary volunteering spirit.

For this action, the Medal of Distinguished Service was awarded to him

Iyar 5735, May 1975, **Mordechai Gur, Lieutenant General, GHQ Chief of Staff**

Major Garson Gabriel, 499300

Description of action:

On October 13 1973, during an offensive on the Golan Heights, Captain Gabriel Garson's jet was hit and he was forced to abandon over enemy territory. He reached the ground safely and escaped toward the mountains with Syrian soldiers in pursuit. When he saw that he could not escape, he hid his radio communicator and surrendered. He underwent extreme torture while in the Syrian prison but managed to hold on for several days and did not divulge any information. On the verge of collapse he gave out only minor information. During the interrogation he lost the feeling in his legs. He suffered serious pain, mainly in his left leg, but refused to receive medical aid for fear that it would be exploited for continued interrogations and pressures. As a result, his gangrenous leg had to be amputated. In his behavior he exhibited bravery and exemplary loyalty.

For this action, the Medal of Distinguished Service was awarded to him

Iyar 5735, May 1975, **Mordechai Gur, Lieutenant General, GHQ Chief of Staff**

Lieutenant Dal Yitzhak of blessed memory 2010318

For manifesting bravery and dedication

Description of action:

On 10 October 1973 Lt. Yitzhak Dal of blessed memory served as an operating room technician in a field hospital in the Golan Heights in the El Al region. When a heavy bombardment began on the helicopter evacuation point all the men in the field scattered to take cover. In spite of explicit warnings not to get up during the heavy artillery fire—Lt. Yitzhak Dal of blessed memory returned and treated the wounded in the tent. During this action he was injured and killed. In this action Lt. Yitzhak Dal of blessed memory exhibited bravery and dedication to his role.

For this action he was awarded: the Chief of Staff Citation

Tishrei 5736, September 1975, **Mordechai Gur, Lieutenant General, GHQ Chief of Staff**

Corporal Dalal Emanuel, 2070639

For manifesting bravery and camaraderie

Description of action:

On October 10 1973, Corp. Emanuel Dalal served as a driver in a medical forward company unit on the Golan Heights, in the El Al region. As the company prepared for advance, with vehicles parked crowdedly on the road heavy artillery fire was shed on the region. Everyone dispersed heading for cover and there were many casualties. Corp. Emanuel Dalal handed medical equipment to the medics and helped treat the wounded. He started up an ambulance that was hit, helped bring the wounded on board and evacuated them. All his actions were done under heavy artillery fire. In this action Corp. Emanuel Dalal exhibited bravery and comradeship.

For this action the Chief of Staff Citation was awarded to him

Tishrei 5736, September 1975, **Mordechai Gur, Lieutenant General, GHQ Chief of Staff**

Master Sergeant Hedvati Ran, *310292*

For manifesting bravery and resourcefulness
Description of action:

On October 10 1973, at the Petroleum Road—Gonen road junction, an ammunition convoy was bombed by Sukhoi Su-20 jets. One ammunition truck caught fire and the tires of the truck next to it began burning. Sgt. 1st Class Ran Hedvati boarded the truck with the burning tires and drove it away from the burning trucks that exploded a few minutes later. He made sure that the convoy's men scatter their vehicles, thus saving men and vehicles. In this action, Sgt. 1st Class Ran Hedvati exhibited bravery, prudence, and resourcefulness.

For this action the Chief of Staff Citation was awarded to him

Tishrei 5736, September 1975, **Mordechai Gur, Lieutenant General, GHQ Chief of Staff**

Lieutenant Colonel Hankin Ehud, of blessed memory, *457272*

Description of action:

Lt. Col. Ehud Hankin of blessed memory, served as a Phantom jet pilot and Captain Shaul Levi of blessed memory, was a navigator. On October 7, 1973 they led a flight of Phantom jets to attack a missile battery in Syria. In the process of identification of the target they found it to be much closer to their plane at a different location. Nevertheless, knowing the importance of the operation they decided to dive in and attack the target. Though they bombed the target, due to their descent to a lower altitude apparently caused their jet to be hit by anti-aircraft fire, and they crashed. In this action Lt. Col. Ehud Henkin, of blessed memory and Captain Shaul Levi, of blessed memory exhibited bravery, prudence and tenacity.

For this action, the Medal of Courage was, posthumously, awarded to him

Iyar 5735, May 1975, **Mordechai Gur, Lieutenant General, GHQ Chief of Staff**

Captain Heffetz Uriel, *140056*

Description of action:

When battles broke out, Captain Uriel Heffetz did not belong to any specific unit. Of his own initiative he went up to the Golan Heights front and evacuated wounded—often under heavy fire and while risking himself. He brought the wounded to the medical battalion. The battalion commander asked him to stay with them but he always went back to the foremost medical evacuation battalions and continued his actions. In these actions, he exhibited an exemplary volunteering spirit, bravery, and prudence.

For this action, the Medal of Distinguished Service was awarded to him

Iyar 5735, May 1975, **Mordechai Gur, Lieutenant General, GHQ Chief of Staff**

Lieutenant Yudkovitch Shalom Yitzhak, of blessed memory, 2125949

Description of action:

On October 11 1973, Lt. Shalom Yudkovitch of blessed memory, served as an aerial observation officer in a task assisting the ground forces during their breakthrough on the Golan Heights. During the operation, in order to complete the task, it was necessary to take risks far beyond the call of duty. When the aircraft he was on board reached the front it was hit by a missile. The aircraft crashed and Lt. Shalom Yudkovitch of blessed memory was killed. In this action Lt. Shalom Yudkovitch, of blessed memory exhibited bravery and exemplary tenacity.

For this action, the Medal of Distinguished Service was awarded to him posthumously

Nisan 5736, April 1976, **Mordechai Gur, Lieutenant General, GHQ Chief of Staff**

Lieutenant Dr. Yalon Dan, of blessed memory, 484920

For manifesting bravery and dedication

Description of action:

On October 10 1973, Lt. Dr. Dan Yalon, of blessed memory served as a field hospital physician on the Golan Heights in the El Al region. A heavy bombardment on the helicopter evacuation point caused all men in the field to scatter and take cover. In spite of explicit warnings not to get up during the heavy artillery fire, Lt. Dr. Dan Yalon, of blessed memory, returned and treated the wounded in the tent. During this action he was injured and killed. In this action Lt. Dr. Dan Yalon, of blessed memory, exhibited bravery and dedication.

For this action the Chief of Staff Citation was, posthumously, awarded to him

Tishrei 5736, September 1975, **Mordechai Gur, Lieutenant General, GHQ Chief of Staff**

Major Dr. Cohen David, *419369*

Description of action:

Maj. Dr. David Cohen arrived at a battalion as the replacement battalion physician, on the second day of the breakthrough battle into Syria. On October 15 1973, near Tel Shams, the last company commander of the entire division was evacuated to the Medical Evacuation Unit, with both hands amputated and clinically dead. With tenacity and diligence, Dr. David Cohen decided to save him. After many infusions and applying tourniquets, he managed to restore his breathing and immediately evacuated him to the Safed hospital, with his hand hanging in only by a piece of skin, preserved in a way that allowed for its later placement and restoration to proper functioning. In this action, he served as a professional example for the possibility of field revival. His diligence and stubbornness saved a human life.

For this action, the Medal of Distinguished Service was awarded to him

Iyar 5735, May 1975, **Mordechai Gur, Lieutenant General, GHQ Chief of Staff**

Captain Lev Amnon, *50955*

Description of action:

At dusk on October 9 1973, when most tanks of the battalion were unfit, Captain Amnon Lev, the battalion ordnance officer, exchanged barrels and other parts, transferring guns and functioning parts from damaged tanks to other damaged tanks—all without proper tools. From October 11, 1973, he engaged in rescuing damaged tanks and restoring them to service—at times under heavy fire. Within a short period he and his ordnance men restored about forty tanks to service. On the morning of October 19 1973, Captain Amnon Lev left with his armored ordnance vehicle to rescue wounded in the Umm-Butna region. He passed the forward line of tank positions to rescue wounded from a burning tank in open territory. His armored vehicle was hit. At a certain stage of the war, when most of the battalion's commanders were injured, he commanded the battalion for several hours, despite his lacking adequate training. Captain Amnon Lev, a volunteer who had passed the age of service in a combat unit, did all this in spite of his wounds—he was injured on October 9, 1973, and fled from the hospital. In his actions, he exhibited extraordinary resourcefulness, initiative, bravery, and dedication.

For this action, the Medal of Courage was awarded to him

Iyar 5735, May 1975, **Mordechai Gur, Lieutenant General, GHQ Chief of Staff**

Major Levi Shaul, of blessed memory *969141*

Description of action:

Captain Shaul Levi, of blessed memory was a navigator of a Phantom jet flown by Lt. Col. Ehud Henkin, of blessed memory. On October 7, 1973, they led a flight of Phantom jets to attack a missile battery in Syria. During the target identification process they discovered it to be in a different location than planned and very close to the jet. Nevertheless, knowing the importance of the operation they decided to dive in and attack the target. Though they bombed the target, their descent to a low altitude apparently caused their jet to be hit by anti-aircraft fire, and they crashed. In this action Lt. Col. Ehud Henkin, of blessed memory and Captain Shaul Levi, of blessed memory, exhibited bravery, prudence, and tenacity.

For this action, the Medal of Courage was awarded to him posthumously

Iyar 5735, May 1975, **Mordechai Gur, Lieutenant General, GHQ Chief of Staff**

Captain Lior Elazar, *2030635*

For manifesting tenacity, bravery, level-headedness, and superior execution skills

Description of action:

On October 9, 1973, Lt. Lior Elazar led a flight, as navigator, in an offensive against the Syrian GHQ in Damascus. The flight encountered severe weather conditions, making the task nearly impossible. Lt. Lior Elazar participated in the decision to continue and lead the flight over the clouds, though this involved the risk of early discovery by the enemy. He later navigated the flight toward the successfully attacked target. In his actions, Lt. Lior Elazar exhibited tenacity, bravery, prudence ,and superior performance skills.

For this action the Chief of Staff Citation was awarded to him

Nisan 5736, April 1976, **Mordechai Gur, Lieutenant General, GHQ Chief of Staff**

Lieutenant Colonel Lanir Avraham, of blessed memory, *179741*

Description of action:

On October 13, 1973, during a combat flight on the Golan Heights, Lt. Col. Avraham Lanir's plane was hit and he was forced to abandon over enemy territory. Lt. Col. Avraham Lanir, of blessed memory, parachuted and reached the ground alive, was captured and taken prisoner. Lt. Col. Avraham Lanir, of blessed memory was tortured to death by his interrogators and did not divulge any information. In his actions, Lt. Col. Avraham Lanir of blessed memory exhibited bravery, loyalty, and supreme sacrifice.

For this action, the Medal of Courage was awarded to him posthumously

Nisan 5736, April 1976, **Mordechai Gur, Lieutenant General, GHQ Chief of Staff**

Major Lapidot Arnon, 932922

Description of action:

On October 9 1973, Maj. Arnon Lapidot led a flight in an offensive against the Syrian GHQ in Damascus. The flight encountered severe weather conditions, making the task nearly impossible. Maj. Arnon Lapidot decided to continue and lead the flight over the clouds, though this involved the risk of early discovery by the enemy. The task was carried out efficiently and the target was successfully attacked. In his actions, Maj. Arnon Lapidot exhibited bravery, prudence, superior performance skills, and exemplary tenacity.

For this action, the Medal of Distinguished Service was awarded to him

Nisan 5736, April 1976, **Mordechai Gur, Lieutenant General, GHQ Chief of Staff**

Sergeant First Class Maman Yosef, of blessed memory, 491072

Description of action:

During the Yom Kippur War Sgt. 1st Class Yosef Maman, of blessed memory, served as a vehicle technician in a mechanized infantry company fighting in the Golan Heights battles. Before the company went up to the Golan Heights Sgt. 1st Class Yosef Maman, of blessed memory prepared the vehicles diligently and within a short period of time restored them to combat service. On October 8, 1973, in a scanning task in the El Al region, during bombardment, a half-track got hit. The combatants took cover, but Sgt. 1st Class Yosef Maman, of blessed memory, moved quickly to the spot and repaired the malfunction under enemy fire. On October 12, 1973, during battle, a malfunction occurred in the company commander's half-track and all the soldiers took cover. Sgt. 1st Class Yosef Maman, of blessed memory went out under heavy enemy artillery fire to repair it. He was injured and fell while working. In these actions, Sgt. 1st Class Yosef Maman, of blessed memory, served as a model of dedication, bravery, and superior professional performance.

For this action, the Medal of Distinguished Service he was, posthumously, awarded to him

Nisan 5736, April 1976, **Mordechai Gur, Lieutenant General, GHQ Chief of Staff**

Staff Sergeant Samuel Binyamin, of blessed memory, *298747*

Description of action:

On October 11 1973, aerial scout Staff Sgt. Binyamin Samuel, of blessed memory, went on a task assisting the ground forces during their breakthrough on the Golan Heights. During the operation, it was necessary to take risks above and beyond the call of duty. When the aircraft he was on board reached the front, it was hit by a missile and crashed. Staff Sgt. Binyamin Samuel, of blessed memory, was killed in this operation. In this action, Staff Sgt. Binyamin Samuel, of blessed memory, exhibited bravery and exemplary tenacity.

For this action, the Medal of Distinguished Service was, posthumously, awarded to him

Av 5737, August 1977, **Mordechai Gur, Lieutenant General, GHQ Chief of Staff**

Sergeant Abad Sami, *2177577*

For manifesting dedication and camaraderie

Description of action:

On the night of October 6–7 1973, Corp. Sami Abad served as an APC driver in a gun battery. When the battery was hit by the Syrian enemy tank fire and the Israeli forces retreated, Corp. Sami Abad noticed one of the soldiers was injured. He carried the soldier on his back and supported him for two days until he brought him to safety. In this action Corp. Sami Abad exhibited dedication and comradeship

For this action the Chief of Staff Citation was awarded to him

Tishrei 5736, September 1975, **Mordechai Gur, Lieutenant General, GHQ Chief of Staff**

Sergeant Friedman Moshe, *959979*

For manifesting bravery and tenacity

Description of action:

On October 10 1973, Sgt. Moshe Friedman served as a medic in a Medical Unit forward company on the Golan Heights in the El Al region. When the company organized for movement a heavy artillery bombardment began in the region. All the people scattered in the field to take cover and there were many casualties. Sgt. Moshe Friedman was wounded in his head, but refused evacuation in spite of his injury, treated the wounded, and assisted in their evacuation. In this action Sgt. Moshe Friedman exhibited bravery and tenacity.

For this action the Chief of Staff Citation was awarded to him

Tishrei 5736, September 1975, **Mordechai Gur, Lieutenant General, GHQ Chief of Staff**

Captain Snir Avraham, of blessed memory, *2088963*

For manifesting bravery, level-headedness, and dedication

Description of action:

Lt. Avraham Snir, of blessed memory served as an artillery support officer in a tank battalion which participated in the holding battles on the Golan Heights and the breakthrough into Syrian territory. Throughout the fighting he was in the battalion's first tanks and exhibited bravery and resourcefulness. He attempted to arrange artillery batteries for the battalion and would jump out of the tank under heavy artillery fire to measure accurate azimuths for field targets with great dedication. Lt. Avraham Snir, of blessed memory, was killed in the battle over Mazraat Beit Jann. In these actions, he exhibited bravery, prudence, and dedication.

For this action the Chief of Staff Citation was, posthumously, awarded to him Tishrei 5736, September 1975, **Mordechai Gur, Lieutenant General, GHQ Chief of Staff**

Quantitative Summary of the War on the Northern Front

The Yom Kippur War, in the northern front against the Syrian Army and the Arab expeditionary forces, lasted nineteen days, from October 6–24th when the ceasefire went into effect after the liberation of the Hermon outpost.

Forces from three divisions participated in this fighting arena, under the Northern Command Headquarters, along with additional units including artillery, engineering, Air Force support and Special Forces operating in the depths of enemy territory.

The Israeli Air Force carried out about 3,000 combat sorties of them 1,100 attack sorties on the front as part of the task to participate in the ground battles; about 200 attack sorties against missile batteries; 300 sorties against airfields and radar installations, about 100 sorties against strategic targets and about 1,300 sorties to patrol, escort, and defend the field. Forty-nine Israeli Air Force jets fell in Syria during the Yom Kippur War. Thirty additional jets were hit by anti-aircraft fire landing safely, repaired and continued operational activity. Sixteen aerial crewmembers were killed, 24 were captured and fifteen were rescued.

The Israeli Navy, which prepared for the war in advance, operated as a GHQ force against the Syrian Navy in sea and ports and hit targets on the Syrian shore.

The Syrian enemy, its forces on the front and rear, and the expeditionary forces assisting it suffered about 3,300–4,300 dead and about 5,600 wounded. Some 358 of its combatants were taken prisoner. Many Syrian Army and expeditionary forces weapons were hit, including 1,200 tanks, 460 APCs, and 300–400 artillery guns. There were 951 tanks, as well as many APCs and guns, captured by Israeli forces. The Syrians lost 153 aircrafts during the war. Ninety-seven of them were intercepted in dogfights, nine destroyed in offensives on airfields, twenty-four shot down by IDF missiles, guns, and artillery fire, and twenty-three hit by Syrian friendly missiles and guns.

The Syrians, who wished to capture the Golan Heights by surprise, reached slopes over the Jordan Valley and the Sea of Galilee in a number of sectors but retreated to their defensive lines following the command forces counter attack. In the offensive beyond the border, the command forces created an enclave inside the Syrian Golan Heights, from which they posed a threat to Damascus, where they also pushed back counter offensives by the Syrian military units, operating in coordination with the expeditionary forces of Iraq, Jordan, Saudi Arabia, and Morocco. Throughout this period, terrorist organizations continued operating in the secondary front of the Lebanese border.

Many of the combatants were injured during the fighting on the northern front. There were 783 commanders and soldiers who fell in the battle, 2,904 were wounded, and sixty-one combatants were taken prisoner.

The war ended after Israel restored all of the assets following the Six-Day War, to which the enclave regions were added. Following the ceasefire and separation agreements, in July 1974, the Northern Command forces returned to their defensive alignments on the Golan Heights, where they have been deployed for over thirty years along a continuously calm border.

AFTERWORD

MAJOR GENERAL (RES.) URI SIMCHONI

A Personal Look at the War and its Lessons

"All at once, right in the face."

It is customary to say that we cannot know what the next war will look like, but this saying is only partially true. To a large extent, the war would be influenced by decisions and actions made in the period between wars, and since periods between the wars much longer than the wars themselves, we will have the outcome in the beginning.

All at once.

Right in the face.

This is as true today as it was then.

The crushing victory of the Six-Day War served as the basis for the concept of security, the doctrine building and for the way we view the enemy in the six years' period from the end of the Six-Day War to the onslaught of the Yom Kippur War. The Six-Day War had been one on its first day in the preemptive aerial maneuver. The ground strenuous battle following were merely exploiting the success. There were those who did not comprehend that without this opening gambit ground battles would have looked vastly different.

All of our plans, both defensive and offensive, were based on a similar scheme, that is—intelligence warning, reserve forces mobilization, preemptive aerial strike on the SAM alignment and a ground battle. The IDF never planned to start a war with holding of the regular army, without mobilization of reserves, and without a preemptive aerial attack, the implication of which was the outright relinquishing of aerial support for the ground battle later on.

The IF concept does not exist in history, therefore my inner belief that had we done what we planned for years and mobilized the reserves just 12 hours earlier, landed the preemptive aerial strike on the Syrians on the morning of October 6 when it was already known that war was breaking out erupting, not only would this book never have been written but the whole region would have looked different—an internal belief that will forever remain a mere conjecture.

How do such serious errors recur?

We should differentiate between simple errors for which we pay an immediate price—traffic accidents, work accidents, navigation mistakes—and conceptual errors, strategic errors. These errors do not occur in a single given moment they grow and develop slowly like a child grows. Whoever's close by doesn't notice the slow rate of growth, from discussion to discussion, from one situation assessment to another, from one year to the next the basic assumptions diverge and stray from the basic truths, until the image of reality is completely distorted. A war preparation seems like an exercise, you think you can forgo a preemptive aerial strike and the mobilization of reserves is delayed, due to different considerations that dwarf in comparison to the uncalculated risk of the country's fate.

This book does not deal with conclusions and lessons, though some are still relevant today. It tells the story of the command from the viewpoint of those who were there. What won the battle in the north was not one big decision. The battle was won thanks to hundreds of little commanders and soldiers actions at decisive points. The victory was made possible thanks to speed, courage, and improvisational skills of the reserve units, the tenacity and resolve of the regular alignment that withstood the war's opening maneuver and thanks to the actions and preparations accomplished by the command before and during the war.

The bottom line is as true today as it was then.

Israel does not have, did not have, and will not have the capacity to absorb the first strike—it is not Russia. Any military plan not based on a preemptive strike is a gamble over the country's fate. There is no alternative, and there will be no alternative to the size and fitness of the reserve units, which is the basic army and damaging its fitness is favoring a short term interest at the expense of security and the future.

On October 24, the firing ceased and a few days later the first heavy rain came washing away the dust of war.

"The Agranat Investigative Committee"—A Personal View [32*]

Committees are the least successful and least efficient tool for learning lessons, and no committee would really assist improvement. My first exposure to the committee process was during the "Agranat Committee." I was not personally offended by the committee's report and conclusions but a sense of bitterness stayed with me for a long time afterwards. My feeling then—which grew stronger over time—was that the yardstick of logic, the tool by which things should be measured and examined, was inexplicably bent and twisted. There were intrigues and schemes and things that have not yet been exposed, and might never be. And what was made crooked could not be straightened again.

There were mistakes, certainly. In every war—as in every labor—there are many mistakes. We never considered ignoring or hiding them. To the contrary, we talked about them every chance we had. The war was large scale and difficult, many problems were revealed and important points had to be studied in depth, which we did. But the "Agranat Committee" behaved in part as a judicial committee

32 *Segments from Uri Simchoni's book: *White Whale*, Glory Publishing, Binyamina (2006) pp. 47-48, 104-112

and in part as a command committee for drawing lessons and both tasks were incomplete, deficient, and done in a leaning manner while mixing up the two fields.

The War of Attrition that followed the Yom Kippur War was a daily clash. The period was complicated and intense, with a lot of firing and the parallel necessity to reconstruct the outposts which were seriously damaged and in some cases utterly destroyed along the southern line. It was a cold and rainy winter. The political storms happening in the rear following the war did not concern us. We were busy with our own affairs.

One day a Colonel in polished paratrooper uniform arrived at the Command Headquarters at Nachal Geshur and presented himself as Col. Yehoshua Nevo, an investigator on behalf of the "Agranat Investigative Committee." Back then I had no idea what an investigative committee was. I had a casual and frank conversation with him over a cup of coffee in the kitchenette. I shared impressions, experiences without a touch of formality, a totally free talk. He finished and left.

In the evening, I got a call from my friend, Col. Gidon Mahanyimi. I told him that a certain paratrooper, Colonel Yehoshua Nevo, visited me. Gidon, with the instincts of a veteran intelligence man, tensed up.

"What did you tell him?" he asked.

"What are you worried about?" I responded. "He wanted to hear about the war, how things went and so on. We just talked."

"Why are you talking to people without consulting?" Gidon scolded me. "Do you have any idea of who he is? Do you know what he wants? This is an investigative committee, they want heads to roll. How can you deliver a testimony in this way without consulting, without planning? Don't you understand that he came to you to collect evidence and find out who could be hung at the town square? An investigation is against, not for."

"What do I care?" I answered, "What can he collect? What do I

need to plan for? I've been through dozens of inquiries. What's the problem, why should I mind telling him what was, what I thought and what I did?"

"Uri!!!" he practically yelled. "You're naïve. You don't know where you live. An investigative committee is not an inquiry. Every word you said will be used against you in the future. Remember what I told you."

And indeed, time passed and I forgot all about it. We were in a brigade training exercise in the south, between Yeruham and Mitzpe Ramon, when I was suddenly ordered over the phone to appear at a certain address in Jerusalem the next day in order to submit my testimony before the "Agranat Investigative Committee."

I recalled my conversation with Yehoshua Nevo, but did not place too much importance on the matter. It was a long time before and I was deep in the issues of the brigade's summer training. It seemed no more than a nuisance to me. We'll go there, talk for half an hour over a cup of coffee, and come back quickly. My entire knowledge regarding the field of investigating incidents was based on the operational inquiry following the return from battle. I've been through dozens of those. Up to that point I had never met a lawyer and didn't know a thing about the judicial system. It was like Chinese to me, not even a single familiar word. I didn't think I had to prepare. In order to tell the truth you don't have to prepare, consult, or swear on a Bible.

I got to Jerusalem, late, unshaven, and dusty, after a sleepless night, in the middle of a battalion exercise. I parked the brigade command jeep—a lump of light Negev dust—right on the sidewalk outside the front door. I told the driver to stay put since I'd be right back, and went up in a narrow slow elevator.

I entered a strange elongated room. At one end, were five solemn people in dark clothes sitting behind a high bench. A small chair stood at the other end of the room, as far away as possible. This was the chair intended for me. I identified the former GHQ Chiefs of staff Yadin and Laskov from photographs I had seen in the past. The names of the others—Agranat, Landau, and Nebenzahl—I learned later. I thought that, as in an operational inquiry, I should begin recounting things as I remember them. I said two sentences before being interrupted: "Only answer the questions directed at you." Oops. And then they began asking questions—but from the middle, not from the beginning. I wondered why they were asking me about unimportant things, at least as far as I was concerned. I tried to delve into my memory and reply. I am not a loud speaker by nature, I cannot produce a shout, and they—due to their age and distance—had difficulty hearing.

Agranat leaned forward and asked: "Could you speak up?"

"This is my voice," I responded. "May I bring the chair closer?"

"No," Agranat said, "Sit where you are."

I slowly realized that they were not interested in the full story. They had heard a lot of people before me and had already formulated an opinion. They had already drawn their conclusions, the target was already marked, and now they just wanted to get something out of me—I didn't know what it was—to reinforce their conclusions. I was flooded by questions one following the other: who said what to whom, in what situation, at what moment... and I gradually became flustered, I can't respond, I can't recall things in this order and at this level of detail. On the table in front of them the books I knew so well were stacked—the command G3 Branch's green operations logs. "Look," I tried to explain, "All the answers are in the logs before you. These logs were written in real time. The operations NCOs sit in the CCP and diligently transcribe everything of importance, every event, every report and every order. What is this now? An examination about the operations logs?" Who even reads an old operations log? It's all for the record. Many months had passed since the war. Everything ran through my mind, I tried to make sense of what was happening there. I had already exchanged two brigade commander positions by then and went through attrition in the south of the Golan Heights with a reserve brigade and attrition in the Syrian enclave with the Golani Brigade. It had been months since we completed the inquiries in the command. We know the good and the bad, the failures and successes, where we were right and where we were wrong. We know exactly what happened.

But the questions weren't about that. They went around in circles. What do they want to prove? Are they looking for someone? They gave me suspicious looks. "Try to recall better," one of the committee members prodded me. I felt insulted. They don't believe me. What's going on here? And then they began asking questions about the Command GOC, about "Haka," Maj. Gen. Yitzhak Hofi: about what he did at this hour and what he said at another. UI repeatedly answered that I didn't know. I didn't remember exactly. I was aware of the fact that this sounded strange—it was strange for me as well. I was **there**. *I remember every detail related to the war perfectly. But I can't recall what they're asking. What the hell do they want with "Haka"? He was absolutely amazing.*

I understood that someone told stories and slander and they wanted to confirm it through me. But in my head things were organized in a totally different manner, as they had occurred in the field, and I couldn't discuss the first days of the war in hours and minutes like they wanted. How can it be explained to someone who has never been through a war? The first days of the war were one long day for me and at every minute many things happened in different places. The minute the firing began I was connected to the radios, listening and talking on a lot of different networks at once, seeing only code maps, aerial photographs, operational maps and signal diagrams, and blue and red arrows symbolizing the movement of our force and the movements of enemy forces, marked and erased and marked again.

"What are you hiding?" someone shook me out of my reverie, "Why are you covering for your GOC?"

"I'm not hiding anything," I responded. "I have nothing to hide.

I can't answer because I don't remember at such a level of detail. You have all the war written material and you have the operations logs. For anything that I recall and doesn't fit what's written you'll say I'm lying. I can't treat matters this way."

The questions moved on to intelligence. They held a paper in their hands, inspected it thoughtfully and moved their heads toward each other in a slight movement reserved for gentlemen who are keeping a secret, as in the movies. "Did you see a Aman intelligence report that was issued six months before the war?" this was the Aman document regarding the exercise carried out by the Syrian military which included penetrating the Golan Heights through the Qudna—Rapid region. Thoughts were racing through my head: did I see it of didn't I? How can I tell? What is it supposed to prove? The document is a year and a half old. I must have seen a thousand documents since, maybe more. How can I answer that?

There are a lot of intelligence documents that say a lot of things. Sometimes one thing contradicts another and mentions every possible mode of operation. This is the nature of intelligence. Then why are they asking me about this particular document and not about others, which certainly state other things? Every possible scenario is covered by G2's summaries. Intelligence produces countless assessments and evaluations and the army practices all possible modes of operation. The investigation could only use intelligence documents if it gathered all the summaries, all the situation assessments, and all the exercises together. But to fish, out of a sea of documents, the only document that fits a theory that someone came up with and is now trying to prove—this was something that's not to be done, a shallow, charlatan and misleading act.

"I can't recall," I responded for the umpteenth time. "I've seen hundreds of documents. I can't remember whether I did or did not see this one." This was the truth, but the committee did not buy it. "Did you see it or didn't you?" they demanded resolutely. The suspicious glances could not have been harsher.

"I can't recall," I insisted, "but," I attempted to offer a reasonable way out of this awkward situation, "secret documents such as these go through a round of signing. You have the document, you can check. If my name is signed on the margin then I have seen it and if it isn't there—I didn't see it. Beyond that, I don't know."

The investigation went on and on, questions about the defensive plan, intelligence, and gossip.

Nebenzahl had already fallen into a deep sleep, his long chin leaning on his chest. Agranat gathered up in his chair, entirely passive. Landau listened curiously. Yadin and Laskov took over the investigation. Now came the main part for me. "You decided to operate the 7th Brigade on Saturday at 14:45, 45 minutes after the war had broken out. Why did you act this way?"

I ran through the opening hours in Nafah in my head. "What do you mean why? The 7th Brigade saved the Israeli nation. This is what everyone believes, it's well known. How could it have done that if it wasn't in the right place at the right time? What do you mean why I operated it there?" I saw the looks and understood from the tone that white is black and black is white. How can I explain such basic things when the listeners are not interested in the answers and just ask for the sake of asking? I'm confronting something that I know nothing about, something hidden. They're holding incriminating papers—God knows whose. What could be written there? Why don't they just say what they want? Instead they're going around in circles, and when I don't give them the answer they want—they get angry, hand around another document, and shake their heads at each other as if sharing some secret.

Can I explain anything as trivial as operating the 7th Brigade toward the Quneitra salient to them? None of them knows the field. They have never been to the Golan Heights and perhaps have never even crossed the Bnot Yaakov Bridge. The maneuver was right. This has been discussed many times over in the analyses made after the war in the command and the division. "Haka" thinks so, Yanush with his brilliant mind thinks so even the strict Raful thinks it was the right thing to do so. It has been said and discussed and written so many times since the war that the 7th Brigade saved the State of Israel. Then how does this fit in with the logic that to send the brigade (which saved to country, to the place where it saved it) was a wrong move?

"But the main Syrian effort was in the south, not the north," Yadin said. "Then why did you operate the 7th Brigade in the south?"

Now *I understood the intelligence document and the papers passing from one to the other, the little head nods and all the questions. Why didn't he say it an hour ago? Until that moment, ten months after the war, I had never heard that the main effort was in the south. I recalled the talk with Gidon Mahanyimi, the wise Gidon. Everything was different, but the stone that Nevo tossed was already deep in the well, and ten wise men could not get it out.*

"There was no main Syrian effort," I insisted. "But when our line in the southern Heights was broken through and the northern effort was blocked, the Syrians directed the forces designated to exploit the success through the openings. This was part of the battle developments. This is how it's done. Had we sent the 7th Brigade south—the Syrians would have penetrated in the north and what would have stopped them from reaching the Galilee Panhandle? And then you would have asked me why I sent the 7th Brigade south?"

Following the embarrassing investigation I understood that any sentence beginning with "why" or "if" is meaningless. These are always questions asked in retrospect, when the maneuver outcomes carried out are already known. Since something else did not happen it is clear that the number of "whys" and "ifs" is endless. It's a speculative question, because every additional "if" and "why" has more "ifs" and "whys" branching off. Therefore, the assumption that had you done something would have entailed the occurrence of something specific but since you didn't do this then this happened—is a meaningless sentence. But these were belated insights

I had reached many years later. At that moment there was a great embarrassment.

It went on and on in this manner. I try to explain that the Quneitra salient is the vital area of the Golan Heights, and that it remained in our hands because the 7th Brigade stood there and fought bravely, and they say that the south was broken through because the main Syrian effort was there, and because the 7th Brigade was not sent there. I said:"You could look at the half filled glass and argue whether it's half empty or half full forever. It depends on the point of view of the beholder but it doesn't give us more water."

"Anyway," Yadin said, bringing up another idea, "There were five tank battalions on the Golan Heights; two were deployed on the line and three concentrated in the rear. Why didn't you send one to the north, one to the south, and leave the third as a reserve?" I listened and could not believe my ears. I mean, this man was once the GHQ Chief of Staff. "It's exactly the opposite," I tried to explain. "Today, with the wisdom of hindsight, it is evident to me that we should have gone back and entered into a brigade locality in the Hushniya region with the two battalions in the south—the 53rd Battalion and the 82nd Battalion—instead of fighting in this split manner over each outpost. There are two important principles of war: the first—maintain the integrity of the force, avoid splitting up; and the second—capture the key positions; meaning, don't allow the enemy to capture the field from which the campaign could be won. In the north we acted properly, so the line held. In the south we didn't act properly, so the line collapsed. If I had acted as you said, we would have been weak all over, and we would have lost the Golan Heights."

"Why didn't you wait longer? What was on the haste?" Yadin continued.

"What was I supposed to wait for?" I tried to protest, "For the Syrians to capture the controlling positions in the Quneitra salient and then carry out a counterattack against them? Do we need to

wait for everything to fall first, and only then respond? There was no reason to wait. Each minute was critical."

"You were a Lieutenant Colonel," Yadin said, "You weren't the most senior position holder there. Did you get an official appointment?"

"What does the official appointment matter? We don't sit in some air-conditioned room and cover up with papers for backup."

"Who authorized you?" Yadin asked.

"I wasn't appointed," I replied. "Ben Shoham was, but as the command G3 officer I had to take command in the situation that had formed."

"Why didn't you consult with the GOC or the GHQ Chief of Staff?" Yadin continued.

"At that time the GOC was on his way from Tel Aviv to the Golan Heights," I responded, "and the GHQ Chief of Staff was 200 kilometers away. But the accurate answer is that there was nothing to ask, because the situation was clear. In the units were I was educated I was taught to take responsibility, and not to pass it on upwards, and certainly not downwards. I saw what was happening, I was in the right place, and I did what I thought should be done. What's unclear here?"

The tone was escalating. I came from a reality where personal honor is strictly maintained, a world that does not loathe thinking in terms of physical strength. I sit there and take hits. To what point do I have to keep taking it? This is humiliating. How should I respond?

"What is your military training?" Yadin asked, "Did you go to the School of Staff and Command?"

"I went to the School of Staff and Command."

"What was your final grade?" he asked.

"A B," I responded. This was already too much. "What courses did you take to become GHQ Chief of Staff, a squad commanders' course in Juara?" I asked him. I knew from experience that those who like to injure, can never take an injury themselves.

"Get out of the room!" Yadin said angrily.

"Fine," I said and got up to leave. As I thought, the balloon had emptied in a moment. By the door I heard Yadin calling me back to my seat. I returned.

"Erase everything," he instructed someone who sat in the corner writing the whole time.

Yadin calmed down and Laskov began. To my amazement he opened up the book "Armored Warfare" and began reading from it out loud the chapter on counteroffensives. I looked and could not believe it: he's reading a lesson from a training manual, with the serious countenance of a preacher, making sure to pronounce every word. He wrote it dozens of years ago when he was in the training department, and he expects others to take it with them wherever they go. We're talking about fundamental problems in operating a regional command in an all-inclusive war. He can't even differentiate between theoretical frames of reference and real-time problems and solutions in the field. What a pathetic occasion.

I was in the committee room for many hours. When I went out on the street evening had already settled. The jeep remained at the entrance. The driver was bundled up in his seat, not daring to close his eyes because of the weapons and communicators in the vehicle.

"What happened?" he asked. "Where were you?"

"Good question," I replied, "I don't know where I have been. I need to think about it."

Writers and Their Contributions

Part I—Preparation for War

Brig. Gen. (res.) Dr. Dani Asher; Col. (res.) Hagai Mann—the Syrians before the war

Col. (res.) Moshe Givati—preparation in the Hermon and the Syrian plan to capture it

Col. (ret.) Roland Aloni; Brig. Gen. (res.) Dr. Dani Asher; Brig. Gen. (res.) Avraham Bar David; Lt. Col. (res.) Avraham Zohar; Col. (res.) Hagai Mann; Lt. Col. (res.) Yossi Abboudi; Maj. Gen. (res.) Uri Simchoni—the Northern Command before the war

Col. (res.) Ilan Sahar—the 7th Brigade

Col. (res.) Dr. Hanan Shai (Schwartz)—the 188th Brigade

Part II—From a Desperate Holding to an Offensive Toward Damascus

Brig. Gen. (res.) Dr. Dani Asher—the Syrian Army attacks; the Northern Command defensive against the Syrian attack (with sections from the research by Lt. Col. (res.) Avraham Zohar); the command during the counterattack—8–10 October—the section includes comments by Lt. Col. (res.) Avraham Zohar, as well as segments from the research by Col. (res.) Yehuda Wegman—the second battle over the Golan—the containment stage, the counterattack and restoring the situation to its previous condition, 7–10 October 1973; the Syrian Army delays against the defensive alignments east of the Purple Line; the command toward and during the breakthrough into Syrian territory—the section includes comments and segments from the research by Lt. Col. (res.) Avraham Zohar and the research by Lt. Col. (res.) Dr. Amiad Bresner regarding the capture of the "Syrian enclave" 11–12 October; Syrian Army defensive alignment; Northern Command forces establishing in the Enclave and thwarting counterattacks—the section incorporated comments by Lt. Col. (res.) Avraham Zohar and segments from the article by Benny Michelson—the effort to exploit the breakthrough and the threat on Damascus; the Syrian Army's counterattacks with the assistance of the delivery forces

Lt. Col. (res.) Dr. Amiad Bresner and Col. (res.) Ilan Sahar—capturing the Syrian enclave—11–12 October—fighting at the unit level—based on their researches

Col. (res.) Moshe Givati, *The Battles over the Hermon until its Recapture*, based on the first of its kind comprehensive research conducted by him within the history department of the IDF.

Col. (res.) Yehuda Wegman—The activity at the forces' level during the counter attack phase—based on his research—the second battle over the Golan—the containment phase, the counter attacks and restoring the conditions, October 7–10 1973.

Col. (res.) Benny Michelson—The effort to exploit the breakthrough and threat over Damascus at the unit level.

Col. (res.) Ilan Sahar—The 7th Brigade's fighting during the defensive battle.

Col. (res.)Dr. Hanan Shai—The Golan Heights defense during the first two days of combat.

Part III—Operating the Command Systems at War

Describing preparations and activity in the command branches and departments toward the war and during, written by:

Operations—**Maj. Gen. (res.) Uri Simchoni**

Intelligence—**Col. (res.) Hagai Mann**

Artillery—**Brig. Gen. (res.) Avraham Bar David** and **Brig. Gen. (res.) Dr. Dani Asher**

Engineering—**Brig. Gen. (res.) Dr. Dani Asher**

Air Force—**Col. (res.) Yossi Abboudi**

Logistics—**Col. (ret.) Roland Aloni**

Ordnance—**Brig. Gen. (res.) Dr. Dani Asher** (based on Maj. Ofer Golinski's work at the School of Staff and Command, Later Col., Commander of Training Base No. 20)

Medical Corps—**Dr. Danny Nadav** (Medical Corps historian)

Military Police—**Brig. Gen. (res.) Dr. Dani Asher**

Adjutant Corps—**Brig. Gen. (res.) Aharon Ophir**

Control and communication—**Col. (res.) Avraham Kayam** and **Brig. Gen. (res.) Dr. Dani Asher**

Afterword—**Major General (res.) Uri Simchoni**

Bibliography

Brig. Gen. (res.) Dr. Dani Asher—The Syrian Army

Asher, Dani, *All Out War—Limited in Its Dimensions*, Ph.D. Thesis, Haifa University, October 2002

Asher, Dani, "Breaking the Concept," *Maarchot*, Tel Aviv, September, 2003.

Later published in the U.S.A. as *The Egyptian Strategy for the Yom Kippur War*, McFarland, 2009.

Asher, Dani, "The Egyptian Plan for the Yom Kippur War," *Maarchot*, issue 361, November 1998, pp. 2–13;

Asher, Dani, "The Story of a Map," how the Syrians planned to operate the second armored rank during the Yom Kippur War, *Maarchot*, issue 366–367, October 1999, pp. 76–78

Haber Eitan, and Ze'ev Schiff, Dr. Dani Asher (sub-editor), *The Yom Kippur War Lexicon*, Zmora-Bitan/Dvir, 2003

Mayzel, Mati, "Conquering the Golan Heights during the Six-Day War; June 1967," *Maarchot*, 2001

Maoz Moshe, *Assad the Sphinx of Damascus*, Dvir, 1988

Speech by Assad, *Radio Damascus*, December 5, 1970.

Seale Patrick, "Assad," *Maarchot*, 1993

Interview with Mustafa Tlass published in *Al-Ba'ath* and *Tishreen*, October 5–6, 1975

El-Shazly Saad, "Crossing the Channel," *Maarchot*, 1978

Ofer Zvi Lt. Col. (res.), "Syrian Offensive Campaign in the Golan Heights During the Yom Kippur War," *Maarchot*, issue 314, p. 22

"The Iraqi Army in the Yom Kippur War," *Maarchot*, Tel Aviv, 1986

Col. (res.) Dr. Hanan Shai (Schwartz)

Kahalani Avigdor, *Oz 77*, Schocken, Tel Aviv, 1975

Lt. Col. (res.) Dr. Amiad Bresner

Orr, Ori, *These Are My Brothers*, Tel Aviv, 2003

Kahalani Avigdor, *Oz 77*, Schocken, Tel Aviv, 1975

Col. (res.) Yehuda Wegman

The Agranat Investigation Committee Report on the Fighting in the Northern Command, 1975

Wegman Yehuda Col. (res.), *The Syrian Failure in the Second Battle Over the Golan Heights*, 1999

Wegman, Yehuda Col. (res.), "Chaos in Nafah," in: Hagai Golan, Shaul Shai (eds.) *War Today*, *Maarchot* / Ministry of Defense, 2003 pp. 311–358

Postovski Sarah (ed.), Carta Atlas, *The Third Decade*, Jerusalem 1983.

Kahalani Avigdor, *Oz 77*, Schocken, Tel Aviv, 1975

Col. (res.) Benny Michelson

Oren Elchanan, *The Yom Kippur War*, Training and Doctrine/ History, 2004

The Iraqi Army in the Yom Kippur War, *Maarchot*, Tel Aviv, 1986

Maj. Alexander, "Four Days Four Battles," *Maarchot* (234–235), January 1974

Shai Avi Lt. Col. "The Iraqi Delivery Corps during the Yom Kippur War," *Maarchot* (258–259), October-November 1977

Bar-Kochva Moshe Col., "The Armored Campaign against the Iraqis during the Yom Kippur War," *Maarchot*, (258–259) October–November 1977

Lt. Col. David, "The Jordanian Army during the Yom Kippur War," *Maarchot*, (266) October–November 1978

Cohen Ben Ami Maj. *The Story of the Training Base No. 9 Battalion No. 9 during the Yom Kippur War*

Researches by Col. Prof. Eran Dolev

Col. (ret.) Roland Aloni—Logistics

Aloni Roland Col. (ret.), "The Logistics of the Ground Forces during the Yom Kippur War," *Maarchot*, issue 361, November 1998

Dr. Daniel Nadav—Medicine

Orr, Ori, *These Are My Brothers*, Tel Aviv, 2003

Gordon Shmuel Col. (res.) Dr. "30 Hours in October," *Maariv*, Tel Aviv, 2008

Haber Eitan, and Ze'ev Schiff, Dr. Dani Asher (sub-editor), *The Yom Kippur War Lexicon*, Zmora-Bitan/Dvir, 2003

Meeting with Prof. Dineri in Tel Aviv, on 5.8.2005

Interview with Brig. Gen. (res.) Prof. Dan Michaeli in Tel Aviv, on 4.8.2005

The description by Dan Michaeli was presented during a seminar regarding the ground forces during the Yom Kippur War, conducted by the Center for Defense Studies in Ramat Efal, on 6.7.2000

Adjusting Sights (2003). A film based on the book by Haim Sabato, combatant in the 679th Brigade

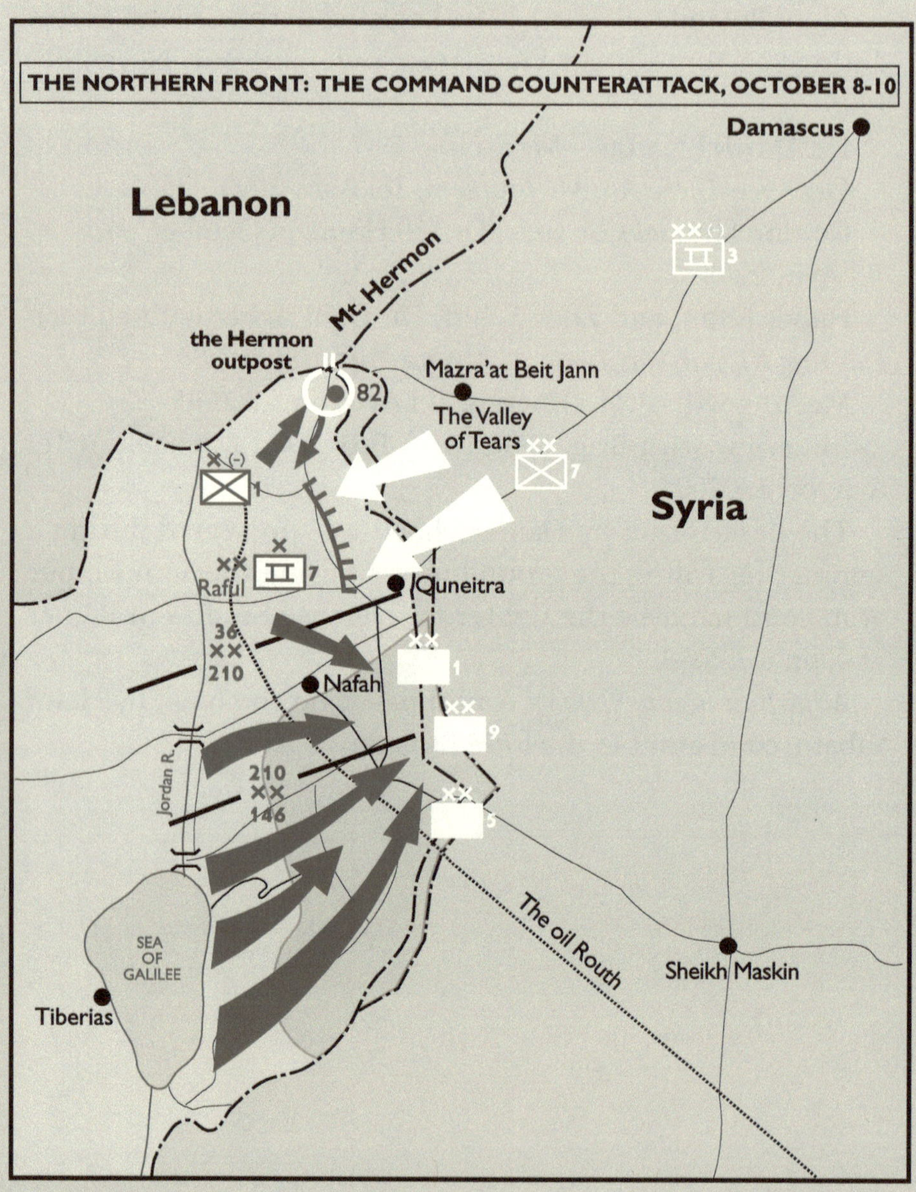
THE NORTHERN FRONT: THE COMMAND COUNTERATTACK, OCTOBER 8-10
Damascus
Lebanon
Mt. Hermon
the Hermon outpost
82
Mazra'at Beit Jann
The Valley of Tears
7
3
Syria
1
Raful
7
Quneitra
36
210
Nafah
1
9
Jordan R.
210
146
5
The oil Routh
Sheikh Maskin
SEA OF GALILEE
Tiberias

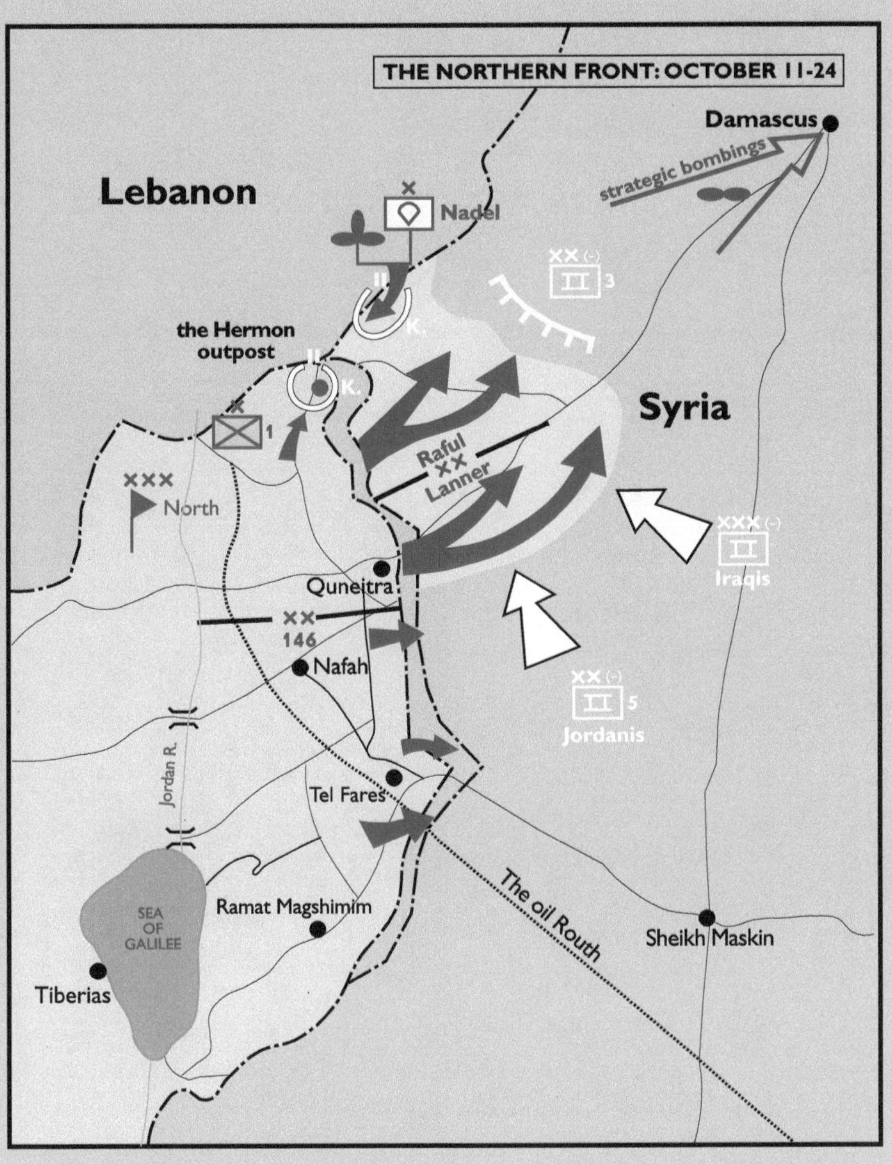
THE NORTHERN FRONT: OCTOBER 11-24
Damascus
strategic bombings
Lebanon
Nadel
the Hermon outpost
K.
3
Syria
1
Raful
Lanner
North
Iraqis
Quneitra
146
Nafah
5
Jordanis
Jordan R.
Tel Fares
The oil Routh
SEA OF GALILEE
Ramat Magshimim
Sheikh Maskin
Tiberias